A HISTORY OF
THE CATHOLIC CHURCH

A HISTORY OF
THE CATHOLIC CHURCH

For the Use of Colleges, Seminaries, and Universities

By

DOM CHARLES POULET

Benedictine Monk of the Congregation of Solesmes

AUTHORIZED TRANSLATION AND ADAPTATION FROM
THE FOURTH FRENCH EDITION
BY
THE REV. SIDNEY A. RAEMERS, M.A., PH.D.

VOLUME I

*THE ANCIENT CHURCH — THE MIDDLE AGES — THE BEGINNINGS OF
THE MODERN PERIOD*

Volume 1 originally translated from the fourth French
edition by Rev. Sidney A. Raemers
© B. Herder, 1941

Reprinted by Arouca Press 2020

978-1-989905-30-2 (paper)
978-1-989905-31-9 (cloth)

Arouca Press
PO Box 55003
Bridgeport PO
Waterloo, ON N2J3G0
Canada
www.aroucapress.com
Send inquiries to info@aroucapress.com

To the
Cardinals, Archbishops, and Bishops
of the Catholic Church
in the United States
This Adaptation of a Classical Work
is Most Respectfully Dedicated

ROMANAE ECCLESIAE

PROPTER POTENTIOREM PRINCIPALITATEM

"History is the living tissue of facts. In this tissue, the thoughts and actions of God and men blend, unite, at times appear at variance, cross each other, and even impede each others's course, the final result being a wonderful mosaic, of which the most outstanding feature is the undying love of God for the human race."

(Pope Pius XI)

Written in a dignified style (of which the translation has lost nothing), and nicely paragraphed, this Church History is a fine combination of completeness and conciseness. The inclusion of documents and questions was a happy thought, and the bibliographies are perhaps the most up-to-date of any such work. To ecclesiastical students especially it should be an immense boon, as it provides an excellent ground to work on.

(Rev.) Myles V. Ronan, C.C., M.R.I.A.

Dublin, Ireland
July 15, 1934

AUTHOR'S PREFACE

The task of condensing the History of the Church within a few hundred pages is a delicate one. We have undertaken it in the hope that our efforts will benefit both seminarians and college students.

Our chief concern throughout has been clearness, precision, and brevity, and for this reason we have carefully eliminated unnecessary details. On the other hand, we have thought it our duty to stress the dogmatic controversies as well as the development of Christian institutions, and hence we have attached more importance to certain decisive epochs in the history of dogma. In this matter we willingly subscribe to the opinion of a very competent judge, who writes: "The history of the second and third centuries of the Church has its special interest, because of the sublime heights reached by so many holy emotions and passions, and because of the early confusion that reigned among a host of new and fecund ideas. But we must confess that the period of one hundred and twenty-five years, extending from the Council of Nicaea to the Council of Chalcedon (325–451), is far more important to one who would obtain a comprehensive view of Christianity, and that ignorance concerning the spirit of that time might lead one into serious error. In those days, in the midst of incredibly bitter doctrinal struggles, the authentic formulas of the great Trinitarian and Christological dogmas, which constitute the nucleus of present-day Catholic belief, took on explicit and definitive form."

In the matter of a bibliography, we have shown some reserve, preferring to omit entirely a number of books now considered out of date, and indicating others which, in our judgment, are more useful, besides being more recent.

In closing, we beg to extend our thanks to Canon Leman, professor of Church History at the Catholic University of Lille, who read our manuscript and suggested a number of valuable corrections.

Fr. Charles Poulet

St. Paul's Abbey, Wisques, P. de C.

AUTHOR'S NOTE TO THE FOURTH EDITION

This new edition is not an exact reproduction of the first. We have added an Introductory Chapter on the general sources of Church History, one on Contemporary Protestantism, and another on more recent events.

The bibliography has been brought up to date, and the text corrected, nay, in some instances, completed. The principal changes are of a general nature, and have to do with dogma and ecclesiastical institutions. Thus, we have expanded our treatment of Severian Monophysitism, the origin of rural parishes, the Gregorian ideas, the various aspects of the Crusades, the political controversies of the sixteenth century, etc.

AUTHOR'S NOTE TO THE ENGLISH TRANSLATION

We willingly recommend to the English-speaking public this translation of our Church History as a clear and faithful version of the original. We shall be most happy if this modest work proves of service to our American brethren in making better known and proportionately loved Our Mother, the Holy Roman Church.

Fr. C. Poulet

St. Paul's Abbey, Wisques, P. de C.
July 1, 1934

TRANSLATOR'S PREFACE

In offering to the English-speaking public a translation of the *Histoire de l'Eglise* by Dom Charles Poulet, Benedictine Monk of the Congregation of Solesmes, the translator has endeavored, within the limits of his ability, to render a service to students and professors of Church History especially, and to the Catholic clergy and laity at large. The fact that the original was written by a member of an Order whose reputation for research and scholarship has stood the test of fifteen centuries, should be ample proof of the worth of the text; the additional fact that the book issues from the world famous monastery of Solesmes, should be an *a priori* argument in its favor. In the words of the well-known Dom Cabrol, "this is not just another history of the Catholic Church, for it recommends itself to the reader by its clearness, order, arrangement, and perfect balance, as well as by the sobriety and conciseness of its exposition."

This History of the Catholic Church does not claim to be an exhaustive treatment of the subject. The present curriculum of our colleges and seminaries forbids such a treatment. Students who are engaged in the pursuit of the arts and sciences, and seminarians who must give a large portion of their time to philosophy, dogma, moral, liturgy, canon law and pastoral theology need a text that will enable them, in a few hours each week, to cover the history of the Church from the call of St. Peter to the pontificate of the present gloriously reigning Pope. A historian acquainted with these conditions, who concerned himself with details, would at once doom his work to failure.

The educated Catholic layman is invited to peruse these pages. He now can learn the essentials of the history of his Church condensed into two handy volumes, and feel quite certain that the presentation of the facts is both impartial and scholarly. The ordinary Catholic layman knows too little about the glories and triumphs of the Catholic Church, his knowledge being generally limited to a few incidents he has culled from Bible and profane history. While the original French work was not primarily intended for the layman, it is to be hoped that in its English dress it will find a place in his home, and that its reading will awaken him to some of the true beauties of an institution which is both God-given and God-giving.

A considerable amount of space has been reserved in this text for theological discussions and the history of institutions. The nature of the subject called for this arrangement, because, while the history of the Catholic Church is necessarily bound up with the profane history of States and nations, her real history is identical with the growth and development of her dogmas and the rise and purpose of her foundations.

We have made bold to introduce a number of changes in the English translation, which is really more an adaptation than a literal version. Thus we have, especially in the second volume, eliminated a great deal of material that would be of interest only to a European student and at times only a student in attendance at a French seminary or university. In place of this material we have inserted chapters dealing with questions with which American and English students should be more familiar. Hence, in the first volume, we have made place for a chapter on "The Beginnings of Christianity in Ireland"; and in the second for additional chapters on "The Reformation in Ireland," "The Catholic Church in the United States," "The Catholic Church in Canada," "The Church in Scotland," etc. Also, for the sake of uniformity, and to supplement the material given in each chapter, we have added Texts and Documents where they were missing in the original, together with suitable lists of questions to guide the teacher, the student, and perhaps even the general reader.

Because the work recommends itself to such a large and diversified class of readers, it was deemed advisable to leave the bibliographies of the author intact and merely add to already long lists a number of selected English works. After all—and this is regrettable and somewhat of an indictment of English and American scholarship—most of the research work in this particular field has been done by either German or French savants, and so, even if a student wished to make a more thorough study of some particular question, he would have to consult literature written in one or other of these foreign languages. Finally, we have eliminated the charts and some of the synoptic tables supplied by the author, as being superfluous and at times cumbersome.

It is to be hoped that these two volumes will receive a hearty welcome. The history of the Catholic Church is a glorious one, and while we are not denying that there have been serious abuses and scandals within her fold in the course of centuries, we are emphatic in saying that no institution or society has rendered such invaluable services to the world and done more to correct the vices and sins of men and bring them nearer to God. Any history of the Catholic Church must of necessity be objective, but if in addition it is impartial, it will establish beyond cavil that the Church of Christ is One, Holy, Catholic, and Apostolic.

In dedicating this translation to the Cardinals, Archbishops, and Bishops of the Catholic Church in the United States, we make the sincere wish that Christ, who founded the Church, will continue to give them the physical and spiritual strength to "carry on" as they have done so nobly in the past. Their history in the United States is almost without a blemish, and their work has ever been a source of admiration to the entire Catholic world. May God bless them in their earnest endeavors, and in future raise up more apostles like them to rule and defend His holy Church.

In conclusion, the translator must extend his heartfelt thanks to the following persons who gave their services so unstintingly. In the first place, to the Reverend Myles V. Ronan, M.R.I.A., of Dublin, Ireland, for his scholarly contribution on "The Reformation in Ireland"; secondly, to Father Ryan, S.J., D.Litt., for his assistance with the chapter on "The Beginnings of Christianity in Ireland"; thirdly to the magnanimous and scholarly Brother Leo, of the Brothers of the Christian Schools, for his kind encouragement amidst adversity and his generous "Foreword" to the work; fourthly to the humble Brother Cornelius, of the Brothers of the Christian Schools, for his artistic work on the design for the cover; and finally to the Rev. James Butler, C. S. C., of the Department of History in the University of Notre Dame, who was kind enough to re-read the translation of the first volume. The translator must also thank most sincerely Miss Mary McKenna of Portland, Ore., who typed and checked the MS., and last but not least Mr. and Mrs. John Fleming of Santa Barbara, Cal., without whose kind generosity the work could not have been completed.

The translator would be extremely grateful to professors and instructors of Church History if they would forward him their criticisms, so that mistakes and omissions may be rectified in future editions. No work is perfect, and the translator is far from entertaining the idea that this work is an exception to the rule.

With these prefatory remarks we commit this work to the English speaking public. We can only wish that the favor it shall receive may be somewhat proportionate to the labor expended in its preparation. We confidently trust that we have conscientiously and faithfully fulfilled the promises of the title of this work; it is for others to appreciate the execution of the task; but, like Samuel Johnson, we confess that "we look with pleasure on our book, however defective, and deliver it to the world with the spirit of a man that has endeavored well."

S. A. RAEMERS

FOREWORD BY BROTHER LEO, F.S.C.

It is beyond dispute that education in this country has nearly everything except what matters most, and that is a unifying principle, a catalyzing agent, a subject of study which will put books and life, the world and the individual, the past and the present, into pattern and proportion. Correlation—a word, for aught I know, contemned by current educationists—really means something. It means that you do not educate either yourself or your child or your candidate for the doctorate merely by accumulating information irrespective of its utility and significance; and it means that unless you have some principle of selection, some standard of values, some study which manages to touch and elucidate all other studies, then the most you can get is an intellectual junk-shop or an educational piggly-wiggly plant.

At this point generality generators devoted—at a measurable distance from the classroom—to specifically Catholic education will eloquently assure us that the teaching of religion keeps our Catholic schools from becoming mere department stores of learning, that the "catechism" counteracts textbooks written by atheistic pedagogues, and that vocal prayers and holy pictures and visits to the Blessed Sacrament create and foster the needed unifying process. Such is the accepted theory, a sound theory as far as it goes; but in actual daily practice, from Catholic grade schools all the way up to Catholic universities—both the few that are such and the many that are so-called—religion exerts less influence than our oratorical apologists suppose.

For this unfortunate condition there are at least a dozen reasons, including a ridiculous admiration on the part of some Catholic teachers for psychology without a soul and pedagogy without God; an unintelligent, misproportioned and distinctly anti-Christian devotion, in certain high schools and men's colleges, to specialized, spectacular, money-making games, and a servile respect on the part of some Catholic school administrators for admission boards and sundry secular agencies, a respect which ought to get into litany form, "North Central Association, we beseech thee to hear us!" But, more than all else—for some reason or for no reason—our schools fail to include or to emphasize several studies, any one of which, properly taught, would bring into all studies the desired unity and Catholicity.

One such study is the history of the Catholic Church. It makes all European history intelligible—which isolated and sectional historical studies certainly do not. It gives the student of whatever grade a sense, a conviction of the spiritual solidarity of all Western peoples. It makes clear the practical truth that in the development of our civilization battles have counted for less than Church councils, and men like St. Benedict and Abélard have counted for more than men like Arius and Joseph of Austria. It serves to draw that all-important distinction between what a man is culturally, morally, religiously, and what office he holds through the inscrutable grace of God and the favor of the Apostolic See.

Like Bacon's commendable ambition, Church History takes all learning for its province. It constitutes a pervasive background for literature and the arts. In its purview philosophy ceases to be a languid lady on a pedestal or a series of abstruse propositions in a book and becomes a synthesis of ideas whereby men live abundantly. Without Church History we could appreciate neither the Butter Tower in Rouen nor the Ghost in "Hamlet." It is indispensable for any ordered understanding of education, for in its account of the monastic schools, the guild institutes, the Jesuit colleges, and the foundations of St. de la Salle, it reminds a forgetful world that education is not a static thing, but a dynamic process. At every point it is associated with science, with discovery, with the development of arts and crafts, with sociology and economics, with problems of civil government.

Most important of all, Church History, in ampler measure than any other subject of study, discloses the complete nature of man. It shows that he has always been a beast; and it shows that always he has been more than a beast. It impartially unfolds the tragic story of his greed, his pride, his sloth; the story likewise of his heroism, his charity, his faith. Church History is like an uninterruptedly flowing river along whose banks men have builded their cities and tilled their farms, fought their battles and pondered the courses of the stars.

Brother Leo

Saint Mary's College,
California

INTRODUCTION BY PROFESSOR R. H. LORD

No more important historical subject could be presented to the attention of readers than that which is set forth in this work.

That the Catholic Church is the most extraordinary institution the world has seen and something not only incomparably great, but absolutely unique and *sui generis,* has been admitted by the most competent non-Catholic historians.

The late Viscount Morley, in his volume on *Politics and History,* declared: "Well may the Roman Church be described as the most wonderful structure that the powers of human mind and soul and all the elemental forces at mankind's disposal have yet reared." The best known of all recent Protestant Church historians, Professor Adolph Harnack, described the Catholic Church as "the greatest religious and political creation known to history." Lord Bryce once affirmed that of all subjects in history the Catholic Church was the one most worth studying. And in a celebrated passage Macaulay wrote: "There is not, and there never was on this earth, a work of human policy so well deserving of examination as the Roman Catholic Church. The history of that Church joins together the two great ages of human civilisation. No other institution is left standing which carries the mind back to the time when the smoke of sacrifice rose in the Pantheon, and when camelopards and tigers bounded in the Flavian amphitheatre. The proudest royal houses are but of yesterday, when compared with the line of the Sovereign Pontiffs. . . . The Papacy remains, not in decay, not a mere antique, but full of life and youthful vigour. The Catholic Church is still sending forth to the farthest ends of the world missionaries as zealous as those that landed in Kent with Augustine, and still confronting hostile kings with the same spirit with which she confronted Attila. . . . Nor do we see any sign which indicates that the term of her long dominion is approaching. She saw the commencement of all the governments and of all the ecclesiastical establishments that now exist in the world; and we feel no assurance that she is not destined to see the end of them all. She was great and respected before the Saxon had set foot on Britain, before the

Frank had passed the Rhine, when Grecian eloquence still flourished at Antioch, when idols were still worshipped in the temple of Mecca. And she may still exist in undiminished vigour when some traveller from New Zealand shall, in the midst of a vast solitude, take his stand on a broken arch of London Bridge to sketch the ruins of St. Paul's."

This marvellous society in unique in a great many ways.

It is not only the oldest of Christian churches, but it is the original church, the only one which can trace its authority and commission with sureness back to a Divine Founder, who said: "As the Father hath sent me, I also send you."

It prides itself on having preserved itself always essentially the same: the same in its faith, its worship, its organization and government. Development there has been, of course, but it is the kind of development found in the growth of the acorn into the oak or of the grain of mustard into the tree whose branches overspread the earth—not the kind of development that consists in rejecting what you have previously believed or in believing to-day the opposite of what you believed yesterday.

The Catholic Church is universal, as is no other Christian society. In the past she has shown a striking ability to adapt herself to all races, to all kinds and conditions of men, and to all changes in civilization. And to-day, still showing that same power, she is everywhere. She has always been by far the largest of Christian societies; more than half the Christians in the world are her children (over 300,000,000); and no other body of Christians is so uniformly extended in every part of the globe and among all races of men.

She has a matchless unity. Wherever the Catholic goes, he finds the same teaching, the same worship, the same institutions with which he is familiar at home: from Canada to Cape Town, from Hongkong to Buenos Ayres. And the present-day Catholic would have just about this same sense of familiarity, of perfect unity with those around him, could he be wafted back in time and be present with St. Francis in the church at Assisi in the 13th century, with St. Ambrose or St. Augustine in the 4th century, or at the Mass celebrated by St. Peter among the first Christians at Rome.

Of all the influences that have moulded European civilization, the Church is incontestably the greatest. Indeed, she made "Europe." For what do we mean by "Europe," i. e., the nations of European civilization, except that group of peoples who were converted, civilized, and brought into a permanent cultural unity by the Catholic Church? "There is no aspect of our modern life"—government, law, education, literature, art, science— "which has not at some period passed through the mould of the Catholic Church" (Arnold Lunn). Nearly all the great cathedrals were built by Catholics. Nearly all Christian religious art is Catholic. So is most of the best religious music. John Ruskin discovered that "all beautiful prayers were Catholic, and all wise interpretations of the Bible." What other body of Christians has a system of theological and moral teachings so complete, coherent, and scientific as that of the Catholic Church? What other religious body has ever drawn forth from its adherents on so large a scale and through so long a period of time the passionate loyalty, the self-sacrifice, the limitless devotion that the Catholic Church evokes from her children? What other religious body has such a roll of illustrious thinkers, great mystics, saints, martyrs, heroes and heroines of the spiritual life?

But there are two points about the Catholic Church, above all, which excite the attention of all outside observers.

The first of them is her absolute self-confidence, her unshakable faith in her own authority and the truth of her teachings. She speaks with a calm assurance such as no other religious body possesses, and she receives from her children an unfaltering trust and obedience such as no other religious body elicits. And that is because she makes a claim that no other religious society in all history has ever made: the claim to infallibility, *i. e.,* the claim that when she speaks authoritatively upon a question of religion or morals, she is divinely safeguarded from error. This is, of course, a claim which the "modern man" outside the Church does not particularly relish. We do not like individuals that we meet who seem to think themselves infallible. But at a time when outside the Church religious opinions are in a state of flux or disintegration, when the trumpet, if called upon to blow, so commonly gives forth but the most uncertain sound, people are beginning to realize, I think, the advantage a church has when it knows its own mind and absolutely believes what it teaches. And even those non-Catholics who most dislike infallibility must admit that if a man or a society should happen to have a revealed message from God to transmit, any doubt or hesitation about delivering that message would be singularly out of place.

The second point about the Church that most arrests the attention of outside observers is her mysterious and almost uncanny strength and vitality. She is the oldest institution in the world to-day, and yet as young in spirit, as active and alert, as if created only yesterday. In her long history she has faced every kind of formidable opposition—the power of imperial Rome, the barbarians, the Mohammedans, the Hohenstaufen, the religious rebels of the 16th century, the French Revolution, Napoleon, Bismarck. She has never been vanquished. Over and over again she has faced crises so severe that her enemies have celebrated her inevitable demise and thanked whatever deities they had that she at last was done for. Chesterton has an essay on "The Five Deaths of the Faith." But in every crisis the Church has pulled herself together, renewed her strength, and come forth rejuvenated and reinvigorated from what ought, humanly speaking, to have killed her. The tremendous political and intellectual revolutions of the past century and a half, the fierce onslaughts directed upon her by modern "Liberalism," Anticlericalism, rationalism, and infidelity have only demonstrated anew that storms and perils galvanize the Church into new life. To-day, when almost everything around her is quaking, tottering, or collapsing, she stands firm. Indeed, under the admirably efficient leadership that emanates from Rome, she is multiplying and intensifying her activities all over the world as seldom before in her history. The appeal that she makes to contemporary minds, and to minds of the highest intelligence, is shown by the long roll of recent illustrious converts in England, Holland, Germany, France, Scandinavia, and the United States. It seems, in fact, no exaggeration to say that the position and prestige of the Church are stronger to-day than at any previous time since Martin Luther began the great revolt against her. Small wonder, then, that acute outside observers are driven to admit that, for better or for worse, the Catholic Church is an institution quite unique of its kind, incomparably great and fruitful in many ways, and endowed with unparalleled strength, vitality, and indestructibility.

Now such a phenomenon demands an adequate explanation. The explanations once current in non-Catholic books—fortunate combinations of circumstances, machine-like perfection of organization, the statecraft of Roman ecclesiastics, or the incurable propensity of the human mind to bow blindly to authority—are pitifully inadequate. To Catholics there seems to be only one explanation commensurate with the facts. It is that the Catholic Church is something absolutely *sui generis* in her nature, her claims, her strength, her vitality, because she is the only society on earth that has had God for its founder and because He has granted to her an authority and an unfailing guidance and support that were never promised to any other institution. It is because, though not unmixed with human elements and human imperfections, the Church is essentially a divine society, the "kingdom of God" on earth. To Catholics the Church is, above all, in St. Paul's phrase, the mystical "Body of Christ," in which and through which through all the centuries since His Ascension He has lived and worked upon earth; when she speaks on the subjects committed to her they recognize in her voice His voice; her cause is His cause, her losses are His losses, and her victories His triumphs. From this point of view the history of the Church is the direct continuation of Our Lord's public ministry, and the late Monsignor Benson in a brilliant book drew an elaborate parallel between Christ's life in His human Body in Palestine and His life through these nineteen centuries in His mystical Body, the Church.

At all events, whether the history of the Catholic Church be regarded from this standpoint or viewed only as that of "the most wonderful structure that the powers of human mind and soul have yet reared," it is a subject which no educated and reflecting mind can afford to ignore.

· · · · · · · · ·

When the History of the Church by the eminent Benedictine, Dom Charles Poulet, of the Congregation of Solesmes, first appeared in France, in 1926, it attracted favorable attention as a scholarly, well-rounded, and very readable exposition of a great theme. Its two volumes offered a happy medium between the brief, hurried, and often desperately dry accounts in the ordinary one-volume manuals of Church History and the inordinate demands upon a reader's time made by the longer and fuller works in seven or more volumes. Dr. Raemers has rendered a notable service in bringing out Dom Poulet's work in English translation, with some additions and adaptations to render it more useful to American readers. In this form it is particularly to be commended to teachers and students in colleges and seminaries; but it should also draw the attention of far wider circles, of all those readers, Catholic and non-Catholic, who desire, through a thoroughly reliable, always interesting, fairly detailed but not too prolix textbook, to familiarize themselves with the unique history of the Catholic Church.

ROBERT HOWARD LORD
(Sometime Professor of History at Harvard University)
St. John's Seminary,
Brighton, Mass.

TABLE OF CONTENTS

SECOND PERIOD

THE PAGAN EMPIRE
FROM TRAJAN'S RESCRIPT TO THE EDICT OF MILAN (111–313)

SECTION I

THE SECOND CENTURY. PERIOD OF THE ANTONINES

SECTION II

THE THIRD CENTURY. END OF THE PERSECUTIONS (203–313)

THIRD PERIOD

THE CHRISTIAN EMPIRE
FROM THE CONVERSION OF CONSTANTINE TO THAT OF CLOVIS (313–496)

SECTION I

THE FOURTH CENTURY

PART II

THE MIDDLE AGES

FIRST PERIOD

THE MEROVINGIAN EPOCH (496–714)

SECTION I

THE SIXTH CENTURY

PART III

BEGINNINGS OF THE MODERN PERIOD

FIRST PERIOD

THE GALLICAN CRISIS
FROM THE ADVENT OF BONIFACE VIII TO THE OPENING OF THE COUNCIL OF
FLORENCE (1294–1438)

SECOND PERIOD

THE BEGINNINGS OF THE RENAISSANCE (1438–1517)

TEXTS AND DOCUMENTS

PART I

INTRODUCTORY CHAPTER

I. THE CHURCH

The Church is a living thing: she is the Man-God uniting the entire human race with Himself by grace. In the words of Bossuet, "the Church is Jesus Christ, but Jesus Christ overflowing and communicating Himself to men."

The Church is the only institution in this world that will not die, because eternity itself is her life-giving principle. She is vested, moreover, with power to renew the face of the earth. History is ever attesting the fact that the marks of the Church point to the presence in her constitution of the supernatural and the divine, and that these marks demonstrate her absolute supremacy in satisfying those innate intellectual cravings which all men have for religion.

Holiness, which is the purpose and basis of all the other marks of the Church, finds its natural habitat within her precincts. The succeeding centuries have always known the Church to be indissolubly united to her Head. They have watched her gather to her bosom all the nations of the earth, in unity of belief, government, and worship. They have seen her push forward where men hesitated to tread, turn to her own advantage almost insurmountable obstacles, and accomplish feats that no purely human power could achieve. The protection and favor of the great is no explanation of her success, for all arguments to the contrary are merely superficial or more apparent than real. She has imposed her theological views without resorting to violence, and yet, throughout all her dogmatic and moral controversies, she has maintained an attitude of relentless intransigence. She alone knows human nature, and she alone has succeeded in dealing with it. Established upon a foundation which, in the eyes of the world, was the quintessence of weakness and instability, she became almost at once the undisputed ruler of the universe and the guide of its destinies. Countless persecutions have not been able to shake the God-given confidence which her members had in final victory. "All things exist for the sake of the Church." This principle will shed an explanatory ray of light on many of the events that have taken place in the course of her existence. In retracing the different steps of her growth and development, we shall be forcibly reminded of the luminous comparisons made by her Founder: "The kingdom of heaven is like to a grain of mustard seed, which a man took and sowed in his field. . . . To a leaven, which a woman took and hid in three measures of meal, until the whole was leavened." [1]

The Church is still growing. It has been correctly remarked that she re-enacts throughout the course of her existence the successive stages in the life of her Founder, of whom the Gospel tells us that "He advanced in wisdom, and age, and grace with God and men." [2] It is not that the Incarnation of the Son of God admits of stages, because the Incarnate Word was perfect from the very beginning, but rather that the God-Man communicated the fruits of His sacred humanity to man only in time.

We can observe a parallel growth in the Church. The young plant develops into a tree, and the child attains to manhood without undergoing any substantial change. Both advance towards perfection in the measure warranted by their essence. Christianity is of God. It is the authentic and definitive religion of man on earth, and the end of time will be but a complete vindication of this fact. Religion is the relation between man and God. But God is immutable and human nature cannot change its essence. Hence, the Christian religion must have been, and actually was, perfect in its origin, but perfect with that relative perfection which is paralleled in the human perfection of the newly-born babe. And though, in the opinion of the Doctors of the Church, the fruits of grace were more abundant in the first centuries than they will ever be again, the Church is still endowed with the ability to grow in perfection. She grows and develops precisely because the human element in her is susceptible of being perfected. Narrowing down our statement to dogmas, and so brushing aside, by one sweep, all the tenets of the pernicious doctrine of Modernism, we can rightfully affirm that she grows and develops in the terms of a truth which becomes better and better known as the years come and go.

[1] Matt. 13, 31 and 33.
[2] Luke 2, 52.

The outstanding purpose of a History of the Church is to assemble the testimony of this very evident and very mysterious growth, to enrich Christian wisdom with the experience of the past centuries, and to light up the ways of Divine Providence, which, if they are followed, are sure to lead man to his eternal destiny.

II. DIVISIONS OF CHURCH HISTORY

We could discuss this subject indefinitely, but shall immediately set aside as purely arbitrary all the classical divisions. The fall of Rome does not mark the end of Christian antiquity, nor does that of Constantinople bring the Middle Ages to a close. Events such as these belong rather to secular history. Moreover, they were virtually realized long before the dates indicated.

Christian antiquity may be divided into three periods:

1. The Primitive Church.
2. The Pagan Empire, the period of the persecutions, from the rescript of the Emperor Trajan to the edict of Milan (111-313).
3. The Christian Empire, embracing the period of the great heresies, from the conversion of Constantine to that of Clovis (313-496).

The Baptism of the Frankish chieftain heralded the conversion of the barbarian races, and at the same time inaugurated a new epoch in the history of the Church, because these new races were quick to fill the place left vacant by the peoples of the old Byzantine world.

The Middle Ages may be divided into four epochs:

1. The Merovingian Epoch (496-714).
2. The Carolingian Epoch (714-887).
3. The Feudal Epoch (tenth and eleventh centuries).
4. Christendom (twelfth and thirteenth centuries).

The conflict between Boniface VIII and Philip the Fair ushered in the modern period. The tragedy of Anagni both symbolized and demonstrated the victory of the civil over the ecclesiastical power. The blow administered to the aged Pontiff by Colonna signalized secular emancipation. Thereafter, the Middle Ages and the Sovereign Pontiff were both in the throes of death.

Modern Church History may be divided into four periods:

1. The Fourteenth and Fifteenth Centuries (1294-1517).

2. The Beginnings of the Reformation (1517-1559).

3. The Wars of Religion (1559-1648).

4. The Seventeenth and Eighteenth Centuries.

The Contemporary Epoch of Church History opened with the year 1789.

Church histories are not lacking either in this country or abroad. But nearly all have their drawbacks as well as their excellencies. The chief merit of German texts seems to lie in their sound critical sense and their authentic information. But they are desperately dry, and their method is analytic and genetic rather than synthetic. In one bulky chapter they cover a lengthy period of four or five centuries, their chief aim being to give cross-sections of the external life of the Church, heresies, institutions, liturgy, and art. It is easy enough to follow the steps in the evolution of each subject, but it is rather difficult to form anything like a precise impression of one century or one generation, and to perceive at a glance the synchronism of men and events.

The chief merit of French texts, like all other works undertaken by writers of this nation, seems to lie in their precise method. Their texts are scholarly, but if we may be permitted to point out one defect, it is that of provincialism.

There is a better pedagogical method than these. It follows the chronological order, and endeavors to give comprehensive views of periods not exceeding a span of fifty years. An effort is made to concentrate upon one definite epoch of Church History coinciding with the life of some one of the great saints, as, for instance, St. Augustine, or upon one pontificate, such as that of Gregory the Great, or Nicholas I. This is the plan followed by the more lengthy manuals, and even by high-school text-books of secular history. It would appear to be the only logical method for a course in Church History that aims at something more than a mere tabulation of dates and events.[1]

III. SOURCES OF CHURCH HISTORY

1. Collections of Inscriptions and Christian Paintings. J. B.

---

[1] Professor Jordan, of the Sorbonne, scores a popular method of teaching history which, if carried to excess, may finally become a veritable scourge in high-school and college education. It consists in completely isolating the great questions of history, and in taking them out of their setting for the purpose of studying them in their logical development. No regard is had for the fact that historical events are in a constant flux, and that, if we are influenced by the past, we are influenced even more by the events in the midst of which we live.

DE ROSSI, *Inscriptiones christianae urbis Romae VII saeculo antiquiores*, 2 vols., Rome, 1861–88; Suppl. edit. J. GATTI, fasc. I, Rome, 1915; Nova series, edit. A. SILVAGNI, t. I, Rome, 1922.—E. LE BLANT, *Inscriptions chrétiennes de la Gaule*, 3 vols., 1856–92 (re-edit. 1923).—J. B. DE ROSSI, *Roma Sotteranea*, 3 vols., Rome, 1864–77.—J. WILPERT, *Die Malereien d. Katakomben Roms*, 2 vols., 1903; *Die röm. Mosaiken u. Malereien der altkirchl. Bauten vom 4–13 Jahrh.*, 4 vols., 1916–17.—F. CABROL and H. LECLERCQ, *Dictionnaire d'arch. chrét. et de liturgie*, since 1907.

2. **Pontifical Acts and Documents. Biographies of the Popes.** *Pontificum Romanorum a S. Clemente I usque ad S. Leonem M. Epistolae genuinae*, edit., P. CONSTANT, 1721, edit., SCHOENEMANN, Gottingae, 1796; *a S. Hilario usque ad S. Hormisdam* (461–523), edit., Thiel, Braunsberg, 1867.—*Regesta Pont. Rom. ab condita Ecclesia ad a. 1198*, edit., PH. JAFFÉ, 1851; edit. 2, cur. F. KALTENBRUNNER, P. EWALD, S. LOEWENFELD, 2 vols., 1885–88; ab a. 1198 ad a. 1304, edit., A. POTTHAST, 2 vols., 1874–75.—Supplement to Jaffé: J. V. PFLUGK-HARTTUNG, *Acta Pontificum Romanorum* (up to the year 1198), 3 vols., 1881–88.

The registers of the Popes of the thirteenth and fourteenth centuries have been published in part by the members of the French College in Rome.— For the contemporary period, *Acta Apostolicae Sedis*, Rome (from 1909 on). —*The Bullarium Romanum*, edit. Coquelines (19 vols., Rome, 1739–44) extends as far as the year 1740, and even as far as the reign of Pius VIII, if we add the supplement to this work, 15 vols., Prato, 1843–67.—For the biographies of the Popes see *Liber Pontificalis*, edit., TH. MOMMSEN in the *Monumenta Germaniae*, 1898; edit., L. DUCHESNE, 2 vols., 1886–1892 (in process of reprinting).—*Vitae Pontificum Romanorum ab ex. saec. IX usque ad finem saec. XIII*, edit., WATTERICH, 2 vols., Leipzig, 1862.—P. F. KEHR, *Regesta Pontificum Romanorum*.

3. **Collections of Councils.** LABBE and COSSART, *Sacrosancta Concilia*, 17 vols., Paris, 1674; edit., Coleti, 23 vols., Venice, 1728–34; suppl., 6 vols. (up to the year 1720), edit., Mansi, Lucae, 1748–52. J. HARDOUIN, *Acta Conciliorum et epistolae decretales ac constitutiones Summorum Pontificum*, 12 vols. (up to the year 1714), Paris, 1715.—J. D MANSI, *Sacrorum conciliorum nova et amplissima collectio*, 31 vols. (up to the year 1439), Florence and Venice, 1759–98; new edition continued down to the time of the Vatican Council, 52 vols., Paris, 1901–24. (For an estimate of the value of Mansi's collection, see DOM H. QUENTIN, *Mansi et les grandes collections conciliaires*, 1900).—*Collectio Lacensis, Acta et Decreta S. Conciliorum recentiorum*, 7 vols., (1682–1870, 1870–90. See HEFELE-LECLERCQ, *Histoire des conciles*, 16 vols., 1907–21.

4. **Liturgy.**—E. RENAUDOT, *Liturgiae orient. collectio*, 2 vols., 1716.— L. A. MURATORI, *Liturgia Romana vetus*, 2 vols., Venice, 1748.—J. A. ASSEMANI, *Codex liturgicus ecclesiae univ.*, 13 vols., edit. nova, 1922.—DURAND,

Rationale divinorum officiorum, Naples, 1866.—MARTÈNE, *De antiquis eccl. ritibus*, 4 vols., Antwerp, 1736.—CABROL and LECLERCQ, *Monumenta ecclesiae liturgica*, 1 vol., 1900.—*Auctuarium Solesmense*, Series liturgica, 1 vol., Solesmes, 1900.—U. CHEVALIER, *Repertorium hymnologicum*, 6 vols., Brussels, 1892–1920.

5. **Acts of the Martyrs and Lives of the Saints.** SURIUS, *De probatis sanctorum vitis*, 6 vols., Colon., 1570–75; Ratisbon, 1859.—B. MOMBRITIUS, *Sanctuarium seu Vitae sanctorum* (1477), edit. nova, 2 vols., 1910.— BOLLANDUS, etc., *Acta Sanctorum*, Antwerp, 1643 ff. The biographies are arranged according to the order followed by the Roman Calendar; from 1882, *Analecta Bollandiana*, critical review of hagiography. (See H. DELEHAYE, *A travers trois siècles. L'oeuvre des Bollandistes*, Brussels, 1920).—The Bollandists have edited *Bibliotheca Hagiographica Latina*, 2 vols., Brussels, 1898–1901; suppl., 1911 (list of all the lives of the saints published in Latin); also, *Bibliotheca Hagiographica Graeca*, 1909; *Bibliotheca Hagiographica Orientalis*, 1910.—J. MABILLON, *Acta SS. O. S. Bened.*, 9 vols., (500–1100), 1688–1701. *Martyrologium Hieronymianum*, editions by de Rossi and Duchesne (*Acta Sanct.*, Nov. t. II), 1894.—*Martyrologium Romanum*, edit. typica Vaticana, Rome, 1914; edit. prima post typ., Rome, 1922 (See *Anal. Boll.*, t. XLII, 1924, pp. 387–406).—LECLERCQ, *Les Martyrs*. Collection of authentic documents on the martyrs from the earliest times.—F. G. HOLLWECK, *Biographical Dictionary of the Saints*, St. Louis, 1924.

6. **Patrology.** *Maxima Bibliotheca Veterum Patrum* etc., 27 vols., Ludg., 1677–1707 (up to the XVI century).—*Bibliotheca Veterum Patrum*, edit. A. GALLAND, 14 vols. (up to the year 1200), Venice, 1765–81.—*Patrologiae Cursus Completus*, accurante J. P. MIGNE: 1. *Patrologia Latina*, 221 tomi (218–21 Indices) *usque ad Innocentium III*, 1844–64; 2. *Patrologia Graeca*, 161 tomi, *usque ad s. XV*, 1857–66; F. CAVALLERA, *Patr. Cursus Compl.*, series graeca, Indices, 1912.—*Corpus Scriptorum Latinorum*, edited by the Vienna Academy since 1866.—*Monumenta Germaniae Historica, Auctores antiquissimi*, Berlin, 13 vols., 1877–1898.—*Die griechischen christlichen Schriftsteller der ersten drei Jahrhunderte*, edited by the Berlin Academy at Leipzig, since 1897.—*Texte und Untersuchungen zur Geschichte der altchristlichen Literatur*, a collection gathered under the direction of the Leipzig Academy, 1st series 1882–1897, 15 vols.; 2nd series, 1896–1906, 15 vols.; 3rd series (A. HARNACK and C. SCHMIDT) 1907 ff. *Texts and Studies*, a collection undertaken and directed by the Cambridge Academy (J. A. ROBINSON), Cambridge, 1891 ff.—*Patrologia Syriaca*, by R. GRAFFIN, 2 vols., 1894 ff.— *Patrologia Orientalis*, by R. GRAFFIN and F. NAU, Paris, 1903 ff. (a continuation of the preceding one). *Corpus Scriptorum Christianorum Orientalium*, by J. B. CHABOT, J. GUIDI, H. HYVERNAT, B. CARRA DE VAUX, 1903 ff.

For collections of more popular Acts of the Martyrs and Lives of the Saints: *Textes et Documents pour l'étude historique du christianisme*, by H.

Hemmer and P. Lejay, 1904 ff. (texts, translation, introduction and notes).—
SS. *Patrum Opuscula Selecta,* by H. Hurter, Innsbruck, 1st series 1868–1885,
48 vols.; 2nd series 1884–1892, 6 vols.—*Cambridge Patristic Texts,* A. Mason,
Cambridge, since 1899, etc.

7. **Collections for the Use of Special Histories.**—*Rerum Italicarum Scriptores,* edit. L. Muratori, Med., 1723–51, 25 vols.; re-edit. Carducci
and Fiorini, Citta di Castello, 1900.—*Recueil des historiens des Gaules et de
la France,* Dom Bouquet, 1738, 23 vols.; new edit. by L. Delisle, 19 vols.,
1869–90; new series, 1899–1906, 7 vols.—*Monumenta Germaniae Historica,*
edit. G. H. Pertz.—*Rerum Britannicarum Medii Aevi Scriptores,* London,
1856–96.—*Corpus Script. Historiae Byzant.,* edit. Niebuhr etc., 50 vols., 1829–
97.

Certain collections will be of help in directing the reader to source ma-
terials. A. Potthast, *Bibliotheca Historica Medii Aevi,* 1867–68; 2nd edit.
1896.—W. Wattenbach, *Deutschlands Geschichtsquellen im M.-A. bis zur
Mitte des 13. Jahrhunderts,* 1858, 2 vols.; 7th edit., 1904.—F. C. Dahlmann,
Quellenkunde d. deutschen Gesch., 8th edit. 1912.—O. Lorenz, *Deutschlands
Geschichtsquellen im M.-A. von d. Mitte d. 13. Jh. bis z. Ende d. 14. Jh.,*
2 vols., 1886–87.—U. Chevalier, *Répertoire des sources hist. du moyen âge.
Bio-bibliographie,* 2 vols., 1905–07; *Topo-bibliographie,* 2 vols., 1894–1903.—
G. Monod, *Les sources de l'histoire de France,* 1888.—A. Molinier, *Les
sources de l'histoire de France:* 1st part: *The Origins of the Italian Wars,*
6 vols.; 2nd part: *The Sixteenth Century,* 4 vols.; 3rd part: *The Seventeenth
Century,* 5 vols.—Ch. Gross, *The Sources and Literature of English History*
(up to the year 1485), 2nd edit., 1917.—H. Hurter, *Nomenclator Literarius
Theologiae Catholicae,* Innsbruck, 3rd edit., 1903.

8. **Recent Enchiridia.** H. Denzinger, *Enchiridion Symbolorum, defi-
nitionum et declarationum de rebus fidei et morum,* Friburgi B.—C. Kirch,
Enchiridion Fontium Historiae Ecclesiasticae Antiquae, Freiburg i. B., 1910.
—M. J. Rouët de Journel, *Enchiridion Patristicum,* Freiburg i. B., 5th edit.,
1922.—E. Cavallera, *Thesaurus doctrinae catholicae ex documentis magisterii
ecclesiastici,* 1920.—E. Amann, *Le dogme catholique dans les Pères de l'Eglise,*
1922.

IV. GENERAL BIBLIOGRAPHY OF CHURCH HISTORY

1. **Auxiliary Sciences.**—Mabillon, *De re diplomatica,* 1681; 2nd edit.,
1709.—E. Reusens, *Eléments de paléographie,* Louvain, 1899.—M. Prou,
Manuel de paléographie latine et française, 4th edit., 1924.—A Giry, *Manuel
de diplomatique,* 1894.—De Mas Latrie, *Trésor de chronologie, d'histoire et
de géographie pour l'étude et l'emploi des documents du moyen âge.*—Ch.
du Fresne du Cange, *Glossarium ad scriptores mediae et infimae latinitatis,*
1678; edit. Favre, 10 vols., Niort, 1882–87.—D. de Sainte Marthe et B.

HAURÉAU, *Gallia Christiana*, 16 vols., 1715–1865;—J. H. ALBANÈS and U. CHEVALIER, *Gallia Christiana Novissima*, 7 vols., 1899–1920.—L. DUCHESNE, *Fastes épiscopaux de l'ancienne Gaule*, 3 vols., 1907–15.—M. LE QUIEN, *Oriens Christianus*, 3 vols., 1740.—L. LEMMENS, *Hierarchia Latina Orientis* (1622–1922), 2 vols., Rome, 1923–24.—BEAUNIER, *Recueil historique des évêchés, abbayes et prieurés de France*, new edit., (*Archives dearchévêchés, la France monastique*), 1906.—P. GAMS, *Series Episcoporum ecclesiae catholicae*, Ratisbonae, 1873 (Supplement 1879 and 1886).—C. EUBEL, *Hierarchia Catholica medii aevi*, 3 vols., Monast., 1898–1910.—K. HEUSSI and H. MULERT, *Atlas zur K.-G.*, 2nd edit., 1919.—O. WERNER, *Kath. Missionsatlas*, 1885; *Kath. Kirchenatlas*, 1888; *Orbis Terrarum Catholicus, sive totius ecclesiae cath. conspectus geographicus et statisticus*, 1890.—K. STREIT, *Kath. Missionsatlas*, 1906; *Atlas Hierarchicus, descriptio geographica et statistica S. Romanae Ecclesiae*, 1913.

2. **Dictionaries.**—*Dictionnaire de Théologie*, published since 1903 by A. VACANT, continued by E. MANGENOT, then by E. AMANN.—*Dictionnaire d'Archéologie Chrétienne et de Liturgie*, published by F. CABROL and H. LECLERCQ (since 1907).—*Dictionnaire d'Histoire et de Géographie Ecclésiastiques*, published by A. BAUDRILLART, A. VOGT, and M. ROUZIÈS (since 1912).—*Dictionnaire Apologétique de la Foi Catholique*, published by A. D'ALÈS (since 1911).—*Kirchenlexikon oder Encyklopädie der Kath. Theol.*, re-edit. by J. HERGENRÖTHER and F. KAULEN, 12 vols.; new edit., *Lexikon für Theologie und Kirche*, Freiburg i. B., 1930 ff. *Realencyklopädie für Protestantische Theologie und Kirche*, edit. by A. HAUCK, 21 vols., 2nd edit., 1913.—*The Catholic Encyclopedia*, 15 vols., New York, 1907–14; supplement 1922.—W. SMITH and H. WACE, *Dictionary of Christian Biography, Literature, Sects and Doctrines*, 4 vols., London, 1877–87.

3. **Collections of Monographs.**—*La Bibliothèque de l'enseignement de l'histoire ecclésiastique.—Les Saints.—La Pensée Chrétienne.—La Bibliothèque de théologie historique*, published under the direction of the professors of the faculty of theology of the Catholic Institute of Paris.—*Les Études de Théologie historique*, annexed to the above collection.—*Science et Religion.—Les Moralistes Chrétiens* (Texts and Commentaries).—*La Bibliothèque Catholique des Sciences Religieuses*.

4. **Reviews.**—*Revue d'Histoire Ecclésiastique*, University of Louvain, since 1900 (abundant and very methodical bibliographies).—*Revue de l'Histoire de l'Eglise de France*, since 1910.—*Revue des Questions Historiques*, since 1866.—*Revue de l'Orient Chrétien.—Echos d'Orient* (by the Assumptionist Fathers), since 1897.—*Bulletin d'Ancienne Littérature et d'Archéologie Chrétienne*, by P. DE LABRIOLLE, since 1911.—*Bulletin de Littérature Ecclésiastique*, Institut Catholique de Toulouse, since 1899.—*Revue Bénédictine*, since 1884.—*Revue d'Histoire et de Littérature Religieuses*, 1896–1907.— *Analecta Bollandiana*, since 1882.—*Revue des Sciences Religieuses* (Faculty

of Catholic Theology at Strasbourg), since 1921.—*Recherches de Science Religieuse* (Jesuits), since 1910.—*Revue Apologétique*, since 1905.—We might add a few secular reviews such as the *Moyen Age* and the *Revue Historique*.

5. **General Encyclopedias of History.**—E. Lavisse and Rambaud, *Histoire Générale du IVe siécle a nos jours*, 12 vols.—*Peuples et Civilisations*. —*Histoire Générale*, published under the direction of L. Halphen and Ph. Sagnac.—*Histoire du Monde*, published under the direction of E. Cavaignac. —*Bibliothèque de Synthèse Historique.*—*L'Évolution de l'Humanité*, published under the direction of H. Berr, 25 vols.—*Histoire Générale*, published under the direction of C. Glotz.—*The Cambridge Medieval History.*—*The Cambridge Modern History.*

6. **General Encyclopedias of Church History.**—Le Nain de Tillemont, *Mémoires pour servir a l'histoire ecclésiastique des dix premiers siècles*, 16 vols., Paris, 1693 (of unquestioned utility).—Rohrbacher, *Histoire Universelle de l'Eglise Catholique*, 29 vols., 2nd edit., 1849–1853; continued up to 1889 by J. Chantrel and Dom Chamard, 9th edit., 1903 (a little out of date).—Darras, *Histoire Générale de l'Eglise*, 25 vols., 1857; continued by Bareille and Fèvre, 1879–1907 (not quite up to date).—Fern. Mourret, *Histoire Générale de l'Eglise*, now in process of being translated by Rev. Newton Thompson (*A History of the Catholic Church*), Herder, St. Louis.— J. Hergenröther, *Handbuch der allgemeinen Kirchengeschichte*, 6th edit., revised by J. P. Kirsch, 4 vols., Freiburg i. B., 1924 ff.—G. Goyau, *Vue Générale de l'Histoire de la papauté dans le Vatican; Les Papes et la Civilisation*, by G. Goyau, A. Pératé, and P. Fabre.—A Dufourcq, *L'Avenir du christianisme: Histoire Ancienne de l'Eglise*, 5 vols.; *Histoire Moderne*, 2 vols.

Among the Histories of the Ancient Church we have: L. Duchesne, *Histoire Ancienne de l'Eglise*, 3 vols., 1907–1910; *The Early History of Christianity* (of questionable value).—Ayer, *Source Book of Ancient Church History.*—H. M. Gwatkin, *Early Church History* (up to the year 313), 2 vols., London, 1909 (Protestant).—B. J. Kidd, *A History of the Church to* A. D. *461*, 3 vols., Oxford, 1922 (Protestant).—J. Zeiller, *L'Empire Romain et l'Eglise*, 1928 (in *Histoire du Monde*, under the direction of E. Cavaignac).— H. von Schubert, *Geschichte der christlichen Kirche im Frühmittelalter*, 2 vols., Tübingen, 1917–21 (Protestant).

Among the Histories of the Church in Germany, we have the classical work of A. Hauck, *Kirchengeschichte Deutschlands*, 6 vols., Leipzig, 1887–1912 (Protestant).

Among the Histories of the Church in England, we have *A History of the English Church*, edit. by W. Stephens and W. Hunt, London, 1901 ff. (Protestant).

Among the Histories of the Church in France, we have: Jager, *Histoire de l'Eglise Catholique de France*, 19 vols., 1862–1873 (out of date).—P. Lelièvre, *Histoire de la France Catholique*, 1926.—G. Goyau, *Histoire Re-*

ligieuse, in *Histoire de la Nation Française,* under the direction of G. Hanotaux.

Among the Histories of the Church in the United States we have: J. G.
Shea, *History of the Catholic Church in the United States,* 4 vols.—Spauld-
ing, *Catholic Builders of the Nation,* 5 vols.—Murray, *Popular History of
the Catholic Church in the United States* (out of date).—P. Guilday, *The
Roman Catholic Church in the United States; National Pastorals of the
American Hierarchy; The Life and Times of John England; The Life and
Times of John Carroll; A History of the Councils of Baltimore,* etc. Dr.
Guilday is also the author of the following: *Church Historians, Introduction
to Church Historians,* and the *English Catholic Refugees on the Continent,*
1558–1795.

For a general bibliography we suggest the following: J. Alzog, *History of
the Church* (transl. Pabisch and Byrne) 3 vols.—F. S. Betten, *Ancient and
Medieval History.*—B. L. Conway, *Studies in Church History.*—Funk-
Cappadelta, *A Manual of Church History,* 2 vols.—H. Grisar, *History of Rome
and the Popes during the Middle Ages,* 3 vols.—A. Guggenberger, *A General History of the Christian Era,* 3 vols. (out of date).—Lingard-Belloc,
The History of England, 11 vols.—H. K. Mann, *Lives of the Popes in the
Early Middle Ages,* 13 vols.—J. H. Newman, *Historical Sketches,* 3 vols.—
L. J. Paetow, *Guide to the Study of Medieval History.*—R. Parsons, *Studies
in Church History,* 6 vols.—L. Pastor, *Lives of the Popes from the Close of
the Middle Ages,* 16 vols.—G. Stebbing, *The Story of the Catholic Church,*
4th edit.—J. J. Walsh, *The World's Debt to the Catholic Church* and *The
Thirteenth, Greatest of Centuries.*—T. Gilmartin, *Manual of Church History,*
2 vols., Dublin.—James MacCaffrey, *History of the Catholic Church in the
Nineteenth Century* (1789–1908), 2 vols.

PART I

The Ancient Church

FIRST PERIOD

The Primitive Church

CHAPTER I

THE BIRTH OF CHRISTIANITY; THE EVANGELIZATION OF THE PALESTINIAN JEWS

I. The Setting : Palestinian Judaism. Christianity was first preached in Judaea, and then throughout the Roman Empire, which comprised the civilized countries of the world, grouped around the great Mediterranean basin.

Palestine is a strip of land reaching out between North Africa on the one side, and Asia on the other. Its geographical position, however, made it a very desirable possession for all the conquerors in ancient times. For a number of years it was torn between an Egyptian alliance on the south, and an Assyrian alliance on the north, and its history was one of continual unrest. But never once did Jahveh relinquish His hold on the Jewish people, and never once did He cease to give them His protection. In the year 590 B. C. a great catastrophe befell the Jews: they were carried away into captivity by the Assyrians and the Chaldeans. Their misfortune was of short duration, however, for the Persians soon loomed on the horizon as the saviours of Israel. In the year 539 B. C., Cyrus captured the city of Babylon, set the Jews free, and permitted them to rebuild their Temple. The Greek rule of the Ptolemies and the Seleucidae proved no less generous, but Antiochus Epiphanes (164 B. C.), seemingly in an attempt to Hellenize the Jews, made a complete break with the political methods of the past. Under the leadership of the Maccabees, the Jews rose in rebellion, and succeeded in enforcing their rights. Judaea was freed and continued to be governed by the Maccabees (Asmonean dynasty) up to the time of the Roman intervention.

In the year 39, Antony substituted Antipater, the Idumean, in place of the Maccabees. His son, Herod the Great, succeeded him, and married Mariamne, granddaughter of Hyrcanus II, the last Asmonean king. Herod made an attempt to restore the national religion of the Jews to its former splendor. Under the insulting protection of the Romans, he rebuilt the Temple, in one of the angles of which he erected the *Turris Antonia,* surmounted by a golden eagle. At the death of Herod the Great (4 B.C.) Palestine was divided between his three sons: Archelaus assumed control of Judaea; Herod Antipas, of Galilee and Perea; and Philip, of Iturea. A number of complaints, apparently coming from some of the subjects of Archelaus, reached the ears of the Emperor in Rome. Augustus annexed Judaea to the Empire, and subjected it to the authority of a procurator, who took up his residence at Caesarea. Save for a short period of three years (Herod Agrippa, 42–44), Judaea remained in this state up to the time of the destruction of Jerusalem by Titus, in the year 70 A. D. The sceptre had really gone out from Judaea, therefore, and according to the prophecy, the Messias was soon to come. Rome seemed willing to allow her subjects some sort of autonomy, and so we witness the revival of the authority of the Sanhedrin, the supreme court of justice, presided over by the high priest and made up of seventy members taken from among the priests and the ancients or scribes. The ever-growing importance of this Jewish tribunal and the particular care taken by the Roman procurators not to ruffle the spirit of Jewish religious nationalism, explain, in part, the turn of events at the time of the Passion of Christ.

If we except the Essenes, a sect of strict ascetics who gathered in cenobitic groups around the shores of the Dead Sea, two factions ruled the Jewish masses: the Pharisees and the Sadducees. Recruited from among the learned and the scribes, the Pharisees were the conservatives. As their name indicates (*Perushim* = separated), the Pharisees were the personification of Jewish particularism. Hence, their attachment to the literal practice of the law in its minutest details. Hillel and Shammai had respectively commented on this law, the former with severity, the latter with grace and indulgence. The Pharisees were the zealous defenders of the Jewish traditions, but they were so zealous that these traditions now existed in a state of heartless rigor and routine.

The Sadducees were the liberals. Recruited from among the more prominent priestly families, they grouped themselves into a levitical aristocracy, the distinctive characteristic of which was a grasping spirit for the office of the high priest and the principal functions of the Temple.

Satisfied with a régime which protected their interests, they sought to diminish the distance separating the Jews from the Romans, and to minimize Jewish national particularism.

The Herodians, too, were opportunists. They looked for the return of a native dynasty under Roman protection. The Jewish race was forced to establish a number of necessary contacts with other races, and yet it always maintained a spirit of relentless separatism. Imperial worship obtained admission everywhere else, but never gained an entrance into Jerusalem, because of rescripts granted in favor of the Jews.

II. The Preaching of the Gospel. The Community at Jerusalem. The Jewish ideal would admit of no foreign admixture, and yet it was far from being clear and explicit. The Jews expected a warlike Messias, who would place them at the head of the nations. Shortly before the year 750 A. U. C., however, Jesus was born at Bethlehem in Judaea, set about preaching the Kingdom of Heaven, and stipulated conditions for entrance into this kingdom which the Jews had not anticipated. These conditions were the reception of the Sacraments and the practice of the three virtues of poverty, humility, and charity. Peter recognized Him as "the Messias, the Son of the living God," and his belief was shared by the other Apostles and disciples, even though they still retained hope in some earthly and national prosperity. Hated by the Pharisees, whose hypocritical formalism He was forever scoring, and whose disregard for a suffering Messias He openly condemned; and marked by the Sadducees as an agitator who would finish by arousing the suspicions of the Roman authorities, Jesus was condemned by the Sanhedrin, presided over by the high priest, Caiphas. Pontius Pilate, the Roman procurator, upheld the Roman policy of neutrality in matters of this kind, but not being able to withstand the popular demand, condemned Jesus to die on the Cross.

Two great events explain the success achieved by the early Church: the Resurrection of Christ and the Descent of the Holy Ghost on Pentecost Day. If Christ had not risen from the dead, no one would have believed in Him; and if the Holy Ghost had not descended upon the Apostles, they would not have had the courage to go out and preach the new religion. Assembled in Jerusalem from all the countries of the world, to celebrate the feast of Pentecost, the Jews flocked together at the noise of the mighty wind which accompanied the descent of the Holy Spirit. Peter delivered such a touching speech on this occasion that 3000 embraced Christianity, and when, a few days later, the same Apostle cured a lame man at the gate of the Temple, the community increased to 5000.

The early converts still adhered to Jewish ideals and practices, but they were strong in their affirmation that Jesus was the Messias, and based their belief on His Passion and Resurrection. In religious matters, therefore, they were revolutionaries. Summoned to appear before the Grand Council, Peter and John were charged to hold their peace, but their only answer to all threats was: "We cannot but speak of the things which we have seen and heard." [1] Fearing a new insurrection, the Grand Council set them free. A few days later, all the Apostles were cast into prison, but during the night they were delivered by an angel, at once resumed their preaching, and were arrested and dragged before the Sanhedrin. Through Peter, their mouthpiece and head, they emphatically declared: "We ought to obey God rather than men." [2] Thanks to the weighty influence of Gamaliel, they escaped with their lives, but not until they had been scourged. Shortly afterwards, Stephen, the deacon, formulated his profession of faith in the divinity of Jesus before these same Jews, fulminating his accusations and reproaches against this "race of stiffnecks and uncircumcised in heart and ears." He was stoned to death, and his execution marked the first act of a bitter persecution. The Apostles remained in Jerusalem, but the faithful scattered throughout Judaea, Samaria, and even Phenicia and Syria. Philip preached the Gospel in Samaria, and conferred Baptism upon many souls, among them Queen Candace's treasurer, an Ethiopian eunuch, whose home at Caesarea became one of the centers of the new faith.

In the year 42, the persecution was resumed with new vigor. Herod Agrippa, a grandson of Herod the Great, had been made king of Judaea by favor of the Emperor Claudius. In an effort to gain popularity, he delivered the faithful into the hands of the Jewish orthodox party. James the Greater suffered martyrdom, and Peter was to be executed after the feast of the Passover, but was miraculously saved by an angel. Herod Agrippa died in the year 44, and the procurator Cuspius Fadus, who succeeded him, put an end to the persecution. Rome had not yet taken sides against the Church as such, which she regarded as merely another syna-

[1] Acts 4, 20.
[2] Acts 5, 2.

gogue in need of her protection. James the Less governed the Church of Jerusalem. This small community already possessed its hierarchy: Simon Peter was regarded as the head, and next in order of rank came the other Apostles. In their first fervor, the early Christians possessed their goods in common, but although they were "one heart and one soul, there arose a murmuring of the Greeks against the Hebrews, because their widows were neglected in the daily administration." [1] Then the Apostles chose seven men to care for the material welfare of the brethren, preferring to give themselves over continually to prayer and the ministry of the word. This step marked the institution of the order of deaconship. A little later, an intermediary order was created, and the persons who received it were termed *presbyteri*. They consisted, as the word indicates, of elderly members of the flock, and their chief duties were to assist the Apostles, and to act in the capacity of an advisory body.

III. The Jewish Question: The Baptism of Cornelius. The question of the evangelization of the Gentiles very soon came up for solution, and it involved another of equal importance. Was circumcision to remain the necessary condition for Christian as well as for Jewish initiation? This question had a doctrinal aspect, because, if circumcision remained necessary, faith in Jesus Christ was not sufficient for salvation; and if it was no longer necessary, Judaism as a religion was manifestly relegated to the background. Moreover, if Christianity subjected its followers to the practice of circumcision, it could no longer lay claim to catholicity, for the Greeks and the Romans would never consent to adopt the practices of a people who were as contemptible as they were insignificant. In this dilemma, Christ spoke to the head of His Church. About the year 40, Peter moved his headquarters to Jaffa. Here it was made known to him in a vision that the Jewish law which forbade the use of food considered impure was abolished, and also that the pagans could be purified. After this revelation the voice of God commanded Peter to repair to the house of Cornelius, the centurion, in Caesarea. Cornelius was received into the Church with his entire family. For the first time in history, a Gentile was made a member of the Church without entering through the doors of the Synagogue. The incident caused some consternation among the faithful. Peter had to explain, and he strongly insisted that he had only acted in accordance with the orders of the Lord. The

[1] Acts 6, 1.

community in Jerusalem accepted his explanation and the incident filled them with happiness and joy.

TEXTS AND DOCUMENTS

THE DEATH OF HEROD AGRIPPA

Herod Agrippa was exhibiting shows at Caesarea in honor of Claudius. On the second day of the shows he put on a garment made wholly of silver, of wonderful texture, and came into the theatre early in the morning. There the silver, lit up by the beating of the sun's first rays upon it, shone forth marvelously, and, by its flashing, cast fear and terror upon those who gazed at him. And straightway his flatterers cried out, one from one place, and another from another (not for his good), addressing him as a god; and they added: "Deal kindly with us; if hitherto we have revered thee as a man, yet henceforth we confess thee superior to mortal nature." The king rebuked them not, nor rejected their impious flattery. . . . A great pain arose in his belly, from the outset most violent. Looking, therefore, upon his friends, he said: "I, your god, am now bidden to depart this life, for so Providence confutes the lying words even now spoken of me; and I who was by you called immortal, am now hurried away to death."

JOSEPHUS, *The Jewish Antiquities*, 18, 8.

QUESTIONS

1. Who were the Maccabees?
2. Which prophet foretold that the sceptre would go out from Juda?
3. What is the difference between a Hebrew, a Jew, and an Israelite?
4. Indicate the terms used to designate Roman representatives in foreign lands, and distinguish between them.
5. What was the authority of the Sanhedrin?
6. What was the end of Pontius Pilate?
7. What do you know of the shrine of St. James at Compostella in Spain?
8. Were there any Sacraments in the Old Law, and was circumcision one of them?
9. How does the Communism of the primitive Church differ from the Communism of the present day?
10. What was the *agape*?

BIBLIOGRAPHY

The Jewish World: E. BEURLIER, *Le monde juif au temps de J.-C. et des apôtres.*—E. STAPFER, *La Palestine au temps de J.-C.,* 1892.—DÖLLINGER, *Paganism and Judaism; The Gentile and the Jew* (transl. N. DARNEL); *The*

First Age of Christianity and the Church (transl. Henry Nutcomb); *Gentile and Jew in the Courts of the Temple of Christ.*—Lagrange, *Le Messianisme chez les Juifs.*—Cohen, *Les Pharisiens,* 2 vols., 1877.—Montet, *Essai sur les origines des partis sadducéen et pharisien,* 1883.—Narbel, *Etude sur le parti pharisien,* 1891.—Prat, art. *Pharisiens,* in *Dict. de la Bible; The Theology of St. Paul,* pp. 33-44 (transl. John L. Stoddard).—Lafaye, *Les Sadducéens,* Lyons, 1904.—Hölscher, *Der Sadducäismus,* Leipzig, 1906.—Lesêtre, art. *Sanhédrin,* in *Dict. de la Bible.*—L. Dennefeld, art. *Judaisme,* in *Dict. de Théol.* —*Cath. Encyl.,* arts. *Pharisees, Sadducees, Essenes.*—Josephus, *The Jewish Antiquities.*—F. Gavin, *Pre-Christian Types of the Sacraments.*

Jesus: Fouard, *The Christ, the Son of God,* (transl. W. Hickey), 2 vols. —Didon, *Jesus Christ,* (transl. B. O'Reilly).—H. Lesêtre, *N.-S. dans son Evangile,* 1892.—Pègues, *J.-C. dans L'Evangile,* 1898.—Jacquier, *Hist. des livres du N. T.,* 2 vols., 1906.—Lepin, *Jésus Messie et Fils de Dieu,* 1907.— Batiffol, *Orphéus et l'Evangile,* 1910; *The Credibility of the Gospel,* (transl. Pollen).—Levesque, *Nos quatres Evangiles,* 1917.—J. Lagrange, *The Gospel according to St. Mark; according to St. Luke,* 1921.—De Grandmaison, art. *Jesus Christ,* in *Dict. d'Apol.*—Dom Delatte, *L'Evangile de N. S. J.-C.,* 2 vols., 1923.—J. Lagrange, *L'Evangile selon saint Jean; selon saint Mathieu; Synopsis Evangelica,* 1927; *L'Evangile de Jésus-Christ,* 1928.—De Grandmaison, *Jesus Christ,* 3 vols., 1930 ff.—Pinard de la Boulaye, *Jésus et l'histoire,* 1929.—Le Camus, *The Life of Christ* (transl. W. Hickey).—Elliott, *Life of Christ.*—Meschler, *The Life of Our Lord Jesus Christ,* 2 vols.

The Primitive Church—The Community at Jerusalem: Döllinger, *The First Age of Christianity and the Church* (French transl. Bayle), Tournai, 1863.—Fouard, *St. Peter and the First Years of Christianity,* 1893.— H. Lesêtre, *La sainte Eglise au temps des apôtres,* 1896.—Le Camus, *L'oeuvre des apôtres,* 3 vols., 1905.—J. Lebreton, *Les origines du dogme de la Trinité.* —Batiffol, *L'Eglise naissante et le catholicisme,* 1909.—Y. De La Brière, art. *L'Eglise,* in *Dict. d'Apol.*—Dublanchy, art. *Eglise,* in *Dict. de Théol.*— Tixeront, *L'Eglise,* in *Conférences apologétiques de Lyon,* 1910.—Janssens, *L'Eglise, fondation historique de Christ* (Coll. *Etudes religieuses,* no. 9).— Fillion, *Saint Pierre* (Coll. *les Saints*), 1906.—E. Jacquier, *Les actes des Apôtres* (Coll. *Etudes bibliques*), 1926.—J. Viteau, *L'institution des diacres et des veuves,* R. H. E., XXII (1926), pp. 513-537.—J. Lebreton, *La vie chrétienne au premier siècle de l'Eglise,* 1927.—A. Lelong, art. *Apostoliques* (Pères), in *Dict. de droit canonique.*—Duchesne, *The Early History of Christianity.*—Shahan, *The Beginnings of Christianity.*—Harnack, *Mission and Expansion of Christianity.*—Gigot, *Outline of New Testament History.*— Rivière, *The Expansion of Christianity in the First Three Centuries,* 1915.— I. Lanslots, *The Primitive Church.*—H. J. Heuser, *From Tarsus to Rome,* 1929.

CHAPTER II

The problem seemed solved. When the Christians scattered before the persecution of the year 42, several among them repaired to Antioch and there converted many Gentiles. The event caused no scandal, and, what is more, Barnabas, a native of Cyprus, was despatched from Jerusalem to assist in the work. Barnabas at once recruited the services of Paul, who was born at Tarsus in Cilicia, but had come to Jerusalem when still a young man to study law at the feet of Gamaliel. Paul inherited none of his Master's spirit of moderation; on the contrary, he was impetuous enough to take part in the martyrdom of Stephen during the persecution of the year 33. When on his way to Damascus with letters from the high priest empowering him to persecute the Christians, he was thrown from his horse, and Christ appeared to him in His risen and glorified Humanity. All this happened in the year 34. Three days after the above-mentioned incident, Paul received Baptism at the hands of Ananias. For a while, he preached in the synagogues of Damascus, but very soon retired into Arabia. It was in the solitude of this country that Christ prepared him for his great mission. After his return to Damascus, he was forced to quit the city very soon in order to escape the persecution of the Jews. He then paid a visit to Jerusalem, where Barnabas introduced him to the faithful, many of whom had assumed an attitude of diffidence towards him. Upon his return to Tarsus, he preached the Gospel in Cilicia and Syria. About the year 42 or 43, Barnabas called him to Antioch to collaborate in the conversion of the Gentiles. "And they conversed there in the church a whole year; and they taught a great multitude, so that at Antioch the disciples were first named Christians."[1] In point of fact, they could no longer be called Jews, since they had renounced the Jewish ceremony of initiation. Paul and Barnabas then resolved to undertake a first apostolic journey, which lasted over a period of four or five years (45–49).

[1] Acts 11, 26.

I. The Environment: The Jews of the Dispersion. Jews who ventured beyond the boundaries of their own native land, met in almost every place with their compatriots grouped in small colonies and scattered throughout the civilized world. The ensemble of all these colonies went under the generic name of the Jews of the Dispersion (διασπορά). At times, these groups assumed very large proportions, and, as a rule, they were to be encountered in sea-ports like Thessalonica, and larger cities like Alexandria and Rome. With their almost inborn understanding of business matters, the Jews of the Dispersion had become extremely rich and influential, so much so that the Roman State, especially after the death of Caesar, did not hesitate to confer upon them very extensive privileges, and even to grant them freedom of worship. The Jews of the Dispersion were still mindful, however, of their home city, and always endeavored to keep in close touch with the Palestinian Jews of Jerusalem. These large and small Jewish ghettos served as so many stopping-off places for Paul and Barnabas, who obtained the use of the synagogues for their sermons and discourses.

A regular clientele of religious devotees grouped themselves around each one of these Jewish communities, apparently attracted hither by the worship of one God. Opposed as they were to circumcision and to the legal prescriptions of Judaism, these persons were labelled merely as "God-fearing" or "God-worshipping men" (φοβούμενοι, σεβόμενοι τὸν θεόν) and since they were regarded by the Jews as still unclean, they could not be admitted beyond the first enclosure of the Temple, and so were called "proselytes of the gate." Some among them, forgetting their natural prejudices, and accepting the law in all its integrity, including even the rite of circumcision, were allowed to share in all the privileges of the race. These were called "proselytes of justice." There is no doubt that these various groups showed themselves more disposed to receive the message of Christianity than any other persons.

The mission of Paul was at once both to benefit and to suffer from the migration of the Jews to the lands of Greece and Italy. Setting out from Antioch, Paul and Barnabas preached the Gospel in the island of Cyprus, where they succeeded in converting the proconsul Sergius Paulus. From there they passed into Asia Minor, where they founded a community at Antioch of Pisidia. Driven out of the city, they made their way to Iconium and to Lystra, where Paul was stoned, dragged outside the town, and abandoned as dead. He quickly recovered, however, and, still accompanied by Barnabas, repaired to the town of Derbe. After quite a lengthy stay in the different cities of Pamphylia, Pisidia, and Lycaonia, the Apostles returned to the metropolis.

Although this first journey lasted four or five years, its field of action remained restricted. St. Paul really entered on the major portion of his work at Antioch of Pisidia, and the distance from this city to Derbe is only about ten days' march. The Apostle was forced to narrow the field of his activities because of the number of difficulties he encountered.

II. Judaeo-Christian Opposition. Against this authentic evangelization some Jewish converts objected: "Except you be circumcised after the manner of Moses, you cannot be saved." [1] These recalcitrant judaizers were early converts to Christianity who retained something of the Pharisaic mentality. "When Paul and Barnabas had no small contest with them, they determined that Paul and Barnabas and certain others of the other side, should go up to the Apostles and priests of Jerusalem about this question." [2] The heads of the Church convened, and the foremost places were taken by Peter, John, James, Paul, and Barnabas. Such was the First Council of the Church, and Peter upheld Paul and Barnabas in their decision that the Christians were to be freed from the ritual and ceremonial obligations of the law. He went so far as to refuse to make an individual concession to the judaizers in the matter of the circumcision of Titus.

The Council of Jerusalem had decreed that converts from paganism were no longer to be subjected to the observance of the Jewish law, but the further question as to whether the Jews themselves were freed from this law, still awaited solution. The dissension at Antioch was to bring about the desired settlement of the question. Reaching Antioch before the advent of certain of the followers of James, Peter seated himself and began to eat in the company of newly converted pagans. Upon the arrival of the followers of James, Peter changed his whole attitude and withdrew from them. His conduct as such was not deserving of reproach, since the observance of the ceremonial obligations was not necessary for salvation, and he might have thought it best not to conform to them for the sake of the weak. Under the circumstances, however, his behavior was

[1] Acts 15, 1.
[2] Acts 15, 2.

tantamount to a definite approval of the attitude of the judaizers, and a formal recognition of their superiority over the Gentiles. Paul severely reprimanded Peter for such an indiscreet act of condescension, stressing the fact that faith in Christ suffices for all men to be saved. His contention was that the Jewish converts had professed belief in Jesus Christ in order to be justified by faith in Christ, and not by works. The School of Tübingen, given over to higher Scriptural criticism, viewed this dissension in the light of a veritable schism. According to them, Peter and Paul were the respective leaders of two opposite factions—Petrinism and Paulinism. The first of these favored the Judaeo-Christian party; the second, the newly organized Church at large. As a matter of fact, there is not the slightest evidence of the existence of so marked a disagreement between the two Apostles. In the course of his journeys, Paul continued to collect money for the poor in Jerusalem, and in his Second Epistle, Peter was not sparing in his praise for Paul, whom he calls "our most dear brother" (2 Pet. 3, 15). All ancient documents, moreover, including the Letter of St. Clement of Rome and that of St. Ignatius to the Romans, represent the two Apostles as equal sharers in the love and veneration of the faithful, and only towards the end of the second and the beginning of the third century do we meet with the version of an early schism as set forth by the descendants of the judaizers.

III. **The Missionary Labors of St. Paul.** With the seal of approval unreservedly placed upon his teachings by the Council of Jerusalem, Paul left Antioch, accompanied by Silas, in the summer of the year 50, on a second missionary journey. Their way led through the same countries which Paul had evangelized in his first journey, but this time the Apostle decided to take the land route. He revisited Derbe, Lystra, Iconium, and Antioch, and at Lystra found a very reliable helper in the person of Timothy. His plans were to evangelize Asia and Bithynia, but he was directed by the "Spirit of Jesus" to change his course and enter Europe. Upon his arrival at Troas, he was joined by Luke, the "beloved physician," who was destined later on to become his biographer. Interpreting as a command from the Master a vision, in which a man from Macedonia besought him to visit that country, he set sail from Troas, landed at Neopolis, and journeyed on foot to the chief city of Macedonia, Philippi. All four evangelized Philippi, where they were scourged, chained, and thrown into prison as a result of an uprising among the people. Set free the next day by the magistrates of the city, who were almost beside them-selves when they learned that the men whom they had scourged were Roman citizens, they passed on to Thessalonica, where they converted a large number of persons. But here a second uprising took place, and they withdrew by night to Berea.

Always pursued by the Jews, who never lost an opportunity to stir up a rabble against him, Paul separated from his companions at Berea, and fled, first to the coast, and then by sea to Greece. At Athens, he de-livered his famous speech before the Areopagus, to which the wise and learned philosophers listened with skeptical smiles. His efforts were not all lost, however, for a few embraced the new faith, among them Dionysius the Areopagite and a very worthy woman named Damaris. During the autumn of the year 51, Paul moved on to Corinth. Here he was met by his three companions, with whom he founded a small community, and remained there until the year 53. We know that all this time he stayed at the house of Aquila, a Jew from Pontus, and Priscilla, his wife, who, like himself, were tent-makers, and that from their humble home he despatched his two letters to the Thessalonians. Incensed with anger at his success, the Jews again arrested him, this time dragging him before the tribunal of the Proconsul L. Junius Gallio, a brother of the famous Stoic philosopher, Seneca. Gallio refused to lend an ear to their re-monstrances, and in the spring of 53, Paul quit Corinth, accompanied by Aquila and Priscilla. After a short sojourn at Ephesus, the Apostle went up to Jerusalem to fulfill a vow he had made. The period covered by this second missionary journey is marked by the greatest results and achievements, because it effected the foundation of stalwart communities at Philippi and Thessalonica in Macedonia and Corinth in Greece. From these first Christian centers in the pagan world, the new faith was soon to spread to its uttermost confines.

After a brief stay at Antioch, Paul proceeded on his third missionary journey. His main purpose this time seemed to be to strengthen and consolidate what he had already achieved, rather than to enlarge upon his work by new conquests. First, he visited the churches of Galatia and Phrygia, arriving at Ephesus in the spring of 54. Until the autumn of 56, he remained at Ephesus, where he composed his First Epistle to the Corinthians. It was during his stay at Ephesus that the tumult among the silversmiths occurred. Early in the year 57, he embarked from Troas to revisit his Christian foundations in Europe, first proceeding to Macedonia, where he composed his Second Epistle to the Corinthians. From there he pushed on to Corinth, to judge for himself the effects of his letter, and write his great Epistle to the Romans. This Epistle was meant principally to pave the way for a visit to the capital of the Empire and to the Christian community established there. The Apostle had contemplated this visit for a long time. But before going to Rome, he wished first to go up to Jerusalem by way of Philippi, Troas, Miletus, and Tyre, to deliver in person the money he had collected from his converts for the relief of the poor. His farewell address to the heads of the Christian centers of Asia Minor is a masterpiece of pathos.

Paul arrived in Jerusalem around the Feast of Pentecost of the year 58. It was not without apprehension that he re-entered the Holy City. Jerusalem was still the stronghold of the old conservative party, whose leaders had commissioned a number of emissaries to trail the Apostle and counteract his teachings by advocating a return to legal Judaism and the rite of circumcision. In an effort to offset their influence, Paul had written two epistles during his second missionary journey. In his letter to the Corinthians he had been content to oppose only certain noncommissioned missionaries who had openly stated that they were in the possession of letters of recommendation signed by the great Apostles; but in his Epistle to the Galatians he boldly unmasked the judaizers, by clearly defending the thesis of salvation for all men, in a manner that augured well for the calm yet forceful attack he was to renew in his Epistle to the Romans. According to the Pauline thesis, all men, both Jews and Gentiles, are sinners. They attain to salvation through faith alone,[1] as evidenced in the case of Abraham, the "father of believers." The law never saved any one; formerly, it was nothing more than a rampart or a parapet; now, its utility even as such had become obsolete. Henceforth, the gap between Pauline universalism and Jewish particularism could never be breached.

A few days after his arrival in Jerusalem, Paul was threatened with death. He was rescued by the Roman tribune, Claudius Lysias, who in an attempt to force a confession of guilt, ordered him to be scourged.

---

[1] The stand taken by St. Paul does not militate in favor of the Lutheran position. The Apostle was merely intent, in this instance, upon contrasting the saving power of faith with the futile character of the law (*Transl.*).

Paul appealed to his rights as a Roman citizen and was sentenced to appear before the Sanhedrin. This second attempt to impeach him also proved unsuccessful, Paul very cleverly giving them the lead in a discussion on the resurrection of the dead, dividing the Pharisees and the Sadducees in their views, and diverting any possibility of harm to himself. Firmly convinced that it was impossible to reach some kind of settlement, and fearing that his prisoner might be the object of foul play on the part of the Jews, Lysias sent him in chains to Caesarea, where the Jews brought forward their accusations against him at the tribunal of Felix, the procurator of Judea. Felix found no cause for condemning him, but kept him a prisoner for two years in the hope that he himself or his friends would purchase his freedom with a bribe (58-60). Portius Festus succeeded Felix in the year 60 and Paul appealed to Caesar. Festus' answer was: "Hast thou appealed to Caesar? To Caesar thou shalt go." Foiled in their plans, the Jews sought to wreak their vengeance on James the Less, head of the Church in Jerusalem, and so taking advantage of the vacancy created in the procuratorship, the high priest Ananias summoned him to appear before the Sanhedrin, as a transgressor of the law, and ordered him to be stoned to death, together with several other Christians.

TEXTS AND DOCUMENTS

St. Clement on the Spirit of Faction at Corinth

Take into your hands the Epistle of the blessed Paul the Apostle. What did he first write to you, at the outset of the Gospel-preaching? Of a truth he wrote to you in the Spirit concerning himself and Cephas [Peter] and Apollo, because even at that time you had made factions. But that first one, indeed, involved less guilt on you; for you were partisans of Apostles of high reputation, and of a man to whom they had borne witness. But now reflect who they are that have perverted you, and have diminished the august name of your world-renowned fraternity. It is a shameful report, beloved, exceedingly shameful and unbecoming the conversation that is in Christ, to hear that the established and ancient church of the Corinthians is in a state of revolt against the Elders by reason of one or two persons.

I, *Ep. ad Corinthios*, XLVII, 1 ff.

QUESTIONS

1. Outline the character of St. Paul as revealed in the Acts of the Apostles and in his own Epistles.

2. Locate the cities of the Roman Empire in which the Apostles preached the Gospel.
3. Name the most prominent of the companions of St. Paul, and discuss their characters.
4. What was the sum and substance of the speech delivered by St. Paul before the Areopagus?
5. Who were the judaizers and why were they so opposed to the teachings of St. Paul?
6. What is the importance of the First Council of Jerusalem?
7. Who were the Jews of the Dispersion?
8. What is meant by Jewish particularism?

BIBLIOGRAPHY

St. Paul.—FOUARD, *St. Paul and His Missions.*—PRAT, *The Theology of St. Paul,* 2 vols.; *Saint Paul* (Coll. *Les Saints*), 1922.—C. TOUSSAINT, art. *"Saint Paul,"* in *Dict. de la Bible; Epitres de saint Paul,* t. I, 1909.—TOBAC, *Le problème de la justification dans saint Paul,* Louvain, 1908.—P. CLERISSAC, *De saint Paul à Jésus-Christ,* 2nd edit., 1920.—LEMONNIER, *Epitres de saint Paul,* transl. and comp., 1907-08.—P. LAGRANGE, *Epitre aux Romains,* 1916; *aux Galâtes,* 1918.—P. DELATTE, *Les Epitres de saint Paul,* 1924.—E. TOBAC, *Le problème de la justification dans saint Paul et dans saint Jacques, R. H. E.,* XXII (1926), pp. 797-806.—A. TRICOT, *Saint Paul,* 1928.—BANDAS, *The Master Idea of St. Paul's Epistles on the Redemption,* Bruges, 1925.—LATTEY, *Introduction to the Epistle to the Romans.*—T. F. BURKE, *St. Paul, the Apostle of the Resurrection,* Paulist Press.—McSORLEY, *School of St. Paul.*—FINK, *Paul, Hero and Saint,* Paulist Press.—LYNCH, S. J., *The Story of the Acts of the Apostles.*

The Jewish Question.—Besides the works of PRAT and BATIFFOL, *oper. cit.,* J. THOMAS, *L'Eglise et les judaïsants, la réunion de Jérusalem,* in *Rev. quest. hist.,* XLVI (1899), pp. 400-460; *La question juive à l'âge apostolique, après le concile de Jérus., ibid.,* XLVII (1890), pp. 313-407.—COPPIETERS, *Le décret des apôtres, Rev. biblique,* 1907, pp. 34-58, 218-239.—HEFELE, *History of the Councils,* t. I, app. I.—L. MARCHAL, art. *Judéo-Chrétiens à l'âge apostolique,* in *Dict. de Théol.*—SCHURER, *History of the Jewish People in the Time of Jesus Christ.*—GIGOT, *Outlines of the New Testament History.*—DUCHESNE, *Early History of the Christian Church.*—BELLOC, *The Jews.*—CHESTERTON, *The New Jerusalem.*—KURTH, *The Church at the Turning Points of History,* transl. DAY.—BATIFFOL, *Primitive Christianity.*

CHAPTER III

THE COMMUNITY AT ROME

I. The Environment: The Graeco-Roman World. While St. Paul was evangelizing the countries of the East, one power alone held sway over the entire world, and one supreme master held the fate of both Senate and armies in his hand. That power was Rome, and that master, the Emperor. The Emperor was acclaimed by the people as a god, provided he continued to give them bread and games (*panem et circenses*); no wonder, then, that the centralization of such vast and unrestrained power finally degenerated into unprecedented tyranny. Impiety and immorality of the worst kind quickly followed in the wake of riches and luxury, so much so that we find the Roman religion in full decadence during the reign of Augustus. In vain did that Emperor try to restore religion to its primitive splendor by embellishing the temples, re-instating the electoral colleges, and encouraging new forms of worship; all his efforts to instill a new life into the fast disintegrating religion proved unsuccessful; it was becoming a laughing-stock even for the illiterate, who regarded it as a mere mixture of Latin traditions and Greek fables.

The influence of religion on private morals was nil. There is no disputing the fact that the strong organization built up during the times of the Republic had greatly contributed to the welfare and prosperity of Rome. In the ancient city the father was the absolute master of the household. The wife commanded her husband's respect, but was completely subject to him. She, in turn, had authority over the children, who nevertheless remained under the tutelage of the father. Finally, the love and respect for ancestors and the worship of the fireside gods made for the protection of family interests. But with victories and conquests came riches and pleasures. Sallust, Livy, Pliny, Seneca, and Tacitus are equally strong in denouncing the decay of morals. Men no longer entered into marriage contracts, or, if they did, were not concerned in perpetuating their name. The stability of the marriage bond was held in ridicule, and so women sought divorce for the slightest reasons, some among them not even hesitating to profess polyandry. The law Pappia-Poppaea, enacted by Augustus for the purpose of conferring special privileges upon married citizens, particularly upon those who had three children (*jus trium liberorum*), went the way of all other legislation, and instead, the Roman nation sank deeper and deeper into the quagmire of iniquity and vice. Everything about their civilization acted as a contributing cause to this evil state of affairs. The education of children was entrusted to slaves whose very influence was corrupting; the literature, the arts, and the theatre rivalled with one another in obscenity; the existing conditions reduced slaves to the level of puppets and playthings in the hands of their masters. Scaurus, the father-in-law of Sylla, had 8000 of these poor unfortunates, who were often ill-treated and condemned to the rudest kind of manual labor. The most severe forms of punishment were inflicted upon these human beasts of burden: they were handcuffed, constrained to wear yokes, and cruelly scourged. The master exercised the right over life and death of his slaves.

In spite of all this, some writers insist that the world as a whole was moving towards a state of amelioration. As proofs of their contention they point first to certain examples of heroic virtue; secondly, to the ever increasing influence of Stoicism; and thirdly, to the growing popularity of the Oriental religions recently imported into Rome. According to them, Christianity merely followed in the wake of a moral reaction which was already well under way, and which, in any event, would have attained the goal without its assistance.

No statement could be more false. True, it is possible to point to outstanding examples of virtue, such as that of Aurelia, wife of Caesar, and Paulina, wife of Seneca; but the testimony of contemporary writers proves that these were exceptions. Secondly, at the time referred to by these writers, Stoicism was far from being the passive, proud, and assertive system of philosophic thought into which it was finally moulded by Epictetus and Marcus Aurelius. These philosophers standardized it as a religion of forbearance and abstinence, but in the days of Seneca it was nothing more than a vague sort of doctrine, bearing more than one resemblance to the lay morality of our time. In an effort to prop up its tottering walls, Seneca composed his famous treatises: *De tranquillitate animae, De clementia* (On Peace of Mind, On Indulgence), etc. Then he and other writers in philosophy wrote letters of direction, but treatises and letters were of no avail, and even Seneca proved himself unwilling to bear patiently his affliction and opened his own veins, thus ending his troubles by death. Finally, the Stoics recruited their members among the elite; hence, as a religion Stoicism would not appeal to the masses. Thirdly, although the people felt a natural inclination towards Oriental rites, such as that of Isis, Aphrodite of Byblis, the celestial Virgin of Carthage, etc., which had an air of mystery about them, they were attracted to their altars in Rome more on account of the magical and immoral practices connected with the cult, than because of any impelling force behind it. The literati continued to cling to the more ideal doctrines of Pantheism.

However, we are not denying that Christianity was preceded by some form of preparation, for no matter how inefficacious the teachings of philosophy or how futile the attempt at transfusion of Oriental rites into the fast corrupting blood of Roman and Greek religions, they evidenced one and all the existence of higher aspirations among thinking people, as well as a vague sense of disgust for religion in its present dress. This fact accounts sufficiently for the success of Jewish proselytism, especially among the matrons. Moreover, strange rumors were current; a Messias was expected, not only in Palestine, but also in foreign lands. Pagan writers were foretelling the approach of new and better days. Suetonius wrote: "The idea was fast spreading throughout the entire East, that, in the unwritten pages of fate, leadership in the world was to be transferred to men coming from Judaea." According to Tacitus, "Many had faith in a prophecy, formulated in ancient writings, which foretold that men from Judaea would gain possession of the Empire." Finally, the material conditions of the world also helped the spread of Christianity. The entire universe was at peace, all the nations of the earth were gathered together under one rule, the fine Roman roads made travelling easier and safer, and the diffusion of the Greek tongue had bound the nations together by a closer tie. Nevertheless, Christianity did not forge ahead without opposition. "Casting a superficial glance at the history of the primitive Church," writes Paul Allard, "we seem to find Christians wellnigh everywhere; we find them in countries bordering on the birthplace of the new religion and in the countries farthest removed from it. . . . We might thus gather that Christianity at once leapt to the position of the universal religion. This impression may not be altogether false, but it requires some correction. There were such things as degrees and inequalities in the rapid spread of Christianity." [1] The greatest obstacle encountered was the new code of Christian morality.

II. The Christian Community at Rome. The origins of Christianity at Rome are veiled in obscurity. No doubt it was introduced by Roman proselytes, who had heard Peter's preaching in Jerusalem; then by soldiers of the *cohors italica civium romanorum voluntariorum,* a body of volunteers who resided at Caesarea within call of the governor of Palestine; and finally, perhaps, by Cornelius, the centurion, an officer of this legion, and a number of other converts among the military, who, upon returning to Rome, had hastened to spread the "good news." It may well be, also, that Peter paid his first visit to Rome in the reign of Claudius, between 41 and 44, and remained there about six years, when an imperial edict banished all Jews. The community gradually made progress in growth and development. In 57, an illustrious recruit, Pomponia Graecina, joined its ranks. In the following year it had already attained sufficient proportions to warrant Paul writing his Epistle to the Romans. In the salutations with which the letter closes, we remark the predominance of Roman names, a positive proof that the community had spread beyond the restricted Jewish quarters. And yet, when St. Paul arrived there in chains, in the year 61, the "brethren" came to meet him in the Forum of Appius, a proof that their number was still rather small. As yet little prejudice existed against the Christians, who were frequently confused with the Jews. Paul was, no doubt, able to take advantage of the situation, because, although in the continual custody of a Roman soldier, he received many visitors and even preached the Gospel abroad. Under his direction the community must have made rapid progress, for Tacitus avers that in the year 64 the Christians already comprised an immense multitude (*"ingens multitudo"*). When these words were penned, Paul had been set free and had left Rome to undertake several journeys.

No writer to-day raises any doubt concerning this departure of Paul from the Eternal City, and no one contests the fact that the Apostle was put to death after a second arrest in the year 67. His captivity, as described by himself in his Epistle to the Philippians, is very different from that described in his Second Epistle to Timothy. When he wrote the former of these Epistles, his quarters were comfortable and he was

[1] Allard, *Ten Lectures on the Martyrs,* p. 8.

allowed to receive visitors; when he wrote the latter, he was lying in chains and treated like a criminal. Moreover, the Acts of the Apostles end abruptly with the statement that Paul remained two years in Rome in the custody of a soldier; if he had been put to death soon after, St. Luke would surely have made mention of the fact.

During the time that elapsed between the two captivities, St. Paul made a journey into Spain. This fact is certainly historical, for thirty years after his death, Pope St. Clement mentioned in a letter to the Corinthians that Paul had travelled "to the farthest corners of the West," and a list of saints compiled at Rome towards the year 170 in express terms mentions his journey into Spain. Paul also re-visited his Christian communities in the East, as is evidenced by his so-called pastoral letters to Titus and Timothy.

The Roman community was not without a shepherd during this time, for St. Peter had come to the city about A. D. 63 or 64. The earliest proof of this statement is the testimony of the Apostle himself, who dates his First Epistle from Babylon. Now, it is not at all likely that Peter made a trip to Mesopotamia. The city of Babylon was no longer in existence, hence the name here is used symbolically to designate Rome, which had often been called the Babylon of the West.

In his Epistle to the Corinthians, despatched from Rome in the year 96 or 97, Pope St. Clement recalls to the minds of his readers the martyrdom of the two Apostles Peter and Paul, as well as the courage they displayed while "amongst us." Similarly, in his Epistle to the Romans, St. Ignatius begs his friends not to put any obstacle in the way of his martyrdom, and not to plead his cause with the Emperor. He adds with great reserve: "This is only a request. I do not command you as Peter and Paul; they were Apostles; I am only a condemned man." Such expressions would be without meaning, if Peter had not come to Rome.

In the course of the second century, the proofs for our contention become even more categorical. In two distinct instances, St. Irenaeus, a disciple of St. Polycarp, who in turn was a disciple of St. John, explicitly states that Peter and Paul founded the Church of Rome. His testimony, dating as it does from the very era of the Apostles, suffices to put an end to all controversy. "Matthew," says Irenaeus, "composed his Gospel whilst Peter and Paul were preaching Christ in Rome and laying the foundations of the Church." Clement of Alexandria (150–215) speaks of the Gospel as preached in Rome by Peter and transcribed by Mark. Towards

side the Walls" now marks the spot of his burial. St. Peter was martyred in the Vatican, and according to Origen's testimony crucified head downwards. In close proximity to his mangled remains were buried the bodies of his successors from St. Linus to St. Victor (202). In keeping with a very ancient tradition, the Church at the beginning of the fourth century instituted one common feast for the two Apostles, fixing the date at the twenty-ninth of June.

The persecution of Nero ended with the death of this tyrant († 69); but his edict against the Christians was not recalled, and so the Christians were still at the mercy of the very first incident that might direct the attention of the Emperor to them. The dynasty of the Flavians had succeeded that of the Caesars, and under its first two representatives, Vespasian (69–79) and Titus (79–81), the Christians were not molested; but in the reign of *Domitian* (81–96) they were again made to feel the effects of the Neronian edict. From the day Titus captured the city of Jerusalem (A. D. 70) the Jews were compelled to pay tribute to their conquerors. Domitian, in an attempt to replenish the public treasury, which was depleted by his many foolish extravagances, made the payment of the tax binding even upon those "who lead the Jewish life." But the Christians regarded the fact of being counted on a par with the Jews in the matter of taxation as tantamount to an attempt to make them abjure their faith. On this occasion the distinction between the two religions again became official, just as it had been at the time of the burning of Rome. The Neronian edict was once more put into force, and new arrests were made. Domitian's anger knew no bounds when, in the year 95, he learned that members of the imperial family had joined the infamous sect. The consul Flavius Clemens, a son of Flavius Sabinus, the eldest brother of Vespasian, was denounced, accused of "indolence," and made to suffer the death penalty. His wife, Flavia Domitilla, was exiled to the island of Pandataria. Acilius Glabrio, who had been consul in 91, was also arrested as a plotter of things new (*"molitor novarum rerum"*). The persecution spread to the provinces, as far as Asia Minor, Smyrna, and Pergamum. St. John was brought to Rome and plunged into a caldron of boiling oil in front of the Porta Latina. According to the testimony of St. Irenaeus, he was later banished to the island of Patmos, where he composed the Apocalypse.

Towards the end of his life, Domitian ceased to persecute the Christians. He had invited the relatives of Jesus to come to Rome from Judaea, and, after questioning them, had decided they were peaceful and inoffensive. He soon fell a victim to a revolution within his own palace, and not, as some have averred, to the vengeance of the Christians. The truth of the matter is that Stephen, a freedman, and the Empress Domitia, having discovered their names on the proscription tablets, saved their lives by putting the tyrant to death.

At the end of the first century, and during the life-time of the last of the Apostles, there existed a great number of Christian communities. Begun at Jerusalem, the preaching the Gospel had spread to Samaria, Syria, and Cilicia. Thanks to the indefatigable labors of St. Paul, it reached all the countries bordering on the eastern shores of the Mediterranean: Asia Minor, Macedonia, and Greece. Through the ministrations of Titus, it forged its way to the coast lines of Illyria and Dalmatia. In the West, it gained a foothold in the Roman metropolis, whence it spread to the commercial seaport of Marseilles and the ancient Roman colony of Narbonne. Finally, the work was carried by St. Paul into the far western province of Spain.

In certain instances, these early Christian foundations rested on a solid basis. In Asia Minor, St. John had set up such a body of bishops that Pliny complained to the Emperor Trajan that the provinces of Bithynia and Pontus were infested with the new sect. Already the Christian religion had overflowed the limits of the Roman world. St. Thomas preached in the kingdom of the Parthians, situated between the Tigris and the Euphrates, and despatched Thaddeus to Abgar, King of Edessa. St. Simon is reputed to have penetrated to Babylonia and Persia. St. Andrew labored in Scythia. St. Bartholomew journeyed as far as India. St. Mark, the Evangelist, is credited with the founding of the Church of Alexandria in Egypt, and after the death of St. Paul, Luke carried the Gospel to different parts of Achaea, and finally suffered martyrdom in Thebes.

TEXTS AND DOCUMENTS

The Neronian Persecution According to Tacitus

In order to stifle the rumor that he had himself set Rome on fire, Nero falsely accused and punished with the most fearful tortures the persons commonly called Christians, who were hated for their wicked practices. Christus, the founder of that name, was put to death as a criminal by Pontius Pilate, procurator of Judaea, in the reign of Tiberius; but the pernicious superstition, repressed for a time, broke out again, not only throughout Judaea, where the mischief originated, but also in the city of Rome, whither all horrible and disgraceful things flow from all quarters as to a common receptacle, and where they are encouraged. Accordingly, first those were seized who confessed; next, on their information, a vast multitude were convicted, not so much on the charge of burning the city, as of hating the human race.

In their very deaths they were made the objects of sport: for they were covered with the hides of wild beasts, and worried to death by dogs, or nailed to crosses, or set fire to, and when the day waned, burned to serve for the evening lights. Nero offered his own garden for the spectacle, and exhibited a Circensian game, indiscriminately mingling with the common people in the dress of a charioteer, or else standing in his chariot. For this cause a feeling of compassion arose towards the sufferers, though guilty and deserving of exemplary capital punishment, because they seemed not to be cut off for the public good, but were victims of the ferocity of one man.

TACITUS, Annales, XV, 44.

QUESTIONS

1. What were the conditions of the Graeco-Roman world at the time of the first spread of Christianity in the West?
2. What is meant by the expression *"panem et circenses"*?
3. Contrast the state of woman under Roman law and under the Christian economy.
4. Define Stoicism as a system of moral philosophy.
5. Indicate some of the obstacles to the spread of Christianity.
6. Indicate some of the helps of which the first missionaries were able to avail themselves.
7. Which are some of the possible origins of Christianity in Rome?
8. What proof have we that Paul journeyed to Spain?
9. What proofs have we that St. Peter was in Rome, and what is the significance of this fact?
10. What difference is there between an edict and a rescript?

BIBLIOGRAPHY

The Graeco-Roman World.—BONETTY, *Documents historiques sur la religion des Romains*, 1867.—DÖLLINGER, *Paganism and Judaism*.—BOISSIER, *La religion romaine d'Auguste aux Antonins*, 4th edit., 1892.—C. MARTHA, *Les moralistes sous l'empire romain*, 1865.—G. KURTH, *Les origines de la civilisation moderne*, 5th edit., 1903, t. I, Ch. I.—LAURAND, art. *Romains (Religion des)* in *Dict. d'Apol.*—V. CHAPOT, *Le monde romain* (Coll. *L'Evolution de l'humanité*), 1927.—J. P. MAHAFFY, *The Greek World under Roman*

Sway.—G. Finley, *Greece Under the Romans.*—S. M. Best, *Glorious Greece and Imperial Rome.*

St. Peter's Advent to Rome.—Paul Martin, in *Rev. quest. hist.,* 1873, 1874, 1875.—M. Leclercq, *De Romano sancti Petri episcopatu,* Louvain, 1888.—C. H. Turner, in *Journal of Theological Studies,* Jan., 1900.—J. Chapman, *La Chronologie des premières listes épiscopales de Rome,* in *Rev. bénéd.,* 1901, pp. 399–417; 1902, pp. 13–37, 145–170.—J. Guiraud, *Questions d'hist. et d'archéol. chrét.,* 1906, pp. 215–271.—P. Monceaux, *L'Apostolat de saint Pierre à Rome,* in *Rev. hist. litt. rel.,* 1910, pp. 216–220.—L. Vouaux, *Les Actes de Pierre,* 1912.—A. d'Alès, art. *Pierre (saint) à Rome,* in *Dict. d'Apol.*—Guignebert, *La Primauté de Pierre et la venue de Pierre à Rome;* refuted by F. Flamion, *Saint Pierre à Rome,* in *Rev. Hist. éccl.,* 1913 (XIV).—Lietzmann, *Petrus und Paulus in Rom,* Bonn, 1915.—Fouard, *St. Peter and the First Years of Christianity,* trans. F. X. Griffith.—T. E. Moore, *Peter's City; An Account of the Origin, Development, and Situation of the Roman Question.*—M. Creighton, *Mind of Peter.*—C. J. O'Connell, *The Catholic Church, True Church of the Bible.*

The Persecutions of Nero and Domitian.—Healy, *"The Literature of the Neronian Persecution,"* Cath. Univ. Bull., Washington, 1904, X, pp. 357–370.—L. De Combes, *La condition des juifs et des chrétiens à Rome et l'édit de Néron,* Rev. cath. des inst. et du droit, t. XXXIII (1904), pp. 47 ff.—Gsell, *Essai sur le règne de l'empereur Domitien,* 1893.—P. Allard, *Les chrétiens ont-ils incendié Rome sous Néron?* (Coll. *"Science et Religion"*), 1904; *Ten Lectures on the Martyrs.*—H. Leclercq, art. *Incendie de Rome,* in *Dict. d'Arch.*—J. Rivière, *Expansion of Christianity in the First Three Centuries according to the Conclusions of Harnack.*—A. J. O'Reilly, *Martyrs of the Coliseum.*

The term "Apostolic Fathers" is applied to several authors who wrote towards the end of the first and the beginning of the second century. Their writings so faithfully echo the teachings of the Apostles that they are reckoned among the most valuable documents of Christian antiquity. In more than one instance they won the distinction of being classified with the literature that was read in public in church assemblies. We particularly consider the *Didaché*, or Doctrine of the Twelve Apostles, and the *Shepherd of Hermas* as witnesses of sacramental development; and the Letter of St. Clement and the Epistles of St. Ignatius as witnesses to the existence of a hierarchy.

I. **The Witnesses of Sacramental Development: The Didaché and The Shepherd.** The Didaché or Doctrine of the Twelve Apostles (Διδαχὴ τῶν ἀποστόλων) was discovered in 1883 in the library of the monastery of the Holy Sepulchre at Constantinople by Philotheos Bryennios, metropolitan of Nicomedia. The discoverer was of the opinion that the manuscript had borrowed from the Letter of Barnabas and the Shepherd of Hermas and estimated the date of its composition to be somewhere between the years 120 and 160. As a matter of fact it is the Letter of Barnabas that has borrowed from the *Didaché*, the original copy of which dates back to the year A. D. 80 or 90. The *Didaché* is a work of considerable importance because it treats of the organization of the primitive Church. The first part opens with an exhortation to the newly baptized and expounds the doctrine of the Two Ways: that of life and that of death; that of the essential precepts and that of the capital sins. Here we find short treatises on Baptism, fasting, prayer, and the Holy Eucharist, as well as the formulas used in connection with each. The second part is a disciplinary instruction concerned with the welcome to be given to missionaries and prophets, the sanctification of the Sunday, etc. The conclusion is a warning to be vigilant because the end of the world is near.

The whole work is a sort of small catechism and prayer-book for the use of the faithful.

"Apart from its dogmatic content," writes Tixeront, "the *Didaché* gives us a pretty accurate picture of what was, in those early times, the interior life of the Christian communities from the point of view of moral teaching, the practices they observed, and the form of government under which they lived. Some authors have seen in this work the most ancient of Christian rituals; it is perhaps more exact to characterize it as a kind of 'Vade Mecum' for the faithful and a directory for the use of the church officials." [1]

According to indications in the Canon of Muratori, Hermas was the brother of Pope Pius I (c. 140–155). His book is entitled *The Shepherd* from the name of the Angel of Penance, who plays the principal part in the second division of the book and who appears to the author in the guise of a shepherd. *The Shepherd* comprises five visions (ὁράσεις), twelve precepts (ἐντολαί), and ten similitudes (παράβολαι). Above all the book is a treatise on Penance. Hermas is conscious of grave disorders and even scandalous actions that have crept into the Church of Rome, but he is confident that the merciful Lord will call the perpetrators of these crimes to forgiveness. In opposition to the rigorists, the writer stresses the necessity and efficaciousness of Penance, and the different symbolical visions which fill *The Shepherd,* are all made to converge towards this one idea. A second-rate mind and a very mediocre writer, Hermas was an excellent moralist, endowed with good common sense.

II. The Witnesses to the Existence of a Hierarchy: St. Clement and St. Ignatius. The Epistle of St. Clement dates back to the end of the first century. Its purpose is to remind the Corinthians of their duty of obedience to the local ecclesiastical authority. According to a very primitive custom in the Church, the Epistle introduces itself as a letter "from the Church of God which is in Rome to the Church of God which is in Corinth." And yet it is undoubtedly the work of Pope Clement himself, as the constant tradition of the ages attests. The writer contrasts the former prosperous state of Corinth with the miserable conditions prevailing there as a result of the schism. In an attempt to rehabilitate the community in a spirit of concord, he exhorts its members in the first part to flee the occasions of jealousy and to practice charity, penance, obedience,

---

[1] Tixeront, *Handbook of Patrology,* transl. Raemers, p. 20.

and humility. In the second part he penetrates to the very core of his subject. The ecclesiastical hierarchy, he says, is of divine institution. Christ appointed the Apostles. They appointed bishops and deacons, who in turn, as the need was felt, chose other men to succeed them. To these men the faithful owe submission and obedience. The authority of Clement's Letter was so great that we find it appended in several ancient manuscripts of Holy Scripture to the canonical Epistles of the Apostles.

The success which greeted this first letter was the signal for the rise of a whole pseudo-Clementine literature. The most ancient work of this kind is the so-called Second Epistle of St. Clement. In point of fact, it is neither a letter nor a formal epistle, but a homily, and bears some resemblance to the *Shepherd,* so that some have not hesitated to ascribe it to a writer of the same period. "The analogy, however," writes Tixeront, "is not very pronounced." [1] The author recalls to the faithful the practice of good works and penance in view of the approaching *parousia.*

We might also call attention in this place to the two letters *Ad Virgines,* which contain a eulogy of virginity and forbid the cohabitation of clerics with women. The composition of these letters must be placed somewhere during the course of the third, and perhaps even the fourth century. The pseudo-Clementine writings were none the less objects of great veneration on the part of the faithful, and sometimes were given the honor of being read in public.

In the course of his journey to Rome, where he was to be thrown to the wild beasts, St. Ignatius, the Martyr, composed seven letters. The first four were written at Smyrna and addressed to the Ephesians, the Trallians, the Magnesians, and the Romans. The last three are dated from Troas, and addressed to the churches of Philadelphia and Smyrna, and to St. Polycarp. These letters, in which St. Ignatius speaks of his approaching martyrdom, are documents of great value, because by their recommendation to the faithful to group themselves around their bishops, they constitute a categorical proof of an already existing partition of the clergy into bishops, priests, and deacons. Protestants were quick to perceive this fact and dated the letters from the middle of the second century, but the emphatic testimony of St. Polycarp, St. Irenaeus, Origen, and Eusebius make their assertions unacceptable. "The style of the Ignatian Epistles," writes Batiffol, "is rude, obscure, enigmatic, and full of

[1] *Ibid.*

repetitions and entreaties, but it is always very energetic, and here and there strikingly magnificent," while the Letter of St. Polycarp to the Philippians, on the occasion of the sojourn of St. Ignatius among them, is only a second-rate homily.

Two authors of much less importance must also be ranged among the Apostolic Fathers, namely: *Pseudo-Barnabas* and *Papias*. Modern critics unanimously deny the genuineness of the letter attributed to Barnabas, which has sometimes been compared to the Epistles of St. Paul. The letter was intended for a Christian community threatened by the influence of the judaizers, and is a violent "speech for the crown" against the Mosaic observances, which, the author declares, have been completely abrogated. The letter was probably composed at Alexandria, towards the end of the first or in the beginning of the second century. "The author," writes Tixeront, "goes farther and asserts that these traditional observances in reality never existed in the sense in which the Jews understood them. The precepts relating to fasting, circumcision, the Sabbath, the Temple, etc., which they had interpreted in a gross material sense, were to be understood spiritually of the mortification of the passions and the sanctification of the interior temple, which is the soul." [1]

The author of "The Explanation of the Sayings of the Lord" is Papias, bishop of Hierapolis in Phrygia, who wrote during the second half of the second century. We possess only a few fragments of the work, which seems to be a first attempt at exegesis applied to the Gospel. It contains important information on the value of oral tradition and the composition of the Gospels of SS. Matthew and Mark.

TEXTS AND DOCUMENTS

The Shepherd of Hermas
(Extract)

After a few days I saw him in the same plain where I had also seen the shepherds; and he said to me, "What do you wish with me?" I said to him, "Sir, that you would order the shepherd who punishes to depart out of my house, because he afflicts me exceedingly." "It is necessary," he replied, "that you be afflicted; for thus," he continued, "did the glorious angel command concerning you, as he wishes you to be tried." "What have I done which is so bad, Sir," I replied, "that I should be delivered over to this angel?" "Listen," he said, "your sins are many, but not so great as to require that you be de-

[1] *Ibid.*

livered over to this angel; but your household has committed great iniquities and sins, and the glorious angel has been incensed at them on account of their deeds; and for this reason he commanded you to be afflicted for a certain time, that they also might repent, and purify themselves from every desire of this world. When, therefore, they repent and are purified, the angel of punishment will depart." I said to him, "Sir, if they have done such things as to incense the glorious angel against them, yet what have I done?" He replied: "They cannot be afflicted at all, unless you, the head of the house, be afflicted; for when you are afflicted, of necessity they also suffer affliction; but if you are in comfort, they can feel no affliction." "Well, Sir," I said, "they have repented with their whole heart." "I know, too," he answered, "that they have repented with their whole heart; do you think, however, that the sins of those who repent are remitted? Not altogether, but he who repents must torture his own soul, and be exceedingly humble in all his conduct, and be afflicted with many kinds of affliction; and if he endures the afflictions that come upon him, He who created all things, and endowed them with power, will assuredly have compassion, and will heal him; and this will He do when He sees the heart of every penitent pure from every evil thing; and it is profitable for you and for your house to suffer affliction now. But why should I say much to you? You must be afflicted, as that angel of the Lord commanded, who delivered you to me. And for this give thanks to the Lord, because He has deemed you worthy of showing you beforehand this affliction, that, knowing it before it comes, you may be able to bear it with courage." I said to him, "Sir, be thou with me, and I will be able to bear all affliction." "I will be with you," he said, "and I will ask the angel of punishment to afflict you more lightly; nevertheless, you will be afflicted for a little time, and again you will be re-established in your house. Only continue humble, and serve the Lord in all purity of heart, you and your children, and your whole house, and walk in my commandments, which I enjoin upon you, and your repentance will be deep and pure; and if you observe these things with your household, every affliction will depart from you. And affliction," he added, "will depart from all who walk in these my commandments."

QUESTIONS

1. What is the difference between a catechumen and a neophyte?
2. What was the Canon of Muratori?
3. What is the meaning of the term *"parousia"*?
4. Were there any conditions prevailing in Corinth that would make for the almost constant state of schism in which we find this city in Christian antiquity?
5. What is meant by a pseudo-writing?
6. What were the apocrypha?

BIBLIOGRAPHY

Didaché.—Sources: In a general way for the Apostolic Fathers, FUNK, *Patres Apostolici*, 2 vols., Tubingae, 1901, re-edited by F. Diekamp in 1913.— For the *Didaché*, edit. HEMMER and A. LAURENT, in Texts and Documents: *Les Pères Apostoliques*, 1907.—E. JACQUIER, *La Doctrine des Douze Apôtres* (text, version, and commentaries), 1891.—Works: JACQUIER, art. *Apôtres (La Doctrine des Douze)*, in *Dict. de Théol.*—C. TAYLOR, *An Essay on the Theology of the Didaché*, Cambridge, 1889.—VON RENESSE, *Die Lehre der Zwölf Apostel*, Giessen, 1897.—BARDENHEWER, *Patrology; The Lives and Works of the Fathers of the Church*, transl. SHAHAN.—J. A. ROBINSON, *Barnabas, Hermas, and the Didaché.*—SCHLECHT, *Die Lehre der Zwölf Apostel in der Liturgie der Katholischen Kirche*, Freiburg i. B., 1906.

Hermas.—Sources: edit. A. LELONG in Texts and Documents. *Les Pères Apostoliques, IV: Le Pasteur d'Hermas*, 1912.—Works: A. RIBAGNAC, *La Christologie du Pasteur d'Hermas*, 1887.—A. D'ALÈS, *L'édit de Calliste*, 1914.— C. TAYLOR, *The Shepherd of Hermas.*—J. A. ROBINSON, *ibid.*—*The Works of the Ante-Nicene Fathers*, A. Roberts and J. Robinson, editors, vol. II.—P. BATIFFOL, *Hermas et le problème moral au second siècle*, in *Etudes hist. et théol. positive*, 6th edit., 1920.—A. BAUMEISTER, *Die Ethik des Pastor Hermas*, Freiburg i. B., 1912.

St. Clement.—Sources: H. HEMMER, *Les Pères Apostoliques*, II, 1909.— Works: J. B. LIGHTFOOT, *Clement of Rome*, 2nd edit., 1909.—R. KNOPF, *Der erste Clemensbrief*, Leipzig, 1899.—W. SCHERER, *Der erste Clemensbrief an die Korinther*, Regensburg, 1902.

St. Ignatius.—Sources: Special edition by A. LELONG in Coll. Texts and Documents: *Les Pères Apostoliques*, III, *Ignace d'Antioche*, 1907; and J. B. LIGHTFOOT, *The Apostolic Fathers*, part II, 2nd edit., 1889-90.—Works: H. DE GENOUILLAC, *L'Eglise Chrétienne au temps d'Ignace d'Antioche*, 1907.—M. RACKL, *Die Christologie des hl. Ignatius von Ant.*, Freiburg i. B., 1914.— J. CHAPMAN, *S. Ignace d'Antioche et l'Eglise Romaine*, in *Rev. bénéd.*, XIII (1896).—ORR, *The History and Literature of the Early Church.*

Pseudo-Barnabas.—Sources: Special edition of G. OGER and A. LAURENT, Texts and Documents, *Les Pères Apost.*, I, 1907.—Works: In a general way for Greek literature, P. BATIFFOL, *La littérature grecque*, 4th edit.—The works of MSGR. FREPPEL, especially, *Les Pères apostoliques et leur époque*, 4th edit., 1885.—J. TIXERONT, *Handbook of Patrology*, transl. RAEMERS.—P. LADEUZE, *L'Epitre de Barnabe*, Louvain, 1900.—PH. HAEUSER, *Der Barnabasbrief neu untersucht und neu erklärt*, Paderborn, 1912.—PUECH, *La littérature grecque chrétienne*, 2 vols., 1928.

CHAPTER V

I. The Early Christian Community. Membership in the Christian Church meant a complete break with pagan customs. The first Christians were not only forbidden to attend the theatre and the public games, but they were also strictly enjoined to shun the many idolatrous practices woven into the very fibre of every-day pagan life. As a consequence, the faithful experienced a sense of security only when intrenched within the parapets of their own community. True, they continued to fulfill their various civic obligations, respecting the laws of the State, paying taxes, etc., but they were forbidden to enter into the marriage contract except with coreligionists. The Christian family presented a picture very different from that of the pagan home. Virtues hitherto unheard of flourished among them, including uprightness, respect of women, mutual love, and, what was an inexplicable riddle to the pagan mind, unbounded hospitality.

The public religious life of the early Christians was modelled on that of the Synagogue. To the Bible readings were added the Christian manifestations: the Eucharist and the charismata or effusions of the Holy Ghost. The Eucharistic service usually took place after the agape or love-feast. Among the charismata, the most remarkable were prophecy and glossolalia. Prophecy was the revelation of hidden things, more particularly of the secrets of the heart. Glossolalia was not the gift of tongues as possessed by the Apostles on Pentecost Day, but the ability to speak, without understanding it, a language of praise and thanksgiving which only an inspired interpreter could transmit to the faithful.

It is regrettable that these early Christian practices gave rise to abuses. The agape sometimes degenerated into an ordinary meal, and so an attempt was made to simplify it, with a view to separate it completely from the Eucharistic synaxis. Prophecy and glossolalia could easily give rise to intemperance of speech, and so, without being completely prohibited, they were excluded as charismata from Christian gatherings and replaced by the homily. The practice of improvising still existed, but it was reserved to members of the hierarchy. The Eucharistic synaxis was held in private houses, preferably on Sunday, which commemorated Christ's Resurrection from the dead, and replaced the Jewish Sabbath at a very early date.

II. **The Episcopate.** As the work of preaching the Gospel progressed, the Apostles appointed in the different communities which they founded colleges of πρεσβύτεροι whose business it was to carry out the functions of divine worship and administer the spiritual and material goods of the churches. The terms "bishops" (overseers) and "presbyters" (ancients) were at that time, synonymous, and so we read of St. Paul calling together at Miletus the "priests" of the church of Ephesus, and recommending to their care the recently founded church over which the Holy Ghost had appointed them "bishops." These "ancient overseers" composed the "presbyterium"; they imposed hands, administered the Sacraments, and presided over Christian gatherings. It was only towards the beginning of the second century that one of them was selected as the depositary of all the powers of Orders and jurisdiction and the term ἐπίσκοπος took on the meaning which it has to-day.

Yet the Apostles did communicate the plenitude of the power of Orders to a few chosen disciples like Titus and Timothy, in order to insure the Apostolic succession. In the majority of cases these first bishops were missionaries and founders of churches; the stable episcopal see was the exception rather than the rule. The first episcopal see we meet with is that of St. James at Jerusalem. St. Peter founded the see of Rome, and St. Mark, in all probability, that of Alexandria. After the death of St. Paul, some of those upon whom he conferred the plenitude of the power of Orders established themselves in permanent sees. An instance in point is St. Dionysius, who set up his at Athens. Throughout the entire first century, however, most of the churches were governed, not by one bishop, but by a college of ἐπίσκοποι-πρεσβύτεροι, i.e., a gathering of priests who ministered to their needs under the proximate or remote supervision of one of the Apostles or his delegate.

During the closing years of the first century, we witness a multiplication of fixed episcopal sees by St. John in Asia Minor. This step must not be interpreted as an innovation. In the beginning the Apostles had deemed it wise to reserve to themselves the direction of newly-founded Christian communities, which counted only neophytes. After the death of the Apostles, it was but natural that the episcopate as an institution should take on a more definite and stable form in the different Christian communities and that the individual heads of each community, consecrated by them, should exercise the plenitude of authority previously reserved to the Apostles. The episcopate is an Apostolic institution which in course of time tended to spread more and more widely.

In the opening years of the second century, the episcopate, as an institution in which one bishop heads a well-defined Christian community, is an accomplished fact accepted by all. The first great witness to this truth is St. Ignatius of Antioch, in his Letters to the Ephesians, the Magnesians, the Trallians, the Philadelphians, and the Smyrnaeans. Writing to the Ephesians he says: "You must all be in perfect accord with your bishop;" to the Magnesians: "I had the honor of seeing you in the person of Damascus, your bishop." Pointing to the origin of episcopal unity, he declares: "There is only one flesh of Our Lord Jesus Christ, just as there is only one bishop with the college of priests and deacons." And again: "Wherever the bishop is, there let the people be, as where Jesus is, there is the Catholic Church." Finally: "Respect the bishop as a type of God, and the presbyters as the council of God and the college of the Apostles. Apart from these, there is not even the name of a church."

Later writers like St. Justin and Hegesippus confirm this testimony. We have, moreover, the names of many of the early bishops: Papias of Hierapolis, Melito of Sardis, Polycrates of Ephesus, etc.

III. The Roman Primacy. Our Lord Jesus Christ conferred the primacy of jurisdiction in His Church on St. Peter in such unmistakable language that there could be no controversy as to its meaning. Moreover, without this primacy, the primitive Church would have been a truncated institution, in open contradiction with the explicit teachings of the Gospels, copies of which were already in circulation. And so we find the Roman Church, the see of St. Peter, assuming from the very start, first place among the churches, taking precedence over even the more ancient and, at that time, more illustrious churches of Asia Minor. St. Paul conceded this high rank to the Roman Church when he wrote in his Epistle to the Romans: "Your faith is spoken of in the whole world." [1] The presumption is that if the Apostle felt himself obliged to despatch to the

---

[1] Rom. I, 8.

Church of Rome the Epistle which contains his great doctrinal synthesis, it was because he conceded to that embryonic community an exceptional importance. And so when, later on, he resolved to journey to Rome and end his career within the precincts of that city, he gave further evidence of his conviction that the Church of Rome was the center of Christian unity.

Before the close of the first century (between A.D. 95–98), and during the life-time of St. John the Apostle, the bishop of Rome intervened as arbiter between factions abroad in his capacity of supreme head of the Church. Controversies had arisen at Corinth; the Christian element in the city was divided, because some had refused to submit to the presbyters who presided over them. The Church of Rome authoritatively intervened. "You would be a source of great joy to us," wrote St. Clement, bishop of Rome, "if, obedient to what we have written you in the Holy Ghost, you would cut short the unjust outburst of your anger. Behold, we have sent you men both faithful and wise. They shall be the witnesses between ourselves and you." The faithful of Corinth did not regard the intervention of St. Clement as an intrusion; on the contrary, his letter reestablished peace and quiet in the local church, and his efforts were so sincerely appreciated by the Corinthians that seventy years later they still continued to read this message in the assembly of the faithful.

A few years later, explicit testimony is borne to the supremacy of the Roman Church by *St. Ignatius of Antioch,* a disciple of the Apostles, according to whose letter this Church is the "president of the society of love" ($\pi\rho o\kappa\alpha\theta\eta\mu\acute{e}\nu\eta$ $\tau\tilde{\eta}s$ $\alpha\gamma\alpha\pi\tilde{\eta}s$). In other words, St. Ignatius regards the Roman Church as the head of all Christians, united among themselves by the bond of charity. Commenting upon this same epithet, St. Ignatius continues: "You have never deceived any one; you have taught others; it is my wish that whatever you prescribe by your teaching be not contested." The testimony of St. Ignatius derives additional weight from the fact that it proceeds from the great metropolis of Antioch, which had a prior claim to be a see of Peter (*cathedra Petri*).

We have another witness to the same fact in *St. Irenaeus,* an Asiatic bishop and disciple of St. Polycarp, who in turn was a disciple of St. John. "All other churches," he writes, "where the Apostolic tradition is preserved through the care of those who come from all parts, must group themselves around this Church [*i.e.,* the Roman Church] because of her special authority." [1]

Moreover, Rome was already a veritable center, attracting Christians from all parts of the Empire. Justin and Tatian journeyed to Rome; St. Polycarp visited the city when he was eighty years old, and St. Irenaeus and countless others also came. Among these Roman pilgrims we may point in particular to Bishop *Abercius* of Hieropolis in Phrygia. In an epitaph which he composed for his own tomb, he has given us a very enthusiastic picture of the Church of Rome, which he describes as a "queen clothed in a stole and sandals of gold, in which dwells a people who possess the effulgent seal." This seal is to be interpreted as meaning the confession of the Catholic faith.

All doctrinal and disciplinary questions were referred to Rome, and her decision was always accepted as final. The appearance of Montanism, a well-defined heresy, furnishes an instance in point. Some of the members of the church of Lyons were Asiatics, and professed the false doctrines of Montanism. The brethren of Gaul "informed Eleutherius, bishop of Rome, of this state of affairs, in order to restore peace to the churches." Ten years later, Irenaeus, bishop of Lyons, sought anew the advice of the Pope on this same question, and Praxeas arrived in Rome from the East to obtain the condemnation of the Montanist heresy. The striking feature of this whole procedure is that the communities abroad did not appeal to the Apostolic cities of Ephesus and Antioch for the solution of an Oriental difficulty, but to the bishop of Rome. Instances of appeals of this kind are plentiful in the first centuries, and the heretics themselves formed no exception to the rule. Persuaded that a victory was scored for their teachings if they encountered favor in the eyes of the Roman authorities, heresiarchs one and all hastened to Rome to plead their cause. Marcion, who journeyed thither from Pontus, and Valentine, who came from Egypt, are only two instances in point.

Towards the end of the second century, an intervention on the part of the Church of Rome, even more remarkable than any we have so far cited, failed to cause any resentment on the part of the other Christian communities. In regard to *the date of Easter,* two traditions existed side

[1] *"Ad hanc enim ecclesiam* [*sc.* Romanam] *propter potentiorem principalitatem necesse est omnem ecclesiam convenire, hoc est, eos qui sunt undique fideles, in qua semper ab his, qui sunt undique, conservata est ea quae est ab apostolis traditio."*

by side: one, Oriental; the other, Roman. The first of these two traditions reckoned the date of Easter according to the manner of the Jews, the 14th of the first Jewish month, or the 14th Nisan, no matter on what day of the week this date fell. Rome, on the other hand, reckoned the date of Easter in a more Christian manner, always setting the date on the Sunday following the 14th Nisan. For the Asiatics, Easter was the anniversary of the death of Christ; for the others, it was the anniversary of His Resurrection. Thus there arose a serious liturgical conflict. The minds of the Asiatics were not completely at rest on this score, because, finding themselves at variance with Rome on this question, they petitioned St. Polycarp, bishop of Smyrna, to repair to the Eternal City and debate the question with Pope Anicetus (c. 154). The attempts on the part of St. Polycarp to win the Pope over to his side proved unsuccessful, but the epilogue to the drama is even more significant. Victor I, Bishop of Rome (190–198), resolved to settle the question. He issued orders for all the churches of the West and the East to assemble in synods and expound their different opinions. We know from the writings of Eusebius that the results of these debates were recorded in synodal letters, and we have the verdict of the bishops of Pontus (in the neighborhood of Amastris); that of the churches of Osrhoene (in the neighborhood of Edessa); that of the bishop of Corinth; that of the synod of Palestine, and that of the churches of Gaul. All of these took issue against the practice of fixing the date of Easter according to the Jewish manner of reckoning, siding with the Roman practice; but the Asiatics held out, protesting that the Roman custom was not in accord with the Apostolic tradition, and declaring that they would never concede the point. When matters came to this pass, Pope Victor did not hesitate, but fulminated against the rebels a sentence of excommunication, manifestly conscious as he was that the Church of Rome embodied all Christendom, and could sever from her communion persons who were recalcitrant to her decisions. True, some persons, in particular St. Irenaeus, regarded the punishment as legitimate, though excessive; as a matter of fact, the decision carried the day and the practice of celebrating Easter on Sunday prevailed. The controversy regarding the date of Easter is significant also because it provides an additional proof of the far-reaching influence of a Church which already in the second century could concern herself with so secondary a question.

TEXTS AND DOCUMENTS

The Primacy of the Roman Church
(Irenaeus, *Haeres.*, III)

It is within the power of all, therefore, in every church, who may wish to see the truth, to contemplate clearly the tradition of the Apostles manifested throughout the whole world; and we are in a position to reckon up those who were by the Apostles instituted bishops in the churches, and [to demonstrate] the succession of these men to our own times; those who neither taught nor knew of anything like what these [heretics] rave about. For if the Apostles had known hidden mysteries, which they were in the habit of imparting to "the perfect" apart and privately from the rest, they would have delivered them especially to those to whom they were also committing the churches themselves. For they were desirous that these men should be very perfect and blameless in all things, whom also they were leaving behind as their successors, delivering up their own place of government to these men; and these men, if they discharged their functions honestly, would be a great boon [to the Church], but if they should fall away, the direst calamity.

Since, however, it would be very tedious in such a volume as this to reckon up the successions of all the churches, we do put to confusion all those who, in whatever manner, whether by an evil complacency, by vainglory, or by blindness and perverse opinion, assemble in unauthorized meetings; [we do this, I say] by indicating that tradition derived from the Apostles, of the very great, the very ancient, and universally known Church founded and organized at Rome by the two most glorious Apostles, Peter and Paul; as also [by pointing out] the faith preached to men, which comes down to our time by means of the successions of the bishops. All other churches, where the Apostolic tradition is preserved through the care of those who come from all parts, must group themselves around this Church [*i.e.*, the Roman Church] because of her special authority.

The blessed Apostles, then, having founded and built up the Church, committed into the hands of Linus the office of the episcopate. Of this Linus, Paul makes mention in the Epistles to Timothy. To him succeeded Anacletus; and after him, in the third place from the Apostles, Clement was allotted the bishopric. This man, as he had seen the blessed Apostles, and had been acquainted with them, might be said to have the preaching of the Apostles still echoing [in his ears], and their traditions before his eyes. Nor was he alone [in this], for there were many still remaining who had received instructions from the Apostles. In the time of this Clement, no small dissension having occurred among the brethren at Corinth, the Church in Rome despatched a most powerful letter to the Corinthians, exhorting them to peace, renewing their faith, and declaring the tradition which it had lately received from the Apostles, proclaiming the one God, omnipotent, the Maker of

Heaven and earth, the Creator of man, who brought on the deluge and called Abraham, who led the people from the land of Egypt, spake with Moses, set forth the law, sent the prophets, and who has prepared fire for the devil and his angels. From this document, whosoever chooses to do so, may learn that He, the Father of our Lord Jesus Christ, was preached by the churches, and may also understand the Apostolic tradition of the Church, since this Epistle is of older date than these men who are now propagating falsehood, and who conjure [into existence] another god beyond the Creator and the Maker of all things that exist.

The Episcopate

(The First Epistle of St. Clement)

The Apostles have preached the Gospel to us from the Lord Jesus Christ. . . . Our Apostles also knew, through our Lord Jesus Christ, that there would be strife on account of the office of the episcopate. For this reason, therefore, inasmuch as they had obtained a perfect fore-knowledge of this, they appointed those [ministers] already mentioned, and afterwards gave instructions, that when these should fall asleep, other approved men should succeed them in their ministry. We are of the opinion, therefore, that those appointed by them, or afterwards, by other eminent men, with the consent of the whole Church, and who have blamelessly served the flock of Christ in a humble, peaceable and disinterested spirit, and have for a long time possessed the good opinion of all, cannot be justly dismissed from the ministry. For our sin will not be small, if we eject from the episcopate those who have blamelessly and holily fulfilled its duties. Blessed are those prebyters who, having finished their course before now, have obtained a fruitful and perfect departure [from this world]; for they have no fear lest any one deprive them of the place now appointed them. But we see that ye have removed some men of excellent behaviour from the ministry, which they filled blamelessly and with honour. . . . Your schism has subverted [the faith of] many, has discouraged many, has given rise to doubt in many, and has caused grief to us all. And still your sedition continueth.

QUESTIONS

1. Define charismata, and draw up a list of them.
2. What is meant by the "Eucharistic synaxis"?
3. What was the ceremony of the imposition of hands?
4. Prove that the words ἐπίσκοποι and πρεσβύτεροι are identical in meaning when used in reference to the establishment of the episcopate.
5. What Scripture texts can you quote in support of the view that Christ conferred upon Peter not only the primacy of honor, but also the primacy of jurisdiction?

6. What historical proof can you give that the bishop of Rome was vested with supreme authority in matters of jurisdiction?
7. What was the heresy of Montanism?
8. How was the date of Easter computed by those who followed the Jewish calendar?
9. What reasons influenced Pope Anicetus in refusing to yield to St. Polycarp on the question of the date of Easter?

BIBLIOGRAPHY

Origins of the Episcopate.—BATIFFOL, *L'Eglise naissante,* ch. III.—DE SMEDT, *L'Organisation des églises chrétiennes jusqu'au milieu du IIIe siècle,* in *Rev. quest. hist.,* t. XLIV and L (1888 and 1891).—DOUAIS, *Origines de l'épiscopat,* in *Mélanges litt. et hist. relig.,* I, 1899.—MICHIELS, *L'Origine de l'épiscopat,* Louvain, 1900; art. *"Evêques,"* in *Dict. d'Apol.*—J. H. BARBOUR, *Beginnings of the Historic Episcopate.*—R. S. THOMPSON, *Historic Episcopate.* **The Roman Primacy.**—Sources: I CLEM., 58.—IGN., *Ep. ad Rom.,* 3.—IRENAEUS, III, 3.—On the paschal controversy, EUSEBIUS, *H. E.,* V, 24.—Works: MSGR. DUCHESNE, *The Churches Separated from Rome.*—MSGR. FREPPEL, *Saint Irénée.*—DUFOURCQ, *Saint Irénée* (Coll. *"Les Saints"*) and (Coll. *"La Pensée Chrétienne"*).—J. CHAPMAN, *La Chronologie des premières listes épiscopales à Rome,* in *Rev. bénéd.,* XVIII (1901), pp. 399-417; XIX (1902), pp. 13-17, 145-170.—G. BARDY, *L'église romaine sous le pontificat de saint Anicet, R. S. R.,* XVII (1927), p. 481-511.—RIVINGTON, *Roman Primacy.*—BATIFFOL, *L'Eglise naissante,* ch. III, and especially, ch. IV: *Le catholicisme de saint Irénée.*—L. SPIKOWSKI, *La doctrine de l'Eglise dans saint Irénée,* 1926.—A. FORTESCUE, *The Early Papacy,* 1920.—J. CHAPMAN, *Studies on the Early Papacy.*

CHAPTER VI

I. Baptism. The postulant in the early Church was first instructed in the traditional teachings. The Apostles' Creed furnished him with an excellent summary of all the dogmas. The *Didaché* contained the moral portion of his instruction and rounded out this primitive course of catechetics. An immediate preparation of one or two days of fasting was then imposed upon the aspirant, who, after fulfilling this last condition, was led to a stream of water and there received the Sacrament of Baptism by a triple immersion. We find references, however, to a triple pouring of water on the head of the candidate, and this way of administering Baptism remained in force until the time when baptismal *piscinae* were annexed to all churches and Baptism by immersion or quasi-immersion became the general practice.

II. The Holy Eucharist. Early belief in the Holy Eucharist is explicitly attested, not only by numerous Scriptural texts, but also by several writings of the primitive Church. The three principal witnesses to this doctrine are the *Didaché,* St. Ignatius, and St. Justin.

The testimony of the *Didaché* has been the subject of much discussion, yet the work clearly indicates that the celebration of the Eucharist comprised a breaking of the bread, Communion, and thanksgiving. "On the Lord's Day assemble together and break bread and give thanks, having confessed your transgressions, in order that your sacrifice be not defiled."

St. Ignatius is very explicit. True, when speaking of the Body and Blood of Christ, his language is often figurative, but one passage in his Letter to the Smyrnaeans is manifestly Eucharistic in meaning. "The Docetae," he writes, "abstain from the Eucharist and from prayer, because they refuse to admit that the Eucharist is the flesh of our Lord Jesus Christ, flesh which suffered for our sins and which the Lord deigned to raise from the grave." Thus, the Docetae alone refuse to align themselves with the general belief of the faithful in the Eucharist.

St. Justin's statement is even more emphatic: "For it is not as common bread or common drink that we receive these, but as by God's word Jesus Our Saviour became flesh and blood for our salvation, so also have we been taught that the food made Eucharist by the word of prayer that comes from Him, is both flesh and blood of that Jesus who was made flesh." The words of St. Justin clearly express formal belief in the fact that the presence of the Body and Blood of Jesus under the appearances of bread and wine is as real as His Incarnation. Moreover, a special importance attaches itself to his testimony because, in refuting the accusations brought against the Christian mysteries, the apologist enters into a very minute description of the Mass. He distinguishes between: (1) The preparation for Mass, or the reading of the memoirs of the Apostles and the books of the prophets; (2) The offertory; (3) The Eucharistic narrative, in the course of which the consecration takes place; and (4) Communion. "Bread and a cup of water and wine are brought to the president of the brethren, and he takes it and sends up praise . . . and gives thanks at great length. When he has completed the prayers and the thanksgiving, the whole people present respond, saying 'Amen.' When the president has given thanks and all the people have responded, the deacons, as we call them, give to each of those present to partake of the consecrated bread and wine and water, and they take some away for the absent."

III. Penance. In the early days of the Church the Christians, being in constant danger of death and expecting the Second Coming (*parousia*) of the Lord, lived exemplary lives. This unfortunately developed in some a tendency towards an excessive sort of rigorism, termed *Encratism*. Certain religious zealots required of the faithful the practice of absolute perfection, and refusing to see any distinction between precepts and evangelical counsels, admitted only precepts. Moreover, the adepts of Encratism prohibited the use of heavy foods, especially meat and wine, looked upon marriage with disapproval, and endeavored to constrain all Christians to practice virginity. Vestiges of these exorbitant demands are to be met with in many of the earlier apocryphal writings, and in particular in the Gospel according to the Egyptians, the *Acta Thomae,* the *Acta Pauli et Theclae,* and the *Acta Petri cum Simone.*

As a measure to insure purity of life the doctrine of Encratism was held in favor in many places, although the spirit of moderation which prevailed in most communities made sounder minds look at it with suspicion. In its stead a more orthodox kind of morality soon loomed on the horizon, and well-balanced ascetical practices, such as bodily mortification, fasting, and almsgiving, quickly took its place. At a very early date, two days or "stations," Wednesday and Friday, were set aside each week for fasting. Explicit reference is made to them in the *Didaché,* and on these days the Christians partook of only one sparse meal after sunset. Continence is also regarded as one of the early forms of primitive asceticism, although its observance was not enjoined upon anyone. Continent persons of both sexes remained in the world, and endeavored to give themselves over more completely to the exercise of prayer.

Primitive moral asceticism finds its most authorized expression in *The Shepherd of Hermas.* This work was composed by a brother of Pope Pius I (140–155), and expresses the ideas of the papacy and the Roman presbyterium in these matters. Hermas professes "the redemption from sin by sincere repentance," and stresses the idea that pardon for past offenses is obtainable, provided the sinner have contrition. But Hermas is quite conscious of the fact that the preaching of such a doctrine in his time might savor of undue indulgence, and hence places the proofs for his thesis upon the lips of an aged woman, the personification of the Church, and declares that this pardon can be granted only once in the form of an extraordinary concession, or "a kind of jubilee." All sins can be forgiven and even the adulterer, the homicide, and the apostate are susceptible of redemption. Redemption comprises two parts: *conversion* (μετάνοια), which is the work of the sinner; and *cure* (ἴασις), which is a gift of God. Between the two, the penitent is required to undergo a laborious sort of purification, a forecast of future penitential discipline. St. Irenaeus speaks of fallen women who cease not to wail and repent for their sins.

TEXTS AND DOCUMENTS

The Didaché on Baptism and the Holy Eucharist
(Extracts)

VII. Concerning Baptism, baptize thus: Having first said all these things, baptize in the name of the Father, and of the Son, and of the Holy Spirit, in running water. But if thou hast no running water, baptize in other water; and if thou canst not in cold, then in warm. But if thou hast neither, pour out water thrice upon the head in the name of the Father, Son, and Holy Spirit. But before the Baptism let the baptizer and the baptized fast, and any others who are able; but thou shalt order the baptized to fast one or two days before.

IX. Now concerning the Eucharist, hold Eucharist thus. First, concerning the cup: We thank Thee, our Father, for the holy vine of David, Thy servant, which Thou didst make known to us through Jesus, Thy Servant; to Thee be glory for ever. And concerning the broken bread: We thank Thee, our Father, for the life and knowledge which Thou didst make known to us through Jesus, Thy Servant; to Thee be glory for ever. Even as this broken bread was scattered over the hills, but was gathered together and became one, so let the Church be gathered together from the ends of the earth into Thy kingdom, for Thine is the glory and the power through Jesus Christ for ever. But let no one eat or drink of your Eucharist except those who have been baptized in the name of the Lord; for concerning this also the Lord did say: Give not that which is holy to the dogs.

X. But after you are satisfied, thus give thanks: We thank Thee, O holy Father, for Thy holy name which Thou didst cause to tabernacle in our hearts, and for the knowledge and faith and immortality which Thou didst make known to us through Jesus, Thy Servant; to Thee be glory for ever. Thou, Lord almighty, didst create all things for Thy name's sake, and didst give food and drink to men for their enjoyment, that they might give thanks to Thee; but to us Thou didst freely give spiritual food and drink, and eternal life through Thy Servant. Above all we thank Thee for that Thou art mighty; to Thee be glory for ever. Remember, Lord, Thy Church, to deliver it from all evil and to make it perfect in Thy love, and gather it together from the four winds to Thy kingdom, which Thou hast prepared for it; for Thine is the power and glory for ever. Let grace come, and let this world pass away. Hosanna to the God of David! If any man is holy, let him come! If any man is not, let him repent: Maran atha. Amen. But suffer the prophets to hold Eucharist as they will.

XI. Whosoever, then, comes and teaches you all these things that have been said before, receive him. But if the teacher himself be perverted and teach another doctrine to the destruction of this, hear him not; but if he teacheth so as to increase righteousness and the knowledge of the Lord, receive him as the Lord. . . . But he shall not remain more than one day; or if need be, a second as well; but if he stay three days, he is a false prophet. And when an apostle goeth forth, let him accept nothing but bread until he lodgeth; but if he asks for money, he is a false prophet. . . . And not every one that speaketh in the Spirit is a prophet; but only if he holds to the ways of the Lord. Therefore, from their ways shall the false prophet and the true prophet be known. And no prophet who orders a meal in the Spirit shall eat of it; otherwise he is a false prophet; and every prophet who teaches the truth, if he do not what he teacheth, is a false prophet. But no prophet, who has been tried and proved true, working unto the mystery of the Church in the world, yet not teaching others to do what he himself doeth, shall be judged by you: for he has his judgment with God; for so also did the prophets of old. But whosoever shall say in the Spirit: "Give me money, or something else," you shall not listen to him; but if he tell you to give on behalf of others in need, let no one judge him.

XIV. On the Lord's day come together, break bread, and hold Eucharist, after having confessed your transgressions, that your sacrifice may be pure. But let no one who is at variance with his fellow join in your meeting, until he be reconciled, that your sacrifice may not be defiled. For this is that which was spoken by the Lord: "In every place and time offer me a pure sacrifice, for I am a great King," saith the Lord, "and my name is wonderful among the heathen."

XV. Appoint, therefore, for yourselves bishops and deacons worthy of the Lord, meek men, and not lovers of money, and truthful and approved; for they also render to you the service of prophets and teachers. Therefore, despise them not, for they are your honorable men, together with the prophets and teachers. And reprove one another not in wrath, but in peace, as you find it in the Gospel; and let no one speak with any who has done wrong to his neighbor, nor let him hear a word from you until he repents. But your prayers and alms and all your acts perform as you find it in the Gospel of our Lord.

XVI. Watch over your life. Let not your lamps be quenched, nor your loins unloosed; but be ready, for you know not the hour in which our Lord cometh. But be often gathered together, seeking the things which are profitable for your souls: for the whole time of your faith shall not profit you, except you be found perfect in the last time.

The Sacrifice of the Eucharist According to St. Justin
(I Ap., 65–67)

And on the day of the sun [Sunday] all who live in cities or in the country gather together in one place, and the memoirs of the Apostles or the writings of the prophets are read, as long as time permits; then, when the reader has ended, the president by his words instructs and exhorts all to imitate the good things just read. After which we all rise together and pray, and when our common prayer is ended, bread, wine, and water are brought, and the president offers to God prayers and thanksgivings, according to his ability, and the people assent, saying *Amen.* Then follows the distribution of the consecrated food, some of which is carried by the deacons to those who are absent.

QUESTIONS

1. Describe the conversion and initiation of an early convert to the Church.
2. Who were the *Docetae?*
3. What was Encratism?
4. Do you think that Church discipline regarding the celibacy of the clergy is traceable to the remote influence of the Encratites?
5. How is the work of Redemption effected according to the *Shepherd of Hermas?*
6. Define Christian asceticism.

BIBLIOGRAPHY

The Eucharist.—Sources: *Didaché,* IX.—IGNATIUS, *Ep. ad Smyrn.,* VII, i, VIII, 1–2; *Eph.,* XX, 2; *Philad.,* IV; *Rom,* VII, 3.—JUSTIN, *Apol.,* LXV–LXVI, 3 passages of Dial. with Trypho, XLI, LXX, CXVII.—Works: G. RAUSCHEN, *L'Eucharistie et la Pénitence durant les six premiers siècles,* 1910—G. BAREILLE, art. *Eucharistie* (according to the Fathers) in *Dict. de Théol.*—LEBRETON, art. *Eucharistie,* in *Dict. d'Apol.*—MSGR. RUCH, *Eucharistie* (according to the Holy Scriptures), in *Dict. de Théol.*—BATIFFOL, *Etudes hist. et théol. pos.,* second series, *l'Eucharistie,* new edit., 1920.—WARREN, *The Liturgy and Ritual of the Ante-Nicene Church,* 1897.—A. FORTESCUE, *The Mass: A Study in the Roman Liturgy.*

Penance in the Early Church.—TERTULLIAN, *De paenitentia.*—BATIF-FOL, *Etudes d'histoire,* 1904.—RAUSCHEN, *Euch. u. Buszsakr.,* 1908.

CHAPTER VII

I. Jewish Gnosticism. The heresies that made their appearance during the life-time of the Apostles originated in Jewish or Judaeo-Christian soil. The alarm in their regard was first sounded by St. Paul in his Letters to the Ephesians and the Colossians, written in his prison at Rome, and addressed to communities situated on the boundary lines of Phrygia, in the valley of the Lycus. In these Epistles the Apostle strongly denounces a Christology in which the person of the Saviour is unduly minimized, and exaggerated importance is attached to the angels. By way of contrast, St. Paul brings out clearly the true rôle of Christ as the author and end of all creation and the head of the Church.

In these same parts of Asia, another group of heretics is singled out by St. John in his Apocalypse. They were called the *Nicolaites* and purported to have been founded by a deacon named Nicholas. Their teaching led to immoral practices.

We know, too, through the testimony of St. Irenaeus, that St. John opposed the teachings of *Cerinthus,* an Egyptian Jew of the school of Philo, who conceded that Our Lord was a prudent and truly wise man, but refused to acknowledge His divine character. According to him, the true God neither created the world nor issued the law to the Jews. The angels created the world, and the Angel of the law was the God of the Jews. These first discoveries of a series of angels intermediary between God and the world comprise what is known as Jewish Gnosticism; they presaged the advent of a complete philosophical system known as Gnosticism.

But the birthplace of the first real heresy was Samaria. *Simon Magus* was the first to attempt to bribe the Apostles with money to obtain possession of the power of working miracles *(simony)*. The Apostles rejected his offer with scorn, but Simon was not so easily discouraged. Soon he set himself to sketching the bold outlines of a complete gnosis, in which he was the supreme God and his concubine, Helen, the first goddess, his Thought (ἔννοια) incarnate like himself. In Samaria he was the Father, in Judaea, the Son, and among the heathens, the Holy Ghost. St. Irenaeus has given us a description of his theological system. "There is," he says, "one Supreme Power, to which corresponds a feminine power, known as the Thought. This Thought emanated from the Father, and created the angels, who in turn created the world. But because they did not want to appear what they really were, *i.e.*, creatures of *Ennoia,* the angels sought to obtain possession of Thought, succeeded in subduing her, chained her to a feminine body, and by a process of metempsychosis made her pass from one woman to another." The intervention of God in the affairs of this world has for its purpose the deliverance of *Ennoia* and the punishment of the wicked angels.

The answer to all this verbiage—whether direct or indirect it matters not—was formulated by the great Apostle St. John. Paul had successfully refuted the Judaeo-Christians in his explanation of justification by faith; John dealt a deadly blow to Gnosticism by his Christian conception of the Logos. In more instances than one, the Logos had no more significance with the Greeks than that of some intermediary being, half-way between God and the world. He was a sort of demiurge, or, as the Gnostics later on called him, an eon: the highest of all creatures, but still a creature. The term was shrouded in the same vagueness that beset the word "reason" in the eighteenth, and the word "science" in the nineteenth century. St. John completely clarified the meaning of the expression by declaring that the Logos was the living and personal Christ, the perfect mediator between God and man. "What is there about this prologue," writes Fouard, "that might not have emanated from the mind and fallen from the lips of this Apostle? John was a man gifted with sublime visions; no eye has pierced farther into the vast deeps of the celestial life: thereof his Apocalypse is witness. Instinctively, as it were, and as a familiar friend he goes straight to the very heart of the Godhead." [1]

II. The End of Judaeo-Christianity. The Gnostic heresies were cradled in Samaria or Asia Minor, and are traceable to the Jews of the Dispersion. As for *Palestinian Judaism,* its influence was dwindling fast; as a religious sect it was doomed. The uncompromising attitude of the Zealots was everywhere fomenting a spirit of revolt, when in the year

---

[1] Fouard, *St. John,* p. 179.

66, under the reign of the Emperor Nero, the trouble finally came to a head. An insurrection was unleashed, the Roman garrison was completely wiped out in a horrible massacre, and open warfare began to spread throughout the length and breadth of Judaea. Appointed to repress the sedition, Vespasian was about to lay siege to the Holy City, when Nero's death paved his way to the imperial throne. The newly installed Emperor entrusted the expedition to his son Titus. Jerusalem suffered all the horrors of a siege, which lasted five months, and the city was forced to capitulate on the 8th of September, A. D. 70. The cruelties of the reprisals were unprecedented. Men, women and children, who had huddled together like cattle in the precincts of the Temple for protection, were butchered unmercifully, and those who escaped slaughter were carried away into slavery. The deicide city was completely gutted and its remains left to smoulder until the day when the Emperor Hadrian founded there the colony of Aelia Capitolina, with its pagan sanctuaries. A statue of Jupiter was erected on the hill where the Temple had stood, and on Mount Calvary, a temple of Venus.

Before these troubles broke out, the Christian Jews had withdrawn from the city and taken refuge at Pella beyond the Jordan, where, completely isolated from the rest of Christendom, they developed a spirit of particularism destined to grow and finally split them into two groups, as distinct as the principles from which they emanated. The first of these groups were the Nazarenes; they were simply schismatics. The second were the Ebionites; they were real heretics. The *Nazarenes* would have been Christians, had they not persisted in the obstinate observance of the Jewish law and Jewish practices. They took up their quarters in the villages of Palestine; their legalism, like their language, sequestered them from the rest of society; they led their own lives and never meddled in the affairs of others, and so, little by little, they disappeared from the face of the earth. The *Ebionites,* on the contrary, aimed at spreading their influence. We find them scattered throughout the Empire and located even in the large cities like Rome and Alexandria. They are, so to speak, the Diaspora of Judaeo-Christianity. All attempts at finding a founder by the name of Ebion have proved futile. In point of fact, the name of the sect signifies "the poor." To their way of thinking, Jesus Christ was merely the last of the prophets, the humble son of Joseph and Mary. Scrupulous practice of the law had brought him justification, and so we, too, they argued, shall be justified, if, like him, we observe the law: circumcision, the Sabbath, etc. In later years the Ebionites entered into relationship with the Essenes. From this contact with "the higher forms of Jewish life" resulted a mixture of Essenian, Jewish, and Christian elements. The practices borrowed from the Essenes were more of an ascetical nature: daily ablutions, a vegetarian diet, celibacy, etc. Essenian Ebionitism is best known to us through the "Clementine Romances," written by members of the sect, and comprising twenty homilies and the so-called *Recognitiones* in ten books. Essenian Ebionitism in turn was to produce a very bizarre kind of offspring, termed the doctrine of Elkesai, so named after its problematical founder, El Kasai. It consisted in the preaching of a new Baptism, capable of remitting all sins, that was administered in conjunction with incantations and magical formulas of all kinds. The spirit of Ebionitism was too narrow to acquire any universal and lasting influence. Judaeo-Christianity could never survive the blow dealt the sect by the mighty pen of St. Paul.

TEXTS AND DOCUMENTS

THE SIEGE OF JERUSALEM

And now all hope of escape was cut off from the Jews, together with their liberty of going out of the city. Then did the famine widen its progress, and devour the people by whole houses and families; the upper rooms were full of women and children that were dying by famine, and the lanes of the city were full of the dead bodies of the aged; the children also and the young men wandered about the market-places like shadows, all swelled with the famine, and fell down dead wheresoever their misery seized them. As for burying them, those that were sick themselves were not able to do it; and those that were hearty and well, were deterred from doing it by the great multitude of those dead bodies, and by the uncertainty there was how soon they should die themselves; for many died as they were burying others, and many went to their coffins before that fatal hour was come. Nor was there any lamentation made under these calamities, nor were any mournful complaints heard; but the famine confounded all natural passions; for those who were just going to die, looked upon those who were gone to their rest before them with dry eyes and open mouths. A deep silence, and a kind of deadly night, had seized upon the city; while yet the robbers were still more terrible than these miseries were themselves; for they broke open those houses which were no other than graves of dead bodies, and plundered them of what they had, and carrying off the coverings of their bodies, went out laughing, and tried the points of their swords on their dead bodies; and, in order to prove what mettle they were made of, they thrust their swords through some of those that still lay alive on the ground; but for those that entreated them to lend them their right hand, and their sword to despatch them, they were too proud to grant their requests, and left them to be consumed by the famine. Now everyone of these died with their eyes fixed upon the Temple. Children pulled the very morsels that their fathers were eating out of their mouths, and what was still more to be pitied, so did the mothers do as to their infants; and when those that were most dear were perishing under their hands, they were not ashamed to take from them the very last drops that might preserve their lives; and while they ate after this manner, yet were they not concealed in so doing; but the seditious everywhere came upon them immediately, and snatched away from them what they had gotten from others; for when they saw any house shut up, this was to them a signal that the people within had gotten some food: whereupon they broke open the doors and ran in, and took pieces of what they were eating, almost up out of their very throats, and this by force; the old men, who held their food fast, were beaten; and if the women hid what they had within their hands, their hair was torn for so doing; nor was there any commiseration shown either to the aged or to infants, but they lifted up children from the ground as they hung upon the morsels they had gotten, and shook them down upon the floor; but still were they more barbarously cruel to those that had prevented their coming in, and had actually swallowed down what they were going to seize upon, as if they had been unjustly defrauded of their right. They also invented terrible methods of torment to discover where any food was, and a man was forced to bear what is terrible even to hear, in order to make him confess that he had but one loaf of bread, or that he might discover a handful of barley-meal that was concealed; this was done when these tormentors were not themselves hungry; for the thing had been less barbarous had necessity forced them to it; but it was done to keep their madness in exercise, and as making preparation of provision for themselves for the following days.

JOSEPHUS, *Bell. Jud.*, V, ix, 1.

QUESTIONS

1. Define Gnosticism, both as a philosophical and a theological system of thought.
2. Give a definition of simony.
3. What is a gnosis?
4. What were the eons?
5. Who were the Nazarenes?
6. Who were the Ebionites?
7. What were the *Clementine Romances?*
8. How was Gnosticism the precursor of Arianism?

BIBLIOGRAPHY

The First Heresies.—The Enchiridia published by Herder contain a complete collection of the principal historical or dogmatic texts: DENZINGER-BANNWART, *Enchiridion Symbolorum*, 1927; C. KIRCH, *Enchiridion fontium historiae ecclesiasticae antiquae*, 1910; M. J. ROUET DE JOURNEL, *Enchiridion Patristicum*, 1913.—Works: G. BARDY, *Cérinthe*, in *Rev. bibl.*, July 1st, 1921, pp. 344-374.—ERMONI, *L'Ebionisme dans l'Eglise naissante*, in *Rev. ques. hist.* LXVI (1899), pp. 481 ff.—L. CERFAUX, *La gnose simonienne, nos principales sources*, R. S. R., 1925, pp. 489-512; 1926, pp. 5-21; pp. 265-286; pp. 481-504.— ST. ALPHONSUS, *The History of Heresies and their Refutation*, transl. J. T. MULLOCH.—ST. IRENAEUS, *Treatise Against the Heresies*, transl. HITCHCOCK.

St. John.—KNABENBAUER, *Evangelium secundum Joannem*, 1898.—TH. CALMES, *L'Evangile selon saint Jean*, 1904 (abridged edit., 1906).—J. LE-BRETON, *op. cit.*, pp. 374-429.—LEPIN, *L'origine du quatrième Evangile*, 1907; *La valeur historique du quatrième Evangile*, 1910; art. *Evangile*, in *Dict. d'Apol.*—MANGENOT, *Jean l'Evangéliste*, in *Dict. de la Bible.*—J. LABOURT, *De la valeur du témoignage de saint Irénée sur la question johannine*, in *Revue biblique*, t. VII.—E. BREHIER, *Les idées philosophiques et religieuses de Philon d'Alexandrie*, 1908.—LOUIS, *Philon le Juif*, 1911.—PIROT, *Saint Jean* (Coll. Les Saints), 1923.—J. LAGRANGE, *Evangile selon Saint Jean*, 1925.—A. DURAND, *Saint Jean et ses devanciers*, in *Etudes*, April 20, 1927, pp. 129-142.—FOUARD, *St. John and the Close of the Apostolic Age.*—BAUNARD, *The Life of the Apostle St. John.*—FILLION, *St. Jean l'Evangéliste, sa vie et ses écrits*, 1909.— J. BELSER, *Das Evangelium des hl. Johannes*, Freiburg i. B., 1905.

SECOND PERIOD

The Pagan Empire

From Trajan's Rescript to the Edict of Milan (111–313)

SECTION I

The Second Century. Period of the Antonines

CHAPTER I

THE PERSECUTIONS

I. Trajan's Rescript. The dynasty of the Antonines ruled Rome throughout almost the entire second century (96–192). With the exception of Commodus, its last representative, it furnished the Empire with excellent administrators. Nerva reigned only one year (96 to Jan. 25, 98), and was succeeded by *Trajan*. This Emperor was above all a soldier, gifted with practical common sense. In the beginning he paid little or no attention to the Christian religion, although Nero's edict forbidding its practice was still in force. The legal position of the Christians at this time is clearly indicated for us by a letter addressed to the Emperor by Pliny, governor of Bythinia. Persons charged with practicing the new religion had been arraigned before his tribunal. Upon obtaining their admission of guilt, the young governor had desisted from making any further inquiries concerning their conduct in other matters, and had condemned them to death. Was not the mere profession of the Christian religion *ipso facto* a juridical crime punishable by death? The question was not even debatable. But Pliny soon found himself deluged with denunciations of all kinds, many of which were anonymous. Moreover, several of the accused expressed themselves as willing to renounce their faith. In this twofold dilemma, he was undecided whether or not they should be condemned, and so referred the matter to the Emperor.

Trajan replied like a true politician versed in the law: (1) Christianity must remain proscribed as a religion. Unquestionably, membership in the sect is not a crime that must be sought out and prosecuted—*Christiani conquirendi non sunt*—but in due respect for a prohibitive law antedating his reign, the Christians must be punished if brought to justice and the offense proved—*Si deferantur et arguantur, puniendi sunt.* (2) And since only the name Christian is deserving of reprehension, Trajan refuses to associate the sect with revolutionists and common criminals. Hence, anyone who denies he is a Christian is no longer guilty. Apostates are to be pardoned, therefore, on their own recantation. (3) For the same reason, there is no need of enacting against the Christians a sort of law of suspects, or to take account of anonymous denunciations.

In maintaining the tenor of the Neronian Edict, while limiting its application, these measures gave proof of unprecedented shrewdness and cunning on the part of the Emperor. By befriending the apostates, Trajan was making use of a good weapon against Christianity, and by refusing to give a hearing to anonymous accusations, he was safeguarding public peace and tranquillity. The rescript of Trajan was none the less an immoral piece of machinery. It showed itself favorable to apostasy and, moreover, was overtly unjust in punishing the Christians and at the same time forbidding that they be hunted. "The Christian is punishable," wrote Tertullian, "not because he is guilty, but because he is discovered, although he is not to be sought out."

The importance of Trajan's rescript is considerable. In interpreting the *Institutum Neronianum,* it determined for a lengthy period of time the tenor of all future persecuting legislation. Its practical conclusions follow from the principle: The profession of Christianity is the crime of Christians. Mommsen is in error, therefore, when he traces the cause of the persecutions to the *jus coercendi,* in virtue of which Roman magistrates could institute police measures to insure public order and safety. If such were the case, why did the governors deem it necessary to refer the matter of persecuting the Christians to the Emperor? Equally without foundation is the theory, advanced by other historians, that the Christians were persecuted because by lewd actions and magical practices they committed breaches against the penal laws of the State, and much less the reason alleged by Le Blant, that they were punished for the crime of *lèse majesté, i. e.,* refusal to sacrifice to the gods and to the Emperor. Trajan's rescript leaves no doubt as to the nature of their crime; it is the Christian name; and with the disavowal of this name all culpability ceases.

In practical life, legislation of this kind placed the Christians at the complete mercy of the governors of the provinces and their subordinates, the *curatores civitatis,* who, beginning with the reign of the Antonines, took the place of the municipal authorities in every city of the Empire. If these officials had no particular grievances against the Christians, they could invoke the authority of Trajan's rescript and not persecute them; on the other hand, if popular sentiment and prejudice clamored for victims, or their attention was called to the actions of some Christian or Christians, they could wreak vengeance upon them. Hence the local character of the persecution under the Antonines.

The principal martyrs during Trajan's reign were St. Clement and St. Ignatius of Antioch. According to the acts of his martyrdom, Clement was condemned to the mines (*ad metalla*), exiled to the Tauric Chersonesus (Crimea), thrown into the Black Sea with a heavy stone around his neck, and then buried on one of the islands off the coast. St. Ignatius of Antioch was arrested in 107 and cast to the lions in the amphitheatre at Rome. A striking example of the condition of the Christians under the Antonines is seen in the fact that the bishops of the different localities which Ignatius traversed on his way to the Eternal City were unmolested when they came out on the road to greet him. Another martyr of this period was St. Simeon of Jerusalem.

II. Strict Application of the Rescript under Hadrian, Antoninus, and Marcus Aurelius. Hadrian (117–138) and Antoninus (138–161) assumed the attitude dictated by Trajan's rescript in regard to the Christians. A consummate dilettante, an indefatigable traveller, Hadrian whiled away his time sipping from the beauties of nature, revelling in the new mysteries of Oriental religions, and despising Christianity. But more conscientious governors who were in the lists grappling with the religious difficulties were constantly referring matters to him. Mob uprisings were everywhere creating situations both abnormal and illegal, and so, swamped with accusations on both sides, the magistrates were undecided whether to offer resistance or yield. In 123 or 124, Hadrian answered them in his letter to Minucius Fundanus, proconsul of Asia. The authenticity of this document has been contested, but it is really beyond dispute. If Tertullian does not speak of it, his silence is amply compensated by the mention made of it by St. Justin, who wrote only fifteen years later and cited the text in its entirety. Hadrian's rescript made no substantial changes in that of his predecessor. Like Trajan, the new Emperor required that the accusations be listed according to a regular form; hence it was unjust to sacrifice the Christians to the clamors of the angry rabble.

Hadrian's letter failed to temper popular fanaticism; the martyrdom of St. Polycarp under his immediate successor is positive proof of that. In the year 155, at the public festivals, the cry was suddenly heard: "Death to the atheists! Arrest Polycarp!" The proconsul at once issued orders that the homes of the Christians be searched. Arraigned before the judge, Polycarp refused to insult God. "Eighty and six years I have served Him," he explained, "and He never did me anything but good." At these words the multitude surged into the stadium, a pyre was hastily erected, Polycarp was fastened to the stake, and in a few minutes his charred body fell amidst smoke and flames.

It is hard to conceive of a more illegal procedure; and so we find Antoninus issuing orders in a letter addressed "to all the Greeks" that similar uprisings against the Christians cease. This Emperor, however, adopted the very same attitude towards the new religion as his predecessors. An excellent ruler and administrator from every other angle, he was ultra-conservative and irrevocably wedded to the past in the matter of religion, and would have considered himself as lacking in piety towards the gods as well as towards his adoptive father, Hadrian, had he taken a different course of action. Among the many martyrs who fell as victims to the persecution of the Emperor Hadrian, we may single out Pope Alexander I, Eustachius and Theopista with their three sons, and Symphorosa and her seven sons. The most outstanding of the martyrs under the reign of Antoninus were St. Polycarp and Popes Telesphorus, Hyginus, and Pius I.

Marcus Aurelius is perhaps the most vaunted man of all Roman antiquity. "Morality for him," according to Renan, "was the final word in all human existence, and the object of his unceasing application." In the light of this assertion, how are we to explain that the nineteen years of his reign were the most cruel the Church had so far experienced? In his own pride as a man of learning, and in the intimacy of his own mind, he had nothing but feelings of contempt for this religion of the *simpliciores;* but in the eyes of the philosophers of his immediate entourage, a Fronto, for instance, the new religion was gradually assuming all the proportions of a dangerous rival, and so they did not hesitate to sound a note of warning to the debonnaire Emperor. Marcus Aurelius resolved to fall back upon the legislation of Trajan, and in adopting this measure, was firmly convinced that he was serving the best interests of the State. Moreover, public scourges in the form of invasions, deaths, and epidemics were sweeping the Empire and stirring public opinion to the highest pitch. Marcus Aurelius, himself not immune from superstition, adopted an attitude of *laissez-faire*. He intervened only in the case of the *Martyrs of Lyons*.

In the year 177, during the preparation of a solemn public festival to be celebrated at Lyons in Gaul, the populace suddenly began to vent its long pent-up fury against the Christians. Several of them were arrested, and many more hunted out and driven from their homes. Frightened by the awful tortures inflicted on their companions, several denied their faith, while others confessed the perpetration of horrible crimes at their secret meetings. If such were their mode of living, were they not all, apostates included, to be prosecuted as guilty of incest, infanticide, and other such monstrous crimes? Upon being consulted, Marcus Aurelius immediately limited the governor's actions to the strict terms of Trajan's rescript. Taking no account of accusations based on the common law, he persisted in regarding the case of Christianity as a mere crime *propter nomen:* "Let those who profess to be Christians be condemned to death; but let those who deny the faith be released." The court procedure began. All the Christians showed heroic courage, headed by their ninety-year-old bishop, St. Pothinus, a disciple of St. Polycarp. Those who had apostatized returned to the faith. St. Blandina, a young slave girl, exhibited remarkable fortitude and power of endurance. She was the last to suffer; after being scourged, and seated in a fiery chair, she was thrown before a wild bull, who tossed her with his horns, gored her, and trampled her to death.

All the details of these heroic scenes have been preserved for us in a letter addressed by "the servants of Christ, dwelling in Vienne and Lyons in Gaul, to the brethren in Asia and Phrygia." Mention should be made also of St. Justin and of St. Felicitas and her seven sons. According to De Rossi, the reign of Marcus Aurelius witnessed also the martyrdom of St. Cecilia, a noble lady of the *gens Caecilia,* who, married against her wishes to the pagan Valerian, persuaded him to respect her virginity, and finally converted both him and his brother Tiburtius.

Under the reign of *Commodus,* the persecution abated, especially after the Emperor married Marcia, who was a Christian or at least a catechumen. Moreover, law-court procedures held no interest for this "good-natured boy," who preferred to give exhibitions of his strength and skill as a gladiator to following the philosophical pursuits of his father. Marcia requested from Pope Victor a list of the confessors condemned to the mines and obtained from her husband that they be recalled from exile. And yet Pope Eleutherius fell victim to a persecution, as well as the senator Apollonius, who delivered an apology of Christianity before the senate in full session. The death of the Scillitan martyrs at Carthage, who proudly refused a delay of thirty days to reconsider their decision and apostatize, must also be placed at this time. Local governors still continued, therefore, to enforce the measures dictated by Trajan's rescript.

III. The Christian Literary Reaction: The Apologists of the Second Century. After examining the religious policies and persecuting tactics of the Antonines, it becomes quite apparent that, in entrenching themselves behind the technicalities of the law in their warfare against the new religion, the Emperors at least showed they did not share the prejudices of the common *plebs.* Encouraged by this fact, and believing that the authorities could be converted to a policy of tolerance, certain among the Christians set about composing apologies, some of which were dedicated to the Emperor himself. The first of these writers was a veteran Greek missionary, *Quadratus,* who presented a defense of Christianity to the Emperor Hadrian on the occasion of his visit to Athens. A small fragment of his work is cited by Eusebius. We are indebted to the same Church historian for information concerning *Aristo* of Pella, author of a dialogue between an Alexandrian Jew and Jason, a Jewish Christian. This writer confutes the tenets of Judaism, and at the same time answers all the current objections of the pagans.

The Athenian philosopher *Aristides* is the oldest apologist whose work has been preserved. He dedicated his apologies not to Hadrian, as claimed by Eusebius, but to the Emperor Antoninus Pius. The human race, he explains, is divided into four distinct categories. The Barbarians worship the forces of nature; the Greeks deify the passions of man; the Jews indulge exclusively in external and superannuated forms of worship; the Christians alone worship God in spirit and in truth. Aristides brings his apology to a close with a touching picture of the life of the early Christians. Intrepid and at times daring in character, the work is written in a grave and dignified style, well calculated to convince the addressee.

Tatian is the "father of the virulent apology." His criticism of Greek civilization is partial, bitter, excessive, and merciless. From every aspect it is in marked contrast with the sublime Christian doctrine of creation and redemption. This worthy precursor of Tertullian was lacking in both common sense and mental equilibrium. He proved it by severing relations with the Church and joining the forces of Encratism.

While in Rome, Tatian had been the disciple of the most illustrious apologist of this whole period, *St. Justin.* Born between the years 100 and 110 of Greek heathen parents at Flavia Neapolis, the ancient Sichem and the modern Nablus, Justin spent many years in search of truth at the different schools of philosophy then in existence. He finally found peace of mind in the Christian religion, journeyed to Rome during the reign of Antoninus, and became the founder of a very famous school. We have from his pen an apology addressed to the Emperor, another addressed to the senate, and finally a dialogue with the Jew Trypho. Until then the apologists had sought only to refute the slanderous accusations directed against the Christians and to quell popular prejudice; St. Justin was fearless in his attacks upon juridical prejudice, which condemned them solely because of the name they bore without any basis for criminal charges: "We are condemned for crimes which no one has proved should be laid to our charge." The Dialogue with Trypho the Jew is an account of a lengthy dispute which Justin is supposed to have had at Ephesus with a learned rabbi. The purpose of the work, inspired perhaps by the former writing of Aristo of Pella, is to offer a refutation of Judaism, prove the caducity of the old Mosaic law, and convince the opponent of the Messiaship of Jesus Christ and the vocation of the Gentiles.

From a theological point of view the works of St. Justin are exceptionally valuable, because they give us a fairly good account of the development of Christian dogma in the early Church. Since, however, the science of both philosophical and theological terminology was still in its infancy, the expressions of this well-meaning layman are not always quite orthodox. Thus, he seems to believe in a sort of subordination of the Son to the

Father, is of the opinion that the angels have aërial bodies, and is a devotee of the doctrine of Millenarianism. Critics are generally agreed that his style is very defective and that his composition is devoid of all plan.

In point of fact, the efforts of the apologists failed to achieve results. The scepticism and thoughtlessness of Hadrian were insurmountable barriers to their arguments, and the devotion of Antoninus Pius to the national religion prohibited him from giving them a hearing.

Under the reign of Marcus Aurelius a second generation of apologists was born. Christianity was now the target, not only of mob frenzy and legal vexations, but also of the literary onslaughts of the pagan men of letters, philosophers and rhetoricians who grouped themselves around the Emperor. It was at this time that the imperial tutor Fronto of Cirta composed his discourse against the Christians, and Lucian of Samosata caricatured the death of the martyrs in his work *On the Death of Peregrinus.* In the year 178, *Celsus* wrote his *True Discourse* or better, *Demonstration of Truth,* no longer extant to-day, but preserved almost in its entirety for us by Origen in the following century in his famous treatise *Against Celsus.* It may be said in truth that all the objections formulated against Christianity from the time of Porphyry down to that of Voltaire are already to be found in the work of Celsus.

With the appearance of this new type of opponents, the apologists broadened their line of attack, carrying the debate into the political field, at that time the logical forum of controversies. In the eyes of the judges, the guilt of being a Christian was confined merely to the name; prohibition to have that name must have been prompted by public interest; therefore, the votaries of this new religion are "the enemies of the human race" and the contemners of rightfully established authority. The new apologists bend every effort, therefore, to prove that the faithful are loyal and law-abiding subjects, and that they love the Emperor and pray for him. The thesis defended is the same as that subscribed to by SS. Peter and Paul, for whom "the Roman Empire is the stable order of things decreed by God and one with the providential order of the universe," for even when the Emperor's name was Nero, St. Peter wrote: "Honor the Basileus." Beginning with the reign of Marcus Aurelius, the Christian apologists featured the spirit of loyalty shown by the Christians.

These new characteristics are met with in the treatise of Melito of Sardis, in the *Legatio pro Christianis* of Athenagoras, and in the three books *Ad Autolycum* of Theophilus of Antioch. To the same period belongs *Octavius,* a Latin work by *Minucius Felix,* in which the author carries on a dialogue between Caecilius, "the devil's advocate," and Octavius, a Christian. The latter tries to prove that the splendor of Rome is by no means attributable to polytheism, and in doing so lays bare the whole politico-religious conflict which prompted the great persecutions of the third century. The *Letter to Diognetus* bears many a resemblance to *Octavius,* and like the character in *Celsus,* Diognetus endeavors "to present an apology of Christianity to a pagan who is desirous of obtaining a knowledge of it."

But the prejudices of men of letters towards Christianity were not only political but also philosophical in character. Hence the apologists, and St. Justin in particular, set out to prove that there exist points of contact between the wisdom of the ancients and the Gospel. Before becoming incarnate, the Divine Logos was already acting in the world, among the Jews by theophanies, and among the pagans by philosophical research and discovery. Moreover, the pagans knew of the writings of the Old Testament, a fact which explains the fund of truth common to Plato, the Stoics, and the Gospel. The results of the efforts of this second generation of apologists were also very meagre. The most they succeeded in achieving was a sketch of the compromise which culminated in the Christian gnosis of a Clement or an Origen.

TEXTS AND DOCUMENTS

PLINY'S LETTER TO TRAJAN

It is my custom, Sir, to refer to you in all cases where I am in doubt, for who can better clear up difficulties and instruct me? I have never been present at any legal examination of Christians, and I do not know, therefore, what are the usual penalties passed upon them, or the limits of those penalties, or how searching an inquiry should be made. I have hesitated a great deal in considering whether any distinction should be drawn according to the ages of the accused; whether the weak should be punished as severely as the robust, or whether the man who has once been a Christian gained anything by recanting? Again, whether the name of being a Christian, even though otherwise innocent of crime, should be punished, or only the crimes that gather around it?

In the meantime, this is the plan which I have adopted in the case of those

Christians who have been brought before me. I ask them whether they are Christians; if they say Yes, then I repeat the question for the second time, and also for a third—warning them of the death-penalty involved; and if they persist, I order them to be executed. For I do not doubt that—be their admitted crime what it may—their pertinacity and inflexible obstinacy surely ought to be punished.

There were others who showed similar mad folly, whom I reserved to be sent to Rome, as they were Roman citizens. Later, as is commonly the case, the mere fact of my trying such cases led to a multiplying of accusations, and a variety of cases were brought before me. An anonymous pamphlet was issued, containing a number of names of alleged Christians. Those who denied that they were or had been Christians and called upon the gods with the usual formula, reciting the words after me, and those who offered incense and wine before your image—which I had ordered to be brought forward for this purpose, along with the regular statues of the gods—all such I considered acquitted, especially if they cursed the name of Christ, which it is said a real Christian cannot be induced to do.

Still others there were, whose names were supplied by an informer. These first said they were Christians, then denied it, insisting they had been, but were so no longer, some of them having recanted many years ago, and more than one, full twenty years back. They all worshiped your image and the statues of the gods, and cursed the name of Christ.

But they declared their guilt or error was simply this: On a fixed day they used to meet before dawn and sing hymns to Christ, as though he were a god. So far from binding themselves by oath to commit any crime, they swore to keep from theft, robbery, adultery, breach of faith, and not to deny any trust money deposited with them when called upon to deliver it. This ceremony over, they used to depart and meet again to take food; but it was of no special character, and entirely harmless. They had ceased from this practice after the edict I issued, by which, in accord with your orders, I forbade all secret societies.

I then thought it the more needful to get at the facts behind their statements. Therefore, I placed two slave-women, called deaconesses, under torture, but I found only a debased superstition carried to great lengths, so I postponed my examination, and immediately consulted you. This seems a matter worthy of your prompt consideration, especially as so many people are endangered. Many of all ages and both sexes are put in peril of their lives by their accusers; and the process will go on, for the contagion of this superstition has spread, not merely through the towns, but into the villages and farms. Still I think it can be halted and things set right. Beyond any doubt, the temples, which were almost deserted, are beginning to be thronged with worshipers; the sacred rites, which long have lapsed, are now being renewed, and the food for the sacrificial victims is again finding a sale, though up to recently it had almost no market. So one can safely infer how vast numbers could be reclaimed, if only there were a chance given for repentance.

TRAJAN'S REPLY TO PLINY

You have adopted the right course, my dear Secundus, in examining the cases of those cited before you as Christians; for no hard and fast rule can be laid down covering such a wide field. The Christians are not to be hunted out. If brought before you, and the offense is proved, they are to be punished, but with this reservation: if any one denies he is a Christian, and makes it clear that he is not, by offering prayer to our gods, then he is to be pardoned on his recantation, no matter how suspicious his past. As for anonymous pamphlets, they are to be discarded absolutely, whatever crime they may charge, for they are not only a precedent of a very bad type, but they do not accord with the spirit of our age.

HADRIAN'S LETTER TO MINUCIUS FUNDANUS

I am in receipt of a letter from your predecessor, the worthy Sicinius Granianus. It is a matter well worth your attention to put an end to vexatious suits, and to furnish informers with no opportunity to carry on their base trade. If, then, the people subject to your authority have any accusations to make against Christians, and agree to prove these accusations publicly, so that Christians may be given a chance to defend themselves, it is your duty to arraign the accused before your tribunal, and not allow yourself to be swayed by the requests and shouts of the mob; because it is for you, and not for the people to judge of the merits of the case. If, therefore, the informer can furnish proof that Christians have violated the law, you will punish the accused according to the nature of their crime. If, on the other hand, you are convinced that the accusation is nothing more than a malicious charge, you will condemn and punish as an action of this sort deserves.

QUESTIONS

1. What was the legal position of the Christians during the reign of the Emperor Trajan?
2. Why was Trajan's rescript unethical in character, even from the standpoint of a purely legal document?
3. Why were the persecutions of this century chiefly local in character?
4. What might have been the origin of the accusations of immorality formulated against the early Christians?
5. Give a short account of the persecution in Gaul under Marcus Aurelius.
6. What is the character of this Emperor's philosophy?
7. What was the task of the early apologists, and how did they acquit themselves of it?

8. Discuss the character and style of St. Justin's works.
9. Indicate the evolution in the character of the accusations launched against primitive Christianity.
10. How were these accusations met by the apologists?

BIBLIOGRAPHY

The Persecutions in General.—P. ALLARD, *Histoire des persécutions*, 5 vols., 1892; *Le christianisme et l'empire romain; Dix leçons sur les martyrs.*— LE BLANT, *Les persécuteurs et les martyrs aux premiers siècles de notre ère*, 1893.—DE CHAMPAGNY, *Les Césars; les Antonins*, 3rd edit., 1859.—DUFOURCQ, *Etude sur les Gesta Martyrum romains*, 1900.—K. J. NEUMANN, *Der römische Staat und die allgemeine Kirche bis auf Diocletian*, Vol. I, Leipzig, 1890.— G. UHLHORN, *The Conflict of Christianity with Heathenism*, 1899.

The Right to Persecute.—P. ALLARD, *La situation légale des chrétiens pendant les deux premiers siècles*, in *Rev. quest. hist.*, 1896, t. LIX, pp. 5–49; 1912, pp. 106–117.—BATIFFOL, *L'Eglise naissante et le catholicisme*, pp. 26 ff. —G. BOISSIER, *La Lettre de Pline au sujet des chrétiens*, in *Rev. d'Arch.*, 1876, t. XXXI, p. 119; *Les premières persécutions, les chrétiens devant la législation romaine*, in *Rev. des Deux-Mondes*, April 13, 1876, pp. 787–821.—C. CALLEWAERT, *Les premiers chrétiens furent-ils persécutés par édits généraux ou par mesure de police?* in *Rev. hist. eccl.*, 1901, t. II, pp. 771–797; 1902, t. III, pp. 5–15, 324–348, 601–614; *Le délit de christianisme dans les deux premiers siècles*, in *Rev. quest. hist.*, 1903, t. LXXIV, pp. 28–55; *Les premiers chrétiens et l'accusation de lèse-majesté*, same review, 1904, t. LXXVI, pp. 5–28; *Question de droit concernant le procès d'Apollonius*, same review, 1905, t. LXXVII, pp. 349–375; *Les persécutions contre les chrétiens dans la politique religieuse de l'Etat romain*, t. LXXXII, pp. 5–19; *Le rescrit d'Hadrien à Minucius Fundanus*, in *Rev. hist. et litt.*, 1903, t. VIII, pp. 152–189; *La méthode dans la recherche de la base juridique des persécutions*, in *Rev. hist. eccl.*, 1911, t. XII, pp. 5–16, 633–651.—L. GUÉRIN, *Etude sur le fondement juridique des persécutions dans les deux premiers siècles*, in *Nouvelle rev. hist. du droit français et étranger*, 1895, t. XIX, pp. 601 ff., 713 ff.—E. LE BLANT, *Sur les bases juridiques des poursuites*, in *Comptes-rendus Acad. Insc. et B. L.*, 1866, t. II, p. 358.

The Persecution of the Second Century.—I. ANTONINUS: *Martyrdom of Saint Polycarp.*—G. LACOURT-GAYET, *Antonin le Pieux et son temps.*— J. RÉVILLE, *De anno dieque quibus Polycarpus Smyrnæ martyrium tulit; Etude critique sur la date du martyre de S. Polycarpe*, in *Rev. hist. des religions*, III (1881), pp. 369–81.—LOUIS SALTET, *L'Edit d'Antonin*, in *Rev. hist. et litt. relig.*, I, p. 383.—II. MARCUS AURELIUS, *The Martyrs of Lyons.*— DARTIQUE-PEYROU, *Marc-Aurèle dans ses rapports avec le christianisme*, 1897. —A. DE BARTHÉLÉMY, *Les assemblées nationales dans les Gaules*, in *Rev. quest. hist.*, July, 1868, pp. 14–22.—LE BLANT, *Les actes des martyrs et les supplices* *déstructeurs du corps,* in *Rev. d'Arch.,* 1874, pp. 178–194.—Dom Leclercq, *Les martyrs,* t. I, pp. 90 ff.—III. Commodus, *The Martyrdom of Apollonius.*—Works: Celeuneer, *La favorite de Commode,* in *Rev. quest. hist.,* t. XX (1876), p. 156.—Bassani, *Commodo e Marcia,* Venice, 1905.—Callewaert, *Question de droit concernant le procès d'Apollonius,* in *Rev. quest. hist.,* t. LXXVII (1905), pp. 349–375.—Prince Max of Saxony, *Der heilige Märtyrer Apollonius von Rom,* Mayence, 1902.

Apologists.—Sources: *Corpus Apologetarum Christianorum saeculi secundi,* edit. De Otto, t. I and II, 3rd edit., Ienae, 1886–87.—St. Justin, *Apologies,* edit. L. Pautigny, 1904, and *Dialogue with Trypho,* edit. G. Archambault, 1909 (in Texts and Documents, Coll. Hemmer and Lejay).—*The Apology of Aristides,* edit. J. Rendel Harris and J. Armitage Robinson, in Texts and Studies, I, Cambridge, 2nd edit., 1893.—*Letter to Diognetes,* edit. Funk, *Patres Apostolici,* I, 1901.—Works: Freppel, *Les Apologistes Chrétiens au II*^e *siècle,* 2 vols., 1860.—Aubé, *De l'apologétique chrétienne au II*^e *siècle,* 1861. —Bareille, art. *Apologistes (Pères)* in *Dict. de Théol.*—J. Martin, *L'Apologétique Traditionnelle,* 1905.—L. Laguier, *La méthode apologétique des Pères dans les trois premiers siècles,* 1905.—A. Puech, *Les apologistes grecs du II*^e *siècle de notre ère,* 1912; *Recherches sur le Discours aux Grecs de Tatien,* 1903.—M. Picard, *L'Apologie d'Aristide,* 1892.—M. G. Lagrange, *Saint Justin* (Coll. Les Saints), 1914.—L. Feder, *Justinus des Märtyrers Lehre von Jesus Christus,* Freiburg i. Br., 1906.—J. Lebreton, *Le conflit religieux au II*^e *siècle,* in *Revue Apol.,* t. XL (1925), pp. 65–83, 257–278.—G. Bardy, art. *"Justin,"* in *Dict. de Théol.; The Christian Latin Literature of the First Six Centuries* (transl. Mother Mary Reginald, O. P.).

Minucius Felix.—Sources: *P. L.,* t. III, col. 239–376; *C. V.,* II (1867), by Halm; J. P. Waltzing, Louvain, 1903, with French translation and commentary.—Works: O. De Félice, *Etude sur l'Octavius,* Blois, 1880.—G. Boissier, *La fin du paganisme,* t. I.—Monceaux, *Hist. litt. Afr. chr.,* t. I.— G. Hinnisdaels, *L'Octavius de Minucius Félix et l'Apologétique de Tertullien,* Brussels, 1924.

CHAPTER II

I. Doctrinal Dangers Arising from a Pagan Environment: Gnosticism. In the eyes of intellectual and cultured pagans, Christianity was the religion of the illiterate and uncouth; in an attempt to enrich it with treasures chiefly of the mental order, some of the early enthusiasts invented what is known as gnosis. Gnosticism may be defined as an effort on the part of intellectual Christians to graft upon dogma notions borrowed from ancient philosophies and Oriental religions, and thus substitute for the simple faith of the common people (πίστις) a higher form of theological knowledge (γνῶσις). The aid of the pantheistic theories of the Greeks was enlisted as well as that of the theogonic and cosmogonic theories of ancient Egypt, Chaldea, Persia, and even India; and finally, less pure sources were tapped, such as the mysteries of pagan rites and superstitious, demiurgic, and magical practices originating in neo-Platonism. Armed with this incongruous mass of material, the Gnostics boasted they could throw light on all the leading questions of Christian dogma: the nature of God, the nature of man, the origin of evil, etc., and although the various schools which comprised the system exhibited distinctly different points of view, they were generally agreed upon these fundamentals. Gnosticism was a monopoly effected by Christianity which resulted only in an advantage to the syncretism of pagan worship.

The Gnostics professed belief in one supreme God, Father of all things, but completely isolated in His grandeur. Between Him and the inferior world there exists a whole spiritual world of real beings or personified passions which have emanated from Him and are called eons because they existed in God from all eternity. The sum-total of the eons goes to make up what is known as the Ogdias or Pleroma or Upper Heaven. From one of the inferior eons issues creation or evil, contemptible matter; if this matter is evil, the eon or *demiurge* who presided over its formation is equally evil. Some of the Gnostics contended that this eon was the God of Judaism, that exclusive religion so opposed to the true and broad gnosis. And yet creation has not been irrevocably condemned, because God has communicated to it a spark of life, a sweet scent of the spiritual world. Men have permitted themselves to be more or less impregnated with this life-giving energy. Hence three distinct classes among them: (1) The πνευματικοί, or *spirituals,* in whom the spiritual element predominates and whose salvation is assured; (2) the *psychics,* who have succeeded in establishing an equilibrium between mind and matter, and who, being just ordinary Christians are free to save or lose their souls; and (3) those in whom the *material* element predominates, and who are condemned in advance (pagans and Jews).

Subject to the domination of matter from the time of the fall, the spark of life was to be freed by Jesus, the Redeemer. Although a mere eon, he was made up of two beings—the one human, the other divine. The *Dualists* taught that the first of these beings was merely the container of the second; the *Docetae,* more logical in their contention that Christ should be completely emancipated from the powers of evil, opined that the container was one of appearance only. The saving influence of Christ is not traceable, therefore, to His sufferings and death, but to His knowledge or gnosis: to know the Father and delve into the hidden mysteries of His life—there lies the secret.

Thus, since religion is a matter of knowledge only, morality is of little importance. True, some of the Gnostics chastised their bodies because they considered them evil, but equally certain is the fact that some adopted an attitude of indifference. The result was a multiplicity of sects and, in some cases, barefaced profligacy without precedent. But why show any concern? In the end, the truly spiritual will be saved and the material world will crumble. This will mark the return of all the luminous particles to the Pleroma (ἀποκατάστασις or universal renovation). The whole superstructure of the doctrine rested on forms of worship, often quite superstitious in character, borrowed at random from the Christian religion, the pagan mysteries, and the Oriental rites. Such forms of worship comprised the use of all kinds of magical formulas, images, and bizarre medals, and so, prevented by their lack of education from penetrating into the secret depths of the gnosis, the common people eagerly clung to these practices.

The countless schools of Gnosticism are reducible to two principal systems: the *Syrian gnosis* and the *Alexandrian gnosis*. The first of these two systems borrowed its essential points of doctrine from the Syrian, Chaldaic, and Persian religions, and counted as its outstanding exponents: Menander, Saturninus, the Ophites and the Cainites. The compatriot and successor of Simon Magus, Menander, taught substantially the same doctrines as the notorious magician from Samaria. A more sullen and morose prophet, Saturninus, regarded marriage as a diabolical institution. The Ophitic system worshipped the serpent (ὄφις), because, by revolting against the demiurge, this animal had brought knowledge into the world. The Ophites degenerated into several other equally extravagant sects. However, for the Cainites, the truly spiritual men were the infamous characters of the Old and New Testament, in particular Cain and Judas Iscariot, and an individual named Justin effected such a perfect mixture of Greek mythology and Judaism that he succeeded in having Hercules accepted as one of the prophets. In fine, the Syrian Gnostics were charlatans, who peddled their tinsel to gullible buyers in the form of eccentricities and eons with high-sounding names.

The Egyptian Gnostics were shrewd and clever doctors, who fitted out these drolleries in philosophical dress and adjusted them to the taste of the sages of Alexandria. Their high priests were Basilides, Valentinus, and Carpocrates. We are introduced to Valentinus by St. Irenaeus; his nuptial gnosis is replete with marriages and births, while the eons of Basilides are celibates. The success of all three masters in Egypt itself was incalculable, but outside this province, it was chiefly the influence of Valentinus that was felt, and this in wellnigh every place. He even journeyed to Rome, only to be driven out by the community. The intellectual and moral superiority of the school of Alexandria in the second century was real and unquestionable; in the third century, we find the different systems blending together and philosophy gradually receding before the approach of strange rites and mysteries. In the end, it stooped to the level of the infamies of the Oriental religions.

Despite the extravagant notions peculiar to the different systems, Gnosticism as a whole constituted a serious temptation of intellectual pride to the early Christians. It was the first attempt at a systematic concept of religion, of "a Christian philosophy in relation to Judaism and paganism." From the methodological standpoint especially, we remark the substitution of individualism for the teaching of the Apostles. The Church had no right to impose her magisterium except upon ignorant souls (*simpliciores*); the Gnostics, on the other hand, in elaborating its teachings, sought to give a personal touch to religion. And so the refutation of all these errors was also launched from a methodological point of view. The Church did not seek to combat these second-century modernists by a rational synthesis of her faith, but contented herself with invoking her hierarchical and Apostolic tradition; the successors of the Apostles, she insisted, have the deposit of the faith, firstly among them the bishop of Rome, which is the first of all the churches. Harmony and conformity with the religion of Rome, therefore, is the criterion of all religious truth, and any departures from this religion must necessarily be treated as errors.

St. Irenaeus, bishop of Lyons, stresses this same argument in his treatise *Adversus Haereses* (Against the Heresies), the proper title of which is *The Detection and Overthrow of the Pretended but False Gnosis.* Written between A. D. 174 and 199, this work comprises five books, of which only a Latin version has reached us. In the first book St. Irenaeus exposes the system of Valentinus, the boldest and most thorough of all the Gnostics. The second book offers a detailed refutation of Gnosticism, based on a complete examination of its own gratuitous hypotheses, absurdities, and principles of immorality. In the third and most important book, the Saint widens his line of argument, laying special stress on tradition. He argues that the rule of Catholic faith is to be found in the writings of the Apostles, as preserved in its integrity by the churches, especially the Roman Church. In the fourth book the argument is confirmed by the words of Jesus Christ, and in the fifth and last he opposes Christian eschatology to the teaching of the Gnostics. In his exposition of the Gnostic systems, St. Irenaeus is well informed, his dialectic is strong and in places caustic, his style appears diffuse and awkward in the Latin translation only because the latter is literal to a fault.

The argument from tradition was at once so simple and peremptory that it sufficed of itself to refute the Gnostics, and the Church never felt the need of convoking councils against them. These early heretics failed to establish themselves in the midst of Christian communities because the unusual character of their theories quickly attracted attention and usually reprobation. Hence, they were forced to group themselves into autonomous communities, which could recruit their membership only from among "weak and restless minds, greedy for occult science, for initiation, and for mysteries." On the other hand, Gnosticism furnished the occasion for the appearance of such terms as οὐσία, ὁμοούσιος, ὑπόστασις, etc., a first step in the construction of a theological terminology.

II. Doctrinal Dangers Arising from Within: Millenarianism, Montanism, and Marcionism. The first Christians lived in expectation of the *parousia,* but gradually the idea of an earthly triumph of Christ found its way into their concept of His second appearance. The Jews had hoped for a temporal reign of the Messias, and since Jesus had not fulfilled their hopes in His first advent, many Christians looked for a second return and set the duration of this second victorious advent at one thousand years (Millenarianism), after which time the general judgment would take place, together with the eternal triumph of the Son of God. Such eschatological dreams made their appearance in many writings of that period, and especially in the Book of Henoch, whose authority in the second century was very considerable. Millenarianism, moreover, based its claims upon an interpretation, evidently quite narrow, of certain passages of the Apocalypse, and the measure of its success can be gauged to some extent by the fact that it not only won over heretics like Cerinthus, who was its first exponent towards the end of the first century, but also orthodox Catholics like Papias, St. Justin, and St. Irenaeus. True, the concept of this second advent was very different in the two cases: for Cerinthus, the temporal reign of Christ was a time of carnal pleasures and earthly rejoicings; for the Fathers, it was a time of great spiritual uplift.

Encratism was a mere tendency; Millenarianism nothing but an opinion, spread throughout the Christian communities; but Montanism was a rigorous and enthusiastic sect which made its appearance in the second half of the second century. It bore some resemblance to the other two movements. The origin of the prophecies of the Phrygian Montanus (c. 172) and his two women associates, Maximilla and Priscilla, is singular enough. Seized with fear at the idea of the *parousia,* they set about preparing the world for the approaching judgment by rigorous ascetical practices and exaggerated forms of moral severity. On general principles, they absolutely refused forgiveness for grievous sins. Might not the descent of the Heavenly Jerusalem upon the little town of Pepuza be expected any day? Up to that time there were to be no more marriages, no family life, no earthly interests; but only a community of possessions. As a prelude to the *parousia,* the Holy Ghost was to descend into their midst, and so Montanus introduced himself as the living incarnation of the Paraclete. His fantastic prophecies were intended to impart a clearer knowledge of the New Covenant and supplement the Gospel message, and both he and his associates uttered their oracles while languishing in unusual and ecstatic reveries. At bottom, Montanism was an attempt to substitute private judgment for hierarchical teaching, just as Gnosticism had been an endeavor to supplant the latter by individual knowledge.

Montanism, enlisting in its cause only a scattered minority of religious fanatics, soon laid itself open to suspicion. It owed most of its success in Asia Minor to the leadership of Alcibiades, Theodotus, Themiso, a pseudo-confessor, and a robber named Alexander, all very suspicious characters. When the Heavenly Jerusalem failed to realize, the Montanists hastened to transform Pepuza into an earthly Jerusalem, calling it the metropolis of the Holy Spirit. The movement made very few converts outside of Asia Minor, and invariably they were men of harsh and unbalanced temperament. Tertullian, himself a very severe man, fell a prey to their snares and grouped around him a small community of followers. Condemned by Rome, Montanism took refuge in Phrygia and Africa, where for a long time it was able to keep up a front as a schismatic oddity.

The complicated character of Gnosticism had succeeded only in establishing "lodges of initiates of high and low degree." Montanism was essentially an individualistic and extra-hierarchical movement. Marcionism created a church and formulated a practical doctrine accessible to all men. Marcion professed belief in a Redeemer, who, commissioned by the Good God to save the human race, underwent the sufferings of the Cross. His body, however, was one of mere appearance, and its life began only at the time of His preaching. The moral teachings of Marcion are clearly encratic in character: believers must abstain from marriage and use only so much and such nourishment as is necessary to sustain life. All these teachings are based upon his interpretation of the Gospel of St. Luke and the Epistles of St. Paul, the rest of Holy Scripture being regarded as non-existing. In fine, Marcion's doctrine is nothing more than a truncated and distorted Catholicism, and hence it is a mistake to reckon it among the Gnostic sects. In the year 155 Marcion repaired to Rome, and succeeded in establishing a small community there. From the Eternal City the movement spread, establishing churches here and there. It even had some martyrs among its members, and for many years offered stolid resistance to the Catholic Church.

TEXTS AND DOCUMENTS

THE APOSTOLIC TRADITION AND THE ARGUMENT FROM PRESCRIPTION
(TERTULLIAN, *De Praescript. Haeret.*, 20–21)

They then in like manner founded churches in every city, from which all the other churches, one after another, derived the tradition of the faith and the seeds of doctrines, and are every day deriving them, that they may become churches. Indeed, it is on this account only that they will be able to deem themselves Apostolic, as being the offspring of Apostolic churches. Every thing must necessarily revert to its original for its classification. Therefore, these churches, although so many and so great, are but the one primitive Church, [founded] by the Apostles, from which they all [sprung]. In this way all are primitive, and all are Apostolic, whilst they are all proved to be one, in [unbroken] unity, by their peaceful communion, and title of brotherhood, and bond of hospitality—privileges which no other rule directs than the one tradition of the selfsame mystery.

From this, therefore, do we draw up our rule. Since the Lord Jesus Christ sent the Apostles to preach, [our rule is] that none other ought to be received as preachers than those whom Christ appointed; for "no man knoweth the Father save the Son, and he to whomsoever the Son will reveal Him." Nor does the Son seem to have revealed Him to any other than the Apostles, whom He sent forth to preach—that, of course, which He revealed to them. Now, what that was which they preached—in other words, what it was which Christ revealed to them—can, as I must here likewise prescribe, properly be proved in no other way than by those very churches which the Apostles founded in person, by declaring the Gospel to them directly themselves, both *viva voce,* as the phrase is, and subsequently by their Epistles. If then, these things are so, it is in the same degree manifest that all doctrine which agrees with the Apostolic churches—those moulds and original sources of the faith— must be accepted as truth, as undoubtedly containing that which the [said] churches received from the Apostles, the Apostles from Christ, Christ from God. On the other hand, all doctrine must be prejudged as false which contradicts the truth of the churches, of the Apostles, of Christ, and of God.

QUESTIONS

1. Give a summary of the teachings of Gnosticism.
2. What are the principal differences between the Syrian and the Alexandrian gnoses?
3. Compare Montanism and Marcionism.

4. Give summaries of the doctrines of Millenarianism, Montanism, and Marcionism.

5. Show the relationship existing between these false theologies.

6. What is meant by the hierarchical and Apostolic tradition, and what is the value of the argument in refuting Gnosticism?

BIBLIOGRAPHY

Gnosticism.—Sources: Fragments of Gnostic writings in *P. G.*, VII, 1263. —St. Irenaeus, *Adversus Haereses.*—Works: Mansel, *The Gnostic Heresies,* London, 1873.—E. de Faye, *Introduction à l'histoire du Gnosticisme,* 1903.— E. Buonaiuti, *Lo Gnosticismo,* Rome, 1907.—Tixeront, *op. cit.,* I, p. 187.— Bareille, art. *"Gnosticisme,"* in *Dict. de Théol.*—E. de Faye, *Gnostiques et Gnosticisme. Etude critique sur les documents du Gnosticisme chrétien aux IIᵉ et IIIᵉ siècles Bibl. de l'Ecole des Hautes Etudes,* fasc. XVIII, 1913.— L. Duchesne, art. *"Gnosticisme,"* in *Dict. d'Apol.*

St. Irenaeus.—Sources: *P. G.,* t. VII.—Works: J. Chapman, *Le témoignage de saint Irénée en faveur de la primauté romaine,* in *Rev. bénéd.,* XII (1895).—A. Camerlinck, *Saint Irénée et le canon du Nouveau Testament,* Louvain, 1896.—A. Dufourq, *Saint Irénée* (Coll. *"Les Saints"*), 1904; (Coll. *"La Pensée Chrétienne"*), 1905.—Batiffol, *L'Eglise Naissante et le Catholicisme,* ch. IV, *Le catholicisme de saint Irénée.*—Funk, *Der Primat der römischen Kirche nach Ignatius und Irenaeus,* in *Kirchengeschichtl. Abhandl. und Untersuch.,* Vol. I, 1897.—J. Tixeront, *op. cit.,* t. I, p. 247.—J. Lebreton, *Histoire du dogme de la Trinité des origines au concile de Nicée,* t. II, *De saint Clément à saint Irénée,* 1928.

Montanism.—Sources: Tertullian, *De corona militis; De fuga in persecutione; De exhortatione castitatis; De virginibus velandis; De monogamia; De jejunio; De pudicitia.*—S. Epiphanius, *Haer.,* XLVIII, XLIX.—Works: Funk, art. *"Montanismus,"* in *Kirchenlexikon* of Freiburg.—V. Ermoni, *La crise montaniste,* in *Rev. quest. hist.,* t. XXII (1902), pp. 61–96.—De Labriolle, *La crise montaniste,* 1913; *La polémique anti-montaniste,* in *Rev. hist. et litt. rel.,* XI (1906), pp. 97–145.—A. D'Alès, *Tertullien,* pp. 345 ff.—J. Tixeront, *op. cit.,* 210.—R. Janin, *Le Millénarisme et l'Eglise grecque, Echos d'Orient,* 1928, pp. 201–210.—G. Bardy, art. *"Millénarisme,"* in *Dict. de Théol.*

Marcionism.—Sources: St. Justin, *Apologia,* I, 26, 58; *Dialog.,* 35.— Tertullian, *Adversus Marcionem libri quinque.*—Works:—Meyboom, *Marcion en de Marcioneten,* Leyden, 1888.—V. Ermoni, *Le Marcionisme,* in *Rev. quest. hist.,* January, 1910.—A. D'Alès, *Marcion, La réforme chrétienne au IIᵉ siècle,* in *R. S. R.,* 1923 (XII).—E. Amann, art. *"Marcion,"* in *Dict. de Théol.*—A. Von Harnack, *Marcion, Das Evangelium vom fremden Gott,* Leipzig, 1924; *Neue Studien zu Marcion,* 1923. Harnack makes Marcionism the precursor of Protestanism, a thesis refuted by Msgr. Batiffol.

CHAPTER I

THE PERSECUTIONS OF THE THIRD CENTURY

I. Intermittent Persecution of the Church in the Interest of Public Safety. In the third century new relations were set up between Christianity and the Roman Empire. In keeping with the ordinances of Trajan's rescript, the profession of the Christian religion had up till then been regarded as a judicial crime; with the numerical growth of its members, the new sect began to constitute a menace to the State. Hence, the task of prosecuting the Christians was no longer left to the discretion of the local governors, but more general measures were devised to rid the Empire of them in the interest of public safety. Fortunately, lulls occurred here and there, and so we must not be astonished at finding a tolerant and almost favorable ruler succeeding an infuriated and implacable persecutor.

The African Emperor *Septimius Severus* had quelled to his satisfaction the military uprisings which followed immediately upon the fall of the Antonine dynasty, and at first showed himself favorably disposed towards the Christians. But with their ever increasing numbers, the Emperor became alarmed for the cause of the official religion and the safety of the Empire, which, to his way of thinking, was intimately bound up with that of religion. And so he resolved to cut short any further schemes of propaganda by prohibiting all conversions to the faith. Henceforth it was forbidden to become a Christian or to induce others to accept the Christian faith. The special class of new converts was to be hunted out everywhere. To them the *"conquirendi non sunt"* of Trajan was no longer to be applied (edict of the year 202). This measure explains why the majority of the martyrs of this period were neophytes or catechists. In Egypt, we may mention St. Potamiana, but especially SS. Felicitas and Perpetua, and St. Saturus with their respective companions. The major portion of their Acts has been preserved for us in the form of an autobiography written by St.

Perpetua while in prison. According to St. Gregory of Tours, the martyr-dom of St. Irenaeus also occurred during this persecution.

In those days, the forms of official worship awakened an attitude of scepticism in the minds of men. The tendency was towards some superior sort of philosophism that would end in a fusion of all religions and the worship of one transcendental Being. The aspirations of a pagan syncretism were in the direction of monotheism. Already in the reign of Septimius Severus and that of his son, Caracalla, the Empress Julia Domna, a Syrian by birth, presided over meetings at which it was resolved to group all the ancient gods around one supreme God. The philosopher Philostrates was commissioned to write the life of Apollonius of Tyana, a mysterious per-sonage who had established himself in Asia as an ascetic and a wonder-worker, and whose philosophy had finally resolved itself into a sort of solar monotheism. It would seem, however, that this small group of haughty philosophers purposely ignored the Christian religion.

In consequence of another military revolution, the sister of Julia Domna, Julia Moesa by name, succeeded in having her two grandsons Heliogabalus and Alexander Severus raised to the throne. With the advent of these two princes, the new spirit of religiosity again gained favor, although attempts at syncretism took quite opposite directions.

Heliogabalus, a native of the Levant, placed at the head of Olympus his Syrian god, Baal of Emesus, represented under the figure of a black stone. The rites attendant upon this form of worship were filled with obscenities and fits of sacred frenzy. The most that can be said in favor of this pro-longed religious orgy is that, by its lack of concern for the defence of the national religion, it afforded the Christians some respite, and permitted them to live for a while in peace.

With the advent of *Alexander Severus* (222–235) [1] an honest attempt at

[1] *Syrian Dynasty*

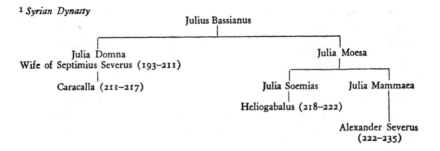

syncretism issued in real tolerance for Christianity. A pious and meek young man, Alexander, gave orders to place in his domestic *lararium* a bust of Jesus Christ, side by side with those of Orpheus and Apollonius of Tyana, *"animae sanctiores."* It is even said that his mother Mammaea was a Christian. At any rate the dispositions of the new Emperor were responsible for measures of great importance, for he abolished the *Institutum Neronianum,* and, according to Lampridius, let the Christians alone (*"Christianos esse passus est"*). Legislation of this kind conferred upon the faithful the right to hold meetings and own property, and so we find them in litigation with the tavern-keepers of Rome concerning a piece of land, appealing their case to the Emperor and winning the decision. It is certain that churches appeared here and there during this reign, because Origen observes that the next Emperor, Maximinus, ordered them to be destroyed by fire.

Moreover, in the beginning of the third century several Christian communities possessed their own cemeteries. How are we to account for this fact? We know that Septimius Severus had issued an edict authorizing the establishment of burial societies, syndicates of humble folk (*collegia tenuiorum*), formed with the view of guaranteeing respectable burial for their kin. Is it possible that Christian communities sought to shield themselves behind such legislation as groups of poor people, possessing their patrons in the person of rich Christians? Did they not guarantee a fitting burial for their members? Duchesne and Batiffol object to this view on the ground that an attempt of this kind on the part of Christians to camouflage their true position would have deceived no one. Burial societies were few in number, whereas great churches like those of Rome, Carthage, and Alexandria, counted thousands of members. Would it not be more in keeping with the facts to say that the origins of Christian property are to be sought in the very principle of life which animated its organism and prompted its growth, and not in any law of authorization? Alexander Severus did nothing more than sanction a practice already in existence; some of his successors continued his policy, others annulled the right.

Alexander Severus fell victim to an army revolt in 235. His death inaugurated a period of military anarchy which saw the appearance of the vanguard of the barbarian invasions. *Maximinus Thrax* (the Thracian), an uncouth barbarian of herculean strength and a roaming soldier, finally succeeded in imposing his authority upon the mob (235-238) and by way of reaction to the policies of his predecessor, resolved to strike at the heart of the Christian religion by hunting down its chiefs and teachers. By his orders, Pope Pontianus and the famous priest Hippolytus were banished to Sardinia, and Pope St. Anterus, the successor of Pontianus, was put to death. In Pontus, where terrific earthquakes had aroused the fury of the people, a violent persecution was inaugurated by the local governor, Serenianus.

Peace returned with the Gordians, particularly under *Philip the Arabian* (244-249), who practiced the Christian religion privately, together with Severa, his wife. We have the Emperor's correspondence with Origen, and we also know that it was he who permitted Pope Fabian to transfer the relics of his predecessor, St. Pontianus, in solemn procession from Sardinia to Rome. However, this sudden reversion to the spirit of tolerance of Alexander Severus was destined to be short-lived.

A stubborn conservative, *Decius* set out to annihilate Christianity, which he considered the enemy of ancient paganism. With his accession to the throne, the former political grievances again appeared in the foreground with renewed strength. His first step was a general persecution of the Christians as a measure of public safety. All were given the alternative to apostatize or to die, and in order that none might escape, a commission was established in every city and village, before which all the inhabitants were to be arraigned. Each individual had to prove either that he was not a Christian or that he no longer intended to remain one, first, by offering to the gods a victim or at least a few grains of incense sprinkled upon burning charcoals; secondly, by denying the divinity of Christ according to a set of blasphematory formulas; and thirdly, by partaking of a pagan repast. All those who complied with the conditions received a certificate (*libellum*) attesting to the fact; those who refused were thrown into prison. A preliminary test of this kind immediately singled out certain Christians as belonging to an élite who had performed a first act of courage. To force these to deny the faith, the judge did not leave a stone unturned: tortures, seductions of honor and virtue, long drawn-out court procedures, imprisonment—no method was overlooked. St. Cyprian informs us that "those who wanted to die could not succeed in having themselves put to death." After weeks and sometimes months of delay, the sentence was finally passed, the Christian's goods were confiscated, and he was either banished or put to death. The Emperor's purpose was not so much to execute the Christians, as to induce them to apostatize and become good Roman citizens. So much pressure was brought to bear that relapses into paganism were frequent, especially among the rich. Among those who suffered martyrdom we may mention Pope Fabian in Rome, St. Denis of Paris, and finally St. Polyeuctus, an Armenian soldier, immortalized by the French poet Corneille.

The Decian persecution was of short duration (250–251), but left behind it unforgettable memories. Seven years later it was resumed by Valerian. With the example of his predecessor still before his eyes, the new Emperor perceived the futility of trying to exterminate Christianity by forcing its adherents into apostasy, and so he set out to deal it a more deadly blow by sapping its very foundations as a society. Accordingly, in the year 257, he issued an edict directed against the heads of the Christian communities (bishops and priests), giving them the choice between apostasy or exile. He also declared all church corporations and burial societies illicit and forbade the faithful under pain of death to frequent the cemeteries or places of worship banned by the State. And woe to those who made any attempt to reorganize a meeting that had been dissolved! They ran the risk of being surprised near the entrance of the catacombs, like St. Tarsicius, or trapped and buried alive while at prayer. But when even exiled bishops like St. Cyprian of Carthage, St. Denis of Alexandria, and St. Stephen of Rome, continued to encourage the faithful, and persons whose goods had been confiscated were offered shelter in the funeral domains of the aristocracy, the Emperor issued a second edict (258), much more stringent than the first. The death penalty was substituted for exile, and degradation and decapitation fulminated against senators, noblemen, and army captains. Noble women of the same rank were condemned to exile. Valerian was too economical to suppress the attendants of the imperial household, but he enslaved them and confiscated all their goods.

In overthrowing Christianity, Valerian hoped to replenish the coffers of the State with the spoils. One of the instigators of the persecution, indeed, was none other than his favorite, Macrian, secretary of the treasury. Among the many victims of the persecution we must reckon Pope St. Stephen; Pope Sixtus II, who together with his clergy was surprised in the cemetery of Praetextatus and decapitated while seated upon his pontifical throne; the deacon St. Lawrence; in Africa, St. Cyprian of Carthage; and at Utica, one hundred and fifty-three Christians who were thrown into quick-lime and hence named "the white mass" (*massa candida*).

Valerian's punishment came when he was captured and made a slave by the Persians. His successor *Gallienus,* whose wife, Salonina, was perhaps a Christian, put an end to the persecution. But whereas his predecessors had remained content to cease prosecuting the faithful, Gallienus repealed the edicts, decreeing that religious freedom be restored to the bishops, "the magistrates of the word," that the places of worship be given back to them, and official recognition be accorded to their persons. This edict was a semi-recognition of the Church, and, as it were, a prelude to the peace of Constantine.

From 260 to 300 the Christians enjoyed a relative tranquillity, although the persecution continued to rage in certain provinces, where the imperial authority was too weak to assert itself. It is true that *Aurelian* (270–275) in his fanaticism for the sun-god, towards the end of his reign issued a bloody edict, ordering a general persecution, but the Emperor's assassination prevented its enforcement. The closing years of the third century were years of prosperity. *Diocletian* (284–305) was surrounded by Christians at his court in Nicomedia, and in many towns the sky-line appeared dotted with basilicas and churches.

II. The New Paganism, a Rival of Christianity. Paganism had made an abortive attempt in the second century to rehabilitate itself in the philosophy of the Stoics, but this movement reached only an intellectual minority. Public calamities, profound anxieties, and innate cravings on the part of men for some sort of belief, prompted the appearance in the third century of certain rejuvenated forms of paganism, all reducible to Neo-Platonism, Mithraism, and Manichaeism. All three proved formidable obstacles to the expansion of Christianity.

Neo-Platonism may well be called the last attempt on the part of the searching mind of Greece to explain the mystery of the cosmos. *Plotinus,* its founder, professed a Pantheistic doctrine of emanation that bore more than one resemblance to Gnosticism. The Infinite, the Absolute, the Omnipotent can give of His substance without suffering any diminution in His own being. In point of fact, He engenders a second principle, who in turn engenders a third, and so on, down to matter and evil. That is the way in which we are derived from the One Being, which constitutes the true substratum of the human soul. The whole purpose of Plotinian spirituality, therefore, was to unite men intimately with this One Divine Being, and raise them by a succession of purifications to the contemplation of Being, and even to ecstasy. Yet, no matter how transcendent the spiritual theory of the Neo-Platonists was, it did not exclude such gross religious doctrines of traditional paganism as polytheism, myths, and magic. All these elements have their part to play in the conversion of man from the material to the immaterial and ineffable. Thus the gap between ancient paganism and philosophy was successfully bridged over; it was the fond hope to salvage the latter by the former.

It is easy to see why Neo-Platonism could have no sympathy for the Christian religion. This lack of sympathy developed into positive antagonism with *Porphyry,* a disciple of Plotinus, who between the years 290 and 300 composed fifteen books "Against the Christians." This work is most perfidious in character, because, while recognizing the beauties of the religion of Jesus, its author bent every effort to uncover flagrant contradictions and incongruous improbabilities in its message. Porphyry was the first inventor of a Paulinism directly opposed to Petrinism. Yet, Neo-Platonism remained first and last an intellectual movement, incapable of influencing the masses.

From the latter point of view, the religion of Mithra constituted a far more serious menace. An offshoot of Persian Mazdaism, *Mithraism* was essentially the worship of the sun-god, but being very impartial, and in fact cosmopolitan in character, it sought to incorporate into its creed the Syrian myths and the Hellenic divinities, and even to enter into an alliance with all the then existing priestly castes. It might be said that Mithraism was an attempt to rally all the forces of polytheism against Christianity. While effecting this work, it did not fail to cater to the element of the new, susceptible as this was to allay in men the ever increasing spirit of religious unrest. Hence, in the examination of the credentials of this new religion, we meet with a certain number of moral precepts, symbols of expiation like the taurobolium and a series of initiations and mysteries. And since it enjoined upon its followers neither austere practices nor staunch virtues, it had everything that would appeal to their imagination and at the same time curry favor with their passions.

Mithra counted a number of worshippers, especially among the military, although the many innovations of the sect themselves constituted the greatest obstacle to the success of the movement in Egypt, Syria, and Greece. The religion of Mithra, the Neo-Platonism of Porphyry, and, we might add, the attempt at a syncretism put forth by the Severi, were so many efforts on the part of a fast disintegrating paganism to purge itself of polytheistic tendencies and lift itself to the high level of monotheism. The theory of one supreme God (*summus Deus*) was becoming *à la mode;* it was a final intellectual challenge on the part of paganism to Christianity, which, in spite of the worthy attempts of the apologists, had not yet discarded its swaddling clothes.

Another export from the Orient was the doctrine of *Manichaeism*. Born between the years 214 and 218, Mani set out at the age of twenty-four to preach in Babylonia and Persia a bizarre kind of a doctrine, that might be described as a mixture of Babylonian religion, Parsism, and Mazdaism. The Manichaeans believed in two kingdoms: one of light, ruled by God, the other of darkness, ruled by Satan. To resist Satan, God emanated an eon, the Mother of Life, who in turn emanated Primitive Man. Vanquished by Satan, this eon, man, was set free by God, but not before the Evil One had left upon it the imprints of a terrific struggle. This fact explains the constant battle waged in man's soul between good and evil, in which we see him pulled in opposite directions by the demons and by the angels and their messengers: Zoroaster, Buddha, Jesus and especially Mani, "the ambassador of light." To emerge from darkness into light, man must follow the triple moral teaching of Mani: *signaculum oris,* abstention from impure foods and strict abstinence; *signaculum manus,* abstention from the handling of certain unclean objects; and *signaculum sinus,* abstention from all sexual relations. The *electi* keep these commandments to the letter, and after death, return to the kingdom of light; the *auditores* do their best, but the matter of their salvation is problematical. Nothing here savors of Christianity, so that, if we stigmatize the movement as heretical, it is only because it later on introduced certain Christian ceremonies, like Baptism and the Holy Eucharist, and certain Christian feasts, like that of Pentecost. Manichaeism had a considerable following. From its cradle in Persia it spread into Armenia, Cappadocia, and even India and China. It was the forerunner of the Albigensian heresy.

TEXTS AND DOCUMENTS

DECIAN LIBELLI

One of the *libelli* issued to a Christian who had satisfied the authorities of his submission to Decius's edict was found in the Fayum district in Egypt. It is written on a papyrus leaf and reads as follows:

"To the Commissioners of Sacrifice of the Village of Alexander's Island. From Aurelius Diogenes, the son of Satabus, of the village of Alexander's Island, aged 72 years:—scar on his right eyebrow.

"I have always sacrificed to the gods, and now, in your presence, in accordance with the edict, I have sacrificed, and poured the drink offering, and tasted of the sacrifices, and I request you to certify the same. Farewell! Handed in by me, Aurelius Diogenes.

"I, Aurelius Syrus, certify that I saw Diogenes sacrificing.

"Done in the first year of the Emperor, Caesar Gaius Messius Quintus Trajanus Decius, Pius, Felix, Augustus: the second of the month of Epiphi" (Nov. 250).

QUESTIONS

1. What was the policy pursued by Septimius Severus in reference to Christianity?
2. Explain the statement: The aspirations of a pagan syncretism were in the direction of monotheism.
3. Contrast the religious policies of Heliogabalus and those of Alexander Severus.
4. What are the different theories advanced in explanation of the origins of Christian property?
5. Why would you say that the persecution of the Emperor Decius was the most systematic of all the persecutions?
6. Which are the principal tenets of Neo-Platonism?
7. What reason can you give for the religion of Mithra obtaining favor among the military?
8. Define Manichaeism and show that it was the forerunner of the error of the Albigenses.

BIBLIOGRAPHY

The Persecutions of the Third Century.—I. Syncretism.—Réville, *La religion à Rome sous les Sévères*, 1866.—G. Bareille, art. *"Apollonius,"* in *Dict. de Théol.*—Batiffol, *La paix constantinienne*, ch. I, and *Excursus A, Sol invictus.*—Duviquet, *Héliogabale*, 1903.—II. SS. Felicitas and Perpetua. —A. D'Alès, *L'auteur de la Passio Perpetuae*, in *Rev. hist. eccl.*, VIII (1907), pp. 5–18.—Monceaux, *Hist. litt. Afr. chr.*, I, p. 72.—A. Audollent, *Carthage romaine.*—A. Pillet, *Histoire de sainte Perpétue*, Lille-Paris, 1885.—A. Robinson, *The Passion of St. Perpetua*, in *Texts and Studies*, I, fasc. 2, 1891.

Neo-Platonism.—E. Vacherot, *Hist. critique de l'école d'Alexandrie*, 1846–1851.—Rodier, art. *"Plotin,"* in *La Grande Encyclopédie.*—Louis, *Doctrines religieuses des philosophes grecs*, (*Bibl. Hist. des Religions*), 1909, ch. VIII.

Mithraism.—Franz Cumont, *Textes et documents relatifs au culte de Mithra*, 2 vols., Brussels, 1896–99.—A. D'Alès, *Mithracisme et catholicisme*, in *Rev. prat, apol.*, Feb. 1, 1907; *Mithra (La religion de)* in *Dict. d'Apol.*— Martindale, *Mithra*, in *Christus*, pp. 383–405.—Lagrange, *Les religions orientales et les origines du christianisme*, in *Correspondant*, July 25, 1910, pp. 209–241.—Franz Cumont, *Les mystères de Mithra*, Brussels, 1913; *Les religions orientales dans le culte romain*, ch. VI, 1907.—A. Valensin, *Jésus-Christ et l'étude comparée des religions*, 1912.

Manichaeism.—F. Rochat, *Essai sur Mani et sa doctrine*, Geneva, 1897. —Tixeront, *op. cit.*, I, p. 433.—G. Bardy, art. *"Manichéisme,"* in *Dict. de Théol.*

I. The Sacramental Controversies. 1. The Question of Unforgivable Sins. At the outset of the third century we begin to note the appearance of certain rigoristic tendencies in several Christian centers. While not denying that God has the power to remit all sins, some churches refused canonical absolution to three classes of criminals: apostates, adulterers, and homicides. To state the matter differently, the excommunication fulminated against these three sins was perpetual. St. Irenaeus refers to sinful women who spend their whole lives doing public penance, and others who, discouraged by such rigorism, decide to sever relations with the Church. In an attempt to remedy a situation of this kind, Pope Callixtus (217-222) issued a disciplinary decree, admitting great sinners, and especially the unchaste, to ecclesiastical absolution, and re-instating them in the Church after a period of public penance. The legislation was no sooner formulated than the rigorists cried out scandal. The leaders of the opposing faction were Tertullian and the Roman priest Hippolytus.

Already a Montanist, *Tertullian* launched his *De Pudicitia* (On Chastity), in which, without any regard for the stand he had taken fifteen years previously in his *De Paenitentia* (On Penance), he denied that any forgiveness could be accorded sinners of this type. *Hippolytus* formulated his protestations in his *Philosophoumena,* at the same time accusing Pope Callixtus of errors concerning the dogma of the Trinity. He even went so far as to pose as anti-pope, although, to be fair to him, his opposition was born of an indiscreet zeal tinged with exaggerated mysticism. Later in life he repented of his sin, renounced his schismatic doctrines, and suffered martyrdom during the persecution of Maximinus.

The edict of Pope Callixtus had re-opened the doors of the Church to the repentant unchaste; circumstances were slowly arising that induced the Church to follow the same policy in regard to apostates. The persecution of the Emperor Decius, which began in the year 250, resulted in a number of relapses into idolatry. The fallen (*lapsi*) were divided into two classes: those who had sacrificed to the idols (*sacrificati*), and those who had bribed the officials and obtained from them bogus certificates (*libellatici*). In the absence of *St. Cyprian*, bishop of Carthage, who was hiding in a secret retreat, the *lapsi* began to besiege confessors and martyrs in an effort to obtain from them certificates of confession (*libelli pacis*), and upon presentation of these certificates to the priests, they were reconciled to the Church. The matter was a very delicate one from two points of view, because it quite naturally gave rise to the double question: Could the Church absolve apostates? and: Did the martyrs possess such powers of intercession? When asked his opinion of this whole matter, St. Cyprian admitted the principle of reconciliation, since the decision issued by him was to the effect that *lapsi* in danger of death who presented a certificate of confession could be reconciled to the Church in the absence of the bishop. On the other hand, he decided that the martyrs had usurped a power reserved to others, and refused to concede to them any other right than that of recommending certain *lapsi* for reconciliation. The bishop alone was the judge as to who was actually deserving of forgiveness, and he himself would examine all particular cases upon his return to Carthage.

Decisions of this kind caused dissatisfaction among confessors and *lapsi,* and in several cities were the occasion of brawls and riotings. Felicissimus Novatus and a number of other priests declared themselves in open revolt against Cyprian and proceeded to welcome back into the Church all those who presented certificates of confession (*libelli pacis*). They even went so far as to appoint a schismatic bishop named Fortunatus. St. Cyprian appealed his case to the Roman clergy, who at that time (since the death of St. Fabian, January 20, 250), were without a bishop and through the medium of a priest named *Novatian,* the mother-Church issued an answer completely approving the stand taken by him. Then the persecution suddenly came to an end; Cyprian re-entered the city, and in the early days of April, 251, convoked a council. Here it was decreed, first, that the sin of apostasy was not unforgivable, but that a lengthy penance would be imposed upon the *lapsi* who should seek forgiveness at the feet of their bishop. He alone would pass judgment upon each individual case. And since the bishop had now returned to his flock, there was no need of *libelli pacis;* consequently, no account would be taken of them. Secondly, a difference was established between the *libellatici* and the *sacrificati*. The first class of *lapsi* could be reconciled to the Church after the facts of their case had been examined; the second could be absolved from excommunication only at the hour of death. Thus, the African decision of Bishop Cyprian was a compromise, yet in complete accord with that of Pope Callixtus.

But the opposition was not to be so easily foiled. Headed by Novatus, it sought to enlist in advance the support of the future pope. Novatus journeyed to Rome, but all his plans and intrigues were completely frustrated. The choice of the clergy fell, not upon his candidate, Novatian, but upon the priest *Cornelius,* who, not being acquainted with African affairs, convoked a Roman council which set its mark of approval upon all the decisions of St. Cyprian. Thwarted in his ambitions, *Novatian* headed a schismatic movement, with Novatus as his acolyte. The new schismatics had to have matter for schism, and so they seized upon the question of the hour, the position of the *lapsi*. Novatian was a rigorist, hence he took a stand that was the very opposite of that of his friend Novatus, who, however, experienced no qualms of conscience in completely reversing his former views. Thus both he and Novatian began to advocate the permanent exclusion of all *lapsi* from the Church, even at the hour of death. The disgruntled candidate then had himself elected pope by his followers and thus became one of the first antipopes in history.

Novatian's error, already implicitly condemned, was again denounced by a council of sixty bishops, presided over by Pope Cornelius. Scholarly writings supported the verdict of the Sovereign Pontiff, in particular the beautiful treatise *De Unitate Ecclesiae* (On the Unity of the Church) of St. Cyprian. In it, the holy bishop of Carthage defends unity, which he considers an authentic mark of the true Church. To his way of thinking, the worst enemy of Christianity is not the persecutor, who can be overcome by constancy, but the schismatic, who seeks to rend the seamless robe of Christ.

2. The Question of the Baptism of Heretics. Cyprian derived much inspiration from all these conclusions in his new controversy with a layman named Magnus. This time, however, the debate shifted to other ground, being concerned now with the Baptism of heretics. The question put by Magnus was the following: Must converts from paganism, who have been baptized by heretics, be baptized anew before being re-admitted into the Church? Consistent with his doctrine of total exclusivism, St. Cyprian replied that, being outside the Church, heretics could not confer a Sacrament of the Church. "We do not rebaptize," he wrote, "but we baptize those who come to us from among the heretics. They can have received nothing from the heretics, since the latter have nothing." Theologically speaking, and pushed to its logical conclusions, the error of St. Cyprian was a serious one. Baptism, and for that matter all the Sacraments, produce their effects *ex opere operato,* and to hold a different opinion would be tantamount to conceding that the character of the priesthood may be lost through schism, heresy, or even mortal sin. One would then have to admit the existence of an invisible Church dependent upon the interior dispositions of minister and subject. In a word, the error of St. Cyprian was the forerunner of Wiclifism and Puritanism.

When the controverted question was carried to the tribunal of Pope *St. Stephen I,* the latter did not view it in the same light in which we regard it to-day, after the Protestant Reformation. Pope St. Stephen saw only this one phase of the matter: In Rome, as well as in Jerusalem and Alexandria, Baptism was never repeated, but heretics were reconciled to the Church either through the imposition of hands *in poenitentiam,* or through the anointing with oil (*consignatio*). The Roman custom should prevail, because it embodied the tradition of the Church. "If some one comes to you from among the heretics," he replied in substance, "you must refrain from introducing any innovations which run counter to duly constituted tradition (*nihil innovetur nisi quod traditum est*). Remain content, therefore, to reconcile him through the imposition of hands *in poenitentiam.*" To the Pope's way of thinking the whole question was purely one of discipline, similar in every respect to the controversy regarding the date of Easter in the second century.

Cyprian insisted on his right as a bishop to decide the matter for himself. "Each one of the heads of the Church," he wrote, "is free to conduct his own affairs as he sees fit." Accordingly, in the year 256, he convoked a second council of African bishops, this time numbering 87, who, "smarting under the sharp rebuke administered by the Bishop of Rome to the Bishop of Carthage," set their mark of approval upon the action of St. Cyprian.

Cyprian's cause was sponsored also by Firmilian, bishop of Caesarea in Cappadocia, who assured him that the whole of Asia Minor was on his side. But as Pope Stephen had already signified his opinion to all Christendom, relations were suspended for the time being between the churches of

Africa and Asia Minor on the one hand, and the Church of Rome. It is a significant proof of the Pontiff's patience and meekness that he did not fulminate excommunication against Cyprian and his followers, but this may have been due in part to the influence of a new Irenaeus in the person of Denis of Alexandria. Harmony was re-established when Pope Stephen, who suffered martyrdom, was succeeded by Pope Xystus II; but it was not until after the Council of Arles (314) that the Church of Africa gave up its ancient practice.

It would be a mistake to conclude from this misunderstanding that St. Cyprian, the apostle of unity, was opposed to the primacy of the pope; he calls Rome *"locus Petri"* (the see of Peter), and again *"ecclesia principalis, unde unitas sacerdotalis exorta est"* (the principal Church, the birthplace of sacerdotal unity).

II. The Trinitarian Controversies. 1. Monarchianism. Expressed in the simplest formulas, early belief in the Blessed Trinity was in no immediate peril. But already in the second century the mystery began to raise doubts in the minds of scientific inquirers, and the danger was felt that in attempting explanations of the mystery, theologians might exaggerate either the divine unity, Modalism, or the trinity of persons, Adoptionism.

Praxeas had journeyed to Rome from Asia to denounce Montanism, and particularly its false conception of the rôle of the Holy Ghost. By way of reaction, he minimized the part played by the Holy Spirit to the extent of absorbing His personality and that of the Son in the one personality or monarchy of the Father (Monarchianism). The next inference was logical enough: the Son was the Father incarnate, suffering and crucified (Patripassianism). It would appear, however, that, after journeying from Rome to Africa, Praxeas came under the influence of Tertullian and retracted his errors.

The first known representative of Modalistic Monarchianism was Noëtus of Smyrna. He formed a Patripassian school, to which belonged Epigonus, Cleomenes, and Sabellius. These three set up their headquarters in Rome, where they caused such a commotion that, according to Tertullian, the subject matter of every conversation seemed to be Monarchianism (*"Monarchiam, inquiunt, tenemus"*). The heresy was strenuously opposed by Tertullian, Hippolytus, and Pope Callixtus. Hippolytus' views were so stringent that he did not hesitate to accuse even the Pontiff of slackness, although the latter condemned Sabellius outright. The truth of the matter is that the papal condemnation spelled the end of Monarchianism in the West, even though the error did continue to eke out an existence in the East, especially in Egypt and Pentapolis. But in these countries, the Patripassian doctrine of Sabellius (Sabellianism) underwent considerable modification: it was no longer the Father who suffered, because He would cease to be the Father by incarnating Himself as the Son: and He would cease to be the Son by appearing as the Holy Ghost. The only possible explanation, therefore, was that God was a simple and indivisible monad, susceptible of different successive modes of being (Modalism).

Denis of Alexandria opposed Modalism, but his terminology could be interpreted as favoring the opposite error. He placed such strong emphasis on the distinction of persons in God that he seriously compromised the doctrine of the unity of nature. His namesake, Pope Denis, called him to order, but the explicit answer of Denis of Alexandria leaves no doubt as to his orthodoxy.

2. Adoptionism. Like the Monarchianism of Praxeas, the opposite error of Adoptionism was the outcome of circumstances. *Theodotus,* a rich Christian of Byzantium, had apostatized during one of the persecutions, and, on a visit to Rome, sought to excuse his conduct by stating that in denying Christ he had not denied God, since Jesus was only a human creature, born of a virgin, who, flooded with divine grace on the day of his Baptism, had been able to carry out His Messianic mission, although, in becoming the adoptive son of God, He had not ceased to be a man like ourselves (*Adoptionism*). This error also went under the name of *Subordinationism,* because it completely subordinated the Son to the Father, putting the same distance between them as there is between the Creator and the creature.

Excommunicated by Pope Victor towards the year 190, Theodotus, called "the Ancient," organized a schismatic community, which resembled a literary circle more than a church, and in which Plato and Aristotle were given the places of honor. But, if Jesus Christ was a mere man, was there not a possibility of His being surpassed by some other creature? A second Theodotus, termed "the Younger," settled this question by making Melchisedech "the greatest power," "the celestial virtue and the principal grace," son of God and mediator between God and man.

Adoptionism was vigorously opposed by St. Hippolytus. It scored but little success in the West, although an individual by the name of Artemon sought to revive it in Rome towards the year 235. The error was doomed to failure because it challenged truths too deep-seated in the minds of men to be shaken.

And yet, in the year 260, Paul of Samosata, bishop of Antioch, resuscitated the same heresy by giving it an intellectual twist and a new dress in the theory of the Logos. The Logos or Word, he held, was merely an attribute of God: divine reason manifested itself through Moses and the Prophets, but especially through Jesus, the son of the Virgin, who was only a man superiorly inspired by the Logos, but "little by little merited in some way to be divinized." Paul of Samosata based his Christology on such Scripture texts as: "My father is greater than I" and "Jesus advanced in wisdom, and age, and grace before God and men." Patronized by Zenobia, queen of Palmyra, whose Oriental and anti-Roman policies he favored, Paul succeeded in defending himself against charges proffered by Firmilian of Caesarea, Denis of Alexandria, and Gregory Thaumaturgus. In the end, however, he was condemned by a council of 70 bishops, who had convened at Antioch from all parts of Asia Minor and Syria. His doctrine was destined to revive towards the beginning of the fourth century in the form of Arianism, to the great injury of the whole Christian Church.

TEXTS AND DOCUMENTS

Decision of St. Cyprian in the Matter of the Baptism of Heretics
(Epist., 69)

We judge and hold for certain that no one can be baptized outside the Church, since there is but one Baptism appointed in the holy Church. And it is written in the words of the Lord: "They have forsaken me, the fountain of living water, and hewed them out broken cisterns, which can hold no water." And again, Sacred Scripture warns, and says: "Keep thee from the strange water, and drink not from a fountain of strange water." It is required, then, that the water should first be cleansed and sanctified by the priest, that it may wash away by its Baptism the sins of the man who is baptized; because the Lord says by Ezechiel the prophet: "Then will I sprinkle clean water upon you, and you shall be cleansed from all your filthiness; and from all your idols will I cleanse you: a new heart also will I give you, and a new spirit will I put within you." But how can he cleanse and sanctify the water who is himself unclean, and in whom the Holy Spirit is not, since the Lord says in the Book of Numbers: "And whosoever the unclean person toucheth shall be unclean." Or how can he who baptizes give to another remission of sins, who himself, being outside the Church, cannot put away his own sins?

But, moreover, the very interrogation which is put in Baptism is a witness of the truth. For when we say, "Dost thou believe in eternal life and the remission of sins through the holy Church?" we mean that remission of sins is not granted except in the Church, and that among heretics, where there is no Church, sins cannot be put away. Therefore, they who assert that heretics can baptize, must either change the interrogation or maintain the truth; unless indeed they attribute a church also to those who, they contend, have Baptism.

It is also necessary that he should be anointed who is baptized; so that, having received the chrism, that is, the anointing, he may be anointed of God, and have in him the grace of Christ. Further, it is the Eucharist whence the baptized are anointed with the oil sanctified on the altar. But he cannot sanctify the creature of oil, who has neither an altar nor a church; whence also there can be no spiritual anointing among heretics, since it is manifest that the oil cannot be sanctified nor the Eucharist celebrated at all among them. But we ought to know and remember that it is written: "Let not the oil of a sinner anoint my head," which the Holy Spirit before forewarned in the Psalms, lest any one going out of the way and wandering from the path of truth should be anointed by heretics and adversaries of Christ. Besides, what prayer can a priest who is impious and a sinner offer for a baptized person, since it is written, "God heareth not a sinner; but if any man be a worshipper of God, and doeth His will, him He heareth." Who, moreover, can give what he himself hath not, or how can he discharge spiritual functions who himself has lost the Holy Spirit? And therefore, he must be baptized and renewed who comes untrained to the Church, that he may be sanctified within by those who are holy, since it is written, "Be ye holy, for I am holy, saith the Lord."

But it is to approve the Baptism of heretics and schismatics, to admit that they have truly baptized. For therein a part cannot be void, and part be valid. If one could baptize, he could also give the Holy Spirit. But if he cannot give the Holy Spirit, because he that is appointed without is not endowed with the Holy Spirit, he cannot baptize those who come; since both Baptism is one and the Holy Spirit is one, and the Church founded by Christ the Lord upon Peter, by a source and principle of unity, is one also. Hence it results that, since with them all things are futile and false, nothing of that which they have done ought to be approved by us; we who are with the Lord, and maintain the unity of the Lord, and according to His condescension administer His priesthood in the Church, ought to repudiate and reject and regard as profane whatever His adversaries and the antichrists do.

If any one shall come to you from any one of the heresies, there must be no innovation, but the tradition is to be observed and hands imposed upon him in penance. Moreover, the heretics themselves do not baptize strictly speaking those who come to them, but merely administer Communion. There is no need of investigating the person of the one who baptizes, because he who has been baptized may obtain grace through the invocation of the three Persons of the Blessed Trinity: the Father, the Son, and the Holy Ghost. It is the name of Christ which produces the effect of Baptism, in such wise that he who has been baptized in any place, may also obtain the grace of Jesus Christ. In this place we follow this tradition which we have received from the Apostles.

QUESTIONS

1. Who were the *lapsi,* the *libellatici,* and the *sacrificati?*
2. How do you account for the fact that St. Cyprian was ignorant of the *ex opere operato* manner in which the Sacraments produce their effects?
3. Which were the unforgivable sins, and how would you account for their having been regarded as unforgivable by the early Christians?
4. What was the fallacy in St. Cyprian's argument against Baptism administered by heretics?
5. Contrast the error of St. Cyprian and that of the Gallican hierarchy of a later period.
6. Whence did the heresy termed Monarchianism derive its name?
7. Contrast Monarchianism and Modalism?
8. Trace the origin and development of the heresy of Adoptionism.
9. Who was Paul of Samosata?

BIBLIOGRAPHY

The Penitential Question in Rome under Callixtus.—Sources: TERTULLIAN, *De poenitentia, De pudicitia,* edit. P. DE LABRIOLLE, Coll. Hemmer and Lejay.—Works: A. D'ALÈS, *Tertullien et Calliste,* in *Rev. hist. eccl.* (1912), t. XIII, pp. 5-33, 221-256, 441-449, 621-639; *La théologie de Tertullien,* 1904; *La théologie de saint Hippolyte,* 1906; *L'édit de Calliste.*—BATIFFOL, *L'Eglise naissante,* pp. 340-353.—P. GALTIER, *Le véritable édit de Calliste,* R. H. E., 1927, pp. 465-488.

The Penitential Question at Carthage under St. Cyprian.—Sources: CYPRIAN, *Letters, Ad Novatianum,* edit. G. VON HARTEL, C. V., t. III.—Works: Msgr. FREPPEL, *Saint Cyprien et l'Eglise d'Afrique au IIIe siècle.*—E. HAVET, *Cyprien évêque de Carthage,* in *Rev. des Deux-Mondes,* 15 Sept.,

1885.—LE PROVOST, *Etude sur saint Cyprien*, 1889.—P. MONCEAUX, *Hist. litt. de l'Afr. chrét.*, t. II, 1902.—AUDOLLENT, *Carthage romaine*, 1901; art. *"Afrique,"* in *Dict. d'Hist.*—L. CHABALIER, *Les lapsi dans l'Eglise d'Afrique au temps de saint Cyprien*, 1904.—BATIFFOL, *L'Eglise naissante*, pp. 420–457.— A. D'ALÈS, *La Théologie de saint Cyprien*, 1924.—A. D'ALÈS, *Novatien, Etude sur la théologie romaine au milieu du IIIe siècle*, 1925.

The Baptismal Controversy.—Sources: ST. CYPRIAN, *Letters* and *Liber de rebaptismate*, edit. G. VON HARTEL, *C. V.*, III.—Works: Besides the works cited, G. BAREILLE, art. *"Baptême des hérétiques,"* in *Dict. de Théol.*, II, col. 219–233.—A. D'ALÈS, art. *"Baptême des hérétiques,"* in *Dict. d'Apol.*, I, col. 390–418; *La question baptismale au temps de saint Cyprien*, in *Rev. quest. hist.*, t. LXXXI (1907), pp. 353–400.—J. DELAROCHELLE, *L'idée de l'Eglise dans saint Cyprien*, in *Rev. hist. et litt. relig.*, t. I, 1896.—P. BATIFFOL, *L'Eglise naissante*, pp. 458–484.—*Saint Cyprien et la papauté*, in *Etudes*, 5 Nov., 1908. —G. BARDY, *L'autorité du siège romain et les controverses du IIIe siècle, R. S. R.*, 1924, pp. 255–273, 385–411.

Trinitarian Errors. 1. Patripassian Monarchianism.—Sources: TERTULLIAN, *Adversus Praxeam*.—ST. HIPPOLYTUS, *Contra Noëtum; Philosophoumena*, IX, 7–12; X, 27.—Works: A. D'ALÈS, *La théologie de Tertullien*, 1904; *La théologie de saint Hippolyte*, 1906.

2. Adoptionism.—Sources: *Philosophoumena*, VII, 35, 36; X, 23; IX, 3, 12; X, 27.—*Traité contre Artémon*, in Eusebius, *H. E.*, V, 28.—Saint Hippolytus, *Contra Noëtum*, 3.—Saint Epiphanius, *Haer.*, LIV, LV.—*Pseudo-Tertullian*, 23, 24.—On PAUL OF SAMOSATA: A. RÉVILLE, *La Christologie de Paul de Samosate (Bibl. des Hautes Etudes, sect. sciences relig.*, t. VII), 1896. —P. GALTIER, *L'Omoousios de Paul de Samosate*, in *Rech. de sciences relig.*, 1918 (VIII).—G. BARDY, *Paul de Samosate (Spicilegium Lovaniense)*, 1924.

CHAPTER III

I. Eastern Christian Literature: Clement and Origen. Already in the middle of the second century a catechetical school existed at Alexandria. In the beginning, its purpose was primarily an apologetic one, its aim being to effect some sort of reconciliation or compromise between pagan philosophy and the Christian religion, by means of an orthodox gnosis. In point of fact, it was the first school to attempt a theological synthesis of the data of revelation. Unfortunately, however, its leaders took Plato in preference to Aristotle as their guide in the field of philosophical and theological research. The inevitable result was Origenism.

The first master of the Alexandrian school of whom we have any knowledge was Pantaenus. None of his works are extant to-day. His disciple *Clement* (150?–215?), is best known to us through a famous trilogy which comprises the *Protrepticus*, the *Paedagogus*, and the *Stromata*. In the *Protrepticus*, or *Exhortation to the Greeks*, Clement demonstrates the superiority of Christianity over all systems of pagan philosophy, and conducts his readers through the darkness of pagan thought to the light of Christian belief. In the *Paedagogus* he initiates his pupil, already converted from pagan ways, into the practice of Christian morality, and in a lofty and sprightly chat leads him, with Jesus Christ as his teacher, through the paths of Christian discipline. Among other things, the *Paedagogus* contains a very fine description of the virtues and the vices. In the *Stromata* he initiates his pupil into the secrets of the spiritual and mystical life, and paints for him a living portrait of the true Gnostic, *i. e.,* the perfect Christian. Clement displays an erudition that is truly prodigious, His style is fluent and florid, but marred in places by an absence of order. Then, too, he often lacks precision, and his writings contain many inaccuracies which heretics have seized upon to misinterpret his true teaching.

Origen was the most famous of Clement's pupils. Born in Egypt around the year 185, he was selected at the age of eighteen to be his successor in the headmastership of the school. From 204 to 230, he taught at Alexandria. As a consequence of a heated discussion, followed by a breach with his bishop, Demetrius, he took a similar position at Caesarea in Palestine. During the Decian persecution, he was cast into prison and underwent many tortures, which hastened his death at Tyre in Phoenicia in 254.

Origen was a veritable prodigy of erudition. He is often referred to as *Adamantius, i. e.,* "the Man of Steel." His writings resemble an ecclesiastical encyclopedia in 800 volumes, touching upon every known topic: apologetics, the spiritual life, Holy Scripture, and positive theology. He was above all a commentator of the Bible, or better perhaps "a biblicist who formulated almost all his theological doctrines while explaining Holy Scripture." In his *Hexapla* (sixfold Bible) he made a supreme attempt at biblical criticism by arranging the Old Testament in six parallel columns, according to six different versions, a method which favored comparative study. St. Jerome made use of the *Hexapla,* which he found in the library of Caesarea, as the basis of his own exegetical work.

But Origen was not satisfied with external criticism of biblical texts; he attempted textual explanations in his commentaries and scholia, the latter being brief notes, often of a purely grammatical character, on the more difficult passages. Unfortunately, his interpretation of Holy Writ is excessively allegorical, at times purely arbitrary, and hence dangerous. Thus he informs us that the Garden of Eden never did exist, but is a mere figure of Heaven. The school of Antioch reacted against this exegetical subjectivism.

Another fault of Origen is that he rested his theological considerations upon the unexpurgated philosophy of Plato. His *De Principiis* is a veritable manual of theology, but the author's description of Christianity tallies only too closely with what might be termed a Platonic gnosis, from which men of a later age insidiously constructed a system of error of widespread influence, which the Church condemned under the name of Origenism. The works of Origen had an influence on all Greek thought, but especially on that of the Cappadocians.

II. Western Christian Literature: Tertullian, St. Cyprian, and St. Hippolytus. Up to the end of the second century, the Greek language was the only one in use in the Church. Tertullian was the first writer of note to employ Latin. *Tertullian* saw the light of day at Carthage in the year 160; his conversion to Christianity took place around the year 195. We have it on the authority of St. Jerome that he was ordained to the priesthood. Energetic in mind, independent in character, and an implacable logician, he was a born polemist. His style is warm, colorful, crisp, and rich in antitheses.

The *Apologeticum* is the most remarkable of all his polemical writings. Written in the year 197, it proves the innocence of the Christians and the unfairness of the laws of Trajan. Tertullian also waged war against the heretics. Towards the year 200, he wrote his *De Praescriptione Haereticorum,* a general refutation of all dogmatic innovations, in which he follows the method used by St. Irenaeus, urging the faithful to abide by the authority of tradition and of the Church. Such, he remarks, is not the conduct of heretics. They manipulate the Scriptures to suit their own fancy and pretend to amend the rule of faith by appealing to Holy Writ. But the Scriptures are the property of the Church, which has come by them through lawful inheritance. By the laws of logic, therefore, heretics must not be permitted to argue from the Scriptures, and any proof advanced by them as issuing from this source can be of no avail. This is the famous argument from prescription.

But Tertullian was above all a moralist, harsh and severe; he set out to solve, in every detail, the multiple disciplinary and moral questions which arose from the constant association of Christians with the pagan world. In his *De Cultu Feminarum* he laid down rules governing feminine dress. In his *De Spectaculis* and *De Idololatria* he fulminated prohibitions: Christians may not frequent the theatre, the circus, the stadium, the amphitheatre, and other official spectacles; they may not even be tradesmen, teachers, soldiers, office-holders.

Such was Tertullian, "the inexorable intransigent," and when he fell prey to the snares of Montanism, his rigidity changed into Puritanism. From that time on, the uppermost questions in his mind were: flight in times of persecution, second marriage, fasting, and penance. Formerly, Tertullian had held to the opinion that flight from persecution was at times permissible; now, in his *De Fuga in Persecutione* (203), he condemned it without restriction. Formerly, he had merely advised widows against re-marriage (*Ad Uxorem*); now he forbade the practice under pain of adultery (*De Monogamia*). Formerly, he had counselled fasting; now he prescribed it strictly (*De Jejunio*). Formerly, he had assented to the absolution of the Christians who had fallen into grievous sin (*De Poenitentia*); now he disputed the right of the Church to absolve them (*De Pudicitia*).

Elsewhere in his writings, Tertullian endeavored to prove that the new theory of the Paraclete was contained in germ in Holy Writ and declared that precedence should be given to the spiritual masters of the new prophecy over those constituted in Sacred Orders. He even went so far as to found a sect within Montanism itself, which went by his name (Tertullianism). But at that, he is the most important witness we have of the ancient tradition: the Christian world in his day, its relations with paganism, its public and private life, its theology and discipline.

St. Jerome informs us that *St. Cyprian* (210–258) was such an assiduous reader of the writings of Tertullian that in calling for them he was in the habit of saying "Give me the Master" (*Da magistrum*). And yet, what a difference there was between the violent and passionate apologist and the charitable and prudent bishop! St. Cyprian is above all a shepherd, and his chief purpose in writing is to be of service to his readers. All his works are dictated by circumstances, and their contents are subordinated to the instruction of the faithful. Hence, they are filled with accurate analyses, which give proof that the author was a learned moralist. The purpose he had in writing led him to discard the rhetorical form and logical precision of his master Tertullian, and to seek the proof for his arguments in the supernatural testimony of the Bible. "In every one of his books," writes Monceaux, "three elements are always found combined: citations from the Bible, commentaries on these texts, and application of them to existing circumstances."

We know the events which prompted the two principal writings of St. Cyprian. The *De Lapsis* (251) imposes upon apostates the obligation of doing penance; the *De Unitate Ecclesiae* (251), directed against the African schismatics, stresses the outstanding characteristic of the true Church, which is unity. Among his apologetical writings we may cite the *Ad Donatum* (246), which depicts the moral transformation effected in his friend by Baptism; and the *Ad Demetrianum* (251), in which he takes a pagan magistrate to task for calumniating the Christians. The real cause of the plagues that have devastated Africa, he writes, is not the Christians, who are law-abiding citizens, but the vices of obstinate heathens. The three books of *Testimonia ad Quirinum* are a compilation of diverse theses substantiated by biblical citations. The first deals of the provisional character of the Jewish law and the vocation of the Gentiles; the second, of the divinity of Christ; and the third, of the moral obligations of Christians. The success of these *Testimonia* was tremendous, because they furnished polemical writers with a methodical repertoire of facts and proofs. The *Ad Fortunatum de Exhortatione Martyrii* (257) is another collection of Scriptural texts calculated to inspire courage in the soldiers of Christ. The temperament of the Bishop of Carthage led him to favor the homily as a vehicle of thought. His *De Habitu Virginum* (249) is a eulogy of virginity; his *De Immortalitate* is an admirable treatise on Christian suffering and death. Besides these he wrote: *De Opere et de Eleemosynis, De Bono Patientiae,* and *De Zelo et Livore.*

St. *Hippolytus* was a Roman priest and scholar, who headed a schism against Pope St. Callixtus. After being exiled to the island of Sardinia together with Pope Pontianus during the persecution of Maximinus, he re-entered the true fold and died a martyr. Inferior to Origen in erudition and fecundity, he resembles him in this, that his mind embraced all domains of sacred science: exegesis, apologetics, dogma, moral, discipline, history and geography. His taste for allegorical interpretation makes for another resemblance with Origen, although Hippolytus is soberer and more rational, and careful to advert to the historical sense. Of his many homilies, most of which were written on the books of the Old Testament, there remain to-day only a few fragments. This may be due in part to the fact that at the time Hippolytus wrote, Latin was fast displacing Greek as the language of the Roman Church, and in part to the fact that the memory of his unhappy schism discouraged the reading of his works. The principal work that has come down to us is the *Philosophoumena,* "A Refutation of all the Heresies." More of a jurist than a metaphysician, St. Hippolytus displays a love of precision which often leads him to become unduly vague and intransigent.

TEXTS AND DOCUMENTS

Extract from Hippolytus' Refutation of all Heresies

The Stoics themselves also imparted growth to philosophy, in respect to a greater development of the art of syllogism, and included almost everything under definitions, both Chrysippus and Zeno being coincident in opinion on this point. And they likewise supposed God to be one originating principle of all things, being a body of the utmost refinement, and that His providential care pervaded everything; and these speculators were positive about the existence of fate everywhere, employing some such example as the following: that just as a dog, supposing him attached to a car, if indeed he is disposed to follow, both is drawn, or follows voluntarily, making an exercise also of free power, in combination with necessity, that is fate; but if he may not be disposed to follow, he will altogether be coerced to do so. And the same, of course, holds good in the case of men. For though not willing to follow, they will altogether be compelled to enter upon what has been decreed for them. [The Stoics], however, assert that the soul abides after death, but that it is a body, and that such is formed from the refrigeration of the surrounding atmosphere; wherefore, also, that it was called psyche (*i. e.,* soul). And they acknowledge likewise, that there is a transition of souls from one body to another, that is for those souls for whom this migration has been destined And they accept the doctrine, that there will be a conflagration, a purification of this world, some say the whole of it, but others a portion, and that [the world] itself is undergoing partial destruction; and this all but corruption, and the generation from it of another world, they term purgation. And they assume the existence of all bodies, and that body does not pass through body, but that a refraction takes place, and that all things involve plenitude, and that there is no vacuum. The foregoing are the opinions of the Stoics also.

QUESTIONS

1. Outline the history of the catechetical schools of Alexandria.
2. Criticize the works and style of Origen.
3. Contrast the characters of Origen and Tertullian.
4. Which are the chief errors of these two early Christian writers?
5. What is the famous argument from prescription?
6. Discuss Tertullian as a moralist, as an exegete.
7. Describe the character and works of St. Cyprian.

BIBLIOGRAPHY

Christian Literature.—General Works: O. Bardenhewer, *Patrology,* tr. Shahan.—Tixeront, *Handbook of Patrology* (transl. Raemers).— Msgr. Batiffol, *La littérature grecque,* 1901.—P. de Labriolle, *Histoire de la littérature latine chrétienne,* 2nd edit., 1924.—A. Puech, *Histoire de la littérature grecque chrétienne,* 2 vols., 1928.—P. Monceaux, *Histoire de la littérature latine chrétienne* (Coll. Payot), 1924.—F. Cayré, *Précis de Patrologie,* t. I, 1927.—G. Bardy, *Littérature grecque chrétienne,* 1928.—Orr, *The History and Literature of the Early Church.*

Clement of Alexandria.—Sources: *P. G.*, VIII–IX; and above all the edit. of O. Staehlin, in the Collection *Christliche Schriftsteller* of Leipzig, 1905–1909.—Works: FREPPEL, *Clément d'Alexandrie*, 1865.—E. DE FAYE, *Clément d'Alexandrie*, 2nd edit., 1906.—J. PATRICK, *Clement of Alexandria*, Edinburgh, 1914.—G. BARDY, *Clément d'Alexandrie* (Coll. "*Les Moralistes Chrétiens*"), 1926.

Origen.—Sources: *P. G.*, XI–XVII; of the edit. of the *Schriftsteller* of Berlin, 5 vols. have appeared.—Works: FREPPEL, *Origène*, 1884.—Ch. BIGG, *The Christian Platonists of Alexandria*, Oxford, 1886.—F. PRAT, *Origène* (*La Pensée Chrétienne*), 1907.—G. BARDY, *Recherches sur l'histoire du texte et des versions latines du de Principiis*, Lille, 1924.—E. DE FAYE, *Origène*, 2 vols., 1928.—DE LABRIOLLE, *Latin Christianity* (transl. H. WILSON).

Tertullian.—Sources: *P. L.*, I–III.—F. ŒHLER, Q. S. F.: *Tertulliani quae supersunt omnia*, Lipsiae, 1853–1854.—*C. V.*, XX and XLVII (incomplete).—*De pudicitia, De poenitentia* (1906), *De praescriptione haereticorum* (1907), edit. G. DE LABRIOLLE, coll. Hemmer-Lejay.—*Apologeticum*, text and translation by J. P. WALTZING, Louvain, 1910.—Works: FREPPEL, *Tertullien*, 1864.—G. BOISSIER, *La fin du paganisme*, I, 259–304.—G. MONCEAUX, *Hist. litt. de l'Afrique chrétienne*, I, 1901.—A. D'ALÈS, *La théologie de Tertullien*, 1905.—DOM LECLERCQ, *L'Afrique chrétienne*.—G. DE LABRIOLLE, *La crise montaniste*, 1913 (Bibliography, pp. vii–xx); *Tertullien jurisconsulte* in *Nouv. Rev. hist. du droit français et étranger*, Jan.-Feb., 1906.—DE LABRIOLLE, *op. cit.*

St. Cyprian.—Sources: Edit. G. HARTEL, in *C. V.* III; *P. L.* III and IV.—Works: FREPPEL, *Saint Cyprien*, 1865.—MONCEAUX, *Hist. litt. Afr. chr.*, t. II, 1902.—S. CYPRIEN (Coll. "*Les Saints*"), 1914.—P. GODET, art. *Cyprien*, in *Dict. de Théol.*, t. III, col. 2459–2470.—E. W. BENSON, *Cyprian, his life, his times, his work*, London, 1897. Also the works and articles already cited.

St. Hippolytus.—Sources: Edition of Fabricius, in *P. G.*, X, very insufficient. For Scriptural works, edit. N. Bonwetsch and H. Achelis. *Hippolytus Werke.* I in the *Schriftsteller* of Berlin, Leipzig, 1897. For the *Philosophoumena*, edit. P. Cruice, 1860, or *P. G.*, XVI, or again P. Wendland in *Hippolytus Werke*, III. Band. Leipzig, 1916. For the chronicles, edit. Bauer (*Texte und Unters.*, XXIX, I), Leipzig, 1905.—Works: A. D'ALÈS, *La théologie de saint Hippolyte*, 1906.

CHAPTER IV

I. Diocletian, Galerius, and Maximinus Daja. With the ever-
threatening attitude of the barbarian hordes, *Diocletian* very soon realized
the futility of trying to cope with difficulties single-handed. Authority
could become effective only on condition that the links connecting the
Empire's boundaries were strengthened and the person of the Emperor
was multiplied in direct ratio with them. And so, in the year 285, Diocletian associated Maximian Hercules with himself in the government, giving him the title of Augustus and the Western portion of the Empire to
administer. In the year 293, he created two Caesars: one, Galerius, his son-
in-law, to act as his own representative in the East; the other, Constantius
Chlorus, to divide the government of the West with Maximian. Diocletian established himself at Nicomedia, and took as his share of the
Empire Thrace and Asia; Galerius took up his residence at Sirmium and
received as his portion the Balkan Peninsula and the Danubian Provinces;
Maximian Hercules moved to Milan and proceeded to administer the
affairs of Italy, Spain, and Africa; Constantius Chlorus established the
seat of his government at Treves, and ruled over Gaul and Britain. In
spite of the fact that two of the reigning officials were vested with the title
of Augustus and the other two with that of Caesar, each one of the four
emperors was sufficiently master of his own affairs to have the undivided
ministration of his share of the Empire. And so we need not wonder
at encountering persecution of Christians in the East, while Rome and
Gaul enjoyed a period of peace and tranquillity.

There still existed an old political party in Rome with members scattered throughout the Empire, for whom the safety of the nation depended
not only on the successful checking of barbarian invasions, but also on
the maintenance of internal unity through the persecution of Christians.
Galerius was the first of the four emperors to be won over to this camp.

Commissioned as he was to protect the most seriously threatened frontiers of the Empire, the Danubian Provinces, he believed he could enhance military discipline and patriotism by making attendance at the services of official pagan worship compulsory. The Christian soldiers refused to comply with his orders and were reprimanded; a few protests of a more energetic nature resulted in capital punishment for the offenders. It was the prelude to a new persecution. Almost all the *Acts* of Christian soldiers date back to this period. We have those of St. Maurice and the Theban legion, twice decimated at Agaune on the banks of the Rhine by order of the Emperor Maximian; as well as those of St. Sebastian, tribune of the pretorian guard at Nicomedia, who was pierced to death with arrows.

From a spirit of sectarianism rather than from any reason of State, Galerius then brought pressure to bear on Diocletian to obtain the promulgation of a general edict of persecution. By his advice, the extremely superstitious Emperor consulted with Apollo of Miletus, who strongly denounced the Christians. Diocletian yielded on condition that no blood be shed, and in 303 issued a first edict. The terms of the document ordered first, the destruction of all Sacred Books and places of worship; and second, public abjuration by all Christians under pain of civil death for the nobility, and slavery for the common people. The persecution now began in earnest, and a new class of *lapsi* appeared upon the scene in the *traditores,* who voluntarily surrendered the Sacred Books they had in their possession. The destruction of valuable archives is attested by the many omissions which occur at this time in the Acts of the Martyrs, calendars, and martyrologies.

An unbloody persecution of this kind failed to satisfy the fanaticism of Galerius, who continued to besiege the timid Diocletian, this time renewing against the Christians the calumny with which Nero had besmirched their name. On two successive occasions a fire had broken out in the imperial palace; Galerius persuaded the Emperor that the Christians had kindled it, and a local persecution was begun at Nicomedia. With even more cunning and shrewdness Galerius aroused the Emperor's political misgivings on the occasion of popular upheavals in Syria and Roman Armenia, the result being that Diocletian gave orders for a bloody persecution. A second edict appeared in the same year (303), commanding that all clerics be imprisoned; and a third gave them the option of either sacrificing to the gods or being subjected to torture. Finally, after a brief respite, granted on the occasion of the twentieth anniversary of Diocletian's advent to the throne, a fourth edict appeared, pronouncing the death penalty against Christians of every class who refused to offer sacrifice. According to Eusebius, "the prisons were so filled with bishops and priests that there was no place left for criminals." Different means were resorted to in an effort to track down the followers of Christ. In public places, and even in stores, statues were erected to which everyone was required to pay homage, and at times all commodities were conse-crated to the idols before being put on sale. The number of martyrs who sealed their fate with their blood is wellnigh incalculable. We might make mention in passing of St. Agnes in Rome and St. Lucy in Syra-cuse, both of whom were miraculously preserved from attacks upon their virginity.

In the year 305, a thunderbolt shook the Empire to its very founda-tions. Yielding to the pressure of Galerius, Diocletian and Maximian Hercules abdicated. The two Caesars immediately assumed the title of Augustus, Galerius in the East, and Constantius Chlorus in the West. Resolved to redouble the measures of violence, Galerius associated with himself in the government a man whom he could trust to carry out his plans. This man was none other than his nephew, *Maximinus Daja*, who was appointed governor of Egypt and Syria. An edict issued in the year 306 resulted in a persecution as systematic as that of the Emperor Decius. The head of each family was summoned by name in every city and given the option to sacrifice or die. New and more complicated means of torture were devised; many bodies were refused burial and allowed to rot in the open; the outskirts of the city of Caesarea resembled a charnel-house; the prisons were filled to overflowing; no room was left for fresh chain gangs in the mines; at the quarries of the Thebaid, and in the mines of Cilicia, Palestine, and Cyprus, long trains of Christians arrived every day and were subjected to every kind of hardship and outrage. But the persecutor was the first to tire of it all. Stricken with a dreadful and protracted malady, Galerius sought to obtain a cure from the God of the Christians by issuing, in the year 311, a decree in which he granted the faithful the right to hold meetings, provided they did not disturb the public peace.

Galerius finally succumbed, and Maximinus Daja succeeded him as master of the East. He resumed the task of persecuting the Christians, but resorted to different methods in attaining his end. Precursor of Julian the Apostate, he fully realized that the entire strength of a religion is bound up with the quality of its priesthood, and in consequence he combined all his efforts against the bishops and priests. At the same time, he sought to instill new life into official pagan worship by reorganizing its administration, modelling his changes upon the then existing Christian hierarchy. At the head of the local pagan clergy he placed a provincial high priest selected by the more worthy magistrates. At the same time he inaugurated a libelous campaign against the character of Christ, flooding the book shops with copies of the pseudo-Acts of Pontius Pilate, which parodied the Gospel narrative. These stories were taught to the children in the schools; they were also made the subject matter of public debate in the forums. Unlike the persecution of Decius, undertaken merely as a measure to insure public safety, the persecution of Maximinus Daja quickly assumed all the characteristics of a real religious warfare. Daja's attention was diverted from the scenes of conflict only by the worries of a disastrous expedition undertaken in Armenia. In the meantime, Constantius Chlorus died, and it was soon learned that the West was ruled by a protector of the Christian religion, Constantine.

II. The Edict of Milan. Ever since Maximian Hercules, colleague of Diocletian, had abdicated, the West had enjoyed a period of tranquillity. Constantius Chlorus, and his son Constantine, who succeeded him in the government of Britain and Gaul, both adopted an attitude of religious tolerance. But the division of the Empire between two Augusti and two Caesars, which was intended to secure stability, resulted in strifes of all kinds, and even open warfare. Rival claimants arose, who plunged the Empire into civil war. Severus was the first. He usurped the place left vacant by the abdication of Maximian Hercules; and his action resulted in old Maximian again taking up the purple. Severus was defeated, but Maximian ended his career shortly afterwards by hanging himself. Maxentius succeeded, and later on Licinius announced himself as the colleague of Constantine in the East. All these moves finally resulted in clearing the field for the four Augusti: Maximinus Daja, Maxentius, Licinius, and Constantine.

In the year 312 the most decisive event of all took place, when Maxentius declared war on Constantine. The young Emperor of Gaul quickly crossed the Alps and gave him battle at the *Milvian Bridge,* on the banks of the Tiber. Victorious, he entered Rome, Oct. 29, 312. The matter would have resolved itself into a mere political victory of one tolerant pagan over another tolerant pagan, and not a complete triumph for Christianity, had not an event of considerable importance, which took place in the course of the expedition, changed the whole situation. This event was the conversion of Constantine.

Eusebius has recounted the incident for us in his *Vita Constantini,* the official version certified by the Emperor himself. "It was after midday; the sun was sinking; the Emperor beheld in the heavens, above the sun, a cross of light, around which were woven the words: 'In this sign thou shalt conquer (Τουτῳ νικα).' He began to ask himself the meaning of this apparition. That night, Jesus Christ appeared to him in a dream, bearing the emblem he had seen in the heavens, and commanding him to make of it a military standard. The Emperor sent for silversmiths and commanded them to reduplicate the pattern in gold and precious stones (*labarum*)." Like Clovis in later years, Constantine saw in his victory an intervention on the part of the Deity, and so the words *"instinctu divinitatis"* were engraved by his orders on the Arch of Triumph erected on this occasion, and still standing amongst the ruins of the City of the Caesars. The Emperor was soon to give positive proof that he had championed the cause of Christianity by issuing the famous Edict of Milan, in which he formulated the principle of absolute tolerance: Christians were afforded protection, and pagans were shielded from harm. It was decided, furthermore, that ecclesiastical property, including all goods and land that had been alienated, was to be returned in full and without litigation to its rightful owners. If, as a consequence of such action, the present owner suffered any notable loss, he was to be indemnified by the State. Thus all previous acts of confiscation were revoked by an act of generosity on the part of the Emperor which even the Concordat of 1801 did not have the courage to imitate. A clause of this kind was evident proof of the will of the State to liquidate the past and to settle all accounts with the Christians. And yet, if we take a closer view of the edict, it held out hope for even greater advantages and favors. Objectively tolerant, and nothing more, it was intended by Constantine to be even kind and benevolent. It is clear, indeed, that his only concern was for the Christians, for they are the only ones mentioned by name in the document. Moreover, it is explicitly stated that the tolerance conceded to other religions is only a consequence of that granted to Christianity. The future conduct of the Emperor justified this view.

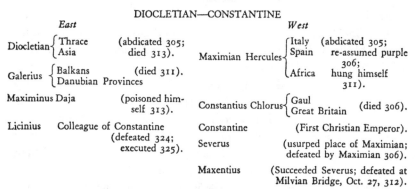

THE ROMAN EMPIRE

DIOCLETIAN—CONSTANTINE

East				West	
Diocletian	Thrace Asia	(abdicated 305; died 313).	Maximian Hercules	Italy Spain Africa	(abdicated 305; re-assumed purple 306; hung himself 311).
Galerius	Balkans Danubian Provinces	(died 311).			
Maximinus Daja		(poisoned him- self 313).	Constantius Chlorus	Gaul Great Britain	(died 306).
Licinius	Colleague of Constantine (defeated 324; executed 325).		Constantine	(First Christian Emperor).	
			Severus	(usurped place of Maximian; defeated by Maximian 306).	
			Maxentius	(Succeeded Severus; defeated at Milvian Bridge, Oct. 27, 312).	

III. The Final Struggle. 1. The Last of the Apologists: Arnobius and Lactantius.

The persecution gave rise to the last of the apologists: Arnobius and Lactantius. *Arnobius* was a distinguished rhetorician who taught at Sicca, a small town in Proconsular Numidia. He was a declared enemy of Christianity, but around the year 295, was led rather suddenly to embrace the new religion. His action was such a surprise to those who knew him, that the bishop to whom he applied for admission into the Church, first exacted a proof of his sincerity. Arnobius furnished this proof by composing a long apologetical treatise in seven books, entitled *Adversus Nationes* (Against the Pagans). In the first two books he answered the calumnies of those who would make Christianity the cause of all the evils which devastated the Roman Empire; in the other five he endeavored to prove that the anger of God is aroused by the crude conception the pagans have of the Divinity. The whole treatise is positive proof that Arnobius knew very little of the religion he was defending. He never refers to Holy Scripture, and, to his way of thinking, Christianity is nothing more than an expurgated form of deism. His style is frequently pompous and redundant, like that of a rhetorician, and yet the whole work constituted in its day a powerful weapon against the claims of paganism. The realistic imagination of Arnobius is exceptionally vigorous. His greatest achievement is to weigh this or that metaphysical hypothesis, or this or that popular form of belief, and then with impeccable logic and precision to deduce from his investigation the rather nonsensical conclusions contained therein.

Lactantius, a pupil of Arnobius, was converted to Christianity around the year 300. In his *Divinae Institutiones,* a calm and serene piece of work, he purposed to give a complete compendium of Christian doctrine, written in literary style for the use of those among the more cultured who held Christianity in contempt. The treatise *De Ira Dei* (On the Anger of God) is intended as a complement to the *Institutiones,* and establishes the principle that God is the avenger of crime. After the triumph of Constantine, Lactantius wrote his treatise *De Mortibus Persecutorum* (On the Death of the Persecutors). From the historical point of view this work is a faithful picture of the ten years of persecution from the first decree of the Emperor Diocletian down to the battle of the Milvian Bridge (303–313). From the apologetical point of view, it ventures the opinion that the tragic deaths of the imperial tyrants were a just punishment for their cruelties. Lactantius is not a deep thinker, and his knowledge of theology is but mediocre. He is above all a classicist, who endeavors to imitate as closely as possible the great models of Latin antiquity, especially Cicero. His *De Mortibus Persecutorum* exhibits a vividness and color of style not to be met with in his other works, having been composed in an intensely emotional period. The pictures are sketched with dramatic sobriety, interspersed with master strokes of wit and pungency.

2. The Last Persecutor: Licinius. Upon assuming his share of the Roman Empire, Constantine found himself in a peculiar predicament. As emperor, he was the head (*pontifex maximus*) of the official religion; as victor in the battle of the Milvian Bridge, he was forced to acknowledge that his sympathies were for the Christian religion. Constrained to humor his colleague Licinius, he endeavored, up to the year 323, to adhere as strictly as possible to the spirit of the Edict of Milan, placing the Christians on an equal footing with the pagans. If he declared Catholic priests exempt from all municipal obligations, permitted the filing of wills in favor of churches, and allowed the foundation of trusts for the construction of basilicas, he was only granting the same privileges to the Christian religion as to pagan forms of worship.

Meanwhile Licinius, who had never made a secret of his hostility to the Christians, had commenced to persecute the Church. New martyrs were added to the old, chief among whom were the Forty Martyrs of Sebaste. In the spring of 323, a state of open warfare was declared between Constantine, the champion of Christianity, and Licinius, the defender of paganism. Licinius was twice defeated, once at Adrianople and afterwards at Chrysopolis (Scutari), but Constantine at first spared his life, merely imprisoning him at Thessalonica. Later, however, he gave orders for his execution, because of a charge of treasonable correspondence with the enemies of the Empire.

Constantine successively published two edicts. The first, addressed to the bishops of Palestine, was an act of reparation by which honors and goods were restored to the victims of Licinius; the second was in the form of a proclamation, a veritable hymn of thanksgiving to God, through whom victory had come to Constantine. It is in this second edict that we fully discern the new attitude of the Emperor. Having become sole ruler of the Empire, he wanted it to be known that he would continue the policy of tolerance proclaimed in 312. And yet, if he abided by the letter of the Edict of Milan, he certainly did not allow himself to be hampered by its spirit. In this respect he speaks the same language as when writing to a bishop or a council. And if he respects the conscience of infidels, it is primarily because he deplores their "obstinacy." He authorizes them to maintain their rites, but is careful to add that these rites and ceremonies are the results of an erroneous belief.

3. **The Last Result of the Persecutions: Donatism.** The last result of the persecutions was *Donatism*. In the year 311, Mensurius, bishop of Carthage died, and the archdeacon *Caecilian* was elected as his successor. This action aroused the ire of jealous rivals, who prevailed upon a council of some 70 bishops from Numidia to declare his episcopal consecration invalid on the ground that his consecrator, *Felix of Aptunga*, had been a *traditor* during the recent persecution, and hence had lost his power of Orders. A wealthy widow by the name of Lucilla seems to have been at the bottom of the whole controversy, and, for a consideration, she even succeeded in having the council ratify the election of her servant, the lector Majorinus, and consecrate him bishop of Carthage. Her action plunged the whole city into a state of schism.

But graver consequences were in store. To state that Felix of Aptunga could not have validly consecrated Caecilian was tantamount to affirming that priests who had betrayed their trust could not validly administer the Sacraments, and hence no longer belonged to the Church. From a practical point of view, the argument reached out to more persons than Felix of Aptunga; the whole of Africa soon found itself under the jurisdiction of bishops and priests whose administration of the Sacraments was considered invalid. In instituting proceedings against the Catholicism of Africa in the matter of her hierarchy and her Sacraments, *Donatism* dealt the Church a deadly blow by calling into question her very existence.

The Donatists, who derived their name from their leader *Donatus,* surnamed the Great, and successor of Majorinus, went so far as to assert that they alone constituted the true Church, and when it was objected that they were ostensibly lacking in the mark of Catholicity, they would reply that the word "Catholicity" merely signified purity, holiness, and full possession of the Sacraments.

The strange part of this whole matter is that the efforts of the Donatists were crowned with success. From the standpoint of religious theory, the doctrine bears marked resemblances to the teachings of St. Cyprian on the invalidity of Sacraments when conferred by heretics. And so, the error which St. Cyprian seized upon to combat schism was turned into a weapon in defense of schism against his lawful successor. Donatism was soon to become the rendezvous for all disgruntled schismatics; it was first and last the religion of a band of wild fanatics, among whom Donatus succeeded in establishing some sort of order and organization.

The Donatists appealed to the Emperor Constantine, who promptly referred the matter to *Pope Miltiades.* At a council held in the Lateran (Oct. 2, 313) the objections of the enemies of Caecilian were overruled. An investigation revealed that Felix of Aptunga had never been a *traditor,* and when this accusation had been disproved, the schism soon lost much of its leverage. In the following year a similar verdict was pronounced by a council held at Arles, which declared that clerics ordained by *traditores* were validly ordained, and that converts from heresy should not be rebaptized. But the Donatists remained irreconcilable and were so importunate in their demands that Constantine himself resolved to judge their cause. At Milan, Donatism was again condemned, and the innocence of Caecilian vindicated. From that time on Donatism assumed the character of a politico-religious faction. Constantine sought at first to subdue the rebels by force, but this only caused them to rejoice in persecution. Then he had recourse to kindness, but this only encouraged them to attack Catholics, burn their churches, and spread terror throughout Africa. The decisive blow was dealt to this heresy by St. Augustine.

By his hesitant attitude Constantine strengthened the schism rather than favored the progress of peace; and by establishing himself as the arbiter of a religious controversy he took the first step toward Caesaro-papism. His policy in dealing with the Donatists foreshadowed the Arian policy of his successors.

TEXTS AND DOCUMENTS

DEATH OF GALERIUS

When Galerius was in the eighteenth year of his reign, God struck him with an incurable plague. A malignant ulcer formed itself low down in his secret parts, and spread by degrees. The physicians attempted to eradicate it, and healed up the place affected. But the sore, after having been skinned over, broke out again; a vein burst, and the blood flowed in such quantity as to endanger his life. The bleeding, however, was stopped, although with difficulty. The physicians had to undertake their operations anew, and at length they cicatrized the wound. In consequence of some slight motion of his body, Galerius received a hurt, and the blood streamed more abundantly than before. He grew thin, pallid, and feeble, and the bleeding then stanched. The ulcer began to be insensible to the remedies applied, and a gangrene seized all the neighboring parts. It diffused itself the wider, the more the corrupted flesh was cut away, and everything employed as means of cure served but to aggravate the disease.

Then famous physicians were brought in from all quarters; but no human means had any success. Apollo and Aesculapius were besought importunately for remedies: Apollo did prescribe, and the distemper augmented. Already approaching its deadly crisis, it had occupied the lower regions of his body: his bowels came out, and his whole seat putrefied. The luckless physicians, although without hope of overcoming the malady, ceased not to apply fomentations and administer drugs. The humors having been repelled, the distemper attacked his intestines, and worms were generated in his body. The stench was so foul as to pervade not only the palace, but the whole city; and no wonder, for by that time the passages from his bladder and bowels, having been devoured by the worms, became indiscriminate, and his body, with intolerable anguish, was dissolved into one mass of corruption.

They applied warm flesh of animals to the chief seat of the disease, that the warmth might draw out those minute worms; and accordingly, when the dressings were removed, there issued forth an innumerable swarm: nevertheless the prolific disease had hatched swarms much more abundant to prey upon and consume his intestines. Already, through a complication of distempers, the different parts of his body had lost their natural form: the superior part was dry, meagre, and haggard, and his ghastly-looking skin had settled itself deep amongst his bones; while the inferior, distended like bladders, retained no appearance of joints. These things happened in the course of a complete year; and at length, overcome by calamities, he was obliged to acknowledge God, and he cried aloud, in the intervals of raging pain, that he would rebuild the Church which he had demolished, and make atonement for his misdeeds.

Lactantius, De Mortibus Persecutorum, passim.

The Edict of Milan

I, Constantine Augustus, and I, Licinius Augustus, came under favorable auspices to Milan, and took under consideration all affairs that pertained to the public benefit and welfare; these things among the rest appeared to us to be most advantageous and profitable to all. We have resolved among the first things to ordain, those matters by which reverence and worship to the Deity might be exhibited.[1] That is, how we may grant likewise to the Christians, and to all, the free choice to follow what mode of worship they may prefer. That whatsoever divinity and celestial power may exist, may be propitious to us and to all that live under our government. Therefore, we have decreed the following ordinance, as our will, with a salutary and most correct intention, that no freedom at all shall be refused to Christians, to follow or to keep their observances or worship. But that to each one power be granted to devote his mind to that worship which he may think adapted to himself.[2] That the Deity may in all things exhibit to us his accustomed favor and kindness. It was just and consistent that we should write that this was our pleasure. That all exceptions respecting the Christians being completely removed, which were contained in the former epistle, that we sent to your fidelity, and whatever measures were wholly sinister and foreign to our mildness, that these should be altogether annulled; and now that each one of the Christians may freely and without molestation pursue and follow that course and worship which he has proposed to himself: which, indeed, we have resolved to communicate most fully to your care and diligence, that you may know we have granted liberty and full freedom to the Christians, to observe their own mode of worship; which as your fidelity understands absolutely granted to them by us, the privilege is also granted to others to pursue that worship and religion they wish. Which it is obvious is consistent with the peace and tranquillity of our times; that each may have the privilege to select and to worship whatsoever divinity he pleases. But this has been done by us, that we might not appear in any manner to detract anything from any

---

[1] *"Haec enim in primis ordinanda esse credimus quibus divinitatis reverentia consuleretur."*
[2] *"In colendo quod quisque diligeret habeat liberam facultatem."*

manner of religion or any mode of worship. And this we further decree, with respect to the Christians, that the places in which they were formerly accustomed to assemble, concerning which also we formerly wrote to your fidelity, in a different form, that if any persons have purchased these, either from our treasury, or from any other one, they shall restore them to the Christians, without money and without demanding any price, without any superadded value or augmentation, without delay or hesitancy. And if any have happened to receive these places as presents, that they shall restore them as soon as possible to the Christians, so that if either those that purchased or those that received them as presents, have anything to request of our munificence, they may go to the provincial governor, as the judge; that provision may also be made for them by our clemency. All which, it will be necessary to be delivered up to the body of Christians,[1] by your care, without any delay. And since the Christians themselves are known to have had not only those places where they were accustomed to meet, but other places also, belonging not to individuals among them, but to the right of the whole body of Christians, you will also command all these, by virtue of the law before mentioned, without any hesitancy, to be restored to these same Christians, that is, to their body, and to each conventicle respectively.[2]

The aforesaid consideration, to wit, being observed, namely, that they who as we have said restore them without valuation and price, may expect their indemnity from our munificence and liberality. In all which it will be incumbent on you to exhibit your exertions as much as possible to the aforesaid body of Christians, that our orders may be most speedily accomplished, that likewise in this provision may be made by our clemency for the preservation of the common and public tranquillity. For by these means, as said before, the divine favor with regard to us, which we have already experienced in many affairs, will continue firm and permanent at all times. But that the purpose of this our ordinance and liberality may be extended to the knowledge of all, it is expected that these things written by us, should be proposed and published to the knowledge of all, that this act of our liberality and kindness may remain unknown to none.

EUSEBIUS' *Ecclesiastical History,*
(Transl. by C. F. CRUSE, pp. 407 ff.)

QUESTIONS

1. Trace the imperial succession from Diocletian to Constantine.
2. Who were the *traditores?*
3. What is the significance of the phrase *"instinctu divinitatis"?*
4. Contrast the Edict of Milan of 313 with the French Concordat of 1801.

[1] *"Corpori christianorum."*
[2] *"Ad jus corporis eorum."*

5. Give a brief literary criticism of Lactantius' *"De Mortibus Persecutorum."*
6. Tell the story of the Forty Martyrs of Sebaste.
7. Trace the origins of Donatism.
8. What was the importance of the battle of the Milvian Bridge?
9. What is meant by Caesarianism or Caesaro-papism?

BIBLIOGRAPHY

Diocletian.—Batiffol, *La paix constantinienne,* ch. III.—De Broglie, *L'Eglise et l'Empire romain au IVe siècle.*

St. Agnes.—Jubaru, *Sainte Agnès,* 1907.—P. Allard, art. *"Agnès,"* in *Dict. d'Arch.*—Dufourcq, art. *"Agnès,"* in *Dict. d'Hist.*—Butler, *Lives of the Saints,* vol. I, revised by H. Thurston, S. J.

The Conversion of Constantine and the Edict of Milan.—Desroches, *Le Labarum,* Critical and archeological study, 1894.—Lejay, *Rev. hist. et litt. relig.,* t. X (1906), p. 27.—J. Maurice, *Numismatique constantinienne,* 1908.—Dutouquet, art. *"Constantin (conversion de),"* in *Dict. d'Apol.*—Batiffol, *La paix constantinienne,* ch. IV.—G. Boissier, *L'Edit de Milan,* in *Revue des Deux-Mondes,* Aug. 1, 1887, p. 528.—E. Chénon, *Les rapports de l'Eglise et de l'Etat,* ch. I. 1913.—R. Pichon, *L'Edit de Milan, Rev. des Deux-Mondes,* 1913.—J. Maurice, *Constantin le Grand,* 1925.

Arnobius and Lactantius.—Sources: for Arnobius, *P. L.,* V, edit. Reifferscheid, in *C. V.,* IV; for Lactantius *P. L.,* VI, and VII; edit. Brandt, in *C. V.,* XIX and XXVII.—Works: P. Monceaux, *Hist. litt. Afr. chr.,* III, 1905. —Freppel, *Commodien, Arnobe et Lactance,* 1893.—R. Pichon, *Lactance,* 1901.—F. Gabarrou, *Arnobe, son œuvre,* 1921.—G. Boissier, *La fin du paganisme,* 1891.—E. Amann, art. *"Lactance"* in *Dict. de Théol.*

Donatism.—Sources: Acts of the Conference of 411; the refutations by Saint Optatus, *De schismate donatistarum, P. L.,* XI, and Saint Augustine *P. L.,* XLIII.—Works: Msgr. Duchesne, *Le dossier du donatisme,* in *Mélanges d'archéol. et d'hist.,* published by l'Ecole française in Rome, t. X (1890), pp. 589–650.—F. Martroye, *Une tentative de révolution sociale en Afrique,* in *Rev. quest. hist.,* t. LXXVI (1904), pp. 353–406; LXXVII (1905), pp. 5–53.— Monceaux, *L'Epigraphie donatiste,* in *Rev. de philologie,* t. XXXIII (1909), pp. 112–161.—Audollent, art. *"Afrique,"* in *Dict. d'Hist.*—G. Bareille, art. *"Donatisme,"* in *Dict. de Théol.*—Monceaux, *Hist. litt. de l'Afrique chrét.,* t. IV.—Batiffol, *La paix constantinienne,* ch. V; *Le catholicisme de saint Augustin,* 2 vols., 1922.—F. Martroye, *La repression du donatisme et la politique religieuse de Constantin et de ses successeurs en Afrique,* 1914.

CHAPTER V

I. The Sufferings of the Martyrs. At a very early date in Church History exact records of the sufferings of the martyrs were made, and sometimes the contents of these records were communicated to neighboring churches. Such is the origin of the "Acts of the Martyrs," our most valuable source of information for all that concerns the persecutions. The Acts may be divided into three categories. The first comprises the official court proceedings, transcribed by the clerks of the court and sometimes copied by Christians. Ordinarily these documents are very brief. The fact that it must have been quite difficult to gain possession of them explains why only a few copies have come down to us. We may cite as examples the Acts of St. Justin and those of St. Cyprian. The second category comprises accounts written by contemporary Christians and sometimes eye-witnesses. More often than not these narratives fairly breathe with an enthusiasm at once temperate and stirring: instance the letter of the churches of Lyons and Vienne to the churches of Asia in 177, or the autobiography of St. Perpetua. The authentic character of these writings is beyond dispute. Finally, the third category comprises accounts drafted some time after the events themselves. This is where discrimination is needed, because in many instances the truth is rather disconcertingly obscured by legend. It would be nothing short of temerity, however, to reject certain Acts of Martyrs *en bloc* because this or that legendary trait can be detected in them. The number of Acts of Martyrs that will stand the test of a just and fair criticism is sufficient to furnish us with a clear concept of the persecutions themselves, and also of the principal martyrs who suffered and died.

It is a relatively easy matter to reconstruct the ordinary process of dealing with a martyr from his arrest to his execution. The first step was what we might term "preventive imprisonment," which could assume two different forms. By way of exception, a Christian who had been accused could continue to live and roam at large under the direct surveillance of a soldier. This was the *custodia militaris* or *custodia libera*—the form of imprisonment to which Saint Paul was subjected during his first sojourn in Rome. As a general rule, however, the accused was immediately confined to a public prison, *custodia publica,* where, loaded down with heavy chains, he often suffered all the tortures of hunger and thirst. His condition became even more pitiable when he was condemned to the *nervus,* since in this case he was commanded to lie on his back and allow his feet to be drawn through a beam drilled with holes. At times he was thrown into a lower and darker gaol (*carcer inferior*). Imprisonment, therefore, was a sort of preliminary torture, by which the judge sought to break down the courage of the accused. During the Decian persecution, when representatives of the Emperor sought to make apostates rather than martyrs, the time of this imprisonment was prolonged indefinitely.

The Christians emerged from prison for the *interrogatio,* which more often than not took place in public. Neither witnesses nor defenders were present, but the Christian himself was the witness, and could gain freedom by apostatizing. A striking feature of this part of the procedure is that there exists no record of a Christian appealing his case to a higher tribunal: the faithful valued the grace of martyrdom too much to run the risk of losing it. Some of the penalties enacted by law were banishment, deportation, and hard labor. Many Christians condemned to the mines (*ad metalla*) were employed in the mines and quarries of Sardinia, Africa, Egypt or Palestine. The death penalty for martyrs, strictly so-called, assumed diverse forms. Chief among them were fire, the amphitheatre, and crucifixion. Under the reign of Diocletian another form of death was invented, known as judicial drowning.

Christians who confessed their faith before the civil judges were accorded the title of "confessors." The faithful frequently visited them in prison and supplied them with food, and priests and deacons administered the Holy Eucharist to them. After his death, the martyr was not forgotten, but special honors were paid to him at the place of his burial, on the anniversary of his martyrdom (*natale, dies natalis* or *natalitium*). On occasions of this kind the Holy Eucharist was celebrated, followed by a "love feast," at which the poor were fed at the expense of the rich. The veneration of relics originated at this time: cloths were soaked in the blood of martyrs, pieces of their clothing were secured, and bones from their bodies collected, even at the risk of death.

II. The Burial Place of the Martyrs: The Catacombs. The bodies of martyrs were buried in catacombs or Christian cemeteries. A catacomb is a net-work of narrow subterranean passages, intersecting one another (*ambulacra*), with rectangular side recesses (*loculi*) or recesses in the form of arches (*arcosolia*), destined to serve as tombs. These recesses were sealed with a marble slab or a small partition of masonry. Some of the passages led into chambers or vaults (*cubicula*), or opened upon large crypts and veritable churches.

The history of the catacombs is a most interesting one. At the outset, and up to the third century, they remained the property of rich Christian families, who had had them excavated in suburban property belonging to them. This fact explains the discovery in certain ancient parts of the catacombs of names of such famous Roman *gentes* as Pomponii, Caecilii, Acilii Glabriones, etc. The cemetery of Domitilla derives its name from a certain Flavia Domitilla, who was related to the Flavii. By authorization of the ancient law decreeing the inviolable and absolute right of private property (*jus utendi et abutendi*) these wealthy Christians afforded hospitality in their private cemeteries to their less favored co-religionists. The information garnered by J. B. de Rossi suggests the important conclusion that it is not true, as has often been maintained, that primitive Christianity recruited its membership solely from the ranks of the poor slaves, freedmen, and laborers.

In the third century, with the ever increasing number of Christians, several cemeteries became the property of the community and passed into the control of the Church. The first and most famous of these is the Cemetery of St. Callixtus, acquired by the Christian community in Rome during the reign of Septimius Severus. Situated in close proximity to the Appian Way, beside the crypt of Lucina, it is called the Cemetery of Callixtus from the name of the deacon to whom Pope Zephyrinus intrusted its care. It is the same Callixtus who was later on raised to the dignity of Sovereign Pontiff.

From this time on private cemeteries began to disappear, because it was the wish of all Christians that their remains be buried in cemeteries owned by the community. Then too, Christianity was becoming powerful enough to condemn the ancient family worship of the dead, as well as to break down the barriers of social prejudice by according the same burial honors to the slave and the master, the poor and the rich. The increase in the number of cemeteries, and the need of enlarging those already in existence by the addition of new galleries, are conclusive proofs that the number of Christians in those days was quite large. At times there were as many as five galleries superimposed upon one another and connected by means of staircases. The first gallery usually lay about twenty-two to twenty-four feet below the ground, whereas the last descended as low as eighty feet. The existence of large quantities of porous stone in the subsoil of the Roman campania greatly facilitated the work of excavation at such depths. This work was carried on by *fossores* (grave diggers), who buried the dead in the *loculi* (oblong niches large enough to hold from one to three bodies). The religious character of the work of the *fossores* conferred upon them the privilege of being affiliated with the clergy, of which they constituted a sort of inferior Order for whose needs the Church provided.

The *loculi* which held the bodies of the martyrs were surrounded with special care. It is very difficult, however, to identify them to-day. The palm, the crown, and the monogram of Christ inscribed over a tomb are not a sure proof that it contained the body of a martyr. Our only certain proof is the word "Martyr," which occurs but rarely. Nevertheless, it is quite certain that the martyrs were honored by the early Christians in the catacombs. Lamps were kept burning near their tombs, and the adjacent *loculi* were coveted burial places. Some went so far as to destroy paintings or scratch out inscriptions in an effort to secure a resting place behind their tombs (*retro sanctos*).

The veneration of the martyrs was given a new impetus with the advent of Constantine, when basilicas were raised above the most famous of their shrines. Pope St. Damasus (366–384) sought out the burial places of the martyrs, and issued orders that inscriptions, beautifully carved in marble and of special design, be affixed to their tombs. These inscriptions often help to identify a martyr; they are silent witnesses to the ancient belief in Jesus Christ, the Blessed Trinity, and the Communion of Saints. As dogmatic and historical monuments they rank high.

The fifth century inaugurated a new period in the history of the catacombs, which ceased to be cemeteries and became sanctuaries. The *graffiti* traced by pilgrims and the editing of *itineraria,* which belong to this epoch, prove of valuable assistance to modern investigators. At the threatened invasion of the Saracens in the eighth century, the popes transferred the relics of the martyrs to the principal basilicas of the city, and soon the catacombs were completely abandoned.

In 1578 the accidental discovery of immense burial grounds on the *Via Salaria* attracted the attention of archeologists. Antonio Bosio made a study of them and sketched the elements of their history in his "Roma Sotteranea" (Underground Rome). The greatest discoveries, however, were made in the nineteenth century by the famous Roman archeologist, J. B. de Rossi. Basing his study on the *itineraria* and the inscriptions of Damasus, this learned scholar succeeded in retracing the topography of the catacombs. As a result of his work we are able to distinguish four principal centers: 1) on the *Via Ostia,* the Cemetery of Lucina, no longer in existence to-day, but formerly occupying the site of the present Basilica of St. Paul Outside the Walls, where the Apostle of the Gentiles is buried; 2) on the *Via Ardeatina,* the Cemetery of St. Domitilla; 3) between the *Via Ardeatina* and the *Via Appia,* the Cemetery of St. Callistus (containing the crypts of Lucina, of Pope Cornelius, of the popes of the third century, and of St. Cecilia) and the Cemetery of St. Sebastian; 4) on the *Via Salaria Nova,* the Cemetery of Priscilla, with the hypogeum of the Acilii Glabriones.

III. Some Results of the Persecutions. 1. The Number of the Martyrs and the Value of Their Testimony. It is impossible to determine even approximately the number of the martyrs. Tacitus and St. Clement speak of an immense multitude (*"ingens multitudo"*) of Christians massacred under the reign of Emperor Nero in the year 64; while Dio Cassius states that many perished under Domitian. Eusebius informs us that "an immense number" fell victims to popular fanaticism under the Emperor Trajan, and this number does not include those who perished in the ordinary way. The persecution of Septimius Severus was so diabolical in character that the faithful believed that anti-Christ would soon appear. Decius spared "neither age, nor sex, nor condition." Finally, Lactantius, Sulpicius Severus, and Eusebius are unanimous in stating that the ten years of persecution under Diocletian were more bloody than any war.

And yet the persecutions rendered a real service to the Church by preserving among the faithful that spirit of generosity and self-sacrifice which made for numerical increase. "Afflict us, torment us, crucify us," wrote Tertullian, "in proportion as we are mowed down, we increase; the blood of Christians is a seed." [1] In matter of fact, religious communities lost much of their primitive fervor towards the end of the third century, when the Church entered upon a ten-year period of peace and tranquillity. Moreover, the testimony of the martyrs constituted an apologetical argument of the first order. The word "martyr" itself is Greek, meaning "witness." The Apostles, who were contemporaries of Christ, the immediate disciples of the Apostles during the second century, like St. Ignatius, St. Polycarp, and even St. Irenaeus, one and all attest the truth of Christianity. Historically speaking, therefore, their testimony has a quasi-documentary value, based as it is on a direct knowledge of the facts. On the other hand, the most impressive phase of this whole matter was the moral endurance of thousands and thousands of martyrs, which constituted a problem in the minds of pagans. "Whoever is a witness to our courage and constancy," writes Tertullian, "is given a real shock. He wants to know what there is real about this whole matter (*quid intus in re sit*)." The answer, of course, is that the martyrs derived their strength from above and that their heroism is in itself a moral miracle. Thus the blood of martyrs became the seed of new Christians.

2. **The Spread of Christianity.** The condition of Christianity at the time of the Emperor Constantine is positive proof that the Church had thrived on persecutions. Already in the third century there existed in *Italy* a large body of bishops, united under the authority of the Bishop of Rome; so great was their number that Pope Cornelius was able to convoke a council of sixty bishops. It is only fair to add, however, that the faithful in the central and southern parts of the peninsula far outnumbered those of the north.

The same holds true of *Gaul*. In the district of Narbonne and central Lyons, Christianity gained an easy footing thanks to the commercial relations of Gaul with the East; but in the east and the north, in the land of the Celtic tradition, in Aquitania, a large portion of the Lyonnaise and in Belgium, progress was slower, because, as in northern Italy, the cities were surrounded by vast stretches of farming country, where the worship of the national gods continued to hold sway (*pagani:* countrymen, pagans). And yet, the large number of Christians at the court of Constan-

[1] Tertullian, *Apolog.*, 50.

tius Chlorus, and the benevolent attitude of this Emperor and his son Constantine, show that Christianity had taken firm root in Gaul.

In *Spain*, the Catholic religion was wide-spread in the south, but sparse in the north and east. Great ravages were committed in the southern part by the persecutions of Decius and his successors. Spain continued for many years to be a stronghold of idolatry, because of the attachment for pagan worship which the traditions of the Empire had inspired in the tenacious and ultra-conservative Spanish people.

Northern Africa was divided into three districts: Proconsular Africa corresponded to present-day Tunisia; Numidia to Algeria; and Mauretania to Morocco. No conversions to Christianity are recorded in this part of the continent until the middle of the second century. It was not long, however, before African Christianity, in 180, gave proofs of positive strength by withstanding the shock of a bloody persecution. From that time on, Carthage possessed a perfectly organized Christian community, and towards the end of the second century it was the site of a council of seventy bishops, convened from all parts of Proconsular Africa and Numidia.

In the *East*, we already have evidence during the second century of large and well organized groups of Christians, destined to become targets for the popular furor. The communities of Greece and Macedonia drew down upon themselves the fanatical hatred of the rabble to the extent that Antoninus was forced to intervene. The seeds of the faith, sown by St. Paul in *Asia Minor*, began to bear such abundant fruit that, in the words of Pliny the Younger, Bithynia and Pontus were infested by the new sect, and the pagan temples were deserted. To the south of Bithynia, Phrygia gives evidence of many conversions to the faith by its numerous Christian epitaphs (*e. g.*, the Inscription of Abercius). To the west, the countries bordering on the Aegean Sea (Mysia, Lydia, and Caria) were governed by strong bodies of bishops, as is evidenced by the letter of the proconsul Granianus to Hadrian, and the latter's answer. In the interior, Cappadocia numbered many followers of the new religion, although the vast expanse of the land constituted a serious geographical impediment to the uniform spread of Christianity.

Generally speaking, the province of *Syria* showed itself much less disposed to welcome Christianity than Asia Minor. In northern Syria, however, the zeal of the converts was no doubt very fervent, and Antioch, the capital, was one of the strongholds of eastern Christianity; but Phoenicia, with the exception of its maritime portions, remained obstinate in its attachment to pagan worship. Palestine itself remained almost impervious: the Christian religion was merely vegetating in Jerusalem, Galilee was still completely given over to Judaism, while Gaza, in the south, was plunged in the most sensuous forms of Oriental worship. Caesarea, which for almost a quarter of a century had been made by Origen the center of Christian learning, was the lone exception to this general rule. If, therefore, we leave out Antioch in the north and Caesarea in the south, the province of Syria appears as the refuge of Orientalism. From Syria, in effect, proceeded the last efforts, in the third century, to establish Oriental religions in Rome and throughout the Empire.

Egypt, on the contrary, showed itself very hospitable to the Christian faith. In the second century, Alexandria became the seat of one of the most famous theological schools. The persecutions numbered many victims among the Egyptians, and, towards the year 250, Monarchianism obtained a foothold in the Thebaid. Episcopal sees were quite numerous; the Acts of St. Peter of Alexandria mention that between A. D. 300 and 311 he consecrated fifty-five bishops in Lower Egypt.

In the second, but especially in the third century, Christian missionaries made an attempt to spread the influence of the Gospel beyond the confines of the Empire. The countries bordering on the western boundaries showed themselves at first little disposed to receive their message, while in Britain and along the banks of the Rhine and the Danube, the cult of Mithra, so wide-spread among the Roman legions, constituted an almost insurmountable obstacle. The lands on the right side of the Danube, however, had energetic and growing Christian centers during the last of the persecutions. The churches of Africa and Egypt were arrested in their development by the impassable desert, although *Abyssinia* was evangelized already during the reign of Constantine. Frumentius and Aedesius, two Christian youths who had been educated by Meropius, a Christian philosopher of Tyre in Phoenicia, were carried away as slaves to the court of the king of Ethiopia, where they acquired such influence that they were given positions of trust. Later on, Frumentius was consecrated bishop of Axuna, the royal city, by St. Athanasius; he baptized King Aizana and converted the entire nation.

To the flourishing Christian centers of Asia Minor was especially entrusted the charge of preaching the faith to the barbarians. The provinces bordering on the Asiatic side of the Black Sea fairly swarmed with Christian settlements, which were just as numerous among the Goths dwelling between the Danube and the Dniester, as in Chersonesus Taurica (Crimea), whose kings, before the end of the third century, had the cross engraved on all their coins.

St. Gregory, surnamed "Illuminator," was the first apostle of Armenia. Forced to migrate from his country at the time of the Persian invasion, he withdrew to Caesarea in Cappadocia, where he was converted to Christianity. Upon his return to his native land, in the year 261, he succeeded in persuading King Tiridates II, that it would be a measure of public interest to abandon Armenian forms of worship, affiliated as they were with those of their hereditary enemy, Persia. By royal decree, Christianity was declared the religion of the State; a supreme bishop or *katholikos* was placed at the head of the Armenian Church, which successfully combated Parseeism (fire-worship of the Persians).

Christianity did not merely penetrate into the north of Asia Minor; towards the middle of the second century, caravans of Christians were already beginning to make their way into central Asia. From Antioch, the influence of the new religion spread to the little kingdom of *Osrhoene,* situated on the left bank of the river Euphrates. King Abgar VIII, a contemporary of Septimius Severus, was converted to Christianity, and Edessa, the royal city, became a center of Christian worship. From Edessa, Antioch, and Armenia, the new religion spread into Mesopotamia and then into the *Persian Empire.* This immense country, which extended as far as the Persian Gulf, the Caspian Sea, and the Indus, already numbered some Christians in the opening years of the third century, and towards A. D. 250, the Mesopotamian countries bordering upon the Empire boasted of churches in as flourishing a condition as those of Asia Minor. Many Christians fled to Persia to escape persecution, and were afforded hospitality by the Persian kings, who were hostile to Rome. They succeeded in organizing a congregation. Towards the beginning of the fourth century Persia had quite a number of episcopal sees, with the *katholikos* of the twin-city of Seleucia-Ctesiphon as their supreme head. His suffragan bishops were scattered along both sides of the Persian gulf, and spread the influence of Christianity to the island of Socotora, Ceylon, and the coast of Malabar. Finally, Christianity gained some followers among the inhabitants of the islands which stretched from Tartary to the very heart of China.

TEXTS AND DOCUMENTS

COURT PROCEDURE IN THE TRIAL OF ST. JUSTIN MARTYR

The Prefect (to Justin): Hearken, you who are called learned, and think that you know the truth: if you are scourged and beheaded, do you believe that you will ascend into Heaven?

Justin: I hope that if I endure these things, I shall have this privilege, for I know that with all who have thus lived, there abides the divine favor until the consummation of the world.

The Prefect: Do you suppose that you will ascend into Heaven to receive such a recompense?

Justin: I do not suppose it, but I am fully persuaded of it.

The Prefect: But let us come to the matter in hand, which must be speedily settled. Let all of you sacrifice to the gods.

Justin: No one who is in his right senses will pass from piety to impiety.

The Prefect: If you do not obey, you will be punished unmercifully.

Justin: It is our heart's desire to be martyred for our Lord Jesus Christ, and then to be happy forever.

Thus also said the other Christians: Do what you will, for we are Christians, and do not sacrifice to idols.

Thereupon the Prefect pronounced sentence, saying, "Let those who have refused to sacrifice to the gods and to obey the command of the Emperor, be scourged and led away to suffer decapitation according to the law."

QUESTIONS

1. What is meant by the "Acts" of the Martyrs, and what is their historical value?
2. Which were the different forms of imprisonment resorted to in the days of persecution?
3. Name some of the instruments and means of torture.
4. What is meant by the expressions: *"Ad metalla," "Ad lupanar"*?
5. Prepare a summary of the description of the catacombs as given by Wiseman in his *Fabiola* and Newman in his *Callista*.
6. Explain the terms *loculi, arcosolia, cubicula, graffiti, itineraria*.
7. What have been some of the estimates regarding the number of martyrs during the first three centuries?
8. Synopsize the articles in the *Catholic Encyclopedia* on Syria, Egypt, Abyssinia, Africa, Armenia and Persia in reference to the topics discussed in this chapter.

BIBLIOGRAPHY

Acts of the Martyrs.—Ruinart, *Acta sincera.*—Dom Leclercq, *Recueil de pièces authentiques sur les martyrs.*—Leblant, *Les acta martyrum et leurs sources,* in *Nouv. rev. hist. du droit franç. et étr.,* 1879; *Les Actes des martyrs,* supplement to the *Acta sincera* by Dom Ruinart, *Extr. des Mémoires Ac. des. Inscript.,* 2nd Part, t. XXX (1882).—Dufourcq, *Etude sur les gesta martyrum romains,* 6 vols.—H. Delehaye, *Les légendes hagiographiques,* 1906; *Les origines du culte des martyrs,* 1912.—Dufourcq, art. *"Actes des martyrs,"* in *Dict. d'Hist.*—Dom Leclercq, art. *"Actes des martyrs,"* in *Dict. d'Arch.*—H. Delehaye, *Sanctus; Essai sur le culte des saints dans l'antiquité,* Brussels, 1927.—P. Monceaux, *La vraie légende dorée (Relations de martyre traduites).* 1928.—H. Delehaye, *Les passions des martyrs et les genres littéraires,* 1927.

Catacombs.—J. B. de Rossi, *Inscriptiones christianae Urbis Romae saeculo septimo antiquiores,* 1861, 1888; *La Roma Sotteranea,* 1864.—Henri de l'Epinois, *Les Catacombes de Rome,* new edit., with several appendices added by P. Allard, Paris-Brussels, 1893.—Marucchi, *Eléments d'archéologie chrétienne,* 2 vols., 1907.—Pérаté, *L'archéologie chrétienne,* 1892.—A. Baudrillart, *Les Catacombes de Rome,* 1903.—M. Besnier, *Les Catacombes de Rome,* 1909.—Msgr. Wilpert, *Roma Sotteranea, Le pitture delle catacombe romane,* Rome, 1903.—T. Spencer Northcote, *Subterranean Rome,* 2nd edit., 1877; art. *"Catacombes,"* in *Dict. d'Apol.*—Dom Leclercq, art. *"Catacombes"* and art. *"Catacombes (Arts dans les),"* in *Dict. d'Arch.*—A. Silvagni, *Inscriptiones christianae Urbis Romae septimo saeculo,* Nova series, I. *Inscriptiones incertae originis,* Roma, 1922.—Marucchi, *The Evidence of the Catacombs; Christian Epigraphy.*—A. Kuhn, *Roma: Ancient, Subterranean and Modern Rome.*—A. S. Barnes, *The Early Church in the Light of the Monuments,* Longmans, 1913.

The Expansion of Christianity.—Works: P. Allard, *Ten Lessons on the Martyrs,* 1st Lesson.—Msgr. Duchesne, *Les Eglises séparées,* 1896; *Fastes épiscopaux de l'ancienne Gaule,* t. I, pp. 1-33.—J. Labourt, *Le Christianisme dans l'Empire perse (224-632),* 2nd edit., 1904.—Msgr. Petit, art. *"Arménie,"* in *Dict. de Théol.,* I col. 1892.—J. Zeiller, *Les origines de la province romaine de Dalmatie,* 1918.—Harnack, *Die Mission und Ausbreitung des Christentums in den ersten drei Jahrhunderten,* Leipzig, 1902.—Rivière, *The Expansion of Christianity in the First Three Centuries,* Herder, 1915.—Guiraud, *Atlas de géographie historique,* map XIV, no. 2.

CHAPTER VI

I. The Ecclesiastical Hierarchy. It would be a mistake to regard early Christian society as a group of scattered communities. A close bond united them to Rome, and their provincial life manifested itself in the *election of bishops*. When a see became vacant, the neighboring bishops met and elected a new titulary in the presence of, and in union with, the local *plebs*. St. Cyprian describes this practice as a "divine and Apostolic tradition." The election and ordination of a bishop was a so-called synodal act. At the head of this embryonic council we find the metropolitan; no one can become a bishop without his suffrage (*sententia*), and in the election itself he has a kind of veto.

At a very early date we meet with *synods* properly so called. The Easter controversy in the closing years of the second century reveals their existence, though only by way of exception; for if bishops had been in the habit of holding such meetings, Polycrates of Ephesus would not have excused himself for holding one on the ground that he had orders from Rome. In the opening years of the third century, when the Church began to enjoy a short period of peace under the reign of Alexander Severus, bishops convened from one province, or several neighboring provinces, to discuss disciplinary and doctrinal matters and to pass sentence on individual cases. This was the practice in Rome, Africa, Alexandria, and Phrygia. Towards the beginning of the fourth century, the Bishop of Alexandria appears to have been vested with some sort of religious authority over Egypt, similar to the civil authority of a prefect over a province. He gathered around him a body of bishops numbering approximately one hundred, who met in synod at Alexandria. He himself had ordained them. Canon 6 of the Council of Nicaea (325) compares the provincial authority of the Bishop of Alexandria in Egypt with the universal authority of the Bishop of Rome in Italy, but we find no such comparison between this church and that of Antioch, whose primacy is one of honor rather than of jurisdiction. The latter see comprised the vast Diocese of the Orient (Cilicia, Isauria, Phenicia, Palestine, Cyprus, Arabia, and Mesopotamia), whose very magnitude contributed most to its weakness, not to mention the fact that it comprised a number of naturally proud and independent churches. As these were opposed to ecclesiastical centralization, the bishops of the East finally, in the fourth century, sought their center of gravity in the person of the Emperor.

At this time, a new but transitory element found its way into the ecclesiastical hierarchy, *viz.*, the so-called choir episcopate. Canon 13 of the Council of Ancyra (314) mentions "country bishops" (χωρεπίσκοποι). This institution must have originated in the third century, when Christianity began to spread rapidly from the cities to the country, because the *chorepiscopi* were missionaries and nothing more. The same canon 13 of the Council of Ancyra formally prohibits them from ordaining either priests or deacons without the special permission of their bishop, a prohibition which was renewed by the Council of Antioch in 341. Ordained and appointed by the nearest city bishop, the *chorepiscopi* were placed in charge of scattered communities, to whose needs they administered, subject to his jurisdiction. The institution of the *chorepiscopi* did not necessarily involve a menace to the Church's monarchical form of government, though individual encroachments could and actually did bring about such a state of affairs. It was this condition which the Council of Sardica was evidently attempting to correct when it decreed that no *chorepiscopus* should be ordained in a village, or even in a small town, where an ordinary priest sufficed. The institution of the *chorepiscopi* was destined to be short-lived. At the time of the Council of Sardica (343) traces of it could be found only in the Orient.

II. The Moral Life of the Faithful. Christianity effected a complete transformation of marriage. Up to the time of Christ, marriage was a frail and selfish agreement bordering on free union; now it became a symbol of the intimate relation of Christ with His Church. Women were urged to be mindful of the dignity conferred upon them in Baptism. Tertullian asked them to lay aside all vain ornaments, if only to safeguard others against the dangers of temptation. Moreover, in these heroic times, everyone had to be ready always: "Be on the watch, lest the tortures [of the executioner] find you unprepared and little inured to hardships. Accustom yourselves to a hard and severe life, *meditemur duriora.*"

However, the most manifest change effected by the Church was in regard to the position of the slaves. The slave ceased to be a mere chattel and became a person, in whom men respected Christ. Christianity did not imprudently wish to subvert the social order, but it served a gentle master, from whom St. Paul had learned that there is no difference between a freeman and a slave because all men are one in Jesus Christ. From the very outset the Church abolished slavery within the limits of her own jurisdiction by granting the same rights to slave and master in the matter of receiving the Sacraments. In some cases it even happened that the slave was a fully initiated Christian while his master was still a catechumen. Moreover, the slave could aspire to the highest dignities in the Church; witness the example of Callixtus, who was elected to the papacy, and the inscriptions of the catacombs which make no distinction between classes.

The Christians were always careful not to convey the impression that they formed a society by themselves. "We Christians," wrote Tertullian, "do not live apart from the world; like you, we frequent the forum, the baths, the artists' shops, the booths, the markets, the public places. We put our labor and industry at your service." As a Roman citizen, the Christian respected the emperor and prayed for him. He did not seek to be excused from military service, provided he was not asked to sacrifice his faith or virtue. A letter written by Marcus Aurelius contains high praise for Christian soldiers.

But the antagonism between Christianity and paganism was too deep-seated not to manifest itself on many occasions. And first, no real intimacy could exist between pagans and Christians, since any compromise with paganism in the family circle was prohibited. Christians were vehemently dissuaded from marrying pagans, and sometimes they were absolutely forbidden to form such alliances. Legislation of this kind must have required many a meritorious sacrifice; for as the Church of the first three centuries was quite poor, good marriage prospects among her children were relatively few.

Even outside the family circle Christians were required to avoid pagan customs and pastimes. Tertullian was very severe in this regard. As a result, Christians were regarded as strangers and suspicious characters, and the pagans were accustomed to speak of them as *"infructuosi in negotiis."*

Among themselves, on the other hand, the Christians exhibited the greatest cordiality. They called one another by the endearing names of "brother" and "sister." They cared for the poor, the orphans, and the widows; they proffered assistance to the weak, the sick, slaves, prisoners, and persons condemned to the mines; and in times of famine and great calamities they came to the rescue with extraordinary assistance. Reserve funds for the altar and its ministers, burial associations which guaranteed at least a *loculus* to people of ordinary means, information and employment bureaus to assist the unemployed and those in distress—all these institutions sprang up over night in the early Christian Church under the sweet and beneficial sway of charity. Nor were this charity and these institutions provincial and confined to individual churches. By mutual assistance, frequent correspondence, and the welcome reception of pilgrims and travellers, the churches maintained a close bond of union among themselves. The example set by individual Christians and societies was so compelling that the pagans were forced to exclaim: "See how they love one another!"

Some of the early converts resolved to consecrate themselves to the service of God by perfect continence, prayer, and fasting. They were called ascetics, confessors, *monazontes,* virgins, deaconesses, holy widows, and are mentioned as early as the second century. Though fully consecrated to God, they remained in the world. They led a retired life, prayed, fasted, and practiced other austerities, some of them going so far as to segregate themselves from the rest of men and give all their possessions to the poor. All held a place of honor in their community and enjoyed universal esteem. If we are to believe St. Cyprian, the virgins were showered with honors, and were placed next in rank to the clergy in liturgical gatherings.

With the decline of their first fervor, the ascetes sought to impose the recitation of the Divine Office, which, contrary to the practice of the first community at Jerusalem, not all were faithful in saying. In the fourth century we meet with ascetes and virgins who carried out this function in the great Christian centers of the East: Alexandria, Jerusalem, Antioch, and Edessa—an almost positive proof that the institution dates back to a much earlier period in Church history. In the fourth century, the *Peregrinatio Sylviae,* which is an account of an early pilgrimage to the Holy Land, tells of ascetes and virgins celebrating their daily vigils and singing at the break of dawn the *"Deus, Deus meus,"* the *"Benedicite,"* and the *"Gloria in excelsis."* These same ascetes and virgins met at different hours of the day to continue their songs of praise. Very soon, great churches made it their business to carry on this work, under the direction of the clergy. Inaugurated at Antioch, this practice was introduced at Caesarea by St. Basil, at Milan by St. Ambrose, and was generally observed at Jerusalem. At that time those who were perfect, *i. e.,* had consecrated their lives to God, frequently rendered incalculable services to the cause of evangelization by remaining out in the world. From among the consecrated virgins deaconesses were selected, who visited the sick and the poor and assisted the clergy in instructing persons of their own sex.

Asceticism was destined to perfect itself more and more as time went on. In the third century it already possessed all the germs of monasticism, which made its first formal appearance in Egypt, where asceticism was most fervent.

The clergy by their very vocation were constrained to have a high regard for the virtue of chastity. In the early Apostolic age St. Paul had required that the bishop be "a man of one wife," and the Church had legislated accordingly, which did not, however, deprive married bishops of their matrimonial rights.[1] It would be wrong to say, therefore, that celibacy was imposed definitely by law in the Primitive Church. "Whoever draws a distinction between a married and an unmarried priest, and says that it is not fitting to share in the oblation made by the former: let him be anathema," decreed the Council of Gangra in the middle of the fourth century. The early Church historian, Socrates, relates that, during one of the sessions of the Council of Nicaea, a few bishops "undertook to propose a new law. They intended to forbid married bishops, priests, and deacons to have conjugal relations with their wives after ordination. Paphnutius, a venerable bishop from Upper Egypt, who for himself had always been a celibate, observed that it would be very imprudent to impose such a burden of continence not only on clerics, but also on their wives, and that it would be enough to abide by the ancient tradition of the Church and forbid clerics to marry after ordination. . . . His authority carried the day."[2] Hence, there was no legislation in existence requiring priests and deacons who were married at the time of their

[1] Tim. 3, 2, 12; Tit. 1, 6.
[2] Socrates, *Hist. Eccles.,* I, 2.

ordination to lead a celibate life; but it was too late to think of marriage after the reception of Holy Orders, unless the deacon made express mention of his desire to marry to the bishop at the time of his ordination.

So much for the law. In practice, a considerable number of priests vowed to observe perfect continence. The testimony of the early Fathers is most explicit in this respect. This disposition finally induced the Church to enact the law of sacerdotal celibacy in the fourth century. A provincial council held at Elvira (Granada) had, already in 306, commanded married bishops, priests, and deacons to abstain from sexual intercourse with their wives, but towards the end of the fourth century more definite and universal legislation was enacted. A Roman Council held under Pope Siricius in 386 and two councils of Carthage, held respectively in 390 and 401, enjoined continence upon all priests and deacons. Thus what was at first a generally observed counsel became a strict duty, at least in the West. The Church was anxious to safeguard the reputation of her clergy. In the beginning, certain widows and virgins had placed themselves under the protection of a cleric (*virgines subintroductae*), but this practice was strongly discouraged in the third century and later on strictly forbidden.

To the practice of chastity the clergy added the pursuit of knowledge. Following the example of Christ, the Apostles instructed their disciples, who in turn trained their successors. The most famous bishops and ecclesiastical writers did this; for instance, St. Justin at Rome, Tertullian in Africa, and St. Irenaeus, who taught Caius and Hippolytus. Soon great Christian schools were founded at Alexandria, Antioch, Rome, Edessa, and Jerusalem. Candidates were promoted to higher functions and dignities in the Church only on condition that they distinguished themselves in piety and science while in lower Orders. And so, when the shrewd persecutors of the third century attacked the hierarchy, they found both priests and bishops ready and eager to accept martyrdom.

TEXTS AND DOCUMENTS

LIFE OF THE PRIMITIVE CHURCH

How utterly at sea are those who fancy that, in the centuries when the sword of persecution was ever hanging over the Church, the faithful constituted merely a frightened little flock whose only concern was to escape the threatened danger. The *latebrosa et lucifugax natio*, as the pagans sometimes contemptuously styled the Church, was a mere figment of their fancy. The truth is that it existed in the full light of day and never adopted the practices of a secret society; what I have just said of the councils is a sufficient proof. These frequent gatherings, which necessitated so much travelling and brought so many people together to the places in which they were held, could not pass unperceived. In spite of all precautions, whether due to modesty or to prudence, they would be noticed at any time, and especially at the time of which we are speaking. Since the establishment of the Empire little room had been left for the public discussion of politics. Citizens saw all their efforts of this nature confined to the petty deliberations of municipal councils, with occasionally a merely formal provincial assembly thrown in. It was only at the Christian councils that new ideas were broached and serious discussions took place on legal and doctrinal questions of real interest (*per quae et altiora quaeque in commune tractantur*). There alone it was that ideas were exchanged, points of doctrine settled, and laws drawn up which afterwards were enforced on the Christian millions, who were also citizens. In fact we may say, without being suspected of paradox, that the councils alone dealt with politics. To use Tertullian's expression, they were the parliaments of Christianity (*ipsa repraesentatio totius nominis Christiana*), and this quite openly, making no effort to conceal either their existence or character. Yet— and this is the most curious point—they appear to have never been molested by the Roman authorities; with all its animus against individual Christians, Rome hesitated to do anything which might appear at variance with the respect it professed, during imperial times, for the right of association.

ALLARD, *Ten Lectures
on the Martyrs,* pp. 77–78.

QUESTIONS

1. Describe the election of a bishop in the early Church and contrast it with that of a bishop in modern times.
2. What is the difference between a "council" and a "synod"?
3. What was the function of the *chorepiscopi?*
4. What was the attitude of the early Church towards slavery?
5. Define "asceticism"; what are the characteristics of orthodox versus unorthodox asceticism?
6. Trace the early history of ecclesiastical celibacy.
7. State the arguments for and against celibacy in the Church.

BIBLIOGRAPHY

Hierarchy, Choir Episcopate.—Works: P. BATIFFOL, *La paix constantinienne,* ch. II.—HEFELE-LECLERCQ, *Hist. des conciles,* I and II.—DOM PARISOT, *Les chorévêques,* in *Revue de l'Orient chrétien,* t. VI, pp. 157 ff.—

JUGIE, *Les chorévêques en Orient*, in *Echos d'Orient*, t. VII, 1904, pp. 236 ff.—
BERGÈRE, *Etude sur les chorévêques*, 1905.—DOM LECLERCQ, art: *"Chorévêques"*
in *Dict. d'Arch.*—IMBART DE LA TOUR, *Les paroisses rurales du IVe au XIe siècle*,
1900.—MSGR. DUCHESNE, *Origines du culte chrétien*, ch. I.—TIXERONT, *Holy
Orders and Ordination* (transl. RAEMERS).

Moral Life. The Ascetics.—Works: A. D'ALÈS, *Tertullien*, 1900.—J.
HUBY, *Christus. La religion chrétienne*, new edit., 1921.—DOM BERLIÈRE.
Les origines du monachisme et la critique moderne, in *Rev. bénéd.*, Jan. and
Feb., 1891; *Le monachisme. Des origines au XIIe siècle* (Coll. *"Pax,"* 1921).—
J. MAYER, *Die Christliche Aszese*, Friburgi Brisg., 1894.—E. DUBLANCHY, art.
"Ascétisme" in *Dict. de Théol.*—DOM LECLERCQ, art. *"Cénobitisme,"* in *Dict.
d'Arch.*—DUCHESNE, *Origines du culte chrétien*, pp. 404–408.—THOMAS, *Ascétisme oriental et ascétisme chrétien* (Coll. *"Science et Religion"*).—DOM H.
LECLERCQ, art. *Instruction publique; Hôpitaux; Hospice; Femmes; Fiançailles*
in *Dict. d'Arch.*—T. W. ALLIES, *The Formation of Christianity*, London, 1875.

Ecclesiastical Celibacy.—VACANDARD, *Origines du célibat ecclésiastique*, in *Rev. clergé français*, Jan., 1905 (XLI), pp. 252–289; *Etudes de
critique et d'hist, relig.*, 1905, pp. 71–120; art. *"Célibat ecclésiastique,"* in *Dict.
de Théol.*—LEA, *History of Sacerdotal Celibacy* (Protestant).

THIRD PERIOD

The Christian Empire

From the Conversion of Constantine to that of Clovis
(313–496)

SECTION I

The Fourth Century

CHAPTER I

ARIANISM FROM CONSTANTINE TO JULIAN THE APOSTATE

I. Origin and Definition of Arianism. In the closing years of the third century we see two rival theological schools in the East: the Alexandrian idealists and the Antiochian realists. In exegetical matters, the Alexandrians stressed the allegorical, the Antiochians the literal sense of Scripture; in theological matters, the Alexandrians gave precedence to problems of the divine essence and unity over those of the three Persons, whereas the Antiochians delved into speculations regarding the Blessed Trinity and the human nature in Christ. At the outset, these differences were differences in point of view only, and justifiable on either side. Unfortunately, in either unwittingly or intentionally opposing each other, the adherents of the two schools began to exaggerate their theories and, as a result, lapsed into heresy.

Subordinationism was hatched in Antiochian centers. According to this doctrine, the Word is inferior to God. The priest Lucian was largely responsible for the spread of this error. True, he recanted before he died, but his heresy survived him and could boast of scattered followers throughout Asia and particularly of the school of the *Collucianists,* which gave to the world the future leaders of Arianism: Eusebius of Nicomedia, Maris of Chalcedon, Leontius of Antioch, and Arius.

Despite the fact that *Arius* was a priest of Alexandria, he favored Subordinationism, seeking to find a basis for it in philosophy, and to establish it as a complete system of thought and creed. In doing so, he began with a principle which he thought invulnerable, *viz.,* that the Father, being a transcendental and unique Being, is incapable of communicating Himself except through creation, since any process of generation would presuppose that He was composite, divisible, mutable or, in other words, corporeal. As a consequence of this attribute of absolute incommunicability, the Father alone possesses the divine nature, the Son is on a lower plane, and the mystery of the Blessed Trinity is entirely suppressed.

But if we are not permitted to call the Son "God," how are we to define Him? Arius answered this question by expounding his theory of the Logos, according to which there are in God force-ideas, instruments of His action in the world. The sum total of all these forces or powers is the Word or Logos. God could not create the world in a direct manner, because His perfection prevented Him from coming in contact with matter. Therefore, He created it through the intermediary of a demiurge, called Logos. Thus Arius explained by a philosophic theory the problem of creation, which the Gnostic sects had sought to solve by an indefinite and bizarre series of eons.

Arianism may hence be defined as a Subordinationist explanation of the Blessed Trinity and a demiurgical solution of the problem of creation. The consequences were inevitable: the Son is neither equal to, nor consubstantial with, the Father, but a being intermediary between God and creatures. He Himself, therefore, is a creature; the greatest indeed and the oldest of all creatures and Himself a God, but still created. He is not eternal, but created before time and before the centuries (ἀχρόνως). The Logos is mutable and fallible. If He perseveres in the good, it is only by a free effort of His will, meriting by repeated acts of virtue the external honors of divinity, and also our redemption. The Logos cannot perform a theandric act, yet He can save us through His moral influence and the power of His example.

Arianism struck at the divinity of both the Son and the Holy Ghost by reducing them to the rôle of eminent creatures. It contained the germs of all subsequent heresies. In Christology, Arius conceded that the Logos assumed a body, but it was a body without a soul, for what need would there be of a soul in a body already informed by the Logos? Why two spirits informing one and the same body? Here we have Apollinarianism and Monophysitism. On the other hand, the idea of a progressive divinization of the person of Christ paved the way to Nestorianism. Finally, the theory of a redemption effected through the sole example of Christ heralded Pelagianism.

An undermining influence in the field of theology, Arianism was also a dangerous enemy by reason of the methods to which it resorted. Its teachers excelled in the art of concealing the true meaning of their language behind vague formulas, subterfuges, and misunderstood phrases. "With an abundance of words and a store of false erudition at their command, they succeeded admirably in moulding the vacillating and superficial minds of the majority of those who had breathed the atmosphere of Hellenism. They flattered their pride by admitting them to the elaboration of theological theories, and hence met with their greatest success in worldly and fashionable circles. To profess Arianism was positive proof of intellectual culture." (G. Kurth).

The result was that this heresy spread rapidly. Deposed by Bishop Alexander, Arius appealed to public opinion. A rigid ascetic and a wizard at disputation, he gathered around his person both the ignorant and the learned. Soon a whole community of men of learning, virgins and common people, for whom he had the cunning to compose hymns, sponsored his cause. In 320, Alexander convoked a council, which was attended by over one hundred Egyptian and Lybian bishops. Arius was condemned and forced to go into exile.

II. Nicaea (325). Arius retained the support of all the Collucianists, headed by Eusebius, Bishop of Nicomedia, who later energetically entered the lists in his behalf and invited Arius to make his home with him. Arius accepted and while a guest of Eusebius, composed a book, partly in prose and partly in verse, which he entitled *Thalia,* and which was calculated to propagate his errors. With no very definite understanding of the bearing of the conflict, the Emperor Constantine, official protector of the Church, intervened. Through Bishop Hosius of Cordova (Spain), his personal friend and adviser, he despatched letters to Alexander and Arius, bidding them to cease disturbing the peace of the Church. The attempt proved futile. When the situation began to take a serious turn, and the breach between Arius and the Church assumed the proportions of a veritable schism, Constantine suggested a general council. It convened under imperial protection at Nicaea in Bithynia and was presided over by Hosius of Cordova, assisted by two Roman priests, Vitus and Vincent.

The deliberations of the council soon showed that there were not two, but three factions. The majority stood for orthodoxy and was anxious to condemn Arius. A small minority—22 in all—supported the heresiarch. Between these two factions there was a third, which sought to save Arius by modifying his formulas. The leader of the third faction was Eusebius of Nicomedia, one of the cleverest and most cunning ecclesiastics of his day. He was assisted by the theologian, Eusebius of Caesarea, whence the term "Eusebian" often given to this party. Each of the two Eusebius' presented symbols of faith, vague enough to avoid being controversial. The council finally adopted a creed couched in very precise terms and including two famous expressions relative to the nature of the Son: ἐκ τῆς οὐσίας τοῦ πατρός and ὁμοούσιος τῷ πατρί, consubstantialis Patri.

The theological victory was complete. The term *homoousios* became the watchword of Catholics in their struggle against the Arians because it signified that the Son was of the very same essence as the Father. If, indeed, we break up the term into its constituent parts, it can easily be seen that οὐσία designates in the Father that which is fundamental and essential, as opposed to that which is individual and special, and that this οὐσία is numerically the same (ὅμος) in the Father and in the Son. The word could not possibly savor of Sabellianism, because, according to the observation made at a later date by St. Basil, "a thing can never be consubstantial with itself, but only with some other thing." Hence, the term *homoousios* implies both unity of nature and distinction as to persons.

With the exception of two bishops, Theonas of Marmarica and Secundus of Ptolemais, the Creed was signed by all the bishops present, and, to all appearances, peace was once again restored to the Church, especially since Constantine posed as the intransigent champion of the *Nicaenum*. For when Eusebius of Nicomedia, Theognis of Nicaea, and Maris of Chalcedon refused to recognize the condemnation of Arius, though they had appended their signatures to the Creed, he banished them to Gaul.

III. The Anti-Nicene Reaction. First Phase: The Trial and Exile of St. Athanasius. Nevertheless an Anti-Nicene reaction soon set in. Yielding to the incessant entreaties of his sister, Constantia, the Emperor finally (in 328) pardoned both Eusebius of Nicomedia and Theognis of Nicaea and, upon the presentation of an ambiguous profession of faith, allowed Arius to return to Alexandria the following year. Thirsting for revenge, the bishops stationed at the imperial court plotted the exile of the orthodox bishops, and by slanders and calumnies succeeded in wresting from the Emperor a decree demanding the immediate banishment of Eustathius of Antioch, Asclepias of Gaza, and Eutropius of Adrianople.

At this juncture, a formidable opponent to Arianism entered the lists in the person of *Athanasius,* the new Bishop of Alexandria, who in this struggle had the undivided support of all the bishops of Egypt and of the great army of monks and hermits of the desert. From this moment on, the history of Arianism was largely the history of St. Athanasius. Against him was unleashed the furor of the entire Eusebian faction when, in spite of strict orders from Constantinople, he absolutely refused to allow Arius to re-enter Alexandria. He was successively accused of having murdered Bishop Arsenius and cut off his dead hand for magical purposes, and of having had relations with an immoral woman. After refusing to appear before an assembly at Caesarea, which was prepared to condemn him on *a priori* grounds, he journeyed in the company of fifty Egyptian bishops to Tyre, where he was confronted with new accusations and deposed from his see after a mock trial. Athanasius then hastened to Constantinople to demand a just inquiry into his case, but here a new charge was raised against him, namely, that he had tried to stop the corn ships from sailing to Constantinople from Alexandria. The gullible Emperor believed the charge and banished the prelate to Treves, in 335. In the following year, Arius, after appearing at Alexandria, was triumphantly escorted into the city of Constantinople, when he died suddenly of a stroke of apoplexy (336). The people saw in his death the just punishment of God.

Constantine died in 337. He had rendered important services to the Church, even though on his deathbed he did receive Baptism from the hands of the Arian bishop, Eusebius. As Msgr. Batiffol has well put it: "Catholicism is completely justified in reproaching him for having regarded the primacy of Rome as non-existent, allowed himself to be swayed by the pernicious teachings of Arianism, permitted oligarchy to sit in judgment as if it were qualified to speak in the name of the Catholic Church and to domineer that Church with the physical support of the prince." Byzantium, whither he had removed the seat of his government, soon became the headquarters of a State religion.

In the year 337, Athanasius returned to Alexandria, where he was received with great enthusiasm. The Eusebian party again resumed hostilities, and, notwithstanding the pronouncements of a provincial council held at Alexandria, which acquitted the prelate of all the charges preferred against him, the patriarchal see was delivered into the hands of an intruder, Gregory of Cappadocia, who was installed by force. But all of a sudden the situation changed completely. Constans, the eldest of the three sons of Constantine and ruler of the western portion of the Empire, took a Catholic stand and referred the matter to the papacy. His action marked a complete departure from the policy of his father, who had always tried to be the supreme arbiter in both Church and State issues. The case was laid before Pope Julius I (337–352), who convoked a council at Rome. Only too conscious of their weak position, the Eusebians pretended to be unable to attend on account of war in Persia. Athanasius, on his part, appeared before the council, with the official decisions of former councils, supplemented by testimonies from his suffragan bishops and the diocesan clergy. He was unanimously acquitted of all the charges lodged against him. Pope Julius made known the decision of the council to the Eusebians, at the same time formulating a complaint against offenders who had acted "contrary to custom" by condemning the Patriarch of Alexandria without first consulting the Bishop of Rome.

At a council held in the fall of the year 341, on the occasion of the dedication of the basilica of Antioch (*in encoeniis*), the Oriental episcopate struck back, first, by confirming the intruder Gregory of Cappadocia in the see of Alexandria, and secondly, by rejecting the Nicene *homoousios* as unscriptural. In their indecision the Eusebians formulated four different creeds within a few months. Meanwhile, Eusebius of Nicomedia, the leader of the opposition, who had been installed bishop of Constantinople in 339, died.

The attitude of the eastern episcopate was a clear indication of serious schismatic tendencies. An unbiased observer might have easily been led at the time to think that there were actually two Christian churches, one subject to the Emperor in Constantinople, the other subject to the Bishop of Rome. To remedy the situation, the Western Emperor, Constans, convoked a great council at Sardica (Sophia in Bulgaria). In this city, situated on the confines of both Empires, were debated these two burning questions: (1) the judgment of Athanasius and (2) the formulary of the true faith. Engaged at the time in a war with the Persians, Constantius, ruler of the Eastern Empire, did not dare oppose his brother's plans, but this fact did not make the Easterners desist from their intransigent schismatic stand. From the very outset they laid it down as a necessary postulate that the condemnation of Athanasius was definitive and irrevocable. And when the Fathers of the Council refused to accept their claims, the Eusebians moved to Philippopolis in Thrace and placed themselves under the protection of their Emperor. From this city they issued an encyclical letter, in which they condemned not only Athanasius, but also all those who received him into their communion, and first of all "Julius, of the city of Rome, the author and cause of all evils (*principem et ducem malorum*)."

Meanwhile, the Fathers of Sardica continued the regular sessions of their council. After a re-examination of the case of Athanasius and a new proclamation of his innocence, they proceeded to depose the patriarch who had usurped his see and excommunicated all the leaders of the Eusebian faction. In doctrinal matters, the council rejected any new formulary, but abided by the *Nicaenum*. Finally, it made bold to request of the two Emperors that "no civil judge, whose jurisdiction comprises only material things, take it upon himself to pass sentence upon clerics, and that all be free to profess the Catholic faith without being subjected to persecution."

The decisions of the Council of Sardica were not welcomed by the states ruled by Constantius, and so when, at the death of his brother (350), he became supreme ruler of the Empire, he set out at once to revive the old Roman policy of divinizing the person of the Emperor, proclaiming himself supreme pontiff and declaring all ecclesiastical matters to be subject to his sovereign power, or, to quote his own words, "to his eternity." He permitted Athanasius to re-enter the city of Alexandria after the Council of Sardica, but made it very clear that this favor was not accorded him in virtue of its decisions, but solely "through the will of God and by our decision." He gathered around his person all the eastern bishops who, in 351, met at the imperial residence at Sirmium in

Pannonia, and after composing a vague profession of faith (the so-called First Formula of Sirmium), condemned Photinus, the disciple of Marcellus of Ancyra, one of the most ardent supporters of the Nicene Creed, who had become compromised by the use of expressions which savored of Sabellianism.

In the system of *Marcellus of Ancyra* the personality of the Logos was not sufficiently stressed. He taught that God is an indivisible monad which unfolds itself in a threefold manner: (1) by creating the world, (2) by penetrating the human nature in the Incarnation, and (3) by producing the Holy Ghost on Pentecost day, and in this way expanding into a trinity. The *Homoousians* condemned Marcellus at Constantinople as early as 335, and at their request Eusebius of Caesarea had refuted his error in his *Contra Marcellum* and his *De Ecclesiastica Theologia*. And now, his Modalism, which could not have been so apparent—his person had been defended by the Council of Sardica, Pope Julius I, and St. Athanasius (at least up to the year 344)—was again placed in jeopardy by his compatriot and disciple *Photinus*. According to the latter, the Logos is at first only the impersonal Reason of God. By a second extension it becomes the Son of God, who, by penetrating the humanity of Jesus with its divine influence, raises him to the level of an adopted son of God. By condemning Photinus at the Council of Sirmium, the Eusebians hoped to discredit not only Marcellus of Ancyra, but the entire Nicene party, which had too long upheld Marcellus without requiring an explicit recantation of the errors imputed to him.

This attempt to shift the blame was clever enough, but it did not succeed in shaking the two pillars of orthodoxy—the Bishop of Rome and the Bishop of Alexandria. The only course left to the heretics, therefore, was to obtain a condemnation of the latter by the former. For this purpose, Constantius convoked the *Council of Arles*. But since the bishops of Gaul who appeared there were firm adherents of the Nicene Creed, the Emperor forbade all dogmatic discussions, and through the Eastern bishops, Ursacius and Valens, "two old stagers of Arianism," he issued orders that the Council make it its exclusive business to try Athanasius. He went so far as to publish an edict threatening with exile all the prelates who refused to pass a sentence of condemnation. All the bishops except Paulinus of Treves acceded to his wishes, including even the two legates of Pope Liberius.

St. Athanasius refused to recognize the sentence passed upon him and appealed to the decision of a new council, which met at Milan in the spring of 355. Here, in the presence of an orthodox majority, the same tactics were resorted to as at Arles. "And when," in the words of St. Athanasius himself, "the bishops protested, the Emperor lost patience and exclaimed: 'My will is the canon law in this matter; the bishops of Syria are not so recalcitrant when I speak; either obey my commands or depart into exile!'" He even went so far as to draw his sword and brandish it before them. Stricken with terror, the majority yielded. Only a few noble characters stood firm, among whom we must mention Hilary of Poitiers, Lucifer of Cagliari, Eusebius of Vercelli, Dionysius of Milan, and Hosius of Cordova.

The strongest protest issued from the lips of Pope Liberius. "You have three days wherein to make up your mind," was the threat made by the Emperor. "Three days will not change my decision," replied the Pontiff; "exile me to any place you please." He was exiled to Berea in Thrace, and orders were given to arrest Athanasius. A band of five thousand soldiers despatched for this purpose encircled both the prelate and his people during a divine service (Feb. 9, 356), but as they entered the church, Athanasius mysteriously disappeared, and thanks to the good will of the monks, remained in hiding in the desert. The Arian, George of Cappadocia, was immediately installed in the see of Alexandria.

IV. Second Phase: The Doctrinal Struggle and the Formularies of Sirmium. Fortunately, the Arians, who had been so united in their attacks, quickly disbanded in their victory and split into three distinct factions.

On the extreme left were the *pure Arians,* under the direction of Aetius, Eunomius, and Eudoxius of Constantinople. Strong supporters of Arianism in its primitive form, they professed the *heterousios* doctrine, declaring the Son to be unlike in all things to the Father (ἀνόμοιος). Hence their name, "Anomeans" or "Heterousiates" (ἐξ ἑτέρας οὐσίας).

On the extreme right was the *homoousios* group. They claimed to be orthodox, but were rather diffident about the new *homoousians,* whom they declared to be unscriptural and savoring of Sabellianism. Their suggestion was that in the place of *homoousios* the term *homoiousios* be substituted, a word meaning "of a similar nature" to that of the Father. In a spirit of mere prejudice against the term *homoousios,* several good bishops sided in with this party, chief among whom was St. Cyril of Jerusalem. There is no doubt, however, that the very imprecise character of the term *homoousios* enabled the more initiated to imply a certain subordination of the Son to the Father by substituting likeness (*homoiousios*) for identity of substance (*homoousios*).

Between these two groups there was a third, which curried favor with the imperial court and was ready for any emergency. Its adherents adopted a formula so vague that they could recant at will and at the same time rally the anti-Nicene faction to their side should there be need for unity. The *homoios* group acknowledged the Son to be like the Father, an admission which even a good Arian would be ready to make *lato sensu*. The term "Homeans," therefore, was applied to the party; they were also called "Acacians," from the name of their leader, Acacius of Caesarea.

To sum up. Three terms designated the three parties: *heterousios* ("unlike" the Father), *homoiousios* ("of a similar substance" as the Father), and *homoios* ("like" the Father). The orthodox *homoousios* meant "of the same substance" as the Father.

Under the protection of Constantius, the pure Arians seemed at first to have the advantage. At a synod held at Sirmium in 357, a creed was launched, forbidding the use of the terms *homoousios* and *homoiousios,* and advocating the crudest form of Subordinationism. "There is no doubt," it was decreed, "that the Father is greater; He surpasses the Son in honor, dignity, and glory, whence His name Father" (the second formula of Sirmium). To all appearances, therefore, Arianism was to become the religion of the State, and the appointment of Eudoxius, an out-and-out Anomean, to the see of Antioch could only confirm that opinion.

These and other measures roused a volley of protests. Around Easter, 358, Basil of Ancyra convoked a council in his own episcopal city, where, in a long manifesto the semi-Arian group declared the Son to be like unto the Father in substance (ὅμοιος κατ᾽ οὐσίαν). Moved with indignation at the blasphemous utterings of the extreme left, the more moderate among the opposing faction appeared willing to sponsor the cause of orthodoxy. Basil repaired at once to the Emperor, and at his request another council was convoked at Sirmium, where the semi-Arians scored one more victory (the third formula of Sirmium).

To make this victory complete, however, it was imperative to win over the western Consubstantialists with their head, the Bishop of Rome. "If we win Liberius over to our side," observed the unionists, "we shall make short work of all the others." For this purpose the Pope was recalled from exile and brought to Sirmium. It appears that Liberius did join in condemning those who had resorted to the term *Consubstantialis* to defend Sabellianism. On the other hand, he was insistent that Basil and his group should pledge themselves to pronounce anathema against all who claimed that the Son is not like unto the Father in substance and in all things. Hilary of Poitiers adopted a similar attitude, and by these new tactics it was hoped to re-establish harmony and good will. This hope, however, was frustrated. "The party of conciliation," writes Batiffol, "was led to attribute to its opponents a good will which they completely lacked. St. Hilary and Pope Liberius were certainly the victims of this noble illusion. . . . It does not follow that because a *homoousian* like St. Hilary was sincerely in accord with a *homoiousian* like Basil of Ancyra in condemning Anomeism, that Anomeism was not Arianism or that the *homoiousians* were not somewhat Arians themselves." The term *homoousios* should never have been sacrificed, since it was the only term that left no loophole for the heterodox party. Liberius' mistake must be restricted to an over-generous attempt to win over all opponents by a change in tactics. The enthusiastic reception accorded him on his return by the Roman populace is ample proof that he did not default. We might add that his conduct both before and after the Council of Sirmium affords additional testimony in favor of his orthodoxy.

Basil of Ancyra needed nothing more now than the ratification of an ecumenical council that would condemn pure Arianism on the one hand, and, on the other, reject the rather undesirable term *homoousios* and adopt in its stead the more attractive term *homoiousios*. He succeeded in having the Emperor call such a meeting of the bishops at Nicaea.

But suddenly, on the eve of triumph, he lost favor with Constantius. Taking advantage of his position, Basil had exiled the leaders of the Arian party: Eudoxius, Aetius, and Eunomius. The political bishops protested, arguing that such rigorous measures were compromising to unity, that Basil was an intransigent character, and that the only key to the solution was a formula vague enough to be accepted by all who loved peace. During the night of May 22, 359, a new creed was formulated (the fourth formula of Sirmium). It professed the doctrine that the Son is like unto the Father according to the Scriptures (ὅμοιος κατὰ γραφάς). A broad formula of this kind, it was hoped, would reunite the Christian world, and with this object in view, an eastern council was convoked at Seleucia in Isauria, and a western one at Rimini, on the shore of the Adriatic Sea.

At both assemblies, the majority of the bishops upheld the term *homoousios,* but the same measures were used against them, as were resorted to at Arles and Milan to condemn St. Athanasius. At Rimini, shameless pressure was brought to bear on the members of the council by the prefect Taurus, who succeeded in wresting their signatures to an Arian formula. At Seleucia, the majority of the bishops grouped themselves around Basil of Ancyra and remained firm in their attitude. Meanwhile the Emperor was awaiting their decision, and so, seeing the delegates at Rimini yielding under threat, the bishops assembled at Seleucia signed the semi-Arian formula to escape imprisonment and exile. In January, 360, a council held at Constantinople ratified these results, and unity seemed to be re-established.

Such were the beginnings of that "sham orthodoxy" which, until the advent of the Emperor Theodosius, was upheld in the East by a large body of "politically-minded bishops." To make clear the issue, Basil of Ancyra and Cyril of Jerusalem were deposed, and the leaders of Arianism, Eudoxius and Eunomius, were installed, the first at Constantinople, the second at Cyzicus. In the words of St. Jerome: "The world was astonished to find itself Arian." Its surprise was, however, destined to be short-lived, for in the following year (361) the death of the Emperor Constantius marked the beginnings of a return to orthodoxy.

V. The Champions of Orthodoxy: St. Athanasius and St. Hilary. For the rest, Catholicism was not without its defenders in this acute crisis. In the East, the outstanding figure was St. Athanasius; in the West, the leading champions were Liberius, St. Hilary of Poitiers, and Lucifer of Cagliari.

Forced into exile in the year 357, Athanasius did not remain idle. The four years he passed in the desert were perhaps the four most strenuous of his doctrinal apostolate. It was during this period that he wrote his great polemical works, *Ad Constantium, Apologia de Fuga sua,* and *Historia Arianorum,* composed for the monks.

The *Apologia ad Constantium* was addressed to the Emperor, but in reality intended for the public at large. It is a fearless plea, in which

Athanasius reiterates his allegiance and loyalty to his imperial majesty, but at the same time stigmatizes the action of the Arians of Alexandria, who had not hesitated to scourge virgins consecrated to God. In the *Apologia de Fuga sua* he justifies his conduct under persecution. Written in the heat of the fight (357–358), these works expose the methods and tactics of the Arians. The *Historia Arianorum* is the masterpiece of this whole historico-polemical literature. In it Athanasius does not hesitate to place the entire blame of the trouble on Constantius, and goes so far as to call him Antichrist.

In the opinion of the Maurists, it was during his exile in 357 that Athanasius edited his three famous *Orationes contra Arianos*. His main purpose was to defend the definition of Nicaea against the Arians. In the first and second orations, he answers objections; in the third, he shows how the Father and the Son are one—not morally, but physically. He also includes a clear exposé of the fundamental distinction existing between the divinity and the sacred humanity of Christ—a distinction which offset the Arian objections on the infirmities and ignorance sometimes attributed to Christ in the Scriptures. The work refutes not only the outstanding tenets of Arianism, but also the principles underlying the Christological errors of the fifth century. Similar in character to the *Orationes* is the correspondence of Athanasius with Serapion of Thmuis, in defence of the divinity of the Holy Ghost. Athanasius also composed at this time (359) his *De Synodis,* a treatise which might as well be entitled, "Vicissitudes of the Arian Church," and in which he takes secret delight in contrasting the multiple professions of faith according to the Arian heresy with the indefectible creed formulated at Nicaea.

Arius had founded his theory of the Logos on a false conception of the work of creation; Athanasius takes for his starting-point the idea of redemption. This work, according to him, is nothing more than the elevation of human nature to the plane of divine filiation, a feat which would be impossible were not the Word really and truly God. "If the Logos," he argues, "were God only by participation, He could not deify others, since, *ex hypothesi,* He Himself would have to be deified by the Father." Then, too, no one but a Divine Person could have atoned for the infinite offence given to God by sin. Athanasius bases these assertions on Sacred Scripture and to the Arian philosophy of the Logos opposes text after text from Holy Writ proving the consubstantiality of the Word.

As a thorough and painstaking exponent of doctrinal development, and a compiler of exact and pertinent Scriptural evidence, he has no superior.

The chief defender of orthodoxy in the West was St. Hilary. Born at Poitiers about the year 315, he was converted by the study of the Bible. Like Athanasius, Hilary was above all a man of action, although his methods were different. Thoroughly familiar with the sophistry of the Arians, he met them on their own ground, and in so doing penetrated dogmatic questions more profoundly than Athanasius. When exiled to Phrygia by Constantius, he used his enforced leisure to compose two treatises, *De Trinitate* and *De Synodis*. *De Trinitate,* in twelve books, is a scientific discussion of the Divinity of the Second Person of the Trinity. It is perhaps the most profound product of Nicene theology. The *De Synodis* comprises two distinct parts. The first is a sort of historical memoir addressed to the bishops of the Western Empire, on the changes wrought in the East by Arian synods and formularies. The second is an appeal to the semi-Arians belonging to the party of Basil of Ancyra, urging them to accept the homoousios. When the heretics prevailed, Hilary addressed several letters of protest to the Emperor (360). His *Placet ad Constantium* only merited for him the title of "Disturber of the East" and caused his return to Gaul. There he set about building up a defence against Arianism, which was condemned at several provincial councils, notably at that of Paris, in 361. In co-operation with Eusebius of Vercelli he undertook to purge Italy, holding a conference at Milan with the semi-Arian Bishop Auxentius, who put him out of his diocese (*Contra Auxentium*). He died at Poitiers after composing a *Tractatus super Psalmos* and a *Liber Mysteriorum,* the latter being an explanation of the Messianic types of the Old Testament.

Among the eastern opponents of Arianism we should mention *Marius Victorinus,* a converted pagan from Proconsular Africa, who wrote several treatises *De Generatione Divini Verbi,* four books *Adversus Arium* (359), and a small work entitled *De Homoousio Recipiendo* (360). Couched in an obscure style, in which the Greek terminology is clumsily translated into Latin, these works are attempts at justifying the dogma of the Trinity by means of the Neo-Platonic philosophy. For the use of the Latin-speaking people of the West, Victorinus devised a new philosophical language destined to be of great service to the logicians and metaphysicians of the Middle Ages.

Defended by such worthy champions, orthodoxy held firm. The Arian party admittedly owed its success to the protecting influence of Constantius. After his death, the party split into two factions: the Anomeans grouped themselves around Aetius, while the mitigated Arians rallied to Bishop Eudoxius of Constantinople.

TEXTS AND DOCUMENTS

Exposition of the Teachings of Arius
(Alexander of Alexandria to Alexander of Constantinople)

It is no longer possible for you to doubt, my dear brethren, and I must clearly expose to you their perfidy. They say that there was a time when the Son of God did not exist, that He began to be, while before He was not, and that, when He was born, He was made in the same manner as all men. For, they aver, God made all things out of nothing. In this manner they include the Son of God Himself in this creation of all intelligent and unintelligent beings. As a consequence, they assert that the Son of God possessed a nature subject to change and equally capable to do good and evil . . . and having made this supposition, that He was made out of nothing, they undermine the teachings of Holy Scripture, which proclaims the immutability of the Word, the divinity of Wisdom, of the Word, *i. e.,* Christ.

These wicked men go farther and claim that we ourselves can become sons of God just as He did. For it is written: "I have engendered sons, and I have reared them." And when it is objected to them that the rest of the text, which reads: "But these sons have despised me," cannot apply to the Saviour, whose nature is immutable, they cast to the winds all sentiments of piety and reply: "God in His foreknowledge had foreseen that the Son would not despise Him, and hence He selected Him among all others. Not that by His nature He possessed any prerogatives which the other sons of God did not enjoy, for no one, they say, is the Son of God by nature. Nor that He possessed any special quality which brought Him particularly near to God. But God selected Him because, being free and subject to change, the Son had at heart moral perfection, and did not permit Himself in any way to be turned towards evil. In reality, therefore, if Peter or Paul had made the same efforts, their filiation would not differ in any respect from His." As a proof of this insane doctrine, they point to what is said of Christ in the Psalms: "Thou hast loved justice and hated iniquity, and that is why thy God has marked thee with an oil of joy, preferring thee to all thy companions."

(Cfr. E. Amann, *Le Dogme Catholique dans les Pères de l'Eglise,* pp. 129–130).

QUESTIONS

1. Trace the scholastic origin of Arianism.
2. Explain the definition: "Arianism is a Subordinationist explanation of the Blessed Trinity and a demiurgical solution of the problem of creation."
3. Explain how Arianism contained the germ of all subsequent heresies.
4. Who were the "Collucianists"?
5. What was the heresy of Basil of Ancyra?
6. Carefully distinguish between the terms ὅμοιος, ὁμοούσιος, and ὁμοιούσιος.
7. What was Anomeism?
8. Can it be said that Pope Liberius defaulted in sacrificing the term ὁμοούσιος?
9. Write a short appreciation of the character of St. Athanasius.
10. Who was St. Hilary?

BIBLIOGRAPHY

History of Arianism.—Sources: The historians Eusebius, Socrates, Sozomen, Theodoret, Gelasius of Cizica, St. Epiphanius, Philostorgius, Sulpicius Severus; the historico-dogmatic works of the Fathers of the fourth century, especially St. Athanasius, St. Hilary, the Cappadocians, Didymus, St. Jerome, St. Ambrose.—Works: DE BROGLIE, *L'Eglise et l'Empire au IV⁰ siècle*, 1867.—NEWMAN, *The Arians of the Fourth Century*, 4th edit., London, 1876.—KÖLLING, *Geschichte der arianischen Häresie*, Gütersloh, 1874-1883.—GWATKIN, *Studies of Arianism*, Cambridge, 2nd edit., 1900; *The Arian Controversy*, London, 1889.—SNELLMAN, *Der Anfang des arianischen Streites*, Helsingfors, 1904.—ROGOLA, *Die Anfänge des arianischen Streites untersucht*, Paderborn, 1907.—P. BATIFFOL, *La paix constantinienne et le catholicisme.*—LE BACHELET, art. *"Arianisme,"* in *Dict. de Théol.*—F. CAVALLERA, art. *"Arianisme,"* in *Dict. d'Hist.*—A. D'ALÈS, *Le dogme de Nicée*, 1926.

The Teaching of Arius.—Sources: (1) His own writings: Letter to Eusebius of Nicomedia, in St. Epiphanius, *Haer.*, LXIX, 6, and in Theodoret, *Hist. eccl.*, I, 4; Letter of Alexander of Alexandria, in St. Athanasius, *De Synodis*, 16, and in St. Epiphanius, *Haer.*, LXIX, 7, 8; Fragments of *Thalia* in St. Athanasius, *Contra Arianos, Or.*, I, 5, 6, 9; *De Synodis*, 15; Profession of faith of Arius to Constantine, in Socrates, *Hist. eccl.*, I, 26; in Sozomen, *Hist. eccl.*, II, 27; citations by St. Athanasius, *Epist. encycl. ad episcop. Aegypti*, 12, and *De Sententia Dionysii*, 23.—(2) Exposition of the Doctrine of Arius by St. Alexander, *Epistula encyclica*, 3, reproduced by Socrates, *Hist. eccl.*, I, 6.—(3) In general, the historians Socrates, Sozomen, Philostorgius, etc.

St. Athanasius.—Sources: MIGNE, *P. G.*, 25-28.—Works: Besides the general treatises on Arianism, MOELLER, *Athanase le Grand*, 3 vols., 1840.—BÖHRINGER, *Athanasius und Arius*, Stuttgart, 1874.—FIALON, *Saint Atha-*

nase, 1897.—ROBERTSON, *Select Writings and Letters of Athanasius*, 1892.—
A. STUELCKEN, *Athanasiana*, Leipzig, 1899.—F. CAVALLERA, *Saint Athanase*,
Coll. *"La Pensée Chrétienne,"* 1908.—G. BARDY, *Saint Athanase*, Coll. *"Les
Saints,"* 1921.—X. LE BACHELET, art. *"Athanase"* and art. *"Cyrille de Jéru-
salem,"* in *Dict. de Théol.*—A. D'ALÈS, *Le schisme mélétien d'Egypte*, R. H. E.,
XXII (1926), pp. 5-26.—E. AMANN, art. *"Mélète de Lycopolis,"* in *Dict. de
Théol.*—VOISIN, *La doctrine christologique de saint Athanase*, R. H. E., I
(1900), pp. 226 ff.—G. BARDY, *Le symbole de Lucien d'Antioche et les formules
du synode in encœniis*, R. S. R., III (1912), p. 139-155, 230-244.—L. ROUGIER,
Le sens des termes οὐσία ὑπόστασις *et* πρόσωπον in *Les controverses trinitaires
postnicéennes*, *Rev. hist. rel.*, 1916-17.

Marcellus of Ancyra.—Sources: The fragments of his work: *Liber de
subjectione Domini*, collected in *Eusebius Werke*, Bd. IV, edit. E. Kloster-
mann, Leipzig, 1906, pp. 185-215; EUSEBIUS, *Contra Marcellum* and *De
ecclesiastica theologia*; ST. EPIPHANIUS, *Haer.*, LXXII.—Works: Th. ZAHN,
Marcellus von Ancyra, Gotha, 1867; F. LOOFS, *Die Trinitätslehre Mar-
cells v. Ancyra und ihr Verhältnis zur älteren Tradition*, Berlin, 1902; TIX-
ERONT, *History of Dogmas*, Vol. II.—CHENU, art. *"Marcel d'Ancyre,"* in *Dict.
de Théol.*

Pure Arians.—Sources: The 47 propositions of Aetius in St. Epiphanius,
Haer., LXXVI, II; the Ἔκθεσις πίστεως of Eunomius presented to Theodosius, in the notes of Valois to Socrates, *Hist. eccl.*, V, 10; the *Apologetic*, by
the same author, *P. G.* (XXX. 835); The treatises of St. Basil and St. Gregory
of Nyssa against Eunomius and St. Epiphanius, *Haer.*, LXXVI.

Liberius.—Sources: SAINT ATHANASIUS, *Historia Arianorum ad mon-
achos; Apologia contra Arianos*, 89; ST. HILARY, *Contra Constantium*, II;
ST. JEROME, *Chronica*, 380-385; *De viris illustribus*, 89. Letters of Liberius
regarding which there is some controversy, in St. Hilary, *Fragm.*, VI, 5-11.
Concerning the good reputation of Liberius, see the letter of Anastasius to
Venerius of Milan, written in 400-401, edit. by J. VAN DEN GHEYN, in *Rev.
hist. et litt. relig.*, t. IV (1899), pp. 1-12.—Works: BATIFFOL, *La paix constantinienne*, pp. 465-481, 488-494, 515-521.—DOM CHAPMAN, *The Contested
Letters of Pope Liberius*, *Rev. bénéd.*, t. XXVII, 1910.—MSGR. DUCHESNE,
Libère et Fortunatien, in *Mélanges arch. et hist.*, t. XXVIII, pp. 31-78, 1908.—
SALTET, *Les lettres du pape Libère de 357*, in *Bull. litt. eccl.*, 1907, pp. 279-
289; *La formation de la légende des papes Libère et Félix, ibid.*, 1905, pp.
232-236.—DOM WILMART, *La question du pape Libère*, *Rev. bénéd.*, t. XXV,
1908, pp. 360-367.—ZEILLER, *La question du pape Libère*, in *Bull. anc. litt.
et arch. chrét.*, t. III, pp. 1-32, 1913.—A. D'ALÈS, art. *"Libère,"* in *Dict. d'Apol.*
—ZEILLER, *Les origines chrétiennes dans les provinces danubiennes de l'Empire
romain*, Bibl. Ecoles françaises d'Athènes et de Rome, fasc. CXII, 1918.—
Catholic Dict., art. *"Liberius."*

St. Hilary.—Sources: *P. L.*, IX and X; *C. V.*, LXV.—Works: DORMAGEN,

Saint Hilaire de Poitiers et l'Arianisme, 1864.—P. LARGENT, *Saint Hilaire*, Coll. "*Les Saints*," 1902.—L. FEDER, in *Stimmen aus Maria Laach*, 1911, pp. 30–45. —J. A. QUILLACQ, *Quomodo lingua latina usus sit S. Hilarius*, 1903.—X. LE BACHELET, art. "*Hilaire*," in *Dict. de Théol.*—H. JEANNOTE, *Le psautier de saint Hilaire de Poitiers*, 1917.—L. FEDER, *Studien zu Hilarius von Poitiers*, 3 vols., Vienna, 1910–1912.

Victorinus.—Sources: *P. L.*, VIII, 1019–1236.—Works: KOFFMANE, *De Mario Victorino*, Breslau, 1880.—P. MONCEAUX, *Histoire litt. de l'Afrique chrétienne*, III, 1905.—DE LABRIOLLET, *Hist. litt. lat. ch.*, p. 346.

CHAPTER II

The new Emperor, *Julian the Apostate,* recalled the bishops exiled by his predecessor with the sinister intention of causing more divisions and greater confusion in the Church. In point of fact, the result of his action was quite the opposite. In the year 362 Athanasius and Eusebius of Vercelli convoked a synod at Alexandria, which marked the initial steps in the return of the world to orthodoxy. Very soon other councils, convening respectively in Gaul, Spain, and Greece, followed suit. Almost the entire Western portion of the Empire repudiated Arianism, while in the East, former Homoiousians, headed by St. Cyril of Jerusalem, staunchly defended the Nicene Creed. Arianism, which could have become a powerful weapon in the hands of Julian, was thus dealt a mortal blow.

Constantius had not forgotten paganism. The aim of the legislation of his day seemed to be the total suppression of all pagan rites. A law enacted in 341 read: "Let superstition cease, and let the folly of sacrifices be abolished." Another, issued in 351, ordered all temples to be closed. This policy, so contrary to the Edict of Milan, did not impair paganism in points where it was still strong, but it hastened its ruin where it was already in process of disintegration, sowed in the souls of pagans germs of hatred, which sprouted forth under Julian, and thus retarded rather than advanced the inevitable ruin of the ancient cult.

From one point of view it was quite natural for Julian to hate the religion of Constantius, who had been the murderer of Julian's father Julius Constantius. But what inclined him even more towards paganism was his education at the hands of his teachers. As long as Eusebius of Nicomedia had charge of his religious training, his tutor Mardonius bent every effort to mould him into a perfect Hellenist, inclined to pagan ideas. The Neo-Platonic doctrines taught in the universities which he attended later, were responsible for the final and complete perversion of his mind. As a matter of prudence, however, he feigned piety, going so far as to affect monastic ways.

Upon his accession to the throne, Julian immediately began to stamp out Christianity and rebuild the dismantled temples of the gods. In an endeavor to realize the dream of the Neo-Platonists of the school of Porphyry, he favored a sort of compromise between philosophy and the popular religions, between monotheism and polytheism, enhancing his scheme with very pompous and expressive rites, and magic incantations. His next step was to establish a universal pagan church with a hierarchy modelled on that of the Christian Church. The high priest of each province was made a sort of metropolitan under the sovereign protection of a Supreme Pontiff, who was none other than Julian himself. His efforts to mimic Christianity became even more apparent when he gave orders for the establishment of pagan theological schools, and the institution of a pagan liturgy, including a complete penitential system. Julian went even farther. He sought to infuse a new soul into paganism, modelled, of course, on the soul of Christianity, by creating a pagan charity to erect hospitals and care for the sick and the poor. But Julian was appealing to a virtue and a devotion that were purely illusory. "Men and women," says St. John Chrysostom, "who but a moment before were dying of starvation, criminals, ex-convicts, and reprobates, were suddenly raised to the dignity of priests and soothsayers, and surrounded with all manner of honors." Such a ridiculous structure was manifestly doomed to destruction.

Judging the Christians by his own standards, Julian sought also to make apostates. He took a personal interest in this matter, promising positions and honors to those who would repudiate their faith, and promoting discussions with prominent members of the Christian Church. Among the many who resisted his efforts were three officers: Jovian, Valentinian, and Valens, all three destined to become emperors one day.

On the other hand, the Apostate inaugurated a policy of legal intolerance. Paganism was again proclaimed the official religion of the Empire; judges and magistrates were one and all compelled to offer sacrifice to the gods; the Christian clergy were deprived of their immunities and Christian bishops were forced to surrender Church property and Church valuables to indemnify pagan priests, whose rights in these matters had been infringed upon under the reign of his predecessors. The Emperor also published an edict forbidding Christian professors to teach classical literature in their schools, his purpose being to bring about the mental degradation of the "despicable Galileans" by closing to them the avenues of culture and learning. This is only one instance of the many ways by which he sought to vex and annoy the faithful.

In the year 362, Julian went to war with the Persians. He established the base of his campaign at Antioch, and while there, thought to confute the prophecy of Christ by rebuilding the Temple of Jerusalem. By divine intervention, the attempt proved a complete failure. Globes of fire burst forth repeatedly from the earth close to the foundations, impeding all further progress with the work.

Julian also recalled from exile both Arians and anti-Arians, with the hope that they would exterminate one another. Foiled in this plan also, he offered imperial protection to the Anomean Aetius and banished St. Athanasius. Then, too, he furthered the interests of the pagan movement by his negligence in correcting abuses. Finally, he himself persecuted at times, but always under some legal pretext. Thus he ordered the execution of Christian soldiers, giving as his reason that they had threatened to rebel.

There is no denying that some Christians did apostatise, both in the army, as a result of the discipline, and among the people, for motives of personal interest. The majority, however, offered staunch resistance.

Julian was killed in 363, while retreating before an attack of the Persian cavalry. "The words attributed to him when dying: 'Galilean, thou hast conquered,' are just as true as any other historical words. In all probability they were never pronounced by the wounded Emperor, but came from the conscience of the people. Amid the terrible disasters of the Persian retreat, *Jovian* was elected in all haste to succeed him. He had only to say the word for all the soldiers to return to Christianity. Apostates on all sides sought to be re-instated and requested permission to do penance. An edict soon re-established religious freedom, and things were gradually brought back to the position they occupied under the Emperor Constantine. Paganism ceased to be the official religion of the State and was relegated to the plane of a tolerated cult. Christianity, on the contrary, once again became the religion of the Emperor and of the majority of his subjects, and seemed destined in the very near future to become the religion of the State." [1]

[1] P. Allard, *Julian the Apostate.*

TEXTS AND DOCUMENTS

PORTRAIT OF JULIAN THE APOSTATE

Most persons only knew Julian after he had made himself known by his actions and by his abuse of absolute power; but I knew him from the time of our acquaintance at Athens, and I never found a trace of goodness in him. He rolled his eyes from side to side, and had a ferocious aspect. He could not keep his limbs at rest, he was continually distending and contracting his nostrils, in sign of anger or contempt, and he was constantly addicted to sharp sayings and cool buffooneries. His laugh was a bellow. He would at the same moment grant or refuse a favor with equal ease, talked without rhyme or reason, put inopportune questions, and gave answers far from the point. But why do I enter into such detail as to his exterior? . . . Those who were with us [at Athens] can bear witness that, when I noted his characteristics, I said that the Roman State was nourishing a very dangerous viper. So I said, hoping, at the same time that I was deceived; and without doubt, it were better that I had been, and the earth had not been desolated by so many evils.

ST. GREGORY OF NAZIANZUS, *Two Philippics
Against Julian the Apostate, passim.*

QUESTIONS

1. What was the direct effect of the edict of Constantius?
2. Trace the influence of Julian's education on his conduct in later life.
3. What were the general outlines of the new religion proposed by Julian?
4. Tell something about the personal characteristics of Julian.
5. What happened under Jovian?

BIBLIOGRAPHY

Julian the Apostate.—Sources: *Opera,* edit. Hertlein; *Libanius, Epitaphios Juliani,* edit. Reiske; BIDEZ and CUMONT, *Juliani Opera,* G. Budé, 1922–1924; *Amm. Marcell.,* XVI, XXV.—Works: P. ALLARD, *Julien l'Apostat,* 3 vols., 1903.—NAVILLE, *Julien l'Apostat et sa philosophie du polythéisme.*— G. BOISSIER, *La fin du paganisme,* t. I, 1891.—DE BROGLIE, *L'Eglise et l'Empire romain,* t. III.—FR. CUMONT, *Etudes syriennes; La marche de l'empereur Julien,* etc., 1917.—J. VITEAU, art. *"Julien l'Apostat,"* in *Dict. de Théol.*—DOM LECLERCQ, art. *"Julien l'Apostat,"* in *Dict. d'Arch.*—THEODORET, *Ecclesiastical History,* III, pp. 24 ff.—E. J. MARTIN, *The Emperor Julian; An Essay on His Relations with the Christian Religion.*

CHAPTER III

After the death of Julian, Arianism again loomed as a danger on the horizon. *Valentinian,* an orthodox Catholic, succeeded the Emperor Jovian, stricken by sudden death, but unfortunately took as associate in the East his brother *Valens,* as determined an Arian as Constantius had been, and a strong advocate of the latter's politico-religious tactics. In 365, Valens issued a general edict, banishing all the bishops who had recently returned from exile. He struck at Catholics and Arians alike, seeking in this way to reach the incumbents of the principal sees: Athanasius at Alexandria, Meletius at Antioch, and Evagrius at Constantinople. The result of his persecution, however, was purely external. Arianism was on the wane, and the abuses of the Anomeans no less than the dogmatic intolerance of the Emperor contributed towards driving the semi-Arians into the orthodox camp.

I. The Conciliatory Party: The Three Cappadocians. Meanwhile, new champions were rising who endeavored to effect a reconciliation with their pen. The most renowned of these were the three so-called *Cappadocians:* St. Basil, St. Gregory of Nazianzus, and St. Gregory of Nyssa. These writers propounded a new method of solving the problem, without compromising the Nicene Creed. There are two ways of presenting the dogma of the Trinity. The first lays special stress on the unity of substance; the second emphasizes the trinity of persons. It was the second of these two methods which the three great Cappadocians adopted. With St. Basil they affirmed that there is a Father, a Son, and a Holy Ghost, all three of whom have one and the same substance, whereas the Fathers of Nicaea, influenced by the Latin Fathers, had stated that there is not a divine concrete substance of the Father, the Son, and the Holy Ghost. The difference was one in point of view only, dictated by the prevailing circumstances. At Nicaea it was necessary to oppose Arius by adopting an anti-Subordinationist formula, and, therefore, to stress the unity of substance. Now the goal was to reconcile the heterodox party. Hence, it was necessary to allay all suspicions of Sabellianism, stress the trinity of persons, and keep the unity of nature in the background. It must be admitted that there was nothing unorthodox in this stand.

At the same time, the Cappadocians hit upon a terminology that was most appropriate. One of the chief causes of misunderstanding in connection with the term *homoousios* arose from the indefinite meaning of the word οὐσία (nature), which some confounded with ὑπόστασις (person). Such equivocation could easily change the homoousios into an ultra-Sabellian formula and make it signify: there is but one person in the Trinity. Basil and his school insisted that οὐσία signified *nature* and ὑπόστασις, *person,* and proposed a conciliatory formula which read: τρεῖς ὑποστάσεις (three persons), μία οὐσία (one substance). In this way the heterodox party was denied the opportunity of discussing indefinitely the meaning of terms which formerly had been inadequately defined.

Born at Caesarea in Cappadocia, *St. Basil* (329-379) frequented the schools of Athens in company with Julian the Apostate and St. Gregory of Nazianzus. After a visit to the solitaries and monks of Palestine and Syria, he returned to his native land and organized a small religious community on the banks of the river Iris. In 364, he was ordained to the priesthood by the archbishop of Caesarea, whom he succeeded in the see of that city in 370. His principal dogmatic writings are a treatise against Eunomius, in which he refutes that Arian writer, and a treatise on the Holy Ghost, in which he confutes the *Pneumatomachi.* We shall have occasion to speak of his ascetical writings later. He also wrote several homilies, the most famous of which is the *Hexaëmeron,* a literal account of the six days of creation.

Being an energetic and well-balanced man, endowed with good common sense, Basil was "a Roman among the Greeks." His friend, *Gregory of Nazianzus* (330-390), on the contrary, was a very sensitive and impressionable soul, made not for action, but rather for contemplation. For a time he lived with St. Basil on the banks of the river Iris, but was forced to give up this life of solitude to assist his aged father, the bishop of Nazianzus, in the administration of his diocese. Consecrated bishop of Sasima by St. Basil, in 372, Gregory refused to take possession of his see, and after the death of his father, he withdrew to a retreat in Isauria.

Yielding finally (379) to the insistent requests of the Catholics of Constantinople, he again took up the duties of an active life and was installed as their bishop. Owing, however, to difficulties raised at the Second General Council, Gregory resigned and returned to Nazianzus. While at Constantinople, he delivered his famous discourses on the Trinity (XXVII–XXXI). He was a born orator, and though at times he betrays too close an acquaintance with the art of oratory, his Funeral Orations have become classics.

St. Gregory of Nyssa, a younger brother of St. Basil, was above all a thinker and a philosopher, whose ideas are tainted here and there with Neo-Platonism. He followed the example of his brother by writing a treatise against Eunomius in twelve books. He also composed an *Oratio Catechetica Magna,* which is a doctrinal synthesis of the fundamental teachings concerning the faith, the Trinity, the Incarnation, the Redemption, and the Sacraments.

The three Cappadocians have been aptly characterized by saying that Basil was the arm which acted, Gregory of Nazianzus the mouth which spoke, and Gregory of Nyssa the head which did the thinking.

II. The Exclusivism of the Luciferians. The attempts made by the Cappadocians to effect a reconciliation in doctrinal matters were somewhat thwarted by the immoderate zeal of certain writers representing an unorthodox reaction against Arianism, who held firmly to the view that penitent Arians should not be directly reconciled with the Church, but made to do penance and merit that favor. A council held at Alexandria in 362 condemned their views, deciding that heretics should merely be requested to repudiate the Arian doctrine and subscribe to the Nicene formula. Members of the opposing faction grouped themselves around Lucifer of Cagliari, and the orthodox party rather maliciously dubbed them "Luciferians."

Lucifer's writings are purely invective in character and their titles betray his spirit of intransigence. He held that orthodox Christians should have no social intercourse with heretics (*De non conveniendo cum haereticis*) and no mercy should be shown the enemies of God (*De non parcendo in Deum delinquentibus*). The principal followers of Lucifer of Cagliari were Gregory of Eliberis and the Roman deacon Hilary, who even demanded that all repentant Arians be rebaptized.

At Antioch, the former stronghold of Arianism, new dissensions arose. As early as 330, the local bishop, *Eustathius,* had been accused of Sabellianism and deposed from his see by the Eusebians, who sought to revenge themselves for the zeal he had displayed in defending the Nicene Creed. The Eustathians refused to acknowledge the Arian bishops, and more specifically *Meletius,* a semi-Arian prelate, who had been converted to orthodoxy and exiled by Constantius in 360. To Meletius they opposed the priest Paulinus, whom Lucifer of Cagliari recommended as their bishop, and in this move they received the approbation of the city of Alexandria and, finally, even that of Rome. Paulinus and Meletius immediately proceeded to nominate rival titular bishops to the various suffragan sees. It was thus that the *Schism of Antioch* was born. The gap was partially bridged in 417 under the episcopal rule of Alexander, but not completely closed until towards the end of the fifth century, when, during the administration of Bishop Calendio, the relics of St. Eustathius were brought to Antioch.

III. The Final Triumph at Constantinople (381). Despite all these bitter contentions, the orthodox party gradually became victorious. In 379, Meletius convoked at Antioch a synod of 153 Oriental bishops, all of whom subscribed to the Nicene formula. Meanwhile St. Gregory of Nazianzus had returned to Constantinople and established himself in a humble dwelling surnamed by him "Anastasis" (Resurrection), where he delivered his famous theological discourses. After the death of Valens (378) Arianism began to lose favor at the imperial court, until orthodoxy regained all its former power with Gratian in the East and Theodosius in the West. In 380 Theodosius promulgated the *Edict of Thessalonica,* which enjoined faith upon all in the godhead of the Father, the Son, and the Holy Ghost, as taught by Bishops Damasus of Rome and Peter of Alexandria.

At the Second Ecumenical Council, convened at Constantinople in 381, the Trinitarian error assumed a new form, it being argued by some that, if the Son is a creature, the Holy Ghost must *a fortiori* be such. This corollary of Arianism had thus far passed unnoticed, but from 360 on certain bishops of the homoiousian party represented the Paraclete as a mere angel or a simple messenger from Heaven. This heresy spread rapidly throughout Thrace, Bithynia, and the Hellespont, under the authority of *Macedonius* of Byzantium and *Marathonius* of Nicomedia; whence the name Marathonians, and especially Macedonians, is often used to designate these "Pneumatomachi."

Perceiving that their cause was hopeless, the Macedonian minority quietly withdrew from the council. The assembly then declared itself in complete accord with the Fathers of Nicaea (canon 1), and formulated a creed to complement that of the Nicene Council in matters pertaining to the Holy Ghost: "We believe in the Holy Ghost, who reigneth and quickeneth, who proceedeth from and must be honored like the Father, who hath spoken through the Prophets." The terminology was not sufficiently precise, and as a result the procession of the Holy Ghost was described differently: in the West by the formula, *"A Patre Filioque procedit";* in the East by the formula, *"A Patre per Filium procedit,"* according to the theory of St. Gregory of Nyssa, who compared the Father, the Son, and the Holy Ghost to three burning torches, of which the first communicates its light to the second, and through the second *(per Filium)*, to the third. These differences gave rise to the memorable disputes regarding the word *Filioque.* Nevertheless, the year 381 marked the end of Arianism in the Empire.

The disciplinary decisions of the Second General Council were far less felicitous. The third canon decreed that "the Bishop of Constantinople must have pre-eminence of honor after the Bishop of Rome, because this city is the new Rome." The wording of this canon not only relegated Alexandria to second place in the East, but also constituted a direct threat to the primacy of the Roman See. The inferior position of Constantinople in regard to the see of Rome was reckoned only in terms of seniority, and the pre-eminence of the Eternal City was regarded as political in character, being due, not to St. Peter's residence there, but to the fact that Rome was the former seat of the Caesars. The argument was distinctly anti-Christian in character and a disquieting omen for the future. Would the religious position of the two cities follow the vicissitudes of their political fortunes?

In point of fact, Byzantium after the year 381 entered upon a period of extraordinary growth, and tried to centralize all Eastern affairs under the supreme jurisdiction of the Emperor. This was the main purpose of the so-called permanent synod (σύνοδος ἐνδημοῦσα), which, under the presidency of the Bishop of Constantinople, settled all pending ecclesiastical questions. Supreme in matters theological, infallible in matters of Church law, and generous in the distribution of ecclesiastical dignities, it became the supreme religious judge in the East. Byzantinism later assumed the proportions of an institution, placing the patriarch on a level with the Pope, and the Emperor above both.

TEXTS AND DOCUMENTS

The Edict of the Emperors Gratian and Theodosius Abolishing the Toleration of Arianism (Feb. 28, 380)

We will that all the peoples who are ruled by the authority of our clemency shall hold to the religion which the Divine Apostle Peter delivered to the Romans, and which is recognized by his having preserved it there until the present day, and which it is known that the Pontiff Damasus follows, and Peter, Bishop of Alexandria, a man of Apostolic holiness; that is to say, according to the teaching of the Apostles and the doctrine of the Gospel, we should believe in one Godhead of the Father, Son, and Holy Ghost, in coequal majesty and Holy Trinity. We order those who follow this law to take the name of Catholic Christians; all others, mad and insane, we condemn to the infamy of heresy, and they will be punished in the first place by divine vengeance, and also by our penalties, wherein we follow the will of Heaven.

QUESTIONS

1. Compare the characters of the three Cappadocians.
2. How did they approach the problem of orthodoxy?
3. What was their outstanding achievement in this respect?
4. Who were the *Pneumatomachi?*
5. What was the error of the Luciferians?
6. What is to be understood by Byzantinism?

BIBLIOGRAPHY

The Cappadocians.—The opinion stating that they were only semi-Arians in disguise is sustained by Harnack, *Lehrb. der DG.*, II, 252.—Loofs, *Leitfaden,* 4th edit., pp. 257 ff.—Seeberg, *Lehrb. der DG.*, I, p. 187.—Gwatkin, *Studies of Arianism,* 2nd edit., pp. 247–270.—Refutation by Bethune-Baker, *The Meaning of Homoousios in the Constantinopolitan Creed* (*Texts and Studies*), Cambridge, 1901.—See also G. Rasneur, *L'homoiousianisme dans ses rapports avec l'orthodoxie,* in *Rev. hist. eccl.,* t. IV, 1903.—J. Lebon, *La position de saint Cyrille de Jérusalem dans les luttes provoquées par l'arianisme,* in *Rev. hist. eccl.,* XX (1924), pp. 184–210, 357–386.

St. Basil.—Sources: *P. G.*, t. XXIX–XXXII.—Works: L. Roux, *Etude sur la prédication de Basile le Grand*, Strasbourg, 1867.—E. Fialon, *Etude historique et littéraire sur saint Basile*, 1869.—A. Bayle, *Saint Basile, archevêque de Césarée*, Avignon, 1878.—E. Scholl, *Die Lehre des hl. Basilius von der Gnade*, Freiburg i. B., 1881.—A. Kranich, *Der hl. Basilius in seiner Stellung zum Filioque*, Braunsberg, 1881.—Vasson, *Saint Basile le Grand, ses œuvres oratoires et ascétiques*, 1894.—P. Allard, *Saint Basile* (Coll. "Les Saints"), 1899; art. *"Basile"* in *Dict. de Théol.*—Clarke, *St. Basil the Great, a Study in Monasticism*, Cambridge, 1913.—Batiffol, *La littérature grecque.*—J. Rivière, *Saint Basile* (Coll. "Les Moralistes Chrétiens"), 1925.—Cardinal Newman, *The Church of the Fathers.*

St. Gregory of Nazianzus.—Sources: *P. G.*, t. XXXV–XXXVIII.—Works: A. Benoit, *Saint Grégoire de Naziance, sa vie, ses œuvres, son époque*, 2nd edit., 1885.—C. Ullmann, *Gregorius von Nazianz der Theolog*, 2nd edit., Gotha, 1866.—K. Huemmer, *Des hl. Gregor von Nazianz des Theologen Lehre von der Gnade*, Kempten, 1890.—E. Dubedout, *De D. Gregorii Naz. Carminibus*, 1901.—M. Guignet, *Saint Grégoire de Naziance et la rhétorique*, 1911.—Dräseke, *Neuplatonisches in des Gregor von Naziance Trinitätslehre*, in *Byzantinische Zeitschrift*, 1906., t. XV, pp. 141–190.—R. Gottwald, *De Gregorio Nazianzeno, platonico*, Breslau, 1906.—F. Boulanger, text and transl. of funeral orations, in Coll. Hemmer-Lejay.—P. Godet, art. *"Grégoire de Nazianze,"* in *Dict. de Théol.*—P. Batiffol, *La littérature grecque*, pp. 237–240.

St. Gregory of Nyssa.—Sources: *P. G.*, t. XLIV–XLVI.—Works: J. Rupp, *Gregors, des Bischofs von Nyssa, Leben und Meinungen*, Leipzig, 1834.—Diekamp, *Die Gotteslehre des hl. Gregor von Nyssa*, Münster, 1896.—Vollert, *Die Lehre Gregors von Nyssa vom Guten und Bösen*, Leipzig, 1897.—Aufhauser, *Die Heilslehre des heil. Gregor von Nyssa*, Munich, 1910.—Batiffol, *La littérature grecque*, pp. 288–292.

The Luciferians and the Schism of Antioch.—Sources: Works of Lucifer of Calaris, in *P. L.*, XII, 765–1038; *C. V.*, t. XIV.—Works: Saltet, *Les fraudes littéraires des schismatiques lucifériens aux IVe et Ve siècles*, in *Bull. de Toulouse*, Oct.-Nov., 1906.—Cavallera, *Le schisme d'Antioche*, 1905.—E. Amann, art. *"Mélèce d'Antioche,"* in *Dict. de Théol.*

Macedonius.—G. Bardy, art. *"Macedonius et les Macédoniens,"* in *Dict. de Théol.*

CHAPTER IV

THE END OF PAGANISM IN THE EMPIRE

While Arianism was disappearing in the East, paganism received its death blow in Rome. *Valentinian,* brother of Valens and Emperor of the East, had merely put back the Christians into the position which they had occupied before Julian, and although himself a Christian, had adopted a policy of neutrality. Accordingly, he allowed the pagans to carry on their worship, but in order to appear neutral, turned over to the State the temples that had been confiscated by Constantius to the profit of the Christians, but later returned to the pagans by Julian. Valentinian reminds us strongly of Constantine: like him, he adhered scrupulously to the Edict of Milan.

Gratian was the first Emperor to sever the official bond which linked paganism to the imperial power. He refused to accept the insignia of the *Pontifex Maximus.* "Such a garment," he said, "is not becoming to a Christian." He even went so far as to place himself under the direction of *St. Ambrose,* Bishop of Milan (340–397), and, at the latter's instance no doubt, resolved to eradicate paganism. He argued that if the Emperor refused to be the official head of the pagan religion, it was merely a private form of worship and not entitled to any further financial assistance from the State. This was the gist of a decree which he issued in 382. In keeping with the same policy, he issued orders for the removal of the Statue of Victory before which the senators were accustomed to burn incense and which had always been considered symbolic of the official preponderance of paganism. The pagan senators resolved to protest his action, but through the intervention of St. Ambrose and Pope Damasus, their Christian colleagues voiced their refusal to associate with them in their purpose. Gratian refused them a hearing (382).

The following year Gratian was assassinated near Lyons by the partisans of Maximus, whom the militia in Britany had proclaimed Emperor. Through the entreaties of St. Ambrose, the usurper consented to let

Valentinian II, a brother of Gratian, rule over Italy, the Danubian provinces, and Africa. The new Emperor was only twelve years of age, a fact which prompted the pagan party in Rome to seek revenge. *Symmachus,* who was prefect of Rome at the time, drew up a petition in favor of paganism, which he described as threatened with death, and secured the signatures of some of the senators. Personifying the city of the Caesars, he placed upon its lips words of supreme majesty and sadness that recounted the many threats with which the venerable traditions had been assailed. The scheme almost succeeded; but St. Ambrose was keeping watch. He formulated his protest in an energetic letter, arguing with reason that the pagans had not the right to inflict the emblem of idolatry upon their Christian colleagues. Ambrose even placed the young Emperor in such a dilemma that he could not possibly yield: "If a contrary decision is reached by your Imperial Highness, you will still be free to repair to the church; but you will find no priest there, or if one be present, he will protest against your action." The Bishop of Milan scored a complete victory. He then went to the trouble of refuting the arguments of Symmachus in an open letter, in which he proved beyond cavil that there was no possible connection between the ancient glory of Rome and the pagan cult.

Up to this time, the policy of the Emperor Constantine was still in force. Paganism had long ceased to be regarded as the official religion of the State, though it was still permitted to carry on its rites and functions. *Theodosius,* the ruler of the East and real protector of the whole Empire, made it his direct and immediate task to exterminate paganism completely. In 381 he issued orders forbidding any Christian to join the ranks of the pagans and making acts of divination punishable by law. This latter measure was calculated to suppress almost in their entirety the bloody sacrifices conducted for the purpose of reading the future in the entrails of the victims. It abolished at one stroke the most attractive aspect of idolatrous rites. Theodosius thus effected the destruction of paganism by degrees. In 391, however, he took a decisive step by forbidding persons to enter pagan temples under pain of fine. In 392 he even forbade the worship of the gods in secret and thus closed all domestic sanctuaries. At the same time, the Emperor gave the ancient temples to the Christians, and when the pagans of Alexandria objected to this, he issued orders to destroy all the pagan sanctuaries of that city, and in particular the famous Serapeion, which was the center of Egyptian worship.

Although Theodosius was intolerance personified in the matter of pagan worship, he was tolerant to a fault towards individuals, never differentiating between pagans and Christians in making appointments to office and in distributing honors and dignities. A whole line of prefects of the pretorium and the City of Rome was avowedly pagan, for instance: Symmachus, Praetextatus, Nicomachus Flavian, and Albinus. But after the Frankish General Arbogast had assassinated Valentinian II and put in his stead the rhetorician Eugene, who, although a Christian, was constrained to yield to the pagan faction headed by the prefect of the pretorium, Nicomachus Flavian, the latter rebuilt the Altar of Victory and gave permission to offer pagan sacrifices. Setting out immediately from the East, Theodosius scored a brilliant victory near Aquileia, in a battle which resulted in the death of Flavian, Arbogast, and Eugene. True to his policy, Theodosius sought no reprisals, but "the gods paid the price," and paganism was once again officially abolished.

St. Ambrose had been the principal figure in the work of overthrowing the pagan religion. He now set about establishing a Christian government, in which the State would be subject to the Church in everything pertaining to religious doctrine and public morality. "In matters of faith," he was wont to say, "the bishops are the judges of the emperors, and not the emperors of the bishops." In 390 a sedition broke out in Thessalonica, in which several illustrious personages met with their death. The infuriated Theodosius ordered drastic reprisals. Huddled together in the circus, almost the entire population was literally massacred by the militia. St. Ambrose immediately despatched a letter to the Emperor, enjoining upon him a public penance under pain of excommunication from the Church. Theodosius submitted to the Bishop's demands.[1]

The internal causes of the decay of paganism are easy to discern. It was a religion based upon falsehood and lived by deception. It contained no definite set of truths, had no hierarchy, catered only to the rich,

---

[1] According to Theodoret, *Hist. Eccles.*, V, XVII (*P. G.*, LXXXII, 1232), Ambrose actually barred the passage to Theodosius when the latter presented himself at the cathedral and was about to enter the building with his retinue. But neither Rufinus, nor St. Augustine, nor St. Ambrose himself speak of any such dramatic scene. It is certain, however, that the Emperor made suitable amendment for his conduct. (See De Broglie, *Les Pères Bollandistes et la pénitence de Théodose, Corr.*, August, 1900, 2nd series, p. 644; Van Ortroy, *Analecta Bollandiana*, t. XXIII, pp. 418 ff.; De Labriolle, *St. Ambroise*, pp. 136–147.)

despised womanhood, favored slavery, and could not quiet the despairing cries of humanity for religious peace and happiness. It was a religion of externals only, took no account of virtue, its highest efforts in this direction resulting only in cold Stoicism, refined Epicureanism, or fantastic Mysticism. For years it basked in the sunshine of imperial favor, and thrived under the protection of the State. Fidelity to the religion of the gods was reckoned synonymous with good citizenship, and the prosperity of the Empire was attributed in more than one instance to the protection and favor of different deities. It is because the Christians refused to acknowledge the gods of Greece and Rome that they were considered enemies of the Empire and a constant threat to its security. But even though paganism enjoyed all manner of earthly advantages, it fell from sheer rottenness. Religion is for the multitude; paganism curried favor with the few. Religion is the moral bond which unites the intellects and wills of men to their Creator; it must be something elevating, something inspiring, something consoling. These elements were sadly lacking in paganism, its mission was something entirely different, and so it finally succumbed.

TEXTS AND DOCUMENTS

THE LAST FORM OF ROMAN PAGANISM

Paganism reached its lowest depth in the Roman Empire, by the deification of the human monsters who ruled the world, and by the crawling servility with which senate and people raised temples and altars, and offered libations and sacrifices to them. The practice of deifying mortal man had come from the kingdoms of Macedonia and Egypt. Rome began the practice by deifying Caesar as a descendant of Venus. He was named Jupiter. His statue with the inscription "To the Invincible God" was placed in the temple of Quirinus during his lifetime. After his death the worship of Caesar became a regular branch of State religion. The first Emperors rather permitted than coveted divine honors. Augustus allowed the erection of temples and altars in his honor only in the provinces, not in Rome and Italy. His worship, however, became universal after his death. His birthday had equal rank with the festival of Mars. Caligula used to array himself in the fashion of Mercury, Apollo, Mars, and Jupiter. He ordered his statue to be publicly adored on the Palatine, and even offered sacrifices to himself. "He ordered the choicest statues of the gods to be decapitated and the heads to be replaced by his own likeness. He caused a temple to be constructed to his own godhead, and instituted priests and victims for the worship to be offered to himself. Priestly positions were offered to the highest bidders, and were eagerly sought by the richest men in Rome." The passionate remonstrance of Herod Agrippa and the fear of political consequences alone induced him to withdraw his order of placing a gigantic statue of himself for adoration in the Temple of Jerusalem. Claudius received the honors of divinity at his death. They were revoked for a time by Nero, but restored by Vespasian. Nero deified his wife Poppaea, for whom he had murdered Octavia and sentenced Thrasia to death because he could not believe Poppaea to be a goddess. On the whole, about forty-three of these deifications or apotheses took place in the long line of emperors and their families, of which fifteen were those of females.

GUGGENBERGER, *General History of the Christian Era*, pp. 26–27.

QUESTIONS

1. Contrast the religious policies of Valentinian, Gratian, and Theodosius.
2. What were the extrinsic and intrinsic causes of the downfall of paganism?
3. Which were the different steps taken to abolish paganism?
4. Describe the character of St. Ambrose, and show the part he played in the abolition of pagan worship.

BIBLIOGRAPHY

The End of Paganism.—G. BOISSIER, *La fin du paganisme*, 2 vols., 1881.—DE BROGLIE, *l'Eglise et l'Empire Romain.*—BEUGNOT, *Histoire de la déstruction du paganisme en Occident*, 2 vols., 1835.—P. ALLARD, *L'Empire romain de Néron à Théodose.*—DE LABRIOLLE, *Histoire de la litt. lat. chr.*, pp. 351 ff.—G. UHLHORN, *The Conflict of Christianity with Heathenism*, 1899.

St. Ambrose.—Sources: *P. L.*, t. XIV–XVII; *C. V.*, XXXII.—Works: TILLEMONT, t. X (1705), p. 78.—A. BAUNARD, *Histoire de saint Ambroise.*— Th. FOERSTER, *Ambrosius, Bischof von Mailand, eine Darstellung seines Lebens und Wirkens*, Halle, 1884.—R. THAMIN, *Saint Ambroise et la morale chrétienne au IVᵉ siècle*, 1895.—A. DE BROGLIE, *Saint Ambroise* (Coll. "Les Saints") 1899.—DE LABRIOLLE, *Saint Ambroise.*—RAUSCHEN, *Jahrbücher der Christlichen Kirche unter Theodosius dem Grossen*, Freiburg i. Br., 1897.—LARGENT, art. "*Ambroise*," in *Dict. de Théol.*—W. E. BROWN, *Pioneers of Christendom.*

CHAPTER V

The Arian controversies had barely subsided when the East became the scene of another battle. This time, however, theological difficulties were relegated to second place and the battles waged around personalities. Instance the conflict between Rufinus and St. Jerome, and that between Theophilus and St. John Chrysostom.

The prestige of Origen in the East was quite remarkable. Following his example, the two great Cappadocians, Basil and Gregory of Nazianzus, attributed an important rôle to reason in the exposition of dogmatic truths. Unfortunately, other disciples insisted rather on airing some of the errors of the great Egyptian writer, chief among them being Gregory of Nyssa and Didymus the Blind. The latter wrote a commentary on the περὶ ἀρχῶν, the most objectionable of all the master's works. The result was an anti-Origenist reaction, unreasonable in its method of procedure, but at bottom quite justifiable.

Intent as he was upon building up a Christian gnosis, Origen in his theological discussions had laid too much stress on the philosophy of Plato. The result was a twofold series of errors: (1) a form of Subordinationism, according to which the Logos and the Holy Ghost are intermediary persons inferior to the Father; and (2) a bizarre sort of eschatology. In the opinion of Origen, the spirits were born equally perfect, but not all remained faithful to God. Their fall is the reason for the actual state of the world, for some of these spirits became angels, others stars or men, and still others, demons. This world is, therefore, nothing more than a place of purification, in which spirits are imprisoned in bodies awaiting their release. After a purification by fire, matter, having played its part, will revert to nothingness, and all the souls of the elect will return to God. In this manner, the primordial unity will be restored (*apocatastasis*).

I. The Latin Phase: St. Jerome and Rufinus. The crisis was reached in 394. *St. Jerome* and *Rufinus* were at that time both leading a cenobitic life in Palestine. One day an obscure monk by the name of Aterbius, imbued with the anthropomorphic errors rampant in several convents, and opposed on that score to the spiritualistic exegesis of the great Alexandrian, visited their place of retreat for the purpose of denouncing Origenism. St. Jerome refused to compromise, while Rufinus openly declared that he wished to remain faithful to the teachings of Origen. A war of intrigues broke out between the two. On Easter Sunday, 397, thanks to the intervention of St. Melania, the two adversaries resolved to forgive and forget, but the battle between them was resumed with renewed vigor when Rufinus undertook the translation of the περὶ ἀρχῶν, which he had previously expurgated from all unacceptable Subordinationist errors. He insidiously justified his course of action on the ground that St. Jerome himself had translated Origen's Homilies. Cut to the quick, Jerome retorted by publishing a complete translation of the περὶ ἀρχῶν. Rufinus wrote an Apologia, and St. Jerome answered him with another; both works were couched in heated terms. In A. D. 400, Pope Anastasius definitely pronounced himself against Origen, his works and his translator. Rufinus retired, first to Aquileia, and then to Rome. St. Jerome resumed his Scriptural studies in the quiet of his retreat at Bethlehem. The Latin phase of the struggle was over.

II. The Greek Phase: St. John Chrysostom and Theophilus.

St. Jerome and Rufinus had no sooner laid down their arms than the battle was resumed with renewed vigor in the East. *Theophilus*, Patriarch of Alexandria, at first an ardent admirer of Origen, took sides against him, for reasons that were not all metaphysical. The decision of the Sovereign Pontiff strengthened him in his convictions. Accordingly, in the year 401, we find him heading a small army of regular soldiers, and giving chase to a number of Origenist monks in the Nitrian desert. The "Four Long Brothers," Dioscorus, Ammon, Eusebius, and Euthymus, who were the leaders of the persecuted monks, fled to Constantinople, where they expected support from the Patriarch, *St. John Chrysostom* (347–407). Chrysostom received and housed them, but prudently refused to admit them to the communion of the faithful until explanations arrived from Alexandria. The Empress *Eudoxia* was not so discreet, but when the Four Long Brothers preferred grave charges against Theophilus, she induced the Emperor Arcadius to summon the latter to Byzantium and have him tried by a synod presided over by St. John Chrysostom. Her action only resulted in fomenting the rivalry which already existed between the two patriarchs. The "ecclesiastical Pharao" considered himself amenable to no one in the East.

In a few months, however, the scene changed. The Empress Eudoxia turned completely against John, as a consequence of a homily on worldliness, in which she imagined she recognized allusions to herself. Theophilus, who had purposely deferred coming to Byzantium, arrived in the meantime. So numerous were the ecclesiastical personages who expressed discontent at the severity and rigidity of Chrysostom, that an episcopal coterie, headed by Acacius of Beraea, Antiochus of Ptolemais, and Severian of Gabala, joined hands with the coterie at court in a united effort to oust Chrysostom. Theophilus formed a coalition of the different anti-Johannite factions and called the *Synod of the Oak* in the neighborhood of Chalcedon. Many charges were raised against the Patriarch, among others, the crime of lèse-majesté. Chrysostom, who refused to attend, was deposed and sent into exile. He had got no farther than Bithynia when the entreaties of Eudoxia, who had been frightened by an earthquake, prevailed upon him to return to the city.

Two months after his return, St. John Chrysostom again found himself at odds with the Empress. This time Eudoxia had caused a silver statue of herself to be erected in front of the cathedral, and Chrysostom protested against such a desecration from his pulpit. He was charged with comparing her Imperial Highness to Herodias demanding the head of John the Baptist. As a result, the Patriarch was again sentenced to exile, despite the protests of his people. An inquiry was instituted, and Pope Innocent I declared the decree of deposition formulated against the Patriarch at the Synod of the Oak null and void, at the same time despatching a letter of reprimand to Theophilus. St. John Chrysostom, however, was not recalled from exile. In matter of fact, his enemies, fearing his influence in the capitol, resolved to visit him with even severer punishments. Accordingly, in the summer of 407, the Emperor issued a rescript banishing him to the northeast coast of the Black Sea. He never reached his destination, but died of fatigue at Comana, in Pontus, on the 14th of September, 407.

As a writer, St. John Chrysostom, by reason of his origin and his style, belongs to the school of Antioch. His forte was not the higher speculations of metaphysics, but illustrations, comparisons, and popular arguments. His

knowledge of the literal meaning of Sacred Scripture was exact, and Holy
Writ always served as the basis of his homilies. Moreover, he never hesitated to dwell upon grammatical considerations, if he felt that they would
help to elucidate a difficult text. Above all, however, he was a popular
orator, and his appeal was first and last practical. No Christian writer
can rival him for purity of language. His discourses were never lacking
in vivaciousness and passion. He had the grace of a true Syrian, and if his
tone was soft at times, it was always elegant and always touching. His use
of images was ever appropriate, and he seemed to have a natural gift for
fitting and striking metaphors. Among his works we must cite all his
exegetical homilies and his discourses, his letters on the monastic life,
virginity, and the priesthood. His epistles are valuable from the historical
point of view. The last of them, two letters to Pope Innocent I, written in
404 and 406, respectively, and the seventeen letters to the deaconess Olym-
pias, praise the beauty and sanctifying virtue of Christian suffering.

TEXTS AND DOCUMENTS

Some of the Charges Preferred against St. John Chrysostom at the "Synod of the Oak"

1. A certain monk, John, had been beaten by order of Chrysostom, and
   chained like a demoniac.
2. Chrysostom had sold many valuable articles belonging to the church.
3. He had reviled the clergy.
4. He had called St. Epiphanius a fool and a demon.
5. He had written a book full of abuse of the clergy.
6. He had consecrated Antonius bishop, although he violated people's
   graves.
7. He did not pray either on entering or leaving the church.
8. He had ordained priests and deacons without an altar (not standing at
   the altar).
9. He had consecrated four bishops at once.
10. He received visits from women without witnesses.
11. No one knew to what purpose the revenues of the church were ap-
    plied.
12. He had treated Acacius (Bishop of Beraea) with arrogance, and refused
    to speak to him.
13. He bathed alone.
14. He had ordained many without witnesses.
15. He ate alone, and as immoderately as a cyclops.

QUESTIONS

1. What was the subject matter of the Origenist controversy?
2. Give some details regarding the eschatalogy of Origen.
3. What is the meaning of the term "Apocatastasis"?
4. Describe the character of St. John Chrysostom.
5. Do you think St. John Chrysostom was too severe in his treatment of the Empress Eudoxia?

BIBLIOGRAPHY

St. Jerome and Rufinus.—J. BROCHET, *Saint Jérôme et ses ennemis*, 1905.—DE LABRIOLLE, *op. cit.*, p. 493.—BARDY, *Recherches sur l'histoire du texte et des versions latines du De Principiis*, 1924.—F. CAVALLERA, *Saint Jérôme (Spicilegium Lovaniense)* 1922.—MACKAIL, *Latin Literature*, p. 278.— P. MONCEAUX, *St. Jerome, the Early Years*, (transl. by F. J. SHEED).—E. K. RAND, *Founders of the Middle Ages*.

St. John Chrysostom.—Sources: *P. G.*, t. XLVII–LXIV.—Works: Th. FOERSTER, *Chrysostomus in seinem Verhältnis zur antiochenischen Schule*, Gotha, 1869.—CHASE, *Chrysostom, a Study in the History of Biblical Interpretation*, London, 1887.—E. MARTIN, *Saint Jean Chrysostome*, 1860.—A. PUECH, *Saint Jean Chrysostome* (Coll. *"Les Saints"*), 1900; *Saint Jean Chrysostome et les mœurs de son temps*, 1891.—Chr. BAUR, *Saint Jean Chrysostome et ses œuvres*, Louvain, 1907.—A. MOULARD, *Saint Jean Chrysostome. Le défenseur du mariage et l'apôtre de la virginité*, 1923.—G. BARDY, art. *"Saint Jean Chrysostome,"* in *Dict. de Théol.*—E. LEGRAND, *Saint Jean Chrysostome* (Coll. *"Les Moralistes Chrétiens"*), 1925.—P. BATIFFOL, *Le siège apostolique* (359–451), 1924, ch. V.—CARDINAL NEWMAN, *Historical Sketches*, II, 234; *The Greek Fathers*.

CHAPTER VI

The two outstanding Latin writers of the fourth century are St. Jerome and St. Ambrose.

St. Jerome (d. 420), who was the most erudite of all the Latin Fathers, knew three languages: Latin, Greek, and Hebrew, and had more than an ordinary acquaintance with Chaldaic and Aramaic. At the request of Pope Damasus he undertook, not a translation of the New Testament, but a simple revision of the text by the aid of Latin translations and some Greek manuscripts. The text was immediately adopted into the liturgy, his Psalter receiving the name of *"Psalterium Romanum."* After taking up his quarters in Bethlehem, St. Jerome resolved to revise the Greek translation of the Septuagint, with the aid of the Hexapla of Origen. Of this work there remains only the Book of Job and the Psalms. The revised text of the Psalms was termed *"Psalterium Gallicanum,"* because it was first adopted in Gaul, and is the one found in our Latin bibles.

At the outset of his work, St. Jerome adopted the attitude that all the then existing translations were faulty and that any critical study of the texts should be based on the original Hebrew (*hebraica veritas*). Between 391 and 405, he undertook the gigantic task of making a new Latin translation of the entire Old Testament. At first, the public took alarm. The Roman clergy protested against the boldness of his Scriptural criticism, arguing that he seemed intent upon suppressing all traditional versions, including even so venerable a text as the Septuagint. But posterity justified his action and acknowledged to the fullest extent the worth of his efforts. Slowly but steadily his translation was adopted by the universal Church. In the Middle Ages his version was termed the *Vulgate* and the Council of Trent ordained "that this ancient and vulgate edition, which by the long use of so many centuries has been approved in the Church, . . . be accepted as authentic." [1]

[1] Sess. IV, *On the Canonical Scriptures:* "*Ut haec ipsa vetus et vulgata editio, quae longo tot saeculorum usu in ipsa ecclesia probata est, . . . pro authentica habeatur.*"

St. Jerome also undertook to write a number of commentaries on the Bible, in which he stressed the heretofore much underrated literal interpretation of the sacred text. Composed hurriedly—his commentary on Ephesians was written at the rate of one thousand lines a day—they are collections of materials rather than the product of careful and independent study. This fact explains the many long drawn out paragraphs, and the sometimes endless exposition of opinions, without any attempt at discrimination.

Finally, St. Jerome was a very influential, austere, but kind director of souls. The spirit of Tertullian seemed to live again in his words, so strongly, clearly, and ardently did he preach the virtues he loved above all others: virginity and mortification. He was a master of clear expression, and his style was polished, supple, and transparent. "The defects of his character are well known. His temperament was by nature immoderate and violent, and led him to uphold obstinately a party he had once embraced; his sensitiveness made him chafe at criticism or contradiction. These defects sometimes prompted him to actions and words that were most regrettable. He realized these faults, without always succeeding in overcoming them." [1]

The place occupied in Christian literature by *St. Ambrose* cannot compare with that of St. Jerome. No doubt he made every attempt to overcome the many disadvantages of a tardy and almost improvised vocation by assiduous reading of the Holy Scriptures and earnest study of the Greek Fathers, especially St. Athanasius and the Cappadocians; but he was so absorbed in his duties as a pastor of souls, that in his discourses he aimed rather at being catechetic, positive, and practical, than metaphysical, literary, and classical. Ambrose was first and above all a Christian moralist. This fact is evidenced especially in the most important of all his works, *De Officiis Ministrorum*, where, in conversational language, he lays down rules for the life of the clergy. The plan of the work is based on Cicero's *De Officiis*, and he discusses the *honestum* and the *utile* and the relations between the two. Despite the clearness of the division, the treatise is carelessly composed and, as a result, is more valuable for the information it affords on the state of Christian morality in the fourth century, than for its general argument. The Bishop of Milan also wrote small ascetical treatises that are real masterpieces of refinement. We must cite in partic-

[1] Tixeront, *Patrology*, p. 255 (transl. Raemers).

ular his two little books, *De Virginitate* and *De Virginibus*. St. Ambrose also composed a number of exegetical works, but in commenting upon the biblical text, he is moved only by his desire to serve souls and expound moral lessons. Thanks to allegorical interpretations discreetly borrowed from Origen, he accomplishes this task quite well.

The dogmatic portion of the Saint's work has neither the same interest nor the same originality. His best known contribution in this field is *De Mysteriis*, probably made up of instructions to catechumens, and similar to those of St. Cyril of Jerusalem. They contain valuable information for the history of sacred liturgy. The same is true of the *De Sacramentis*, an anonymous work composed towards the end of the fourth century, in close imitation of the *De Mysteriis*.

What impresses us most in the writings of St. Ambrose is their harmony, charm, and well-tempered force, all of which traits are very becoming to a moralist. St. Ambrose reminds us forcibly of the holy French Bishop Fénelon. In the light of these facts it is easy to understand why he succeeded in gaining so many souls to the cause of virginity.

Juvencus was the first Christian poet. He has left us an evangelical chant, entitled *Evangeliorum Libri Quatuor*, composed about the year 330. Another Spaniard, *Prudentius*, was considerably more productive. Besides his two books against Symmachus, in connection with the restoration of the Altar of Victory, and his *Psychomachia* (Struggle of the Soul), which describes the allegorical battles waged between Christian virtues and pagan vices, we must cite the *Liber Cathemerinon*, which is a collection of twelve pious odes for the different hours of the day, and the *De Peristephanon* (On the Crown of the Martyrs), a collection of fourteen hymns celebrating the lives and deaths of Roman and Spanish martyrs. The diffuseness and bad taste which we meet with at times in the works of Prudentius must not blind us to the real merits of his poetry. He was a born poet, endowed with a lively imagination, Virgilian grace, and a warm and colorful style. Moreover, he was thoroughly acquainted with the technique of versification. The Church has borrowed several of her hymns from the *Cathemerinon*, e. g., "*Quicumque Christum quaeritis*" (Transfiguration), "*O sola magnarum urbium*" (Epiphany), "*Audit tyrannus anxius*," and "*Salvete flores martyrum*" (Holy Innocents).

St. Paulinus has sung the praises of St. Felix of Nola. As a poet, he is far inferior to Prudentius in originality, strength, richness of diction, and especially imagination, although he is his superior in taste, tact, measure, and calm simplicity of expression. At the outset of the fifth century we meet with the Italian poet *Sedulius,* who in his *Carmen Paschale* extols the miracles of Our Lord.

The historical importance of these Christian poets was very considerable. Their influence spread from Rome into the barbarian countries. The writings of Sedulius and Juvencus in particular made a profound and lasting impression upon the Franks and the Anglo-Saxons.

TEXTS AND DOCUMENTS

The Poetry of Prudentius

O SOLA MAGNARUM URBIUM

Bethlehem, of noblest cities
None can once with thee compare;
Thou alone the Lord from Heaven
Didst for us incarnate bear.

Fairer than the sun at morning
Was the star that told His birth;
To the lands their God announcing,
Hid beneath a form of earth.

By its lambent beauty guided,
See, the eastern kings appear;
See them bend, their gifts to offer,
Gifts of incense, gold, and myrrh.

Solemn things of mystic meaning:
Incense doth the God disclose;
Gold a royal child proclaimeth;
Myrrh a future tomb foreshows.

Holy Jesu, in Thy brightness
To the Gentile world displayed,
With the Father and the Spirit,
Endless praise to Thee be paid.

(Transl. by Father Caswall)

QUICUMQUE CHRISTUM QUAERITIS

All ye who would the Christ descry,
Lift up your eyes to Him on high:
There mortal gaze hath strength to see
The token of His majesty.

A wondrous sign we there behold,
That knows not death nor groweth old,
Sublime, most high, that cannot fade,
That was ere earth and Heaven were made.

Here is the King the Gentiles fear,
The Jews' most mighty King is here,
Promised to Abraham of yore,
And to his seed forevermore.

'Tis He the Prophets' words foretold,
And by their signs shown forth of old,
The Father's witness hath ordained
That we should hear with faith unfeigned.

Jesu, to Thee our praise we pay,
To little ones revealed to-day,
With Father and Blest Spirit One
Until the ages' course is done.

(Transl. by Allan G. McDougall)

QUESTIONS

1. Distinguish between the *Psalterium Romanum* and the *Psalterium Gallicanum.*
2. What is meant by the Vulgate, the Septuagint?
3. What criticism would you make of St. Jerome's biblical translations?
4. Which are the Ambrosian hymns?
5. Translate, for the sake of comparison, one of the hymns of St. Ambrose and one of the poems of St. Paulinus.
6. What was the influence of Sedulius and Juvencus upon the Franks and the Anglo-Saxons?

BIBLIOGRAPHY

St. Jerome.—Sources: *P. L.,* XXII–XXX; Letters in *C. V.,* LIV–LX.— Works: A. Röhricht, *Essai sur saint Jérôme exégète,* 1892.—Largent, *Saint Jérôme,* Coll. *"Les Saints,"* 1898.—L. Sanders, *Etudes sur saint Jérôme,* 1903.— J. Brochet, *Saint Jérôme et ses ennemis,* 1906.—J. Turmel, *Saint Jérôme,* 1906.—G. Krutzmacher, *Hieronymus, eine biographische Studie zur alten Kirchengeschichte,* Berlin, 1906.—P. de Labriolle, *Saint Jérôme: Vie de Paul de Thèbes et vie d'Hilarion; Hist. litt. lat. chr.,* p. 445.—F. Lagrange, *Lettres choisies.*—F. Cavallera, *Saint Jérôme,* 2 vols., (*Spicilegium Lovaniense*) 1923. —J. Forget, art. *"Jérôme,"* in *Dict. de Théol.*—Dom Leclercq, *Saint Jérôme,* Brussels, 1927; art. *"Jérôme,"* in *Dict. d'Arch.*—Monceaux and Rand, *op. cit.*

Prudentius.—Sources: *P. L.,* t. LIX–LX.—Works: A. Puech, *Prudence,* 1888.—Boissier, *La fin du paganisme,* II, pp. 123–177.—De Labriolle, *op. cit.,* p. 596.

St. Paulinus.—Sources: *P. L.,* t. LXI; *C. V.,* t. XXIX–XXX.—Works: F. Lagrange, *Histoire de saint Paulin,* 2 vols., 1877.—André Baudrillart, *Saint Paulin,* Coll. *"Les Saints,"* 1904.—P. de Labriolle, *La correspondance d'Ausone et de Paulin de Nôle,* 1910.—G. Boissier, *La fin du paganisme,* II, pp. 57–121.—P. Reinelt, *Studien über die Briefe des hl. Paulinus von Nola,* Breslau, 1904.—Kraus, *Die poetische Sprache des Paulinus Nolanus,* Augsburg, 1918.—Brochet, *La correspondance de saint Paulin de Nôle et de Sulpice Sévère.*

CHAPTER VII

I. Eastern Monachism and Its Influence on the West. The first form of the monastic life to appear in the Church was anachoretism; the second, cenobitism. St. Paul of Thebes, who inaugurated anachoretism, lived for almost one hundred years in the desert, not far from the Red Sea (✝ 340). St. Antony, his disciple, was constrained by a great number of ascetics to direct their spiritual efforts, and so the first groups of hermits came into existence. These monks did not live in complete isolation, but met once a week for the Eucharistic synaxis, and also to receive instructions in common.

The monks directed by St. Antony were located in the Thebaid desert in Upper Egypt, but in the region bordering upon the Delta or lower Egypt there was a considerable number of smaller groups. One of these was located in the Nitrian desert (5000 monks); another was that of the Cellulae, which gave us such famous saints as Macarius of Alexandria (395), and such illustrious writers as Evagrius the Pontian (399); finally, another was situated in the great desert of Sceta.

A spirit of holy emulation animated all these men, although there was danger that, if left to themselves, they might commit indiscretions in the matter of austerity, or even succumb to temptations of vain-glory. To forestall such possibilities it was deemed advisable to group the cells around a church and stress centralized organization as being the best means of furthering the cause of cenobitic life. This task was undertaken by St. Pachomius, who grouped together as many as 7000 monks in the monastery of Tabennesi in Upper Egypt. And so, while St. Benedict endeavored to imbue western monachism with the spirit of family life, St. Pachomius aimed more particularly at massing an army of ascetics at Tabennesi, dividing this army into legions, and partitioning off the religious duties of the week among them. St. Pachomius has left us, in Coptic, a Rule, the Latin translation of which was made by St. Jerome in the year 404.

From Egypt the influence of monachism spread into the East. St. Hilarion, the disciple of St. Antony, transplanted the eremitic life into Palestine, while St. Epiphanius, the future bishop of Salamina, founded in the same country the first institutions of Pachomian cenobitism. The peninsula of Mt. Sinai was soon transformed into a veritable Thebaid, while Syria and Mesopotamia were both gained to the cause. But whereas Egypt witnessed a gradual evolution from eremitism to cenobitism, the East preferred to follow the pure form of the eremitic life. The foregoing fact explains the character of extraordinary austerity which marked this species of uncontrolled monachism. Here we meet with monks who live off grass and shrubs, or again with hermits loaded down with chains, and stylites living on top of pillars, the most famous among the latter being St. Simon, who performed miracles and converted thousands from the summit of his column.

It was about this time that St. Basil undertook a journey into Egypt to investigate for himself the conditions of monastic life. Upon his return, he conceived a form of cenobitism, which admitted of small groups, and which he attempted to realize in a desert in Pontus, on the outskirts of Neo-Caesarea. He himself lived in this desert until the time of his episcopal consecration, in 370. During these years he composed in catechetical form his Longer Rules (*Regulae fusius tractatae*), followed later on by his Shorter Rules (*Regulae brevius tractatae*). These works were masterpieces of human wisdom and well-tempered austerity, and augured well for the period of intellectual culture which was to follow. The *Regulae* met with the same success in the East as the Benedictine Rule in the West. Even at the present time, they continue to guide the destinies of the monks of the separated churches.

To sum up, three forms of monachism flourished in the East during the course of the fourth century: Antonian eremitism, Pachomian cenobitism, and Basilian cenobitism. The form of prayer, however, was the same for all three, and it was impregnated with joy and confidence. A most important feature distinguished the spirituality of the East from the pious movement initiated by the religious experience of St. Augustine in the West. For just like the Greek theologians, who waged war not against the Pelagians, but the Manichaeans, St. Antony stressed the goodness and kindness of human nature rather than its failings and miseries, the freedom of our actions rather than the deficiencies of our conduct.

Egypt was also instrumental in introducing monachism into the West. During the course of his first exile at Treves, in 335, St. Athanasius spent some time at Rome, and while there, came in contact with a group of ladies, Asella, Marcella, Laeta, and Paula, the future protegees of St. Jerome. His account of the austerities practiced by the monks in the East stirred up a spirit of pious emulation in the Christian centers of Rome. On the other hand, westerners were beginning to undertake pilgrimages into the lands of the East, some of them even sojourning there for a while. Towards the year 372, Rufinus repaired to Palestine together with the patrician, St. Melania the Elder, who founded a monastery at Jerusalem. Some years later the granddaughter of this lady, Melania the Younger, distributed her entire fortune among the poor and set out for the East with her husband, Pinian. Shortly after his Baptism, St. Jerome journeyed to the East and spent three years (375–378) in the solitude of the desert of Chalcis, north of Antioch. Here he wrote the biographies of St. Paul of Thebes, St. Hilarion, and St. Malchus, and induced his protegees, Paula and Eustochium, to take up their abode in Palestine. In 336, they settled at Bethlehem and built several monasteries there, one for men under the direction of St. Jerome, and three for women under the direction of Paula.

An unprecedented wave of generosity swept the souls of holy persons in those days. Besides the migrations just mentioned, pious movements were initiated in Rome itself. Within the precincts of the Eternal City, illustrious Christians like Asella, Marcella, Laeta, and their companions, spiritual daughters and correspondents of St. Jerome, erected a real monastery on Mount Aventine. At Milan, St. Ambrose constituted himself the champion and panegyrist of virginity, and from Plaisance, Bologna, and even Mauritania young girls hastened to him in order to consecrate their lives to the service of God. Christian spouses, too, resolved to practice continence and follow the rules of the monastic life; thus Paulinus, an official attached to the Roman consulate, withdrew to Nola with his wife to practice asceticism, and the Roman senator Pammachius, a son-in-law of Paula, consecrated himself to the service of the sick in the hospital erected by Fabiola.

II. The Reaction of Christian Epicureanism. The spirit of Christian asceticism was not calculated to gain the favor of the old Roman world, which grew indignant at such marked contempt for anything that spelled worldly pleasure. This attitude was more pronounced because of the fact that, although paganism had been routed to all external appearances, it had left a deep-seated impression in many souls. True, thanks to the protection of Christian princes, Christianity had taken almost exclusive possession of the Empire. From the conversion of Constantine to the accession of Theodosius, many laws were enacted in favor of Christian worship and Christian morality. Theodosius, in particular, made special efforts in this direction. He urged that Easter and Sundays be reckoned among the ferial days, forbade marriages between Jews and Christians, prohibited actresses from posing as virgins of Christ on the stage, and waged a deadly warfare against shameful vices. But the large crowd of semi-converts who had joined hands with the forces of Christianity threatened almost constantly to sow the seeds of corruption. In external etiquette the members of society and the court of the Emperor were Christian; in matter of fact, however, they were given over to practices of frivolity and, in more than one instance, to open and unrestrained debauchery. If we are to believe Ammianus Marcellinus, 30,000 dancers were allowed to ply their trade in Rome unmolested. These two contradictory phenomena of libertinism and holiness are to be encountered side by side in the Church of the fourth century. The student cannot hope to comprehend the history of this particular period if he will not attribute the right share to each.

At Milan, protests issuing from different sources had already constrained St. Ambrose to deliver two homilies on virginity (378). Towards the year 384, a layman, *Helvidius* by name, from the city of Milan, sought to justify the stand taken in these matters by worldly Christians by false arguments purported to be based on Holy Scripture. According to him, Mary had had several other children after the birth of Our Lord. St. Jerome refuted him by composing his *Adversus Helvidium* (Against Helvidius), the first Latin treatise ever written on Mariology.

A few years later an unbalanced monk by the name of *Jovinian* went so far as to deny the virginal birth of Christ. The conclusion which he drew was that virgins, widows, and married women were on an equal footing, and that one state of life was not to be extolled over another. Inaugurating a system of Christian Epicureanism, Jovinian favored an easy life. To his way of thinking, there was no essential difference between abstaining from food and partaking of the same in thanksgiving; the reward would be the same for all, provided they kept the faith. It was not long before Pope Siricius condemned the writings of Jovinian and forced him to leave the city of Rome. From Rome he went to Milan, where St. Ambrose anathematized him at a synod held around the year 389. At the instance of his friend Pammachius, St. Jerome composed his treatise *Adversus Jovinianum* (Against Jovinian), in which he refuted the heretic and turned his arguments into ridicule.

Finally, about the year 405, a priest from St. Bertrand de Cominges, by the name of *Vigilantius*, attacked the celibacy of the clergy. To his way of thinking, continence was nothing more than a bait for vice, and priests should be compelled to marry for considerations of ordinary morality. It followed that monachism in all its forms was a social evil that ought to be suppressed. Vigilantius exercised some influence in Spain and Gaul, but St. Jerome crushed him in a pointed refutation, referring to him as "Vigilantius, the avowed enemy of pious vigils" (*Vigilantius Dormitantius*).

Somewhat previous to the appearance of Vigilantius, a rigoristic movement was initiated in Spain by *Priscillian,* who advocated an asceticism based on the supposition that man was composed of two elements—a divine element that was good, and a human element that was bad. By the divine element God and man are of the same nature, the human element and the world from which it is derived are the work of another principle, which is evil. Priscillian recruited his followers mainly from among women and educated persons. He made use of apocryphal books and preached a form of strict Encratism, probably based on Manichaean doctrines. Thus he enjoined complete abstinence from the works of the flesh and from the use of meat and wine. He displayed the inflexible obstinacy of an *illuminé*. Condemned by a council held at the request of bishops Hydatius of Merida and Itacius of Ossonoba, at Saragossa in 380, and banished by a decree of Gratian, he repaired to Italy, where he pleaded his cause unsuccessfully with Pope Damasus. Undaunted by his failures, he sought protection among the opulent and the great, and succeeded in having the decree condemning him to exile annulled. Summoned a few years later to appear before a council assembled at Bordeaux, he appealed to the usurper Maximus. This step proved disastrous. Proceedings were instituted against him at Treves, and he was found guilty of immorality and magical practices, and condemned to death. St. Martin of Tours and

St. Ambrose protested against such excessive rigor, and Priscillian's lead-ing accusers, Hydatius and Itacius, were deposed. The sect survived the death of Priscillian, and St. Augustine fought against it in his treatise *Adversus Mendacium* (Against Lying), in which he takes its adepts to task for their tactics of dissimulation. The final condemnation of the heresy was pronounced in 563 by the Council of Braga.

III. The Monastic Apostolate in Gaul in the Fourth Cen-tury: St. Martin. The progress of Christianity in Gaul had been very slow. In the fourth century it had followers only in the large cities; the peasants or inhabitants of the *pagus* (pagans) remaining attached to the popular form of religion, which was a mixture of national Druidism, Greco-Roman mythology, and mysterious importations from the East. To meet this situation, Providence raised up *St. Martin* (316–397).

Martin was born at Sabaria in Pannonia and in his youth enlisted in the militia. It was during this period of his life that the famous incident at Amiens occurred, when, in mid-winter, he cut his tunic in two with his sword and gave one-half of it to a beggar. He was baptized in 339, and after living as a hermit on a wild and uncultivated island in the Mediter-ranean Sea, set out to visit St. Hilary of Poitiers, and founded the first Gallic monastery about five miles from that town, at a place called Ligugé (*Logoteiacus*). Ligugé quickly became the center of a powerful and ex-tremely fertile apostolate. Candidates for Baptism were welcomed and instructed there, and a veritable army of apostles and missionaries received their training within the walls of the monastery and then went out to preach the Gospel throughout the land. Martin with holy audaciousness directed the main attack against the pagan sanctuaries, ordering their destruction and substituting churches in their place. He seems to have focussed his attention upon the central part of Gaul, evangelizing espe-cially Touraine, Anjou, and Isle de France. Elected bishop of Tours, he founded, about two miles from that city, a monastery called Marmoutier (*Majus monasterium*), which later gave many holy bishops to the Church, for instance, St. Maurilius of Angers, St. Victorius of Mans, etc. It is from this period of intense evangelization that the origin of rural parishes dates in Gaul.

As early as 396, Sulpicius Severus, a nobleman from the province of Aquitania, wrote a life of St. Martin of Tours, which met with great success and stirred up a spirit of holy emulation, so that, at the outset of the fifth century, monachism began to flourish in Provence. In the year 410, a rich Roman by the name of *Honoratus* established a monastery in one of the Lerins islands, south of Cannes, which became a real nursery of bishops for Gaul. We need only cite St. Lupus of Troyes and St. Eucherius of Lyons. Towards the year 415, a priest by the name of Cassian founded the monastery of St. Victor at Marseilles.

Before becoming a monk, Cassian had undertaken numerous pilgrimages into the East, where he composed his *Institutiones* and his *Collationes* (Conferences). Apart from a semi-Pelagian note, which mars these works, they contain a highly spiritualized concept of perfection, Christianity being made to consist essentially not in asceticism and mortifications, but in purity of intention and cleanness of heart. The whole is in marked contrast with the intemperate mortification practiced in the East. Cassian was the precursor of St. Benedict. He was above all, says Huby, a psychologist. Some pages of his writings—his analysis of ennui, for instance—are masterpieces of penetration and subtility, interspersed with agreeable touches of humor.

TEXTS AND DOCUMENTS

LIFE OF THE EARLY MONKS

Amongst the numbers of men and youths who, eager for salvation, went to live with Pachomius, there was naturally a very great variety of capacities, of gifts, and of powers, both of body and soul. Some came to him who were already mortified, and soon reached the highest degree of perfection, others progressed more slowly, and some not at all. But these last were always the exception. In order that all might be properly watched over and guided, they were divided into orders and choirs, and each order placed under the inspection of a superintendent, and these again were under the abbot of Tabenna. The remaining monasteries of the order had each a prior, who was subject to the abbot of Tabenna, although the monastery of Pabau was larger and more considerable than that of Tabenna. The hierarchical form was observed from the first beginning of the monastic life. In the various orders of monks all were distributed according to their various talents and capabilities, the weak in the easy occupations, and the strong in the difficult ones; but all, without exception, had to work. There was an order for each work that was required in the monastery—an order of cooks, of gardeners, of bakers, etc. The sick formed one order, and the porters another, which latter consisted of very circumspect and discreet men, because they had charge of the intercourse with the external world, and the preparatory instruction of those who wished to be received. Each order inhabited their own house, which was divided into cells, and three brethren dwelt together in each cell. But there was only one kitchen for all, and they ate in community, but in the deepest silence, and with their hoods drawn down so low over their heads, that no one could see whether his neighbor ate much or little. The holy abbott practised the same rule about food as about prayer; he was not too severe upon some, whilst he gave free scope to the zeal of others. Their usual meals consisted of bread and cheese, salt fish, olives, figs, and other fruits. Boiled vegetables were also served daily, but none ate of them save old men and children, or the infirm, and these also generally availed themselves of the permission of eating some supper, which was always brought to table, to give the brethren an occasion of self-denial.

On Wednesdays and Fridays each superintendent assembled his order, and gave them an instructive or an admonitory exhortation. On Saturdays the superior of each monastery preached once, on Sundays twice. Each order had also its little library, out of which the brethren were provided with books. Silence was faithfully observed, and speaking was only allowed at certain hours. Hospitality was nobly practised towards all comers. They were lodged and fed in apartments near the gate. They might share at will in the church services of the monks, but could not eat with them or dwell amongst them, not even if they were priests or anchorites. There was a separate building for female guests, in which they were hospitably lodged. And this beautiful virtue of hospitality is an inheritance which the monasteries of the East have faithfully preserved to this day, and which they exercise in an admirable manner towards all travellers.

DALGAIRNS, *The Fathers of the Desert,*
Vol. I, pp. 190 f.

QUESTIONS

1. Define Asceticism, Monachism, Eremitism, Cenobitism.
2. Compare the forms of Eastern and Western Monachism.
3. Contrast Pachomian and Basilian Cenobitism.
4. How would you refute the contention that the Eastern cenobites were psychological freaks and that the stylites were sublimated pole-sitters?
5. Make a comparative study of the rules of St. Basil and St. Benedict.
6. Compare Christian asceticism and unorthodox Hindu asceticism.
7. Account for the rise of Christian Epicureanism.
8. What is the importance of the *Adversus Helvidium?*
9. Define Priscillianism.
10. Discuss the beginnings of monachism in Gaul.

BIBLIOGRAPHY

Monachism.—O. Zöckler, *Aszese und Mönchtum*, 2 vols., Frankfort, 1897.—A. Harnack, *Das Mönchtum, seine Ideale, seine Geschichte*, Giessen, 1881.—Dom Leclercq, *Cénobitisme*, in *Dict. d'Arch.*—Dom U. Berlière, *L'ordre monastique des origines au XII⁰ siècle*, Coll. *"Pax,"* 1921.—Dom G. Morin, *L'idéal monastique et la vie chrétienne des premiers jours*, Coll. *"Pax,"* 1921.—F. Martinez, *L'ascétisme chrétien pendant les trois premiers siècles*, 1913.—P. Pourrat, *La spiritualité chrétienne des origines de l'Eglise au Moyen-Age*, 1919.

Egyptian Monachism.—E. Amélineau, *Saint Antoine et les commencements du monachisme en Egypte*, in *Rev. hist. des religions*, t. LXV, 1912.—P. Ladeuze, *Etude sur le cénobitisme pachomien*, 1898.—Butler, *The Lausiac History of Palladius*, 1898–1904, 2 vols.—A. Lucot, *Histoire lausiaque*, in Coll. Hemmer-Lejay, 1912.—E. Amann, art. *"Macaire d'Egypte,"* in *Dict. de Théol.*

Eastern Monachism.—Dom Besse, *Les moines d'Orient antérieurs au concile de Chalcédoine*, 1900.—H. Delehaye, *Les saints stylites*, 1924.—Morison, *St. Basil and his Rule*, Oxford, 1912.—Clarke, *St. Basil the Great. A Study in Monasticism*, Cambridge, 1915.—P. Allard, *St. Basile*, Coll. *"Les Saints,"* 1899.—Gobillot, *Les origines du monachisme chrétien et l'ancienne religion de l'Egypte*, in *Rev. des sciences religieuses*, t. XII (1921).—Dom Leclercq, art. *"Laures palestiniennes,"* in *Dict. d'Arch.*—Ryan, *Irish Monasticism*, 1st Part.

Beginnings of Western Monachism.—A. Thierry, *Saint Jérôme, la société chrétienne à Rome et l'émigration romaine en Terre Sainte*, 1876.—Lagrange, *Lettres choisies de saint Jérôme*, 1900.—G. Goyau, *Sainte Mélanie*, Coll. *"Les Saints,"* 1908.—Génier, *Sainte Paule*, Coll. *"Les Saints,"* 1917.—Card. Rampolla, *Santa Melania giuniore*, Rome, 1906.—Gorce, *Saint Jérôme et la lecture sacrée dans le milieu ascétique romain*, 1926.—*Cath. Encycl.*, art. *"Monachism,"* by Dom Cuthbert Butler.—C. R. de Montalembert, *The Monks of the West*, 2 vols., 1861–1879.—Ryan, *Irish Monasticism*.—T. W. Allies, *The Monastic Life; From the Fathers of the Desert to Charlemagne*, London, 1896.

Priscillianism.—Sources: The writings of Priscillian in *C. V.*, t. XVIII; eight canons of the Council of Saragossa in 380 in Mansi III, 633.—Works: F. Paret, *Priscillianus, ein Reformator des 4. Jahrhunderts*, Würzburg, 1891. A. Puech, in *Journal des Savants*, 1891, and in *Bull. Anc. Lit. et Arch. chr.*, 1912.—Dom Leclercq, *L'Espagne chrétienne*, 1906.—Babut, *Pr. et le Priscillianisme*, in *Bibl. Hautes Etudes, sect. hist. et phil.*, fasc. 169.—G. Morin, *Pro Instantio*, in *Rev. Bénéd.*, 1913, pp. 158 ff. (G. Morin attributes the Priscillian treatises of Schepps to Instantius).

St. Martin.—Lecoy de la Marche, *Saint Martin de Tours*, 1881.—Bulliot, *Mission et culte de saint Martin, d'après les légendes et les monuments,* in *Mémoires de la Soc. éduenne,* 1888.—A. REGNIER, *Saint Martin,* Coll. *"Les Saints,"* 1913.—BABUT, *Saint Martin de Tours,* 1918; refuted by P. DELEHAYE, *Saint Martin de Tours et Sulpice Sévère,* Paris and Brussels, 1920.—P. MONCEAUX, *Saint Martin,* 1927.—CARDINAL NEWMAN, *Church of the Fathers,* ch. X. —SULPICIUS SEVERUS, *Life of St. Martin* (Engl. transl., Benziger Bros.).—W. E. BROWN, *op. cit.*

CHAPTER I

THE BARBARIAN INVASIONS

I. The Four Great Movements of the Barbarian Tribes: Visigoths (376), Germans (406), Huns (451), Ostrogoths (489). The invasion of the barbarians was not an incident that happened of a sudden; it was heralded by a series of events that foretold its coming unmistakably. For a long time the Germans had been seeking to establish themselves in the Empire, and to achieve their purpose, many had resorted to such lawful means as settling in its provinces as colonists, or enlisting in the Roman armies. This pacific invasion was followed by a sudden irruption, caused by the advance of the Asiatic tribe of the Huns, who, camped between the Ural and the Volga, finally penetrated into Europe. They first attacked the Eastern Germans, descendants of the Gothic race, and, after seizing the territory situated between the Black Sea and the Dniester, constrained the Visigoths to seek the protection of Valens, at that time Emperor of the East. Valens placed two provinces at their disposal, Moesia and Thrace. This was the first invasion of the barbarians into the Empire, and it took place in the year 376. Some of these Visigoths were Christians. As early as 325, indeed, the Greek Theophilus had sat in the Council of Nicaea as bishop of the Goths. His successor, *Ulfila,* was the real apostle of the nation. He was born in Cappadocia; after being captured and adopted by the barbarians, he preached the Gospel to them, and even translated the Bible into their language. This Gothic Bible, the earliest literary document in any Teutonic language, has been preserved in part in the famous *Codex Argenteus,* so-called because it is written in letters of silver on purple vellum. Unfortunately, Valens in welcoming the Goths made it a condition of their admittance that they embrace Arianism. He succeeded in persuading Ulfila that the quarrel was of no importance, as far as dogma was concerned, but involved only the pride of the Latins and the Greeks.

The Goths dragged the Arian heresy along with them in all their invasions. The more intelligent among them succeeded in obtaining important posts in the government of the Empire. One of them, *Alaric* by name, on August 24th, 410, took possession of the city of Rome, while his brother, Aistulf, migrated with his people into southern Gaul and established himself so firmly there that Wallia, his successor, obtained title to the land from the Emperor Honorius. Such were the origins of the kingdom of the Visigoths in Toulouse, through which Arianism took root in the West, and its influence spread rapidly to all neighboring peoples.

Pressed in turn by the Huns, the *Germans,* situated on the banks of the Rhine, finally overflowed the narrow limits of their province and swarmed into Gaul. This was the German invasion of the year 406. While the Franks established themselves on the banks of the Rhine and the Meuse, and the Burgundians settled in the valley of the Rhône, the Vandals passed on into Africa. On account of their contacts with the Visigoths of Toulouse, both Burgundians and Vandals were contaminated by Arianism.

It was not long before a persecution broke out in Africa. The cause was twofold: the Catholic episcopate and aristocracy represented the Roman element that had to be uprooted, and the Vandals were fanatical Arians. Under the rule of *Genseric,* efforts were made to increase the number of apostates, and countless were the defections, especially among the opulent and the great, who feared for their position and property. Hunnic initiated an even more violent persecution, and after barring all Catholics from public office, exiled a number of them into the desert. According to Victor of Vita, 4996 of these unfortunates wended their way into the great African wilderness, the majority among them succumbing before reaching their destination and strewing the route of the caravans with their dead bodies.

Huneric followed the policy of his predecessors, and even surpassed them in cunning and cruelty. After convoking all the African bishops at Carthage for what was presumably to be a conference and a debate, he insisted that they take an oath of allegiance to him. Those who refused were found guilty of the crime of *lèse-majesté* and exiled to the island of Corsica; those who acquiesced were accused of having broken the Gospel precept which forbids the use of oaths, and by an odious and at the same time ridiculous sentence, ordered to be deported. Not one bishop escaped. Deprived of their spiritual heads, the faithful were made to suffer a persecution of unprecedented violence. Novel instruments of torture were invented to force them to accept the new Baptism of the heretics. The persecution counted numerous martyrs, as is attested by the *Historia persecutionis Africanae provinciae* (History of the Persecution in the African Province), a work composed by Victor, Bishop of Vita, an eye-witness and himself an exile for the faith. The Roman Council of 487 laid down very precise conditions for the reconciliation of the *lapsi*. Bishops, priests, and deacons could be reconciled only on their deathbed, but those who had been baptized by ruse or violence were excused from all guilt. Huneric died in the same manner as the Emperor Galerius, "a corrupting mass devoured by worms" (*putrefactus et ebulliens vermibus*). His successor, Gunthamund, restored peace and tranquillity to the Church of Africa for a short time, but *Thrasamund,* surnamed "the Arian Julian," resumed hostilities (496–523). He exiled one hundred and twenty bishops to the island of Sardinia; among them Fulgentius of Ruspe, the opponent of semi-Pelagianism. Intervention from Byzantium in the person of Belisarius, a general of Emperor Justinian, towards the end of the sixth century, finally set northern Africa free, although the weakened condition of Catholicism, as the result of so long a crisis, made Africa an easy victim for the domination of the Arabs. Such were the far-reaching consequences of the German invasion of 406.

After being the cause of the first two migrations, the *Huns* themselves poured down upon the Empire. This was the invasion of the year 451. Being nothing more than a devastating torrent, the event would hold no interest for us from a religious standpoint, did it not show forth the moral strength of resistance of Christianity. After crossing the Rhine, *Attila* swept down upon Champagne. The inhabitants of Paris resolved to take to flight, but a virgin, who later was to become the great St. Genevieve, assured them that Christ would protect their city. As a matter of fact her prediction came true. Attila turned his back upon Paris, and directed his steps towards Troyes, where this time the holy Bishop Lupus inspired the inhabitants with confidence. Continuing his march, Attila appeared at the gates of Orleans, but St. Anianus (Aignan), the bishop of the city, had enlisted the help of the Roman General Aëtius, who defeated the Huns at the battle of the Catalaunic Fields. Meeting with failure on all sides in Gaul, Attila turned his eyes upon Italy, but Pope *St. Leo* went out to meet him in the valley of the Po, and by his firm, uncompromising attitude intimidated the general of the Huns, who, in consideration of a tribute, consented to withdraw.

The Church was the only agency which dared to raise its head against the barbarian invaders. The imperial power no longer existed except in name. True, Ricimer made an attempt to instill new life into its fast disintegrating organism (454-472), but Odoacer, who succeeded him for seventeen years, completely abolished the imperial dignity in the West, vested at that time in a mere child, Romulus Augustulus (476). By this time, however, the Huns had joined hands with the *Ostrogoths,* who soon invaded the peninsula (489). *Theodoric,* their leader, assassinated Odoacer and assumed the title, "King of Italy." Theodoric was very tolerant in his policies, but like all sovereigns of Gothic extraction, was tainted with Arianism. And so all the barbarians professed Arianism, except the Franks, who remained pagans.

II. The Church and the Barbarians. Although the Christians were animated with a spirit of true loyalty towards the Empire, the Church realized that she was instituted for all men and not for one special race or people. And so, faithful to her trust, she resolutely set out to win the rude and proud barbarians to the religion of her Founder. The Christians of Africa were less attached, perhaps, than any others to the traditions of Rome, and hence they were the first to take action. In the "City of God," St. Augustine laid down the thesis that the Empire was nothing more than the ephemeral city of men, but that there was an eternal city, into which God would receive all those who believed in Him. Paul Orosius, a disciple of St. Augustine, in his Seven Books against the Pagans, also expressed the idea that the barbarians could be converted. Finally, Salvianus, a priest of Marseilles, went so far as to prove that their rôle as instruments of Divine Providence was to inject new life and vigor into an aging and almost decrepit world. It is certain that in the second half of the fifth century many bishops adopted this religious policy, the success of which was permanently assured by the conversion of Clovis in the year 496.

III. Origins of Christianity in Germany and Great Britain.

The period of the barbarian invasions was characterized by definite progress on the part of Christianity in the West. At first the work of evangelization did not extend beyond the boundaries of the Roman State, although in the Danubian provinces, inhabited by the Celtic races, progress was more rapid than along the banks of the Rhine, where lived the proud and ferocious Germans. True, St. Irenaeus mentions churches and communities in Germany, but no reliable information on this point is available until the opening years of the fourth century, when we learn of the martyrdom of St. Afra at Augsburg and of St. Florian at Lauriacum (Lorsch) in Norica. Soon after the land was dotted with episcopal sees: at Augsburg, Lauriacum, Tiburnia in Carinthia, Saboria (Seben) in the Tyrol, Emona (Laibach) in Carniola, etc. The whole country situated in the neighborhood of the Alps, Norica and Rhetia, professed Christianity, and St. Severinus († 482) exercised the functions of his ministry throughout the length and breadth of the land. These provinces were dependent upon Italy and stood under the jurisdiction of the metropoles of Aquileia and Milan.

In the Rhenish provinces also we find an episcopate at the outset of the fourth century. Agricius of Treves was present in 314, together with Maternus of Cologne, at the Council of Arles. The sojourn of St. Athanasius at Treves (334–337) and the influence of St. Martin strengthened the inhabitants along the banks of the Rhine in their Christian faith. At Arles, St. Maximin of Treves defended Athanasius and was banished (354); at Rimini, Servatius of Tongres declared himself emphatically an anti-Arian. When, in the opening years of the fifth century, the Franks appeared on the horizon, the churches of Treves, Cologne, and Mayence retained their episcopal sees, but the Christians who fled before the Hunnic invasion and took refuge in the islands of the Meuse, transferred the episcopal see of Tongres to Maestricht (Holland).

The first clash of Christianity in Great Britain was not with the barbarians, but with an advanced civilization, the Celtic or Western. Tertullian is the first to testify to the fact that the "Britons are subject to Jesus Christ." He speaks of Christianity as having penetrated regions of Britain which the Roman legions themselves had not reached. In the course of the fourth century progress was even more rapid. St. Bede informs us that, after the persecution of Diocletian, the Britons erected basilicas in honor of their martyrs, Alban, Aaron, and Julius, and that at Canterbury a church was dedicated to St. Martin. A number of witnesses inform us that the primitive Church in Britain received its discipline from Rome. Three of Britain's bishops signed the decrees of the Council of Arles (314) and adopted the Roman regulations regarding the celebration of Easter. Palladius was consecrated bishop of the Scots of Ireland by Pope Celestine A. D. 431. British episcopal sees existed also in the capitals of various provinces, such as York and London.

Towards the end of the fourth century, when the Romans withdrew from Great Britain, the Picts of Caledonia, the Scots of Ireland, the Saxons and the Franks invaded its shores. Despite this political setback, the Britons continued to make progress in their faith, thanks to the growth of a native monachism, modelled on the constitution of the ancient clan, which it completed in the religious order. The priest, who was the real spiritual head, governed the tribe, just as in Gaul the bishop governed the city.

St. Germanus of Auxerre made two attempts to offset the evil influence of semi-Pelagianism in Great Britain, one with St. Lupus in 429, and another with Severus of Treves in 447. He exercised his apostolate especially in South Wales. His disciple Illtud founded the monastery of Llantwit, and, with the assistance of the Britons David, Gildas, and Cadoc, established a sort of missionary monachism. From Wales, Christianity spread to Amorican Britain.

TEXTS AND DOCUMENTS

THE DEATH OF ST. ALBAN

On the top of this hill, St. Alban prayed that God would give him water, and immediately a living spring, confined in its channel, sprang up at his feet, so that all men acknowledged that even the stream had yielded its service to the martyr. For it was impossible that the martyr, who had left no water remaining in the river, should desire it on the top of the hill, unless he thought it fitting. The river then having done service and fulfilled the pious duty, returned to its natural course, leaving a testimony of its obedience. Here, therefore, the head of the undaunted martyr was struck off, and here he received the crown of life which God has promised to them that love Him. But he who laid impious hands on the holy man's neck was not permitted to rejoice over his dead body; for his eyes dropped upon the ground at the same moment as the blessed martyr's head fell.

At the same time was also beheaded the soldier, who before, through the divine admonition, refused to strike the holy confessor. Of whom it is apparent, that though he was not purified by the waters of Baptism, yet he was cleansed by the washing of his own blood, and rendered worthy to enter the Kingdom of Heaven. Then the judge, astonished at the unwonted sight of so many heavenly miracles, ordered the persecution to cease immediately, and began to honour the death of the saints, by which he once thought that they might have been turned from their zeal for the Christian faith. The blessed Alban suffered death on the twenty-second day of June, near the city of Verulam, . . . where afterwards, when peaceable Christian times were restored, a church of wonderful workmanship, and altogether worthy to commemorate his martyrdom, was erected. In which place the cure of sick persons and the frequent working of wonders cease not to this day.

At that time suffered Aaron and Julius, citizens of the City of Legions, and many more of both sexes in divers places; who, after they had endured sundry torments, and their limbs had been mangled after an unheard-of manner, when their warfare was accomplished, yielded their souls up to the joys of the heavenly city.

When the storm of persecution ceased, the faithful Christians, who, during the time of danger, had hidden themselves in woods and deserts and secret caves, came forth and rebuilt the churches which had been levelled to the ground; founded, erected, and finished the cathedrals raised in honour of the holy martyrs, and, as if displaying their conquering standards in all places, celebrated festivals and performed their sacred rites with pure hearts and lips. This peace continued in the Christian churches of Britain until the time of the Arian madness, which, having corrupted the whole world, infected this island also, so far removed from the rest of the world, with the poison of its error; and when once a way was opened across the sea for that plague, straightway all the taint of every heresy fell upon the island, ever desirous to hear some new thing, and never holding firm to any sure belief.

BEDE, *Ecclesiastical History*, p. 17
(Transl. SELLAR)

QUESTIONS

1. Which causes led up to the invasions of the barbarians?
2. Locate on a map of Europe the exact position occupied by the Visigoths, the Germans, the Huns, and the Ostrogoths.
3. Explain the presence of the Arian heresy in northern Africa.
4. What was the character of the persecution in the province of northern Africa?
5. Trace the history of the early sees of Canterbury, London, and York.

BIBLIOGRAPHY

Invasions.—Sources: St. Jerome; *The Chronicles of Marcellinus* (379–534); Hydatius, (379–468); Prosper (379–455); Orosius, *Historiarum libri III.*— Works: Ozanam, *Etudes germaniques*, 2 vols., 1845–49.—Geoffroy, *Rome et les Barbares*, 1874.—Fustel de Coulanges, *Histoire des institutions politiques de l'ancienne France, l'Invasion germanique*, 2nd edit., 1886.—Kurth, *Les origines de la civilisation moderne*, t. I.—Grisar, *Histoire de Rome et des Papes.*—G. Boissier, *Le christianisme et l'invasion des barbares* in *Rev. des Deux-Mondes*, 1890.—Villari, *Le invasioni barbariche in Italia*, Milan, 1900. —Cardinal Newman, *Historical Sketches*, vol. II, pp. 365–430 and vol. III, pp. 105–129.

The Vandals in Africa.—Dom Leclercq, *L'Afrique chrétienne*, t. II.— F. Martroye, *L'Occident à l'époque byzantine. Goths et Vandals*, 1904; *Genséric, La conquête vandale en Afrique et la destruction de l'empire d'Occident*, 1907; art. *"Genséric,"* in *Dict. d'Arch.*—A. Audollent, art. *"Afrique,"* in *Dict. d'Hist.*

The Church and the Barbarians.—Sources: Orosius, *Historiae adversus Paganos*, P. L., XXXI, 663–1172; *C. V*, V, 1–564.—Salvian, P. L., LIII; M G H, I, I.—St. Augustine, *De Civitate Dei*, P. L., XLI, 11–804, *C. V*, XL.— Works: Kurth, *Les origines de la civilisation moderne*, I; *The Church at the Turning Points of History; Clovis*, Introduction.—G. Boissier, *La fin du paganisme*, II.—E. Méjean, *Paul Orose et son Apologétique contre les païens.* —P. Richard, art. *"Allemagne,"* in *Dict. d'Hist.*—André Baudrillart, *Saint Geneviève*, Coll. *"Les Saints."*—R. Monlaur, *Sainte Geneviève*, 1924.

Germany.—Hauck, *Kirchengeschichte Deutschlands*, t. I, Leipzig, 1898.— P. Richard, art. *"Allemagne,"* in *Dict. d'Hist.*—André Baudrillart, *Saint Séverin, apôtre du Norique* (Coll. *"Les Saints"*).

England and Ireland.—Hunt, *The English Church from its foundation to the Norman Conquest*, London, 1899.—Spence, *The Church of England*, t. I, London, 1897.—Dom Gougaud, *Christianity in Celtic Lands*, 1911.—Dom Cabrol, *L'Angleterre chrétienne*, 1909.—J. Chevalier, art. *"Angleterre,"* in *Dict. d'Hist.*—De Smedt and De Backer, *Acta SS. Hiberniae*, Lille, 1891.—Bury, *Life of St. Patrick and his Place in History*, London, 1905.—Riguet, *Saint Patrice*, Coll. *"Les Saints,"* 1911.—Dom Leclercq, art. *"Irlande"* and *"Iona"* in *Dict. d'Arch.*—J. Healy, *Insula Sanctorum et Doctorum; Ancient Irish Schools and Scholars; The Life and Writings of Saint Patrick.*—T. J. Shahan, *St. Patrick in History*, 1905.—J. M. Flood, *Ireland and the Early Church*, Dublin.—G. Metlake, *Life and Writings of St. Columban.*—E. J. McCarthy, *Montalembert's St. Columban.*—B. Fitzpatrick, *Ireland and the Foundations of Europe.*

CHAPTER II

The conversion of Ireland to Christianity dates from the fifth century. Zimmer's contention that the foundation of the Irish Church was laid by half-Romanized Britons in the fourth century, rests on such feeble evidence that it cannot be defended. A more recent theory, that St. Patrick was, indeed, the apostle of Ireland, but lived in the early third or the late second century, must be described as fantastic. In this connection it should be remembered that the country districts of western and northern Gaul were heathen territory to the end of the fourth century and that Christianity in Britain must have been confined largely to the Latin-speaking population of the Roman towns, down to the collapse of Roman power, about A. D. 410.

That there were Christians in Ireland in 431 is certain, for in that year, Pope St. Celestine I consecrated the Deacon Palladius and sent him as first bishop "to the Irish who believed in Christ." Two years earlier, St. Germanus of Auxerre and St. Lupus of Troyes had been sent by Celestine to Britain to free the Church in that country from the virus of the Pelagian heresy. It is reasonable to infer that when they returned to Gaul and acquainted the Pope with the results of their mission, they added a reference to the neighboring island of Hibernia, and recommended that its struggling Christian communities should receive encouragement and help. It was in consequence of this recommendation that Palladius was commissioned to proceed to Ireland.

The new bishop seems to have sailed from South Britain and landed on what is now the Wicklow coast, whence he wended his way westward through the vale of Glenmalure, to a more popular district about Donard. According to a late Irish tradition, than which, however, no better has been preserved, he made some conversions, established a few churches, and then died "in the territory of the Picts," a phrase which may mean no more than the Pictish territory of the Loigse, a few miles farther west. His place at the head of the mission was taken by the man who, in the mysterious designs of Providence, was to be the apostle of the Irish nation, St. Patrick. It is the clear and unvarying testimony of Irish records that the coming of this Saint as an evangelist to Ireland took place in A. D. 432.

St. Patrick was born in the Roman province of Britain, in 385 or 386. His father, Calpurnius, was a decurion or member of the municipal council of his native town, and thus a responsible officer of local government under the imperial Roman authority. He had likewise been ordained a deacon, as his father, Potitus, had been ordained a priest, according to the custom, still common in the fourth century, of seeking recruits for the clerical state among men distinguished in the conduct of civil affairs. The family enjoyed considerable social prestige, for Patrick speaks more than once of the nobility of his birth, and easy circumstances, for Patrick refers to the paternal *villula* beside the town and the men-servants and maid-servants of the household.

Owing to the growing weakness of the Roman power in Britain, Irish raiders were able to enter that province and carry off rich booty in slaves and property. In a mighty foray, in 401, the boy Patrick was captured and carried to Ireland, where he was sold as a thrall to a Pictish aristocrat near Lough Neagh. "I was then," he writes in his *Confession*, "about sixteen years of age. I knew not the true God; and I went into captivity in Ireland with many thousands of persons, according to our desert. . . . And there the Lord opened the understanding of my unbelieving heart, that even though late, I might call my faults to mind, that I might turn with all my heart to the Lord, my God, . . . who protected me and comforted me as a father does his son." On the Antrim hillsides an extraordinary change took place in the young slave's soul. "After I came to Ireland tending flocks was my daily task, and constantly I used to pray through the day. Love of God and the fear of Him increased more and more, and faith grew and the spirit was moved, so that in one day I would say as many as a hundred prayers and at night nearly as many, so that I used to stay even in the woods and on the mountain [for this purpose]. Before daybreak I used to arouse myself to prayer in snow and frost and rain, and I felt no hurt, nor was there any sluggishness in me, for the spirit was fervent within me."

Six years passed in this manner. Then one night he heard in sleep a voice which whispered: "Thou dost well to fast; soon shalt thou go to thine own country." Some time afterwards came the eagerly awaited "answer": "Behold, thy ship is ready!" He journeyed in much peril, perhaps two hundred miles, to a place on the coast which he had never seen before, and where he knew no man. A ship lay ready to sail, and Patrick asked to be taken on board. The captain at first refused, but quickly changed his mind and admitted the fugitive slave as a passenger. It is curious to note that the cargo consisted of Irish hounds, probably intended for some Gallic mart, for the nobles of that country were passionately devoted to the chase.

The ship arrived, probably in early summer of 407, to find western Gaul cruelly devastated by barbarian hordes. So appalling had the situation become that Patrick and his companions wandered through a "desert" for twenty-eight days, and all but perished of hunger. They had the misfortune, too, of being captured by a roving band, in whose hands they remained for sixty days. Patrick's movements during the next few years are very obscure. It is likely that he visited southern Gaul, Italy, and the "isles" of the Tyrrhenian sea (among them Lerins, where he saw something of the monastic life), before he returned to his own country.

To Britain, at any rate, he returned, according to the "answer" received in the vision of the night during slavery. His family greeted him as a long-lost son and begged him to settle permanently in their midst. This was, naturally, his own desire; but a new and heavenly call began, just then, to agitate his soul. It was God's will, he now realized, that he should return to the land of his slavery and shame, and spend his life preaching the Christian faith to its pagan inhabitants.

Between Britain and Gaul there was, at this period, a traditionally close connection in matters ecclesiastical. It seems, then, that Patrick returned to Gaul to prepare himself for his missionary career. To succeed in this purpose, he would obviously need to engage in serious theological study, secure the guidance of prudent and holy men, and win approval and support from the competent authorities. According to Irish records, he appears to have attached himself to the Church of Auxerre, under that city's celebrated bishops, Amator and Germanus. His desire to undertake missionary work in Ireland became well known; but difficulties lay in the way of its realization—above all his admitted ill-success in study and a kind of general impression made upon those about him that he was hardly the man required for so arduous an enterprise. Yet, when

St. Germanus was in Britain, in 429, and a missionary expedition to Ireland was discussed, Patrick was mentioned by a friend as a suitable person to lead it. Later, however, in Gaul, when the matter came up for formal decision, Patrick was dropped by his friend, and so emphatically rejected that the memory of the incident continued to cause him grievous pain. We may take it that Palladius was the candidate then selected, for it is he who was consecrated by Pope Celestine as bishop for Ireland. Soon afterwards Patrick also received permission to proceed as a missionary to that country, and was already on the way thither when news arrived of Palladius' death. This caused the ecclesiastical authorities to change their plans. Patrick was chosen to succeed the deceased prelate, and was consecrated bishop, probably at Auxerre, before he resumed his journey to Ireland.

Success was to crown his efforts. According to Irish tradition, he first converted the people of eastern Ulster, among whom his youth had been spent as a swineherd. In due course he made his way to Tara, where the High King, Loiguire, had his chief fortress—a near approach, in the circumstances of the time, to a national capital. Loiguire remained a pagan himself, but he raised no objection to a *modus vivendi* which left Patrick free to preach wherever he pleased. It must be said that outside of the rich midland district which was the High King's personal patrimony, such a permission could profit little, unless the good will of the minor kings was also secured. Older dynasts, as a rule, remained obdurate in their paganism, but the younger princes showed a welcome readiness to listen to the Gospel message. This, again, would be of little value unless the freemen of the State accepted the new religion, for the political constitution of Celtic Ireland was democratic in spirit, though monarchical in form. Incessant preaching to the populace was, therefore, necessary. As time went on, the Saint extended the field of his activity to Connacht, where his fast of forty days on Crochan Aigli, Croaghpatrick, became fixed in the people's memory. He also labored in Munster, where Ardpatrick in southern Limerick has claims to rank as his chief foundation. Leinster was evangelized, in the main, by his two episcopal helpers, Auxilius and Iserninus.

A date of importance in the work of conversion is A. D. 439, when three bishops, Auxilius, Secundinus, and Iserninus, were sent to Patrick from abroad, probably from Auxerre. The see occupied by Secundinus lay about five miles south of Tara, and is still called "the church of Secundi-nus," Domnach Sechnaill, in an English dress, Dunshaughlin. Secundinus, before his death in 447, composed a laudatory poem in honor of St. Patrick. He is found associated with his master in one of two remarkable documents connected with the early Irish Church. One is the canon which decrees that "if any difficult questions arise in this Island, they are to be referred to the Apostolic See." The second document is a collection of canons addressed "to the priests and deacons and to all the clergy" by Patrick, Auxilius, and Iserninus, bishops, and probably belongs to the period 447-459, the last-mentioned year being that in which Auxilius died. These documents suggest, too, that as late as 447 there were but four bishoprics in Ireland, those administered by St. Patrick himself and by the three bishops sent to his aid from Gaul.

Treating of the year 441, the Annals of Ulster record that Leo became bishop of Rome and Patrick was approved in the Catholic faith. This is shown by Bury to mean that Patrick, leaving Ireland under the care of the bishops who had recently become his colleagues, made the long journey to Rome and assured the Vicar of Christ that the foundations of the Irish Church had been securely laid. He may also have announced to the Pope his intention of establishing a metropolitan see at Armagh. As a mark of the great Pontiff's approval he received and carried back to Ireland a portion of the relics of Saints Peter and Paul, Stephen and Lawrence, a treasure that was preserved and reverenced at Armagh and numbered for centuries among the chief insignia of St. Patrick's successors.

The foundation of Armagh is chronicled in the Annals under the year 444, after the return of St. Patrick from Rome. He is likely to have chosen this site because of its close proximity to Emain Macha, the ancient capital of the Ulster Kings. The city has ever since remained the ecclesiastical capital of the country.

St. Patrick refers more than once in his *Confession* to the amazing success of his missionary endeavors. His converts were counted literally by the thousands. The ordination of clergy is mentioned no less than three times, nor is the detail omitted that they were ordained "everywhere." They must have been, for the greater part, of native Irish stock. Before St. Patrick died, he conferred the episcopal Order upon some of these. According to a later legend, the number of bishops consecrated by the Saint was two hundred, nay, even three hundred odd, but trustworthy records imply that St. Patrick by no means multiplied sees in such a fantastic manner.

It is evident from the *Confession* that St. Patrick held the monastic state in veneration and thought it a veritable triumph of divine grace when youths and maidens of his flock became monks and nuns. He records himself with joy that "sons of the Irish and daughters of chieftains are seen to become monks and virgins of Christ." These were regarded by him as the fairest fruits of his missionary labors. Even the slave girls showed heroism in their following of the higher vocation; "but the Lord gave grace to many of his handmaids, for, though forbidden to embrace the life of virginity, they insisted bravely on doing so." But whatever the Saint's predilection for the monastic state, he placed the ecclesiastical government of the country in the hands of bishops, not in those of abbots. This is equivalent to saying that he organized the Irish Church like every other church in Christendom.

Points of doctrine on which St. Patrick laid particular stress were the dogma of the Holy Trinity, the necessity of divine aid in all profitable human activity, and obedience to the Apostolic See. A clear exposition of the doctrine of the Eucharist is found in a hymn, *"Sancti venite,"* which tradition ascribes to his helper, Secundinus. This hymn forms part of the so-called Antiphonary of Bangor (compiled about 680), and is the oldest Eucharistic hymn in existence. It was usually sung at Mass during the communion of the priests, just before that of the laity.

St. Patrick, when he aspired to do missionary work in Ireland, was held up to ridicule as a man of defective education and inferior character. Certain of his British countrymen, ecclesiastics and men of learning, continued to speak of him as an unworthy chief pastor of the Irish Church. To vindicate his reputation, he penned, in the years before his death, his *Confession*. In this interesting document he tells the extraordinary story of God's Providence in his regard—how out of the world of men God selected him, a careless boy, in an obscure provincial town, a captive slave, a dull student, to be a marvellously successful worker in a fertile but neglected vineyard. It has been truly said that "this *Confession* is one of the great documents of history and explains to us better than all the historians, how barbarism was tamed and civilization saved. Imagine a young lad of tender years, son of a Roman citizen, torn away by fierce raiders from his parents and people, no doubt amid scenes of bloodshed and ruin; kept for years the despised chattel of a petty chieftain herding flocks in a bleak land of bog and forest. Think that the ruling sentiment that grew out of this pitiful experience was one of boundless love and devotion towards the people that had done him such terrible wrongs, so that, when he had regained his freedom by flight, in nightly visions he heard their voices calling him back to them, and freely and eagerly made up his mind to spend himself altogether in their service. It was this spirit that subdued the ferocity of fierce plundering rulers and warlike peoples."

A second document from his pen is the *Letter Denouncing Coroticus*. This British kinglet ruled on the Rock of Clyde, the fortress of Dunbarton. It happened that some of St. Patrick's converts, who had received Baptism, were massacred on the morrow by a body of fighting forces landed in Ireland by Coroticus, and others carried off into slavery. Efforts to secure their release were derided by the raiders. St. Patrick, justly indignant, addressed a letter to the British clergy and faithful, calling upon them to expel Coroticus and his followers from their communion.

St. Patrick died on March 17, 461, and was buried at Saul, probably within the first church which he had founded. Two treasures connected with the apostle survived into the later centuries—a crozier and a four-sided iron bell. The crozier, said to have been presented to the Saint by Our Lord Himself, and therefore called the "bachall Iosa" (staff of Jesus), was burned as an object of superstition by English Lutherans in 1538. The bell, enclosed in a beautiful shrine made to contain it about 1100, is still preserved. It was rung, after a silence of many generations, at the final High Mass of the Eucharistic Congress held in Dublin in 1932.

The eminent significance of St. Patrick in Irish history has always been recognized. He organized whatever Christianity already existed; he converted the great mass of pagan Ireland, and he brought the Island formally into the brotherhood of Christian nations. When he died, the faith preached by Christ and his Apostles was the religion of the country. He became ere long the hero of the race, and his name continued to be cherished with a fidelity and enthusiasm for which there is no parallel.

From the death of St. Patrick to the end of the fifth century, both Gaul and Britain were overrun by barbarian bands, so that little help could be expected from the Church in these countries. Christian Ireland, as yet almost in its infancy, was thus thrown back upon its own resources.

It is a striking tribute to the manner in which St. Patrick had done his work, that all demands were successfully met. At this time, the monastic life was becoming increasingly popular everywhere in the West. The influence of Lerins was felt as far north as Britain. Nowhere did the monastic ideal find more ardent admirers than in Ireland. In some mysterious way it seemed to make an irresistible appeal to the Irish nature. After A. D. 500, the British Church enjoyed an era of comparative peace, and intimate relations were resumed between that country and Ireland. The result was that monastic establishments began to multiply.

St. Finnian of Clonard seems to have played the biggest part in bringing about this transformation; though St. Enda of Arran, who had been trained in the monastery called *Candida Casa* in Galloway, is also mentioned as a pioneer of Irish monasticism. St. Finnian had been educated by a disciple of St. Patrick, named Fortchern, a man who on his mother's side belonged to the British nation. It was probably through him that St. Finnian came into contact with St. Codoc of Llangarvan, then the leading monastic personage within British territory. St. Finnian's disciples were the "twelve apostles of Ireland," all celebrated abbots and founders of monasteries. Before the end of the sixth century houses of regular religious observance were scattered in immense numbers over the face of the country.

Monasteries well-known to fame were Clonard, Clonmacnois, Derry, Durrow, Clonfert, Birr, Terryglass, Aghaboe, Devenish, Lorrha, Glasnevin, Bangor, Moville, Cloneenagh, Clonfert-Mulloe, Ferns, Lynally, Glendaloch, Tuam, Dromore, Scattery Island, Rosscarbery, Mungret, Roscommon, Cork, Rahan, Lismore, as well as older foundations at Kildare, Monasterboice, and Louth, and possibly still older foundations at Sierkieran in Ossory, Ardmore in Waterford, Beggary Island in Weford Harbour, and Emly in Tipperary. Yet more ancient episcopal churches, like Armagh, Trim, Slane, Sletty, Coleraine, and Ardstraw, were attracted by the movement and passed into the government of prelates who combined the offices of bishop and abbot.

Since the clergy and monks displaced and superseded the native learned class of druids as "philosophers and theologians" of the nation, it was taken for granted from the beginning that they should devote themselves to serious study. Thus, in the lives of sixth century saints application to letters is mentioned as a matter of course. By the year 600, the ancient native learning inherited from the Celtic past, and the new Latin learning introduced with Christianity, were combined in the monastic schools. Having accepted, assimilated, and fostered native culture, the influence of these schools in Ireland was profound; having adopted also classical culture, which the Church saved for Europe, Irish churchmen were able to proceed to the continent and played a considerable part in repairing the intellectual as well as the spiritual losses caused by the barbarian invasions.

In consequence of the fact that the ablest leaders in the country devoted to religion and learning all the energy and ardor displayed by their ancestors in military pursuits; that monasteries and ecclesiastical institutions were numerous and well-filled; that, therefore, an enormous proportion of the population led lives of high and even heroic virtue, Ireland merited in the seventh century the proud title, "Island of Saints and Scholars."

TEXTS AND DOCUMENTS

St. Patrick Receives His Vocation

And again, after a few years, I was in Britain with my kindred, who received me as a son, and in good faith besought me that at all events now, after the great tribulations which I had undergone, I would not depart from them any more.

And there in truth I saw, in a vision of the night, a man named Victoricus, coming, as it were, from Ireland with countless letters. And he gave me one of them, and I read the beginning of it, which was entitled *The Voice of the Irish;* and while I was reading aloud the beginning of the letter, I thought I heard at that very moment the voice of them who dwelt by the wood of Fochlut, which is nigh unto the western sea. And they cried, as with one mouth: We beg of thee, holy youth, to come and walk once more among us. And I was moved to the bottom of my heart and could read no further. And so I awoke. Thanks be to God that after many years the Lord granted to them according to their cry.

QUESTIONS

1. What do you know of the youth of St. Patrick up to the period when he escaped from slavery?
2. Describe St. Patrick's "call" and his selection by his ecclesiastical superiors as apostle to the Irish nation.
3. When, and under what circumstances, was Armagh chosen as the Irish primatial see?

4. Was St. Patrick a successful missionary? Why did he write his "Confession"?

5. Which were the chief monasteries of sixth and seventh century Ireland?

BIBLIOGRAPHY

The Beginnings of Christianity in Ireland.—Dom Louis Gougaud, *Christianity in Celtic Lands; Gaelic Pioneers of Christianity.*—J. M. Flood, *Ireland and the Early Church,* Dublin.—Most Rev. J. Healy, *Ireland's Ancient Schools and Scholars,* New York; *The Life and Writings of St. Patrick.*—T. J. Shahan, *St. Patrick and History.*—Heinrich Zimmer, *The Celtic Church in Britain and Ireland.*—Bury, *Life of St. Patrick and His Place in History,* London, 1905.—B. Fitzpatrick, *Ireland and the Foundations of Europe.*—Riguet, *Saint Patrice,* (Coll. *"Les Saints"*).—J. Healy, *Insula Sanctorum et Doctorum; Ancient Irish Schools and Scholars; The Life and Writings of St. Patrick.*—Mrs. T. Concannon, *St. Patrick, His Life and Mission.*

CHAPTER III

The life of St. Augustine is revealed to us in part in his "Confessions," the most touching book in antiquity because it tells the inner story of a soul. *Aurelius Augustinus* was born November 13, 354, at Tagaste, an insignificant town in Numidia. His father, Patricius, was a heathen, but his mother, Monica, belonged to a Christian family. In consequence of a prejudice current in those days, Monica put off the Baptism of her child. Augustine completed his literary studies at Carthage, a gay city in those days. It was here that he contracted an illegitimate union, which lasted for sixteen years, and joined the sect of the Manichaeans. He taught rhetoric successively at Tagaste, Carthage, and Rome, and through the good offices of the prefect Symmachus, finally obtained a chair of rhetoric in Milan (384). The sermons of St. Ambrose, who was bishop of that city at the time, made such a deep impression upon him that he resolved to study the Christian religion. The crisis came in the month of July, 386, on the day when, hearing a voice crying out to him: *"Tolle, lege"* (Take and read) he opened the Bible at the verse in the Epistle to the Romans, in which St. Paul recommends that we "put on Jesus Christ." After eight months spent in the solitude of Cassiciacum, near Milan, Augustine received Baptism. On his return journey to Africa, he had the misfortune of losing his mother by death at Ostia (387). The recital of his "Confessions" ends here, and his public life begins.

In 391, on a visit to Hippo, he was designated by the voice of the people to become the coadjutor of Valerius, the old and venerable bishop of that city. He succeeded Valerius in 396, and for the next thirty-five years was the outstanding leader of the African hierarchy and arbiter of western controversies: Donatism and Pelagianism.

I. St. Augustine and Donatism. Donatism was not a new heresy at the time of St. Augustine, but had already been in existence for almost a century. It would be hard to explain how a local quarrel, originating in the election of a bishop, could degenerate into what was almost a civil war, if one did not take into account the spirit of independence characteristic of the African mind. The movement quickly assumed the proportions of an insurrection against Roman domination, the Donatists organizing themselves into wild and fanatical bands which spread terror and death. Things came to such a pass that when, in the year 347, the Emperor Constantius sent two officers, Paul and Macarius, to pacify the rebels, a military expedition had to be organized, which apparently succeeded in crushing the opposition.

The Emperor Julian legally rehabilitated the Donatists, and even authorized them to seize basilicas that had been restored to Catholics. They did not wait for a second invitation, but again set about confiscating Christian property at the point of the sword. After the death of the Apostate, they retained their freedom of worship, the State remaining content to offer mere negative protection to African Catholicism by forbidding all proselytizing by heretics. It was this motive which prompted the Emperor Valentinian to prohibit bishops from rebaptizing under pain of being unworthy of the priesthood.

With the advent of the Emperor Theodosius, legislation against the Donatists assumed a more severe form. In 392, a law was passed which imposed a fine of ten pounds in gold upon any heretical bishop who held ordinations. The African Catholics at first refused to make use of such weapons, and followed St. Augustine in his endeavor to win over the Donatists by friendly discussions. The Council of Carthage, convened in 401, suggested that a conference between Catholic and Donatist bishops be held, but the Donatists strenuously objected. By a clever gesture of indignation their leader, Primianus of Carthage, declared that "it would be monstrous to gather together in the same place the sons of martyrs and the race of traitors." From that moment they redoubled their violence, refusing all discussion and even attempting to murder several bishops, among them Augustine himself. This forced the Catholics into action. At a council held at Carthage in 404, a number of bishops requested that the schismatics be made to return to the Church, and in 405 the Emperor Honorius issued an edict which abolished Donatism and condemned all recalcitrants to exile. The edict did not produce its effect, however, and Donatism continued to recruit members from fanatical peasants and slaves. Finally, at the instance of St. Augustine, the Emperor, in the year 411, convoked a conference between Catholic and Donatist bishops at Carthage. The question of personalities, which had been the root of the whole trouble for a century, was completely aired, and the Donatists had to admit that they could not prove that Caecilian had been a traditor. From that moment on, the heresy ceased to be a danger. By grouping around him the African episcopate, Augustine had crushed the enemy with better results than all the imperial armies. The Donatist schism did not, however, fully die out until the Arabic invasion in the seventh century.

II. St. Augustine and Pelagianism. St. Augustine had no sooner disposed of Donatism than he encountered another heresy, which was all the more dangerous as it posed as an ascetic reaction against Epicureanism. The leader and founder of this sect was a British monk by the name of *Pelagius*. Pelagius was a learned man, austere in his manner of living, lacking, however, in moderation, and, as a consequence, extremely severe in his direction of souls. He did not teach that we should plead excuse for our sins on the ground of human frailty, nor that we should seek the remedy in a grace which is stronger than our corrupted nature, but, on the contrary, inaugurated a system in which man was left to his own resources, unlimited power entrusted to his will, and the divine action restricted to mere exterior intervention. In his opinion, as in that of Jean Jacques Rousseau in later years, man is born good and with a wholesome will power. In the very language of the Pelagians themselves, freedom is a perfectly poised balance, the scales of which are affected only by the will. Man, therefore, is naturally impeccable, and, can never sin. According to Pelagius, Adam's sin was personal, and hence human nature is untainted by original sin and so perfectly poised that it can dispense with the divine assistance. As a matter of fact, Pelagius admitted the existence of only external helps on the part of God: graces of instruction and example furnished by the Old Testament, and especially by Jesus Christ, which exert an influence upon us only inasmuch as they are rays of light originating from without. Christ Himself is our model in this, but nothing more; He redeemed us, but only by the example of His holy life.

In the matter of salvation, therefore, we are self-dependent; born with powers as incorrupt as those of our first parents before the Fall, we can reach Heaven by our own spiritual energies. God intervenes only as a guide, who points out the way, or as a paymaster, who apportions salaries according to merit. Pelagianism is a cold and proud system of religion, a form of Stoicism scarcely touched by Christianity, in which Redemption has no purpose or meaning, since the Incarnate Word neither redeems nor quickens us. The Church sensed the danger and immediately sought to meet it. In this work she could find no better champion than Augustine. The whole being of this man, who was so humble in spirit and in whom the sentiment of human corruption and gratitude for the work of grace was so profound, rose up in rebellion against this most degenerate kind of naturalism.

When Rome, in which city they had secretly sown the seeds of their destructive doctrine, was sacked by Alaric, Pelagius and Coelestius fled to Africa. Coelestius preached his heresy at Carthage, but the Deacon Paulinus, the future biographer of St. Ambrose, brought accusations against him and carried to Aurelius of Carthage six propositions which were condemned at a provincial council held in 411. At the same time, Augustine, in answer to many requests and consultations, published in rapid succession his treatises, *De peccatorum meritis et remissione, De spiritu et littera, De natura et gratia* (413), and *De perfectione justitiae hominis.*

The opposition was too strong for Pelagius. Being a former director of consciences, he had come in contact with the illustrious Melania. He resolved, therefore, to imitate St. Jerome and pass over to Palestine, whither his reputation as an ascetic had preceded him. Here, however, he ran afoul of St. Jerome in person, who, accustomed to wielding practical arguments, asked Pelagius what was the purpose of prayer and fasting if there was no such thing as grace. "Why go to so much trouble," he argued, "to obtain something which my will is in a position to give me." Moreover, if there is no original sin, why does the Church baptize little children "for the remission of sins" (*in remissionem peccatorum*)? There can be no question in their case of a sin of the will, and hence they must be tainted with a sin of nature.

Unfortunately, the heresiarch had succeeded in gaining the confidence of John of Jerusalem. A council was convened in the house of the latter, and although Pelagius and Paul Orosius, the delegate of St. Augustine, were brought face to face, Bishop John refused to condemn his protégé under pretext that, since the parties in question were Latins, the trial should be referred to Rome (415). The same equivocal attitude was adopted at another Palestinian council held at Diospolis (Lydda). There were easterners inclined to favor Pelagianism, among them Theodore of Mopsuestia, the ancestor of Nestorianism. Thanks to the protection afforded by these different agents, Pelagianism succeeded in strengthening its position in Palestine, just as Donatism had done in Africa. Already it had its organized bands of robbers and plunderers.

But the West was keeping watch. In the year 416, Africa saw two anti-Pelagian councils, one at Carthage, and another at Milevis. With the approbation of St. Augustine, synodal letters were despatched to Rome, requesting the condemnation of Pelagius. These letters stressed two fundamental errors of the heretics: the uselessness of grace and the inefficacy of infant Baptism. Pope Innocent I confirmed the decision and excommunicated both Pelagius and Coelestius. In vain did the heresiarchs appeal to Zosimus, the successor of Innocent I, submitting to him a retractation of their doctrines and an ambiguous profession of faith. The Church of Africa had been challenged to prove that the heretics were guilty, and so two new councils were convoked. The first concerned itself only with persons, decreed the insufficient character of the retractation of Coelestius, and requested the heretics emphatically and categorically to affirm the necessity of grace. The second, presided over by Augustine, attacked the dogmatic question and condemned the Pelagian errors in nine concise articles. Pope Zosimus then convoked a Roman council, in which Pelagius and Coelestius were declared contumacious, and which issued a long encyclical letter (*epistola tractoria*), which was sent to all the Churches of the West and East. The letter was subscribed to by nearly all the bishops of the world, who joined with the Holy See in condemning Pelagianism and upholding the dogma of original sin and the universal necessity of grace. Julian of Eclanum (Mirabella, near Beneventum) and a few other Italian bishops struck back, but were finally condemned by the General Council of Ephesus, in 431.

III. The Opponents of the Teaching of St. Augustine: Semi-Pelagianism.

St. Augustine was called upon to refute Pelagianism on more than one occasion. In its general outlines, his doctrine was very clear: It is God who saves mankind. He not only dispenses at His discretion the light and power which move the will in its choice, but before choosing between all these helps of the natural and the supernatural order,

He knows what reaction the free will will make to each. The difficulty was in explaining the damnation of those who are not called. St. Augustine stressed the pleasure of God, who predestines one out of mercy, and abandons the other out of justice, dispensing to each enough efficacious and sufficient grace.

Semi-Pelagianism was born of a scandal occasioned by a misinterpretation of the Catholic concept of grace. Its followers were convinced that St. Augustine taught a fatal predestination by God of the damned to sin and the fires of hell, as well as a fatal predestination of the elect to merit and glory, in such wise that God assigned some men to good and others to evil. In such a system there was no human liberty, no sufficient grace, and no divine will that all men be saved, but only fatal predestination, or predestinationism. As a reaction against this pseudo-Augustinian concept of salvation, the Semi-Pelagians professed the complete spiritual equality of all men, and taught the existence of a kingdom of God which was a republic of pure justice without any privileges. Sufficient grace, which is intended for all men, becomes efficacious only in the measure in which it is used by the creature, and only in proportion to his or her acquired merits.

As a consequence the Semi-Pelagians taught: (1) that there is no predestination of the elect, and no gift of final perseverance which gives assurance of salvation; (2) that there are no special and personal graces which guarantee the assent of certain souls, except they be the result of previous good will; and (3) that there is only one grace which is general and common to all men; that, before reaching us, this grace is merited by the right use of our freedom and becomes efficacious only by the good use we make of that same freedom. The Semi-Pelagians did not, therefore, affirm with the Pelagians that we save ourselves without grace, but that we render grace efficacious.

This opposition originated in southern Gaul, and particularly with the monks of St. Victor of Marseilles, grouped around their abbot, *John Cassian*. In the thirteenth of his "Conferences" John placed all initiative to good in the human will; the part played by grace was described as a consequential adjunct (*incrementum*). Faustus, the future bishop of Riez, then abbot of Lerins, and Vincent of Lerins, both took sides against St. Augustine, the first in a treatise entitled *De Gratia Libri Duo,* and the second in a work entitled *Commonitorium.* St. Hilary of Arles and

St. Prosper of Aquitania unmasked the error and reported it to the Bishop of Hippo, who immediately set about writing a refutation in his *De Praedestinatione Sanctorum* and his *De Dono Perseverantiae* (428–429).

After the death of the great African Bishop, which occurred in the year 430, Prosper became the standard bearer and champion of orthodoxy and composed the treatise *De Gratia Dei et Libero Arbitrio* (On Grace and Free Will). It was not long before he set out for Rome, together with St. Hilary of Arles, and obtained from Pope Celestine I a letter which placed the doctrine of St. Augustine above suspicion and silenced the Semi-Pelagian faction. The fight continued, however, and not even the Council of Arles (475) was able to put an end to it. The discussion was resumed between the African Fulgentius of Ruspe, surnamed *Augustinus Abbreviatus,* and Faustus of Riez. The final blow was dealt to the error only at the beginning of the sixth century, when *St. Caesarius of Arles* appealed to Pope Felix IV, who sent him a series of *"capitula"* condemning Semi-Pelagianism. Fifteen bishops, gathered in a synod at Orange for the consecration of a basilica, adopted these *"capitula"* with a few additions. The decrees of this, the second Council of Orange (529), which were confirmed by Boniface II, finally settled the controversy.

The influence of St. Augustine was by no means restricted to the Donatist and Pelagian quarrels. He also refuted all the other errors of his day, especially Manichaeism. His voice was heard throughout the civilized world and indefinitely after his death. In theology he was the supreme teacher (*magister intangibilis*) up to the thirteenth century. There was only one weak point in all his teachings: namely, that he based his arguments on Plato's philosophy of the beautiful, instead of on Aristotle's philosophy of the true, which fact accounts for the Thomistic reaction of the thirteenth century. Finally, St. Augustine exerted a profound influence upon Christian spirituality.

TEXTS AND DOCUMENTS

Canons of the General Council of Africa, or Sixteenth Council of Carthage (418)

Can. 1. If any man says that Adam, the first man, was created mortal, so that, whether he sinned or not, he would have died, not as the wages of sin, but through the necessity of nature; let him be anathema.

Can. 2. If any man says that new-born children need not be baptized, or that they should indeed be baptized for the remission of sins, but that they have in them no original sin inherited from Adam, which must be washed away in the bath of regeneration, so that in their case the formula of Baptism "for the remission of sins" must be taken not literally, but figuratively; let him be anathema, because, according to the Epistle to the Romans (V, 12), the sin of Adam has passed upon all his descendants.

Can. 3. If any man says that the grace of God, by which man is justified through Jesus Christ, is effectual only for the forgiveness of sins already committed, but does not avail for avoiding sins in the future; let him be anathema.

Can. 4. If any man says that this grace only helps not to sin, in so far that by it we obtain a better insight into the divine commands, and learn what we should desire and avoid, but does not also give us the power gladly to do and to fulfill what we know to be good; let him be anathema.

Can. 5. If any man says that the grace of justification was given to us in order that we might the more easily fulfill that which we are bound to do by the power of free-will, so that we could fulfill the divine commands even without grace, only not so easily; let him be anathema.

Can. 6. If any man understands these words of the Apostle: "If we say that we have no sin, we deceive ourselves, and the truth is not in us," to mean that we must acknowledge ourselves to be sinners only out of humility, not because we are really such; let him be anathema.

Can. 7. If any man says that the saints pronounce the words of the Lord's Prayer, "forgive us our trespasses," not for themselves, because for them this petition is unnecessary, but solely for others, and that, therefore, it is, "forgive us," not "forgive me"; let him be anathema.

Can. 8. If any man says that the saints pronounce these words, "forgive us our trespasses," out of mere humility, and not in their literal meaning; let him be anathema.

CANONS OF THE COUNCIL OF ORANGE (529) ON GRACE AND FREE WILL
(Summary)

Can. 1. The sin of Adam has injured not only the body, but also the soul of man.

Can. 2. The sin of Adam has injured not only himself, but also his posterity; and not merely the death of the body, but also sin, the death of the soul, has by one man come into the world.

Can. 3. Grace is not only granted when we pray for it, but grace itself works in us to pray for it.

Can. 4. God does not wait for our desire to be cleansed from sin, but He works this desire in us Himself by means of His Spirit.

Can. 5. As the growth, so also the beginning of faith, the disposition for faith, is wrought by grace, and is not in us by nature. Were this faith naturally in us, then all who are not Christians would necessarily be believers.

Can. 6. It is not correct to say that the divine mercy is imparted to us when we (by our own strength) believe, knock, etc. Rather it is divine grace which works in us, so that we believe, knock, etc. Grace not merely helps the humility and obedience of man, but it is the gift of grace that he is humble and obedient.

Can. 7. Without grace, and merely from natural powers, we can do nothing which belongs to eternal salvation; neither think nor will in a proper manner (*ut expedit*), nor consent to the preaching of the Gospel.

Can. 8. It is not correct to say that some attain to the grace of Baptism by the mercy of God, others by their own free will, which was weakened by Adam's sin.

Can. 9. All good thoughts and good works are gifts of God.

Can. 10. Even the saints need divine aid.

Can. 11. We can vow nothing to God, but what we have first received from Him.

Can. 12. What God loves in us, is God's own gift.

Can. 13. The free will, weakened in Adam, can be restored only by the grace of Baptism.

Can. 14. One who is unhappy can be delivered from his misery only by prevenient divine grace.

Can. 15. The condition of Adam, as appointed by God, was changed by sin; the condition of man brought about by sin is changed in the faithful by the grace of God.

Can. 16. All that we have is a gift of God. If any one fails to recognize in any good whatever, that he has it from God, either he has it not, or it will be taken from him.

Can. 17. That which makes the heathen strong is worldly desire; that which makes Christians strong is the love of God, impressed on our hearts by the Holy Ghost.

Can. 18. Unmerited grace goes before the most meritorious works.

Can. 19. Even if human nature had still the integrity in which it was created, it could not preserve it without the aid of the Creator. If, however, it is unable without grace to preserve the safety which it has obtained, much less can it regain that which it has lost.

Can. 20. God works much good in man without man's co-operation; but man can work no good unless God enables him so to do.

Can. 21. The law does not justify, and grace does not consist, as some maintain, in the natural power of man. The law was there, and did not justify; nature was there, and did not justify. But Christ has died to fulfill the law, and to restore the nature which was corrupted through the sin of Adam.

Can. 22. That which man has of his own is only falsehood and sin; what he possesses in truth and righteousness, he has received from God.

HEFELE, *History of the Church Councils*, Vol. II.

QUESTIONS

1. Why is St. John Chrysostom called "Glory of the Christian Pulpit," St. Jerome, "Doctor of Sacred Scripture," and St. Augustine, "Doctor of Grace"?
2. Which were the principal teachings of the Manichaeans, the Donatists, the Pelagians, and the Semi-Pelagians?
3. Institute a comparison between Pelagianism and Protestantism.
4. Discuss the doctrine of the transmission of original sin.
5. Why is St. Augustine called the Christian Plato?
6. Compare St. Augustine and St. Thomas Aquinas from the standpoint of their approach to philosophy.

BIBLIOGRAPHY

St. Augustine.—Sources: *P. L.*, XXXII–XLVII; *C. V.*, XXV, XXVIII, XXXIII (*Confessions*), etc.—Works: CUNNINGHAM, *S. Austin and his Place in the History of Christian Thought*, London, 1886.—V. WOLFSGRUBER, *Augustinus*, Paderborn, 1898.—THIMME, *Augustins geistige Entwickelung*, Berlin, 1908.—J. MARTIN, *S. Augustin* (Coll. *"Les Grands Philosophes"*), 1901.— HATZFELD, *Saint Augustin*, Coll. *"Les Saints."*—L. BERTRAND, *Saint Augustin*, 1913; *Les plus belles pages de saint Augustin*, 1914.—P. DE LABRIOLLE, *op. cit.*, pp. 517–579.—P. BATIFFOL, *Le catholicisme de saint Augustin*, 2 vols., 1920. —E. PORTALIÉ, art. *"Augustin,"* in *Dict. de Théol.*—AUDOLLENT, art. *"Afrique,"* in *Dict. d'Hist.*—G. COMBÈS, *La doctrine politique de saint Augustin*, 1928.—C. C. MARTINDALE, *History of Religions*, vol. III.—FATHER PAUL, O. S. F. C., *The Doctors of the Church*, London.

Pelagianism.—Sources: The writings of Pelagius, *Commentarium in Épistulas Sancti Pauli*, *P. L.*, XXX; *Epistula ad Demetriadem*, *P. L.*, XXX; *Libellus fidei ad Innocentium*, *P. L.*, XLV.—Works of those who have refuted Pelagius: SAINT AUGUSTINE especially, *P. L.*, XLIV, XLV; MARIUS MERCATOR, *Commonitorium; Liber subnotationum in verba Juliani*, *P. L.*, XLVIII; ST. JEROME, *Dialogus contra Pelagianos*, *P. L.*, t. XXIII; PAUL OROSIUS, etc.— Works: *Der Pelagianismus nach seinem Ursprunge und seiner Lehre*, Freiburg i. B., 1866.—F. KLASEN, *Die innere Entwickelung des Pelagianismus*, Freiburg i. B., 1882.—JACOBI, *Die Lehre des Pelagius*, Leipzig, 1892.—A. BRUCHNER, *Julian von Eclanum*, Berlin, 1897.—TIXERONT, *History of Dogmas*,

II.—PORTALIÉ, art. *"Augustin,"* in *Dict. de Théol.*—TURMEL, *Le dogme du péché originel dans saint Augustin, Rev. hist. et litt. relig.*, 1901, pp. 385–426; 1902, pp. 128–147, 209–231, 289–322, 510–534.—RIVIÈRE, *Le dogme de la Rédemption*, 1905.—JUENGST, *Pelagianismus und Augustinismus*, Giessen, 1901.—BATIFFOL, *Le catholicisme de saint Augustin*, vol. II.—J. FORGET, art. *"Julien d'Eclane,"* in *Dict. de Théol.*

Semi-Pelagianism.—Sources: CASSIAN, *P. L.*, XLIX; *C. V.*, XIII and XVII: Letters CCXXV and CCXXVI of Augustine.—Works: TIXERONT, *op. cit.*, III.—SUBLET, *Le semi-pélagianisme*, Namur, 1897.—WÖRTER, *Beiträge zur Dogmengeschichte des Semipelagianismus*, Paderborn, 1898; *Zur Dogmengeschichte des Semipelagianismus*, Münster, 1900.—J. TURMEL, *Saint Augustin et la controverse semi-pélagienne; La controverse semi-pélagienne après saint Augustin*, in *Rev. hist. et litt. rel.*, 1904, pp. 410–433, 497–518.—J. LAUGIER, *Saint Jean Cassien et sa doctrine sur la grâce*, Lyons, 1908.—JACQUIN, *La question de la prédestination aux Ve et VIe siècles*, in *Rev. hist. eccl.*, VII (1906), pp. 269 ff.—L. VALENTIN, *S. Prosper d'Aquitaine*, 1900.—A. MALMORY, *Saint Césaire d'Arles*, 1894, pp. 143–153.—PORTALIÉ, art. *"Augustin,"* in *Dict. de Théol.*—LÉONCE COUTURE, *Saint Prosper d'Aquitaine*, in *Bull. de litt., eccl.*, Toulouse, 1900.—J. RIVIÈRE, *Le dogme de la Rédemption dans saint Augustin*, 1927.

CHAPTER IV

In the fifth century, the theological conflict shifted from Trinitarian to Christological doctrines. Idealistic in its principles, the Christology of the Alexandrians stressed more particularly the divine nature of Christ, defining Him as "an incarnate God" (θεὸς ἔνσαρκος), while the Christology of the Antiochian school emphasized His human nature, defining Him as "a man-God" (ἄνθρωπος θεός). The difference in these two points of view is quite apparent in the earliest stages of both Christological heresies.

I. **The Precursors: Alexandrian Apollinarianism and Antiochian Duopersonalism.** Towards the end of the fourth century there lived at Laodicea in Syria—*i. e.,* in the very center of Antiochian activities—a bishop who, through his father, *Apollinaris the Elder,* born in Egypt, had become associated with the school of Alexandria. In opposition to the Syrian school, which laid special stress on the duality of natures in Christ, he insisted on the personal unity of the Man-God. His reaction to the teachings of his opponents unfortunately led him to affirm the unity of nature in Christ. Juggling away the human nature of Christ by entirely suppressing His rational soul, he taught that the Divine Logos united Himself to a mere human body, and that Christ was nothing more than the Divine Nature clothed with flesh (μία φύσις σεσαρκωμένη). The sacred humanity of the Man-God was thereby reduced to an equivocal and incomplete humanity, in such wise that Christ could no longer redeem us by sharing in our nature. The whole doctrine of the Redemption was thus compromised. True, the Council of Alexandria, held in 362, condemned these doctrines, but it did not succeed in exterminating them.

In the opposite camp, Diodorus of Tarsus and his disciple, Theodore of Mopsuestia, were so intent upon bringing out the integrity of the two natures that they distinguished two separate persons in the Saviour: the Son of God and the son of Mary.

This error continued to spread without meeting with very much opposition, until the day when *Nestorius,* Patriarch of Constantinople, championed it and forced the Church to take action. "One day," writes the historian Socrates, "the priest Anastasius recommended that the faithful cease calling Mary mother of God ($\theta\epsilon o\tau\acute{o}\kappa o\varsigma$), for the simple reason that she was a creature, and God could not be born of a creature." Asked for his opinion in the matter, Nestorius upheld Anastasius. "Mary," he said, "merely engendered the man in which the Word became incarnate. . . . Jesus is God, however, because He contains God. I worship the vase because of its contents, and the vestment because of him whom it clothes."

II. Nestorianism: Its Definition. St. Cyril and the Antiochians. The whole Nestorian heresy was contained in the words just quoted. Nestorius clearly distinguished the man and the God in the Saviour. Arguing from the philosophical principle that an intellectual nature is by that very fact a person, he concluded that there are two persons-natures: the divine and the human. "No complete nature," he said, "is in need of another nature in order to exist. The humanity [of Christ] is complete, and in no need of union with the divinity to be a man." Thus, in Christ, the human nature subsists by itself. It follows that, "as long as there are two subjects of attribution, two egos, we cannot attribute to God the Word, the properties and actions of the human person, and vice versa." The communication of idioms was thus thrown into the discard, and the soteriological consequences were disastrous: In Christ, it was only the man who suffered, and His passion therefore, had not a theandric and infinite value; the Passion of Christ did not effect the Redemption of mankind.

It is true that Nestorius admitted a union between the two natures in Christ, but this union was purely moral. "The two natures are separated in essence," he wrote, "but united in love." Love has stood the test of trials and temptations and has been increased by moral victories; it is now invincible. It was useless, however, for Nestorius to insist on this moral union of friendship and love: the result was merely an artificial person; the whole scheme involved deception.

A necessary corollary of Nestorianism was, of course, the denial of the divine maternity of Mary. For, if there are two distinct persons in Jesus Christ, Mary is the mother of the human person only. Very soon the whole controversy centered around this one point. In his Easter homily for 429, *St. Cyril of Alexandria* protested against the new ideas, and vigorously upheld the doctrine of the θεοτόκος. When Nestorius remained obstinate, Cyril appealed to the Pope. Celestine I condemned the teaching of Nestorius at a Roman Council held in August, 430. The heresiarch was asked to retract, but he refused, feeling that he had the support of Emperor Theodosius II and also that of the Antiochian theologians, Andrew of Samosata and Theodoret of Cyrus, who had attacked St. Cyril. Though orthodox like St. Cyril himself, they viewed the Christological problem from a different angle. Prejudiced by the traditions of their school, and somewhat diffident of Apollinarianism, they stressed above all the distinction between the two natures, whereas St. Cyril, as a reaction against Nestorianism, laid special emphasis on the indissoluble character of the union between the divinity and the humanity of Christ. In the twelve anathematisms which St. Cyril required Nestorius to sign as a proof of his orthodoxy, the Bishop of Alexandria spoke of ἕνωσις φυσική, *i. e.,* real unity, as opposed to the relative, accidental, and purely moral union taught by Nestorius. At once the diffident Antiochians interpreted his thought in a Monophysitic sense, imagining that he postulated one sole nature after the union.

III. **The Condemnation: The Council of Ephesus, 431. The Edict of Union, 433.** Both St. Cyril and Nestorius requested that a council be held to settle the controversy. The Emperor Theodosius II convoked a council to meet at Ephesus on June 7th, 431, and the Holy See appointed two legates to preside at its meetings. In vain did St. Cyril try to win over Nestorius. "Never," he said, "will I recognize as God a child who was two months old, three months old, etc." He even refused to appear before the assembled Council. Bishop John of Antioch and his group were slow in arriving, and so St. Cyril proceeded with the meeting. At his instigation, the Council anathematized Nestorius and condemned his doctrine. The decision was nothing more than an echo of that of the Roman Council. In their enthusiasm, the Ephesians escorted the Fathers to their respective homes in the city by torchlight, proclaiming in loud voices the Theotokos.

Finally, however, John of Antioch arrived at Ephesus, together with forty-three Oriental bishops. He immediately convoked a counter synod, which deposed St. Cyril. Confident that it had the support of the legates, the orthodox Council continued its sessions and condemned the Pelagian heresy, basing its decision on the *Tractoria* of Pope Zosimus. The Emperor Theodosius II, however, hesitated to give his decision. He first had Cyril and Nestorius thrown into prison, but after giving both parties a hearing, was won over to the truth. The deposition of Nestorius was ratified, and he was relegated to Antioch.

The Antiochians, however, continued to distrust St. Cyril, and so, anxious to come to some peaceful agreement, the Bishop of Alexandria issued a series of explanations, so clear and explicit that they placed him above all suspicion of Apollinarianism. Very soon an understanding was reached between him and John of Antioch, which resulted in the *Edict of Union* of the year 433. Out of a spirit of friendship and good will, St. Cyril sacrificed his favorite expression: ἕνωσις φυσική, and, as a reward, witnessed the complete triumph of his doctrine. The edict read that "there is in Christ a union of two natures in one Lord" and that "the Blessed Virgin is the mother of God (Theotokos)." Pursued vigorously by the Emperor Theodosius II and John of Antioch, Nestorianism was completely routed. It took refuge in Persia, and was successively headed by Barsauma of Nisibis and Babai the Great, who succeeded in establishing an autonomous Nestorian church. The Empire was rid of the heresy forever.

TEXTS AND DOCUMENTS

The Christology of Nestorius

I. Two natural or physical persons: The divine person and the human person. Any nature that is complete has no need of another nature in order to exist and live, because it possesses in itself, and has received all that is necessary for its existence. . . . How then, can you maintain that two complete natures form one nature, since the humanity is complete and has no need of union with the divinity to constitute man?

II. An artificial or moral person: The prosopon of union. The union of the prosopons takes place in prosopon, and not in essence or in nature. An essence must not be conceived without hypostatis, as if the union (of essences) took place in one essence, and that one prosopon resulted from one essence. But the other natures subsist in their prosopons, and in their nature, and in the prosopon of union. As to the natural prosopon of the one, the other uses the same in virtue of the union. Thus, there is only one prosopon for the two natures. The prosopon of one essence uses the very prosopon of the other. But what essence can you obtain without prosopon? That of the divinity or that of the humanity? But then you can no longer maintain that God the Word is flesh, and also that the flesh is the Son.

If you attribute two natures to God the Word: God and man, and that man is nothing, we can only think of you (as follows): Either you acknowledge only an apparent humanity, which might have served to designate the Word; or you maintain that the humanity had no part to play, by its nature, in the prosopon of the economy; or you insist that God the Word manifested Himself to undergo human sufferings against His will.

In an effort to explain the prosopon of union, Nestorius offered the following comment on the well known text of the Epistle to the Philippians: "Taking the form of a servant, being made in the likeness of men, and in habit found as a man" (Phil. 2, 7–8): "He took the form of a servant; the essence of the man was not the form of the servant, but he who took it, made it his image and his prosopon. . . . He who was taken had the essence and the nature of man; but he who took was found man by his appearance without taking the nature of man. For he did not take the nature, but the form, the form and the appearance of man in everything required by the prosopon. Speaking of the humility of his appearance, the Apostle says: "He humbled himself, becoming obedient unto death, even to the death of the cross" (Philip. 2, 8), in order to show in the nature the humility of the form of the servant and to prove the opprobrium which He suffered at the hands of men. For they despised Him, who was humbled to the very depths. He also reveals to us the reason why He took the form of a servant, when under the appearance of men He was found in appearance as a man: He humbled himself unto death, even to the death of the cross. It was not in His nature that He suffered all these things, but He made use of him who suffers naturally, in his form and in his prosopon, in order to impart to him through grace in his prosopon a name which is above all names, before which every knee shall bow, in Heaven, on earth, and under the earth. And every tongue shall confess it (Philip. 2, 9–11), in order that, through his likeness with God, and in accordance with the dignity of God, He may be recognized as the Son, He who took the form of a servant, who was in the form of man, who was in appearance as a man, who humbled himself unto death, even the death of the Cross, and was exalted because a name was given to Him which is above all names, under the appearance of the form of a servant, which form was taken and united to the Godhead. The man, as opposed to the Word, is the form of the servant, not in appearance, but by essence, and this form was taken for the form and the appearance and the humiliation unto the death of the Cross. This is why it was exalted and was given a name which is above all names.

The Apostle says first: "The form of God," which is the likeness of God, and then: "He took the form of a servant," not for the essence, nor for the nature, but for the likeness and the prosopon, to share in the form of a servant, and also, in order that the form of the servant might share in the form of God, so that there would be only one prosopon with the two natures. The form, indeed, is the prosopon.

III. The ineffable friendship between God, the Word, and the man Jesus. Never has anyone been known to use the prosopon of God in his own prosopon, either among the prophets, or among the angels. But Christ, our Lord, has said: "I and the Father are one." (John 10, 30).—"He that seeth me, seeth the Father also." (John 14, 9).—"I do the works of my Father" (John 10, 37), etc. No one among the prophets or the angels ever dared to speak in that way.

The Twelve Anathematisms of St. Cyril of Alexandria

1. If any one does not confess that Emmanuel is true God, and that, therefore, the holy Virgin is the Mother of God, since she bore, after the flesh, the incarnate Word of God; let him be anathema.

2. If any one does not confess that the Word of God the Father hypostatically united Himself with the flesh, and is one Christ with that which has become His own flesh, God and man together; let him be anathema.

3. If any one separates the Hypostases as to their unity in the one Christ, connecting them only by a mere association of dignity or authority and power, and not rather by a conjunction in *physical union;* let him be ananathema.[1]

4. If any one divides between two Persons or Hypostases, the expressions which are used in the Evangelical and Apostolic writings, or again by the saints, or by Christ Himself, and ascribes the one class to the man, separated from the Word of God the Father, and the others to the sole Word of God the Father; let him be anathema.

5. If any one ventures to say that Christ is a man who bears God (θεοφόρος), and not rather, that He is true God, as the One Son in nature in accordance with the expression: "The Word was made flesh," and partook like us of flesh and blood; let him be anathema.

6. If any one ventures to say that the Word of God the Father is the God and the Lord of Christ, and does not confess that Christ Himself is at once God and man, since according to the Holy Scripture, "The Word was made flesh"; let him be anathema.

7. If any one says that Jesus is moved as man by the Divine Word, and that the glory of the Only-begotten Son has been superadded to Him as to one distinct from the only Son; let him be anathema.

---

[1] This expression was the most equivocal of all those used in the anathematisms, because it could lead one to believe that this natural physical union resulted in the confusion of the two natures in Christ (Monophysitism). In some of his later explanations, St. Cyril stressed the distinction of the two natures after the union.

8. If any one ventures to say that the man assumed by the Word is to be adored, and glorified, and acknowledged as God, along with the Divine Word, as if one were separate from the other (for the word *with* [σύν] suggests the idea of duality), and does not rather honor Emmanuel in *one* adoration, and direct *one* praise to Him, as the Word made flesh; let him be anathema.

9. If any one says that the *one* Lord Jesus Christ is glorified by the Holy Spirit, that in using the power of the Holy Spirit He uses a power foreign to Himself, and that He has received from the Spirit power over evil spirits and miraculous power for the good of man, and does not rather regard the Spirit by whom He wrought miracles as His own; let him be anathema.

10. Holy Scripture says that Christ became our High Priest and Apostle, and that He offered Himself in the odor of sweetness to God. If, therefore, anyone says that our High Priest and our Apostle is not the Word of God Himself, made flesh and man like us, but another than He, a man distinct from Him and born of a woman, or else that He gave Himself as a sacrifice not for us alone, but also for Himself, notwithstanding the fact that He, as the sinless One, needed no sacrifice; let him be anathema.

11. If any one does not confess that the flesh of the Lord is life-giving, and belongs to the Divine Word as His own, but pretends that it belongs to another external to Him, who is united with Him merely in dignity, or only participates in the divine indwelling; and does not rather hold it to be life-giving, for this reason, as we have said, that it belongs to the Word, who can make all things live; let him be anathema.

12. If any one does not confess that the Word of God suffered in His flesh, was crucified in His flesh, and tasted death in His flesh, and then became the first-born among the dead, since He as God is life and life-giver; let him be anathema.

The Formula of Union, 433

We profess therefore [1] that Our Lord Jesus Christ, the only Son of God, is true God and true man, constituted by a body and a rational soul; that He was engendered by the Father before all time as to His divinity, and as to His humanity, was born of the Virgin Mary in time for us and for our salvation; that He is consubstantial with the Father in His divinity, and consubstantial with us in His humanity; for one union was effected by the two natures, and so we acknowledge only one Christ, one Son, one Lord. Because of this union, which is free from all admixture, we also acknowledge that the Blessed Virgin is the Mother of God, because God the Word was made flesh, was made man, coalesced with the Temple [His humanity],

---

[1] Anxious to make peace, Cyril became reconciled with the "Orientals," *i.e.,* the Antiochians, and accepted as an explanation of the anathematisms their formula, which stresses the distinction of natures even after the union. This formula was probably drawn up by Theodoret himself.

which He took from her.[1] Concerning the Evangelical and Apostolic expressions which have reference to Christ, we are aware that theologians apply some of them to the two natures, because they are addressed to one person only, whereas they distinguish the others, because they are addressed to one of the two natures.[2] Expressions that are becoming to God are attributed to the Divinity, whereas those which refer to the abasement, are addressed to the humanity.

QUESTIONS

1. Contrast Antiochian Christology and Alexandrian Christology.
2. Define Apollinarianism and Duopersonalism.
3. What is meant by the expression, "Communication of idioms"?
4. Give a summary of the doctrinal views of Nestorius.

BIBLIOGRAPHY

Apollinarianism.—Sources: The writings of Apollinarius, in the edition of H. Lietzmann, *Apollinaris von Laodicea und seine Schule*, I, Tübingen, 1904.—*Contra Apollinarium, P. G.,* XXVI, 1903 ff.—St. Epiphanius, *Haer.,* LXXVII.—St. Gregory of Nyssa, *Antirrheticus adversus Apollinarium, P. G.,* XLV.—St. Basil, *Epist.,* CXXIX, CCLXIII.—St. Gregory of Nyssa, *Epist.,* CI, CII, CCII.—Theodoret *Eranistes, Dial.* V; *Haeretic. fab. Compendium,* IV, 8.—St. Vincent of Lerins, *Commonitorium,* 12.—Socrates and Sozomenus.—Works: Tixeront, *op. cit.,* vol. II.—Voisin, *L'Apollinarisme,* Louvain, 1901; *La doctrine christologique de saint Athanase,* in *Rev. hist. eccl.,* I (1900), pp. 226 ff.—G. Godet, art. *"Apollinaire,"* in *Dict. de Théol.*—Draeseke, *Apollinarius von Laodicea,* Leipzig, 1892.—Aigrain, art. *"Apollinarisme,"* in *Dict. d'Hist.*

Nestorianism.—Diodorus, *P. G.,* XXXIII, 1559.—Theodore, *P. G.,* LXVI. —Nestorius, *Letters and Discourses* collected by F. Loofs, *Nestoriana,* Halle, 1905; *Le livre d'Héraclide de Damas,* Syriac edition by Bedjon, 1910.—E. Schwartz, *Acta conciliorum œcumenicorum,* t. I, vol. V, *Concilium universale Ephesinum,* Berlin-Leipzig, 1924–26.—Works: Tixeront, *op. cit.,* III, *Des concepts de nature et de personne dans les Pères des Ve et VIe siècles,* in *Rev. hist. et litt. relig.,* 1903, p. 583, cited in *Mélanges de Patrologie et d'Histoire,* 1920.—M. Jugie, *Nestorius et la querelle nestorienne,* 1912.—Fendt, *Die Christologie des Nestorius,* Kempten, 1910.—V. Ermoni, *Diodore de Tarse*

---

[1] It will be observed that in the second anathematism, St. Cyril condemned those who spoke of the flesh as being the abode of the Divinity. By subscribing to the profession of faith of the Orientals, he showed that this expression is susceptible of an orthodox interpretation.

[2] This last sentence is certainly aimed at the fourth anathematism. The distinction is approved between expressions which concern the divine nature and those which concern the human nature, provided they are not predicated of two distinct persons. St. Cyril had said practically the same thing

et son rôle doctrinal, in *Le Muséon,* 1901, pp. 424–444.—F. Nau, *Nestorius d'après les sources orientales,* 1911.—Pirot, *L'œuvre exégétique de Théodore de Mopsueste,* Rome, 1913.—V. Grumel, *Un théologien nestorien: Babaï le Grand,* in *Echos d'Orient,* 1924 (XXVII).

St. Cyril.—Sources: *P. G.,* LXVIII–LXXVII.—Works: Largent, *Saint Cyrille et le Concile d'Ephèse,* in *Rev. quest. hist.,* July, 1872, t. XII, pp. 5–70: *Etudes d'histoire ecclésiastique,* 1892.—Weigl, *Die Heilslehre des hl. Cyrill von Alexandrien,* Mainz, 1905.—Nau, *Saint Cyrille et Nestorius,* in *Rev. Orient chr.,* 1910, XV, pp. 365–391, 1911. XVI.—Mahe, *Les anathématismes de saint Cyrille,* in *Rev. hist. eccl.,* July, 1906, pp. 505–542; art. *"Cyrille"* in *Dict. de Théol.*—J. Lebon, *Le monophysisme sévérien,* Louvain, 1909.—Jugie, art. *"Ephèse,"* in *Dict. de Théol.*—P. Batiffol, *Le siège apostolique,* ch. VI. —A. Fortescue, *The Greek Fathers.*

The Papacy.—Sources: *Liber Pontificalis,* edit. Duchesne.—Jaffé, *Regesta Rom. Pontif.,* 2 vols., edit. Loewenfeld, Kaltenbrunner, Ewald, Leipzig, 1885–1888.—Works: Grisar, *Rome et les papes au moyen âge.*—Goyau, Fabre, Pératé, *Le Vatican, les Papes et la civilisation,* 1895: 1st Part: G. Goyau, *Vue générale de l'histoire de la papauté.*—Batiffol, *Le Siège apostolique,* 1924.—W. Rade, *Damasus, Bischof von Rom,* Freiburg i. B., 1882.— Chapman, *Studies on the Early Papacy.*

CHAPTER V

St. Cyril died in the year 444 and was succeeded by *Dioscorus,* an extremely violent and ambitious man, who insisted on the pre-eminence of Alexandria over Constantinople and Antioch, and never missed an opportunity to molest the old friends of Nestorius, like Theodoret of Cyrus and Ibas of Edessa. He succeeded in grouping around him a large clientele. The zelanti, indeed, had never believed in the sincerity of the conversion of the defenders of Nestorius, and so, after the death of St. Cyril, they began to view the acts of the Council of Ephesus and the Edict of Union as a dangerous transaction. On the other hand, they placed so much stress on personal unity in the Godhead, that they ended by asserting a natural union or its equivalent. It was in this way that Monophysitism was born.

I. The Monophysitic Systems. A first system taught the absorption of the humanity by the divinity, somewhat as objects are absorbed or consumed by fire. "Just as objects that are thrown into the fire, become like unto the essence of fire, so human nature is received into the divine, enclosed in it, changed into it, and made one with it without division in essence or prosopon." The necessary implication of this theory was Theopaschitism, or the doctrine which attributes the sufferings and death of Christ to the Divine Nature, since this Nature alone existed after the union. It issued also, it would seem, in Docetism, because if the humanity of Christ is absorbed, some appearance of it must remain which falls under our senses.

A second theory taught the absorption of the divinity by the humanity, in such wise that the Word ceased to be really God and became man. It was argued, by way of analogy, that "whether waters are running or frozen, they do not form two essences of water."

A third system was Monophysitism, properly so called, which did not suppress either nature, but blended both in such a way that a *tertium quid* was obtained—a new nature comprising neither the divinity nor the humanity. Oxygen and hydrogen combine in about the same way to form water.

The intransigence of the new heretics was all the more arrogant as they claimed to be defending the Church against the still formidable Nestorians, and based their views on literature contributed by outstanding men in the field of theology, such as Athanasius, Gregory Thaumaturgus, Julius of Rome, etc. They were mistaken in this last point, because, as a matter of fact, they were quoting from the pseudo-epigraphs of Apollinaris of Laodicea, which were circulated under the names of orthodox writers.[1]

II. The Struggle: The Council of Constantinople, The "Robber Synod" at Ephesus, and the Council of Chalcedon. A very strong anti-Nestorian party had been organized at Constantinople, which recruited its members especially from the monasteries. Its leader was the archimandrite *Eutyches,* a man of mediocre intelligence, completely lacking in real culture, and, to make matters worse, hatefully stubborn. He formed a committee for Church welfare, which issued its decisions from different vantage points: through Uranius of Himeria Eutyches agitated against Ibas of Edessa, and through the Syrian monk Barsumas, he launched an attack upon Theodoret and Domnus of Antioch. It should be added that Eutyches' influence at the court of Constantinople was very considerable, due to the fact that his godchild, the eunuch Chrysaphius, resided there.

But orthodoxy was keeping watch. Theodoret had foreseen that constant appeal to Cyril and exaggerating his authority would drive the Alexandrians into Monophysitism, and so, in 447, he composed his work entitled *Eranistes* (The Beggar), a theological treatise in dialogue form, in which he established successfully against Monophysitism that the Word remained unchanged in the Incarnation, without admixture, and impassible. The arguments with which he defended his thesis were more philosophical than theological, but were based, one and all, upon the testimony of the Fathers.

After the theoretical refutation came the direct attack. Denounced by Eusebius of Dorylea in a provincial council held at Constantinople,

[1] See Tixeront, *Handbook of Patrology,* p. 147 (transl. Raemers).

Eutyches was summoned to appear before it. He refused to renounce his errors, however, arguing that, to anathematize them would be to anathematize the teaching of Athanasius and Cyril. The Council excommunicated him, but he appealed his case to Pope St. Leo (440–461), to St. Peter Chrysologus, to Dioscorus, and even to the Emperor Theodosius II. Dioscorus hastened to absolve him from the excommunication, and the Emperor convoked a council at Ephesus to reconsider his case. Flavian, Patriarch of Constantinople, forwarded detailed information to Pope St. Leo, who issued precise instructions to his legates in the famous *Epistola Dogmatica ad Flavianum* (Dogmatic Epistle to Flavian).

The doctrinal teaching of this Epistle may be summed up as follows: (1) Jesus Christ is only one person; (2) but in this one person there are two natures, without confusion and mixture; (3) each of these two natures has its own faculties, its own proper operations, which it does not carry on independently of the other, and outside the union which is permanent, but of which it is the immediate principle: this is the consequence of the duality of natures; (4) the unity of person, on the other hand, results in the communication of idioms. These are the broad outlines of the Christological doctrine which Pope Leo championed, and which he hoped would triumph at the Council of Ephesus.

But the stage was set for a victory of error. Theodoret and those who had passed sentence upon Eutyches were refused admission to the Council; the presidency was tendered to Dioscorus, who would not even allow the papal legates to read the Epistle of St. Leo; and finally, the archimandrite Barsumas arrived, a sort of barbarian, who had gone so far as to train his retinue of fanatical monks to give chase to the opponents. The Council was at once converted into a scene of tumult and violence. Eusebius of Dorylea, the accuser of Eutyches, was literally covered with maledictions: "Away with Eusebius!" they cried: "Burn him alive!" Eutyches was acquitted of heresy and re-instated into office; his enemies were one and all deposed. The papal legates were grossly insulted, and Flavian was treated with such violent outrage that he died three days after, from the effects of the wounds he had received. The bishops were constrained to sign, at the point of the sword, and in this way 135 signatures were obtained. A few indignant persons protested the action of the Council; the recriminations of Flavian and Eusebius of Dorylea reached the ears of the Pope, through his legates, who had managed to make their escape.

When Pope St. Leo received the reports of what had happened at Ephesus, he referred to the Synod as a *"Robber Synod" (latrocinium)*, a name that has clung to it ever since. Immediately he convoked another council, to cancel the decisions of Ephesus. In the meantime, Theodosius II died (450), and was succeeded by his sister, Pulcheria, who married General Marcian. Both were strong supporters of the orthodox faith—the result being a sudden and complete change of policy. Anatolius, the new patriarch of Byzantium, condemned Eutyches, and subscribed to the "Epistle to Flavian." Things seemed to be taking such a decided turn for the better that Pope St. Leo deemed a new council unnecessary. However, Marcian insisted that it be held.

And so the Fourth General Council convened at Chalcedon, under the presidency of the papal legates. Six hundred and thirty bishops attended. The "Epistle to Flavian" was loudly acclaimed, and a symbol decreed, which read: "We confess one and the same Christ Jesus, the Only-begotten Son, whom we acknowledge to have two natures, without confusion, transformation, division or separation between them. The difference between these two natures is not suppressed by their union; on the contrary, the attributes of each nature are safeguarded and subsist in one person." Such terminology spelled ruin for both Monophysitism and Nestorianism. Unfortunately, the work of interpretation was not carried far enough, for no one even dreamed of demonstrating that the decisions of Chalcedon did not contradict the decisions of Ephesus or the teachings of St. Cyril. A terrible misunderstanding resulted, and a large party continued to believe that the Council of Ephesus had been condemned by the Council of Chalcedon, and the Christology of St. Cyril by the letter of St. Leo. This was too much for minds embittered against Nestorianism, minds which could not bear even a semblance of legislation issuing from the West. The quarrel was increased by the rivalry of the two patriarchates: the Monophysite patriarchate of Alexandria and the orthodox patriarchate of Byzantium.

The Monophysite controversy continued in this way for almost a hundred years. In the end all those parts of the Eastern Empire which spoke a language other than Greek, severed relations with the Roman Church, and remained in schism, even to the present day: to wit, the Copts in Egypt, the Jacobites in Syria, the Armenians, and the Abyssinians—about four million in all.

III. The First Reactions to the Council of Chalcedon: The "Henoticon" and the Acacian Schism.

The Council of Chalcedon had deposed the Patriarch Dioscorus, but the Monophysites soon succeeded in establishing their candidates in the great sees of the Empire. The monk Theodore was installed in the see of Jerusalem, Timothy Aelurus (The Cat) in that of Alexandria, and Peter Fullo in that of Antioch. The latter added to the Trisagion, an ancient hymn of the Church, the words: "Who was crucified for us," to stress against the Nestorians that Jesus is truly one of the three Persons of the Trinity. The Emperor Leo (457-473) combated these prelates for a time, and even had them deposed; but when the usurper Basiliscus gained possession of the throne, he thought it good policy to recall them and to annul the decisions of the Council of Chalcedon by issuing his *Encyclicon* (476), dedicated to Timothy Aelurus. Five hundred Egyptian and Syrian bishops subscribed to the formula "with as much freedom as joy," and Monophysitism was firmly established at Alexandria. After the death of Timothy Aelurus, the patriarchate passed, without any opposition whatsoever, into the hands of his friend, Peter Mongus (The Stammerer).

Moved by a spirit of rivalry, more than by solicitude and care for orthodox doctrine, Acacius, the ambitious Patriarch of Constantinople, formulated a protest. A revolution at the court of Basiliscus turned the tide in his favor. Sinister consequences, however, had already taken place—Egypt and Syria had been lost to the cause of orthodoxy, and perhaps even to the Empire. Acacius suggested to the new Emperor, Zeno, that he inaugurate the disastrous policy of conceding points to the Monophysites, and sacrificing the decisions of Chalcedon, in order to win the heretics back to the orthodox faith. The proposed formula, known as *Henoticon* (Formula of Concord), was quite orthodox and sinned by omission rather than by direct statement of any error. It acknowledged the formularies of faith of Nicaea and Ephesus, but regarded the decisions of the Council of Chalcedon as null and void, at the same time carefully avoiding the controverted expression, "in two natures." The Monophysites had no possible means of escape, and the same game played by the Eusebians after Nicaea was re-staged in an attempt to hit upon a formula vague enough to satisfy all parties. The leaders of this movement depended, moreover, on the support of Peter Mongus, the Patriarch of Alexandria, with whom Acacius had had an understanding; but the orthodox party made known their apprehensions to Rome, and Pope Felix III excommunicated both Acacius and Peter Mongus, and requested the Emperor Zeno to withdraw the *Henoticon*.

It was at this point that the Acacian Schism broke out, which was destined to disturb the inner life of the Church for thirty-four years (484–518) and establish Byzantine autonomy on a firm and solid basis. Anastasius, the successor of Zeno, in his open warfare against Rome went so far as to try to elect the Archdeacon Lawrence pope, after the latter had promised that he would recognize the *Henoticon*. He gave orders to have the revamped Trisagion inserted in all liturgical texts, and installed in the see of Antioch the patriarch Severus, an exalted Cyrillian, a harsh character, and a master of dialectics. The results can easily be surmised: the breach between Byzantium and Rome was widened, and the triumph of Monophysitism in Syria and Egypt definitely assured.

Post-Chalcedonian Monophysitism was not a coarse and gross Eutychianism, although it still survived, without, however, having any notable representatives. Severian Monophysitism, on the other hand, could claim such exponents as Dioscorus, Timothy Aelurus, and Severus, whose teaching was the exact reproduction of that of St. Cyril, and adhered closely to material orthodoxy, although, by refusing to subscribe to the terminology of Chalcedon, it upheld a verbal Monophysitism (*una natura Verbi incarnati*), contrary to the teachings of the Church, who alone has the right to impose certain formularies and reject others. The Anti-Chalcedonian opposition certainly brings out the rivalry between the patriarchates and the spirit of particularism of Egypt and Syria, but it would be incorrect to affirm, as Harnack does, that the intervention of these political factors suffices to account for the course of events. As a matter of fact, the battle was first and last a doctrinal one, in which convictions were sometimes defended even to the point of religious fanaticism.

About the year 520, a rupture took place at Alexandria, which split the Monophysites into two sects, termed, respectively, the Severians and the Julianists. The Julianists derived their name from Julius, Bishop of

Halicarnassus, their leader, who, it was claimed, asserted that the divinity of Christ was so closely united with the human nature, that Christ was not subject to human passions or exposed to the changes of a corruptible nature. Severus accused Julius of reducing Christ to the mere appearance of humanity, suffering and death, of letting his imagination run wild, and of aligning himself with Eutyches. As a matter of fact, however, by *aphtharsia* or the incorruptibility of Christ, Julian merely understood the absence of original sin and its consequences, suffering and death, so that he freely took these things upon Himself. In other words, Christ was incorruptible by nature, but passible by His own free choice.

Other schisms spent themselves in endless logomachies and divided the Monophysites still further, so true is it, as has been said, that outside the Catholic Church there is not even a semblance of unity.

TEXTS AND DOCUMENTS

The Epistle of St. Leo to Flavian (Epistle 28)

I. In Jesus Christ there are two natures without confusion or mixture. . . . Since then the properties of both natures and substances remained intact, and united in one person, lowliness was assumed by majesty, weakness by strength, mortality by eternity. In order to pay our debt, the impassible nature was united to the passible, so that, as our salvation required, the one Mediator between God and men, the man Jesus Christ, on the one hand could die, and on the other hand could not die. In the inviolate and perfect nature of a true man, true God was born, complete in His own nature and complete in ours. I say, "in ours," and I mean, as the Creator formed our nature in the beginning, and as Christ wills to restore it. For there was no trace in the Redeemer of that which the tempter brought into us. He participated in our infirmities, but not in our sins. He took upon Himself the form of a servant, without the stain of sin, and He raised the human nature without impairing the divine. For the emptying of Himself, by which the Invisible became visible, and the Lord and Creator of the world willed to become one of the mortals, resulted in no loss of power, but was rather a manifestation of His compassion. He who in the form of God had made man, became man in the form of a servant. Each nature preserves its property inviolate, and as the form of God did not annihilate the form of a servant, so the form of a servant in no way impaired the form of God.[1]

---

[1] With the precision of a lawyer and the skill of a theologian, the Pope expresses in admirable language the doctrine of the Incarnation: two natures in the unity of one person; two true natures, acting each in its own sphere, but in complete harmony and full co-operation. The position taken by the Pope is the same as that taken by the Act of Union of 433. He is

II. Each of these natures has its own faculties. . . . The Son of
God came into the world, therefore, in a new order of things, and in a new
kind of birth. In a new order of things, because He who is in His own nature
invisible, became visible in our nature; He who is incomprehensible, willed to
be comprehended; He who existed before all time, began to exist in time;
the Lord of all, veiling His majesty, took upon Himself the form of a servant,
the impassible God did not disdain to become a passible man, and the Immortal subjected Himself to the law of death. But then, again, it was by a
new kind of birth that He came into the world, since the inviolate Virgin,
without experiencing concupiscence, furnished flesh to the Son of God. The
Lord assumed from His mother nature, not guilt, and as His birth is wonderful, so is His nature different from ours. For He who is true God, is at
the same time true man, and in this unity there is no lie, for the lowliness
of man and the loftiness of God have interpenetrated. As God is not changed
by His compassion, so neither is man consumed by the divine dignity. Each
of the two natures effects in communion with the other that which is proper
to it, since the Word performs that which is of the Word, and the flesh that
which is of the flesh. The first of them shines forth in miracles, the other sub-
mits to insults. And as the Word does not recede from the equality of the
glory of the Father, so does the flesh not abandon the nature of our race. For,
as must be often repeated, He who is one and the same, is truly Son of God
and truly Son of man. God in this, that "in the beginning was the Word, and
the Word was with God, and the Word was God;" man in this, that "the
Word was made flesh, and dwelt among us;" God in this, that "all things
were made by Him, and without Him nothing was made;" man in this,
that He was made of a woman and under the law. The birth of the flesh is
the revelation of human nature; the being born of a virgin is the sign of His
divine power. The weakness of the child is evidenced by the lowliness of
the cradle; the glory of the Highest is proclaimed by the voice of the angels.
. . . As it does not belong to one and the same nature to bewail a deceased
friend with deep compassion, and to call him back to life when he has been
four days dead, by the mere command of His Word, or to hang upon the
Cross and change the night into day; so it does not belong to one and the same
nature to say: "I and the Father are one," and "the Father is greater than I."
For, although in Jesus Christ there is only one person of God and man, yet
the common glory and the common lowliness of the two natures have a different source. From us He has the manhood, which is inferior to the Father;
from the Father He has the Godhead, which is equal to the Father.

**III. The Unity of person results in the communication of id-
ioms.** Because the two natures constitute only one person, we read that the Son
of man came down from Heaven (John 3, 13), while the Son of God took

even more explicit, not having to contend with party remonstrances. The Council of Chalcedon,
held in the year 451, harks back to Leo's letter to Flavian as a call to arms for the cause
of orthodoxy.

flesh of the Virgin; and also that the Son of God was crucified and buried, while He suffered not in the Godhead, according to which He is the only-begotten Son, co-eternal and consubstantial with the Father, but in the weakness of human nature. For this reason we say in the Creed that the only-begotten Son of God was crucified and buried. . . . These things were written that we might know that He possessed the properties of the divine and human natures undivided, and that we, without identifying the Word and the Flesh, should confess that the Word and the Flesh are one Son of God. This mystery of the faith was quite foreign to Eutyches, who acknowledged our nature in the only begotten Son of God, neither in the humiliations of His death, nor in the glory of His Resurrection.

(E. Amann, Le Dogme Catholique
d'après les Pères, pp. 344–352.)

PROFESSION OF FAITH OF THE COUNCIL OF CHALCEDON

After a literal repetition of the Creeds of Nicaea and Constantinople, the Council goes on to say:

These two creeds had sufficed for many years to give us a complete knowledge of faith and confirmation of religion, for they teach everything with reference to the Father, and the Son, and the Holy Ghost, and the Incarnation of the Saviour to those who receive it in faith. Since, however, some who would do away with the preaching of the Church have devised vain expressions through their own heresies, and, in one instance, have dared to destroy the mystery of the Incarnation of our Lord and rejected the designation of Mary as Mother of God, and, in another instance, introduced a sort of mixture or confusion of natures, imagining, contrary to reason, that there is only one nature of the flesh and of the Godhead, and irrationally maintaining that the divine nature of the only-begotten Son had, by the admixture of humanity, become passible; therefore, the holy, great, and ecumenical Council decrees that the faith of the three hundred and eighteen Fathers shall remain inviolate, and that the doctrine afterwards promulgated by the one hundred and fifty Fathers at Constantinople on account of the Pneumatomachi shall have equal validity, being put forth by them, not in order to add to the creed of Nicaea anything that was lacking, but in order to make known in writing their belief concerning the Holy Ghost against the deniers of His glory.

On account of those, however, who endeavor to destroy the mystery of the Incarnation, and who, boldly insulting Him who was born of Mary, affirm that He is a mere man, the holy Synod has adhered to the synodal letters of St. Cyril to Nestorius and the Orientals in opposition to Nestorianism, and has added to them the letter of the holy Archbishop, Leo of ancient Rome, written to Flavian, of sacred memory, for the overthrow of the Eutychian errors, as agreeing with the doctrine of the great Apostle Peter and as a pillar against the heretics.

The Synod, therefore, opposes those who seek to rend the mystery of the Incarnation into a duality of sons, excludes from her communion those who venture to declare the Godhead of the Only-begotten capable of suffering, opposes those who imagine a mingling and a confusion of the two natures in Christ, excludes those who foolishly maintain that the servant-form of the Son, assumed from us, is from a heavenly substance, or any other (than ours), and anathematizes those who claim that before the union there were two natures of our Lord, but after the union only one.

Following, therefore, the Holy Fathers, we all teach with one accord one and the same Son, Our Lord Jesus Christ, perfect in His Godhead and perfect in His manhood, true God and true man, consisting of a rational soul and of a body, of one substance with the Father as touching the Godhead, and of one substance with us as touching the manhood, like unto us in everything except sin; according to the Godhead, begotten of the Father before all time, but in the last days, for us men and for our salvation; according to the manhood, born of the Virgin Mary, the God-bearer, one and the same Christ, Son, Lord—Only-begotten, confessed in two natures, without confusion, without change, without rending or separation; while the difference of the natures is in no way denied by reason of the union, on the other hand, the peculiarity of each nature is preserved, and both concur in one Person and Hypostasis. We do not confess One separated into two persons, but one and the same Son and Only-begotten and God the Logos, the Lord Jesus Christ, . . . as the prophets announced of Him, and He Himself taught us, and the Creed of the Fathers has handed down to us.

QUESTIONS

1. Draw up a list of the General or Ecumenical Councils, and state the doctrine defined in each.
2. Make a list of the great heresies which disturbed the peace of the Church during the first five centuries. Name the authors of these heresies, and their orthodox opponents. Which of these heresies resulted in permanent schisms?
3. What were the beginnings of the rivalry between Byzantium and Alexandria?
4. Define Monophysitism.
5. What is the importance of the "Dogmatic Letter to Flavian"?
6. What were the origins of the Acacian schism?
7. Which phases of the Christological controversies bring out the fact that the Holy See is infallible in its *ex cathedra* dogmatic and moral teachings?

BIBLIOGRAPHY

Eutychían Monophysitism.—Sources: Mansi, *Concil.*, VI, VII.—P. Martin, *Le brigandage d'Ephèse*, according to the recently discovered acts of the council, in *Rev. quest. hist.*, 1874, XVI, p. 5–68; *Le pseudo synode connu dans l'histoire sous le nom de Brigandage d'Ephèse*, studied according to its acts recently discovered in Syriac, *ibid.*, 1875.—St. Leo, *P. L.*, LIV.—Nestorius, *Le livre d'Héraclide*, 1910.—Theodoret, *Eranistes, Hæreticarum fabularum compendium*, IV, 13, *P. G.*, LXXXIII.—Evagrius, *H. E.*, II, III, *P. G.*, LXXXVI.—Theophanius, *Chronographia, P. G.*, CVIII, etc.—Works: Quesnel and Ballerini, *De causa Eutychis dissertationes*, in *P. L.*, LV.—Krüger, *Monophysitische Streitigkeiten im Zusammenhange mit der Reichspolitik*, Jena, 1884; art. *"Monophysiten,"* in *Realencyclopädie für protest. Theologie*, 1905. XIII.—Loofs, art. *"Eutyches und der eutychianische Streit,"* ibid., 1898, V.; *"Christologie,"* ibid., 1898, IV.—Smits and Wace, *Dictionary of Christian Biography*, II, p. 404.—Voisin, *L'Apollinarisme.*—J. Pargoire, *L'Eglise byzantine de 527–847*, 1905.—Tixeront, *op. cit.*, III.—M. Jugie, art. *"Eutychès et l'eutychianisme,"* in *Dict. de Théol.*—P. Batiffol, *Le Siège apostolique*, 1924.

St. Leo.—Sources: *P. L.*, LIV–LVI.—Works: A. de Saint Chéron, *Histoire du pontificat de saint Léon et de son siècle*, 1846.—Kuhn, *Die Christologie Leo's I. des Grossen*, Würzburg, 1894.—Régnier, *Saint Léon le Grand*, Coll. *"Les Saints,"* 1910.—P. Batiffol, *Le Siège apostolique*, ch. VII; art. *"Léon"* in *Dict. de Théol.*

Chalcedon.—A. Largent, *Le brigandage d'Ephèse et le concile de Chalcédoine*, in *Etudes d'histoire ecclésiastique*, 1892.—J. Bois, art. *"Chalcédoine,"* in *Dict. de Théol.*—A. Fortescue, *op. cit.*

The Henoticon.—Sources: Text of the Encyclical, in Evagrius, *Hist. eccles.*, III, 4, *P. G.*, LXXXVI, 2, col. 2600 ff.—Text of the Henoticon in Evagrius, *Hist. eccles.*, III, 14; Excommunication of Acacius in Evagrius, *Hist. eccles.*, III, 21; S. Félix, *Epist.* VI, IX, X, *P. L.*, LVIII. 921, 934, 936.—Works: J. Hergenröther, *Photius*, Ratisbon, 1867, I, pp. 110–153.—E. Revillout, *Le premier schisme de Constantinople*, in *Rev. quest. hist.*, 1877, XXII, p. 83–134.—E. Marin, *Les moines de Constantinople*, 1897, pp. 228–232, 267–270; art. *"Acace,"* in *Dict. de Théol.*—L. Salaville, art. *"Hénotique,"* in *Dict. de Théol.*; *"L'affaire de l'Hénotique,"* in *Echos d'Orient*, 1918, p. 255.—M. Jugie, art. *"Acace,"* in *Dict. d'Hist. eccl.*

Julian of Halicarnassus.—R. Draguet, *Julien d'Halicarnasse et sa controverse avec Sévère d'Antioche sur l'incorruptibilité du corps du Christ*, Louvain, 1924; art. *"Julien d'Halicarnasse"* in *Dict. de Théol.*

General Survey of Christianity During the Fourth and Fifth
Centuries

CHAPTER I

THE PAPACY

I. The Papacy, the Guardian of Orthodoxy. In the battles
waged against the Trinitarian and Christological heresies, the Popes
proved themselves the champions and best guardians of the faith. Against
the Arians, Sylvester I (314–335) ratified the decisions of the First Council of Nicaea (325). His successor, Julius I, championed the cause of
St. Athanasius and presided through his legates at the Council of Sardica,
where it was expressly declared that "Rome is the see of Peter, to which
all the bishops of every province must refer." Then came Pope Liberius
(325–366). In spite of the decisions reached by the Councils of Arles and
Milan, both of which were influenced by the Emperor Constantius, this
Pope refused to condemn Athanasius, preferring voluntary exile in
Thrace. His successor, St. Damasus (366–384), enriched the papacy with
all its splendor. He rehabilitated ancient Rome and stressed the primacy
of the Holy See most explicitly in that famous declaration: "The Holy
Roman Church is raised above all others, not by decrees of councils, but
by the words of Our Lord, who said, 'Thou art Peter, and on this rock
I will build my church.'" Pope Damasus explained that "by the presence
and victory of Peter, Rome was raised above all other cities." The Eastern
patriarchates are the next in line and owe their origin to their relations
with Peter the Apostle: "The second see was consecrated at Alexandria
in the name of Peter by his disciple St. Mark. It is also on account of the
blessed Apostle Peter that the third see, that of Antioch, must be honored,
because Peter sojourned there before coming to Rome." This assertion of
papal rights did not remain a dead letter. Pope Damasus was the first to

make use of them when he fixed the Canon of the Scriptures by these simple words: "These are the books of the Old Testament, which the Holy Roman Catholic Church accepts." A decision of a council held at Hippo re-echoed this *imperatoria brevitas* by saying: "The confirmation of this list must be settled in accord with the Church beyond the seas."

At the outset of the fifth century, Pelagianism was condemned by Pope Innocent I (401–417). Vain attempts were made to circumvent Pope Zosimus (417–418). Correctly informed by the Africans, he anathematized Pelagius at a council held in Rome. Then Pope Celestine I (422–432) intervened in a Semi-Pelagian debate and placed the doctrine of St. Augustine above all suspicion. And no sooner had St. Cyril called his attention to the heresy of Duopersonalism, than he convoked a Roman council at which Nestorius was requested to retract his teachings. Celestine sent legates to Ephesus and enjoined upon them to appear at the council "in the capacity of judges, and not as controversialists." One of them, the priest Philip, made this statement, which contains the essence of the dogma of papal infallibility:

"It is a fact well-known throughout the ages that the holy and blessed Peter, prince and head of the Apostles, pillar of faith, cornerstone of the Catholic Church, received from our Lord the keys of the kingdom, and the power to bind and loose sins. It is he who to this day and for all time lives and judges in his successors." The Roman primacy is stressed in equally emphatic terms at the Council of Chalcedon. In the letter which he sent by his legate, Paschasinus, St. Leo said: "They must abide by the declaration of faith which we made in our dogmatic letter to Flavian." In vain did the Patriarch Anatolius try to substitute in its stead a vague formula. The legates declared: "If you do not abide by the Epistle of Pope Leo, we shall return home, and hold a council in the West." The bishops at once cried out: "We believe as Leo believes, and not as Dioscorus."

The conditions which made for an ecumenical council were as follows: (1) The Pope must convoke it or permit it to convene. As a matter of fact, the four ecumenical councils of this period were convoked by the Emperor, who sent out notices to the bishops, placed the postal service at their disposal, provided for their food and lodging, and afforded them proper protection at their meetings. But the convocation of these councils implied the consent of the Pope, expressed by the presence of the legates, who presided over the meetings in his name, and were the first to append their signatures to the documents. (2) The entire episcopate had to be represented at the council. The Oriental bishops, it is true, were in the majority, but the West was sufficiently represented by the papal legates. (3) Finally the decisions of the council had to be ratified by the Pope. It was many years before the Council of 381 was recognized as ecumenical.

II. **The Pope, Patriarch of the West and Metropolitan of Italy.** In his capacity as Patriarch of the West, the Pope had under his direct jurisdiction: Italy, Gaul, Spain, Brittany, Germany, the two provinces of eastern and western Illyricum (Macedonia, Crete, Thessaly, the two Epiri, the two Dacias, etc.). We do not meet in the West with episcopal sees which display the ambition of Alexandria and Byzantium, and it was only towards the end of the fourth century, under the reign of the Emperor Theodosius, that Milan began to assume special importance. The fame of St. Ambrose was one of the principal reasons why disciplinary or doctrinal difficulties were often referred to Milan at the same time as to Rome, but the papal primacy was never threatened. In the year 417, Pope Zosimus invested the metropolitan of Arles with powers over all the bishops of Gaul.

The Pope was more especially the metropolitan of Italy. Following the example of Constantine, a number of noble families had made large grants of money and property to the Roman Pontiff. The names of pontifical lands often indicate the sources of these donations (*fundus Cornelii, fundus Constantini, massa Furiana, Varoniana,* etc.). Such were the origins of the so-called "Patrimony of St. Peter." As early as the fifth century the Pope was the largest land owner in all Italy. St. Gelasius (492–496) drew up a list of farms and rents which was still in use in the days of St. Gregory, and safeguarded what was known as "the patrimony of the poor."

III. **Byzantine Opposition.** It was not long, however, before the Byzantine bishops set themselves up as rivals of the Patriarch of the West in Illyricum. These intermediary provinces had belonged to the Western Empire up to the year 379, when Gratian gave them to his colleague Theodosius. It was at this time that Constantinople sought to extend her spiritual jurisdiction so as to include them. To protect its rights, the Holy See, about A. D. 380, established a "Vicar Apostolic" of Thessalonica. In 421, however, the Patriarch Atticus brought pressure to bear on Theodosius

II, and the latter made eastern Illyricum subject to "New Rome." Thanks to the energetic protests of Pope Boniface I, this decision was repealed, but Illyricum remained a bone of contention between Rome and Byzantium until the day when, in 732, Leo the Isaurian avenged himself for the condemnation fulminated against Iconoclasm, and definitively severed these regions from the jurisdiction of the Holy See.

The antagonism between the two sees was again increased when, in an attempt to counteract the Apostolic origin of the see of Rome, a certain legend, borrowed from the works of Pseudo-Dorotheus of Tyre, was circulated in the Orient in the sixth century. According to this legend, St. Andrew, the founder of the see of Byzantium, had installed his disciple Stachys in this see as his successor.

Moreover, the differences in the eastern and western mentalities were becoming more and more pronounced. The intellectual acumen and power of understanding of the classical period was gradually disappearing, and as a consequence of the Orientals discontinuing their study of Latin, and the Occidentals giving up the study of Greek, endless and insoluble difficulties resulted in the field of theology. For two centuries, moreover, schisms raged almost without respite. (1) Arianism, from the Council of Sardica to the advent of Chrysostom (343–398), a period of 55 years; (2) the condemnation of Chrysostom was followed by the schism of the Joannites (404–415), for a period of 11 years; (3) the schism of Acacius and the Henoticon lasted for a period of 35 years.

These causes for rupture were counteracted for a long time by motives for peace, such as the desire for Church unity expressed in the Creed of Nicaea and Constantinople, and introduced almost everywhere through the liturgy of the Mass in the closing years of the fifth century; firm belief in the primacy of the Holy See as the supreme authority in matters of faith and morals, and the highest court in matters of discipline; and, finally, deep veneration for Christian Rome, always the center of pilgrimages, and with an abundance of Greek monasteries.

TEXTS AND DOCUMENTS

POPE DAMASUS AND THE PRIMACY

We will close this short notice of the Roman Primacy under Damasus—the most influential Pope of the fourth century—by dealing with two decisions of his, which contain fresh, and till now unknown, witnesses to the history of Roman supremacy. These two weighty decrees, each a landmark in the development of Church doctrine and legislation, have been but recently ascribed to Damasus by competent critics, having formerly been placed at a later date.

The first decree was promulgated by the Pope at the Roman Council of 374. It is the earliest decision which gives a complete list of the sacred books of the Old and New Testaments, and is, therefore, very important in the history of the canon of the Bible. It serves to prove that, even then, the same sacred books were recognized and read in the Church, as having been written "under the operation of God," as those which are still accepted by Catholics as inspired or canonical to-day. The list begins thus: "The list of the books of the Old Testament, which the Holy Catholic Church accepts and reveres, is as follows," the formula implying that it is a rule of faith based on the earliest traditions, especially of the Roman Church, and teaching mankind in which books the Word of God is contained.

The other pronouncement of Damasus which we wish to mention here concerns the patriarchates of the East and the primacy of the Roman See. In his decree regarding the patriarchates, he touches on the disputes we have just spoken about, concerning the precedence to be accorded to the great eastern bishoprics; possibly, indeed, the decree stands in historical connection with the events spoken of. But what is more important is the Pope's emphatic utterance on the subject of the supremacy of the Roman Church, founded by Christ on Peter—a decree which, so to speak, crowns all previous pronouncements on the primacy. It begins thus: "The entire Catholic Church spread over the globe is the sole bridal chamber of Christ. But the Church of Rome has been placed above all other Churches, not by decree of councils, but by the word of our Lord and Saviour in the Gospel, who gave it the primacy when He said: 'Thou art Peter, and upon this rock I will build my Church, and the gates of hell shall not prevail against it. And I will give to thee the keys of the kingdom of Heaven; and whatsoever thou shalt bind upon earth, it shall be bound also in Heaven, and whatsoever thou shalt loose on earth, it shall be loosed also in Heaven.'"

GRISAR, *History of Rome and the Popes*
Vol. I, pp. 337 ff.

QUESTIONS

1. What is meant by the Roman Primacy?
2. Distinguish between a primacy of honor and a primacy of jurisdiction.
3. Show from the evidence of the first five centuries that Rome enjoyed a primacy of jurisdiction already in those days.
4. Sum up the remote causes of the great Greek schism.
5. Does the spirit of rivalry which existed between the western and eastern

patriarchates sufficiently account for the evolution of the dogma of papal infallibility?

6. Compare the ancient and modern procedure of electing bishops.

BIBLIOGRAPHY

The Papacy.—THOMAS S. DOLAN, *The Papacy and the First Councils of the Church,* Herder, 1910.—CHAPMAN, *Studies on the Early Papacy.*—GRISAR, *History of Rome and the Popes.*—G. GOYAU, *Vue générale de l'histoire de la papauté.*

I. The Bishop: Election of the Bishop. His Auxiliaries. The election of a bishop ordinarily took place as follows: The candidate was proposed by the clergy and the people, and his candidacy ratified by the bishops of the province and the metropolitan. This procedure, however, was not always strictly enforced. Very often the Emperor would meddle with the election and impose his choice. This fact partially accounts for the servility of certain Oriental prelates. Once the election was approved by the metropolitan, the candidate received the episcopal consecration from the hands of three bishops. He was then invested with the distinctive mark of his office, which was the miter, a sort of narrow headband made of thin metal.

Once established for life in his diocese, the bishop surrounded himself with a group of ecclesiastical advisers. In proportion as the spiritual duties of the bishops increased, there were established, especially in the East, a great number of new charges. The archdeacon was a sort of vicar-general, who issued orders to all the clergy. He managed the church goods and provided for the welfare of the poor and the widows. The apocrisiary had charge of all diplomatic relations. Those whom the bishops of Rome despatched to Constantinople, often attained to the high office of the papacy. Instances of such were Vigilius, Pelagius I, St. Gregory the Great, Sabinianus, and Boniface III. Below the archdeacon was the archpriest, who replaced the bishop, when absent, in the exercise of sacerdotal functions. After him came a whole group of church officers: *syncellae,* a sort of private secretaries, who, as their name indicates, shared the bishop's apartments; *treasurers,* who collected and distributed the revenues; *defensores,* who handled all ecclesiastical law suits; *notaries* and *archivists,* who wrote down and preserved the acts; *fossores,* or grave diggers; *mansionarii,* or beadles. All these persons were listed with the clergy and belonged to the ecclesiastical hierarchy, but custom permitted the same cleric to hold a number of offices.

II. The Clergy: Ecclesiastical Celibacy. Revenues and Immunities. The establishment of churches in outlying districts was already a problem in the third century, and in the fourth, with the extraordinary growth of Christianity, it called for immediate solution. The main question at issue was whom to put at the head of these churches. Bishops could not be appointed, for such a procedure would strike a blow at the monarchical episcopate. The institution of the *chorepiscopi,* therefore, was of necessity a makeshift. The councils of Laodicea and Sardica expressly forbade that bishops be nominated to rural parishes. At first, priests were assigned to these places temporarily, but very soon this arrangement was adopted definitively. When parishes began to grow and require the administration of several officiating clergymen and several oratories, they were headed by archpriests. The development of the parish as an institution attained complete maturity in the closing years of the fifth century.

In the West, the Council of Elvira, held around 300, commanded all clerics to abstain from sexual intercourse with their wives. It is a well-known fact, however, that the decisions of this council were very severe and intended only for Spain. The decisions of a council held at Rome under Pope Siricius, in 386, carried more weight. Priests and deacons were held from that time on to practice continence, and St. Leo enforced these regulations, making them binding even on subdeacons. No doubt, objections issuing from local communities, especially in Spain, had to be overcome, but little by little ecclesiastical celibacy spread throughout the West. The Greeks, however, continued to follow the ancient custom. Clerics who had been admitted to higher Orders could no longer contract marriage, but could continue to live in the married state if they had entered it before receiving subdeaconship. Bishops were the sole exception to this rule; they were constrained to observe perfect continence.

The education of the clergy remained about the same as in the early days. The candidate was required to be a free man, but could not be a neophyte. Gradually the bishop took a more direct interest in the training of his clergy. By constraining candidates to exercise successively the different ecclesiastical functions and live in close proximity to the prelate while the latter managed church affairs, he succeeded in getting the best results. Sometimes, the bishop gathered his clerics around him to live a community life with him. St. Augustine adopted this measure at Hippo and St. Eusebius at Vercelli. Cases of this kind, however, always remained the exception. The ordinary procedure followed was the education of young clerics by priests in outlying districts, who in this way trained their successors. This practice was first inaugurated in Italy; a synod held at Vaison introduced it into the province of Arles.

After peace had been restored to the Church, the Emperor Constantine acknowledged the right of Christian communities to receive legacies and bequests. At times, the episcopal church became very rich and divided its revenues into four parts, appropriated, respectively, by the bishop, the clergy, the fund for the maintenance of church buildings, and the poor. Rural parishes also had their revenues, part of which belonged by law to the bishop, in particular one-third of the offerings of the faithful. At times the clergy, especially those residing in the country, were obliged to engage in manual labor. It is still a Church law in the Orient that ministers of the altar remain farmers if they earned their living from the soil before their ordination.

Finally, clerics enjoyed certain immunities. Constantine excused them from all municipal functions, which were gratuitous and often quite burdensome. Constans exempted them, together with their families, from all extraordinary taxes. To these immunities we must add the *privilegium fori*. Already in the fourth century, bishops were not subject to the jurisdiction of civil tribunals, and the third Council of Carthage and the Council of Chalcedon extended this privilege to all the clergy. In the sixth century, Justinian decreed that suits brought against clerics by laymen should be filed in the ecclesiastical courts and sentence passed by the bishops in matters pertaining to their priests, and by the metropolitan and the patriarch, in those pertaining to their suffragan bishops. The penalties imposed were suspension, deposition, lay communion (excommunication), and, in cases of relapse (*recidivi*), complete exclusion from the Christian community. It sometimes happened that clergymen were appointed to be judges in civil cases, replacing the civil magistrates. Constantine decided that, at the request of either party in a law-suit, the case should be referred to the bishop.

TEXTS AND DOCUMENTS

THE POPE AS METROPOLITAN

Two special prerogatives belonged, as we know, to the metropolitan. He had the right of consecrating all bishops elected in his province, and of convoking them to ordinary or extraordinary councils in his own city. Hence the whole body of suffragans of Milan, Ravenna, and also of Rome, were spoken of, sometimes as the episcopate "of the consecration" (*ordinatio*) of the bishops of Milan, Ravenna, or Rome, sometimes as the *concilium* or "synod" of their respective metropolitan.

At Rome the Pope personally undertook the consecration of "his" bishops on certain Sundays in the year. As regards the periodical provincial councils, however, the original rule, observed elsewhere, also held good for Rome, *viz.*, that they should be held twice a year at the appointed season. Alternations, however, occurred in this rule, mainly on account of the numerous exceptional cases which were constantly requiring the bishops to assemble.

Adapted from Grisar, History of Rome
and the Popes, Vol. I, pp. 347 ff.

QUESTIONS

1. Contrast the method of electing bishops in the West with that followed in the East.
2. What were the duties of archdeacons, archpriests, *defensores, fossores?*
3. What traces are there of these offices in present-day ecclesiastical administration?
4. How are we to account for the establishment of rural parishes, and what was the procedure followed?
5. What is meant by "ecclesiastical immunities"?

BIBLIOGRAPHY

The Hierarchy.—Sources: Thomassin, *Vet. et nov. eccles. discipl., lib.* II, c. 21–23, 97–108.—Works: Dom Parisot, *Les chorévêques,* in *Rev. de l'Orient chrétien,* VI, 1901, pp. 157 ff.—Jugie, *Les chorévêques en Orient* in *Echos d'Orient,* VII, 1904, pp. 236 ff.—Bergère, *Etudes sur les Chorévêques,* 1905.—Imbart de la Tour, *Les paroisses rurales du IVe au XIe siècle,* 1900.—Allard, *Le clergé chrétien au milieu du IVe siècle,* in *Rev. quest. hist.,* LVIII, pp. 5–40.

CHAPTER III

We have no lack of documentary evidence regarding ancient liturgical practices. The reader has already been apprised of the importance of such writings as the *Doctrine of the Twelve Apostles* and the works of St. Justin. In the third century, the works of Tertullian and St. Cyprian abound in liturgical data. The *Apostolic Tradition* of St. Hippolytus and the canons which bear his name also contain much information on Baptism, Ordinations, and the Mass. Beginning with the fourth century, some writers wrote *ex professo* treatises on these subjects. Mention should be made of the *Liber de Mysteriis* of St. Ambrose (on Baptism and the Holy Eucharist), but especially of his *De Sacramentis Libri Sex,* in which we find a detailed description of liturgical practices. It was around this time also that the *Peregrinatio Aetheriae* was composed—a sort of diary kept by an abbess of Galicia, which contains interesting details on the liturgy of the Church of Jerusalem. The *Apostolic Constitutions,* written towards the end of the fourth and the beginning of the fifth century, are the work of an interpolator, who tried to mould into one the different documents regarded as being of Apostolic origin, and by clever additions and subtractions succeeded in adapting them to the liturgy of his time. Books II and VIII contain a description, the broad outlines of which reproduce the service of the Churches before the advent of Constantine. Beginning with the fourth and fifth centuries, special collections of formulas of orations and prayers were made, a practice strongly encouraged by the councils. It is to this period that we must ascribe certain parts of the Gelasian Sacramentary.

I. **The Eucharistic Synaxis: The Mass of the Catechumens. The Mass of the Faithful. Private Masses. The Stational Mass.** In the early Church a synaxis was held on Sunday, the first part of which corresponded to the ancient gathering of the synagogue. At this synaxis the faithful listened to readings from the Old and New Testaments, as well as the singing of homilies and hymns. Pliny makes mention of these in his letter to the Emperor Trajan. This synaxis gradually evolved into a distinct vigil and gave rise to the Office of Matins. At Rome it survived in the case of some solemnities, notably Easter and Pentecost. Very soon, however, the Office of Vigils and the Eucharistic synaxis were combined to form the Mass of the Catechumens and the Mass of the faithful.

The Mass of the Catechumens comprised the singing of psalms and the reading of lessons. While the pontiff advanced from the *secretarium,* or sacristy, to the altar, the choir intoned the anthem *ad introitum,* followed by a psalm. This was the custom at Rome from the fifth century onward. The function then began with the salutation of the bishop, *Pax,* or *Dominus vobiscum,* and the collect. At a very early date, the *supplicatio* was inserted at this point. This was a prayer of the faithful, recited by the deacon, which enumerated the principal intentions of the Church. The people responded with *Kyrie eleison.* This acclamation is all that remains of the *supplicatio* to-day. Formerly, this liturgical prayer followed the readings, including the reading of the Gospel, as may still be seen from the Office of Good Friday, the grand orations of which are authentic remnants of this prayer. Then came the two readings from the Old and New Testaments (Epistles). These readings were not yet fixed, but their selection was left to the bishop. Between the readings, psalms were chanted in the form of responses, in other words, with a refrain or response inserted at different places. Sometimes, also, the readings were continued without response or interruption (*in directum*). The final reading was that of the Gospel, selected by the bishop and read to the people by the deacon. This was followed by a commentary. The majority of the homilies written by the Fathers were delivered at this moment. After this first part, gentiles, penitents, and catechumens were dismissed by one formula. This was the *missa, i. e.,* the dismissal of the catechumens.

The assistants still had a part to play in the Mass properly so called: first, in the form of prayers, because it was at the beginning of the Mass that the prayer of the faithful mentioned above was formerly recited; secondly, at the Offertory, where each Christian was required to furnish the matter of the sacrifice, bread and wine, and also to add other gifts for the clergy and the poor. In the course of the fifth century, a psalm was intoned during the Offertory corresponding to the psalm chanted during the Introit. This is the origin of our Offertory.

Finally, came the exclusive part of the celebrant, the Eucharistic prayer, or prayer of thanksgiving. The ancient formula enumerated all the gifts of God: the Creation, the miracles of the Old Testament, the Incarnation, and the Passion. It was quite natural and in keeping with the chronological order to place at this juncture the account of the Last Supper, because of its power of consecration (*vis consecrandi*). Mindful of the divine precepts, the celebrant then recalled the whole sequel of the mystery of Christ and the mission of the Holy Ghost. This was the *anamnesis* and the *epiclesis*. The Greek schismatics later maintained that, as the epiclesis mentioned the work of the Holy Ghost in the mystery of the Eucharist, it possessed the power of consecration. As a matter of fact, there was no question at that time of determining the precise moment when the offerings (*oblata*) were sanctified. It sufficed to know that Jesus Christ acted through the priest. The Canon ended with a Trinitarian doxology, and the faithful answered with an approving *Amen*—the same which precedes the *Pater Noster* to-day. The time between the *Sursum Corda* and the *Pater* was taken up by one continuous prayer of thanksgiving, and formerly this prayer was not interrupted by the *Sanctus,* or Trisagion, or the commemorations placed before the Preface. The exact wording of this long prayer, recited in a loud tone of voice, was at first left to the discretion of the celebrant, but became fixed in the different liturgies towards the third or the fourth century.

After the breaking of the Host, the Holy Eucharist was distributed to the priests, the clergy, and the faithful. The bishop placed the Eucharist in the right hand of the recipient, saying at the same time, *"Corpus Christi."* The recipient answered, *"Amen."* Women received the Host in the same way, but had their hand covered with a piece of linen, called the *dominicale.* The deacon then offered to each the chalice, saying, *"Sanguis Christi, calix vitae."* It was an early custom to intone a psalm during Communion. As in the case of the Offertory, nothing remains of this psalm to-day but the anthem. At the outset, the Christians frequently carried the Holy Eucharist to their homes, and bishops sent it to one another as a token of peace. After the Communion, a prayer of thanksgiving was recited, followed by the formula: *"Ite, missa est"* (Go, you are dismissed).

In the second century the only Mass was the one celebrated by the bishop, and on Sunday only. Very soon, however, Masses commemorating the anniversary of martyrs on the day of their birth (*natale*) were added to this pontifical Mass. It is thus that we are informed by the Roman calendar of the year 354 that the *natale* of St. Cyprian was celebrated in the cemetery of Callixtus. The Bishop of Rome, however, safeguarded the universal character of the Mass. With this purpose in mind, he created the *stations*. On solemn feast-days he went forth in procession with his entire clergy to the church at which Mass was to be offered. This stational Mass was celebrated in the days of Pope Hilary (461–468).

II. The Ceremony of Christian Initiation: The Catechumenate. The ceremony of Christian initiation comprised Baptism, Confirmation, and first Communion. It called for a period of preparation, termed the catechumenate, which was the regular procedure from the beginning of the third to the end of the fifth century.

Admission to the catechumenate presupposed an application made in due form to the bishop, and an investigation conducted by the latter. The postulant was required to effect certain changes in his life before being accepted. Persons who were engaged in work regarded as dishonest or unbecoming, like actors and cabmen, had first to give up their profession.

Admission to the catechumenate was marked by various rites, which, at Rome in particular, consisted in an exsufflation, accompanied by a formula of exorcism, the imposition of the sign of the Cross on the forehead and of hands on the head of the candidate, and the placing on his tongue of a small quantity of exorcized salt. From that moment on the catechumen was regarded as a member of the Christian community, even though he was still called an *auditor* or listener, and took his place at Christian gatherings, not as a mere stranger, like the pagans or the Jews, but as belonging to the congregation. After the Mass of the Catechumens, and before the dismissal, he received the solemn imposition of hands from the bishop. At private gatherings, he was instructed by the catechists.

After this first period of probation, which varied in length in different countries—two years in Spain, according to the Council of Elvira, and three in the Orient, according to St. Gregory of Nazianzus—the catechumen made application for admission into the ranks of those who were directly preparing for Baptism. These persons were called *competentes* (the elect). It sometimes happened that a catechumen indefinitely deferred taking this step until he was near death—a practice which permitted him to retain pagan habits under the cover of the catechumenate.

The Church protested against this abuse, and invited catechumens to have their names inscribed among the *competentes* several weeks before Easter. The candidate then made his confession to the bishop and received an additional catechetic instruction. This was followed by the *traditio fidei,* or placing of the Creed in the hands of the *competentes*—a ceremony which took place in Rome on Wednesday of the fourth week in Lent. Most of the catecheses of St. Cyril of Jerusalem (348) have reference to the Creed. Throughout this period, the "elect" were subjected to impositions of hands and exorcisms, the last and most solemn of which was the *Effeta.*

In the early Church everything of a preparatory nature was accomplished during Lent. Baptism was administered only at Easter and on Pentecost Sunday, in a private chapel called the baptistry. The candidate was baptized by immersion, the officiating minister either placing his head under a faucet of water, or taking water from the piscina and pouring it over his head. The newly baptized Christian was then anointed with a double unction: the first, *chrismatio,* a part of the Sacrament of Baptism and administered by a simple priest; the second, *consignatio,* reserved to the bishop. The latter unction was the Sacrament of Confirmation. This distinction did not exist in the East, where the priest both baptized and confirmed the neophytes, who then assisted at the Easter Mass, at which they received holy Communion. This was followed by the blessing in their honor of milk and honey, which were served immediately after Communion. An allusion to this custom is to be found in the words of the Introit: *"Quasimodo geniti infantes."* The neophytes continued their instructions during Easter week, until the Sunday *in albis deponendis,* when they discarded their white garments.

The reader might ask if Baptism in those days admitted of any substitutes. It was generally agreed that Baptism of blood was efficacious, but the question of the efficacy of the Baptism of desire was controverted. Soon the days on which Baptism could be received were multiplied. At Jerusalem, it was customary to baptize on the anniversary of the dedication of the church of Calvary. Then, too, in the East, the custom was introduced of baptizing on Epiphany, and also, in several churches, on the feast-days of the martyrs. Rome, however, continued to baptize only at Easter and on Pentecost.

According to a decision issued by Pope Stephen on the occasion of his controversy with St. Cyprian, the Western Church recognized the validity of the Baptism of heretics, and this view was imposed on the Africans by the Council of Arles (313). The East was less submissive to Roman directions. The *Apostolic Constitutions* did not admit the validity of such a Baptism. Some distinguished between heretics and heretics. In the fifth century a canon falsely attributed to the Second Ecumenical Council treated as valid the Baptism of Arians and Macedonians, but as invalid that of Montanists and Sabellians.

III. Christian Penance: Private Confession and Public Penance. Our Lord had instituted the Sacrament of Penance, and so, from the earliest times, the Christians considered it a strict obligation to have recourse to this Sacrament. In the beginning it was called *exomologesis,* a Greek word signifying *avowal.*

This Sacrament comprised first of all the accusation of one's faults. It was the duty of the "church officers," *i. e.,* the bishops, to hear confessions and absolve from sins. In the fourth and fifth centuries the Roman Church knew of no other ministers of the Sacrament of Penance, even though she entrusted the task of preparing the *lapsi* for reconciliation to the parish priests. At Constantinople, however, we find a penitentiary priest carrying on his duties as early as the fourth century. Confession was usually private. Public confession was never of obligation; when it occurred, it was the exception and not the rule. St. Leo suppressed the custom, introduced into some provinces of Italy, notably Campania, of drawing up a list of one's sins and reading it aloud in the presence of the Christian assembly; he feared "that many might become estranged from the Sacrament of Penance either by shame or by the fear that deeds punishable by law might be revealed to their enemies."

After the confession properly so called, we read of public works of satisfaction strictly enjoined upon repentant sinners, the most outstanding of which were the prohibition to assist at Mass and the privation of holy Communion. In the East it was customary to distinguish four kinds of penitents: (1) the *lugentes,* who stood at the door of the church and recommended themselves to the prayers of those who entered; (2) the *audientes,* who assisted only at the Mass of the catechumens and were then discharged with the simple injunction, *"Ite missa est";* (3) the *prosternantes,* who, before withdrawing, prostrated themselves at the feet of the bishop to receive the imposition of hands; (4) the *stantes,* who stood near the faithful, but took no part in the Offertory and the Communion. This division was approved by the Council of Nicaea, but in the West there existed only the category of the *stantes,* who were assigned to a special place in church, called the *limen in vestibulo* by Tertullian, and *extra castra* by St. Jerome. It was only after the guilty party had performed his penance that he received absolution in public. Ancient descriptions forcibly convey the impression that penitents, far from considering themselves absolved in the internal forum, strove strenuously and sorrowfully to merit absolution. The solemn reconciliation or communion of the penitent was effected through the bishop. At Rome this took place on Holy Thursday; in the Orient and in Spain, on Good Friday.

As a rule, the penance imposed was a very long one, and seldom renewed. A person who had the misfortune of relapsing into mortal sin could not be re-admitted to the exomologesis, for fear that the remedy might deteriorate from repeated usage. His salvation was not despaired of, however, but he was advised to leave the matter in the hands of God. In the fourth century, the penitential discipline was somewhat mitigated.

In the East, the suppression of the penitentiary priest by Nectarius, Patriarch of Constantinople, in the year 391, had for its effect the abolition of public penance and the different stages of penitents. Public satisfaction became a matter of free choice and was imposed only on rare occasions and to satisfy for grave scandals. In the West, St. Leo still continued to regard public penance as necessary for the expiation of mortal sins. Many of the faithful continued to do public penance from motives of pure zeal, and certain funeral inscriptions recall that the deceased engaged in public penance as a pledge of immortality.

IV. The Liturgical Year. Already in Apostolic times, the first day of the week, being commemorative of Easter and Pentecost, was substituted for the seventh day, or Jewish Sabbath, for the celebration of divine worship. This fact accounts for the expressions: *una sabbatorum, post dies octo,* used to designate the gatherings of the Apostles. The Apostolic Fathers also speak of Sunday as the day on which the Eucharistic synaxis was celebrated. A few continued to cling to the practice of the Saturday observance. In fact, in some liturgies, and notably in the monastic rites recalled by Cassian, Saturday was still observed as a feria with the Eucharistic sacrifice and a special Office. It was soon ousted from that place by Wednesday and Friday, which also had their special services. These days were fast days, and were called station days. On these days, meetings were held and often solemn Mass was celebrated. Saturday in Roman usage became a day of fasting and penance, on which Mass was not celebrated.

From the start there were two great feast-days: *Easter* and *Pentecost*. Easter comprised not only the feast of the Resurrection of our Divine Saviour, but also His Passion and Death. These three days, therefore, constituted one feast and at one time were referred to as the Passover of the Passion, the Passover of the Crucifixion, and the Passover of the Resurrection. Very soon the custom was introduced of placing before this feast a fast which lasted one day, two days, or forty hours. This practice appears for the first time in a letter of St. Irenaeus to St. Victor (189–198), but it dates back much farther. It is not until the time of the Council of Nicaea that we meet with a reference to a real Lent, comprising a fast of six weeks in the West and seven in the East—in reality of equal duration, since the East excepted both Sundays and Saturdays.

Epiphany, which was celebrated in the East on the sixth of January, at the outset recalled in a more particular manner the manifestation of the Messias at His Baptism in the Jordan and at the marriage feast of Cana in Galilee. For this reason it was called Theophany. The first trace of the celebration of Christmas at Rome takes us back to the year 354. The Nativity of Christ was commemorated on the twenty-fifth of December, with a view, perhaps, of counteracting the popular feast of the Sun-God Mithra. More probably, however, that day was selected because astronomers had succeeded in computing the date of the death of Our Lord, fixing it at the twenty-fifth of March. It was argued that His Incarnation also took place on that date "because the years which Christ spent on this earth were complete years, fractions of years being imperfections." The Roman feast of Christmas and the Eastern feast of the Epiphany spread rapidly to include all Christendom. Christmas was ushered in by a preparatory period, Advent, the existence of which is attested in Gaul towards the end of the fifth century.

The *cult of the Blessed Virgin Mary* dates back to the earliest days of antiquity, as may be seen from the writings of the Fathers and the paintings in the catacombs. The attacks upon the dignity of Mary by Jovinian and Helvidius in the West, towards the end of the fourth century, and the far more serious blasphemies of Nestorius and Eutyches, who denied her divine motherhood, contributed to the development of her cult. The great Marian feast-days, however, were not yet in existence. Only the Presentation of Our Lord, or the Purification, is referred to as a local feast-day at Jerusalem by the *Peregrinatio Silviae* in the second half of the fourth century.

Each particular church observed the anniversary of the death of its martyrs (*dies natalis*) by an office celebrated at their tombs and in which their names were commemorated. These feasts date back to the second century. The anniversary of St. Polycarp († 155), for example, was instituted at Smyrna after his death. With the exception of SS. Peter and Paul, however, the Roman calendars do not contain any martyrs prior to the third century. At the outset, these anniversaries were quite naturally celebrated as purely local feasts. Very soon, however, the most famous among the saints were venerated outside of their own country. Some, like St. Xystus and St. Lawrence of Rome, St. Cyprian of Carthage, etc., attained to what was tantamount to universal veneration. The translation of relics added a new impetus to this form of worship.

Special mention must be made of the veneration of SS. Peter and Paul at Rome. The Philocalian Calendar of the year 336 mentions the feast of the 29th of June. This date marked either the anniversary of their martyrdom or that of the translation of their relics to the *Via Appia,* at the place called *"Ad Catacumbas,"* where they awaited the day when Constantine was to enshrine them in basilicas erected near their first resting places in the Vatican and on the *Via Ostia* (St. Paul Outside the Walls). Although the fact of the translation of their bodies is contested, the date of June 29 is still observed. The Philocalian Calendar of the year 354 calls attention to a solemnity entitled *Natale Petri de Cathedra,* celebrated on the 22nd of February, the purpose of which was to commemorate the inauguration of St. Peter's apostolate. The date of February 22 was selected in order to counteract a very popular pagan feast, that of the deceased members of each family. As the 22nd of February often fell in Lent, the feast was transferred in some countries to the 18th of January. This accounts for the double feast-day, although the only day recognized in Rome, previous to the sixteenth century, was February 22. During the pontificate of Sixtus III (432–440), the feast of the dedication of the church of the Apostles on the Esquiline was celebrated August 1. This church preserved the chains of St. Peter, whence the name "St. Peter's Chains" was given to the basilica and to the feast of its dedication (*a vinculis S. Petri*).

V. The Churches: Constantinian Basilicas. The first Christian gatherings took place in the dining rooms of private homes. With the gradual increase in the numbers of the faithful, an entire house had to be set aside for that purpose, comprising a meeting room, a furniture room, and a room for the priests. The old Roman houses, with their porticoes opening into the *atrium,* were well adapted to this purpose. Sometimes the homes of the rich were converted into places of worship. Instances in point in Apostolic times were the house of Aquila and Prisca on the Aventine and the *Ecclesia Pudentiana* on the Viminal.

As soon as civil authority recognized the right of the Church to own property—which happened in the course of the third century—the faithful set about constructing churches. The pagan Porphyry says: "The Christians rival with the builders of our temples and construct spacious houses in which they gather to pray." The basilica was rectangular in form and divided into three naves by two rows of columns. A high roof covered the central nave, which was larger than the other two, and terminated, not in a wall, but in a semi-circular recess called apse. From this description it is evident that the Christian basilica was not, as has sometimes been maintained, modelled on pagan temples, nor on ancient civil structures. Rather, it was an imitation of the Roman mansion, in which the first liturgical meetings had been held. We find in it, indeed, the vestibule, the first court, or atrium, in the center of which was the fountain for the purification of worshippers before they entered the second court, or peristyle, surrounded by columns, in which the catechumens and the penitents congregated; and finally, the nave. Mention must be made in this place of the four great Constantinian basilicas, which because of their extraordinary splendor, were destined to become the *"major basilicas"* of Rome. They were: (1) the ancient mansion of the Laterani on Mount Coelius, which belonged to Fausta, the wife of Constantine, and was donated by her to Pope Miltiades in 313. St. Sylvester gave it the name of Basilica of Our Holy Saviour, and under this caption we celebrate the feast of its dedication on the ninth of October. Many years later, Lucius III consecrated it to St. John the Baptist, and called it St. John Lateran. In the fourth century this basilica had replaced that of St. Peter as the chief religious center in Rome. Penitents were reconciled to God within its porticoes on Holy Thursday, catechumens were baptized there on Holy Saturday, and the Pope officiated at its altar on Easter Sunday and conferred ordinations. Not very far from there, on the same Coelius, was another palace, the *Domus Sessoriana,* home of St. Helena, the mother of Constantine. Upon her return from Palestine, where she had been instrumental in the finding of the Holy Cross, she resolved to dedicate an oratory in her house to the Cross of the Saviour. This is the origin of the Basilica of the Holy Cross of Jerusalem. (2) The Emperor Constantine wished also to honor the first martyrs, the founders of the Roman Church, and with this purpose in mind issued orders that a basilica be erected on the Vatican hill, beyond the Tiber, on the spot where St. Peter had died and was buried. Already in the fourth century this basilica was the center of pilgrimages, like St. John Lateran, and the celebration of the feast of its dedication was made binding upon the Universal Church. This feast took the name of *In Dedicatione Basilicarum SS. Apostolorum Petri et Pauli* (Nov. 18). (3) At the other extremity of Rome, on the *Via Ostia,* Constantine erected another church, to mark the spot where St. Paul's head was severed from his body. This was the church of St. Paul Outside the Walls, which was enlarged under the administration of the Valentinians, towards the end of the fourth century. (4) Finally, Constantine built the basilica of St. Lawrence Outside the Walls, on the spot which marked the burial place of the famous Roman deacon of that name.

The origin of four great Roman basilicas, therefore, can be traced to the Emperor Constantine. To the above-mentioned we must add the Basilica of St. Mary Major, the largest of all churches consecrated to Our Lady. It was built in the first half of the fourth century by Pope Liberius, and was first called the Liberian Basilica, then St. Mary of the Snows, on account of the miracle mentioned in the Breviary on August 5, the day on which its dedication is celebrated. It is also called St. Mary at the Crib (*ad praesepe*), because the crib preserved there is thought to be that in which the Infant Jesus lay. The church itself strikes one as "a sort of Bethlehem in the heart of Rome," as the feast of the Nativity of Our Lord is commemorated there in all its solemnity.

TEXTS AND DOCUMENTS

The Mass in the Early Centuries

The Prayer of the Faithful. Nobody prays; the choir sings a psalm, the bishop and his ministers prepare the Sacrifice. Here then there is an hiatus. In the ancient liturgy this was the moment of a prayer. The faithful stood up, their arms stretched out, their eyes raised to heaven, just like those in prayer who are painted upon the walls of the catacombs; or they prostrated themselves, and prayed in silence. Then the celebrant spoke in the name of the faithful, just as he had in the first collect. . . . Only the faithful now remained in the church. All then stood up, turned to the East, and offered up a prayer called the prayer of the faithful. After this prayer they give each other the kiss of peace, and then the deacon prays for all the needs of the church. This is the litany prayer.

Dom Cabrol, Le Livre de la Prière Antique,
pp. 105 ff.

The Communion and Post Communion. The Pontiff communicated, then the priests, then the assistants. The bishop placed the Eucharist under the form of bread in the open right hand of each of the faithful, saying *"Corpus Christi,* The Body of Christ." The deacon presented the chalice to each, saying: *"Sanguis Christi, calix vitae,* The Blood of Christ, the chalice of life." Thus gradually, in order to avoid any possible irreverence, it became customary for the priest to place the Sacred Host in the mouth of the communicant, and where the Precious Blood was also given, for the Deacon to administer it, and frequently through a golden or silver reed (*calamus*).

Ibid., p. 114.

The Blessing. The Lord through Moses ordered priests to pour forth a blessing on the people. . . . In order to safeguard the honour of the Pontiff, the Sacred Canons have appointed that the bishop should pronounce a longer benediction, and the priest a shorter, saying: "May the peace, faith, and charity, and the communication of the Body and Blood of the Lord be (abide) always with you."

Duchesne, Christian Worship, p. 222.

QUESTIONS

1. What was the Eucharistic synaxis?
2. Trace the origin of the Introit, the Kyrie, the Collects, the Epistle, the Gospel, the Offertory, the Preface, the Consecration, and the Communion of the Mass.
3. What were the anamnesis and the epiclesis?
4. What was the Stational Mass?

5. Account for the origin of the early feasts of the Church.
6. What was the Exomologesis?
7. Give as accurate a description as possible of a Christian basilica.
8. What is the difference between a catechumen and a neophyte? Are catechumens and catechumenates still in existence to-day?
9. How does a vigil in the liturgy of to-day differ from a vigil in the early Church?
10. What was the Discipline of the Secret?

BIBLIOGRAPHY

The Liturgy.—A. Fortescue, *The Mass, A Study of the Roman Liturgy*, Longmans, 1922.—Dom Guéranger, *The Liturgical Year*.—J. O'Brien, *A History of the Mass and its Ceremonies in the Eastern and Western Church*, 15th edit.—W. Lübke, *Vorschule z. St. d. k. Kunst* (English transl: *Introd. to a History of Church Architecture*, 1855).—Duchesne, *Christian Worship*, 2nd edit., 1904.—Cabrol, *Etude sur la Peregrinatio Silviae.*—F. Ernst, *Die Ketzertaufangelegenheit in der altchr. K. nach Cyprian*, 1901.—H. Delehaye, *Legends of the Saints.*

Works on Liturgical Sources.—Dom Cabrol, *Introduction aux études liturgiques*, 1907; *Etude sur la Peregrinatio Silviae*, 1895.—Dom Férotin, *Le véritable auteur de la Peregrinatio* in *Rev. quest. hist.*, Oct., 1903.—Nau, art. *"Constitutions Apostoloques"* in *Dict. de Théol.*—F. X. Funk, *Didascalia et Constitutiones Apostolorum*, Paderbornae, 1905.

The Eucharistic Synaxis.—Dom Cabrol, *Le livre de la prière antique*, 1910, ch. VII: *Les Origines liturgiques; Etudes sur la Peregrinatio*, ch. II.—Duchesne, *Les origines du culte chrétien.*—Dom Cagin, *Eucharistia.*—Batiffol, *Dix leçons sur la messe*, 1919; *l'Eucharistie.*—Rauschen, *L'Eucharistie et la Pénitence durant les six premiers siècles.*—Dom Moreau, *Les liturgies eucharistiques*, Brussels, 1924.—M. de la Taille, *Mysterium fidei*, 2nd edit., 1924.—Dom J. de Puniet, *La liturgie de la messe*, 1928.

Baptism.—Dom J. de Puniet, art. *"Baptême"* and *"Catéchuménat,"* in *Dict. d'Arch.*—G. Bareille, art. *"Catéchèse,"* and *"Catéchuménat,"* in *Dict. de Théol.*; art. *"Baptême d'après les Pères."*—Duchesne, *Les origines du culte chrétien.*—V. Ermoni, *L'histoire du baptême depuis l'Edit de Milan jusqu'au concile in Trullo* in *Rev. quest. hist.*, 1898, LXIV, pp. 313-324; *Le baptême dans l'Eglise primitive*, 1904.—Corblet, *Histoire du sacrement de baptême*, 2 vols., 1892.—Galtier, *La consignation à Rome et à Carthage*, in *Rech. de sc. relig.*, 1911 (II): *La Consignation dans les Eglises d'Occident*, in *Rev. hist. eccl.*, 1912 (XIII).

Penance.—Batiffol, *Etudes d'hist. et de théol. positive*, 1st series, 1920. —Rauschen, *L'Eucharistie et la Pénitence*, 1910.—Vacandard, art. *"Confession,"* in *Dict. de Théol.*—Msgr. Boudinhon, *Sur l'histoire de la pénitence*, *Rev. hist. et litt. relig.*, 1897, pp. 306 ff.; pp. 496 ff.—A. d'Alès, *Limes ec-*

clesiæ, in *Rev. hist. eccl.*, 1906, 16 ff.; *l'Edit de Calliste.*—Tixeront, *op. cit.*, I and II; *La confession est-elle une invention du moyen âge?;* and *Comment se confessaient les chrétiens des premiers siècles*, in *l'Université catholique de Lyon,* 1913 (LXXII).

The Liturgical Year.—Dom Guéranger, *The Liturgical Year, passim.* —Dom Cabrol, *Le livre de la prière antique; Les origines liturgiques,* 1906.— Duchesne, *Les origines du culte chrétien.*—Dom Dumaine, art. *"Dimanche,"* in *Dict. d'Arch.*—Dom Cabrol, *Etude sur la Peregrinatio Silviae,* 1895; *Le Paganisme dans la liturgie* in *Rev. prat. d'Apol.,* 1906–1907 (III–V); *Les Fêtes chrétiennes et les fêtes païennes* (Coll. *"Etudes religieuses,"* No. 63).—F. Cabrol, art. *"Fêtes chrétiennes"* in *Dict. d'Arch.*

Constantinian Basilicas.—H. Leclercq, art. *"Basilique," "Byzance"* et *"Constantin"* in *Dict. d'Arch.; Manuel d'archéol. chrétienne,* 2 vols., *passim.*— H. Grisar, S. J., *History of Rome and the Popes in the Middle Ages* (transl. L. Cappadelta).—P. J. Chandlery, S. J., *Pilgrim Walks in Rome.*—F. Brannack, *Church Architecture.*

PART II

The Middle Ages

FIRST PERIOD

The Merovingian Epoch (496–714)

SECTION I

The Sixth Century

CHAPTER I

FROM THE CONVERSION OF CLOVIS TO THE ELECTION
OF ST. GREGORY THE GREAT (496–590)

At the end of the fifth century all the barbarian kingdoms in the West were either Arian or pagan. The conversion of Clovis, leader of the Franks, was the signal for a complete change.

I. The Franks: Conversion of Clovis. Clovis was first led to show respect for Catholicism from purely political motives. The Gallo-Roman natives had nothing but hate for the pagan invader; it was deemed prudent, therefore, to gain their good will, together with the protection of their episcopate in Gaul, all the more so as the latter enjoyed tremendous influence. St. Remigius, Bishop of Rheims, who was both an Apostle and a diplomat, wrote to Clovis: "If you keep in accord with the bishops, your government will be strengthened thereby." Then, too, the pagan chief was subject to the religious influence of his wife, Clotilda, a Burgundian princess, who, though of Arian parentage, was herself a Catholic. It was mainly due to her example that he consented to have his first child baptized a Catholic, but when the child died, he interpreted its death as a punishment inflicted by the ancient gods of Gaul. These same gods seemed intent on avenging themselves again upon the person of a second child, who had also received Baptism, but when the child survived, the God of Clotilda was acknowledged by Clovis as having equal power. In the year 496, in the very heat of a battle against the Alemanni, he uttered a supreme cry for help to the God of the Christians: "If my troops are victorious," he exclaimed, "I shall believe in Thee and receive Baptism." He was victorious, became the diligent pupil of St. Remigius, and together with 3000 of his warriors was baptized by him on Christmas day in the year 496. From that time on, the Franks were regarded as the liberators of the Catholic population of the rest of Gaul, and Clovis spoke of his campaigns against the Burgundians and the Visigoths of Toulouse as so many crusades. The Visigoths were brought into complete subjection in 507. As to the Burgundians, they were incorporated into the kingdom of the Franks only in 534, although already in the year 517, Prince Sigismund, son of King Gundobald, and the bishops of the province, held a council for the purpose of strengthening ecclesiastical discipline. Henceforth, Gaul was Catholic.

II. Theodoric and the Ostrogoths. In Italy, on the other hand, the barbarians remained stubborn followers of Arianism. Theodoric, a clever politician, showed himself untiring in his efforts to blend the Gothic with the Roman element. He restored the ancient framework, senate and consulate, and assigned to each its respective functions. The Goths were enlisted in the army and the Romans given administrative posts. The barbarian chief, however, was quite tolerant, granting privileges and immunities to the churches, endeavoring to live in peace with Popes Gelasius I (492–496) and Anastasius II (496–498), and even taking for chief advisers the Catholics Boethius and Cassiodorus. At the time of the Roman schism, which broke out on the occasion of the Henoticon, he gave proof of his political wisdom. The imperial coterie was endeavoring to substitute the Archdeacon Lawrence in place of Symmachus, the lawful successor of Pope Anastasius. The immediate result was a state of civil war in Rome. The two candidates then appealed to Theodoric, who, without any partiality, pronounced himself in favor of Symmachus. The quarrel continued to drag, however, and so he appointed a delegate (*visitator*) to settle the matter. At the instance of the Roman clergy he even convoked a council (502), but refused to meddle any further, so that finally Symmachus emerged victoriously from the contest.

The religious question, however, was far from being settled. An ordinary soldier, by the name of *Justin*, now succeeded the Emperor Anastasius, the last representative of the Theodosian dynasty. Taking advantage of his accession to the throne, the people of Constantinople hastened to express their sympathy for the cause of orthodoxy. On the fifth day of July, 518, the feast-day of the Fathers of Chalcedon, they appealed to the Emperor with their cries: "Send the synodal letters to Rome; insert the Four Councils into the dyptics; Leo, the Bishop of Rome, in the dyptics!" Justin acquiesced in their demand, and in order to put an end to the Acacian schism, *Pope Hormisdas* sent legates to Byzantium, who bore a profession of faith in the papal primacy and infallibility. "It is our desire," the formula read, "to follow in all things the communion of the Apostolic See, in which resides the entire and true solidity of the Christian faith, and in which religion has always been preserved without blemish." This formulary of Pope Hormisdas was signed by the entire eastern episcopate.

A campaign was at once started against all the heretics of the Empire, including not only the Monophysites, but also the Arians. They were despoiled of their churches, and forbidden to carry out the functions of their worship. Theodoric interpreted this measure as an attack upon himself, and, believing the papacy an accomplice to it, summoned John I to Ravenna, and with violent threats commanded him to repair at once to the Emperor and obtain from him the withdrawal of the anti-Arian legislation. The Pope was received with honors at Byzantium, Justin going so far as to request the Bishop of Rome to crown him a second time. In addition to this the Emperor granted him permission to wear the imperial insignia. Theodoric was furious, and on the Pope's return, threw him into prison, where he died of ill-treatment (526). The Senator Boethius and his father-in-law, Symmachus, already suspected as Catholics, were involved in a charge of high treason. After a long captivity, during which Boethius composed his admirable treatise, *De Consolatione,* he was executed. Theodoric died the same year as John I (526), but first took the precaution to appoint as his successor Felix III (526–530).

The Romans were thus divided into two camps: the Greek party and the Gothic party. After the death of Felix III, the Goth Boniface II and an individual by the name of Dioscorus contested for the office of the papacy, and only the sudden death of the latter saved the Church from schism. The papacy for a while succumbed to the dominion of the Gothic element, King Athalaric going so far as to claim a tribute of 3000 gold pieces for the privilege of electing the Sovereign Pontiff. But the days of the Gothic dynasty were numbered. Justinian, the successor of Justin, reconquered Italy, and King Theodatus attempted in vain to obtain pardon by despatching to him the new Pope, Agapitus I. Agapitus died while on his mission to Constantinople, without having achieved anything. Belisarius, Justinian's lieutenant, then landed in the peninsula and seized the city of Rome; as a result the papacy passed under the domination of a new oppressor.

III. Justinian: The Three Chapters. Encouraged by his wife, the Empress Theodora, Justinian (527–565) during his entire reign tried to effect a reconciliation between the Catholics and the Monophysites. The latter had concentrated their forces at Alexandria and were a constant threat to the peace and unity of the Empire. Under the administration of Justin, his predecessor Justinian had upheld the Scythian monks despatched to Rome for the purpose of obtaining Pope Hormisdas' approval of the formula: "One of the Trinity was crucified," which, to their way of thinking, corrected the exaggerated expressions of Chalcedon in regard to the distinction between the hypostases. Those who accepted the formula were called "Theopaschites" because they appeared to attribute the Passion to the divinity itself. The formula, though defensible in itself, was open to a Monophysitic interpretation, and hence Pope Hormisdas refused to subscribe to it. From this refusal on the part of the Sovereign Pontiff, certain Byzantine monks, called "Acoemeti," argued that his action was tantamount to an approval of the Nestorian theories. Seeing this, Pope John I finally approved the formula, "One of the Trinity was crucified." The Monophysites subscribed to it, but persisted in their heretical teaching.

Stubbornly pursuing his policy to reconcile the Catholics and the Monophysites, the Emperor Justinian soon ordered Belisarius to substitute in place of the new pope, St. Silverius (536–537), the Deacon Vigilius, a former nuncio at Byzantium. The latter proved himself superior to his reputation, so that when Theodora attempted to rehabilitate the Monophysite Anthimus, deposed by Pope Agapitus in the see of Constantinople, he exclaimed: "Although unworthy, I am the Vicar of Blessed Peter, just like my predecessors, who condemned this man."

Soon new complications set in. For three centuries Origenism had been rampant in the monasteries of Palestine. Sustained by the Apocrisiary Pelagius, the Patriarch Peter of Jerusalem denounced the danger to the Emperor Justinian, who issued an edict condemning Origenism. This condemnation was approved by a council held at Constantinople and ratified by Pope Vigilius. It was at this time that, to divert attention from the main scene of action, a notorious Origenist by the name of Theodorus Ascidas, who was bishop of Caesarea in Cappadocia, suggested that the Emperor inaugurate a theological campaign to win over the Monophysites. There were two persons in the Orient who had always been regarded as dangerous characters: Ibas of Edessa and Theodoret of Cyrus. Both had long opposed St. Cyril and upheld Nestorius. Theodore of Mopsuestia, the precursor of Nestorius, was looked upon as being even more dangerous. It was argued that the condemnation of these three Antiochians would result in the conversion of those Monophysites who had been scandalized by the rehabilitation of Ibas and Theodoret at the Council of Chalcedon. The Emperor Justinian allowed himself to be deceived and issued an edict which anathematized the Three Chapters, as they were called, *i. e.*, (1) the person and writings of Theodore of Mopsuestia; (2) the writings of Theodoret against St. Cyril and the Council of Ephesus; and (3) the letter of Ibas of Edessa to Maris, Bishop of Hardashir in Persia, against the same Cyril.

It was always possible to maintain that the condemnation of these three persons and their writings was directed against them as opposing the Council of Ephesus, but not as having been rehabilitated by the Council of Chalcedon. And yet no one could possibly be mistaken, for why this sudden anti-Chalcedonian movement at the very time when the best interests of the Church called for the vindication of the decisions of the famous Council? Everything was done, however, to secure the approval of the Sovereign Pontiff. Vigilius was summoned to Constantinople, and, although he refused to give in at first, he gradually weakened to the extent of entering into discussions and ended by yielding (548). In his *Judicatum* he subscribed to the edict against the Three Chapters, but was careful to place the authority of the Council of Chalcedon outside the pale of discussion. The episcopate of the West protested his action; the Africans even spoke of excommunicating Vigilius until he regained his senses. In the face of such a storm the *Judicatum* was withdrawn, and in an agreement with Emperor Justinian, Vigilius decided that nothing further should be said concerning the Three Chapters, but that the whole dispute should be referred to a general council.

Goaded on, however, by Theodorus Ascidas, the Emperor broke his promise, and in the year 551 issued a new edict against the Three Chapters. Vigilius braced himself this time and protested against Justinian's action, but feeling that his life was threatened, he fled to Chalcedon, where he proclaimed the deposition of Theodorus Ascidas. The Emperor retreated before this energetic stand, and Vigilius returned to Constantinople on the promise that the matter would be settled by a council. The council convened, but a clever selection of the bishops summoned resulted in all 151 siding with the Emperor. The opposing African bishops were excluded *in globo*. Thereupon, Vigilius refused to attend the sessions, and in his *Constitutum* forbade the condemnation of the Three Chapters. But the Council paid no attention to him and Justinian sent into exile the Latin clerics who opposed his action. Seeing that his solicitude for the dead was causing greater anxieties for the living, Vigilius ended by sanctioning the acts of the synod without restriction, and so the latter took rank as the Fifth Ecumenical Council. Just as he was re-entering the Italian peninsula, Pope Vigilius died, leaving to his successor *Pelagius* (555-560) the task of imposing the condemnation of the Three Chapters upon the West—a task that was all the more unpromising, as Pelagius had been a member of the opposition while serving as nuncio at Byzantium. By clever and tireless maneuverings, however, he finally succeeded, although he was unable to prevent the churches of Tuscany, Liguria, and Istria from plunging headlong into a schism, which lasted over half a century.

Moreover, Justinian had failed to achieve his purpose, for the Monophysites still refused to be reconciled. The Emperor now had recourse to the more stringent measure of deporting the heretical bishops in the southern provinces of the Empire to Constantinople. In spite of all his efforts, however, some Monophysite bishops still remained and succeeded in grouping around themselves many followers. They called themselves Copts, Christians of ancient Egypt, and Melchite Catholics (from Melech = king, *i. e.*, the royal party). In Syria, the wicked Empress Theodora secretly appointed a shrewd and energetic leader for the Monophysite party in the person of an ex-monk, James Jacob Baradai.

He was a high-strung fanatic, who at the risk of every sort of danger, travelled the length and breadth of Syria and the border provinces, clothed like a beggar and consecrating both bishops and priests. He reestablished the Monophysite patriarchate at Antioch and founded the dissenting Church, which went by his name—Jacobite Church.

The reign of the Emperor Justinian was not devoid of glory. This upstart restored the imperial authority in the West, converting reconquered Africa and Italy into two prefectures of the praetorium. Through the famous Justinian Code he accomplished an immortal legislative reform, imbuing the rigor and severity of the ancient Roman law with the spirit of Christianity, and introducing into it an element hitherto unknown, namely, solicitude for social justice, public morality, and human welfare. Because he undertook to do too much, however, he indirectly paved the way for the dangers which the Persian invasions brought upon Christianity.

The least that can be said of Justinian's reign is that wonderful religious monuments survived him. From the accession of Constantine to the advent of Justinian, the East had been groping in its artistic efforts, and had gradually substituted for the straight lines of the Roman basilicas the curved forms of octagonal or circular churches. From the architecture of the Persians it borrowed the cupola. It is thus that a Byzantine art of Asia Minor gradually saw the light in the fifth century (churches at Ephesus, Sardes, Philadelphia) and in the sixth century a Byzantine art arose in Syria (cathedrals of Bosra and Ezra). The climax was reached in Justinian's reign with the construction of the famous church of Santa Sophia of Constantinople, built by Anthemius of Tralles and Isidore of Milet. It is true that the architecture of Santa Sophia appears somewhat heavy, when the basilica is viewed from the outside, because of the many buttresses necessary to sustain the enormous weight of the edifice; but from the inside the cupola gives proof of the prodigious daring of the architects, and lends to the whole a unique spaciousness and simplicity. Byzantine art is remarkable, not only for its use of the cupola, but also for the lavishness of its decorations. A truly Oriental splendor is in evidence everywhere in Santa Sophia: exquisitely carved capitals, many colored marble columns, scintillating mosaics on a gold background, etc. Unfortunately, the mosaics which contained representations of human figures were long completely covered with plaster by the Turks.

The Emperor Justinian had barely disappeared from the scene of action (565), when Greek domination in Italy was again threatened by a migration of barbarian Germans, namely, the Lombards. This invasion forced Pope John III (551–574) to flee from Rome and take refuge in the church of SS. Tiburtius and Valerian. His successor, Benedict I (575–579), was unable to stem the wave of atrocities and sacrileges which swept across the land. It would seem that the overtures made by Pope Pelagius II (579–590) and the gold and silver of the Church were the incentives which finally moved these barbarians to depart from Rome. The Emperor was absolutely powerless to defend his far-distant colony, and so the whole of Italy was over-run by the invaders, with the exception of a few districts which remained in the possession of the Greeks and were called Exarchate of Ravenna (Ravenna, Bologna, Romagna, Venice, Rome, and Naples).

The sixth century was a troubled period for the papacy, during which the Church was torn between the Goths and the Greeks, the former oppressing and persecuting her, while the latter harassed her by baneful and disastrous religious controversies. A pontiff was soon to appear, however, whose influence would restore peace and good order everywhere.

TEXTS AND DOCUMENTS

Cassiodorus' Respect for and Submission to the Pope of Rome

Do not leave the care of the City of Rome to me alone. It derives its security far more from you. You are placed as a watchman over the Christian people; you show a father's love for all. The sphere of our care is limited, but yours is quite universal. Your first duty is indeed to lead the flock to spiritual pastures, but even their temporal concerns you cannot disregard. For as man consists of body and soul, a good father cherishes his children both bodily and spiritually. Yea, his first concern is to avert by prayer those earthly needs which may be a penalty for sin. . . .

Give me counsel how I should fulfill my duty. . . . I am a court official, but for all that I am still your disciple. . . . May the See of Peter, which is the wonder of the whole world, protect me, its reverer; this See was doubtless established for the whole world, but, since it is fixed in Rome, it has special responsibilities towards us who live in the City. Rome has the happiness of guarding in its midst the tombs which all peoples desire to see, and on this account we have both a claim and a pledge for the aid of the Apostles. This, together with your prayers, will overcome the difficulties of our office.

Variar., 9, N. 2, edit. Mommsen.

QUESTIONS

1. What importance had the conversion of the Frankish chieftain, Clovis?
2. Contrast the religious situation of Gaul and that of Italy under the respective leaderships of Clovis and Theodoric.
3. What was the religious policy of the Emperor Justinian?
4. Indicate some early attempts on the part of the Greek and Gothic parties to control the election of the Sovereign Pontiff.
5. What possible profit could the civil power derive from gaining control of this election?
6. What were the "Three Chapters"?
7. What is to be thought of the action of Pope Vigilius in subscribing to the condemnation of the Three Chapters?
8. What is the Justinian Code?
9. Give an analysis of Byzantine art.
10. Who were the Lombards?

BIBLIOGRAPHY

Clovis and the Franks.—Sources: Dom Bouquet, *Recueil des hist. de Gaule,* III and IV.—*Monumenta Germaniae Historica:* the 3 vols. of the *Scriptores rerum Merovingicarum* (especially Gregory of Tours).—Works: Kurth, *Clovis; The Church at the Turning Points of History,* ch. III; *Le baptême de Clovis* in *La France chrétienne,* 1896; *Les origines de la civil. moderne,* II, p. 4; *Sainte Clotilde,* Coll. "Les Saints."—Lecoy de la Marche, *La fondation de la France,* 2nd Part, ch. III, p. 142.—Lavisse, *Histoire de France,* II.—Hanotaux-Goyau, *Histoire de la Nation Française.*—Moehler, *Hist. du moyen âge depuis la chute de l'empire romain jusqu'à la fin de l'époque franque,* Paris and Louvain, 1904.—Msgr. Duchesne, *L'Eglise au VIe siècle,* 1926.

Theodoric.—Grisar, *op. cit.,* II, ch. IV.—Kurth, *Les origines.*—Martroye, *Goths et Vandales,* 1905.—Hodgkin, *Italy and her Invaders,* 8 vols. 1880–95.—Villari, *Le invasione barbariche in Italia,* Milan, 1900.—E. Amann, art. "*Jean I,*" in *Dict. de Théol.*

The Three Chapters.—Sources: Facundus, *Pro defensione trium capitulorum,* P. L., LXVII. The text of the *Judicatum,* P. L., LXIX. iii. The protest in *Epist. clericorum Italiae,* P. L., LXIX, 113, 115. The second edict of Justinian against the Three Chapters, P. G., LXXXVI, i, col. 993-1035. The *Constitutum,* P. L., LXIX, 67-114. The acts of the council, Mansi, IX, 376 ff.—Works: Grisar, *op. cit.,* II, p. 132.—Pargoire, *L'Eglise byzantine de 527–847,* p. 41.—Duchesne, "*Vigile et Pélage*" in *Rev. quest. hist.,* XXXVI, p. 369.—Marin, *Les moines de Constantinople,* p. 278.—J. Bois, art. "Constantinople," in *Dict. de Théol.*—Knecht, *Die Religionspolitik Kaiser Ju-*

stinians, I, Würzburg, 1896.—A. DE MEISSAS, *Nouvelles études sur l'histoire des Trois Chapitres*, in *Annales de Phil. chrétienne*, 1904.—GLAIZOLLE, *Justinien, son rôle dans les controverses*, Lyons, 1905.—P. BATIFFOL, *L'Empereur Justinien et le Siège Apostolique*, 1926.—DOM LECLERCQ, art. *"Justinien,"* in *Dict. d'Arch.*

Byzantine Art.—DIEHL, *Justinien et la civilisation byzantine au VI*^e *siècle*, 1901; *Manuel d'art byzantin;* art. *"Art byzantin,"* in the *Musée d'art*, published under the direction of Eug. Müntz.—BRÉHIER, *Les Eglises byzantines*, Coll. *"Science et Religion,"* 1905.—M. LAURENT, *L'art chrétien primitif*, II, ch. XII and XIII, Brussels, 1911.—BRANNACK, *op. cit.*

CHAPTER II

Gregory I was born in the year 540, of the ancient Roman patrician family of the Anicii. He entered upon a public career, and at the age of thirty was made Prefect of the City of Rome by the Emperor Justinian II (570). Upon the death of his father, Gregory renounced his career, soon afterwards became a monk, and spent his entire fortune in founding seven monasteries: six in Sicily, and one, that of St. Andrew's, in his own palatial residence on the Coelian in Rome. After his ordination (578) he was selected by Pope Benedict I as *apocrisiarius,* or papal nuncio, to the court of the Emperor in Constantinople. In 585 he returned to Rome and the solitude of his cloister. It is said that the sight of a few young Anglo-Saxon slaves in the slave-market inspired him with the idea of evangelizing Great Britain. His presence in Rome, however, seemed indispensable, for he had hardly set out on his contemplated mission, when Pope Pelagius III called him back to the Eternal City. At the death of Pelagius (590) he was literally forced to accept the papacy by the unanimous choice of both clergy and people.

I. The Saviour of Italy. Gregory's Dealings with the Secular Power. Gregory the Great himself has described for us in a few vivid sentences the state of Rome and Italy at this period: "Sights and sounds of war meet us on every side. The cities are destroyed; the military stations broken up; the land is devastated; the earth depopulated. No one remains in the country; scarcely any inhabitants are left in the towns; yet even the poor remains of humankind are still smitten daily and without intermission. Before our eyes some are carried away captive, some are mutilated, some murdered. She herself, who once was the mistress of the world, we behold worn down by manifold and incalculable distresses, the bereavement of citizens, the attack of foes, the reiteration of overthrows. Where is her senate? Where are they who in former days reveled in her glory? Where is their pomp, their pride? Now no one hastens to her for preferment; and so it is with the other cities also; some are laid waste by pestilence, others are depopulated by the sword, others tormented by famine, and still others swallowed up by earthquakes."

The Pope resolved to repair these ruins by as perfect an administration as possible of the patrimony of the Roman Church. The farmers were placed under the direction of *conductores,* who administered the land and collected the rents. Above them were the *rectores patrimonii,* whose duty it was to promote the material and moral welfare of the farmers and laborers. Administered in this way, the patrimony made possible numerous works of charity. At Rome, in close proximity to the principal churches, homes for the poor (*habitacula pauperum*), hospitals (*nosocomia*), and orphan asylums (*phtochia*) were erected. The distribution of alms was carried out in an orderly manner. St. Gregory kept tabulated records of all persons in need of public assistance, in which each one was listed together with his age and status in life. He also undertook a number of sound social reforms. In one instance he would raise a slave to the rank of an independent farmer; in another, he would take under his patronage (*commendatio, defensio*) freemen who, pursued by the Lombards, humbly sought his protection. Finally, his notaries and subdeacons kept him well informed regarding the administration of the Greek governors, who knew they would have to account to him for any exactions they committed. By these various measures Gregory slowly laid the foundations for the temporal power of the papacy, awaiting the day when the latter would be completely emancipated from imperial authority.

Outside, Gregory worked assiduously to overthrow the last of the Arian kingdoms. Agilulf, the chief of the Lombards, was a barbarian who had ravaged Italy and even contemplated laying siege to the city of Rome. Gregory succeeded in deterring the invader from his project by the firm attitude he adopted with him and the presents he bestowed upon him. The wife of Agilulf, Theodelinda, a Bavarian princess, was a Catholic. By an assiduous correspondence Gregory encouraged her in the work of converting her husband. In the year 602, Agilulf received Baptism, and a great many of his subjects followed him into the Church. Theodelinda founded the famous monastery of Bobbio and erected a basilica dedicated to St. John the Baptist at Monza, near Milan. Agilulf placed on its altar an iron crown, upon which was engraved his name, together with the title "King of all Italy." This crown was used later on in the coronation ceremonies of Charlemagne and Napoleon.

After their numerous defeats at the hands of the Franks, the Visigoths transferred the center of their power to Spain. They still remained Arians, however, even though they were surrounded by Catholic peoples. In Galicia, to the Northwest of the peninsula, the Suevi had been converted by the missionary monks, St. Martin and St. Donatus, and in 563, a council held at Braga, the capital of the kingdom, definitively assured the triumph of orthodoxy. In the Northeast were the Franks, and in the South a Greek army occupied a portion of the country, beginning with the year 554.

The many victories of King Leovigild (572–580) finally enabled him to set up his capital at Toledo, from which point, under the instigation of his wife, Galswintha, a fanatical Arian, he issued orders for a general persecution of the Catholics. Out of hatred for the true faith, he even put to death Hermenegild, a son of his first marriage with the sister of St. Leander, later archbishop of Seville. But Recared, a brother of the victim, revenged himself by embracing Christianity. He convoked a council of all the bishops of Spain, both Arian and orthodox, at Toledo, and after listening to the arguments of both sides, abjured Arianism, sent a deputation to St. Gregory, and began a friendly correspondence with him. From that moment on, Spain always showed great deference and respect for the see of Rome, so that when, in 603, two deposed bishops appealed their case to St. Gregory, the latter immediately despatched a legate, who had no difficulty in rehabilitating them. In the seventh century, famous councils convened at Toledo under the direction of St. Isidore of Seville, the brother and successor of St. Leander.

St. Gregory not only took the leading part in the conversion of the Arians, but also endeavored to enter into friendly relations with all princes. He induced Queen Brunhilde to assist in the work of reforming the French clergy. Students of history have sometimes wondered that the Sovereign Pontiff was so lavish in his praise of this would-be domineering and cruel Queen of Austrasia, but recent writers represent Brunhilde in a new light, as a noble ruler and above reproach in her private life. Gregory also wished to signify his loyalty to the Emperor, but not at the expense of the rights of the Church. When, in 592, Maurice prohibited all public officers from entering the ranks of the clergy, Gregory protested; and when John the Faster (*Jejunator*), Bishop of Constantinople, arrogantly assumed the title of Universal Patriarch, he called attention to this "universal danger," and opposed to a title "filled with arrogance and pride" that of "Servant of the servants of God" (*servus servorum Dei*), which his successors have retained to the present day.

II. The Conversion of England: The Mission of St. Augustine. As a simple monk St. Gregory had conceived the plan of evangelizing the Angles; as pastor of the Universal Church, he realized this plan. In the days of Tertullian, Great Britain already counted a number of Christians, but the invasion of the Scots, that of the Saxons in the fifth century, and finally that of the Angles in the seventh century, drove the native Britons into Cornwall and Wales, and Christianity with them. The Anglo-Saxons occupied the rest of the country, and gradually set up seven kingdoms (heptarchy): Kent, Sussex, and Wessex in the South; East Anglia and Essex in the East; Northumbria in the North; and Mercia in the center of the island. In these kingdoms they implanted the blood-thirsty religion of Odin.

The method followed by St. Gregory consisted not in sending to the barbarians a few scattered missionaries, but in setting up in their midst, at the outset, a complete monastery, so that the pagans might have a true picture of the Christian life under their very eyes. The task of evangelizing Great Britain was entrusted, therefore, to forty monks, under the direction of *St. Augustine,* the prior of St. Andrew's. These missionaries left Rome in the autumn of 596, ascended the course of the river Rhone, then that of the Loire as far as Nantes, and finally reached the mouth of the Thames. King Ethelbert, who ruled over Kent at the time, and had married the Frankish princess Bertha, a very good Christian woman, received them with great hospitality, and gave them permission to preach throughout his kingdom. It was not long before several of his warriors embraced Christianity. Augustine established his see at Canterbury, and was greatly encouraged and assisted in his work of organizing the missions by the sage and practical advice of Pope St. Gregory. The latter counselled that Augustine utilize the pagan temples, because "as long as the nations see that their temples are not destroyed, they will remove error from their hearts, and, knowing and adoring the true God, will the more freely resort to the places to which they have been accustomed." He advised, moreover, that the pagan feasts be transformed, but not done away with.

The missionary labors of St. Augustine were crowned with great success. In the year 601, Pope Gregory appointed him "Bishop of the English" and sent him the pallium as a mark of his supremacy over the churches of England. Very soon the kingdom of Essex followed the example of the kingdom of Kent. The capital of this kingdom was London, and the first bishop Melletius. The only dark page in this early history of English Catholicity was the hostile attitude of the Bretons. Converted towards the end of the third century, but almost completely cut off from any contact with Rome, they had adopted certain special customs regarding the date of the celebration of Easter and the manner of conferring Baptism and tonsure. Augustine pleaded with them to accept the Roman tradition on these secondary points, and to come to his assistance in the work of evangelizing the English. They obstinately refused, however, chiefly because of their hatred for the savage Saxons, who had vanquished them.

III. The Literary Efforts of St. Gregory. St. Gregory was above all an ascetical and a mystical writer. From the point of view of literary excellence, he is quite inferior, making no attempt at style and at times showing almost complete indifference to its rules. His writings are marked, however, by a dignified simplicity, and this enables one to follow without the slightest fatigue the gradual unfolding of a thought which is clear, always original, and not infrequently pregnant with meaning. In his exegetical works he lays special stress on the allegorical and the mystical sense. At the time when he was still an apocrisiary, he wrote his *Expositio in Job,* which is such a complete compendium of the principles of Christian ethics that it is usually designated by the name of *Moralia.* Mention should also be made of his twenty-two homilies on Ezechiel, and his forty homilies on the Gospels, many of which were later incorporated in the liturgical lectionaries and still have a place in the Roman Breviary.

The two works of St. Gregory most popular in the Middle Ages were his *Regula Pastoralis* and his *Dialogues.* The *Regula Pastoralis* is a clear and methodical exposition of the duties of the priest and comprises four parts: in the first, *qualiter veniat,* St. Gregory examines the marks of a vocation to the priesthood; in the second, *qualiter vivat,* he gives a description of the virtues indispensable to a pastor; in the third, *qualiter doceat,* he lays down rules for the direction of the faithful, according to their status in life; and in the fourth, *qualiter se cognoscat*, he treats of the interior life.

IV. St. Gregory and the Benedictine Order. In the four books of the *Dialogues*, written in 593, St. Gregory relates a series of miracles and deeds of extraordinary virtue performed by holy persons during his time. The second book is entirely devoted to St. Benedict, whom he is intent upon presenting to his readers as the father of western monachism. St. Benedict was born about the year 480 at Nursia, in Umbria. His parents belonged to the nobility, and so he was sent to Rome to study. Terrified, however, at the sight of the sins and vices of his companions, he fled into the solitude of Subiaco, his sole purpose from now on being "to live there alone with himself under the eye of God." Soon disciples gathered around him, among them two children, Maurus and Placidus. This fact constrained him to establish in the neighborhood of his grotto (*il sacro speco*) twelve little monasteries, each housing twelve monks. When the evil spirit stirred up against them calumnies on the part of the priest Florentius, he moved his establishment to Monte Cassino in Campania, about eighty kilometers from Naples (528).

In the solitude of his new retreat, St. Benedict composed a Rule, which is the result of long experience and stamped with the genius of a Roman organizer. To the abbot, who is commissioned by the Eternal Father, St. Benedict entrusts absolute power over all the monks, who, under his direction, engage in the praises of God. Perfect subordination to the abbot and his assistants, the uniformity of a life in common, and the perpetual bond linking the monk to the cloister where he was professed, were so many guarantees that this legislation would last. They also purged the monastic life of all whimsicalities and of what we might call a "spirit of vagrancy." In the hours consecrated to the praise of God, both manual and intellectual labor had their assigned place. Moreover, the strict vow of poverty barred the monk forever from returning to worldly things; *omnia omnibus sint communia* (all things were held in common). Finally, in all its details the Rule of St. Benedict is marked by a spirit of moderation and discreetness which places it within the reach of all. St. Benedict had legislated above all for his monks at Monte Cassino; the *Dialogues* made his Rule known throughout the West. The names of St. Benedict and Pope St. Gregory are so closely associated in history that they can never be separated.

TEXTS AND DOCUMENTS

THE RULE OF ST. BENEDICT
(Extracts)

CHAPTER III. OF CALLING THE BRETHREN TO COUNCIL

As often as any important matters have to be transacted in the monastery, let the Abbot call together the whole community, and himself declare what is the question to be settled. And, having heard the counsel of the brethren, let him weigh within himself, and then do what he shall judge most expedient. We have said that all should be called to council, because it is often to the younger that the Lord revealeth what is best. But let the brethren give their advice with all subjection and humility, and not presume stubbornly to defend their own opinion; but rather let the matter rest with the Abbot's discretion, that all may submit to whatever he shall consider best. Yet, even as it becometh disciples to obey their master, so doth it behove him to order all things prudently and with justice.

Let all, therefore, follow the Rule in all things as their guide, and from it let no man rashly turn aside. Let no one in the monastery follow the will of his own heart; nor let any one presume insolently to contend with his Abbot, either within or without the monastery. But if he should dare to do so, let him be subjected to the discipline appointed by the Rule. The Abbot himself, however, must do everything with the fear of God and in observance of the Rule: knowing that he will have without doubt to render to God, the most just Judge, an account of all his judgments. If it happen that less important matters have to be transacted for the good of the monastery, let him take counsel with the seniors only, as it is written: "Do all things with counsel, and thou shalt not afterwards repent."

CHAPTER XXXIII. WHETHER MONKS OUGHT TO HAVE ANYTHING OF THEIR OWN

The vice of private ownership is above all to be cut off from the monastery by the roots. Let none presume to give or receive anything without leave of the Abbot, nor to keep anything as their own, either book, or writing-tablet, or pen, or anything whatsoever; since they are permitted to have neither body nor will in their own power. But all that is necessary they may hope to receive from the father of the monastery; nor are they allowed to keep anything which the Abbot has not given, or at least permitted them to have. Let all things be common to all, as it is written: "Neither did any one say that aught which he possessed was his own." But if any one shall be found to indulge in this most baneful vice, and after one or two admonitions does not amend, let him be subject to correction.

Chapter LXIV. Of the Appointment of the Abbot

In the appointing of an Abbot, let this principle always be observed, that *he* be made Abbot whom all the brethren with one consent in the fear of God, or even a small part of the community with more wholesome counsel, shall elect. Let him who is to be appointed be chosen for the merit of his life and the wisdom of his doctrine, even though he should be the last of the community. But if all the brethren with one accord (which God forbid) should elect a man willing to acquiesce in their evil habits, and these in some way come to the knowledge of the bishop to whose diocese that place belongs, or of the Abbots or neighboring Christians, let them not suffer the consent of these wicked men to prevail, but appoint a worthy steward over the house of God, knowing that for this they shall receive a good reward, if they do it with a pure intention and for the love of God, as, on the other hand, they will sin if they neglect it.

Let him that hath been appointed Abbot always bear in mind what a burden he hath received, and to whom he will have to give an account of his stewardship; and let him know that it beseemeth him more to profit his brethren than to preside over them. He must, therefore, be learned in the law of God, that he may know whence to bring forth new things and old; he must be chaste, sober, and merciful, even preferring mercy to justice, that he himself may obtain mercy. Let him hate sin and love the brethren. And even in his corrections, let him act with prudence, and not go too far, lest, while he seeketh too eagerly to scrape off the rust, the vessel be broken. Let him keep his own frailty ever before his eyes, and remember that the bruised reed must not be broken. And by this we do not mean that he should suffer vices to grow up; but that prudently and with charity he should cut them off, in the way he shall see best for each, as we have already said; and let him study rather to be loved than feared.

Chapter LXV. Of the Prior of the Monastery

It happeneth very often that, by the appointment of the Prior, grave scandals arise in monasteries; since there are some who, puffed up by the evil spirit of pride, and deeming themselves to be second Abbots, take it upon themselves to tyrannize over others, and so foster scandals and cause dissensions in the community, especially in those places where the Prior is appointed by the same bishop, or the same Abbots as appoint the Abbot himself. How foolish this custom is may easily be seen; for from his first entering upon office, an incentive to pride is given to him, the thought suggesting itself that he is freed from the authority of his Abbot, since he has been appointed by the very same persons. Hence are stirred up envy, quarrels, backbiting, dissensions, jealousy, and disorders. And while the Abbot and Prior are at variance with one another, it must needs be that souls are endangered by reason of their disagreement; and those who are their subjects, while favoring one side or the other, run to destruction. The evil of this peril falleth on the heads of those who, by their action, have been the cause of such disorders.

We foresee, therefore, that it is expedient for the preservation of peace and charity, that the ordering of the monastery depend upon the will of the Abbot. If possible, let all the affairs of the monastery be attended to (as we have already arranged) by deans, whom the Abbot shall appoint, so that, the same office being shared by many, no one may become proud. But if the needs of the place require it, and the community ask for it reasonably and with humility, and the Abbot judge it expedient, let him himself appoint as Prior whomsoever he shall choose with the counsel of the brethren who fear God. Let the Prior reverently do whatever is enjoined on him by his Abbot, and nothing against his will or command, for the more he is raised above the rest, so much the more carefully ought he to observe the precepts of the Rule.

QUESTIONS

1. Why is Pope St. Gregory deserving of the title of "the Great"?
2. What is meant by the "Patrimony of St. Peter"?
3. What is the importance of St. Gregory's *Regula Pastoralis*?
4. Which are the great monastic Rules in the Church to-day?
5. Give an appraisal of the Rule of St. Benedict; which are some of the situations it remedied?
6. What was the sum and substance of the liturgical controversy in England at the time of St. Augustine, its first missionary?

BIBLIOGRAPHY

St. Gregory the Great.—Sources: *P. L.,* LXXV–LXXIX; the letters in *Mon. Germ. hist., Epist.,* I, II, 1891–1899.—Works: GRISAR, *Saint Grégoire.*— SNOW, *St. Gregory the Great,* London, 1892.—DUDDEN, *Gregory the Great,* London, 1905.—TARDUCCI, *Storia di Gregorio Magno e del suo tempo,* Roma, 1909.—GODET, art. "Grégoire I," in *Dict. de Théol.*—PINGAUD, *La politique de saint Grégoire le Grand,* 1877.—VAES, *La papauté et l'Eglise franque à l'époque de saint Grégoire,* in *Rev. hist. eccl.,* VI, pp. 537–556, pp. 755–784.— DIEHL, *L'administration byzantine dans l'exarchat de Ravenne,* Ecol. franc. Athènes et Rome, fasc. LIII.—DOIZÉ, *Le rôle politique de saint Grégoire pendant les guerres lombardes* in *Etudes,* 1904.—DUCHESNE, *Les origines de l'Etat Pontifical.*—P. VAILHÉ, *Saint Grégoire et le titre de patriarche oecuménique* in *Echos d'Orient,* May 1908; art. "Constantinople (Eglise de)" in *Dict. de Théol.*—DOIZÉ, *Les Patrimoines de l'Eglise Romaine au temps de saint Grégoire.*—DOM H. LECLERCQ, "Grégoire le Grand" (Coll. "Les Saints"),

1928.—E. AMANN, art. *"Martin de Braga"* in *Dict. de Théol.*—P. BATIFFOL, *Saint Grégoire*, 1928.—SNOW-HUDLESTON, *St. Gregory the Great, His Work and His Spirit*, 1924.

St. Gregory and England.—DOM CABROL, *l'Angleterre chrétienne avant les Normands*, 1909.—BROU, *Saint Augustin* (Coll. *"Les Saints"*) 1897.— L. GOUGAUD, *Les chrétientés celtiques*, 1911.—W. STUBBS, *Constitutional History of England.*—HUNT, *The English Church from its Foundation to the Norman Conquest*, London, 1899.—A. HUMBERT, art. *"Angleterre,"* in *Dict. d'Hist.*—LINGARD-BELLOC, *The History of England*, 11 vols., 1912.

St. Benedict.—Sources: *La règle bénédictine*, and *Dialogues de saint Grégoire.*—Works: DOM TOSTI, *Della vita di S. Benedetto.*—DOM A. L'HUILLIER, *Le patriarche saint Benoit*, 1904.—DOM BERN. MARÉCHAUX, *Saint Benoit, sa vie, sa règle, sa doctrine spirituelle*, 1911.—DOM DELATTE, *Commentaire de la Règle de saint Benoit*, 1912.—DOM U. BERLIÈRE, *L'ordre monastique des origines au XIIᵉ siècle*, ch. XII.—DOM BESSE, art. *"Benoit,"* in *Dict. de Théol.* —DOM LÉVÈQUE, *Saint Grégoire le Grand et l'Ordre Bénédictin.*—DOM RYELANDT, *Essai sur la physionomie morale de saint Benoit* (Coll. *"Pax"*), t. XVII, 1924.—DOM CUTHBERT BUTLER, *Benedictine Monachism; Studies of the Benedictine Life and Rule*, 1919.—DOM J. DE HEMPTINNE, *L'ordre de saint Benoit* (Coll. *"Pax"*).—DOM LAURE, *Règle du patriarche saint Benoit, texte, trad. et commentaire*, Chambéry, 1925.—*The Benedictines of Farnborough, The Rule of St. Benedict.*—DOM BRUNO DESTRÉE, *The Benedictines*, New York, 1923.—CARDINAL NEWMAN, *Historical Sketches.*—D. KNOWLES, *The Benedictines*, 1930.

SECTION II

The Seventh Century

CHAPTER I

THE WEST IN THE SEVENTH CENTURY
THE EVANGELIZATION OF THE BARBARIANS

I. In Great Britain. Of the seven Anglo-Saxon kingdoms, only two at first embraced Christianity: Kent and Essex. After the death of St. Augustine, the Roman monks scored more victories. Two kings were converted to the true faith, Edwin of Northumbria, who yielded to the preaching of Paulinus, and Sigebert of East Anglia, who harkened to that of Felix. But the savage chief Penda of Mercia defeated these two Christian princes in battle, and paganism once more became triumphant. It was at this critical juncture that the Celts saved the entire situation. Oswald, a nephew of Edwin, succeeded in reconquering Northumbria, and immediately requested the help of missionaries from the Scots of the great abbey of *Iona,* founded by St. Columba, a native of Ireland (563). These monks established the center of their missionary labors in the island of *Lindisfarne.* Oswald defeated Penda and implanted Christianity in Mercia.

At the very outset, these nascent churches were threatened by a serious danger: Celtic separatism. Strange to say, the movement in the direction of unity originated in Lindisfarne. *Wilfrid,* a native of Northumbria, was a monk in this monastery. He was extremely broad-minded, and in order to investigate matters, undertook a journey to Canterbury and Rome. Upon his return to the island of Lindisfarne, he introduced the Rule of St. Benedict and the Roman tradition. A meeting was called at the monastery of Whitby, in which the leaders of the Celtic and the Roman factions propounded their arguments. Thanks to the eloquence of Wilfrid, the Roman cause carried the day (664).

The task of unifying these two factions was completed by a new group of Benedictine monks despatched to the island by Pope Vitalian (657–672). The leader of this group was the Greek monk *Theodore*, who was later promoted to the see of Canterbury. Despite a regrettable quarrel which arose between him and Wilfrid, who had become Archbishop of York, the evangelization of Great Britain advanced with rapid strides, and intellectual culture received a very important impetus. Together with his learned friend Adrian, Theodore soon established the school of Canterbury, in which literature, prosody, astronomy, and mathematics were taught. It was at this school that St. Aldhelm received his early training. Later on he became bishop of Malmesbury in Wessex and established quite a reputation as a poet. Another companion of Theodore's, Benedict Biscop, founded the monastery of Wearmouth, in Northumbria, and later on that of Yarrow, where the Venerable Bede was trained. From these English schools sallied forth the leaders of the Carolingian reform on the Continent, among them Alcuin.

II. In Germany: The Irish Monks. St. Willibrord. The work of evangelizing Germany proceeded in the beginning at a very slow pace. In the Rhenish provinces, the apostolate remained latent, although the country had already been partitioned off into dioceses. There were three metropolitan sees: Cologne, with the suffragan see of Maestricht; Mayence, with the suffragan sees of Spires, Worms, and Strasbourg; Treves, with the suffragan sees of Metz, Toul, and Verdun. Four barbarian nations had established themselves along the opposite bank of the Rhine: the Bavarians to the south along the upper Danube and the Rhine; the Alemanni on a straight line with Alsace; the Thuringians, more to the north and directly opposite Cologne; the Saxons, neighbors of the Frisians, between Thuringia and the sea.

The Celtic monks undertook the conversion of all these countries. Arriving primarily for the purpose of evangelizing Gaul, where he founded the monastery of Luxeuil, the Irish monk *St. Columban* was exiled for his fearless criticism of Queen Brunhilde, and established himself at Bregentz on the shores of Lake Constance, where his influence and that of his itinerant missionaries was soon felt throughout the trans-Rhenish provinces.

Eustasius, St. Columban's successor in the abbacy of Luxeuil, preached the Gospel to the Bavarians, but conversions were effected on a large scale only towards the end of century by *St. Rupert* of Worms. He preached throughout the land, baptized Duke Theodo, and on the ruins of the Roman city of Juvavium erected the monastic church of Salzburg, the future metropolis of Bavaria. In the meantime, St. Emmeram established the church of Ratisbon, and St. Corbinian that of Freising in Bavaria. The majority of the leading towns in this country owe their origin to the establishment of a monastic church richly endowed by the Duke.

Christianity was preached to the Alemanni by *St. Gall,* a disciple of St. Columban, who established in Switzerland a monastery which bore his name. From this center of piety and learning sallied forth St. Agrestius, St. Trudpert, and St. Fridolinus, founder of the abbey of Säckingen, on the outskirts of the Black Forest. Although no definite organization was set up in these provinces, Christianity had taken root sufficiently for the *Lex Alemanniae,* promulgated in the opening years of the eighth century, to appear entirely impregnated with its teachings.

Thuringia was evangelized by an Irish monk, *St. Kilian,* who preached the Gospel to the inhabitants of the provinces situated along the banks of the river Main, and founded the church of Würzburg. It was not long, however, before he was put to death for having blamed the private life of a duke.

For the rest, the apostolate of the Celtic monks merely paved the way for further attempts in this field. The dukes who had been enthroned by the Merovingians, the Gallo-Roman officials and colonists, and the remnants of the ancient Celtic population which had come under Roman influence, constituted a Christian nucleus, but the masses of the people continued to cling to paganism, and yielded only to an organized plan of evangelization, sustained by the secular power. The apostolate of St. Columban and his companions was lacking in both internal organization and external support. The Irish monks established no hierarchy in the countries which they evangelized, but pressed forward at random without the support and wise counsel of the Sovereign Pontiff; the rulers of Eastern France, or Austrasia, were too much taken up at home with warfare against undisciplined serfs and abroad with warfare against neighboring kings and princes, to be of any effective help to the missionaries.

Merovingian Gaul was united under one head only with the advent of King Dagobert (628–638). Thanks to his protection, *St. Amandus* and *St. Eligius* evangelized the northern portions of the country, Belgium and Batavia. St. Amandus first preached the Gospel in the valley of the Escaut, in the neighborhood of Tournai and Ghent, where he founded the monastery of Elnon, which was named after him. Some time later he was forced to accept the bishopric of Maestricht, and preached the Gospel throughout the valley of the Meuse. His missionary labors led him to the very mouth of the river Rhine, and even into Frisia, the refuge of paganism in its most ferocious form.

Towards the end of the century, an era of permanent results finally began for these northern countries. In the course of one of his journeys to Rome, Wilfrid of York was forced by contrary winds to land on the coast of Frisia. Upon his return to England, he spoke of this land to his monks at Ripon, and twelve years later sent the Frisians his disciple, *St. Willibrord*. The latter placed himself under the protection of the major-domo of the Frankish Palace, Pepin, who had just completed the conquest of southern Frisia as far as the Zuyder Zee. He established himself at Utrecht, built a monastic cathedral, recruited a native clergy, took care to provide shelter for himself and his monks at the monastery of Echternach against possible uprisings in Frisian territory under Frankish rule, preached the Gospel along the banks of the Meuse and the Moselle, and, finally, upon the advice of Pepin, journeyed to Rome to receive investiture and episcopal consecration at the hands of Pope Sergius (687–701). With the sanction of the Pontiff he created a new ecclesiastical province, and for forty years, until 739, he preached the Gospel throughout Frankish Frisia, and finally succeeded in stamping out all traces of pagan worship.

TEXTS AND DOCUMENTS

The Death of St. Columba

Having written the verse, as we have said, at the end of the page, the Saint went to church, to recite the office of Sunday night. This being over, he immediately returned to his cell and spent the remainder of the night on his bed, having for his couch a bare flag, and a stone for his pillow; which at the present day stands as a kind of monument near his sepulchre. It was while reclining there that he gave his last instructions to the brethren, but in the hearing of his attendant alone, saying: "This, dear children, is my last advice to you: that you preserve, with each other, sincere charity and peace; and if you thus imitate the example of the holy Fathers, God, the comforter of the good, will assist you, and I, being with Him, will intercede for you; and He will not only give you sufficient to supply the wants of this present life, but will bestow on you likewise the eternal rewards that are prepared for those who observe the divine precepts."

The brief narrative brings thus far the last words of our venerable patron, as he was about to leave this weary pilgrimage for his heavenly country. After uttering these words, as the happy hour of his departure gradually approached, the Saint became silent. Then, as soon as the midnight bell tolled, rising quietly, he hastened to church, which he reached before the rest, and entering alone, knelt down in prayer near the altar. At this moment his attendant Diarmit, who slowly followed him, saw from a distance that the whole interior of the church was filled with a heavenly light, which fell on the Saint. As he approached the door, the light he had seen, and which was also seen by a few more of the brethren standing at a distance, disappeared. Diarmit, therefore, entering the church, cried out in a mournful voice: "Where are you, Father?" and groping in the dark, before the brethren came with lights, he found the Saint in a recumbent posture before the altar; raising him up a little, he sat down beside him, and supported his saintly head upon his bosom. Meanwhile, the choir of monks came up in haste with their lights, and seeing that their Father was dying, began to weep. And the Saint, as we have been told by some who were present before his soul departed, raised his eyes aloft and looked around, with a wonderful expression of joy and gladness, no doubt seeing the holy angels coming to meet him. Diarmit then raised his holy hand, that he might bless his assembled monks, and the venerable Father himself raised it at the same time, as well as he was able, that, since he could not do so in words, he might at least, by the motion of his hand, bless his brethren as he was dying. And having given them his holy benediction by this sign, he immediately expired. After his soul had left the body, his face still continued ruddy, and wore that wonderful expression of joy which was caused by his vision of the angels; insomuch that it appeared like that, not of a dead man, but of one in a quiet slumber. Meanwhile the whole church resounded with lamentations.

St. Adamnan, *Life of St. Columba.*

QUESTIONS

1. What danger threatened the unity of the early Church in Great Britain?
2. Discuss the part played by St. Wilfrid in warding off this danger.
3. How do you account for the fact that the early evangelization of Germany was undertaken by Irish monks?
4. What was the character of the Irish apostolate in Germanic lands?
5. Give an account of the labors of St. Willibrord.

6. Locate all the countries mentioned in this chapter on a modern map of Europe.

BIBLIOGRAPHY

The Apostolate in Germany in the Seventh Century. Saint Willibrord.—Sources: BEDE, *Hist. ecclesiastica gentis Anglorum,* III, 13; V, 10–11, *P. L.,* XCV.—ALCUIN, *Vita S. Villibrordi libri duo, P. L.,* CI, 693–724.—Works: HAUCK, *Kirchengeschichte Deutschlands,* Leipzig, 1887–1911, I–V.—LAVISSE and RAMBAUD, *Histoire de l'Europe,* I.—MSGR. LESNE, art. *"Amand,"* in *Dict. d'Hist.*—E. DE MOREAU, *Saint Amand (Museum Lessianum),* 1927.—BEDE, *Ecclesiastical History,* Bk. V, cc. IX–XI.—BUTLER, *Lives of the Saints,* new ed. by H. Thurston.

CHAPTER II

I. The Persian Peril: Triumph of Heraclius. The Orient was in quest of a saviour, and so in the year 610 it acclaimed *Heraclius,* son of the exarch of Carthage, who found the Empire in a deplorable state, due to the fact that the Persians had become masters of Mesopotamia, Asia Minor, and Palestine. In 615 they had ransacked Jerusalem, carrying away with them the Holy Cross and many other precious relics. Heraclius was seriously thinking of transferring the center of power to Carthage, when the Empire was suddenly rescued by the energetic efforts of *Sergius,* Patriarch of Constantinople. Taking advantage of a friendly movement on the part of the people, the Patriarch led the "Basileus" into a church, where he made him swear that he would either save his people or lay down his life for them. Heraclius immediately took the offensive, scoring two victories, the first at Ninive, and the second at the very gates of the city of Ctesiphon (628). King Chosroës II was dethroned by a revolution, and the Persians hastened to sign a treaty, the terms of which required that they abandon all their conquests and restore to Heraclius the wood of the true Cross. In this manner, the campaign took on the aspect of a veritable crusade. Soon the Emperor brought back the true Cross to Constantinople amid scenes of great pomp, an event which is still commemorated by the feast of the Exaltation of the Cross (September 14).

II. The Monophysite Danger and the Reaction of Monotheletism. Heraclius had warded off the external danger, but the internal danger of Monophysitism still remained. In an attempt to offset this last-mentioned peril, the Patriarch Sergius invented Monotheletism. According to him, the human will and activity of Christ were not capable of any spontaneous action, but were directed by the command and under the impulse of the divine will, somewhat like an inert object is moved by an external force. This theory was tantamount to a denial of the human activity and the human will of Christ, and also to the suppression of His human nature, because to suppress Christ's human will is to do away entirely with His human nature. Monotheletism, therefore, is nothing more than Apollinarianism in disguise. In the light of these facts it is easy to understand why the Monophysites exclaimed: "It is not we who come to the Council of Chalcedon, but the Council of Chalcedon comes to us." Cyrus, the Patriarch of Alexandria, and his followers sided with Sergius. But *St. Sophronius,* a monk of Alexandria, opposed his teaching as heretical. Failing to win him over to his cause, Sergius wrote a very clever letter to Pope Honorius I, which contained the following explanations: "The expression 'one sole operation' appears strange to several, causing them to suspect that we deny the duality of natures, which God forbid. . . . On the other hand, the expression 'two operations' is a source of scandal for many, because it cannot be found in the writings of the Fathers, and would have as its immediate consequence the admission of two opposite wills in Christ." Sergius argued that it was best not to speak of either one or two wills, but to trust that silence would finally make for peace and harmony. Honorius answered by a letter which is incontestably orthodox in substance, but in which he naïvely sided with the policy of silence suggested by Sergius. In the meantime, Sophronius was made Patriarch of Jerusalem and set himself up as an anti-Monothelite. Honorius again sealed his lips, and in a second letter to Sergius, once more recommended silence.

The pusillanimity of Honorius emboldened Constantinople. In 638, under the name of the Emperor Heraclius, appeared the *Ecthesis,* a sort of theological edict, which permitted the faithful to speak of Christ as having only one will. The rescript was evidently prompted and approved by Sergius. Later on it received the approbation of his successor, Pyrrhus, and of a council of fawning prelates who ranged themselves behind the two patriarchs. Time and time again the Popes remonstrated by ostracizing Monotheletism. This was particularly true of Severinus, John IV, and Theodore I, who went so far as to issue orders to the patriarch of Constantinople to remove the *Ecthesis,* which was still posted on the portals of Santa Sophia. St. Sophronius died in 638, but lived on in the person of the monk St. Maximus, an intransigent adversary of the cause of Monotheletism.

It was at this juncture that the Patriarch Paul suggested to Constans II, successor of Heraclius, that since the *Ecthesis* was meeting with so much opposition, it might not be amiss to substitute in its stead an edict again imposing silence on this question. This is the origin of the *Typos,* which appeared in 648. Acting on the advice of St. Maximus, however, *Pope Martin I* and the Lateran Council issued a condemnation of Cyrus of Alexandria and the three Byzantine patriarchs, Sergius, Pyrrhus, and Paul. Pope Martin was seized and secretly haled to Constantinople, where he was exposed to the insults of the rabble, and after being held prisoner for a long time, was finally exiled to the Chersonesus. It was there that he died, September 16, 655. St. Maximus, arraigned before the Emperor, courageously proclaimed that "the task of formulating definitions belongs to priests, and not to kings." Orders were then issued to cut out his tongue and amputate his right hand, and the same cruel tortures were inflicted upon his disciples. Then, one and all were exiled to the Caucasian mountains, where they died.

The blood of the martyrs soon restored peace and unity to the Church. In 668, the Emperor Constantine Pogonatus, the successor of Constantius II, decided with Pope Agatho to convoke a general council. As a preparation for the event, a synod was held at Rome, in which 125 bishops affirmed the dogma of the two wills in Christ. The *Sixth General Council* met at Constantinople, 680-681, presided over by papal legates and enhanced by the presence of the Emperor. Pope Agatho sent a dogmatic letter (*epistula dogmatica*) to the Fathers of the Council, somewhat similar to the Tome of Pope St. Leo, in which he stressed the existence of two wills in Jesus Christ. To the profession of faith of the Council of Chalcedon the Fathers added the following declaration: "We also proclaim two natural volitions and wills in Him, and two natural operations, without division, without change, without partition, and without confusion, according to the teaching of the Holy Fathers; and not in any sense of the term two natural wills, opposed to each other, as the wicked heretics have averred, but a subordinated human will, which, far from being at variance with the divine and all-powerful will, is subject to it." In its dealings with those who had upheld the contrary teaching the Council was no less categorical: "We anathematize Theodore of Pharan, Sergius, Paul, Pyrrhus, and Peter of Constantinople, and together with them Honorius, the former bishop of Rome, who followed them in their teaching." Pope Leo II, the successor of St. Agatho, ratified the decisions of the Council and anathematized "the inventors of the new heresy . . . as well as Honorius, who, instead of purging this Apostolic Church, allowed the immaculate to be marred by a profane treason." Honorius is here condemned, not as a heretic, but only in so far as he had permitted himself to be duped by Sergius and had proved himself negligent in the matter of preserving the true doctrine. It is his personal honor, therefore, which is at stake, and not the papal infallibility, notwithstanding the contrary opinion of those who opposed the Vatican Council. A careful reading of his two letters to Sergius, one of which is preserved in its entirety, the other in part, leaves the impression on an unprejudiced mind that he was not a Monothelite, although he uses expressions that could easily be misinterpreted, especially if wrested from their context. He adopts the words of Sergius, but understands them in an orthodox sense. It is true that he forbids the use of the expressions "one will" and "two wills," but he nowhere says that he requires all the faithful to accept this decision under pain of separation from the Church. Hence he did not intend to teach *ex cathedra*. Thus ended the last great doctrinal dispute in the East. Monotheletism continued to linger for a while among the Maronites of the Lebanon. At the time of the Crusades the Maronites made their peace with Rome and have been faithful Catholics ever since. They number about 300,000.

III. The Arabian Danger. Arabia had resisted all attempts at evangelization, and continued to cling to the tenets of paganism. The Kaaba, a famous sanctuary, was the center of a bizarre religion, which consisted partly of Jewish traditions and partly of idolatrous rites. It was a small and almost cubical stone building situated in the straggling village of Mecca. The spring where the angel Gabriel slaked the thirst of Agar and Ismael was venerated there, and also a stone whiter than milk, fabled to have been brought there by the angel from Paradise to serve as a pillow for their head, but changed to black by the sins of men. The temple harbored no less than 360 idols of all shapes and forms, each tribe possessing its own.

In the year 571, the illustrious family of the Hachim of the clan of the Quraish, to whom the guardianship of the Kaaba was entrusted, gave to the world a son, whom they called *Mohammed,* a name which signifies "The Glorified." Left an orphan when still a child, he was forced to earn his livelihood by driving camels and herding sheep, and would no doubt have lived and died in poverty, had he not attracted the attention of a rich widow, Kadisha, who first employed him to trade for her and subsequently married him. Mohammed was 25 years of age at the time; his sudden rise to fame and wealth gave him the opportunity he desired to cultivate an inborn taste for quiet meditation. It was while he was giving himself over to this life in a cave on Mt. Hira, that he had a vision, in the course of which the angel Gabriel handed him a piece of parchment, saying: "Read, for thy Lord is the generous One, he who learneth." From that moment on Mohammed believed himself called to overthrow idolatry and to restore the true worship of God. His wife was his first convert; then followed Ali, who had married one of his daughters, the famous Fatima, and Abu-Bekr, his father-in-law.

His programme, which included the destruction of the idols of the Kaaba, drew down upon his head the hatred of the Quraish of Mecca, and so, on the 16th of July, 622, he took to flight and withdrew to Yatreb. This is the date of the Hejira (Flight or Migration), and marks the beginning of the Moslem era. With the rapid growth of his party, Mohammed was soon able to have his revenge. He seized Mecca and purified the Kaaba. When he died, in the year 632, he had won the whole of Arabia over to his cause.

"In judging Mohammed's moral character we must distinguish between the Mohammed of Mecca and the Mohammed of Medina. The hostility to Jews and Christians, the introduction of heathenism into Islam, the institution of the Holy War, the violation of his own lax marriage laws, the instigation of robberies and murders, the defence of his crimes and schemes by pretended revelations—all force us to the conclusion that at Medina we have to do with an unscrupulous politician. At Mecca, on the other hand, as he shows a profound and persevering conviction of the truth of his revelations, the materials for which he had already assimilated, and as his actions are not incompatible with that subjective persuasion, we prefer to attribute his prophetic experiences to his general nervous condition and the epileptic fits with which he was frequently visited." [1]

The tenets of the new religion, Islam, were contained in the Koran, a book revealed to the prophet by the angel Gabriel. Islam comprises *Iman* or dogma and *Din* or moral. The first article of faith is that "there is no other God but Allah, and Mohammed is his prophet," or, rather, "the seal of the prophets," because, being the last and greatest, he completed the

[1] E. Power, S.J., *Lectures on the History of Religions*, Vol. IV, Lecture II.

teachings of the other five: Adam, Noe, Abraham, Moses, and Christ. Beyond this life there is another; after death men cross a bridge narrower than a hair; the wicked will be hurled from this bridge into hell, but the good will be admitted to a paradise of purely sensuous pleasures. The moral teachings of the Koran are based on the false doctrine of fatalism, which throws human freedom and the foundations of morality into the discard. All worship is reduced to acts of formalism; observance of certain hours for prayer (five times a day), almsgiving, fasting every day during the whole month of the Ramadan, and abstention from wine, pork, and games of chance, etc. Moreover, the Koran regards woman as a slave, destined by God to satisfy the sensuous instincts of man.

One of the causes of the rapid spread of Islamism was that the new religion promised its heroes booty and spoils of all kinds on this earth, and material joys in the world to come. Hence, immediately after Mohammed's death, his followers inaugurated a *"Holy War."* In the East, they conquered Persia and Turkestan, and even pushed on into India; in the West, they seized the city of Jerusalem (637) and subjugated Syria, Palestine, and Egypt. It is not true that they set fire to the magnificent library at Alexandria. In all these regions infested with Monophysitism, the feeling against Constantinople ran so high that many preferred to surrender to the Arabs rather than to submit to the imperial yoke. Always pressing forward, the infidels finally succeeded in subjugating the whole of Northern Africa: Tripoli, Algeria, and Morocco. Fifty years after the death of Mohammed they had extended their conquests as far as the Atlantic Ocean (681). In all these countries the conquerors violently persecuted the Christians.

As for the remainder of the Empire, it was becoming more and more estranged from Rome. In the year 692 the Council in Trullo went so far as to treat as abuses certain disciplinary and liturgical details which at Rome or in Africa did not harmonize with Byzantine tradition.

After these important conquests, the infidels clashed with the Visigothic kingdom of Spain. The Church of Spain had been made to feel the influence of the East through the intermediary of the Greek *diaspora* of Boetica (Andalusia). As at Byzantium, the sovereign governed the Church, and the code was at once civil and ecclesiastical (nomocanonical). It was the prince, too, who convoked the councils and proposed to them the subjects for deliberation. Hence, the famous Councils of Toledo were national assemblies as well as ecclesiastical gatherings. After questions of dogma and Church discipline were debated, questions of State polity came in for their part of the discussion, and civil dignitaries took their place beside the bishops at the various meetings. This fact accounts for the decidedly humane character of all Visigothic legislation, which upheld the equality of races and conditions, and sought to replace the judiciary duel by well-conducted investigation and trial before witnesses. Unfortunately, the Church of Spain carried on an isolated existence. Shut off from the main currents of Catholic life, the Spaniards were too prone to confound the interests of the nation with those of religion. The kings nominated the bishops, and they in turn created the kings. This constant interpenetration of State and Church finally resulted in the forces of both being sapped by endless friction. Spain, divided against itself, could not offer much resistance to the Moors, who, assisted by the traitor, Count Julian, crossed the Straits of Gibraltar and defeated King Roderic at the memorable battle of Xeres (711), as a consequence of which the entire peninsula surrendered to the invaders.

TEXTS AND DOCUMENTS

The Ecthesis of the Emperor Heraclius
(Extracts)

In regard to the mystery of the Person of Christ the ἕνωσις κατὰ σύνθεσιν is to be professed without σύγχυσις and διαίρεσις. This doctrine preserves the property of each of the two natures, but shows that only *one* hypostasis and one person of God the Logos is united with the quickened flesh and rational soul, whereby not a quaternity is introduced instead of a trinity, since there is not a fourth Person added to the Trinity, but the eternal Logos of the Trinity, who has become flesh. And not another was He who worked miracles, and another who endured sufferings, but we acknowledge one and the same Son, who is at the same time God and man, having but one hypostasis, one person, suffering in the flesh, impassible in the Godhead; to Him belong equally the miracles and the sufferings which He voluntarily endured in the flesh. . . . We ascribe to one and the same Incarnate Logos all divine and human energy, and render *one* worship to Him, who, for our sake, was voluntarily and truly crucified in the flesh, and rose from the dead, etc.; and we do not at all allow that anyone should maintain or teach *one* or *two* energies of the Incarnate Lord, but demand that there should be confessed, as the holy and ecumenical synods have handed it down, that one and the same only-begotten Son, our Lord Jesus Christ, works both the divine and the human, and that all energy, be it divine or human, proceeds from *one* and the same Incarnate God, the Logos without mixture and without separation, and refers back to one and the same [Person]. Since the expression, *one energy*, although some of the Fathers used it, offends the ears of many, and disquiets them, because they are suspicious lest it should be used in order to set aside the two natures which are hypostatically united in' Christ; and [since] in the same way many take offense at the expression, *two energies*, because it is not used by any of the holy Fathers, and would oblige us to teach two mutually contradictory wills, as if God the Logos, aiming at our salvation, was willing to endure suffering, but His manhood had opposed itself to this His will, which is impious and foreign to the Christian dogma. Even the wicked Nestorius, although he divided the Incarnation and introduced two Sons, did not venture to maintain that these two Sons had two wills, but, on the contrary, taught that they had but one. How, then, can the orthodox, who profess the doctrine of only *one* Son and Lord, admit two, and those mutually opposed, wills? We, following the Fathers in this as in all other things, profess *one* will of our Lord Jesus Christ, the true God, so that at no time His flesh, quickened by reason, was separated from the Logos-God and, of its own impulse (ὁρμή), in opposition to the suggestion of God the Logos, hypostatically united with it, fulfilled its natural motion [that of the flesh], but only at the time and in the manner and measure in which the Word willed it. These dogmas of piety have been taught us by those who from the beginning have themselves seen the Word, and have been with Him, serving Him; and also by their disciples and successors and all later God-enlightened teachers of the Church, or, which is the same, the five holy and ecumenical councils, etc. And we ordain that all Christians shall thus think and teach, without adding or taking away anything.

HEFELE, *History of the Church Councils,*
Vol. V, pp. 62 ff.

QUESTIONS

1. What was the occasion of the restoration of the true Cross?
2. What is the heresy of Monotheletism?
3. Contrast the characters of the Patriarch Sergius and Pope Honorius.
4. What is the significance of the "Ecthesis" of the Emperor Heraclius?
5. How must we interpret the condemnation of Pope Honorius by the Sixth General Council of the Church?
6. How would you go about proving that the early Church professed some sort of belief in the infallibility of the Pope?
7. Describe the character of Mohammed.

8. Why does not the rapid spread of Islam militate in its favor as a divinely inspired religion?

9. What was the character of the early councils of Spain?

BIBLIOGRAPHY

Heraclius.—Drapeyron, *Héraclius*, 1869.—Pernice, *L'imperatore Eraclio*, Florence, 1905.—Diehl, *Histoire de l'Empire Byzantin*, ch. III.

Monotheletism and Honorius.—Sources: Mansi, X and XI.—*Letters of Sergius to Honorius*, Mansi, XI, 533, 536.—*Protestation of Sophronius*, Mansi, XI, 461–509; *P. G.*, LXXXVII, 3, col. 3148–3200.—*Lettres d'Honorius*, *P. L.*, XI, 470–475.—*Ecthesis*, Mansi, X, 992–997.—*Epistula dogmatica* of Agatho. *P. L.*, LXXXVII, 1161–1213.—Works: Hefele-Leclercq, *Hist. of the Councils*, III, I.—G. Owsepian, *Die Entstehungsgeschichte des Monothelismus*, Leipzig, 1897.—G. Krueger, art. "Monotheleten," in *Realencyklop. für protest. Theologie*, XIII.—Pargoire, *L'Eglise byzantine de 527 à 847*, 1905.—A. Chillet, *Le Monothélisme*, Brignais, 1911.—Tixeront, *op. cit.*, III, ch. VI.—Dom Cabrol, art. "Honorius," in *Dict. d'Apol.*, VIII, col. 514–519.—E. Amann, art. "Honorius," in *Dict. de Théol.*—Dom Chapman, *The Condemnation of Pope Honorius*, London, 1907.—V. Grumel, art. "Maxime de Chrysopolis," in *Dict. de Théol.*

Mohammed and Islam.—Works: Carra de Vaux and Palmieri, art. "Coran," in *Dict. de Théol.*—Carra de Vaux, art. "Islamisme," in *Dict. d'Apol.*—Power, art. "Islamisme," in *Christus.*—Carra de Vaux, *La religion de l'Islam.*—Caetani, *Annali dell' Islam*, Milan, 1905.—Montet, *l'Islam*, [Coll. "Payot,"] 1922.—Casanova, art. "Mahomet" and "Mahométisme," in *Dict. de Théol.*—Carra de Vaux, *Les penseurs de l'Islam*, 5 vols., 1921–1926.—R. Aigrain, art. "Arabie," in *Dict. d'Hist.*—Dom Leclercq, art. "Invasion arabe," in *Dict. d'Arch.*—E. Dermenghem, *Mahomet*, 1929.—E. Power, S. J., *Lectures on the History of Religions*, Vol. IV, lect. II.—C. M. Draycott, *Mahomet: Founder of Islam*, New York, 1916.—S. Lane-Poole, *The Speeches and Table-Talk of Mohammed*, New York, 1905.—D. S. Margoliouth, *Mohammed and the Rise of Islam*, New York, 1905.—Muir-Weir, *The Caliphate: Its Rise, Decline, and Fall, from Original Sources*, Edinburgh, 1915.—J. L. Menezes, *The Life and the Religion of Mohammed.*—T. W. Allies, *Peter's Rock in Mohammed's Flood.*—G. Oussani, art. "Mohammed and Mohammedanism" in *The Catholic Encyclopedia*, Vol. X, pp. 424–428.

CHAPTER I

CHRISTIANITY IN MEROVINGIAN GAUL

I. The Episcopate. Before the Merovingian era the clergy and people of a city selected and nominated their bishop; in the course of that period kings inaugurated the practice of recommending their candidates, a procedure which very soon amounted to imposing the persons of their choice upon the electors. It not infrequently happened that in this matter they allowed themselves to be influenced by the great, by women, and by gifts. The Councils of Orleans, 533 and 536, of Clermont, 535, of Tours, 567, vainly protested against this practice. The Council of Paris, 614, achieved some results when Lothaire II issued a decree which made for some regularity in the elections during his reign and that of Dagobert I. It must be conceded, moreover, that, as a general rule, the Merovingian kings selected the best equipped and most virtuous candidates. A partial proof of this statement lies in the fact that several among them, like Eleutherius of Noyon, Audoenus (Ouen) of Rouen, and Leodegar of Autun became great saints and that some of them did not hesitate to score the immorality and cruelty of these princes, who at heart were still barbarians. One instance in point is that of Germanus of Paris, who excommunicated Caribert for marrying a nun.

For the rest, the Church herself imposed certain obligations upon bishops. St. Caesarius has codified them in his *Statuta Ecclesiae Antiqua,* and the councils renewed them from time to time. According to these documents, the power of the bishop is limited, first, by the provincial synod, made up of bishops of the metropolitan circumscription; and secondly, by the *presbyterium,* or council of the priests of the city, who must be consulted in all important matters, such as the compilation of lists of candidates for Holy Orders, the disposal of church goods, etc.

Nevertheless, the influence of the bishop was quite considerable. Long before civil authority was established on a firm basis, he was the first organizer, being frequently obliged to lend his assistance in matters far removed from the spiritual realm. His was the duty to secure and maintain the stock of provisions necessary for the citizens, as well as to see to the upkeep of public highways. The word "bishop" signifies overseer, and "pontiff" (*pontifex*), bridge-builder. The governor ranked second to the bishop, and could incur his disfavor.

On the other hand, the bishop usually was a great land owner. The ecclesiastical goods in his possession were derived in great part from donations made by kings and their families, prelates and clerics, and also by a large number of *tenuiores*. In those days of deep faith, to give to a church or monastery meant to give to the holy patrons of these institutions and thereby to secure their intercession; and in barbarian society, where plundering and violence were still rampant, bequests to the Church were regarded as excellent means of expiating one's sins. To donations we must add the many privileges granted to the Church by the kings: *e. g.,* exemption from indirect taxation, tolls levied on merchandise, exemption from direct taxes, public tributes, imposts and excises. The direct outcome of such privileges was what was termed "immunity," which prevented the kings' functionaries and the counts not only from levying taxes on land owned by the Church, but also from erecting buildings upon them, bringing suit against anyone within their precincts, etc. At times, also, kings granted fiscal rights to certain churches. Thus, they would give permission to this or that monastery either to levy a royal "tonlieu" (sum paid for a stand in the market), or taxes on several *villae*, or even a whole city, and so forth. The rights acquired at this time became permanent customs.

Very soon, however, abuses crept in and unscrupulous persons began to indulge in habits of spoliation. Courtiers obtained from kings the title to valuable pieces of church property, and frequently the bishop was urged to grant to the king's protégés the produce of a certain domain by a precarious tenure (*jure precarii*). On the face of things, abuses of this kind did not appear to be crying wrongs, since the procedure constituted the great, not owners, but merely usufructuaries of the property;

in point of fact, however, these acts were robbery in disguise. It was not long, indeed, before secularizations of this sort were attempted on a large scale, or duly legalized after being effected. And yet very definite religious uses of church goods were commanded by the councils, which ranged these uses under four headings: (1) the support of the clergy; (2) the support of the bishop; (3) the construction and upkeep of churches; (4) the service of the poor.

We must say a special word about this last use. At a time when no public assistance of any kind was forthcoming, the Church defrayed all the expenses in connection with the feeding, clothing, and sheltering of the poor. The destitute, the sick, and in particular the lepers, lived off the *mensa episcopalis* (the bishop's table). These various categories of persons constituted a veritable corporation, the members of which were designated by the name of *matricularii,* because their names were inscribed on a register or matriculation-book. In course of time a hospital was built in every episcopal city to provide for their needs. The bishop offered protection also to the weak and to orphans; he was their guardian, so that even the counts could not bring suit against them without informing him; he appointed his archdeacon to defend them in the civil tribunals. He also took a special interest in prisoners and frequently provided them with food from his table or interceded with the count to obtain their deliverance.

Finally, the bishop, as the representative of the Church, although he did not condemn slavery in so many words—a move that would surely have issued in a social revolution—fought strenuously to suppress its abuses. He visited with excommunication the master who put his slave to death without the permission of the court, or the civil judge; he proclaimed the lawfulness of marriages contracted by slaves—an action that meant an important step forward in the direction of morality—and, finally, he saw to it that they did not fall into the hands of pagans or Jews. Moreover, the Church spoke from her pulpits of the manumission of slaves as a corporal work of mercy, and the act was effected with liturgical ceremony. The master delivered his slave into the hands of the bishop in the presence of the assembled clergy, before the altar, and the slave, when liberated, was placed under the immediate protection of the Church. The liberation of slaves who labored on ecclesiastical estates, however, was a rare occurrence, because they were not estranged from the rest of the community and earned a good living under the protecting influence of the crozier.

The important position held by the episcopate explains why the episcopal office was so frequently conferred upon members of the old Gallo-Roman families, which had become the custodians of culture and civilization.

Another significant characteristic of this period is the importance attached to regional and national councils. For although the supremacy of the Roman Pontiff was not contested, direct relations with Rome were the exception rather than the rule.[1] The Church of Gaul sought to fill this need to the best of its ability by holding periodical meetings of the clergy, in which disciplinary questions, observance of the fast, celebration of feast-days, and suppression of magical and superstitious practices formed the principal objects of discussion.

II. The Clergy. When the Gospel penetrated into outlying country districts, it became necessary to establish religious centers, which were given the name "rural parishes." The priest in charge of such a parish was called the "priest of the people" (*presbyter plebanus* or *parochianus*).

As early as the fifth century we meet with a great number of such parishes, but of different origin. Some of them were founded directly by the bishop in towns or *vici,* and had an archpriest at their head. Besides being the spiritual head of the town, the archpriest also directed the activities of a number of oratories, with the assistance of other members of the clergy, who formed a veritable college, and for whom he was amenable to the bishop and the archdeacon. These first parishes were more frequently than not erected on the sites of destroyed temples, in acknowledgement of the triumphant victory of Christ over the pagan gods, and in an endeavor to purify places formerly consecrated to the evil spirits. Moreover, the people more readily repaired to churches constructed on the very site of temples where they had been accustomed to meet in prayer. Often, too, a church was erected over the burial-place of a saint, who at once became its owner and patron.

Other churches were founded by the wealthy on their own property or *villae,* and served as private oratories for the use of their families. These provided the clerics who served them with "food and clothing." The

---

[1] Roman influence persisted, however, as is sufficiently attested by the correspondence of St. Gregory. See Vaes, *La papauté et L'Eglise franque,* in *Rev. hist. eccl.,* VI (1925).

danger was soon felt, however, that these oratories, erected within the confines of the parish, might in time break loose from duly constituted ecclesiastical authority and fall under the oppressive rule of the proprietor. This seems to be the reason why the Council of Vaison (529) ruled that these clerics could not confer the Sacraments of Baptism and Penance, but only offer the holy Sacrifice of the Mass. The same reason induced the Church to prohibit the ordination of slaves or freedmen who were still dependent upon their former masters; it was illicit for unengaged clerics and priests to recommend themselves for these positions.

By an inevitable law of fate, however, the practice of placing oneself under the patronage of the great (*patronatus*) became more and more widespread during the sixth and seventh centuries. The need for protection induced priests, even parish priests, to place themselves under the "mainbour" of the local ruler, and bishops and abbots of monasteries under the "mainbour" of the king. This step ushered in the lamentable practice of secularizing parishes. The opulent and the great began to usurp the administration of church goods as well as the supervision of the work of the clergy; often they even assumed the title of archpriests.

III. The People. Merovingian society still remained impregnated with barbarism and superstition. The clergy, and they alone, were able to exert an influence on its rough but loyal characters. At a time when anarchical Germanic customs had well-nigh obliterated the notion of the State, civil authority found itself incapable of exercising anything like restraint on the minds of these men. Moreover, its powers of repression were almost nil, the king himself being hardly more than the head of robber bands. Religious faith, on the other hand, created a deep impression on the minds of these barbaric hordes, although, to be truthful in the matter, they were probably moved more by fear than by love. This fact explains why the priests often had to resort to the threat of hell-fire to obtain a hearing. Then, too, superstitious practices were still quite rampant, pagan customs and traditions being obstinately adhered to, and ancient pagan temples and shrines visited and venerated. The worship of streams, rocks, and trees still subsisted; libations were made to lakes, and offerings thrown into them; and not infrequently, and even quite naïvely, ancient pagan ceremonies were combined with new Christian usages. The Church voiced her protest against such abuses through her teachings; but the best solution and cure seemed to lie in substituting Christian feasts and heroes in place of the pagan ones. Here we have the explanation of the extraordinary impetus which the veneration of martyrs and relics and the custom of making pilgrimages received at this period.

IV. **Monachism.** Cenobitism attained a high degree of development during the Merovingian period. In the opening years of the fifth century the monks had shown a marked preference for deserts and waste places; monasteries, and especially *cellae,* were established at random almost everywhere. During the second half of this same century, the precarious conditions brought about by the barbarian invasions constrained the monks to seek refuge within fortified enclosures, and in the sixth century, bishops and kings alike invited them to establish their headquarters in cities and to keep watch over the tombs of martyrs and saints. Towards the end of this century, the Irish monks of St. Columban migrated to Gaul and proceeded to establish monasteries in deserted places. The untilled lands of the north and northeast sections of this country were soon dotted with their institutions, for instance, the monasteries of Elnon (St. Amandus) and Sithiu (St. Bertin) in the north; Echternach in the Ardenne; Moyenmoutier in the Vosges, etc. The monks of these monasteries cleared the land and afforded protection to the rural population round about.

The monks of St. Columban rendered other praiseworthy services. Up to their time, religious communities had no effective organization. In Gaul alone there existed as many as twenty different rules, either in translations from the Greek, or in the Latin original, but they were treatises on asceticism rather than serious attempts at legislation. These conditions gave too free a rein to arbitrariness and anarchy; monastic stability was almost unknown, for in spite of the decrees of such councils as that of Agde, in 506, and Orleans, in 511, the monks were constantly changing their place of residence. St. Columban composed a real rule, which soon gained acceptance everywhere; but it was too severe, as it visited any infraction with proportionate corporal punishment. "The monk will not go to bed," he wrote, "unless he is exhausted from work, and he must be constrained to rise before he has finished his sleep." "Corporal punishment was freely meted out. Six, ten, twelve, or even fifty strokes of the lash were administered for coughing at the beginning of a psalm, or for omitting to pray before setting about the fulfillment of some task, or for offering an excuse when reprimanded." [1]

Such austerities were not in accord with the Rule of *St. Benedict*. The ideal sought by this great Roman took account of the physical strength of the monks, and not to over-burden them, in such wise that the weakest among them would be equal to the task imposed (*omnia mensurale fiant propter pusillanimes*). At first a compromise was established between these two monastic legislations, and together they were accepted as spiritual guides by such great abbeys as Jumièges, Fontenelle, Luxeuil, Corbie, etc. Soon, however, the Benedictine Rule prevailed, it being felt that it possessed the advantage of greater moderation and also supplied what the Rule of St. Columban lacked, namely, practical statutes for any association of monks. It is because of this fact that the great French writer Mabillon regarded the seventh century as a golden age for the wide-spread diffusion of monastic foundations.

TEXTS AND DOCUMENTS

DECREES OF THE SECOND COUNCIL OF VAISON (529)

1. All priests in the parishes must, as is already the wholesome custom throughout Italy, receive the younger unmarried lectors into their houses, and instruct them in the singing of psalms (*psalmos parare*), in the Church lessons, and in the law of the Lord, so that they may have able successors. If, however, such a lector shall afterwards desire to marry, the permission must not be refused him.

2. Priests may preach not only in the cities, but also in all rural churches. If a priest is hindered through sickness, a deacon should read a homily by a Father of the Church.

3. As in Rome, in the East, and in Italy, so also in our churches, the *Kyrie Eleison* must be frequently sung, for the awaking of penitence, as well at matins as at Mass and vespers. Moreover, at all Masses, early Masses as well as at those during Lent and the Masses for the dead, the *Tersanctus* should be said, as in the public Masses.

4. The name of the Pope of the period should be read aloud in the churches (in the diptychs, or in the corresponding part of the liturgy).

5. As at Rome, and in the East, and in all Africa and Italy, on account of the heretics who deny the eternity of the Son of God (Arians), in all the

---

[1] Laux, *Church History*, p. 205.

closing forms after the Gloria there is added, *Sicut erat in principio;* so should it also be in all our churches.

HEFELE, *History of the Church Councils,*
Vol. IV, p. 169.

QUESTIONS

1. Trace the history of the nomination and election of bishops.
2. Indicate the scope and limitations of the bishop's power during the sixth and seventh centuries.
3. Which were some of the privileges granted to the Church by the early Merovingian kings and princes?
4. What was the privilege of immunity?
5. Give proofs of the solicitude of the Church for the welfare of the poor and the slaves in the sixth and seventh centuries.
6. Trace the history of the present-day parish.
7. To what abuses did the foundation of private oratories lead?
8. Contrast the Rule of St. Columban with that of St. Benedict.

BIBLIOGRAPHY

Christianity in Merovingian Gaul.—Sources: *Ecrits historiques et hagiographiques de Grégoire de Tours,* edit. Arnd and Krusch, 1885; *Epistolæ merovingaevi,* 1892; *Passiones vitæque sanctorum ævi merovingici,* edit. Krusch, 1896; *Concilia ævi merovingici,* edit. Maassen, 1893, in *Mon. Germ. hist.*—DOM BOUQUET, II, III, and IV.—LE BLANT, *Inscriptions chrétiennes de la France.*—MOLINIER, *Les sources de l'hist. de France,* 1901, p. 94.— Works: FUSTEL DE COULANGES, *La monarchie franque,* 1888.—HAUCK, *Kirchengeschichte Deutschlands,* I.—P. VIOLLET, *Histoire des Institutions politiques et administratives de la France,* 1890.—PROU, *La Gaule mérovingienne.* —MARIGNAN, *Etudes sur la civilisation française:* I. *La société mérovingienne,* II. *Le culte des saints sous les mérovingiens,* 1899.—LAVISSE, *La décadence mérovingienne; La foi et la morale des Francs,* in *Rev. des Deux-Mondes,* 1885 and 1886:—IMBART DE LA TOUR, *Les paroisses rurales du IVᵉ au XIᵉ siècle,* 1900.—VACANDARD, *Vie de saint Ouen,* 1902; *Les élections épiscopales sous les Mérovingiens, L'idolâtrie en Gaule au VIᵉ et au VIIᵉ siècle,* in *Rev. quest. hist.,* 1898–99.—MALMORY, *Saint Césaire d'Arles,* in *Bibl. Ecole Hautes-Etudes,* fasc. CIII.—HANOTAUX-GOYAU, *Histoire de la nation française.*— LAVISSE-BAYET, *Histoire de France,* II, 1st Part.—G. MOLLAT, art. "Elections épiscopales," in *Dict. d'Apol.*—MSGR. LESNE, *Histoire de la propriété ecclésiastique en France,* t. I, 1916.—DOM PITRA, *Saint Léger,* 1846.—P. CAMERLYNCK, *Saint Léger,* (Coll. "*Les Saints*"), 1910.—P. PARSY, *Saint Eloi*

(Coll. *"Les Saints"*), 1907.—P. BATIFFOL, *Les Eglises gallo-romaines et le Siège Apostolique* in *R. H. E. F.*, VIII (1922), pp. 145-169.—CLOCHÉ, *Les élections épiscopales sous les Mérovingiens* in *Moyen-âge*, Sept.-Dec., 1924, pp. 203-254.—DOM LECLERCQ, art. *"Léger (saint)*," in *Dict. d'Arch.*—DILL, *Roman Society in Gaul in the Merovingian Age*, New York, 1906.

Merovingian Monachism.—DOM BESSE, *Les moines de l'ancienne France* (*Archives de la France monastique*, vol. II), 1906.—MSGR. LESNE, *Histoire de la propriété ecclésiastique en France*, t. I, 1910.—U. BERLIÈRE, *L'ordre monastique des origines au XII⁰ siècle*, 2nd edit. (Coll. *"Pax"*), 1921.—E. MARTIN, *Saint Colomban*, (Coll. *"Les Saints"*).

CHAPTER II

In the East also, the bishop was entrusted with the administration of church property, the responsibility for charitable institutions, and the supervision of the monasteries. The Emperor Justinian ordained that a bishop should be thirty-five years of age and practice continence. The bishop was nominated by election, which admitted two stages: the people and the clergy drew up a list of three candidates, and from these the metropolitan or the bishops of the province selected one. In practice, however—and this was especially true of more important sees—the will of the "Basileus" was the all-deciding factor.

Such procedures made for an intimate union between Church and State. We must admit that the Code of Justinian made Christianity enter directly into civil legislation. It proclaimed the Catholic belief in the mysteries of the Blessed Trinity, the Incarnation, and the Redemption; it forbade prostitution, blasphemy, gambling, nay, even divorce. Moreover, the clergy took a keen interest in the Justinian laws. Some of them were posted on the doors of the churches, and the bishops supervised the work of all civic and military functionaries. It need scarcely be pointed out how dangerous this situation was for the independence of the Church.

And yet we note the presence of excellent elements in the Church of the East. Monachism had reached a high degree of development: in the year 536, the Diocese of Constantinople counted no less than sixty-eight monasteries, and that of Chalcedon, forty. Unparalleled fervor and splendor were displayed in Church ceremonies, and the piety of the people was ardent and expansive. Nothing shows this more convincingly than the importance attached to the veneration of relics and the numerous pilgrimages. Jerusalem always remained the center of all religious outpourings, especially in the spring, on the occasion of the pascal solemnities, and in September, for the dedication of the "Anastasis" and the exaltation of the Holy Cross. Unfortunately, a superficial sort of religiosity was often substituted for true piety and the practice of genuine virtue. In higher circles, cruelty in its most degraded forms basked in the sunshine of Caesarism. To cast their political enemies into the sea, gagged in sacks, to tie them in bunches to foundering barges, to cut off their noses and roast them on a spit, were just a few of the minor pastimes of the eastern despots, while among the "plebs" immorality and superstitious practices were widely rampant. Fortune tellers, astrologers, interpreters of dreams, etc., literally swarmed like vermin. Even monachism, which counted so many followers, was quite often largely illusory. Vocations frequently did not assume a definite form until late in life, after those who deemed themselves called, had drunk long and deep from the cup of worldly pleasures, and had entangled themselves in political obligations. This fact explains the antipathy existing between the monks and the imperial and military power.

TEXTS AND DOCUMENTS

THE MONKS OF PALESTINE AND SYRIA

The Syrian desert, from Lebanon as far as the mountains of Armenia, was full of solitaries. . . . These solitaries led a life still more severe than their brethren of Egypt; some of them were to be found who lived like wild beasts, in the heart of the forest, without any provisions, their only food being uncooked herbs. They were called shepherds ($\beta o \sigma \kappa o i$) by their neighbors—a charitable name, for they might more justly have been described as sheep. Others bound themselves to chains made fast in the rock, carried enormous weights, and gave themselves up to all the extravagances of Indian fakirs. Sometimes the bishops tried to persuade them to moderation; but they were scarcely listened to. As a contrast, the Arabs of the desert and the Syrian peasants had the greatest veneration for these extraordinary beings. Their popularity even extended to the towns. . . . We do not find that the pious extravagances of the solitaries of the East had any definite connection with the movement in Egypt. The Eastern monks were not much inclined to a life in common. The grouping in monasteries or colonies of anchorites was only established amongst them by slow degrees. We never hear of any actual rules by which they were guided. It is not surprising that, having no superiors to direct them, living far from one another, and each according to his own will, they should have allowed themselves to be carried into real excesses.

DUCHESNE, *The Early History of the Church,*
Vol. II, pp. 409–410.

QUESTIONS

1. Contrast the method of electing bishops in the West with that followed in the East.
2. What was the Justinian Code?
3. What would you consider to be the outstanding characteristics of an Easterner as contrasted with those of a Westerner?
4. Do you not think it providential, in view of the character of Greek civilization, politics, asceticism, etc., that St. Peter established the headquarters of the Church at Rome?

BIBLIOGRAPHY

Christianity in the East.—See especially PARGOIRE, *L'Eglise byzantine,* 1907.—S. HERBERT SCOTT, *The Eastern Churches and the Papacy.*—A. FORTES-CUE, *The Orthodox Eastern Churches* and *The Uniate Eastern Churches.*

CHAPTER III

The general character of the literature of this period is a marked taste
for encyclopedic knowledge. Authors display little or no originality, their
sole ambition being to classify and codify the monuments of the past in
an effort to salvage them from destruction at the hands of the barbarians.

St. Caesarius was born in 470 at Chalon-sur-Saône; he entered the
famous monastery of Lerins, and, in 503, was raised to the dignity of the
episcopate. For forty years he ruled the see of Arles and acted as the
Primate of all Gaul. He was first and last "a man of action, a preacher, a
moralist, and a teacher of the barbarians." His best work is a series of
practical homilies. They are written in a clear style, replete with imagery,
and well fitted to strike the imagination of the crude and uneducated
audiences to which they were addressed. In them we find a complete description of society as it existed in his day, its vices and its coarseness, as
well as its superstitious attachment to pagan customs and practices.

In Italy, two Romans who served the Gothic dynasty made noble efforts
to salvage ancient science. *Boethius,* a profound thinker and a lover of
philosophy, translated Aristotle's works on logic. It is from him that the
writers of the Middle Ages learned how to argue in syllogistic form and
how to conduct discussions on the Universals. But the best known of his
works is *De Consolatione Philosophiae,* a treatise written while he was
awaiting death in a prison at Pavia. It gives no evidence of being written
under Christian influence: there are no citations from Holy Scripture, and
the name of Christ is not even mentioned.

Cassiodorus was a practical genius. He turned his back upon the world
in 540 and withdrew to the monastery of Vivarium (Viviers), which he
had founded on his estates in Calabria, devoting himself to the task of
copying manuscripts. Under his direction, translations of the principal
Christian works were made from Greek into Latin. It is thus that Bellator
translated the homilies of Origen, Dionysius Exiguus, certain canonical

documents, and Epiphanius Scholasticus, the Church Histories of Socrates, Sozomen, and Theodoret (*Historia ecclesiastica tripartita*). Cassiodorus afterwards combined these three translations into one, which became the favorite manual of Church History in the Middle Ages. His most important work was the *Institutiones Divinarum et Saecularium Lectionum* in two books, of which the first is an introduction to the study of the theological sciences and especially of Holy Scripture, while the second contains the current teaching on the seven liberal arts.

The works of *St. Isidore of Seville* are "treasure-houses of extracts which are the equivalent of whole libraries." His principal work is entitled, *Etymologiae* or *Origines,* and is divided into twenty books. It begins with a treatise on grammar, then deals with theology, and ends by treating of foodstuffs and domestic utensils.

Venerable Bede lived towards the end of the seventh century in the monastery of Wearmouth in England. His exegetical works, which comprise commentaries on the Old and New Testaments, as well as homilies and sermons, are quite extensive, but devoid of originality. On the other hand, his *Ecclesiastical History of England* [1] and his biographies possess documentary value of a high order.

The works of *St. Gregory of Tours* draw a unique and faithful picture of the history of the Franks in the sixth century. They are devoid, however, of anything like historical criticism, are completely lacking in style, and are at best nothing more than a natural and naïve account of the facts, with no attempt at sequence.

Already in these days the literature of the East was in a state of complete decadence. During the sixth century there was only one real theologian, Leontius of Byzantium, the teacher of Justinian. He was a dialectician of unusual merit and succeeded in demonstrating that there was no contradiction between the decisions of Ephesus and those of Chalcedon. Many monastic memoirs and lives of the saints appeared at this time, but their authors made no attempt at being historically accurate; they merely aimed at edifying the reader. Mention should be made of the *Pratum Spirituale* of John Moschus, "a collection of anecdotes, devotional accounts, instructive and pious remarks and discourses, which the author had heard or witnessed, or which had been related to him in the various monasteries

---

[1] Bede's *Ecclesiastical History of England,* translated by A. M. Sellar, is the best English edition of this invaluable work. (*Transl.*)

he visited." St. John Climacus, abbot of Mt. Sinai (525–600), described in his *Ladder* the thirty steps or rungs which enable the soul to ascend to God. He does not pretend to be original, but merely to give to his readers a synthesis of the traditional doctrine.

TEXTS AND DOCUMENTS

AN APPRECIATION OF VENERABLE BEDE

The Venerable Bede was born about 673 in Northumberland and spent most of his life in the Benedictine abbey of Jarrow on the Tyne, where he died in 735. He was a man of broad learning and untiring industry, famous in all parts of Christendom by reason of the numerous scholarly books that he wrote. The chief of these was his *Ecclesiastical History of the English People,* covering the period from the invasion of Britain by Caesar (B. C. 55) to the year 731. In this work Bede dealt with many matters lying properly outside the sphere of Church History, so that it is exceedingly valuable for the light which it throws on both the military and political affairs of the early Anglo-Saxons in Britain. As an historian Bede was fair-minded and as accurate as his means of information permitted.

F. A. OGG, *A Source Book of Mediaeval History*, p. 68.

QUESTIONS

1. What is to be understood by "encyclopedic knowledge"?
2. Why did the authors of this period display no originality in their writings?
3. Give a few incidents in the life of Venerable Bede.

BIBLIOGRAPHY

St. Caesarius of Arles.—Sources: *P. L.,* LXVII and appendix to the sermons of ST. AUGUSTINE, XXXIX; six inedited sermons published by Dom Morin, in *Rev. Bénéd.,* XIII, p. 97; fifteen others, *ibid.,* XVI, pp. 241, 289 and 337.—Works: A. MALMORY, *Saint Césaire.*—CHAILLAN, *Saint Césaire* (Coll. *"Les Saints"*), 1912.—P. LEJAY, *Le rôle théologique de Césaire d'Arles,* 1906, and in *Rev. hist. et lit. rel.,* 1905, pp. 444–487; art. *"Césaire,"* in *Dict. de Théol.* —HANOTAUX-GOYAU, *op. cit.*

Boethius.—Sources: *P. L.,* LXIII–LXIV.—Works: P. DE LABRIOLLE, *Hist. de la litt. lat. chr.,* pp. 663 ff.—GODET, art. *"Boèce,"* in *Dict. de Théol.*—RAND, *op. cit.*

Cassiodorus.—Sources: *P. L.,* LXIX–LXX.—Works: DOM LECLERCQ, art. *"Cassiodore,"* in *Dict. d'Arch.*—P. DE LABRIOLLE, *op. cit.,* p. 673.—DOM BERLIÈRE, *L'ordre monastique,* ch. II.

Venerable Bede.—GODET, art. *"Bède,"* in *Dict. de Théol.*—DOM CABROL, *L'Angleterre chrétienne.*—BEDE, *Ecclesiastical History of England* (edited by A. M. SELLAR).—FATHER PAUL, *op. cit.*

Gregory of Tours.—Sources: *P. L.*, LXXI, 161–1118, and in *Mon. Germ. Hist., Script. Rerum Meroving.*, I.—Works: G. MONOD, *Et. crit. sur les sources de l'Hist. mérov.*, 1872.—A. LECOY DE LA MARCHE, *De l'autorité de Grégoire de Tours*, 1861.—BONNET, *Le latin de Grégoire de Tours*, 1890.

SECOND PERIOD

The Carolingian Epoch (714–887)

SECTION I

The Eighth Century. From the Advent of Charles Martel to the Death of Charlemagne (714–814)

CHAPTER I

THE WEST UNDER CHARLES MARTEL (714–741)

For a long time the Merovingian kings were the rulers of Gaul in name only; their prime ministers, the mayors of the palaces of Neustria and Austrasia, actually guided the destinies of the nation. Between these two kingdoms incessant wars were waged. In the second half of the seventh century the Neustrian chief Ebroin succeeded in gaining the upper hand, but this cruel barbarian, who had put to death St. Leodegar (678), was later assassinated, and the hegemony passed to the mayoralty of Austrasia, presided over by the illustrious family of the Pepinides. This family gave to the world men and women of exemplary piety, instance: St. Arnould (Arnulph), bishop of Metz, St. Begga, the mother of Pepin of Heristal, and St. Gertrude, his sister.

I. The Evangelization of Germany by St. Boniface. The apostolate of trans-Rhenish Germany was inaugurated by the Anglo-Saxon monk Wynfrid, under the patronage and protection of Charles Martel, son of Pepin of Heristal. Wynfrid emulated the zeal of his compatriot, Willibrord, the apostle of Frisia, and accentuated the twofold characteristic of his Frankish and Roman missions. He received his commission from Rome, whither he had journeyed in the year 719. "Go," said Pope Gregory II to him, "from this moment on thou shalt be called *'Boniface,'* *i. e.*, he who doth good." His mission field was mapped out for him:

Bavaria and the Alemanni had remained more or less faithful to the grace of their first conversion; but farther to the north were Hesse and Thuringia, still plunged in idolatry. St. Boniface penetrated all these countries, and from 719 to 722 engaged in a very fruitful apostolate, the principles of which he has set down in a letter to his old bishop, Daniel of Winchester. His plan of attack, he informs us, consisted in allowing the pagans to expound their religion, gently pointing out to them its many contradictions, and, finally, contrasting it with a general description of the Christian religion, that "they might be confounded rather than exasperated."

After this first exploration, Boniface returned to Rome. Gregory II rewarded his labors by conferring episcopal consecration upon him, thus creating the simple missionary first bishop of Hesse and Thuringia. At the same time he vested him with the authority to reform, in the name of the Holy See, the clergy and the faithful of these regions, where discipline and worship were lacking in organization, because the all too independent Celtic monks had failed to set up unity of guidance. In return, Boniface took an oath "that he would not be a party to anything subversive of the unity of the general and universal Church." Armed with his commission, Boniface set out to score more victories. In Hesse he dealt paganism a final blow when, with his own hands, he felled the sacred oak of Odin at Geismar, near Fritzlar;[1] in Thuringia he succeeded in overcoming the opposition of the resentful Celtic missionaries and the degenerate Frankish clergy. Very soon native disciples swelled the ranks of his English collaborators, Lullus, Wigbert, Wynnebald, Willibald, Burchard, etc., and monasteries for men and women alike were founded in different parts of the land. The direction of these monasteries was entrusted by Boniface to his compatriots Chunitrud, Eadburg, Thecla, and the gentle Lioba. Later on he established several great abbeys, like those of Hildesheim and Fulda, which developed into seminaries as well as centers of prayer and preaching.

[1] The reference here is to a gigantic oak, called the "Tree of Thor," which the pagans of the surrounding country regarded with the deepest veneration. Mighty as the God of the Christians was, so they boasted, he had no power over the Oak of Geismar, and none of his followers would dare to destroy it. The Christians advised Boniface to cut down this tree, assuring him that its fall would shake the faith of the pagans in the power of their gods. Boniface consented, and on the appointed day laid the ax to the tree and cut it down with his own hands. Out of the wood Boniface built a small oratory, which he dedicated to St. Peter. (*Transl.*)

In the year 732, Pope Gregory III named Boniface metropolitan of all Germany. At the same time, he charged him "to consecrate bishops for those parts in which the multitude of the faithful showed the greatest increase," and conferred upon him the pallium, which, "according to the Apostolic prescriptions, he was to use only for the celebration of the solemn service of the Mass, or at the consecration of a bishop." From that moment on, and especially after his third journey to Rome (737-738), he devoted all his time and energy to reform and the work of organizing the hierarchy. At that time Bavaria comprised not only its present territories, but also Upper Austria, the Tyrol, and a part of Styria. This vast country he divided into four bishoprics, with seats at Passau, Salzburg, Freising, and Ratisbon, with accurately defined limits, and selected occupants for each. Then, with the assistance of these titular bishops, he convoked the first German synod for the reform of the morals and discipline of the clergy. Later on the abbey of Eichstädt, ruled over by Willibald, a relative of Boniface, was transformed into a bishopric, taking in Frankish Wortgau as far as the Saale. This territory was to serve as an outpost for future missionary journeys to the Slavs along the river Elbe. Thuringia and Hesse were also divided into three bishoprics: that of Buraburg for Hesse, and those of Erfurt and Würzburg for Thuringia. All these cathedral churches remained in the care of monks.

II. The Victory over the Moors. The material aid of Charles Martel, secured through the intercession of Pope Gregory II, contributed much to the success of St. Boniface, who was wont to say: "Without the protecting influence of the King of the Franks, I could neither govern my people, nor defend the priests, nor forbid the practice of pagan rites in Germany." The Frankish monarch did more, however, than lend assistance to the Apostle of Germany, for to the south of his kingdom he succeeded in completely blocking an invasion of the Arabs from Spain. In 719, Governor El Samah had crossed the Pyrenees and taken possession of the cities of Narbonne, Nimes, and Carcassonne; his armies were halted, however, by Count Eude of Aquitania and completely crushed outside the walls of Toulouse. Yet the Arabs would not acknowledge defeat, but invaded Gaul a second time, under the leadership of Abd-el-Rhaman, seized the city of Bordeaux, and were preparing to advance on Tours, whither they were attracted by the treasures of St. Martin's shrine, when they were annihilated by Charles Martel at the battle of Poitiers, in which their light cavalry could not penetrate the stone wall of the Franks (Oct. 17, 732). A few years later, the Arabs returned to the charge, this time following the valley of the Rhône and threatening the city of Lyons. Charles again hurled them back as far as Septimania, whence his successors later dislodged and completely routed them.

III. Relations with the Holy See. The Church looked to the Franks for still another service: the protection of the papacy. In the opening years of the eighth century, Italy was rapidly falling prey to a twofold tyranny: the proximate tyranny of the Lombards, who plundered the land and oppressed its citizens; and the remote, but no less real, tyranny of the Greek emperors, who, without any solicitude for the welfare of the people, crushed them under the burden of heavy taxation, at the same time making themselves odious by their iconoclastic fury. Left alone and abandoned to his own resources, the Pope was forced to cast around for new protectors. As a consequence, Gregory III (731-741) turned his eyes in the direction of the Franks and sent a delegation to the court of Charles Martel. Charles showered the papal legates with gifts, but declined to take up arms against Luitprand, the king of the Lombards, who had just helped him expel the Saracens from Provence. For this same reason, a second and third delegation also failed of results.

In promising his protection to St. Boniface, as papal legate, Charles Martel had paved the way for an alliance between the Franks and the Holy See. He refused, however, to go any further. The idea of a Christian empire, such as was conceived during the Middle Ages, never occurred to him; the most that can be said is that he unconsciously initiated the movement. Charles was a brutal conqueror, and his methods contributed much to the decadence of the Frankish Church. He looked upon ecclesiastical dignities and benefices as so many means of promoting his own interests and increasing his power, and either sold bishoprics and abbeys or made donations of them to his kin and his courtiers. His nephew, Hugh, for instance, held three bishoprics—Paris, Rouen, and Bayeux—together with three abbeys; Milon, his companion in arms, was created bishop of Treves and Rheims and so completely ransacked these churches and the benefices attached to them, that his clerics were forced to take up a trade to make a living.

TEXTS AND DOCUMENTS

St. Boniface and the Papacy

We should pause for a moment to consider, in this great man, one of those heroic lives that influence the destinies of nations. His life is a compendium of the revolution which fills many centuries. Wrapped in absolute barbarism, the Germans had been surrounded, for four hundred years, by the institutions of Christian society; bishops and monks had vainly endeavored to educate these ignorant tribes. How could the faith become mistress of these intellects enslaved by the senses? How could the faith subdue such irregular wills? Their old instincts were showing themselves in slaughter, in robbery, and in carousals; after thirty Catholic kings, the Franks were returning to idolatry; the sacrifices of Woden reddened the altar of Christ; and perhaps, in a short time, there would have remained only a slight remembrance of the Gospel, as of one more fable in the Mythology of the North. Such would have been the end of Christianity, had it been left to the free genius of the Germans. The Barbarians could be educated only under guardianship. Their unruly spirits would bow only to the ascendancy of a great power; such was that of the Popes, who manifested that paternal character which is derived from their divine institution; who had the strength of ideas, who were accustomed to govern, and who had the prestige of time and distance and the majesty of the Latin name. By these means the Pontiffs had mastered the Franks, and through them, other peoples. It was a decisive moment when Gregory II dictated to bishop Boniface the oath of fidelity. Rome then witnessed the fulfillment of what she had foreseen when Alaric restored, in pomp, the sacred vessels to St. Peter's basilica; she saw her empire again extended over the nations that had overthrown it; she saw a Saxon bishop kneeling, in the name of Germany, at the feet of a Roman citizen, and arising, a legate of the Vatican—a proconsul of the new era, who was to introduce, without the aid of lictors or of soldiery, the legislative genius of the old Senate among his people. For thirty-seven years Boniface carried out the designs of the Roman policy; an active correspondence with the Holy See, and twenty-four letters of Popes Gregory II, Gregory III, and Zachary, show us the fruitful docility of this great spirit. The northerners accepted the beneficent rule, imposed upon them, not by the eagle, but under the symbols of the dove and the lamb.

> Cantù, *History Documents*, art. *SS. Columbanus and Boniface.*

QUESTIONS

1. Give a brief account of the missionary labors of St. Boniface.
2. How did the apostolate of St. Boniface differ from that of the Celtic monks?

3. Why is St. Lioba called "the Woman Apostle of Germany"?
4. What part did Charles Martel play in the conversion of Germany?
5. Just how significant is the rôle played by St. Boniface in the conversion of the northern provinces of Europe?
6. How did Charles Martel cope with the invasions of the Moors?
7. Why was the victory of Charles Martel at Tours the turning-point in the Moslem campaign of conquest?
8. Differentiate between the terms: Arabs, Moors, Saracens, Moslems, and Islamites.

BIBLIOGRAPHY

St. Boniface.—Sources: *Vitæ S. Bonifatii,* by Willibald and Anonym. in *Mon. Germ., Script.,* II.—Works: HAUCK, *op. cit.,* I–II.—KURTH, *Saint Boniface* (Coll. *"Les Saints"*).—DOM U. BERLIÈRE, *L'ordre monastique,* ch. II.—RICHARD, art *"Allemagne,"* in *Dict. d'Hist.*—LAVISSE, *La conquête de la Germanie par l'Eglise romaine,* in *Rev. des Deux Mondes,* 15 April, 1887.—LAVISSE-KLEINCLAUSZ, *Histoire de France,* II, 1st Part, pp. 262 ff.—G. W. ROBINSON, *Life of St. Boniface* (from the original of Willibald of Mayence), Harvard Univ. Press, 1916.

Poitiers.—REINAUD, *Invasion des Sarrasins en France,* 1836.—MERCIER, *La bataille de Poitiers,* in *Rev. hist.,* 1878.—ZOTENBERG, *Les invasions des Arabes en France,* 1872.—LAVISSE-KLEINCLAUSZ, II, 1st Part, p. 259.—IMBART DE LA TOUR, *Les Francs et la défaite de l'Islamisme,* in *France chrétienne,* pp. 47–61.—HERVÉ-BAZIN, *Les grandes journées de la chrétienté,* pp. 103–129.

CHAPTER II

I. The Reform of the Frankish Church. Pepin the Short, a son of Charles Martel, was a loyal and true child of the Church. He was baptized by St. Willibrord and educated at the famous abbey of St. Denis. St. Boniface was the first to sense the danger which threatened the Church of Gaul and to call attention to it. "The majority of the episcopal sees," he wrote to Pope Zachary, "are in the hands of covetous laymen or adulterous clerics. And the incumbents who can boast of not indulging in these vices, are more often than not drunkards, hunters, and soldiers, who spill the blood of Christians and pagans indiscriminately." Invested by the Holy See with plenipotentiary powers, and fortified by the protection of the Frankish chieftain, St. Boniface undertook the work of reform by convoking several councils. It was first decided to restore to the ancient metropolitan sees of Rheims, Sens, and Rouen not only an honorary, but also an effective precedence over all other sees. This step resulted in the re-establishment in Gaul of that well-organized hierarchy that had insured the success of his apostolate in Germany. It was resolved, secondly, to formulate certain disciplinary canons in view of reforming the clergy. The details of these regulations were carefully specified: false and unworthy priests, deacons, and other clerics, were to be deposed, degraded, and subjected to punishment; priests and deacons were forbidden to dress like laymen, hunt, hawk, carry arms or go to war; all clerics were prohibited from possessing ecclesiastical goods, except by "precarious tenure" or under the title of benefices, etc. It was voted, thirdly, to work untiringly at the abolition of numerous superstitious practices inherited from paganism. The principal synods convened to achieve these results were the *Concilium Germanicum Primum* (742), that of Estinnes or Leptines in Hainaut (743), that of Soissons (744), and the *Concilium Germanicum Secundum* (745). To cap this most important work, a national council of the entire Frankish Empire was convoked in the year 745. The synodal decisions had all the force of State decrees, cases of transgression being punished by the secular ruler. Very soon a virtuous and well-instructed episcopate replaced an ignorant and dissolute one, so that it could truly be said that the reform of the Frankish Church prepared the bloom of Carolingian Christianity. To a certain extent we may compare the religious regeneration which was its immediate result to that inaugurated for the Universal Church by the Council of Trent in the sixteenth century. It was also through the efforts of St. Boniface that church property, which had passed into the hands of laymen, was restored to its rightful owners, and a halt was called upon the secularization of ecclesiastical goods. As abuses continued, however, Pepin decided to take an inventory, allotting to each church what was necessary for its maintenance and consigning the remainder to the members of the congregation under the fictitious title of "a letter of precarious tenure," and on condition that they paid a small quit-rent, twice the amount of the tithes levied on its revenues, and a contribution to help defray the expenses of keeping the property in repair.

The final seal of approval was placed on the work of St. Boniface when, in 748, he was appointed archbishop of Mayence by the Pope. That city was thus raised to the dignity of metropolitan see of all Germany, just as Canterbury had been some years previously in England. The Saint then conceived the plan of journeying to the mouth of the Rhine and completing the work of evangelizing Frisia, which had been begun by St. Willibrord. A year later, on June 5, 755, he was slain together with fifty-two of his followers, by an infuriated mob of pagans at Dokkum on the banks of the Borne. His body was carried to Fulda and laid to rest in the abbey church.

II. Union with the Holy See. In 751, Pepin despatched envoys to Pope Zachary, to consult him "on the matter of kings who then lived among the Franks and bore the title of king without possessing royal authority." Zachary's reply was to the effect that "it is better to call him 'king' who is invested with authority than him who is deprived of it." His action was tantamount to a recognition of the existing facts. It also paved the way for future relations, could be interpreted in terms of a reward for services rendered the Church by the Pepinides, and insured powerful protection for the Holy See. Encouraged by the verdict of Pope Zachary, Pepin had himself proclaimed king.

It was not long before the papacy reaped the fruits of this wise political move, when Stephen II, the successor of Pope Zachary, was threatened by Aistulf, king of the Lombards, who, after gaining possession of Ravenna, disclosed his plan to march on Rome. After appealing in vain to the Eastern Emperor for help, Stephen journeyed to France, where he crowned Pepin at St. Denis and at the same time conferred upon him the honorary title of "Patrician of the Romans." In return, Pepin promised his aid against the Lombards, and after vainly requesting Aistulf, "out of respect for the Apostles Peter and Paul," not to march against Rome, he crossed the Alps, defeated Aistulf at Susa, and then laid siege to his armies at Pavia. The Lombard king promised to make full restitution, but went back on his word. In response to the Pope's appeal, Pepin again crossed the Alps and beat back Aistulf. Envoys of the Eastern Emperor vainly tried to induce Pepin to restore Ravenna and the other former Byzantine territories of the "Basileus." Pepin refused, declaring that he had undertaken the campaign for the love of St. Peter. Fulrad, abbot of St. Denis, was commissioned to place Stephen II in possession of twenty-two reconquered towns, comprised within the territory which extends from Comacchio towards the south as far as Sinigaglia and Gubbio, and in the Middle Ages was called the Exarchate and the Pentapolis. The deed of donation which was deposited by Fulrad, together with the keys of these cities, on the tomb of St. Peter, is no longer in existence, although the life of Pope Stephen (*Vita Stephani*) contains an account of it.

After the death of Aistulf, Desiderius, new king of the Lombards, received threats from Ratchis, a brother of the deceased. He secured the Pope's aid by promising to "restore" to the Holy See that portion of the Exarchate which he still retained, and to hand over to the Pope the suzerainty over Spoleto and Beneventum. Once firmly established on his throne, Desiderius carried out only part of his promise; yet he remained indebted to the Pope. At that moment, however, disturbances broke out in Rome, which prevented the Holy See from demanding a settlement.

At the suggestion of the Primicerius [1] Christopher, Paul I, a brother of

---

[1] "The Lateran was the headquarters of the chancellor's office, where the clerks were known as *notarii* or *scriniarii*. These included the seven district notaries, the two most important of whom (*primicerius* and *secundicerius*) were numbered among the great ecclesiastical dignitaries. The *primicerius* of the notaries, together with the chief priest and the archdeacon, made up the triumvirate on which the government of the Roman Church devolved, in the event of the Pope's death or absence. He was also trustee of the archives and manager of the library, though by this time the functions of librarians were beginning to be separated from those of the notaries. As yet, there is no mention of the *primiscrinius* or *protoscrinius*, who later succeeded the *primicerius* as the real head of the chancellor's office" (Duchesne, *The Beginnings of the Temporal Sovereignty of the Popes*, pp. 63–64).

Stephen II, had displayed great severity in his dealings with the turbulent Roman aristocracy. A plot against his life was formed by a certain Duke Toto of Nepi and his three brothers, but it was thwarted by Christopher, who even succeeded in making Toto swear that, although the Sovereign Pontiff was the ruler of the whole duchy, his subjects would have no voice in his election, which would proceed in the proper and ordinary way. When Pope Paul I suddenly expired, however, the Duke straightway broke his oath, forced his way into the Lateran, and proclaimed one of his brothers, Constantine, as pope. Tonsure was immediately conferred on the newly appointed Pontiff, who the following day was ordained a sub-deacon and a deacon without any regard for the intervals required by law. He was consecrated at St. Peter's the following Sunday and governed the Church for thirteen months, during which time he held several ordinations (Constantine II, 767–768). But the opposing party had not reckoned with Christopher, who, feeling his position to be precarious, had sought refuge in the palace of King Desiderius. The latter, who was more than pleased at the opportunity to meddle in the affairs of the papacy, entered the city of Rome, made Constantine a prisoner, and proclaimed as pope in his stead a venerable priest by the name of Philip. Christopher refused to recognize the newly appointed pope, assembled the clergy and lay aristocracy of Rome, and after some discussion, finally appointed a priest of St. Cecilia by the name of Stephen. The new pope was recognized by a Franco-Italian council held at the Lateran, at which it was decreed that cardinal priests or deacons alone should henceforth be eligible for the office of pope, and "laymen, both military and civil," should be excluded from the electoral body.

We note in Rome a twofold influence during the eighth century: that of the pope and the clergy on the one hand, and that of the *exercitus romanus* (Roman army) and the local aristocracy, comprising the duke of Rome, the division commanders, the prefect of the city, and many other civic dignitaries. The latter assumed great importance especially after the fall of the Exarchate of Ravenna, when the election of the duke of Rome became their affair. No wonder, then, that they sought to control the election of the pope and to direct all local affairs. The ecclesiastical element, however, opposed their plans. Many services relative to the edileship, to public supplies and public highways, nay, even to military defence, were entrusted to the pope and especially recommended to his exchequer.

And so, without acting directly through his clerics, he showed real concern for matters far removed from the spiritual, *e. g.,* upkeep of the aqueducts, repairing the ramparts, directing military expeditions, etc. Many State officials received their appointments from him, if not *de jure,* at least, *de facto.* A superior influence of this kind, inspired by sincere loyalty, had rendered important services under the reigns of Popes Gregory II (715–731) and Gregory III (731–741).[1]

The spirit of rivalry which existed between the lay and the ecclesiastical powers explains the many disturbances from which Rome suffered at that time. The Pepinides only intervened in the capacity of friends of the Holy See and without any regard for the lay aristocracy. As a consequence, the latter harbored sentiments of revenge. At first, they were somewhat intimidated by the Carolingian protector of the Holy See; but once the latter was eclipsed, they took the offensive. Wars between them and the Bishop of Rome continued to be waged until the establishment of a strong pontifical government in the fifteenth century.

TEXTS AND DOCUMENTS

The Deed of the Donation Made by Pepin to Pope Stephen II

The exact wording of this deed of gift is no longer preserved to us; but in the life of Stephen II we have the list of territories given up to the Holy See. They include, first of all, Comacchio and Ravenna, and then the tract of land between the Apennines and the sea, from Forli in the north as far as Jesi Sinigaglia in the south. There is no mention of Ancona and the remains of what was known later as the Marches, nor of Faenza, Imola, Bologna, and Ferrara. The papal State had still, therefore, much to acquire north of the Apennines. To the south of the chain, Eugubium (Gubbio) alone appears to be included. Perugia, which was a near neighbor, still belonged to the Romans.

With the exception of Narni, which had formerly been annexed by the duchy of Spoleto, and which was restored in 756, the Lombard king's "restitutions" were what he himself had seized. Rome, though at first satisfied, had not forgotten the time when these provinces had other limits. It was hardly thirty years since the annexation of Bologna in the north and Osimo in the south, and now the Romans began to consider the possibility of recapturing Liutprand's conquests in the same way as those of Astolphus. They had not long to wait for their opportunity. Only a few months after the departure of the Frankish army, Astolphus met his death through a hunting accident.

[1] See Duchesne, *The Beginnings of the Temporal Sovereignty of the Popes, passim.*

There was great rejoicing among the Romans, who thought they saw the hand of Providence in the fact of the king's dying only a year after his last expedition. To make matters still more cheerful, the possession of the throne was disputed by two rivals, neither of them very formidable. They were Desiderius, Duke of Tuscany, and Ratchis, brother of the former king, and at that time a monk of Monte Cassino. Desiderius intimated his willingness to acquiesce in all the Pope's wishes, so Stephen sent him a deputation, consisting of his own brother Paul and the Councillor Christopher, together with the Abbot Fulrad. Desiderius promised to restore to the "republic" the cities which were lacking (*civitates quae remanserant*), *i. e.,* Faenza, Imola, and Ferrara to the west of the Exarchy, and Ancona, Osimo, and Umana to the east of the Pentapolis. An agreement was signed under Fulrad's supervision; and, with a little persuasion, Desiderius promised to give up Bologna as well.

Stephen was beside himself with delight, and poured forth his soul in a letter to Pepin, written in March or April, 757. Thanks to the Frankish protection and Fulrad's vigorous action, the Pope already looked upon himself as the sovereign disposer of Italy. Desiderius, the new king, begged his good offices in recommending him to the favor of the Frankish monarch. The inhabitants of the duchy of Spoleto, who had just elected a new duke, and even those of the duchy of Beneventum, approached him with the same end in view. We may add that the dukes of Spoleto and Beneventum were, in theory at all events, officially connected with the Lombard kingdom.

The Byzantine empire, however, did not join its note to this chorus. It was no longer in a position, as in Zachary's time, to benefit by the diplomatic successes of the Holy See, which, by the way, were not as complete as they had hoped. It was for the Pope to yield first. He sent one of his priests, Stephen, to Ratchis, exhorting him to go back to his monastic life. The Abbot Fulrad sallied forth at the head of his Frankish troops to support the eloquence of the legate. The Roman army was ready to follow him. Ratchis did as he was bidden, and Desiderius was proclaimed king of the Lombards. The situation once conquered, he appeared in no hurry to divide up his kingdom. It is true that Faenza and Ferrara were restored to the Exarchy, but as far as Pentapolis was concerned, no change took place.

Duchesne, *The Beginnings of the Temporal Sovereignty of the Popes*, pp. 46 ff.

QUESTIONS

1. Indicate some of the probable causes of the decline of morality among the clergy in the eighth century.
2. What means were taken by St. Boniface in organizing his work of reform?

3. Why did the pope seek the protection of the Frankish kings in preference to that of the Lombards?

4. Account for the passive attitude of the Eastern Emperor when appealed to for protection by Stephen II.

5. Give instances in the lives of St. Boniface and Pepin the Short in proof of the deep veneration in which St. Peter was held in the early Middle Ages.

6. What was the Exarchate?

7. What were the functions of the Primicerius?

8. Describe the end of Pope Constantine II.

9. What were the beginnings of the temporal power of the pope?

10. Why should the pope be independent of all earthly powers? Is temporal sovereignty necessary for this independence?

BIBLIOGRAPHY

Reform of the Frankish Church under Pepin.—Sources: Boretius, *Capitularia regum Francorum*, pp. 24–41.—Works: Lavisse-Kleinclausz, *op. cit.*—Hanotaux-Goyau, *op. cit.*—Hefele-Leclercq, *Hist. des conciles*, III, (2nd Part).—Hauck, *op. cit.*, II.—Msgr. Lesne, *La hiérarchie épiscopale*, 1905; *Histoire de la propriété ecclésiastique en France*, t. I, 1910.

Pepin and the Holy See.—Sources: *Annales laurissenses majores*, edit. Kurze in *Script. Rer. Germ. in usum scholarum.*—Eginhard, *Vita Karoli*, 1–3. —*Clausula de Pippini consecratione*, in *Script. Rer. Merov.*, I, pp. 465–466.— *Codex Carolinus.*—*Vita Stephani*, in *Liber Pontificalis*, I.—Works: Knaale, *Aistulf, König der Longobarden*, 1880.—Kleinclausz, *L'empire carolingien;* Kleinclausz-Lavisse, II, 1st Part, p. 270.—Fustel de Coulanges, *Les transformations de la royauté pendant l'époque carolingienne*, 1892.—Duchesne, *Les premiers temps de l'Etat pontifical*, ch. IV.—Paul Fabre, *Les Carolingiens et le Saint-Siège*, in *La France chrétienne*, pp. 61 ff.—Hubert, *Etude sur la formation de l'Etat pontifical*, in *Rev. hist.*, LXIX.—Bayet, *Le voyage d'Etienne III*, in *Rev. hist.*, XX.—H. de l'Epinois, *Le Gouvernement des Papes et les revolutions dans les Etats de l'Eglise*, 2nd edit., 1867.

CHAPTER III

I. Struggles for the Freedom of the Holy See: The Pontifical State. Didier nursed the secret ambition of some day annexing the Roman territory to his kingdom, and, to further this end, sought to foment a clash between the papacy and Charles, the new king of the Franks. But Pope Hadrian I (772-795) made a bid for the latter's friendship by purposely avoiding to crown the sons of his deceased brother Carloman. And so, when the Pope petitioned Charles to force the restitution of territories usurped by Didier, the Frankish king declared himself in favor of such a move. He defeated the Lombards, seized their capital, Pavia, and re-annexed their country to the Empire. From that moment on Charles gave proof of his true feelings towards the Holy See. During the siege of Pavia, he set out for Rome, where he arrived on Holy Saturday, April 2, 774. He conducted himself as a pious pilgrim, dismounting from his horse, advancing on foot towards the basilica of St. Peter, and ascending on his knees the great staircase leading to the atrium. At a meeting held in the basilica of St. Peter, he ratified the donation of Pepin the Short, and even enlarged it. Basing their information on the sole document which relates the fact, to wit, the Life of Pope Hadrian in the *Liber Pontificalis,* some writers have erroneously maintained that the gifts in land made by Charles to the Sovereign Pontiff were very considerable, comprising Corsica and peninsular Italy, and excluding only Lombardy, Genoa, and Piedmont. Hemmer, however, regards it as quite probable that Hadrian's biographer practiced deceit by exaggerating certain vague promises made by Charlemagne. The so-called Donation of Charlemagne, just like the forged Donation of Constantine, which also belongs to the second half of the eighth century, is probably nothing more than a means of insinuation to the Frankish chieftain to set up a strong Pontifical State on a solid foundation.[1] The real donation had no such proportions,

---

[1] Hemmer, *"Adrian I,"* in *Dict. de Théol.*

339

and the temporal work of Pope Hadrian was achieved only by a series of gracious concessions made by Charlemagne. After the fall of Pavia, the Pope gained possession of the towns of Imola, Ferrara, and Bologna, formerly wrested from the Exarchate of Ravenna by the Lombards. In 781, on the occasion of a visit of Charlemagne to the Eternal City, the Pope received also Sabina, although Sabina was only part of the Duchy of Spoleto, which Charlemagne annexed to his own dominions. In the same manner he gained possession of the Lombard territories in Tuscany, together with the Duchy of Beneventum. The Pontifical State was thus constituted in the shape in which it existed until the nineteenth century. Charlemagne, through his *missi,* retained in Rome a sort of superior jurisdiction to which people could always appeal. The limits of his power, it is true, were rather ill-defined and could easily have given rise to conflicts between the papacy and the Frankish king, had not the agreement between them been a "pact of love and fidelity."

II. Struggles for the Spread of Christianity: The Saxons, the Moors. Everywhere Charlemagne proved himself to be the champion of the Church; through the conquest of Saxony he added considerably to the results achieved by the apostolate of St. Boniface. Situated between the Upper Weser and the Baltic, and extending from the basin of the Rhine to that of the Elbe, Saxony stood out like a citadel of the pagan god Odin. Its inhabitants entertained a fierce hatred for the Franks because they had deserted the cause of the national religion. This fact accounts for the slight success with which the missionaries met in these countries. During the first half of the eighth century, the two Ewalds, the first surnamed the White, the second, the Black, were put to death. Charlemagne resolved to conquer Saxony, and so to win it over to Christianity. A first expedition was crowned with success. Charlemagne's forces gained possession of the fortress of Eresburg and destroyed the Irmensul, a colossal tree, which the Saxons regarded as the pillar upon which the whole world rested. On the occasion of a great assembly at Paderborn, in 777, a large number were converted to the Catholic faith. Charlemagne then divided the kingdom of Saxony between the Rhenish dioceses of Mayence, Cologne, and Würzburg. The Abbey of Fulda became the center of an apostolate which was first entrusted to Sturm, the beloved disciple of St. Boniface (✝ 778), and later to Willibald. Very soon, however, the Saxons went back on their word of honor which they had given to the Frankish king. They rose up against the Franks, indiscriminately massacred Frankish priests and soldiers, and even set fire to the monastery of Fulda (778). In 782, the revolt assumed larger proportions, and the Saxons completely crushed a Frankish army at Suntal near the Weser. The reprisals were appalling, and even excessive. Charlemagne issued orders for the massacre of 4500 prisoners at Verden. After a campaign of three years, the Saxons were finally forced to surrender (783–785). Widukind, their leader, received Baptism.

The Baptism of Widukind was the signal for new attempts at evangelization and at the same time a guarantee that these attempts would be crowned with success. Willibald founded several episcopal sees: at Münster and Osnabrück for the Westphalians; at Minden, Paderborn, Bremen, and Verden for the Engrians, and at Halberstadt and Hildesheim for the Estphalians. The Diet of Aix-la-Chapelle (797) put the final touches to this civil and ecclesiastical transformation. Conversions to the faith were numerous. The Saxon hostages, reared and educated under the supervision of the Franks, gave proof of such ability and piety that most of the bishops of the country were taken from their ranks. From the very first year of its foundation, the Abbey of Corbie (Somme) received a great number of Saxons within its walls and became the center of missionary labors throughout the North. From its halls sallied forth such men as St. Ansgar (Anscharius), the apostle of Denmark and Sweden. Finally, the work of organizing the Saxon nation paved the destinies of Germany of the Middle Ages, in which the Saxon Ottos played such an important part.

The Frisians were neighbors of the Saxons and shared their fortunes. Vanquished in war with them in 782, they showed themselves more disposed to receive the Gospel message from the hands of another Anglo-Saxon, Gregory, Abbot of St. Martin's of Utrecht. Very soon this see became a powerful hierarchical center. The Lex Frisonum, promulgated towards the end of the century, presupposes the existence of a great Christian community.

Charles waged war also against the Moors of Spain. In 778 he crossed the Pyrenees at the head of an immense army, but suffered defeat before Saragossa. On his return journey the rear guard of his army was completely crushed in the narrow pass of Roncesvalles, where the gallant Roland, immortalized by the epic legend, perished. Charles created the kingdom of Aquitania to protect the frontiers of Gaul, and entrusted it to Duke William, who seized Barcelona, Tarragona, and Tortosa, and converted these cities into a wall against the Moorish invaders. Thus the Franks fulfilled their mission as defenders of Christendom. The memory of these struggles gave rise to certain famous French epic poems, and kept alive that spirit of chivalry which later gave to the world the great Crusades.

III. The Pontifical Alliance: The Holy Empire. So many and such unprecedented services merited a reward, and so the papacy resolved to seal its alliance with the Carolingians, whom it sorely needed also to check the turbulent Roman aristocracy. The authority of *Leo III* (795–816) had been contested by the nephews of his predecessor, Hadrian I. He was even attacked by a troop of armed conspirators and cruelly wounded during the solemn procession on St. Mark's day. The Pope fled from the city and repaired at once to Charlemagne, who was at that time at Paderborn. Immediately upon his election to the pontificate, Leo III had sent him the banner of Rome, together with the keys of the *Confessio* of St. Peter, and had issued orders that the Roman people should swear allegiance to him. The king's suzerainty was, therefore, officially recognized by all, and so it was even more imperative for him to intervene now than before. Charlemagne received the Pontiff with the greatest respect and had him escorted back to Rome by a body guard of Frankish counts and bishops. The following year an investigation was opened, and Charles himself arrived at the gates of Rome. Some days were spent in examining the accusations lodged against Leo by his enemies, but the latter, under oath, completely cleared himself in the presence of the king (December 23, 800).

The following day was the vigil of Christmas, and Charles came into the basilica of St. Peter to attend the celebration of Mass. As he was bowing down to pray in his place before the altar, the Pope placed a precious crown upon his head, while the populace shouted: "To Charles, most pious, most august, crowned by God, great and pacific Emperor of the Romans, long life and victory!" This was the same acclamation which was in use at Byzantium. It might be supposed that the sole purpose which Leo had in mind in increasing the prestige of the defender of the papacy was to impose silence upon the turbulent Romans. In point of fact, however, his action was far more significant. It was tantamount to the

recognition that Charles was the defender of all Christendom and the
associate of the Pope in the task of governing the great Catholic family.
The function of the war-like leader was to protect and administer the
temporal; that of the religious leader, to stand guard over the spiritual.
Both were lieutenants of St. Peter. This new conception of imperial
authority is embodied in the mosaics of the Lateran, in which the Pope
and the Emperor Charlemagne are represented as kneeling at the feet
of St. Peter, who gives to the one the pallium, and to the other the banner. Charlemagne regarded the imperial crown and the right to bequeath
it as belonging to him, and so, a few days before his death, he himself
summoned his only remaining son, Louis, whom he had made king
of Aquitania in 806, to his court at Aix-la-Chapelle, and before a general assembly of the clergy and laity, and with their approval, solemnly declared him his successor and heir to all his dominions.

**IV. The Functions of the Emperor; The Fight Against
Adoptionism.** Charlemagne had a very high idea of his imperial functions. A theological error which originated in Spain furnished him with
the occasion of actively entering upon his rôle of *defensor fidei* (defender
of the faith). Adoptionism was a sort of revival of the old Christological
errors. The Spanish bishop Migetius rejected every distinction between the
Word and Christ, maintaining that the second Person of the Blessed
Trinity did not exist before the Incarnation. This teaching was tantamount to Monophysitism, since it regarded the nature of the Word as
temporal and, therefore, human. The danger which lurks in all anti-
Monophysitic reactions is their tendency to lean towards Nestorianism.
And so, in his refutation of Migetius, Elipandus, Archbishop of Toledo,
strongly stressed the eternal generation of the Son and the elements that
distinguished this generation from the temporal mystery of the Incarnation. He emphasized this point of view so much that his statements
issued, at least indirectly, in a distinction of persons between the divinity
of the Word and the humanity of Christ. In point of fact, he contrasted
two filiations in Jesus Christ: the divine, by which He is the natural
Son of God (*natura atque substantia*), and the human, by which He is
only the adopted Son of God (*non natura, sed praedestinatione et gratia*).
Such an opposition between the two filiations could obtain only on condition that the divine nature and the human nature were isolated from each
other. In this way, a greater or lesser breach was instituted between the

two natures, and, as a consequence, between the two persons. This adopted man, considered apart from the Word, was soon made over into a mere mortal, subject to the infirmities of our poor humanity. The doctrine thus evolved was Nestorianism in a new guise.

While Elipandus lost no time in disseminating his error in Galicia and the Asturias, his disciple Felix, Bishop of Urgel, spread it throughout the length and breadth of Septimania and Languedoc. Within the peninsula, the priest Beatus, and Etherius, Bishop of Osma, raised their voices in protest, and the noise of the battle elicited a condemnation of Adoptionism by Pope Hadrian I. The strength of the opposition, however, was centered in Gaul. Charlemagne convoked three councils against Adoptionism: that of Ratisbon (792), that of Frankfort (794), and that of Aix-la-Chapelle (799). At the same time the Gallo-Frankish theologians, Alcuin, Paulinus of Aquileja, and Agobard issued polemical treatises against Elipandus and Felix. At the Council of Aix-la-Chapelle, Felix admitted defeat, after six days had been spent in discussion, but both he and Elipandus persisted in their error. Once the heresy was discredited, however, it began to lose ground and did not survive its originators.

V. The Encroachments of Charlemagne. Unfortunately, the imperial power soon transgressed its lawful boundaries. In the days of Charlemagne people thought in all sincerity that they were to witness a rejuvenation of the Roman Empire. The confusion which reigned among political and religious ideas, the complete absence, so characteristic of the Middle Ages, of anything like a historical sense, and the ever increasing number of legends circulated about the person of the Emperor, caused men to attribute to the new Augustus an unlimited religious power bordering on that of the pagan Caesars. Charles was carried away by the general current of public opinion, and finally came to regard himself as the incarnation, not only of the idea of the State, but also of that of the Church. This fact accounts for his repeated attempts to meddle in the religious life of the Church, for which he was so fond of making regulations. The bishops came to be looked upon as so many functionaries, and the synods as so many State councils. The Emperor exercised minute control over all church property, and issued regulations regarding the ecclesiastical chant and the sacred liturgy. He even went so far as to impart moral teaching to bishops and priests in his capitularies, reminding them of their obligations in the matter of residence and strictly prohibiting them from carrying arms. He then sought to impose his private theological views regarding the veneration of images on the Holy See, and although his attitude towards the Pope was always deferential and respectful, there is no doubt that he too often relegated him to the status of a suppliant. Hadrian was indebted to Charlemagne for many things, and so did not have the courage to protest. It is even doubtful whether he could have done so without scandalizing public opinion. The seeds of Gallicanism had been sown and were beginning to sprout.

TEXTS AND DOCUMENTS

CHARLEMAGNE'S INTEREST IN RELIGION AND THE CHURCH

Charles cherished with the greatest fervor and devotion the principles of the Christian religion, which had been instilled into him from infancy. Hence it was that he built the beautiful basilica at Aachen, which he adorned with gold and silver and lamps, and with rails and doors of solid brass. He had the columns and marbles for this structure brought from Rome and Ravenna, for he could not find such as were suitable elsewhere. He was a constant worshipper at this church as long as his health permitted, going morning and evening, even after nightfall, besides attending Mass. He took care that all the services there conducted should be held in the best possible manner, very often warning the sextons not to let any improper or unclean thing be brought into the building, or remain in it. He provided it with a number of sacred vessels of gold and silver, and with such a quantity of clerical robes that not even the door-keepers, who filled the humblest office in the church, were obliged to wear their everyday clothes when in the performance of their duties. He took great pains to improve the church reading and singing, for he was well skilled in both, although he neither read in public nor sang, except in low tone and with others.

He was very active in aiding the poor; so much so, indeed, that he not only made a point of giving in his own country and his own kingdom, but when he discovered that there were Christians living in poverty in Syria, Egypt, and Africa, at Jerusalem, Alexandria, and Carthage, he had compassion on their wants, and used to send money over the seas to them. The reason why he earnestly strove to make friends with the kings beyond the seas was that he might get help and relief to the Christians living under their rule. He cared for the Church of St. Peter the Apostle at Rome, above all other holy and sacred places, and heaped high its treasury with a vast wealth of gold, silver, and precious stones.

EINHARD, *Vita Karoli,* 26–27, tr. by S. E. Turner
in Harper's School Classics.

Extracts from the Epistola Synodica ad Episcopos Hispaniae

In the year 794 Charlemagne convoked the Council of Frankfort. A letter from Elipandus was presented to the assembly, and the King had it read aloud. Then Charles delivered a long discourse. A delay of two days was granted to permit each one to state his opinion and submit it to the King. The bishops of Italy drew up their statement separately and gave it the title, *Libellus Sacrosyllabus*. The other bishops issued their decision in the form of two letters addressed to the Spaniards: *Epistola Synodica ad Episcopos Hispaniae*. The acts of the Council of Frankfort against Adoptionism contained four treatises, of which the letter to the bishops of the Spanish peninsula constitutes the third.

"We have inscribed at the head of your exposition what you yourselves have inserted: 'We profess and we believe that the Son of God is truly God, engendered from all eternity, before time was, without beginning, co-eternal, consubstantial, not by adoption, but by nature.' A few lines further on we read in the same passage: 'We profess and we believe that He Himself, born of a woman, and made subject to the Law, is not the son of God by generation, but by adoption, not by nature, but by grace.' Here is the serpent again furtively stealing under cover of the shade of the apple tree in Paradise. Persons not on their guard are apt to be deceived by such terminology.

" . . . As to further additions made by you, we find no trace of them in the Creed of Nicaea, to wit, that in Christ there are two natures and three substances; that He is a deified Man and a humanized God. Is not the nature of man made up of a body and a soul? What is there, therefore, between nature and substance, which constrains us to affirm the presence of three substances, and prevents us from merely stating with the Fathers: 'We profess that Jesus Christ, Our Lord, is true God and true Man in one Person'? The Person of the Son persists in the Trinity. After it assumed human nature, it continued to remain the one Person, God and Man; not a deified Man and a humanized God, but God-Man and Man-God: in virtue of the oneness of Person, the only Son of God is perfectly God and perfectly Man. . . . The tradition of the Church points to the existence of two substances in Christ, that of God and that of Man.

"If, therefore, He who was born of the Virgin is true God, how can He be an adopted son or a slave? For you would never dare affirm that God is a slave or an adopted person. And if the prophet referred to him as a slave, he did not give Him this name because of His original status, but only because of that perfect obedience which led him to submit to the will of His Father until death." [1]

The acts of the Council of Frankfort were for a long time withheld from the public through the treachery of heretics. They were brought to light

[1] B. Dolhagaray, art. *"Francfort,"* in *Dict. de Théol.*

towards the end of the sixteenth century, thanks to the research work of Surius, a learned monk of the Order of St. Bruno. His discovery was an important one, because during the time these documents were not available, several theologians had publicly defended the thesis that Christ could be called the adopted Son of God, *in so far as He is Man*. An assertion of this kind is manifestly out of harmony with the decree of the Council of Frankfort. It would be unfair, however, to classify such theologians as heretics, in view of the fact that they had no knowledge of the decisions issued by this Council.

QUESTIONS

1. Must we regard the actions of Pope Hadrian endeavoring to secure the aid of Charlemagne in the establishment of a Papal State as so many political maneuvers and intrigues?
2. Which countries were converted to Christianity as a result of the direct influence of Charlemagne?
3. Give some incidents in the life of St. Anscharius, the apostle of Denmark and Sweden.
4. What was the *Lex Frisonum?*
5. Who immortalized the military exploits of Roland?
6. What was the *Confessio* of St. Peter?
7. Why is the concept of a temporal and a spiritual ruler of Christendom an impracticable one?
8. Which are the main tenets of Adoptionism, and why do they necessarily issue in Nestorianism?
9. State briefly the mediaeval conception of a Christian Roman Empire.

BIBLIOGRAPHY

Charlemagne and the Holy See.—Sources: EINHARD, *Vita Karoli.*— *Annales laurissenses majores.*—*Annales Einhardi.*—Lives of Popes Stephen III and Adrian I, in the *Liber Pontificalis*, I.—PAULUS DIACONUS, *Histoire des Lombards*, edit. Waitz, 1878, in *Script. Rerum Italicarum*, which form part of the *Monum. Germ. Hist.*—RADBERT, *Vie d'Adalard.*—*Codex Carolinus.*— JAFFÉ, *Regesta Pontificum Romanorum*, I, 1885.—Works: DUCHESNE, FUSTEL DE COULANGES, HUBERT, KLEINCLAUSZ, *op. cit.*—HEMMER, art. *"Adrien I,"* in *Dict. de Théol.*—M. JUGIE, art. *"Adrien I,"* in *Dict. d'Hist.*—DOM LECLERCQ, art. *"Charlemagne,"* in *Dict. d'Archéol.*—JEAN BIROT, *Le Saint Empire.*— J. BRYCE, *The Holy Roman Empire.*—H. W. C. DAVIS, *Charlemagne.*—J. I. MOMBERT, *A History of Charles the Great.*—C. L. WELLS, *The Age of Charlemagne.*—HODGKIN, *Charles the Great.*—Cath. Encycl., art. *"Charlemagne."*— C. E. RUSSELL, *Charlemagne, First of the Moderns.*

The Coronation of Charlemagne (800).—Sources: Life of Leo III, in

Liber Pontificalis, II.—*Chronique de Moissac.*—*Annales laurissenses.*—*Lettres et Poésies d'Alcuin*, edit. Dümmer, *Poetae latini aevi carolini*, I, in the *Mon. Germ. Hist.*—THEOPHANES, *Chronologia*, edit. Boor, 1883–1887.—Works: L. LECLERCQ, *A propos du couronnement de l'an 800*, in *Mélanges P. Frédéricq*, Brussels, 1904.—J. FLACH, *La royauté et l'Eglise en France*, in *Rev. hist. eccl.*, IV, pp. 432–447.—C. BAYET, *Léon III et la révolte des Romains en 799*, in *Annuaire de la Faculté des Lettres de Lyon*, 1883.—BRYCE, *The Holy Roman Empire.*—GASQUET, *L'Empire byzantin et la monarchie franque*, 1888.—LOUIS HALPHEN, *Le couronnement impérial de l'an 800*, in *Rev. hist.*, CXXXIV; *Etudes sur le règne de Charlemagne*, 1922.—P. FABRE, *Les Carolingiens et le Saint-Siège*, in *France chrétienne dans l'Histoire*, 1896.

Adoptionism.—Sources: The writings of ELIPANDUS and FELIX D'URGEL, *P. L.*, XCVI.—The writings of their opponents: *Heterius et Beatus* (792), *P. L.*, XCVI; *Paulinus of Aquileia*, *P. L.*, XCIX; *Alcuin*, *P. L.*, C et CI; *Agobard*, *P. L.*, CIV.—The acts of the councils, Mansi, XIII.—Works: J. BACH, *Die Dogmengeschichte des Mittelalters*, Vienna, 1873, I, 102–146.—TIXERONT, *op. cit.*, III.—G. DUBOIS, *De conciliis et theologicis disputationibus apud Francos Carolo Magno regnante habitis*, Alençon, 1902.—P. VUILLERMET, *Elipand de Tolède*, Brignais, 1911.—FRANZELIN, *De Verbo Incarnato*, thesis XXXVIII.—PESCH, *Praelectiones Dogmaticae*, IV, n. 175–188.—M. JUGIE, art. "*Adoptiens*," in *Dict. d'Hist.*—H. QUILLIET, art. "*Adoptionisme au VIIIᵉ siècle*," in *Dict. de Théol.*

The Encroachments of Charlemagne.—M. DUBRUEL and F.-X. ARQUILLIÈRE, art. "*Gallicanisme*," in *Dict. d'Apol.*—F.-X. ARQUILLIÈRE, art. "*Charlemagne et les origines du Gallicanisme*," in *Université Catholique*, 1909, p. 219.

CHAPTER IV

I. Iconoclasm. The worship of images had assumed large proportions in the Byzantine Empire; it had even become quasi-official. In battle, the images were carried at the head of the armies; in the hippodrome, they were accorded the most prominent place and presided over the circus games. The worship of images had, however, met with some opposition. Outside the Church, Jews, Mussulmen, and Manichaeans (Paulicians) regarded this Christian devotion as idolatry; within its fold, especially among the Christians of Syria and Egypt, some of the faithful had adopted an attitude of diffidence and had replaced the representations of human beauty by geometrical figures, or even by symbols borrowed from the animal and plant kingdoms. Iconoclastic influences of this kind, especially Paulician Manichaeism, espoused largely by soldiers recruited from the provinces bordering on the frontiers of Asia, finally attracted the attention of the Emperor, *Leo III*. It would be a mistake, however, to suppose that the ensuing heresy was the upshot of some puerile sectarian movement. At bottom it was a battle sponsored by the State, which had its mind set on Caesaro-papism, against the Church, above all against the monks, who were fast becoming too powerful and too popular. In short, it was an attempt at laicization.

In 726, Leo issued an iconoclastic edict, but it met with bitter opposition among the people. The destruction of a celebrated image of Christ in the Chalcean quarter resulted in an insurrection, which was, however, quickly suppressed by wholesale bloodshed. The beginnings of a revolution were evident in Greece and the Cyclades. The inhabitants of these lands went so far as to proclaim emperor a man by the name of Cosmas, whose fleet was promptly destroyed. Encouraged by these victories, Leo III issued orders to the Patriarch to countersign his iconoclastic edict, and when he refused, appointed in his stead a certain Anastasius, who drew a great number of bishops into heresy with him.

The action of Leo III encountered the opposition of authorized and well-qualified leaders. In the East, St. John Damascene took up arms against him; in the West, the papacy led the attack. St. John wrote three discourses on Images. He enlarged the scope of the controversy and quite cleverly connected it with the question of the part played by sensible rites and objects in the work of our sanctification. He declared very emphatically that the Emperor had no right to settle a question for which he was devoid of authority. On the other hand, Pope Gregory II (715-731) threatened to depose the Patriarch Anastasius; and at a council held in Rome, his successor, Gregory III (731-741), pronounced excommunication against all who professed Iconoclasm (731). Leo in reply equipped a fleet which he sent to Italy, but which perished in the Adriatic Sea.

The Emperor's enthusiasm was somewhat dampened by this setback, as well as by the opposition which he was encountering among the people, and so he resolved to carry on his work without the aid of persecutions († 740). His son, *Constantine V Copronymus,* adopted the same policy, after his competitor Artabasdus had seized Constantinople in the opening years of his reign and kept him in check for more than a year with the aid of the orthodox party. Ten years later, however, in 752, Constantine renewed hostilities. After purging the hierarchy, he convoked a council at Hieria, at which all the bishops, with slavish obedience, countersigned an edict against Iconoclasm. From that moment on, the Basileus' fury knew no bounds. In the churches the sacred images were destroyed and replaced by landscape paintings or pictures of birds. Bishops and monks alike were given the option to subscribe to the theological views of the Emperor, or suffer the consequences. The bishops yielded, but the monks offered heroic resistance. Copronymus became furious and inaugurated a bitter persecution, which reached its height in 765. Peter Calybites, John of Monagua, Paul of Crete, St. Stephen the Younger, and many others suffered martyrdom. In the words of a contemporary writer, "the government seemed intent on completely extirpating the monastic Orders." The orthodox party, however, continued its protestations. In the West, Pope Stephen III again condemned Iconoclasm in a council held in the Lateran in 769; in the East a council held at Jerusalem, representing the three patriarchates of Antioch, Jerusalem, and Alexandria, took the same action (767).

At the death of Constantine Copronymus, a reaction set in. Despite the fact that the new Emperor, Leo IV, surrounded himself with monks, he adhered to Iconoclasm; but his wife, the Empress Irene, was a confirmed opponent of that heresy, and when, after the death of her husband, she became regent, she set herself to restore the veneration of images. She did not achieve her purpose, however, without encountering serious difficulties; the partisans of Iconoclasm were still numerous among the bishops at the imperial court and the soldiers in the army. Irene succeeded in obtaining the resignation of the Patriarch Paul, whom she replaced by Tarasius. She was also instrumental in winning over to the cause of orthodoxy a number of bishops, who had been inveigled into joining hands with the opposing forces, either through timidity or flattery. Soon she was able to propose to Pope Hadrian I the convocation of an ecumenical council to refute the errors of the synod of Hiera. The council convened at Constantinople, but was at first hampered in its work by a military riot. Irene cleverly disbanded the troops and transferred the assembly to Nicaea (*Seventh General Council, 787*); two legates represented the Holy See. The Fathers of Nicaea defined exactly the veneration which is due to images. It is an adoration of honor ($\tau\iota\mu\eta\tau\iota\kappa\dot{\eta}\nu$ $\pi\rho\sigma\chi\dot{\upsilon}\nu\eta\sigma\iota\nu$) and not the latreutic adoration which is due to God alone.

A passing reaction constrained Irene to yield the throne in favor of her son, Constantine VI, but she was able to regain it in 797, and retained it up to the time of the *coup d'état* of Nicephorus (802).

A strong iconoclastic party still remained, which had the backing of the army. In 813, the members of this organization staged a demonstration at the tomb of the immortal Copronymus, and a military revolution proclaimed the Armenian, *Leo Bardas,* as emperor. He resumed the persecution, despite the objurgations of the patriarch Nicephorus, whom he had deposed, and despite those of the monks of St. John of Studion, headed by their abbot, St. Theodore. Many monks and bishops were maltreated. After the overthrow of the Armenian, his successor, Michael II, called the Stammerer (820–829), put an end to the persecution and sought to reach a compromise. Under the reign of his son, *Theophilus* (829–842), Iconoclasm broke out anew on the occasion of the appointment of John Lecamante to the patriarchal see. A reign of terror was inaugurated in 834. During that year, the island of Aphrusia, situated to the south of the Propontis, was used as a burial place for a large number of confessors of the faith, among whom were two brothers, Theodore and Theophanes, upon whose foreheads an executioner from Constantinople engraved twelve iambic verses (July 14, 836).

A second time the cause of orthodoxy was saved by a woman. After the death of Theophilus, his widow, Theodora, assumed the regency. She received much encouragement in her fight for orthodoxy, for all men of good sense were rapidly growing tired of the useless battle against a devotion so deeply imbedded in the hearts of all Christians. Under the presidency of the Patriarch Methodius, a synod reiterated the decisions of the Seventh Council of Nicaea, and no dissenting voice was heard. A new feast instituted on the first Sunday in Lent, still commemorates the triumph of the orthodox cause (κυριακὴ τῆς ορθοδοξίας).

Iconoclasm left many traces in its wake. From the standpoint of art, it contributed much to the maintenance of a well-nigh stereotyped uniformity in Byzantine iconography, consecrated by the persecution. In this way it hampered, even after its defeat, the flight of religious art in the Orient. From the standpoint of politics, Iconoclasm more or less precipitated the separation of Italy from the Greeks, and finally, it paved the way for the great religious schism.

II. Clashes with the West: The Question of Images and the Filioque. The decisions of the Seventh Ecumenical Council had been sent by Pope Hadrian to the Emperor Charlemagne. They were not very well received by the King or by the Frankish Church, and even became the subject-matter of a bitter polemic, the *pièce de resistance* of which were the *Libri Carolini*. These four books, published in 790, contain an attempted refutation of the decrees of Nicaea. They reveal the spirit of political rivalry which existed between the kingdom of the Franks and the Eastern Empire, and the resentment which the Frankish Church felt at being dictated to in matters of faith by the Church of the East. At bottom, Charlemagne's theologians were opposing an imaginary enemy. The Greek word προσκύνησις, (translated by *adoration,* whereas it really means *prostration*) led them to believe that the Council had authorized the adoration of images, whereas it explicitly reserved latreutic worship to God alone. Pope Hadrian replied in a long letter, in which he affected to see in the transmission of the *Libri Carolini* nothing more than an endeavor to consult the Holy See. At the same time he answered all the difficulties raised against the decisions of the Council of Nicaea. It may well be that this letter did not reach its destination until too late (794);

at any rate it did not prevent the Council of Frankfort from condemning, in the very presence of the papal legates, every sort of adoration rendered to images, such as had been defended, so it was believed, by the Council of Nicaea. The controversy continued and subsided only with the lapse of years. The decisions of the Council of Frankfort were re-affirmed at the Assembly of Paris, in 825. Bishop Claudius of Turin was a professed iconoclast, going so far as to prohibit any sort of veneration of images or relics in his diocese. He was refuted by Jonas of Orleans, Theodomir, and Dungal, a monk of St. Denis.

The question of the *Filioque* furnished material for another dogmatic grievance. The procession of the Holy Ghost from the Father and the Son was clearly taught by the Greek and Latin Fathers of the fourth century, and yet, for reasons of prudence, the Church had shown no immediate desire to define the dogma. Such action on her part might easily have resulted in heretical opposition to her stand; moreover, she felt bound to respect the text of the Nicene Creed, which did not contain the *Filioque*. The expression was, however, not altogether unfamiliar. It is met with in several private professions of faith current in the fourth and fifth centuries; and later on, at a date which probably does not extend beyond the seventh century, the councils of Spain inserted it in the Creed of Constantinople. This addition was accepted at the court of Charlemagne about the year 780, and in a memoir extracted from the *Libri Carolini* and addressed to Pope Hadrian, Charles severely rebuked the Seventh Ecumenical Council for not having professed the *Filioque*. As a liturgical innovation, however, it had not as yet gained acceptance in Rome, where the popes, fully cognizant of the cavilling ways of the Greeks, deemed it advisable to defer action. In the meantime, the Latin monks of Bethlehem, who had begun to sing the *Credo* at Mass with the addition of the *Filioque,* were accused of heresy and threatened with expulsion by the Greeks. They immediately appealed their case to the Pope and to the Emperor. The latter commissioned Theodulphus of Orleans to compose a treatise on the Holy Ghost. He also convoked a council at Aix-la-Chapelle, which placed its stamp of approval on the liturgical use of the *Filioque* (809). The Pope, while approving the doctrine, rejected the formula. Charles refused to yield, and retained the formula, which soon gained acceptance throughout France and Germany. This action was another step in the direction of Gallicanism. Leo III formulated what might be called a spiritual protest by issuing orders that two silver shields be attached to the *Confessio,* carrying, the one in Greek, the other in Latin, the text of the Creed without the addition. The *Filioque* was accepted by the Roman Church only under Pope Benedict VIII, when the conduct of Photius released the Holy See from any further obligation in the matter of deference and regard for the opinion of the Greeks.

TEXTS AND DOCUMENTS

DECISION OF THE SEVENTH ECUMENICAL COUNCIL REGARDING THE WORSHIP OF IMAGES

The figure of the cross and holy images, whether made in colors or of stone, or of any other material, are to be retained. They are not to become objects of adoration in the proper sense, which is given to God alone, but they are useful because they raise the mind of the spectator to the objects which they represent. It is right to salute, honor, and venerate them, to burn lights and incense before them, not only because this is in accordance with the tradition of the Church, but also because such honor is really given to God and His saints, of whom the images are intended to remind us.

QUESTIONS

1. Enumerate the causes which gave rise to Iconoclasm.
2. Who was St. John Damascene?
3. What was the grievance of Constantine Copronymus against the monastic Orders?
4. Why should members of the military be such bitter Iconoclasts?
5. List some of the achievements of the Empresses Irene and Theodora.
6. Mention some of the consequences of Iconoclasm.
7. What is the Catholic stand on image worship, and why should this worship be rendered to inanimate things?
8. What were the *Libri Carolini?*
9. Account for the stand taken by the papacy in the matter of the *Filioque.*

BIBLIOGRAPHY

Iconoclasm.—Sources: Mansi, XII and XIII.—St. John Damascene, *P. G.,* XCIV, and XCV.—Nicephorus, *P. G.,* C.—Theodore Studites, *P. G.,* XCIX.— The Chronicles of Theophanes, *P. G.,* CVIII and CIX; of Leo the Grammarian, *P. G.,* CVIII, etc.—Works: TIXERONT, *op. cit.,* III.—TOUGARD, *La persécution iconoclaste d'après la correspondance de Théodore Studite,* 1897.— BEURLIER, *Les vestiges du culte impérial à Byzance et la querelle des icono-*

clastes, in *Rev. des religions*, 1891, III, p. 319–341, and in *Congrès scient. des cath.*, 1891, II, pp. 167–180.—MARIN, *Les moines de Constantinople.*—LOMBARD, *Constantin V*, 1902.—BRÉHIER, *La querelle des images*, 1904.—PARGOIRE, *L'Eglise byzantine de 527 à 847*, 1905.—C. EMEREAU, art. *"Iconoclasme,"* in *Dict. de Théol.*—GRUMEL, art. *"Images,"* in the same Dictionary.—M. JUGIE, *La vie de saint Jean Damascène*, in *Echos d'Orient*, XXVII (1924), pp. 137–161.—MARIN, *Saint Théodore* (Coll. *"Les Saints"*).—DOM LECLERCQ, art. *"Iconoclasme,"* in *Dict. d'Arch.*—V. LAURENT, art. *"Méthode de Constantinople,"* in *Dict. de Théol.*—A. FORTESCUE, art. *"Iconoclasm,"* in *Cath. Encycl.*

The Caroline Books.—Sources: *P. L.*, XCVIII.—Works: E. BORNET, *La controverse des images en Occident*, Lyons, 1906.—J. MARÉCHAL, *Les livres carolins*, Lyons, 1906.—VACANDARD, art. *"Carolins (Livres),"* in *Dict. de Théol.*—TIXERONT, *op. cit.*, III.

Filioque.—Sources: *P. L.*, XCVIII, 1249.—Mansi, XIII, 829 and *P. L.*, XCIX, 283.—Works: TIXERONT, *op. cit.*, III.—G. DUBOIS, *De conciliis et theologicis disputationibus apud Francos, Carolo magno regnante, habitis*, Alençon, 1902.—A. PALMIERI, art. *"Filioque,"* in *Dict. de Théol.*—MANGENOT, *L'origine espagnole du Filioque*, in *Rev. de l'Orient chrétien*, 1906.

The Ninth Century: From the Death of Charlemagne to the Deposition of Charles the Fat (814–887)

CHAPTER I

THE CHURCH IN THE DAYS OF LOUIS THE PIOUS (814–843)

At the outset, the medieval conception of a Christian empire was not clearly defined. One question that seemed quite unsettled was, whether or not the election of an emperor had to be ratified by the Holy See. In the month of September, 813, at the injunction of his father Charlemagne, Louis the Pious had placed the imperial crown upon his own head before the altar at Aix-la-Chapelle. Three years later, however, in the course of an interview at Rheims, Pope Stephen IV, successor of Leo III, crowned both Louis and his wife. "Peter," he stated in the course of the ceremony, "takes delight in making you this present, that you may guarantee to him the enjoyment of his just rights." The formula was tantamount to a mutual contract. The Pope conferred the crown upon the Emperor, and the latter in return gave his protection to the Holy See. The bishops of Rome upheld these principles, but Louis the Pious sought to break away from them. In the year 817, he crowned his eldest son, Lothaire, king of the Franks at Aix-la-Chapelle, but Pope Pascal I took advantage of a journey which Lothaire made to Rome to consecrate him emperor, on April 5, 823.

Another point that was not very clear was whether or not the Emperor should take any part in the election of a pope and intervene in Roman affairs. Pascal I obtained from Louis the Pious a written document, called the Constitution of 817, according to which the Emperor could intervene in the affairs of Rome only in case of disorders and for the purpose of righting matters. The agreement seemed perfect; in point of fact, however, it created an opportunity for the Emperor to intrude.

In Rome the power of the pope had always been opposed by the local aristocracy. To obviate this difficulty, Pascal I exiled several Roman nobles and confiscated their property. In the general confusion several outrages were committed. Pascal had no hand in these crimes, but out of hatred for the Franks, his political enemies accused him of foul play. Louis despatched imperial delegates to conduct an investigation, and Pope Pascal, like his predecessor, Leo III, was constrained to explain and justify his conduct under oath. The real epilogue to this drama occurred in the pontificate of *Eugene II*. As soon as the latter had notified Louis of his election, the Emperor sent his son Lothaire with orders to draw up a *constitutio romana* that would prevent any abuse of power. This constitution contained four principal clauses. The first decreed protection of the king; the pope could not put to death a protegé of the emperor. By the second, any Roman could select the law by which he desired to be tried, be it the Roman or the Frankish; this was called the personal right. By the third, Frankish control was established in Rome; magistrates were required to inform the emperor of their appointments; two permanent *missi* were to send him a report of their administration and list any complaints which the pope could not settle. Finally, by the fourth, it was decided that the election of a new pope, which, since 769, had been the business of the clergy, should henceforth be conducted with the aid of the laity; the pope-elect was to take the oath of office in the presence of the imperial *missus* and the assembled people. Thus the Constitution of 824 made a breach in the independence of the Holy See and conferred upon the Emperor the right of supreme arbiter and absolutely arbitrary control. It would seem that he could have offered the papacy his protection without seeking to dominate completely.

On the other hand, the unitary plan, whereby the king of the Franks guided the destinies of the whole Empire, was not without its opponents in Gaul. One of the precedents against it was the Germanic custom and acceptance of divisions. At the death of Charlemagne two parties disputed the throne: the one, imperialistic and strictly unitary, the other, royalist. Imperialism, which represented the ideal of Christian unity, was dear to the Church. Its champions were Wala, Abbot of Corbie, and Agobard, Archbishop of Lyons. "If God suffered," wrote Agobard, "in order to bring together in His blood those who were far apart, why does this incredible diversity of laws which prevails on all sides oppose the divine work of unity?" It was Agobard and Wala who inspired the terms of the Constitution of 817, which placed the imperial authority of Lothaire, the eldest son of Louis the Pious, above the kingdoms. Louis, however, had taken as his second wife Judith of Bavaria, who, after she became the mother of Charles the Bald, sought to change the unitary pact to her son's advantage. No less than four ecclesiastical assemblies convened in the year 824 to discuss this problem—at Paris, Mayence, Lyons, and Toulouse. In 829 Judith scored a complete victory at Worms. The partisans of unity were not slow in taking the offensive; but at the very moment when a battle was about to be waged in Alsace between Louis the Pious and his sons (Feast of St. John, 833), Pope Gregory IV intervened in person. He appealed to the Augustinian idea of peace, a motive employed more than once as a lever by the Holy See in those troubled times. "How can you oppose me," he wrote to the bishops who sided with the Emperor, "when I am engaged in a mission of peace and unity which is the very ministry of Christ?" His presence alone sufficed to insure the triumph of the partisans of unity without bloodshed. Louis did public penance at St. Medard de Soissons for having disturbed "the unity of the Empire and the tranquillity of the Church."

The victory of the partisans of unity, however, was of short duration. Wala died in exile; Louis was rehabilitated in 835, and Judith issued orders that her son Charles the Bald be given the whole of Gaul. Louis died two years later, and the war reached its climax when Lothaire, the heir of the Empire, clashed with his two brothers, Louis the German and Charles the Bald. Lothaire was defeated at Fontenay-en-Pusaye, June 25, 840, and by the Treaty of Verdun (843) the Empire was divided into the three kingdoms of Germany, Francia, and Lotharingia. Very soon an anarchical aristocracy replaced the Empire and deprived the Church of a valuable aid. Feudalism was born when the Treaty of Verdun was concluded. A dark epoch began, during which force often prevailed over law. It must be admitted, however, that the Church did all in her power to avert this evil. She endeavored to adjust herself to the new regime inaugurated by the Treaty of Verdun, by grafting upon it another Christian idea—that of concord. She insisted that, despite the fact that three kings were invested with equal rights in the government of the Empire, they should remain "united in charity." A thesis, borrowed from St. Augustine, attributed the recent invasion of the Normans and

Saracens to the quarrels of the Christians, who had disregarded the peace instituted by the "Great Charles." The retreat of the Normans, it was contended, could be obtained as a favor of Heaven only on condition that peace and concord were re-established. To set up this regime, several *fraternal assemblies* were established. In point of fact, however, all these efforts remained useless.

The decrease in the royal power was accompanied with an increase in the authority of the bishops. What a difference between the policy of Charlemagne and that of Hincmar of Rheims! The latter stressed the clean-cut distinction between the episcopal and the royal power: the first is derived wholly from God; the second also, but indirectly, since men choose the candidate by election and the bishops confer consecration upon him. "It is not you who selected me to govern the Church," Hincmar said to Louis III, "but it is I, together with my colleagues and the rest of the faithful, who appointed you to govern the kingdom on condition that you observe its laws." If the king did not fulfill his duties, he could be tried and punished by the priests, and the contract entered into between the king and the people could be nullified by the prelates. These ideas did not prevent Hincmar from being moved by sincerely patriotic motives. As a matter of fact, he rendered a great service to royalty by negotiating the annexation of the province of Lorraine, which extended to the east of France boundaries that were fast becoming too restricted.

About this time, new enemies were pouring into Italy. Setting out from the northern coast of Africa, the Saracens landed in Sicily and soon gained possession of Messina and Palermo (831-832). From that moment the entire Italian coast, including Rome itself, was at their mercy. In 846, under the pontificate of Sergius II, the Saracens advanced to the very gates of the City, plundered the churches of SS. Peter and Paul, which at that time were both situated outside the walls, and defeated an army commanded by the Duke of Spoleto. Upon hearing of these sacrileges, the assembly of the Franks decided upon an expedition against the Saracens; the result was that the invaders were expelled for a time from Italy. It was not long, however, before the peninsula was completely cut off from all imperial aid, besides being considerably weakened by its own divisions into egotistical and quarrelsome principalities. From that moment Italy was constrained to look for help, as at the time of the barbarian invasions, in the direction of the papacy. *Leo IV,* the successor of

Sergius II, repaired the walls of Rome, and in order to prevent another profanation of St. Peter's, encompassed the Vatican suburb, situated on the right bank of the Tiber, with a high wall (848–852). This quarter still retains the name of Leonine City. In the battle of Ostia, fought under the very eyes of the Pontiff, a fleet organized by the Saracens was completely destroyed (849).

Between the reigns of Leo IV (847–855) and Benedict III (855–858) some have sought to interpolate the reign of a female pope, by the name of Popess Joan, whose pontificate is presumed to have lasted two years. The legend is as follows: A young girl, disguised as a man, one day left Mayence in the company of her lover, and, after studying at Athens, became successively a notary of the Roman curia, cardinal, and pope. The fraud is said to have been discovered in the course of a public procession, during which the popess was suddenly seized with the pains of childbirth. Roman justice condemned her to be tied to the tail of a horse and dragged through the streets of the city. The Middle Ages believed the legend, and in the sixteenth century, Protestants exploited and considerably amplified it. In 1562, Cyriacus Spangenberg wrote: "Although to all outward appearances men, the Roman pontiffs were often nothing more than prostitutes." In matter of fact, the legend is absolutely untenable. It may owe its origin to the sad influence which women exercised in the government of Rome under the domination of the house of Theophylact, and the by-word may then have been: "We have women for popes." But all the documents pertaining to this period establish beyond cavil that only a few weeks elapsed between the reign of Leo IV and that of Benedict III. A Roman coin has been discovered which bears the figures of Benedict III and the Emperor Lothaire (Sept. 17, 855). Leo IV died July 17.

TEXTS AND DOCUMENTS

The Popess Joan

Joan is said to have been taken, when yet a girl, to the school of Athens, and to have there acquired a great reputation. Now, where were the famous schools of Athens in the ninth century? What was the condition of Athens? As far back as the year 420, Synesius of Ptolemais wrote: "There is now nothing splendid in Athens but the celebrated names of places, just as, after a sacrifice, nothing remains of the victim but its skin. Wandering around you may gaze upon the Academy and the Lyceum, and the portico which gave name to the sect of Chrysippus. The proconsuls have taken away the artistic productions of Thasius. In our day, Egypt teaches, she who received the seeds of wisdom from Hypatia. Athens was once a city, the home of learned men; now it is occupied only by apiarists." The schools of Athens were afterwards, to some extent, revived, but not during the supposed student-life of Joan. Cedrenus and Zonaras inform us that the Emperor Michael III, after he had removed his mother Theodora from its government, allowed the Caesar Bardas to restore the Athenian gymnasia, but Theodora was not relegated to private life until 856, while Joan is said to have died in that year. Equally absurd is the statement that Joan's talents caused her, a stranger, to be chosen Pontiff. It is certain that for many centuries the custom had obtained of raising to the papacy only a priest or deacon of the Roman Church, one trained, as it were, in view of such a contingency. A departure from this rule would scarcely have been made without grave reasons, and none such could be conjectured as subsisting in the case of Joan. Ridiculous indeed is the assertion that the supposed Pontiff gave birth to a child during a solemn religious function. If it can be believed that stupidity was so rampant, so universal, in the Roman court, that the sex and condition of this person could so long remain hidden, exposed, as every Pontiff must necessarily be, to the scrutiny of prelates, courtiers, physicians, chamberlains and servants, we cannot believe that so successful an impostor, and so arrant a knave, would have possessed so much asininity of mind as to subject herself, at such a time, to the risks of a processional walk from the Vatican to the Lateran. Again, in this very mention of the procession from the Vatican to the Lateran the interpolator of Martin's Chronicle betrays himself. He says that the Pontiffs avoid the street that was fatal to Joan, when they proceed to the Lateran. It is certain that the Popes did not commence to inhabit the Vatican before the reign of Boniface IX, who mounted the throne in 1389.

PARSONS, *Studies in Church History,*
Vol. II, pp. 45 ff.

QUESTIONS

1. Which points were not clearly defined at the outset in the medieval conception of a Christian empire?
2. What was the tenor of the *Constitutio Romana* of Louis the Pious?
3. Define the term "Imperialism" as it applies in this present instance.
4. What was the Augustinian concept of peace?
5. Explain the statement: "Feudalism was born at the Treaty of Verdun."
6. Contrast the policies of Charlemagne and Hincmar of Rheims.
7. Which are the high spots of interest in the Invasion of the Saracens?
8. Summarize the article on the Popess Joan in the *Catholic Encyclopedia.*

BIBLIOGRAPHY

Disintegration of the Carolingian Empire.—Sources: Annals of Lorsch up to the year 829, followed by the Annals of St. Bertin for France and the Annals of Fulda for Germany, in *Script. rerum germanic. in usum scholarum*.—Boretius and Krause, *Capitularia*.—Paschasius Radbertus, *Vie d'Adalard et de Wala*.—Works: Kleinclausz, *L'empire carolingien, ses origines et ses transformations*, 1900.—Himly, *Wala et Louis le Débonnaire*, 1849.—Fustel de Coulanges, *Les transformations de la royauté pendant l'époque carolingienne*, 1892.—Pouzet, *La succession de Charlemagne et le traité de Verdun*, 1890.—J. Guiraud, *Histoire partiale, histoire vraie*, I, ch. XVIII.—J. Calmette, *La diplomatie carolingienne du traité de Verdun à la mort de Charles le Chauve*, Bibl. Hautes Etudes, fasc. CXXXV, 1901.—H.-X. Arquillière, *Etude sur la formation de la "Théocratie pontificale,"* in *Mélanges Ferdinand Lot*, 1925.

I. Nicholas I and the Secular Power: The Lothaire-Walrada Affair. The pontificate of Nicholas I marks the full development of the medieval papacy. In an effort to stave off the disintegration of the States of Lorraine, Lothaire, the nephew of Charles the Bald, in 856 married Teutberga, a daughter of the count of Burgundy, and, as a consequence, was forced to send away his mistress, Walrada. After a while, however, he repudiated his lawful wife, accusing her, among other things, of committing incest with his brother, Hubert. Teutberga completely exonerated herself by the ordeal of boiling water, and the king was forced to take her back. He did so very reluctantly, and soon afterwards convoked a council at Aix-la-Chapelle to obtain grounds for a divorce. The assembly was presided over by Teutgaud of Treves and Günther of Cologne, both creatures of Lothaire. By means of tricks and threats they obtained from the unfortunate Teutberga the confession of a sin which she had never committed, and the assembled bishops issued a sentence in which they enjoined upon Lothaire no longer to regard her as his wife. Teutberga was imprisoned in a convent, but made her escape and appealed to Nicholas I. The Pope was well informed regarding the case, especially through Hincmar, who, in a pamphlet, *De Divortio Lotharii Regis,* protested against the entire procedure. Nicholas I deposed Archbishops Teutgaud and Günther and relegated the Council of Metz "to the same plane as the Robber Synod of Ephesus." Lothaire had his brother, the Emperor Louis II, plead his case with the Pope, but it was to no avail. Louis even journeyed to Rome, but Pope Nicholas I took shelter near the tomb of St. Peter and refused to be moved. Finally, Lothaire was forced to yield and took back Teutberga from the hands of the legate Arsenius. Walrada, who had been required to repair to Rome and do penance, at once interrupted her journey and returned to Lothaire. The latter changed his tactics and intimidated Teutberga into asking for a divorce herself. Pope Nicholas, however, stood by his former decision, and his successor Hadrian II, even though he displayed a more conciliatory attitude, upheld the previous decrees and refused to lift the excommunication until Lothaire had sworn that he had not had any sinful relations with Walrada since his condemnation. The medieval idea that the popes had the right to intervene in the private lives of kings and princes, was taking form.

II. Nicholas I and the Primate Hincmar. Hincmar of Rheims was the metropolitan of a circumscription which comprised the whole of Northern France and a portion of what is now Belgium. Of a naturally autocratic temperament, he devised a theory whereby the metropolitan had the right to intervene directly in the affairs of his suffragans. In 861, at a provincial council, he suspended Rothadius II, Bishop of Soissons, whom he accused of mismanaging the affairs of his diocese. The latter appealed to Rome, was arraigned before a new synod, deposed, excommunicated, and imprisoned in a monastery. Pope Nicholas took up his defence, and in a lengthy epistolary discussion made it clear that Hincmar should have awaited the papal judgment before deposing him. He examined the acts of the provincial council, and solemnly annulled its decisions (vigil of Christmas, 864). Hincmar was forced to re-instate Rothadius and, moreover, to make it known at a council convoked at Troyes that a bishop may not be deposed without the consent of the Holy See. We note the same firm attitude on the part of the Pope in handling the case of Archbishop Ebbo, who was successively deposed and re-instated from purely political motives. At a council held at Soissons (853), Hincmar prohibited clerics ordained by Ebbo from exercising ecclesiastical functions. Nicholas I decided that Hincmar had overstepped his authority, and summoned the parties before his own tribunal.

III. Predestinarianism. The character of Hincmar appears in a more favorable light in a doctrinal controversy which arose about this time. Gottschalk, son of Bernon, a Saxon count, had made his monastic profession at the Abbey of Fulda and then broken his vows. The Council of Mayence released him from his obligations as a Benedictine and authorized him to re-enter the world; but his Abbot, Rhabanus Maurus, compelled him to enter the Abbey of Orbais in the Diocese of Soissons. Gottschalk, who was a great student, claimed that he had found in the writings of St. Augustine the elements of Predestinarianism. According to him, God condemns the damned to the tortures of hell by an absolute decree, which takes no account of any foreknowledge He has of merits, in such wise that they are condemned to suffer without any possible chance to escape. This teaching was pure Calvinism, and bound to produce deplorable practical consequences, for if salvation or damnation were predetermined without any regard to our efforts, why should we strive to do good? The inevitable is bound to happen and God's decree will be carried out. Rhabanus Maurus referred the trial of Gottschalk to Hincmar, his natural judge, who obtained his condemnation at the Council of Quiersy-sur-Oise (849), and, after having him flogged in the presence of the whole assembly, sent him to the abbey of Hautvillers, near Rheims.

The Council of Quiersy proclaimed the true stand to be taken in this matter by stressing, against Gottschalk, the will of God to save and redeem all men. Distinguished theologians, however, like Prudentius of Troyes, Ratramnus of Corbie, and Lupus of Ferrières, objected to its conclusions, inasmuch as, in their attempts to counteract the heresy of Gottschalk, they went to the other extreme and seemed to deny any predestination of sinners to punishment, even *post praevisa merita*. In an attempt to exonerate himself, Hincmar condensed his teaching into four articles, which were promulgated at a second Council of Quiersy (853). However, he made the mistake of calling upon the help of the Irish philosopher, John Scotus Eriugena, a subtle agnostic, whose treatise *De praedestinatione* contains serious errors.

The opposition which Hincmar encountered was perhaps less the result of doctrinal antagonism than of personal enmity for the arrogant metropolitan of Rheims. His principal opponents rallied partly around the metropolitan see of Sens, which had been overshadowed by the lustre of Rheims, and partly around the sees of Lyons and Nîmes, where the influence of Ebbo, Bishop of Grenoble, a nephew of the deposed prelate, was considerable. A league of the bishops of the Southeast was formed, and the canons of Valence composed an answer to the articles of Quiersy. Comparing the two documents, we feel that they contain the same doctrine, but treated from a different angle. Quiersy affirms the universal character of Redemption, which Valence denies in the sense that the sinners of the Old Testament have not been salvaged from hell. After a conference held at Langres, in which the canons of Valence were partially retracted, a reconciliation was effected at the Council of Tusey (near Vaucouleurs), in 860. Hincmar was commissioned to explain in a synodal letter the principles on which all were agreed, to wit, the necessity of grace, the part played by freewill, and the universal goodness of Christ, but no mention was made of predestination *ad mortem*. In point of fact, only one person had been guilty of theological error, and that was Gottschalk.

IV. Pope Nicholas I and Photius. In 817, St. Ignatius was appointed to the see of Byzantium. Almost at once he began to flay the scandalous conduct of the imperial court. Matters came to a head when the regency passed from the Empress Theodora to her brother Bardas, and the latter sought to corrupt the morals of the young Emperor, his nephew, Michael III, called the Drunkard. Ignatius protested and refused fellowship to Bardas. He paid dearly for this courage, for Bardas had him exiled to the island of Terebinthios. *Photius*, who, both from a literary and a scientific standpoint, was probably the most learned man of his time, was installed in his place as Patriarch. Convinced that he was within his rights, the deposed Patriarch refused to listen to any settlement. But Photius could well afford to ignore him, for both the Emperor and the clergy of Constantinople adopted the same attitude. Moreover, a twofold seal of approval was set upon the appointment of Photius to the patriarchal see: (1) episcopal consecration at the hands of his friend Asbesta, an excommunicated bishop; and (2) the approval of a council held at Constantinople, which, in addition, anathematized Ignatius. Immediately after his elevation Photius had sent to Pope Nicholas I a letter in which the facts were distorted almost beyond recognition. After the Council of Constantinople (861) he implored the Pontiff to ratify his election in a petition which is "a masterpiece of hypocrisy." Nicholas I despatched legates to Byzantium to investigate the affair. They were tricked completely by the intriguer and ratified his election. A council was quickly convoked, made up of 318 bishops, who, in obedience to an order from the Emperor, declared Photius to be the lawful patriarch. Pope Nicholas, however, convicted his legates of fraud, and in a Roman synod held in 863, anathematized both them and Photius.

Fuel was added to the flames when the Bulgarians decided to unite with the Latin Church. Photius commenced hostilities by his encyclical letter of 867, addressed to the Eastern patriarchs, as well as by a letter to the Bulgarians. The tactics he resorted to consisted in stressing the theological, canonical, and ritual differences which existed between the Greeks and the Latins, for the purpose of fomenting schism. In his encyclical, Photius enumerated five grievances against the Latins: the Saturday fast; the use of dairy products during the first week of Lent; the celibacy of the clergy; the re-administration of the Sacrament of Confirmation by bishops to those who had already been confirmed by priests; and the addition of the *Filioque* to the Creed, or the doctrine of the procession of the Holy Ghost from both Father and Son. In his letter to the Bulgarians he enumerated five other points: the immolation of a lamb together with the Body of Christ on Easter Sunday; the custom adopted by Roman clerics of shaving their beards; the preparation of Holy Chrism with river water; the direct promotion of simple clerics to the episcopate, and the papal claim to primacy. That same year Photius called together the patriarchs of the Eastern Church at Constantinople and deposed Pope Nicholas I.

The triumph of Photius was that of a civic official backed by his hierarchical chief; a close bond of union existed between his success and the fortunes of the Emperor. And so when Michael III was assassinated by a usurper, Basil the Macedonian, the latter consigned Photius to a monastery, re-entered into communion with Hadrian II, the successor of Pope Nicholas, and recalled Ignatius from exile. With this change in civil and ecclesiastical administration, matters took a complete turn, and the task of ironing out the existing difficulties was referred to Rome. A council was held at Constantinople, which re-instated Ignatius and reduced Photius to the lay state (*Eighth Ecumenical Council, 869–870*). Two shadows, however, marred this scene of reconciliation: the incident of the *Libellus Satisfactionis* and the Bulgarian question. The *Libellus Satisfactionis* was a Roman formula of profession which the former partisans of Photius were required to sign before being admitted as members of the council. Some bishops complained to Ignatius and Basil, that the signing of this document constituted an act of servility toward the Church of Rome, and the signatures were fraudulently withheld and presented to the legates only after a protest. Displeased by the fact that the Pope had not given them the priests of their choice, the Bulgarians applied to the Council and asked if they should abide by the decision of Rome or that of Byzantium. In a supplementary session, the Fathers replied: "By the decision of Byzantium." Pope Hadrian protested against this action and threatened Ignatius, but the latter remained obstinate, and died just as the bull of excommunication was issued against him.

TEXTS AND DOCUMENTS

REVERENCE OF THE GREEK CHURCH FOR THE SEE OF PETER

For the cure of the wounds and ills of the human body, the medical art furnishes us with a great number of physicians; but for the members of the Holy Catholic and Apostolic Church of our God the Saviour, there is only one chosen and universal physician, namely, your Fraternal and Paternal Holiness, constituted by the Supreme and Most Powerful Word of God, when He said to Peter, the supreme and most holy Prince of the Apostles: "Thou art Peter, etc." And these blessed words were addressed to the Prince of the Apostles not simply as conferring a private privilege, but through him they were directed to all the Pontiffs of the Roman See, his successors. Therefore, whenever heresies and corruptions came into existence in the past, the successors in your Apostolic See always extirpated such tares and noxious growths; and now your Blessedness, worthily using the power received from Christ, crushes the enemies of truth, and him who, like a robber, enters the fold of Christ by the window. . . . With the physician's hand of holy and Apostolic authority, you cut him off from the body of the Church, and pronouncing us innocent, who have been so oppressed by his wickedness, you have, like a most loving brother, restored us to our Church.

Letter of St. Ignatius of Constantinople
to Pope Nicholas I.

QUESTIONS

1. Account for the origin and purpose of the ordeals of "boiling water," "hot iron," etc.
2. What is Predestinarianism; contrast it with Calvinism and Jansenism.
3. Who was Rhabanus Maurus, and of what importance is he as a teacher?
4. Account for the sudden rise to power of the intruder Photius; give some proofs of his great learning.
5. What was the *Libellus Satisfactionis?*
6. Account for the fact that the Fathers of the Eighth Ecumenical Council, who condemned Photius, notified the Bulgarians that they should follow the decisions of Byzantium, and not those of Rome.
7. Account for the fact that Ignatius of Constantinople is a saint, yet was excommunicated by the Holy See.

BIBLIOGRAPHY

The Lothaire-Walrada Question.—J. Roy, *Nicolas I* (Coll. *"Les Saints"*).—J. DE LA SERVIÈRE, art. *"Divorce des princes et l'Eglise,"* in *Dict. d'Apol.*, fasc. IV.—PARISOT, *Le royaume de Lorraine sous les Carolingiens*, 1898; *Histoire de Lorraine*, I, 1919.

Hincmar.—Sources: *P. L.*, CXXV–CXX.—Works: J. Roy, *Nicolas I.*—P. FOURNIER, *Hincmar*, in *La France Chrétienne*, 1896.—NOORDEN, *Hincmar*, Bonn, 1863.—LESNE, *Hincmar et l'empereur Lothaire*, in *Rev. quest. hist.*, 1905; *La hiérarchie épiscopale*, 1905.—HEFELE-LECLERCQ, *op. cit.*, IV, pp. 197–206, 220–227, 232–237.—*Hist. litt. de la France*, V, pp. 544–594.—H. NETZER, art. *"Hincmar,"* in *Dict. de Théol.*—HANOTAUX-GOYAU, pp. 144–155.

Gottschalk.—Sources: Mansi, XIV, 994, XV, 337; *P. L.*, CXII, 1530; CXXII, 355; CXXV; CXXVI, 122.—Works: GAUDARD, *Gottschalk, moine d'Orbais*, 1887.—TURMEL, *La controverse predestinatienne au IXe siècle*, in *Rev. hist. et litt. rel.*, 1905, pp. 47 ff.—PORTALIÉ, art. *"Augustinianisme,"* in *Dict. de Théol.*—GODET, art. *"Gottschalk,"* in the same dictionary.

Photius.—Sources: *P. G.*, CII.—*Vita Ignatii, Acta SS. Boll.*, X, Oct., 167–205.—HERGENRÖTHER, *Monumenta Graeca ad Photium ejusque historiam pertinentia*, Ratisbon, 1867–1869.—Works: HERGENRÖTHER, *Photius*, 3 vols.—A. LAPÔTRE, *Le Pape Jean VIII.*—DUCHESNE, *Eglises séparées*, pp. 163–227.—VAILHÉ, art. *"Constantinople (Eglise de),"* in *Dict. de Théol.*—M. JUGIE, art. *"Grecque (Eglise),"* in *Dict. d'Apol.*, fasc. VIII; *Theologia dogmatica christianorum orientalium ab ecclesia catholica dissidentium*, t. I. *Théologiae dogmaticae graeco-Russorum origo, historia, fontes*, 1926.—A. VOGT, *Basile I, empereur de Byzance (867–886) et la civilisation byzantine à la fin du IXe siècle*, 1908.—A. FORTESCUE, *The Orthodox Eastern Church*, London.

CHAPTER III

Pope Nicholas I had been an inflexible guardian of the rights of the Church; John VIII was first and last a compromiser.

I. In the East: The Second Revolt of Photius. After the death of Ignatius (877), Photius regained the favor of the Emperor and reascended the patriarchal throne. His attitude towards the Pope at first was that of a sycophant; he sought to justify himself in his eyes. John VIII, who was above all solicitous for unity, showed himself well disposed. He even let it be known that he would recognize Photius as patriarch of Constantinople on condition that he make public atonement in a synod, become reconciled with the former partisans of Ignatius, and restore Bulgaria to the Roman influence. Photius, in his pride, refused to yield. He insidiously convoked a council at Constantinople (the Eighth Ecumenical Council of the Greeks, the *Pseudo-Synodus Photiana* of the Latins), and in the course of its sessions obtained from the papal legates the annullment of the General Council of 869–870, and, as a consequence, the rehabilitation of his former conduct, which the Pope had insisted that he completely repudiate. This last act convinced John VIII of the duplicity of Photius.

But Photius had the backing of the Emperor, and refused to give up his office. In this second war against Rome he adopted new tactics. Instead of making a direct attack upon the Roman primacy, which was too firmly established to suffer from his opposition, and instead of stressing paltry differences in customs, traditions, and discipline, he centered all his polemical efforts on the question of the *Filioque*. In his "Mystagogy of the Holy Ghost," which is an exhaustive treatise on the subject, he tried to distort the Latin doctrine by all sorts of sophistical arguments and to establish the proposition that the Holy Ghost proceeds from the Father alone, quibbling on the term ἐκπορεύεσθαι, which at that time signified, "to proceed from a principle which has no principle." The "Mystagogy of the Holy Ghost" proved to be a veritable arsenal, from which the Greeks of the following centuries obtained abundant ammunition in their warfare against the Latins. It must be remarked, however, that when Photius was deposed later on by the Emperor Leo the Philosopher (886), the cause of the Greek schism was not yet won: the two churches became reconciled only after the death of the heresiarch.

But their union was not well-cemented, and hence was destined to be short-lived. An unfortunate affair added to the natural prejudices of the Greeks towards the Latins. We refer to the marriage case of Leo VI. This Emperor had contracted four marriages, and it must be admitted that he was prompted by grave reasons. Greek usage, however, permitted only two marriages, and so a conflict arose between the sovereign and his clergy. The latter was headed by a man just as clever and almost as learned as Photius, Nicholas the Mystic. The Emperor thought the matter could be settled by a sort of ecumenical council, and hence invited three representatives of the Eastern patriarchs in Mussulman countries, and induced Pope Sergius III to send legates. These legates sided with the Emperor. Nevertheless the battle regarding the four marriages continued to be waged for many years in the Greek Church.

II. In the West: The Holy Empire of 875. Charles the Bald. In the West, the skillful tactics of Pope John VIII were offset by the weaknesses of the Carolingians. At the death of Louis II, son of Lothaire, the imperial crown was disputed between Louis the German and Charles the Bald. Pope John VIII, thinking the latter would come to his aid against the Saracens, who continued to pillage southern Italy and threatened the Papal State, crowned him emperor, Dec. 25, 875. Charles was a valiant and devoted son of the Holy See, but in his capacity of king of western Francia, he had only a small army at his disposal and, moreover, was being constantly harassed by undisciplined bands of Norman ravagers in his own kingdom. And so, when he finally resolved to organize an expedition into Italy, the Frankish aristocracy refused to lend him their aid. He died while recrossing the Alps, at the base of Mont Cenis (877). Carloman, a son of Louis, ruled for a short time over upper Italy, and then Pope John VIII made another attempt to rehabilitate the Empire in the person of *Charles the Fat*. The latter, however, left it to its own sad fate, and as a result it became torn between internal and external factions. Charles lived through the tempestuous and ephemeral pontificates of Marinus I (882–884) and Hadrian III (884–885) as a passive onlooker, and after he was deposed at the Diet of Tribur, in 887, the Empire was divided into seven kingdoms.

III. The Spoletan Domination and the Trial of Formosus. When things had come to this pass, the problem of who was the most suitable candidate for the high office of emperor became a very acute one. Two powerful houses attempted to gain control of the office— that of Italy, represented by Guy of Spoleto, and that of Germany, heir to the Carolingian tradition and directed by Arnulf, Duke of Carinthia. The former of these two houses, it was thought, was situated in too close proximity and might easily degenerate into a tyranny; the second was too far removed and too busy with its internal affairs to be of any great utility. While the papacy hesitated, the Italian candidate, *Guy of Spoleto,* obtruded himself, and Stephen V crowned him emperor (891). The same circumstances constrained Formosus, Stephen's successor, to recognize the oppressive influence of this house and to crown as emperor, Lambert, the son of Guy, who had been associated with him in power. Sensing the danger which threatened the independence of the Holy See, however, the energetic Pope appealed to Arnulf. It was easy to crown him at Rome, but not so easy to overcome the opposition of the Spoletans. At the death of Guy, his widow, the implacable Agiltrude, and her son Lambert, took up the battle against Arnulf, who, having suffered a paralytic stroke, saw all his hopes crumble, together with those of Pope Formosus. The latter, an octogenarian, died of grief in 896.

In 897, Agiltrude seized the city of Rome. A strong Roman party, whom the Pontiff had perhaps treated with undue severity, shared her hatred of Formosus and even went so far as to contest the validity of his election. In giving up his episcopal see of Porto for that of Rome, they argued, Formosus had violated the bond which united a bishop to his church, as a husband to his wife. By order of Agiltrude, the weak Pontiff, Stephen VI, whose reign lasted only thirteen months, caused the body of Formosus, after it had been buried for nine months, to be disinterred. Clothed in his pontifical vestments, the corpse of the deceased was arraigned before a synodal assembly, judged according to due legal procedure, and condemned. He was deposed; his acts were declared null and void, and, finally, his body handed to the mob, who cast it into the Tiber. But Pope Stephen VI, who had made himself the tool of the house of

Spoleto, himself became the victim of reprisals: shut up in a monastery, he was assassinated some time later.

The incident, however, was far from being closed. An effort was made to rehabilitate Formosus, while the question of the validity of ordinations conferred by him—a question of vital importance for a number of clerics still living and ordained by him—was hotly debated for a period of more than thirty years. The first reaction was in favor of Formosus. *Theodore,* an energetic man, who had succeeded Romanus (whose reign had lasted only one day), had the courage to repair the outrages inflicted on Formosus by solemnly depositing his relics in the Vatican Basilica and proclaiming the validity of his ordinations. His successor, John IX (898–900) also rehabilitated Formosus, and convoked three councils to that effect. Benedict IV, Leo V, and Christopher were only passing figures, but *Sergius III,* who had been anti-pope at the time of Theodore and John IX, when rightfully elected, opposed their policy of conciliation and re-opened the trial of Formosus. It was decided that those whom the former Pontiff had consecrated had no other choice but to submit to re-ordination. Sergius III sullied the office of the papacy by numerous vices and disorders. He was the first of the protégés of the House of Theophylact.

TEXTS AND DOCUMENTS

THE MOCK TRIAL OF POPE FORMOSUS

The withered corpse of the aged Pontiff was dragged from its sarcophagus and exhibited before a synod presided over by the Pope. Still dressed in pontifical garments, it was propped up on a throne, and by its side was installed a deacon, who, pale with terror, had to reply in the name of the deceased Formosus. The legal accounts of this abominable trial were burned the following year, but we get some of the details from contemporary writers. The whole history of his past, his quarrels with John VIII, his oaths, his ambitious conspiracies, the perjuries imputed to him, were all brought up to his disadvantage. They revived old ecclesiastical canons, long forgotten by every one, including the president of this gruesome council, and ended by proclaiming the unworthiness of the accused, the irregularity of his promotion, and the invalidity of his acts, especially his ordinations. On this point, however, they confined themselves to the annullment of the Roman ordinations, continuing to recognize those outside. Not one of the Roman clerks thus deposed was reordained. In accordance with the ancient ceremony, the papal mummy was stripped of its insignia, and of all its clothing, except the haircloth which still clung to the withered flesh. It was then thrown into an unconsecrated tomb, among the bodies of strangers. But the brutal populace, anxious to have a share in those outrages on the man before whom they had long grovelled, had the corpse cast into the Tiber.

DUCHESNE, *The Beginnings of the Temporal Sovereignty of the Popes*, pp. 199–200.

QUESTIONS

1. In what did Photius' second breach with Rome differ from the first?
2. What is the origin of the Greek tradition regarding second marriages?
3. What was the question of the "Tetragamy"?
4. Which were the causes of the sudden disruption of the Carolingian Empire?
5. Account for the sudden rise in power of the Dukes of Spoleto.
6. Describe the character of the Empress-Mother Agiltrude.

BIBLIOGRAPHY

John VIII.—Sources: Letters in *P. L.*, CXXVI, col. 651–966.—JAFFÉ, *Regesta*, I, p. 376–422.—WATTERICH, *Pontificum Romanorum vitae*, I, pp. 27–29, 83, 635–650.—Mansi, XVI and XVII.—Works: DUCHESNE, *Les premiers temps de l'Etat pontifical*, ch. XIV, pp. 130–143; *The Churches Separated from Rome*, London.—HERGENRÖTHER, *Photius*, II, pp. 291–587.—GASQUET, *L'empire byzantin et la monarchie franque*, 1888.—A. LAPÔTRE, *Le pape Jean VIII*, 1895.—Works cited above on the Holy Roman Empire, KLEINCLAUSZ, BRYCE, BIROT.—E. AMANN, art. *"Jean VIII,"* in *Dict. de Théol.*—S. SALAVILLE, art. *"Léon VI le Sage,"* in the same dictionary.—C. DIEHL, *Figures byzantines*, 1st Series, ch. VIII: *"Les quatre mariages de Léon le Sage,"* pp. 181–215.

Formosus.—Sources: *Liber Pontificalis*, edit. Duchesne, II, pp. 164, 165, 175, 183, 185, 227.—John VIII, *Epist.*, XXV, CXXX, *P. L.*, CXXVI, col. 675–689, 781. See E. DÜMMLER, *Auxilius und Vulgarius*, Leipzig, 1866.—Works: DUCHESNE, *Les premiers temps de l'Etat pontifical*, ch. XV.—A. LAPÔTRE, *Hadrien II et les fausses décrétales*, in *Rev. quest. hist.*, 1880, XXVII, pp. 377–431; *Jean VIII*, pp. 25–29, 59–61, 178–191.—L. SALTET, *Les réordinations*, 1907, pp. 143–145, 152, 163.—HEFELE-LECLERCQ, IV, 383–390, 433–443, 611–612, 647–650, 708–719.—F. VERNET, art. *"Formose,"* in *Dict. de Théol.*

I. St. Ansgar in the Northern Countries. The conquest of Saxony had thrown open the gateway to the North. The Danes, the Normans, and the Swedes, who inhabited this section of Europe, were no doubt of Germanic origin and tongue, but they had resisted all efforts to incorporate them into the western civilization. On the contrary, they frequently laid waste the coasts of Great Britain and France, and, sailing up the rivers, pillaged and plundered churches and monasteries. In the midst of this scene of general terror, *Ansgar* (Anskar, Asker, Ascar, Anschar, Anscharius are other spellings of his name), a Frankish monk, undertook to win these barbarians over to Christianity. He first evangelized Denmark, whose king he baptized at Ingelheim in 826, and then passed into Sweden, where he established his compatriot Gosbert as bishop. The missionaries, however, did not receive the Frankish protection upon which they had relied, and as a consequence, their work met with a disastrous setback. The Danes poured down upon Hamburg, which was the center of Ansgar's missionary labors, and the Swedes put their bishop Gosbert to death. Ansgar, however, was not discouraged, but set about uniting the see of Hamburg with that of Bremen. His successors reaped the full benefit of his labors, and a century later, about 948, three bishoprics were erected in Jutland: Slesvig, Ripen, and Aarhus. The work of evangelization was not completed, however, until towards the end of the tenth century by the Scandinavian kings.

As to the Norman ravagers, Charles the Simple signed the treaty of Saint-Clair-sur-Epte with them in 911, and after several parleys between the archbishop of Rouen and their leader Rollo, they embraced Christianity.

II. SS. Cyril and Methodius in the Slavic Countries. In the eastern portion of Europe lived the Slavs, who, being constantly harassed by wild hordes from Asia, were finally constrained to establish themselves in central Europe. They took up residence in the country which extended from the coast of Illyria to the shores of the Baltic Sea. These Slavic peoples may be divided into three branches: the southern branch, which comprises the Illyrians (or Carinthians), the Serbs, and the Croatians; the central branch, which comprises the Moravians, the Bohemians, the Poles, and the Wends; and the northern or Russian branch. Because they were almost continually threatened by the Avars, a people established along the banks of the Danube, the Slovenes of Carinthia had placed themselves under the protection of the Bavarians. In this manner, they together with their suzerains passed under Frankish domination in 788. The Russians were not converted until the tenth century, and hence we shall treat here only of the central branch of the Slavic peoples, especially the Moravians and the Bohemians.

The tribe of the Moravians had established itself in the basin of the Morawa in lower Austria, and on the southern slopes of the Carpathian mountains. They had come into contact with the Franks under the reign of Louis the Pious and had accepted their rule. Missionaries were sent to them from Salzburg, which was a Bavarian see. The Slavs, however, despised these German missionaries, who preached to them in a foreign tongue, brought with them new customs and new laws, and were preceded or followed by bands of pillaging soldiers. Duke Ratislas was very anxious to rid himself of their undesirable influence, and so petitioned the Emperor Michael III, the Drunkard, to send them missionaries. Michael despatched to them SS. *Cyril* and *Methodius,* who were destined to play the same part in the conversion of the Slavs as St. Boniface had in that of the Germans.

These two missionaries were brothers, born at Thessalonica, on the very border of the Slavonian dependencies of the Empire, and had a perfect command of the Slav language as well as a thorough acquaintance with Slav customs. They were both of noble birth and of high scholastic attainments, but instead of aspiring to posts of honor, had preferred to embrace the monastic life. Their reception by the Moravians was enthusiastic, and because they used the Slavonic language in their preaching and celebrated the liturgy in the vernacular, they awakened no animosity. A serious conflict soon arose, however, between them and the German missionaries, who, jealous of their success, opposed to their teaching the tri-lingual argument, which stated that by divine right only three languages could be used in the sacred liturgy: namely, Hebrew, Greek, and Latin, which had figured in the inscription placed above the Cross of Jesus. SS. Cyril and Methodius retorted to their arguments by citing the custom followed in the East, where, dependent upon the locality, the Mass was celebrated in Greek, Persian, Armenian, or Syrian.

The two missionaries then journeyed to Rome to obtain the official approbation of their apostolate (868). At the very hour when Photius consummated his break with Rome, the papacy was gladdened by the sight of the Moravians coming into its pale and thus escaping the baneful influences of Byzantium. Hadrian II settled the dispute in favor of the two brothers, placed the Slavic liturgical books on the altar of St. Mary Major, and had the Slavonic liturgy celebrated in four Roman basilicas. He then created Methodius archbishop of Pannonia and legate of the Holy See to the Slavic nations, giving him as his territory the former diocese of Sirmium, which comprised the two Pannonias, Upper Moesia, and a portion of Upper Dacia.

Before the date set for their departure, Cyril fell sick and died, February 14, 869. Methodius returned alone, only to find that Moravia had again fallen under the domination of the Germans; Duke Ratislas had been betrayed into the hands of Louis the German by his own nephew, Svatopluk. In 870, the bishops of Passau, Salzburg, and Freising convoked a Bavarian council, at which Methodius was tried and, as a result, kept in prison for two years. In 872, John VIII obtained his release and permitted him to continue his preaching in the Slavic tongue, but forbade him to use the Slavic liturgy. This step was destined to have serious consequences. Methodius no doubt believed that the Pope was ill-informed, and so deferred the execution of his orders until an opportunity to explain would present itself. In 880, however, he was denounced to the Holy See by Svatopluk himself, who preferred the Latin tongue as being more traditional and more refined. Methodius again journeyed to Rome, and Pope John VIII, who was fearful of the Byzantine propaganda of Basil I, placed his stamp of approval on the use of the Slavic liturgy, but ordained that the Gospel be first read in Latin at every Mass. The Germans, however, continued to oppose Methodius, so much so that John VIII issued a reprimand to their leader, Wiching (March 23, 881). Methodius died in 885, after completing the translation of a large portion of the Bible.

After his death, Wiching journeyed to Rome and denounced Gorazd, the successor of Methodius, to Pope Stephen V. The *Commonitorium* of 885 abolished the Slavic liturgy. The disciples of Methodius were led into exile and left to their fate near the banks of the Danube. They pushed on towards Bulgaria, where they continued to exercise their apostolate under the protection of Boris and Vladimir. And so the work of Methodius, begun in the territory of the Roman patriarchate, and to all appearances destined to become the best possible means of cementing the union between the Slavs and the Holy See, was abandoned by the same Holy See after brilliant attempts on the part of Hadrian II and John VIII. It ended by conferring a distinct advantage upon the Byzantine Church, and supplied the link destined to unite the Slavs, not with Rome, but with Byzantium.

TEXTS AND DOCUMENTS

THE FAME OF ST. CYRIL

St. Cyril first appears in history in the year 847, when, according to Anastasius the Librarian, he reproved Photius, afterwards the prime author of the Greek Schism, for teaching that there are two souls in man. Cyril insisted, says Anastasius, that it was the animosity of the future schismatic against the legitimate Patriarch, Ignatius, that had dragged the wretched man into the darkness of error. Shortly after this episode in the life of St. Cyril, and some time before Photius supplanted Ignatius and segregated, for a time, the Constantinopolitan patriarchate from the communion of the Holy See, the Khazar Turks, then dwelling in the region between Bulgaria and Moravia, requested the empress-regent, Theodora, to send some missionaries to them. After consultation with St. Ignatius, the empress entrusted the task of converting the Khazars to St. Cyril; in a short time the *chagan* or khan and his principal officers were baptized, and ere long the entire nation followed their example.

PARSONS, *Universal History*, Vol. II, p. 370.

QUESTIONS

1. What was the usual process followed in converting the Germanic and Slavic peoples?
2. How were the Slavic peoples divided, and whence did they originate?
3. Indicate the reasons why the Slavic peoples resented being evangelized by German missionaries.
4. Which were the chief objections to the use of a Slavic liturgy; is that liturgy in use anywhere to-day?

5. Who were the apostles of Sweden, Denmark, Norway, Iceland, Greenland, Moravia, Bohemia, Poland, Croatia, Lithuania, and Hungary?

BIBLIOGRAPHY

Conversion of the Barbarians. St. Ansgar.—Dom U. Berlière, *L'ordre monastique*, pp. 75–77.—L. Bril, *Les premiers temps du christianisme en Suède. Etude critique des sources littéraires hambourgeoises*, in *Rev. hist. eccl.*, XII, pp. 17–37, 231–241.—G. Allmang, art. *"Anschaire,"* in *Dict. d'Hist.*

SS. Cyril and Methodius.—Sources: *Die Pannonische Legende*, published by Dümmler in the *Archiv. f. öster. Gesch.*, XIII.—*La légende de saint Cyrille, Denkschriften der Kais. Acad.*, Vienna, 1870.—*La légende italienne, Acta SS. Mart.*—*Fontes rerum bohemicarum*, I, Prague.—Works: Ginzel, *Gesch. der Slaven-Apostel*, Vienna, 1861.—Leger, *Cyrille et Méthode. Etude historique sur la conversion des Slaves au christianisme*, 1868; *Le monde slave*, 1873.—Höfler, *Bonifatius der Apostel der Deutschen und die Slavenapostel Konstantinos (Cyrillus) und Methodios*, Prague, 1887.—Lapôtre, *Jean VIII*, passim.—Dom U. Berlière, *L'ordre monastique*, pp. 70 ff.—Lavisse and Rambaud, *Histoire de l'Europe*, I, p. 704.—Hauck, *Kirchengeschichte Deutschlands*, III, pp. 150–202.—Martinov, *Saint Méthode, apôtre des Slaves et les lettres des Souverains Pontifes conservées au British Museum*, in *Rev. quest. hist.*, 1888 (XXVIII); *La légende de saint Cyrille et Méthode*, same Review, 1884 (XXXVI).—Petrovic, *Disquisitio historica in originem usus Slavi idiomatis in liturgia apud Slavos et præcipue Croatas*, 1908.—F. Dvornik, *Les Slaves, Byzance et Rome au IXᵉ siècle*, 1926.

SECTION III

Christianity under the Carolingians

CHAPTER I

THE ECCLESIASTICAL HIERARCHY

I. The Bishop, his Election, his Auxiliaries. Under the rule of the Carolingians the choice of bishops was effected in the following manner. The church in mourning addressed a petition to the king, requesting permission to proceed with the election. This was conducted by the clergy and by laymen of distinction, the common people being admitted, as heretofore, in the capacity of witnesses, who signified their consent by acclamation. The newly-elected bishop then received from the king the writ for his benefice and permission to be consecrated. Consecration was conferred by the metropolitan, to whom the candidate promised obedience and from whom, in return, he received the crozier and the ring. The metropolitan had the right of veto, but practically the will of the emperor was the decisive factor. In strict justice to the Carolingians, however, it must be said that they sought to make judicious selections; and although the episcopate was designated more frequently than not by the civil power, it did not become a creature thereof.

The first preoccupation of the bishop was the care of souls. In his visits he saw to it that the clergy faithfully carried out their sacred functions, and the people did their respective duties. To facilitate these inquiries, which by order of Charlemagne were to be conducted annually, seven synodal secretaries were established in every commune. These men were selected from among Christians of exemplary lives and were sworn into office. Upon the arrival of the bishop they convened and appeared before him to give an account of the condition of the parish: Sunday observance, charitable institutions, etc. On the basis of this report the bishop issued a declaration, to which the civil authority enjoined obedience and respect.

Very soon, however, it became impossible for the bishop to handle this work of supervision alone, and this fact explains the transitory appearance of the *chorepiscopi,* who for analogous reasons had flourished in the days of the old Roman Empire. They had episcopal consecration and assisted the bishop in the remote parts of his diocese. With the establishment of ecclesiastical circumscriptions (districts), however, they were replaced by archdeacons. Already in the days of Charlemagne, noblemen sought and obtained these positions and exercised their functions without passing through the diaconate, solely on account of the prestige which thereby accrued to them—an abuse against which both capitularies and councils repeatedly protested.

We have already observed how, in the fifth and sixth centuries, many zealous bishops instituted the practice of grouping together the clerics of their respective cathedrals into a sort of monastic organization under one common rule. This was the policy adopted in particular by St. Augustine at Hippo and St. Ambrose at Milan. In the eighth century, the practice became more wide-spread, being introduced, not only in cathedral churches, but also in a number of others of larger size, which received the name of collegiate churches. The communities were made up of clerics from different Orders, who recited the Office in choir and led a community life. The rule imposed by *St. Chrodegang,* Bishop of Metz, was borrowed largely from that of St. Benedict, and was adopted by many dioceses. In course of time the rule of this holy Bishop was combined with the more detailed prescriptions made by the Council of Aix-la-Chapelle. Unfortunately, however, this institution was not, like monachism, founded on the vow of poverty, which made it very difficult for its members to lead a life of complete renunciation; and so when, in 866, Archbishop Günther of Cologne authorized his canons not only to enjoy, but also to administer their revenues, he established a precedent that was quickly followed by others. It spelled the ruin of community life, which in the tenth century was almost completely abandoned, especially after the joint funds were partitioned off among several prebendaryships with fixed revenues.

Members of the rural clergy were appointed by the bishop, whose powers in this respect were, however, somewhat curtailed by the introduction and development of the right of patronage. The name "patron" was given to the chief benefactor of a church. It not infrequently happened that he administered the goods of the church as if they were his own personal property, bequeathing them in dowry or inheritance to his children, or appropriating to himself tithes and private offerings. The nobility was guilty of still another abuse, inasmuch as its members engaged rather extensively in the practice of building private oratories and requiring the services of a private chaplain to minister to their spiritual needs. Very often the clerics appointed to these posts were constrained by force of circumstances to take part in the domestice life of the castle, and so drifted into ways of living not at all in keeping with their vocation. The councils protested in vain, and in the ninth century, when feudalism became conscious of its power, the extraordinary abuses which were to bring so much grief to the Church were already looming on the horizon.

II. **The Metropolitan: Testimony of the False Decretals.** Perhaps no better evidence of the firm and stable character of the ecclesiastical hierarchy can be cited than the *False Decretals*. This name is given to a collection of canons, comprising decrees of popes and decisions of councils, which appeared towards the middle of the ninth century. They are termed Pseudo-Isidorian, because the compiler took the name of Isidore, in memory of St. Isidore of Seville, the author of a previous collection called *Hispana*. In all justice to this Pseudo-Isidore it must be said that he did not fabricate his materials, but merely antedated them, in order to increase their value, attributing recent canons to the authority of former popes and councils. This fact explains why the Decretals were received without protest by Pseudo-Isidore's contemporaries; they reflect the general situation of the Church at that time. They possess incontestable value, therefore, if, after eliminating spurious insertions and readjusting the dates, we accept them only as reflecting the disciplinary regulations of that period.

Pseudo-Isidore emphatically stresses the monarchical character of the diocese and the oligarchical character of the province, in which the metropolitan is nothing more than the president of ten or twelve suffragans, who form the provincial council. It is true that, according to the ancient canons, the metropolitan exercised a very special surveillance over the province, provided for the administration of churches in the event of vacancies, controlled and ratified episcopal elections, and consecrated newly chosen candidates. But in all matters of importance he was required to act in conjunction with his suffragans.

Because the False Decretals are a plea for the liberty of bishops, many scholars have held that they were fabricated in the region of Rheims, as a protest against the claims of Hincmar. It seems more probable, however, that they were composed in the Province of Tours, most likely in the Diocese of Mans, to combat the encroachments of Nomenoe, Count of Brittany. On the other hand, because the False Decretals invoke the right of appeal to Rome, and the popes in the Middle Ages made use of them in their work of reforming the Church, some have represented their author as a sort of individual ever ready to do anything that would advance the cause of the papacy. But the False Decretals themselves attest, and the welcome they received everywhere is evident proof, that in order to safeguard local ecclesiastical autonomies it was quite natural to appeal to the sovereign authority of the pope. The predominant influence of the papal monarchy, then, was a fad which the crafty forger did not overlook, but quite naturally sought to exploit.

III. The Pope: Origins of the Cardinalate. The existence of the Holy Roman Empire was of short duration, and the structure upon which it was erected soon crumbled to pieces, but the spiritual power remained intact in the hands of the Sovereign Pontiff, who was the moral judge of princes and clerics alike, and the final court of appeal in settling disputes. We have already seen him determine the rightful heir to a crown—Pope Zachary conferred the royal insignia upon Pepin—and we have also watched him intervene, when necessary, in the private life of princes—the example of Pope Nicholas I excommunicating Lothaire was quickly followed in the cases of Robert the Pious, Philip I, and Philip Augustus.

All the machinery of ecclesiastical administration was built around the Sovereign Pontiff, and in constructing it, he made use of the clergy of his diocese. Like all other bishoprics, that of Rome had its own body of priests and its parish limits (circumscriptions) in the interior of the city. They were called titles (*tituli*), and twenty-five such *tituli* were in existence already in the days of the early popes. At that time, a bishop, priest or deacon was called *cardinalis,* when, by reason of his functions, he became permanently attached to some church or title. The church was his *cardo,* or the center of his authority. Clerics appointed to direct one of the parishes in Rome were thus designated as cardinals, and, since they were one and all clothed with the dignity of the priesthood, they were called *cardinal priests.* Very soon they were selected to take charge of the special cathedrals of the four Eastern patriarchs, to wit, those of St. Peter, St. Paul, St. Lawrence, and St. Mary Major.

In the seventh century the popes founded deaconries in Rome. These were charitable institutions, or dispensaries, to which was attached a chapel, and each functioned under the supervision of a deacon. When the dispensary was abolished, the chapel remained, and the deacon who ministered to its needs was also called a cardinal. But there was this difference between the titles of cardinal priests and those of cardinal deacons, that whereas the former, being of very ancient origin, were established on the outskirts of Rome, because of the threat of persecutions, the latter were erected in the seventh century, in the heart of the city. There were eighteen of them. It can thus be seen that, in ministering to the material and spiritual needs of the city, the bishop of Rome was assisted by a considerable body of clerics.

Moreover, in the service of his own basilica, the Lateran, the pope called upon the prelates of his circumscription, those of the Roman Campania (suburbicarian sees), and made it obligatory for each of them to spend a week at the Lateran, the center of pontifical administration. In the eighth century, under the pontificate of Stephen III, we find them definitively stationed there. It follows that they were cardinals, and their number evidently corresponded to that of the Roman bishoprics: Ostia, Albano, Porto, St. Rufina, Sabina, Prenestre or Palestrina, and Tusculum or Frascati. In the twelfth century, Pope Callixtus II combined the bishopric St. Rufina with that of Porto.

Because they were associated in the papal administration, these Roman dignitaries in course of time acquired a sort of jurisdiction over the whole Church. As early as the third century, during the interval which followed the death of St. Fabian, the Roman presbyterium advised St. Cyprian on the important question of the reconciliation of the *lapsi.* Gradually the cardinals became the advisors of the Sovereign Pontiff, and during protracted vacancies of the papal see played an exceptional rôle. It was due to their efforts that the affairs of the Church were not unduly hampered during the troubles of the tenth century.

IV. Material Condition of the Clergy: Real Estate and the Tithe.

With the advent of the Franks the possessions of the Church assumed large proportions, thanks to the donations received from kings, private individuals, and especially bishops, who were obliged to bequeath to their church all the property they had acquired during their episcopate, and often made over to her by will and testament the whole or part of their patrimony. The wealth of the clergy aroused the cupidity of the secular power. Charles Martel even went so far as to claim the right to draw large sums from the coffers of churches and monasteries in order to compensate his soldiers for their services. It is true that, at the Council of Leptinnes (743), both Pepin and Carloman sought to convert all benefices derived from ecclesiastical goods into *precaria,* and decreed that, when the grant expired, the different churches should be free either to renew their contract, or to demand the return of their possessions; but in point of fact, temporary owners at once became permanent proprietors of the goods thus confiscated, and a very large portion of ecclesiastical property reverted to the hands of laymen. Soon the usurpers went farther and claimed the right to take clerics under their patronage and grant them the use of these confiscated church benefices. Their action marked the first step in the direction of investiture and its abuses. Juridically incompetent, like women and children, because they did not carry arms, clerics placed themselves under the protecting influence of a person called *advocatus.* Charlemagne issued orders that every church should have its *advocatus,* freely chosen by the bishop or the abbot; but not infrequently it happened that this person turned out to be but another oppressor, for whose protection the church in question paid dearly and received nothing in return. As a result, churches which did not possess *advocati* were soon regarded as being more privileged than the others.

Besides the rents from their properties, the clergy collected what was known as the *dime* or tithe, *i. e.,* a tax which compelled the faithful to pay to the church ministering to their spiritual needs one-tenth of their revenues. The tithe can be traced to the sixth century, and later on its payment was enforced by civil law. This last measure was voted by the Carolingians in an effort to compensate the Church at least in part for the losses sustained by the transfer of her possessions to secular ownership. The episcopal coffers, however, were required to furnish what we would call the budget for religious worship, public aid, and almost the entire budget for public works. Alms-houses and charitable institutions of all descriptions arose in the episcopal cities, and the monasteries provided for countless numbers of poor and destitute persons. Finally, the bishops and abbots, who held temporal sway over their domains, were compelled to provide the king with men, levy taxes on their lands, and make generous contributions in times of war.

TEXTS AND DOCUMENTS

THE AUTHOR OF THE FALSE DECRETALS

Who was the author of the False Decretals? No author of repute any longer ascribes them to St. Isidore of Seville. As Alexander, after the Ballerinis, observes, that holy doctor could not have been the impostor, for the Collection gives Councils of Toledo (6th to 13th), and one of Braga, which were held after his death. That St. Isidore died in 636, the 26th year of Heraclius, we learn from his *Life,* written by his deacon, Redemptus; from Braulio of Saragossa; from Luke of Tay, and from Mariana. The Collection also gives the *Acts* of the Sixth General Council, which was celebrated in 681, or forty-four years after St. Isidore's death. We also read in it epistles of Popes Gregory II and III and of Pope Zachary, who lived in the eighth century. Therefore, Hincmar of Rheims was deceived when he asserted that "Isidore, bishop of Seville, collected the Epistles of the Roman Pontiffs from St. Clement down to St. Gregory." . . . Some critics have ascribed our Collection to some unknown Isidore, also a Spanish bishop. But it is incredible that an impostor, such as this writer must have been, would have missed the opportunity of glorifying the importance of his own church and country. Now in the Collection there are only one or two Epistles addressed to Spanish bishops. Again, down to the time of Innocent III (1198–1216) this Collection was unknown in Spain, and all of the ninth century MSS. which contain it were written in France or Germany, as is shown by the characters and other signs. The barbarisms of style also indicate that the author was a Franco-German, for impurity of diction was as common in the Rhine countries at that time as it was rare in Spain. Blondel accepts these last two reasons for believing the impostor to have been a Franco-German, a subject of Charlemagne, and adds another excellent argument. It is improbable that any resident of Spain, then groaning under the terrible oppression of the Saracens, would have been inclined, or have found the opportunity, to digest and arrange this mass of documents. Finally, there are many things in the Collection which were evidently extracted from the letters of St. Boniface, which is no slight indication that it was prepared in that part of Germany which was numbered among the Gauls. Many critics, and among them the acute Zaccaria, believe that the Collection must be ascribed to a churchman of Mentz, called Benedict the Levite, who, about the year 845, compiled three books of *Capitularies* of Charlemagne and Louis the Compliant.

Parsons, *Studies in Church History*, Vol. II, pp. 99–100.

QUESTIONS

1. Describe the election of a bishop under Carolingian rule.
2. Account for the short-lived existence of community life among the secular clergy of this period.
3. What is meant by the "Right of Patronage"?
4. What is the precise value of the False Decretals?
5. Account for the origins of the cardinalate.
6. What were the deaconries?
7. Describe the early beginnings of investiture.

BIBLIOGRAPHY

Election of Bishops.—Works: Msgr. LESNE, *La Hierarchie épiscopale, Provinces, métropolitains, primats en Gaule et en Germanie* (742–882), 1905. —IMBART DE LA TOUR, *Les élections épiscopales dans l'église de France du IXᵉ au XIIᵉ siècle*, 1890.—G. MOLLAT, art. "*Elections épiscopales*," in *Dict. d'Apol.* Chorepiscopi and archdeacons.—Works: DOM LECLERCQ, art. "*Chorévêques*" and "*Archidiacres*," in *Dict. d'Arch.*—L. DUCHESNE, *Les origines du culte chrétien.*—A. GRÉA, *Essai historique sur les archidiacres*, in *Bibl. Ecole des Chartes*, 1851, pp. 39–67, 215–247. The Clergy.—IMBART DE LA TOUR, *Les paroisses rurales de l'ancienne France*, 1900.—DOM LECLERCQ, art. "*Chanoines*," in *Dict. d'Arch.*—HEFELE-LECLERCQ, III, 1st Part, pp. 20–25, translation of the rule of the canons.—P. THOMAS, *Le Droit de propriété des laïques sur les églises et le patronage laïque au moyen-âge*, 1906. The False Decretals.—Sources: PAUL HINSCHIUS, *Decretales Pseudo-Isidorianæ et Capitula Angilramni*, Lipsiæ, 1863.—Works: A. LAPÔTRE, *De Anastasio bibliothecario Sedis Apostolicæ*, 1885.—Msgr. LESNE, *La hiérarchie épiscopale*, 1905.—F. LOT, *Etudes sur le règne de Hugues Capet*, 1903; *La question des fausses décrétales* in *Rev. hist.*, XCIV, 1907.—DE SMEDT, *Les Fausses Décrétales, l'épiscopat franc et la cour de Rome*, in *Etudes*, 4th series, VI, 1870.—P. FOURNIER, *Etudes sur les Fausses Décrétales*, in *Rev. hist. eccl.*, VII and VIII, 1906–07; art. "*Décrétales*," in *Dict. d'Apol.*, fasc. III.—A. VILLIEN, art. "*Décrétales*," in *Dict. de Théol.* The Cardinalate.—Works: CHOUPIN, art. "*Curie romaine*," in *Dict.*

d'Apol., fasc. III.—Forget, art. *"Cardinaux,"* in *Dict. de Théol.*—Martigny, *Dict. des Antiquités,* art. *"Titres,"* col. 758–760.—Duchesne, *Notes sur la topographie de Rome au Moyen Age,* II, *Les titres presbytéraux et les diaconies,* in *Mélanges d'Arch. et d'Hist.,* VII, p. 237–239.—Dom Leclercq, art. *"Diaconies,"* in *Dict. d'Arch.*

CHAPTER II

Wealth, the encroachments of lay abbots, and the disastrous consequences of confiscation by Charles Martel were so many contributing causes to the downfall of monasticism. Fortunately, a reaction inaugurated by St. Benedict of Aniane and sponsored by Louis the Pious was effected in the opening years of the ninth century.

Benedict Witiza was a native of the French province of Languedoc, who forsook the court of Charlemagne to embrace the religious life at Saint-Seine near Dijon in Burgundy (773). Some years later he founded an abbey near Montpellier, on the banks of the river Aniane (780). Here he enjoined upon his fellow-monks the strict observance of the rule of St. Benedict, which was revived in all its pristine strength; and in order to give the rule additional authority, he cited in support of its requirements parallel passages from other monastic rules. In drawing up his *Concordia Regularum* Benedict Witiza thus furnished a traditional commentary on the Benedictine text. The good example set by this new Benedict was very quickly followed by a number of monasteries in Aquitania and then throughout the Empire. His reform received the approbation of the Council of Aix-la-Chapelle, which stressed the uniform observance of the rule of St. Benedict in all monasteries throughout the Empire. Benedict of Aniane marks the revival of a new spirit which sought to permeate the monastic life of France and Germany. The adviser of Louis the Pious interpreted all monastic regulations literally. To his way of thinking, the Benedictine monk must live a life of complete seclusion from the world and consecrate himself entirely to prayer and work. And because the monks who had been raised to the dignity of the priesthood should not expend all their energies in the exercise of manual trades, it was imperative to prolong the Divine Office. However, this reform movement was destined to be short-lived, and we witness another relapse in the spiritual life of the abbeys in the closing years of the ninth century.

The people in those days were still rough and uncouth, and preserved more than one characteristic of their former superstitions. In particular, they persisted in clinging to the *Ordeal* or "Judgment of God." This custom was of Germanic origin and consisted in having recourse to God when witnesses or written proofs were lacking or failed. God's judgment was presumably manifested when He granted his protection to the innocent. The best known among these ordeals was the judiciary duel or combat in an enclosed field between the two parties involved; there was also the ordeal by fire, in which the accused person was required to take hold of a red-hot iron, or walk bare-footed over burning charcoals. The ordeal by oath was more reasonable: the person taking the oath was credited with telling the truth if no sign from Heaven contradicted his statement. At the outset, it seems the Church did not disapprove of these ordeals. The miraculous events to which she had been an eye-witness during the first centuries of her history had predisposed her to accept, without challenging them, sensible signs of intervention on the part of Divine Providence in behalf of the innocent. The supernatural character of the ordeals exercised a profound influence on the minds of the people of the Middle Ages, and so we need not wonder that, after adopting them, certain churches sought to regulate their use or even attempted to Christianize them, so to speak, by means of prayers and blessings. This accounts for the changes made in several among them, and for the rise of such ordeals as that of the Blessed Eucharist, the oath on the relics of the Saints, etc. With these modifications, the ordeals were tolerated by the popes, except in ecclesiastical trials. At most, however, the attitude of the Church amounted to a prudent concession. Pope Innocent III abolished the ordeals entirely in the opening years of the thirteenth century.

Despite the vestiges of a superstitious paganism, the society of those days was distinctly Christian. The pilgrimages which sprang up on all sides attracted immense crowds. In France, we can point to such shrines as those of St. Martin of Tours, Mont St. Michel, Notre Dame of Puy, Notre Dame of Vezelai, St. Martial of Limoges, Rocamadour, Ste. Foix-de-Conques, and St. Sernin of Toulouse; outside of France we may mention St. James of Compostella, Rome, Monte Cassino, St. Michael of Gargano, and, finally, the greatest of all—Jerusalem. In those days all the great highways led to these famous shrines, and thousands upon thousands of sick persons were cured there. Penitents from every walk in life joined these long processions, including proud barons who came in all humility to make amends for their plunderings and other misdeeds. Devotion towards the relics of the saints was grafted upon this devotion, and often one of the main purposes of a pilgrimage was to secure and carry back home either some small piece of cloth which had touched the tomb of the saint, or a little dust from his burial place, or, better still, a particle of one of his bones.

TEXTS AND DOCUMENTS

An Ordeal by Cold Water

Now the one about to be examined is bound by a rope and cast into the water because, as it is written, "each one shall be holden with the cords of his iniquity." And it is manifest that he is bound for two reasons, namely, that he may not be able to practice any fraud in connection with the judgment, and that he may be drawn out at the right time if the water should receive him as innocent, so that he perish not. For as we read that Lazarus, who had been dead four days (by whom is signified each one buried under a load of crimes), was buried wrapped in bandages and, bound by the same bands, came forth from the sepulchre at the word of the Lord and was loosed by the disciples at His command; so he who is to be examined by this judgment is cast into water bound, and is drawn forth again bound, and is either immediately set free by the decree of the judges, being purged, or remains bound until the time of his purgation and is then examined by the court. . . . And in this ordeal of cold water whoever, after the invocation of God, who is the Truth, seeks to hide the truth by a lie, cannot be submerged in the waters above which the voice of the Lord God has thundered; for the pure nature of the water recognizes as impure, and therefore rejects as inconsistent with itself, such human nature as has once been regenerated by the waters of baptism and is again infected by falsehood.

Ogg, *A Source Book of Mediaeval History,*
pp. 200–201.

QUESTIONS

1. What was the *"Commendam"*?
2. What was the nature of the reform attempted by Benedict of Aniane?
3. Account for the passive acceptance of "ordeals" by the Church.
4. Give a resumé of the article on ordeals in the *Catholic Encyclopedia.*

BIBLIOGRAPHY

Tithes.—P. Viard, *Histoire de la dîme*, Dijon, 1909.—P. Viollet, *Hist. des inst. pol. et adm. de la France*, I, pp. 375–377, 1890.—Msgr. Lesne, *Hist. de la propriété ecclés.*, II, 1921.—G. Mollat, art. *"Dime,"* in *Dict. d'Apol.*, fasc. IV.

Saint Benedict of Aniane.—Dom U. Berlière, *L'ordre monastique.*—Dom Besse, art. *"Benoit d'Aniane,"* in *Dict. de Théol.*

Ordeals.—Works: Vacandard, *L'Eglise et les Ordalies*, in *Etudes de crit. et d'hist. relig.*, 1905.—De Smedt, *Les origines du duel judiciaire*, *Congrès Scient. Inter. des Cath.*, Brussels, 1895; see *Etudes*, 1891.—F. A. Ogg, *Source Book of Medieval History*, ch. XXII.

Veneration of the Saints.—Works: T. Ortolan, art. *"Canonisation,"* in *Dict. de Théol.*—Dom Quentin, *Les martyrologes historiques au moyen-âge.* —Lavisse-Luchaire, II, 2nd Part, p. 78.—Hanotaux-Bédier, *Histoire de la nation française, Histoire des lettres.*—Kellner, *Heortology, A History of Christian Festivals*, Herder, 1905.

CHAPTER III

I. Christian Teaching. A revival of the ecclesiastical sciences was inaugurated under the rule of Charlemagne. The Frankish chieftain had been very much impressed in his travels through Italy by the wealth of learning which clerics displayed in that land, and being desirous of possessing an equally cultured clergy in his own country, he prevailed upon several learned scholars to accompany him back to his palace at Aix-la-Chapelle. The most prominent among these scholars were the Hellenist Paul the Deacon, the grammarian Peter of Pisa, the poet Theodulph, and especially the Anglo-Saxon Alcuin. With the aid of these savants Charles at once set out to realize his literary ideal, and to this end reorganized the Palatine School and established many episcopal, monastic, and presbyterial schools.

The *Palatine School* was made up of clerics and future dignitaries of the Church. Its direction was entrusted to Alcuin. This distinguished Anglo-Saxon scholar was born at York in the year 735. He made his studies under the direction of Egbert, a disciple of the Venerable Bede, and imported into Gaul the methods in use in the monastic schools of Great Britain. Alcuin possessed in an eminent degree the qualifications necessary to carry out the different functions of his office. Gifted with neither originality nor profundity of thought, he was first and last a pedagogue, who could compose clear and concise treatises on grammar and the rudiments of composition and literature. The Academy of the Palace was affiliated with the Palatine School, and formed a very exclusive literary circle, which prided itself in a culture of an advanced type. From these two centers of learning, as from one great central university, came forth a veritable army of bishops and abbots, who made it their purpose in life to advance the cause of learning. Arno, archbishop of Salzburg, Leidrade, archbishop of Lyons, and Theodulph, bishop of Orleans were all pupils of the illustrious Alcuin, and in turn founded .

393

famous *episcopal schools.* We may cite the episcopal school of Lyons, which flourished under Leidrade, Agobard, and Remy; that of Orleans, which distinguished itself under the direction of Theodulph and Jonas; that of Rheims, which became a noted center under Ebbo, Hincmar, and Foulques; that of Mayence, which attained to heights of learning under Rhabanus Maurus; and finally, those of Metz, Verdun, and Paderborn. As instances of typical monastic schools we may mention that of Fleury-sur-Loire, but especially that of Corbie, in the Diocese of Amiens, which trained such illustrious personages as Paschasius Radbertus, Ansgar, and Ratramnus, and then branched out into Saxony, where it established New Corbie. Other monastic schools flourished in the Diocese of Mayence, which gave us St. Alban and Fulda; in that of Spires, and, finally, in the North, St. Amand, etc. At a later date arose the schools of Chartres, Angers, Cluny, and Le Bec.

Charles issued orders that these different episcopal and monastic schools should also provide instruction for the common people. He showed his willingness to co-operate by establishing presbyterial schools. "Every priest," he remarked, "must see to it that his pupils are given an instruction sufficient to enable them to sing the Divine Office with all due propriety, and to serve Holy Mass." In promulgating the ordinance of the Emperor, Theodulph added this remark: "For imparting an instruction of this kind, priests should demand no fee and accept only what is offered them out of gratitude."

II. Latin Literature. Charlemagne's first care was to set up a harmonious relation between the profane arts and sciences and the different branches of sacred learning, and so he assigned the first place in the two cycles of studies, the *trivium* and the *quadrivium,* to theology. Above all, he stressed the study of the Bible. The first task here was to provide a reliable text. Alcuin worked indefatigably to reconstruct such a text with the help of the Bibles of Cassiodorus; at the same time many copies were issued by the School of St. Martin of Tours, where he had been abbot since 756. Soon the rehabilitated version of St. Jerome was used exclusively by all. Many glosses were written, and some authors, like Rhabanus Maurus and Walafrid Strabo, wrote almost complete Biblical commentaries. More often than not, however, the exegetes of this period were mere compilers.

Among the works of *Alcuin* (735-804) are: a treatise on the Blessed

Trinity; the Lives of St. Waast (Vedast), St. Martin, St. Riquier (Richarius), and St. Willibrord; Questions and Answers for Children, a sort of catechism in dialogue form; a small work on Confession, written in the form of a protest against some of the laity who refused to declare their sins in the confessional; and a treatise on the vices and virtues.

Paul the Deacon was a native of Italy and is best known for his History of the Lombards (*Historia Gentis Longobardorum*). He composed a Book of Homilies for the liturgical office, just as Alcuin had done for instruction and preaching. Written under the eyes of the Emperor, these books, theologically speaking, opened up new paths; it was owing to them that a certain classification was gradually effected among the writings of earlier ages. St. Leo and St. Gregory, who are often cited by Paul the Deacon and by Alcuin, in the tenth and eleventh centuries came to be looked upon as inspired by the Holy Ghost, and for a period of almost three hundred years the monks labored in composing anthologies from the writings of the Fathers.

Paulinus, Patriarch of Aquileia and a friend of Alcuin, was a polemical theologian, who undertook to refute the Adoptionists. His Exhortation written for Eric, margrave of Friaul, derives much of its inspiration from the work of Pomerius on the Contemplative Life.

Theodulph of Orleans (821), a Goth born in Italy, is the great poet of this epoch. He composed four hymns which treat respectively of Jesus Christ, the Last End of Man, the Struggle against Vice, and the Duties of Bishops and Priests. We still sing his *Gloria, laus et honor* during the church services on Palm Sunday.

The Spaniard *Agobard* (779–840), Archbishop of Lyons, was a clever controversialist, who refuted the errors of the Adoptionists and later on combated the enemies of Imperialism. His episcopal school became famous under the direction of the Deacon Florus.

Rhabanus Maurus (776–856), Abbot of Fulda, later on Archbishop of Mayence, was one of the great teachers of the German nation. He was a veritable encyclopedist, having written commentaries on almost every book of Sacred Scripture and composed a treatise entitled, *De Universo.*

Walafrid Strabo (807–849), Abbot of Reichenau, was a pupil of Rhabanus Maurus. He drew up a complete plan of studies for his monastery and rendered the same service to Alemania as his master had to northern Germany.

John Scotus Eriugena is a personage concerning whom there is still much dispute. If he was not an out and out rationalist and pantheist, his Alexandrian Neo-Platonism certainly led him to advance false theories in theodicy and cosmology. This is particularly apparent in his treatise "On the Division of Natures," a philosophical discussion on God, the world, and the mutual relations between them. He is regarded by some as the author of a treatise *De Eucharistia*, which denies the dogma of the real presence of Christ in the Blessed Sacrament.

Hincmar of Rheims, who figured in many controversies, has left us some writings on Predestination, the Holy Eucharist, and Canon Law. His voluminous correspondence has great historical value.

Smaragdus, Abbot of St. Mihiel, wrote a Latin grammar, which he attempted to Christianize by substituting for pagan examples, passages taken from the works of the Fathers. His "Royal Road," a moral treatise for the use of princes and rulers, and his "Diadem of the Monks," a manual of religious perfection, consist of citations that have been patched together piecemeal.

Anastasius the Librarian is responsible for the translation of the Acts of the Seventh and Eighth Ecumenical Councils, as well as for some Lives of Saints and Acts of Martyrs. In his *Historia Tripartita* he combined the works of Nicephorus Callistus, Theophanus, and Syncellus.

III. Greek Literature. The main purpose of the literature which originated in the Orient at this time was to combat Iconoclasm, and hence it was chiefly polemical in character. The foremost places must be given to Nicephorus and St. John Damascene. *Nicephorus* wrote a Small Apologetic against the Iconoclasts, which comprises eighty quotations from the writings of the Fathers; but by far the best refutation of the Iconoclastic errors is contained in the three Apologies of *St. John Damascene*. He was a real encyclopedist, who besides these apologetical writings composed several mystical treatises, like those on Virtues and Vices, and also commentaries on St. Paul, inspired by St. John Chrysostom. His principal work is the Source of Science ($\pi\eta\gamma\grave{\eta}$ $\gamma\nu\acute{\omega}\sigma\epsilon\omega\varsigma$), divided into three parts, of which the third, Concerning the Orthodox Faith (*De fide Orthodoxa*), contains all the author's theological views. St. John, however, is scarcely more than a compiler, who wrote a veritable *Summa,* in which he resumes in clear and unmistakable language the teachings of the Fathers.

We must make mention also of *St. Theodore Studites,* abbot, in whose writings the polemist yields to the mystic. His Small Catechesis contains 134 familiar instructions addressed to his fellow-religious; the Great Catechesis preserves 173 others of the same type. To these instructions we must add several ascetical chapters, and especially 507 letters, all of which were written in exile and constitute the most precious document we possess for the understanding of the souls of men in those days.

Photius (*c.* 815–897) is the last of the great Greek writers. He has bequeathed to us an important theological work, entitled *Amphilochia,* numerous commentaries on Holy Scripture, and a collection called *Bibliotheca,* in which he analyzes and quotes volumes of 280 classical authors, now in large part lost.

TEXTS AND DOCUMENTS

An Appreciation of John Scotus Eriugena

When we come to form an estimate of Eriugena as a philosopher, we must not allow his many brilliant qualities to blind us as to the enormity of his errors. He was, without doubt, the most learned man of his century, he was the first of the representatives of the new learning to attempt a system of constructive thought, and he brought to his task a truly Celtic wealth of imagination and a spiritual force which lifted him above the plane of his contemporaries —mere epitomizers and commentators. His philosophy has all the charm which pantheism always possesses for a certain class of minds. It is subtle, vague, and poetic. When we come to examine its contents and method, we find that it is dominated by the spirit of Neo-Platonism. Through the works of Pseudo-Dionysius and of Maximus, Eriugena made acquaintance with the teachings of Plotinus and Proclus; and when he came to construct his own system of thought, he reproduced the essential traits of Neo-Platonist philosophy—pantheism, the doctrine of intuition, mysticism, and universal redemption.

W. Turner, *History of Philosophy,* p. 256–257.

QUESTIONS

1. Trace the origin and development of the educational programme inaugurated by Charlemagne.
2. Explain the terms "Trivium" and "Quadrivium."
3. Discuss the character and writings of Alcuin.
4. Give an appraisal of the poetry of Theodulph.

5. Account for the pantheistic tendencies of the first of the great scholastics, John Scotus Eriugena.
6. What is the outstanding character of the literature of this period?

BIBLIOGRAPHY

Literary Revival under Charlemagne.—EBERT, *History of Litera-ture in the Middle Ages*, 1883–1889.—L. MAITRET, *Les écoles épiscopales et monastiques de l'Occident depuis Charlemagne jusqu'à Philippe-Auguste*, 1866.—BOURBON, *La licence d'enseigner, le rôle de l'écolâtre au Moyen Age*, in *Rev. quest. hist.*, XIX, 1876.—PORÉE, *L'abbaye du Bec et ses écoles.*—CLERVAL, *Les écoles de chartres au Moyen Age*, 1895.—HANOTAUX-PICAVET, *Histoire de la nation française, Hist. des lettres.*—MOLINIER, *Les sources de l'hist. de France*, I.—LAVISSE-KLEINCLAUSZ, II, 2nd Part, p. 342.—HAUCK, *Kirchengeschichte Deutschlands*, II.—MÜLLINGER, *The Schools of Charles the Great.*—PETIT DE JULLEVILLE, *Histoire litt. de la France*, I.—M. MANITIUS, *Geschichte der lateinischen Literatur des Mittelalters.*

Alcuin.—Sources: *P. L.*, C and CI.—Works: EBERT, *op. cit.*, II, pp. 8–11, 17–43, 377–379.—VERNET, art. *"Alcuin,"* in *Dict. de Théol.*—DOM CABROL, *L'Angleterre chrétienne.*—MOLINIER, *Les sources de l'hist. de France*, I.—F. MONNIER, *Alcuin et Charlemagne*, 1863.—HAMELIN, *Essai sur la vie et les ouvrages d'Alcuin*, Rennes-Paris, 1873.—GASKOIN, *Alcuin, His Life and Work*, London, 1904.—TIXERONT, *op. cit.*, III, ch. XII.—A. F. WEST, *Alcuin*, New York, 1916.—HODGKIN, *Charles the Great*, p. 222.—WILMOT-BUXTON, *Alcuin*, 1922.

St. John Damascene.—Sources: *P. G.*, XCIV–XCVI.—Works: J. LAN-GEN, *Johannes von Damaskus*, Gotha, 1879.—KOLL, *Die Sacra Parallela des Johannes Damascenus*, Leipzig, 1897.—LUPTON, *St. John of Damascus*, Lon-don, 1883.—AINSLEE, *John of Damascus*, 3rd edit., London, 1903.—J. BILZ, *Die Trinitätslehre des hl. Johannes von Damaskus*, Paderborn, 1909.—TIXER-ONT, *op. cit.*, III, ch. XI.—V. ERMONI, *Saint Jean Damascène*, Coll. *La Pensée Chrétienne*, 1904.—M. JUGIE, art. *"Jean Damascène,"* in *Dict. de Théol.*—FATHER PAUL, *op cit.*—A. FORTESCUE, *The Greek Fathers.*—J. M. CAMPBELL, *The Greek Fathers*, 1929.

The Liturgy from the Fifth to the Tenth Century

CHAPTER I

THE SACRAMENTS

I. Penance: Penitentials and Redemptions. Solemn and public penance was often fraught with grave inconveniences. Always rigorous in character and quite frequently long in duration, this penance, moreover, could never be repeated. And even after the penitent had been reconciled with God, he was forbidden to carry arms or make use of his marriage rights. A situation of this kind explains why converts, especially from the ranks of the barbarians, deferred doing penance until the hour of death, just as early Christians had put off the reception of Baptism. The Church perceived that concessions had to be made. The practice of confessing sins in secret was retained, and also, for the time being, the rite of public absolution on Holy Thursday; but the solemn excommunication of the penitent was discontinued, and instead, he was required only to expiate his faults by private and less severe penances. Moreover, the penance imposed upon him could be repeated, if necessary. This was the discipline in vogue in the middle provinces of Gaul in the days of St. Caesarius.

It was about this time that the Irish monks and those of St. Columban introduced the custom of fixing penances for certain crimes, according to set codes. These codes were called *Penitentials* and constitute a whole literature in themselves. These little books contain lists of penances fixed for each species of sin. They were almost necessary in view of the very superficial training which some confessors had received. With the appearance of the Penitentials, the practice of confession became more frequent, and in some instances was enjoined as an annual duty. In the eighth century, St. Chrodegang of Metz (742–766) made it obligatory twice a year for all the members of his clergy.

In the reign of the Emperor Charlemagne, Anglo-Saxon influence was instrumental in inaugurating the practice of compensation or "redemption" of certain penances. Prayer was substituted in the place of fasting, the discipline in the place of a pilgrimage, etc. Very soon the custom was introduced of granting a favor of this kind not only to those who could not perform the penance imposed, but also to all who requested the favor. To offset the possible danger of simony, several synods put confessors on their guard against avarice and cupidity. "Redemptions," as they were called, were the logical precursors of indulgences; from the gracious commutation of a penance to complete remission, was but a step.

II. Baptism. The catechumenate as an institution tended to disappear during the fifth century. The Pelagian controversy had stressed the necessity of baptizing newly-born infants, and, as a natural consequence, had caused parents to show real concern for the spiritual welfare of their children. The Church had never ceased to inveigh against the practice of deferring the reception of Baptism, and Pope Innocent I had even gone so far as to close the doors of the clerical state to candidates who had not been baptized in their infancy. During the Merovingian and Carolingian periods the custom of baptizing newly-born children spread everywhere, and two councils of Toledo, held respectively in the years 693 and 694, enjoined the administration of the Sacrament of Baptism within thirty days after birth. Baptisteries adorned even the smallest rural churches. The Sacrament was conferred by a triple immersion, although St. Ildephonsus obtained from St. Gregory permission for the priests of Spain to confer it by a single immersion, because the Arians contended that the other rite symbolized a triple divine nature. When that heresy was overthrown, this exception disappeared.

III. The Holy Eucharist. When the catechumenate was discarded as an institution, the practice arose of distributing the Holy Eucharist to infants immediately after Baptism. Children received Holy Communion many more times before they reached the age of reason, and it often happened that a special place was reserved for them in church. During Mass they knelt near the altar and received Communion after the clergy and before the rest of the faithful. At Constantinople young school boys consumed whatever was left of the consecrated bread after Mass. The custom of frequent and even daily Communion was in vogue in several places. St. Eutychius distributed Communion at Santa Sophia during six hours on the day he was installed as patriarch of that see. In some countries the faithful were permitted to keep the Sacred Species in their homes and administer Communion to themselves. At one time the lamentable abuse crept in of administering Communion to the dead: several synods, and in particular the Council in Trullo, issued strict prohibitions against it.

The rigoristic view of the Jansenists, therefore, has no precursors. True, neglect in approaching the sacred table was evidenced among the faithful in several places, but already in the year 507, the Council of Agde decreed that those who did not receive Communion at Christmas, Easter, and Pentecost should not be reckoned as Catholics. The Venerable Bede expressed his regret that even the most devout among the faithful received Holy Communion only three times each year. It is a strange phenomenon that in the early days all the faithful received Communion when assisting at pontifical Mass, but that when the custom of offering the Holy Sacrifice daily came into use, the full and complete participation of those present in this same sacrifice became more and more rare. Only one server was required at these private Masses, as we learn from a decree of the Council of Mayence, 813. The practice of saying Mass several times a day was introduced in certain places, and a council held at Dingolfing, 932, issued orders that three Masses be celebrated on each feast-day. Out of sheer piety, Pope Leo III used to say as many as seven Masses a day, and it was only in the eleventh century that Pope Alexander II prohibited the celebration of several Masses on the same day.

According to an ancient custom the faithful administered Communion to themselves, although the law required that the Sacred Bread and the chalice be given to each person by the bishop, the priest, or the deacon. Under the reign of Justinian II, in 691, the bishops declared that the Sacred Particle should be received in the palm of the right hand, placed above that of the left, in the form of a cross, and be carried to the mouth without uncrossing the hands. The Precious Blood was more often than not consumed by drawing it from the chalice with the aid of a reed (*fistula*), but soon the practice of receiving Communion under the species of bread alone became prevalent in many places. The rule of St. Columba stipulated that novices and the more illiterate (*rudiores*) be not admitted to partake of the chalice. In the seventh century the custom termed *intinctio panis* was introduced. It consisted in receiving the Sacred Host dipped in the Precious Blood by means of a small silver or golden spoon. Finally, in the eighth and ninth centuries the practice of using unleavened breads, made in the form of small round discs (hosts), was little by little adopted.

Already during the Carolingian epoch theologians began to compose treatises on the Holy Eucharist. In his work *De Corpore et Sanguine Domini,* written in 831, St. Paschasius Radbertus, a monk, and later on abbot of Corbie, launched an attack upon those who held that only the soul is nourished by the food of the Eucharist. Throughout his treatise he declared emphatically that the true body and the true blood of our Lord are contained under the appearances of bread and wine, and in this way stressed the identity of the Eucharistic and historical bodies of Christ. The assertion of this identity in such unmistakable language must be credited to Paschasius, because before his time the Fathers had made only passing references to it. Paschasius, therefore, is a realist, and although he does not deny the spiritual and figurative aspect of the mystery, he is not concerned with it in his treatment of the subject. Ratramnus and Rhabanus Maurus took exception to his teaching, and while careful to safeguard the Real Presence, deemed it incorrect to state that the Eucharistic body of Christ is the same as that born of the Virgin Mary. Being symbolists rather than realists, they laid greater stress on the differences in mode of being between the historical and the Eucharistic bodies of Christ, than on their identity. In the last analysis, however, the two schools kept within the bounds of orthodoxy, John Scotus Eriugena alone giving an exaggerated and Calvinistic twist to the doctrine of symbolism by maintaining that the Holy Eucharist is only a memorial of the Passion.

TEXTS AND DOCUMENTS

SYMBOLISM AND THE HOLY EUCHARIST

It is well known that the early Fathers delighted in symbolism. This is especially true of the great theologians of Alexandria, and also of St. Augustine. Now the doctrine of the Eucharist lends itself in a special way to symbolical treatment. The connection between the mystical body of Christ and his physical body present in the Eucharist, already noticed by St. Paul (I Cor. X, 17), was a frequent subject of allegorical speculation and caused some of the Fathers to use phrases concerning the Eucharist from which we should carefully abstain at the present day. Not that statements which were true fifteen hundred years ago have now become false. It is not the truth that changes, but the manner of expressing it that varies according to the exigencies of popular devotion and of controversy. In days when the Real Presence was not impugned by heretics, but was tranquilly believed by all Catholics, there was no danger of such symbolical phrases being misunderstood. But since the denial of the Real Presence by the heretics of the Reform, we should hesitate to use any expression concerning the Eucharist which might seem, in the changed circumstances, to exclude the reality by excessive emphasis upon the symbolism that surrounds it.

SMITH, *The Sacrament of the Eucharist,*
The Treasury of the Faith Series, p. 38.

QUESTIONS

1. Account for the origin of the Penitentials.
2. Contrast early and present-day legislation regarding the distribution of the Holy Eucharist to children.
3. Show that the recent decrees on frequent Communion were justified by the practice of the ancient Church.
4. Trace the history of the Communion rite.
5. What difference is there between a symbolist and a realist in reference to the Holy Eucharist?

BIBLIOGRAPHY

Penance and the Penitentials.—Sources: SCHMITZ, *Die Bussbücher und die Bussdisziplin der Kirche,* 1883; *Die Bussbücher und das kanonische Bussverfahren.*—Works: A. BOUDINHON, *Sur l'histoire de la pénitence,* in *Rev. hist. et litt. relig.,* II, p. 496; *La missa pœnitentium dans l'ancienne discipline de l'Occident, ibid.,* VII, pp. 1–20.—P. BATIFFOL, *Etudes d'hist. et de théol. positive,* 1st series, 3rd edit., 1904, pp. 145–194.—LOOFS, *Leitfaden zum Studium der D.-G.,* 4th edit., p. 475.—P. FOURNIER, *Etudes sur les pénitentiels,* in *Rev. hist. et litt. relig.,* VI–IX (1901–1904).—BRAT, *Les livres pénitentiels et la pénitence tarifiée,* Brignais, 1910.—A. MALMORY, *Quid Luxorienses monachi ad regulam monasteriorum atque ad communem ecclesiæ profectum contulerint,* 1894.—A. TEETAERT, *La confession aux laïques dans l'Eglise latine depuis le VIIIᵉ jusqu'au XIVᵉ siècle,* 1926.

Theories regarding the Eucharist.—Sources: PASCHASIUS RADBERTUS, *De corpore et sanguine Domini,* P. L., CXX, 1267–1269.—RHABANUS MAURUS, *Dicta cujusdam sapientis de corpore et sanguine Christi,* P. L., CXII, 1510–1514.—RATRAMNUS, *De corpore et sanguine Domini,* P. L., CXXXI, 403.—Works: ERNST, *Die Lehre des H. Paschasius Radbertus von der Eucharistie,* Freiburg i. B., 1896.—NAEGLE, *Ratramnus und die H. Eucharistie,* Vienne, 1903.—BATIFFOL, *Etudes d'hist. et de théol. positive,* 2nd series, 3rd edit., pp. 351 ff.; art. *"Eucharistie,"* in *Dict. de Théol.*

CHAPTER II

I. The Liturgical Literature: The Sacramentaries. After peace
had been restored to the Church, the liturgies divided into two major
groups: the western and the eastern. The eastern liturgies again split into
two principal branches: the Syrian and Byzantine, and the Alexandrine.
In the eastern liturgies the form of the ritual is almost invariable, whereas
in the liturgy of the West the formulas change with the different feasts.
The latter fact accounts for the large number of well developed collections
of sacramentaries, lectionaries, etc., which appeared at this time.

There are two great Latin liturgies: the Roman and the Gallican. According to some authors, in particular Duchesne, the Gallican liturgy is of
eastern (Syriac) origin. It would seem that Bishop Auxentius, a native of
Cappadocia, imported it into Milan in the fourth century, and because of
the importance of the see of St. Ambrose, it spread into Spain, Great
Britain, and especially Gaul, whence its name, Gallican. According to a
more probable theory, however, all the western liturgies have a common
origin in Rome. This is the view taken by Dom Cagin, Dom Cabrol,
and P. Lucas. According to these writers, the western portions of the Empire received the elements of the sacred liturgy from Roman missionaries.
These elements became more and more diversified as they spread, but
the influence of the papacy in Rome insured their stability.

The rites of the liturgy were preserved in several books. The sacramentaries contained the prayers and orations necessary for the different Masses
and the administration of the Sacraments; the lectionary, which was first
called *comes* or *liber comicus,* comprised all the readings according to
the cycle of the liturgical year; the antiphonary contained the anthems
and responses, together with their musical notes, for the Divine Office and
the Mass. The *Ordines Romani* explained the ceremonies and the rules
governing them. Already in the ninth century the *Pontificale* was a book
distinct from the sacramentary and contained an exposition of the functions reserved to bishops.

The three principal Roman Sacramentaries are the Leonine, the Gelasian, and the Gregorian. In the prayers or orations of the first-mentioned sacramentary, which is the most ancient of the three, appears the *Cursus Romanus,* a sort of prosaic rhythm consisting in regular cadences at the end of the phrases, or even at the end of different parts of the same phrase. A large number of these formulas are still to be found in our present-day Missal. The Gelasian Sacramentary, which is also a Roman collection, is of more recent origin. It was imported into France some time before the reign of Pope Hadrian, and some time after that of Pope St. Gregory. The Gregorian Sacramentary is a great improvement on the other two. It bears the impress of a mighty reformer, bent on using his authority to restrict the number of liturgical pieces. The prefaces and variations of the canon, so numerous in the Gelasian Sacramentary, are reduced to those of the present-day Missal. This Sacramentary comprises: first, the Ordinary of the Mass and the Canon; second, the Ordinations; third, the Proper of the Season and the Saints, overlapping each other, and followed by the Common and the Votive Masses. There has been much discussion as to the name of its author. Some are of the opinion that he was Gregory II (715–731). Others point to Gregory III (731–741). As a matter of fact, the author is none other than St. Gregory the Great, as is proved by the testimonies of St. Egbert of York (678–766) and St. Aldhelm (709). The Gregorian Sacramentary was introduced into England by St. Augustine of Canterbury.

II. The Reform of the Missal. The vicissitudes of this important liturgical book were numerous and varied. The spread of the Gallican liturgies had issued in serious difficulties. There being no common center that would make for uniform practice, each church had its own books and its own customs, the result being individualism of the most arbitrary type. Moreover, the different manuscripts swarmed with errors and alterations. A situation of this sort prompted a reaction in favor of the Roman liturgy. Being a lover of order, Charlemagne requested Pope Hadrian to send him a copy of the liturgical collection in use in Rome. The Sovereign Pontiff sent him a collection, which has since been called, "Hadrian's Gregorian Sacramentary." It is the Gregorian edition brought up to date with the liturgical developments of Pope Hadrian's time. Charlemagne had copies of this collection struck off and gave orders that it be used in all the churches of Gaul. By his wish, however, Alcuin made several additions and inserted a few elements of Gallican origin. Charlemagne himself also introduced a few changes. The *Credo* and the prayers *Veni sanctificator* and *Suscipe sancta Trinitas* are of Gallican origin. Hadrian's collection in its new dress became the official Missal used throughout the Empire. Later on it found its way back to Rome and was adopted by the Mother Church. It is our present *Missale Romanum*. The only other liturgies which exist in the West are the Ambrosian and the Mozarabic liturgy of Spain. The latter was discontinued in the eleventh century, thanks to the efforts of Alexander II and Gregory VII, and is preserved to-day only in one chapel in the city of Toledo.

III. The Reform of the Divine Office. In the first centuries of the Church, ascetics and virgins celebrated the Divine Office in the different churches. These groups disappeared with the advent of monachism, or rather were assimilated by the new movement. The habit, however, was already formed, and hence the councils of the Church began to enjoin upon the clergy the celebration of the hours of both day and night. Clerics attached to the great Roman basilicas were particularly bound by these regulations. St. Benedict was acquainted with the order of the Roman psalmody. Before the time of St. Gregory, the manner of reciting the Divine Office varied from one metropolis to another. The differences were many as regards the distribution of the psalms, the responses, and the lessons. Many also were the books necessary to carry on this form of public prayer, to wit, the lectionary, the hymnary, the psalter, etc. A special collection dealt with the recitation of liturgical prayers, according to the prescriptions of the bishop (*Directorium* or *Breviarium*). Moreover, a series of councils held in Gaul and Spain insisted on a uniform method of reciting the Office. The practice of the monasteries attached to the major basilicas of the Lateran, the Vatican, and St. Mary Major in Rome was chiefly instrumental in bringing unity into this chaos. In the matter of the chant, some writers attribute both the wording and the musical notation of the anthems to St. Gregory. as a matter of fact, however, there was a *Schola Cantorum* established in the two great basilicas of the Vatican and the Lateran, for which different popes composed the Roman melody, or *cantilena* of anthems and responses. St. Gregory combined these compositions into an antiphonary, to which his name has become attached, just as in the case of the sacramentaries. The part he played in this great work was very important, as is attested by the traditional thesis, supported by the testimonies of John the Deacon, Venerable Bede, and Egbert of York.

Towards the end of the sixth century, the Roman Church was in possession of a complete Office, supplemented by pieces set to music, which she sought to spread in every land through the intermediary of her monks. The latter were instrumental in having the practices of the pontifical basilicas accepted by the churches of Great Britain, and Benedict Biscop obtained the authorization of Pope Agatho to bring back with him from Rome the archdeacon of St. Peter's, who assumed the task of teaching "the canonical method of the chant and the Office." The Anglo-Saxons in their turn became the promoters of the Roman practices on the continent. The Carolingians also lent a hand. A capitulary of the year 802 prescribed that, in the course of the bishop's visit, the priests should be instructed in the manner of following the *cursus* of the day and night (Breviary) according to the Roman rite. But Roman influence did not have to wait for the advent of Charlemagne to make itself felt in countries where the Gallican liturgy prevailed. Under Charles Martel, the Gelasian Sacramentary, which in its essence is Roman, was in use at St. Denis. Pepin the Short had even suppressed the Gallican rite by an imperial decree and enjoined the *Liber Sacramentorum* of the Roman Church. Charlemagne, therefore, merely put the final touches to a work that was begun before his time.

It was in those days that the liturgy became a science studied for itself. Contributions in this field have, if not a great historical, at least a great documentary value. The first writer of merit was Alcuin, who undertook to recast the Lectionary and the Sacramentary. Amalarius of Metz wrote *Eclogae de Officio Missae,* a description of the Roman pontifical Mass, *De Ordine Antiphonarii,* and *De Officiis Ecclesiasticis.* He lays undue stress on the allegorical method, but he is the best witness we have, and his efforts were largely responsible for the compromise finally effected between the Roman and the Gallican rites. Amalarius encountered two formidable opponents in Agobard of Lyons and his deacon Florus. The principal liturgical compositions of Agobard are *De Divina Psalmodia, De Correctione Antiphonarii* and *Contra Libros IV Amalarii;* the principal work of Florus is a treatise on the Mass. Rhabanus Maurus wrote *De Officiis Divinis,* and Walafrid Strabo *De Ecclesiarum Rerum Exordiis et Incrementis.* Despite their literary defects, in particular undue length and lack of criticism, these Carolingian writers constitute a real liturgical school, the first in history.

TEXTS AND DOCUMENTS

The Hymns of Terce, Sext, and None

NUNC SANCTE

Come Holy Ghost, Who ever One
Reignest with Father and with Son.
It is the hour, our souls possess
With Thy full flood of holiness.

Let flesh and heart and lips and mind
Sound forth our witness to mankind
And love light up our mortal frame
Till others catch the living fame.

Now to the Father, to the Son,
And to the Spirit, Three in One,
Be praise and thanks and glory given
By men on earth, by saints in heaven.
    Amen.

RERUM DEUS

O God, unchangeable and true,
Of all the light and power,
Dispensing light in silence through
Each successive hour;

Lord, brighten our declining day,
That it may never wane,
Till death, when all things round de-
    cay,
Brings back the morn again.

This grace on Thy redeemed confer,
Father, Co-equal Son,
And Holy Ghost, the Comforter,
Eternal Three in One. Amen.

RECTOR POTENS

O God, who canst not change nor fail,
Guiding the hours as they go by,
Brightening with beam the morning
    pale,
And burning in the midnight sky.

Quench Thou the fires of hate and
    strife,
The wasting fever of the heart;
From perils guard our feeble life,
And to our souls Thy grace impart.

Grant this, O Father, only Son,
And Holy Ghost, God of grace,
To whom all glory, Three in One
Be given in every time and place.
    Amen.

        St. Ambrose's Hymns, translated by
        Cardinal Newman.

QUESTIONS

1. What is the sacred liturgy?
2. What were the Sacramentaries?
3. State in summary form the contents of the Lectionary, the Antiphonary, the Pontifical, the Missal, the Breviary, the Hymnary, and the Psalter.
4. What is the origin of our present-day Missal?
5. Who was John the Deacon?

BIBLIOGRAPHY

Liturgical Reform under Charlemagne.—Works: Dom Guéranger, *Institutions liturgiques*, I, p. 233, 1880.—Dom Cabrol, *"Charlemagne et la liturgie,"* in *Dict. d'Arch.*

The Sacramentaries and the Reforms of the Missal.—Works: Dom Cabrol, *op. cit.; Origines liturgiques.*—Dom J. Baudot, *Le missel romain, ses origines, son histoire,* in Coll. *"Liturgie,"* 1912.—Varin, *Mémoire sur les altérations de la liturgie grégorienne,* in *Mémoires Acad. des Inscript. et Belles Lettres,* II, pp. 665 ff., 1886.—Dom Cabrol, art. *"Alcuin,"* in *Dict. d'Arch.*—Duchesne, *Origines du culte chrétien.*—I. Schuster, *Liber Sacramentorum. Notes historiques et liturgiques sur le Missel Romain,* t. I, *La sainte liturgie, Notions générales,* Brussels, 1925.—Dom P. de Puniet, *Le pontifical romain,* t. I, 1929.

The Reform of the Breviary.—Works: Batiffol, *History of the Roman Breviary.*—Dom Bäumer, *Histoire du Bréviaire,* 2 vols., transl. Dom Biron.—Dom Cabrol, art. *"Charlemagne et la liturgie,"* in *Dict. d'Arch.*—Britt, *Hymns of the Breviary and Missal.*—Baudot, *The Roman Breviary.*—Quigley, *The Divine Office.*

CHAPTER III

I. The "Temporale." In the course of this period, ecclesiastical solemnities began to assume greater importance, especially on the three pivotal feasts of Christmas, Easter, and Pentecost. The octave day of the feast of Christmas was made the feast of the Circumcision, and the period of Lenten preparation gradually expanded to its present proportions. "The thirty-six days of fasting," writes Msgr. Duchesne, "had at first appeared to constitute a perfect number, corresponding to one-tenth part of the year. Later on, the incompatibility between this number and the word 'Quadragesima' was remarked, and in the seventh century, four extra days were added and accepted by all the churches in the West. It was about this time also that the stational Masses in *Septuagesima, Sexagesima* and *Quinquagesima* were instituted, the direct effect of which was the opening of the paschal solemnities nine weeks before Easter." The celebration of Easter, like that of Pentecost, lasted three days.

II. Feasts in Honor of the Blessed Virgin Mary. It was about this time that the great solemnities in honor of Mary, which did not exist in the ancient Church, were introduced. The feast of the Presentation or feast of the Purification was already celebrated at Jerusalem during the second half of the fourth century. In the *Peregrinatio Aetheriae* it was entitled *Quadragesimae de Epiphania* (14th Feb.); but later on this was changed to *Quadragesimae de nativitate* (2nd Feb.). At the outset the celebration was purely local in character, and spread to other churches only in the course of the sixth century. An edict of the Emperor Justinian (542) enjoined its observance at Byzantium. The feast of the Annunciation, March 25th, is mentioned in the *Chronicon Pascale,* which dates back to the first half of the seventh century. About this time we also meet with the feast of the Nativity (Sept. 8th) and the *Dormitio* of the Blessed Virgin (August 15th). But these four great feasts in honor of Mary appeared in the liturgies of the Orient only in the course of the seventh century; they are mentioned in the Gelasian Sacramentary at the beginning of the eighth century. The churches which followed the Gallican rite already celebrated the feast of the Assumption, but in the month of January.

III. Other Feasts. As instances of other feasts, we must cite first the Rogations, which are of Gallican origin. St. Mamertus, Bishop of Vienne, inaugurated this practice in 470, and the Council of Orleans (511) extended it to the whole of Gaul. In Rome the Rogations or *Litania minor* (*Lesser Litanies*) were introduced only during the reign of Pope Leo III, towards the year 800; the Church there possessed another litany, called *Litania major* of April 25, which had been instituted to take the place of the pagan procession of the Robigalia.

The feasts of the Holy Cross also have a twofold origin. The one celebrated on September 14th is the more ancient of the two, and commemorates the discovery of the true Cross by St. Helena at Jerusalem. This solemnity was introduced in Rome during the seventh century, but it was unknown in the Gallican churches, although they celebrated the feast of the Invention of the Cross, May 3rd. Later on it served also to commemorate the return of the true Cross after the victory of Heraclius over the Persians in 629.

Finally, we may call attention to the Roman origins of the feast of All Saints. In the opening years of the seventh century, between 607 and 610, Pope Boniface IV obtained possession of the Pantheon of Agrippa, which he renamed *Sancta Maria ad Martyres,* and presided in person at the dedication ceremonies, May 13th. Rome regarded the day as consecrated to all the Saints. Many churches, however, were already celebrating such a feast, but on a different day, and so, in the interest of uniformity, Gregory IV set the date for Nov. 1st, and prevailed upon Louis le Débonnaire to enjoin the observance of that day throughout his States. The Commemoration of the Dead on November 2nd was inaugurated at the beginning of the next period, at the instigation of St. Odilo.

IV. The Veneration of the Saints: Canonization and Martyrologies. Devotion to, and veneration of, the saints had reached an advanced stage of development at an early date. The foremost among the saints to receive honor were, of course, the martyrs, a fact which has led some writers to assert that the practice of honoring confessors did not yet exist in the beginning of the seventh century. As a proof of their contention they cite the fact that Pope Boniface IV gave to the church dedicated to all the saints, the title *Sancta Maria ad Martyres*. It is an easy matter to dispose of their argument by showing that, in ancient times, the distinction between "martyr" and "confessor" had not yet been made, the term "martyr" meaning nothing more than a witness to, or a confessor of, the Catholic faith. Moreover, it is a well-known fact that veneration was offered to St. Paul the Hermit, and a certain St. Antony in the course of the fourth century, and to St. Athanasius and St. Martin in the fifth, the latter's feast being explicitly attested by the first Council of Tours (461). Very soon provincial synods began to prohibit the veneration of persons other than those recognized by the duly constituted ecclesiastical authorities. The accepted procedure consisted in first conducting an investigation, during which the bishop took careful note of the virtues and miracles of the persons in question, issued orders for their names to be inscribed in the diptychs, and finally sent an account of their virtues and deeds to the neighboring churches.

About this time appeared a whole series of martyrologies, edited for the purpose of cataloguing the anniversaries of the martyrs, and, in addition, indicating those of other saints, and the mysteries of the liturgical year. Already in the third century there existed some local calendars, the principal one of which was the *Depositio Martyrum* of the chronographer of 354 for the city of Rome, Furius Dionysius Filocalus. The letters exchanged between the different churches facilitated the editing of martyrologies, properly so called, by the amalgamation of several calendars. It was in this manner that the compilation termed the "Hieronymian Ferial" was effected about the year 500. It contains very important documents, among others, lists of the martyrs of Rome, Africa, the East and the West, and "Passions" and Acts of a greater or less value.

These "Passions" form the connecting link between the Hieronymian Martyrology and subsequent compositions. Soon more orderly collections were substituted for church readings, and they contained more detailed information about each individual saint. These collections are the *historical martyrologies* of the Middle Ages. St. Bede made extensive use of them, and even though his choice was not always happy, he never failed to exploit his source materials conscientiously.

The element of fiction and fantasy begins to appear in these works with the advent of Ado of Vienne, and his errors, transmitted to posterity by Usuard, a monk of St. Germain-des-Prés, later seeped into the Roman Martyrology. What, then, is to be thought of the value of martyrologies? We can best answer this question by quoting the words of Dom Quentin. "Neither the Holy See," he writes, "nor the bishops ever intervened to direct the choice of compilers. It would be just as imprudent, therefore, to accept unreservedly the information furnished by the Roman Martyrology, the heir of the martyrologies of the Middle Ages, as it would be temerarious to lay the blame for the errors which it contains at the door of the ecclesiastical authority."

V. The Ecclesiastical Dress. The essentials of the Roman civilian costume were an under-garment, with or without sleeves, called a tunic (*tunica*), and a bell-shaped outer-garment, or *penula,* without sleeves, donned by thrusting one's head through an aperture made for that purpose in the center. Some persons wore a more sumptuous tunic or dalmatic above the tunic and beneath the *penula.* The Catholic clergy continued to wear the Roman garb, especially in countries occupied by barbarian tribes, where they could not adopt the German style, and so, little by little, the tunic, the dalmatic, and the *penula* came to be accepted as the three principal pieces of ecclesiastical dress. In time, the *tunica alba linea* became the alb worn by all clerics; the *planeta* or *casula* became the chasuble, and between the ordinary tunic or alb and the chasuble, the pope and his deacons on certain feast-days wore a second tunic with large sleeves called the dalmatic. The monks retained the garb of the simple folk, but instead of the *planeta,* they wore the *cuculla,* or cloak with hood, and with the *tunica,* the *cincture,* which served to hold up the tunic whilst they were engaged in manual labor. This dress finally evolved into the monastic cowl and cord.

The Roman civilian dress comprised also the *mappula* or maniple and the *orarium* or stole. The *mappula* was our present-day handkerchief, and was worn on the left arm, as the maniple is worn at Mass to-day; the *orarium* served to wipe the face and also to protect the head against the heat of the sun. This last-mentioned vestment was reserved to priests and deacons, and was unquestionably a Gallican and Visigothic importation, as we are informed by the Councils of Toledo (633) and Braga (675). "It was only in later years," if we are to believe Msgr. Battifol, "that writers began to place a mystical interpretation on pieces of clothing which were in no respect creations of faith, but which, for the historian, represent vestiges of the Roman world preserved by the Catholic Church."

TEXTS AND DOCUMENTS

CANONISATION OF SAINTS

The first example of a solemn canonisation occurred in 993, when Pope John XV decreed celestial honours to St. Udalric or Ulric, Bishop of Augsburg; although some historians maintain that the first solemn canonisation was that of St. Swibert, by Pope Leo III in 804. There is no exact record of the manner in which the evidence was collected that was submitted to the Pope, but the judgment of his holiness was founded on the information supplied regarding the holy life of the bishop and the miracles worked at his intercession; and these are the two principal points to be examined in every canonization. The second example of canonization by the Pope was that of St. Simeon of Treves by Benedict VIII, in 1042.

MACKEN, *The Canonization of Saints*, pp. 25–26.

QUESTIONS

1. What is meant by the "Temporale"?
2. Trace the development of the feasts of the Blessed Virgin Mary.
3. Account for the origin of the Rogations; what was the nature of the pagan ceremony which corresponded to them?
4. What was the Pantheon of Agrippa?
5. Give an account of the early origins of the canonization process.
6. What were the "Passions" and "Acts" of the martyrs?
7. Which are the principal martyrologies?
8. List some of the symbolic meanings attached to the vestments worn by the celebrant at Mass.

BIBLIOGRAPHY

Canonization and Martyrology.—Works: T. ORTOLAN, art. *"Canonisation,"* in *Dict. de Théol.*—DOM QUENTIN, *Les martyrologes historiques au Moyen Age.*—DOM BAUDOT, *Martyrologe romain.*—J. P. KIRSCH, *Der stationische christliche Fest-Kalender im Altertum,* Münster, 1922.—II. DELEHAYE, *Le culte des martyrs.*—MACKEN, *The Canonization of Saints,* N. Y., 1909.

The Ecclesiastical Garb.—Works: BATIFFOL, *Leçons sur la messe.*—DOM LECLERCQ, art. *"Chasuble,"* in *Dict. d'Arch.*—ROHAULT DE FLEURY, *La messe,* vii.—NAINFA, S. S., *Costumes of Prelates.*

THIRD PERIOD

The Feudal Epoch. Tenth to Eleventh Century

CHAPTER I

THE ITALIAN FEUDAL SYSTEM

Introductory Remarks: The Church and the Feudal Regime.
The independence of the Church was threatened by feudalism during the
first half of the ninth century. Quite frequently, especially in the provinces of Germany, the churches which had been deprived of their independence passed into the hands of private lords, and so gradually found
themselves farther and farther removed from the protecting influence of
the central body. The bishops and abbots became landed proprietors, and
constituted the feudal hierarchy. They were first and above all lords, who
maintained a private escort of soldiers, and distributed part of the church
property among vassals who were under oath to pay them homage and
render them service. At the head of this feudal hierarchy was the king, or
suzerain, invested with the power of supreme dominion (*dominium*).
Pastoral functions were not distinguished from the administration of the
temporal goods with which the liberality of princes and faithful alike
had endowed the churches. Over and above very extensive landed properties, parts of which were derived from the royal fiscus, the ecclesiastical patrimony comprised customs, markets, mintage, judicature, castles,
tracts of land, and sometimes even the earldom of the episcopal city—all
of which were so many "regalia," granted by the sovereign to the Church.
In virtue of what was known as the right of immunity, which exempted
ecclesiastical estates from interference by the king's agents, the bishop was
the sole administrator of the Church's temporal goods, and had to answer
only to the king. As far as his secular power was concerned, he was invested with an authority equal to that of an earl or a count, and the king
looked upon the bishopric as a distinction (*honor*) or benefice (*bene-*

ficium), similar in character to the earldoms and benefices he was in the habit of bestowing upon his faithful supporters.

It was only natural, therefore, that kings should take a special interest in the election and appointment of bishops. According to the rules and regulations of the Church, the bishop was chosen by the clergy and the people, and the king merely confirmed their appointment. In point of fact, however, the wealth and the social and religious influence of prelates were powerful agents, and when, in the tenth century, the prince became the benefactor of churches, ratification by him was transformed into an out and out nomination. *Lay investiture* replaced ecclesiastical investiture, and the choice of the prince, before any religious consecration, received from the prince the emblems of his appointment, ring and crozier. An innovation of this kind was fraught with serious consequences. The king in his choice of bishops and abbots was frequently guided by purely temporal motives, his concern being to secure good vassals, rather than give worthy pastors to the Church. Other abuses also crept in. Kings and rulers who held bishoprics and abbeys in their power, often came to regard them as goods for rent, and gave them to the highest bidder. The appointee then compensated himself for any loss he had suffered in the transaction by selling, in turn, inferior offices, without taking into account the moral qualities of the candidates. Thus from one end to the other of the scale of the ecclesiastical hierarchy, simony became rampant, with all its attendant evils. The bishop was above all a *grand seigneur*. He administered his temporal goods, he engaged in hunting, he sometimes wore a coat of armor, and showed little or no interest in the welfare of souls. Having entered the clerical state with no ecclesiastical vocation, he frequently married, and here, too, custom was not slow in creating a sort of right. Very soon some ventured so far as not only to excuse the marriage of priests, but even to advocate it as a sort of extension of the natural law.

In the ninth and tenth centuries the right of "seignory" was extended, and made to include even the parishes. On the one hand, the establishment of new churches on royal domains, the *villae* of bishops, monasteries, etc., resulted in a number of parishes being erected on private property; on the other hand, the institution of the right of patronage, the close relations set up between the rural clergy and the nobility in the struggle for office, the granting of benefices by the king or bishop, and, finally, usurpations and violent deeds of all sorts continued to transform *vici publici* into private churches. The parishes which escaped the scourge of secularization were closely bound over to the church of the bishop, whose power over clerics and their goods assumed the character of a suzerain right. The submission of the clergy to their head took on the form of complete subjection, in such wise that, in the eleventh century, it could be said in all truth: "No church exists without its lord!" (*Imbart de la Tour*). Thus independent parishes became a thing of the past. In the year 1056 the Council of Tours distinguished only three kinds of churches: (1) those belonging to a bishopric, (2) those administered by a convent or a chapter, and (3) those owned by laymen. The latter were far more numerous than the rest, and ecclesiastical and lay rulers alike soon came to regard the church as just another institution to be exploited by them. They gained possession of the patrimony, seized the revenues, gifts, and offerings, and reserved to themselves the right to administer the Sacraments and grant Christian burial. Ownership of this sort assumed such proportions that the patron of a church could even partition it off among several heirs. It not infrequently happened that some persons held the title to one-half or one-third of a church, and that in one and the same sanctuary the altars belonged to several different lords. In most of these cases, the priest in charge was directly appointed by the proprietor, whose vassal he thus became. In the light of these facts it is easy to see how the clergy were gradually deprived of all liberty of action. The right of patronage exercised in respect to churches very quickly swept religious society into the main current of feudalism.

The evils of lay investiture finally attacked the papacy itself. The nomination of candidates to the Holy See passed into the hands of the Theophylacts in the tenth, and into those of the Tusculans in the eleventh century. Later on, these feudal influences were supplanted by the imperial influence, and the emperor in turn came to regard the patrimony of St. Peter as a personal fief, with the pope as his vassal and vice-administrator. The memory of the Caesarism of ancient days urged him to extend his power and to include within his jurisdiction the administration even of spiritual things, and so, intrenched and held fast by feudal power on the one side, and imperial power on the other, the Church seemed doomed to slavery.

I. The Domination of the Theophylacts. When the Carolingian Empire crumbled, the papacy was deprived of its sole protector. This was the signal for the Roman nobility to raise its head. The ambitious Theodora, wife of the vestiary Theophylactus, was one of the first to take a hand in affairs, and by entering into sinful relations with some of the most influential personages, she succeeded in gaining possession of a number of villas and castles. In the opening years of the tenth century, her daughter Marozzia considerably increased the influence of the family, even going so far as to establish her residence in the Castle of Sant' Angelo, and calling herself Madam Senator (*Donna Senatrix*). For more than fifty years the family of the Theophylacts dominated Rome and imposed the candidates of their choice upon clergy and people.

Sergius III (904–911) owed his appointment to the influence of Theodora, and John X (914–928), another protégé of the family, was indebted for his election to Marozzia. John, however, quite unexpectedly overcame the handicap of his unworthy appointment and, in course of time, distinguished himself by many fine accomplishments. The papal estates were constantly being threatened by the Saracens, who, from their retreat at Garigliano, swept down periodically upon Roman territory. John X succeeded in opposing their hostilities by a powerful league, made up of the feudal rulers of central and southern Italy and the last of the Byzantine chiefs. The Pope himself led the allied armies into battle, surrounded the Saracens in their fortress at Garigliano, and completely annihilated them (916). He showed himself no less resolute in the administration of the affairs of his office, and succeeded in shaking off the yoke of the unholy princesses who ruled Rome. At the death of Berengar, king of the Lombards, whom he had crowned emperor, he even attempted to appoint as his successor Hugh, Duke of Provence, and a recent visitor to Italy. In the meanwhile Marozzia had lost her husband by death and had contracted a new marriage with the powerful Duke of Tuscany. Fearful lest the creation of a new emperor might diminish her influence in Rome, the duchess stirred up a revolt. The insurgents invaded the Lateran, seized and massacred Peter, a brother of the Pope, and threw John himself into prison, where he was smothered to death with a pillow.

Marozzia was now able to control the papacy as she saw fit. She gave it in turn to her puppets, Leo VI (928–929), Stephen VII (929–931), and finally to her own son, who called himself *John XI*. The princess entertained the dream of becoming empress, and hence, after the death of her husband, Guy of Tuscany, resolved to marry Hugh, Duke of Provence, the former candidate for the office of emperor. Marozzia had no doubt that John XI would crown his own mother and stepfather, but she failed to reckon with other factors. She had another son, by the name of *Alberic,* whom Hugh had the misfortune to insult on the day of his marriage to Marozzia. Alberic gathered together a small band of soldiers, laid siege to the Castle of Sant' Angelo, and forced Hugh to flee. Marozzia was taken prisoner and met with a mysterious death. Rome was only changing hands, although, to be fair to Alberic, he showed himself more worthy of his office than had his degenerate mother.

Leo VII (936–939), Stephen VIII (939–942), Marinus II (942–946), and Agapitus II (946–955) were Popes in name only, Alberic ruling the city of Rome under the title of "Prince and Senator of all the Romans" (*Princeps atque Omnium Romanorum Senator*). We must give him credit, however, for re-establishing order in the city, respecting the right of clerics to elect their own candidates, and undertaking, with St. Odo of Cluny, the reform of several Roman monasteries. Unfortunately, he had his own son, Octavian, proclaimed successor of Pope Agapitus II while the latter was still alive. Alberic died in 954, Agapitus II in 955, and Octavian inherited both offices, becoming at once Senator of the Romans and Sovereign Pontiff. He took the name of *John XII*. Unquestionably, this youth of sixteen had absolutely no vocation; we must be on our guard, however, against placing too much faith in the statements of the imperial chroniclers, especially Luitprand of Cremona, who accuse him of scandalous conduct.

II. The Three Ottos. In the midst of these trying times another great power loomed on the horizon. The House of Saxony had attained to a very prominent position in Germany, under the administration of Henry I, surnamed the Fowler (919–936); so much so that his son, *Otto I* (936–973), cherished the plan of rehabilitating the Empire of Charlemagne. As a first step in this direction, Otto had himself crowned king at Aix-la-Chapelle. He crushed a number of dukes, who had risen up in rebellion against him, and then set about establishing his power at home. His most signal triumph was a victory over the Hungarians, which put an end forever to their invasions. He also successfully defended his kingdom against the Danes and the Slavs of the North.

It was at this juncture that, in answer to an appeal for assistance from Pope John XII, whose authority was being threatened by the turbulent Roman aristocracy and Berengar, the Lombard king, Otto set out on an expedition in 961, assumed the crown of Italy at Pavia, and triumphantly entered the City of Rome. As a gesture of gratitude for his pretended services, John XII crowned him emperor, February 2, 962. This is the origin of the "Holy Roman Empire of the German Nation," which, far from affording protection to the Church and Italy, more frequently oppressed both. On this occasion was signed the famous document known as *Privilegium Ottonis*. According to the contemporary copy which we possess, Otto made a grant to the papacy of about three-fourths of the kingdom of Italy. The situation at Rome was regulated in conformity with the constitution of 824; the Pontiff-elect and his subjects were to take the oath of fidelity to the Emperor before the ceremony of ordination, and imperial *missi* were to supervise the administration of justice. The rule of Otto was just another instance of a lay protectorate.

Both John XII and the Romans at once realized that they had surrendered to a new taskmaster, and so the Pope immediately opened negotiations with Adalbert, the son of Berengar, former king of Italy. But Otto re-appeared in Rome to give battle to the opposing faction and completely routed it. As a result of this defeat, John XII took to flight, and on November 6, 963, Otto held a pseudo-council, which pronounced the Pope unworthy of his high office, and elected Otto's secretary, an ordinary layman, in his place. The new candidate was ordained a deacon and a priest on the same day, consecrated pope under the name of *Leo VIII,* and invested with the title of viceroy.

It is impossible to justify a procedure of this kind, because no matter how guilty John XII may have been, he was still the lawful incumbent of the Holy See, and Leo VIII was a mere anti-pope, created by the Emperor. And so at the very outset of the Holy German Empire, the papacy came to be considered as a mere bishopric of Germany, which was conferred by the secular power.

The Romans, however, could not resign themselves to being oppressed in this way. Another revolt broke out as a result of their resentful attitude, but it was quickly suppressed by Otto (January, 964). The Emperor had scarcely left the city, when John XII re-entered it (February 22). The unfortunate Pontiff died a few days later, but the Romans again persevered in their resistance by appointing a new pope in the person of Benedict V. Otto was furious. He hastened once again to Rome, imposed the candidate of his choice, Leo VIII, and carried Benedict away as his prisoner. And because the Romans had broken their oath by electing Benedict, the Emperor exacted additional guarantees. By a decree of his candidate, Leo VIII, the people were from that time on barred from taking part in the papal election. Later on, a forger living in Italy attached to this same decree a list of incredible privileges, supposedly granted by John VIII to the Emperor. As the privileges listed correspond in every detail to the claims urged by the imperial party at the time of the quarrel, the addition must be regarded as apocryphal.

After the death of Leo VIII, Otto proposed as his candidate for the tiara a certain Theophylact, son of Theodora the Younger, a sister of Marozzia. By this political move he reckoned on winning over to his side the most powerful member of the opposing party. His plans were completely frustrated, for the firm attitude which Theophylact, as *John XIII*, adopted in regard to the turbulent Roman nobles led to another insurrection. The Pope was arrested, imprisoned in the Castle of Sant' Angelo, and later on transferred to a fortress in Campania. Otto suppressed the rebellion and this time remained six years in Rome. On Christmas day, 967, he had his thirteen-year-old son, Otto II, crowned as *co-imperator;* in 972 the same Pontiff married the young Caesar to Theophania, daughter of the Basileus Romanus II. Otto's secret ambition in encouraging this alliance was to conquer the entire southern portion of the Italian peninsula, which was still in the power of the Byzantines. His rule seemed firmly established in Italy, when he died, May 7, 973.

The uppermost thought in the minds of the Romans was to rid themselves of the odious yoke of the German oppressor. This time the insurgent noblemen placed at their head Crescentius, a son of Theodora the Younger, and a brother of the deceased Pontiff, John XIII. A revolution broke out as the result of the change in administration; Pope Benedict VI (973-974), successor of John XIII, was strangled; and Boniface Franco, who took the name of Boniface VII, was substituted in his place. But *Otto II* (973-983) suppressed the revolt; the intruder, Boniface VII, fled to Byzantium, and the Bishop of Sutri was elected to the office of the papacy with the consent of the Emperor. He took the name of Benedict VII (974–983) and displayed great zeal for the reform of the Church. After his death, Otto II put up his own chancellor, who took the name of John XIV (983–984). Otto II also made an attempt to conquer lower Italy, but was defeated at Stilo by the Saracens of Calabria, and died shortly afterwards (983). The Slavs meanwhile had taken advantage of his absence to pillage the young Christian communities established by Otto the Great on the eastern boundaries of Germany. In Rome the party of Crescentius strove to assert itself. The ex-Pope Boniface VII arrived from Constantinople and had John XIV thrown into prison, and later on massacred. It was not long, however, before both Boniface VII and Crescentius were themselves overtaken by death.

The new Emperor, *Otto III* (983–1002), was barely sixteen years of age. He was of a dreamy and impractical turn of mind, and conceived the plan of organizing a Christian empire with Rome as its capital. His first move in this direction was to appoint to the office of the papacy a cleric of the royal chapel by the name of Bruno, a grandson of Otto the Great. The candidate took the name of Gregory V and was the first German pope. But the Emperor had scarcely left the city, when the Italian faction, commanded by Crescentius the Younger, rose in rebellion and proclaimed as pope, the Greek Philagathos, archbishop of Plaisance. Upon receipt of the news Otto III undertook an expedition into Italy, deposed Philagathos, who called himself John XVI, seized Crescentius, who had taken refuge in the Castle of Sant' Angelo, and had him beheaded.

After the death of Gregory V, Otto III designated as his successor Gerbert, another of his protégés, who took the name of *Sylvester II*. Born at Aurillac, France, Gerbert had made his studies at the episcopal school of Ausona, the present city of Vich, in Spain. He was graduated from this institution with high honors, and his reputation as a learned scholar, thoroughly versed in rhetoric, philosophy, mathematics, and astronomy, quickly spread abroad. Adalbert of Rheims entrusted to him the direction of his episcopal school, and Otto II summoned him to his court to supervise the education of his son, the future Otto III. In the struggle between the last of the Carolingians and Hugh Capet, Gerbert sided with the latter, and in 999, Otto III sought him out in the metropolitan see of Ravenna and appointed him to the see of Rome.

Sylvester II upheld the papal supremacy on three very important occasions. He deposed the intruder Stephen from the see of Puy; he summoned to his tribunal the unworthy prelate Adelbero of Laon, and he re-instated Arnold of Rheims in his episcopal office because his abdication had not been ratified by the Holy See. Unfortunately, Gerbert was harnessed to a political scheme which had no future. Otto III had established himself in the palace of Mount Aventine in Rome, and made elaborate plans for the restoration of the power of the Caesars. The ancient magistratures were revived, and a prefect of Rome was appointed to carry out the orders of the Emperor and at the same time protect the interests of the Church. These plans, however, savored more of paganism than of Christianity, and Otto III appeared in the rôle of a dictator rather than of a protector. The Roman nobles surrounded him in his palace and forced him to quit the imperial city. A few months later (1002), at the age of 22, he died at the foot of Mt. Soracte. Sylvester II disappeared a year later.

III. **The Beginnings of the Eleventh Century: Henry II and Henry III.** The Roman factions had now obtained mastery of the situation, and the third Crescentius, a son of Crescentius the Younger, at once took the power into his hands. Popes John XVII (1003), John XVIII (1009), and Sergius IV (1012), all owed their election to his influence. But his administration was destined to be short-lived, as a result of the opposition fostered by the rival house of Tusculum, which, to further its own schemes, began to affect a deep interest in the German regime.

Otto III was succeeded by Henry of Bavaria. The new Emperor had been educated at the monastery of the Canons Regular of Hildesheim, and later on trained by St. Wolfgang, Bishop of Ratisbon. *Henry II* was thoroughly familiar with the needs of the Church and at once resolved to give it his powerful protection. He let it be known, however, that he would intervene in the affairs of Italy only in the capacity of a protector and for the greater good of the Church. Henry experienced no difficulty in overcoming Arduin, marquis of Ivree, a claimant to the throne, and upon finding two candidates for the papacy in Rome, another Crescentius by the name of Gregory, and Theophylact, a son of the count of Tusculum, pronounced himself in favor of the latter, who became *Benedict VIII* (1012-1024). An era of peace and harmony was at once inaugurated between the Tusculan Pope and the German Emperor, and both St. Henry II and his spouse St. Cunigundis were invested with the imperial purple in St. Peter's Basilica, February 14, 1014. A decree was promulgated to the effect that all future elections were to be conducted according to the sacred canons, and that the pontiff-elect was to bind himself under oath, in the presence of the imperial legates, to respect the rights of all without exception. It must be said that measures of this sort were justified in view of the chronic interference of the Roman nobility. A programme of reform was at once inaugurated along all lines, and three rulers, Henry II, Robert the Pious, and Rudolph III of Burgundy worked untiringly to multiply leagues and peace assemblies in an attempt to instill true Christian principles into the ever-rebellious feudal dukes and princes. They particularly insisted on the appointment to episcopal sees of upright and worthy candidates, and St. Henry allied himself with St. Odilo of Cluny to reform the monasteries.

Henry was the last of the Saxon Emperors. He was succeeded by Conrad II, the first representative of the Franconian dynasty, which produced some of the bitterest enemies the Church has ever known. In Rome, the papacy became a fief of the Tusculans. Benedict VIII was succeeded by his brother, Romanus, who took the name of John XIX. When he died, his eldest brother, Alberic, entrusted the temporal government, together with the title of *Consul Romanorum,* to his son Gregory, and the papacy to another son, Theophylact, who became *Benedict IX.* The new Pope was only twelve years of age, but so disgraced the chair of St. Peter by his misconduct that the Romans lost patience with him and drove him from the city. In his place they installed Sylvester III. After an absence of a few months, Benedict was brought back by the members of his family and ruled the see of Rome for one more year. Then he sold his office to John Gratian, who took the name of *Gregory VI.* Once master of Rome, Gregory sought to re-establish peace and calm, and with the assistance of two great reformers, St. Peter Damian and St. Odilo of Cluny, resolved to raise the Holy See from its state of degradation. But first he wished to reach an understanding with the Emperor, Henry III. Henry, however, was intent upon appointing German candidates to the see of Rome, and so eliminated not only Benedict IX and Sylvester III, whom he had deposed at the Council of Sutri, but also Gregory VI, whom he forced to abdicate. On the occasion of his visit to Rome, the Emperor imposed upon clergy and people alike the candidate of his choice, Suidger, Bishop of Bamberg, who took the name of

Clement II, and in return for the favor conferred upon him, invested both Henry III and his wife Agnes with the imperial purple. Four German pontiffs in turn now occupied the Roman See: Clement II, Damasus II, Leo IX, and Victor II, and although plans for a reform of the Church were outlined during their administration, the imperial supremacy still continued to be a peril.

IV. The Gallican Revolution of 995. The Roman Church during the closing years of the tenth century had also to contend with Gallicanism. Hugh Capet had made the mistake of appointing as successor to Adalbero of Rheims, the instaurator of his dynasty, not the scholarly Gerbert, but Arnold, a natural son of the last Carolingian, Lothaire, who soon turned traitor. Without waiting for a decision from Rome, the king convoked against him a council at Saint Basle, in the course of which the discussion shifted from a question of persons to a question of principles, and in determining the extent of Roman jurisdiction, the abbots, with Abbo of Fleury, took the part of the papacy, whereas the prelates sided with Arnold of Orleans. The latter launched a fierce attack upon the Holy See. The assembly ruled that it was competent to try the case, and requested the culprit to sign an act renouncing his see. Gerbert was designated to take the place of Arnold by the bishops of the province of Rheims. The papacy repeatedly protested, and Gerbert not only sought to exonerate himself before the papal legate Leo at Mouzon (995), but even published the acts of the Council of Saint Basle. The epilogue to this whole affair was written when Gerbert became Pope under the name of Sylvester II and rehabilitated his rival in the see of Rheims.

About the same time, Robert the Pious (996–1031), the son and successor of Hugh Capet, contracted an unlawful union with Bertha, widow of Count Eudes of Chartres. Gregory V (995–999) excommunicated Robert and enjoined upon him a penance which was to last seven years.[1] The King submitted.

---

[1] This fact alone constitutes a sufficient refutation of the story of the alleged terrors of the year 1000. According to some writers, Michelet in particular, the whole of Christendom was seized with intense fear at the approach of that year. People imagined that the end of the world was near, abandoned their work, and lay prostrate, awaiting "the frightful hope of the judgment of God." The truth of the matter is that, as in all times of trouble and distress, uncommissioned prophets may have come forth and announced the end of the world. In no instance, however, were their assertions approved by the ecclesiastical authority. During these very days a number of synods were convoked, in which the pretended disasters were never even discussed, and at the approach of the year 1000, the construction of several important churches, notably that of Cluny, was begun. The legend no doubt originated in the be-

TEXTS AND DOCUMENTS

THE MILLENNIUM

The Middle Ages were never tainted with Millenarianism; it was foreign both to the theology of that period and to the religious ideas of the people. The fantastic views of the apocalyptic writers (Joachim of Floris, the Franciscan Spirituals, the *Apostolici*), referred only to a particular form of spiritual renovation of the Church, but did not include a second advent of Christ. The "emperor myths," which prophesied the establishment of a happy, universal kingdom by the great emperor of the future, contain indeed descriptions that remind one of the ancient Sybilline and millenarian writings, but an essential trait is again missing, the return of Christ and the connection of the blissful reign with the resurrection of the just. Hence the millennium proper is unknown to them.

J. P. Kirsch, art. *"Millennium"* in *Catholic Encyclopedia.*

QUESTIONS

1. Enumerate the causes which led to the decline of the papacy in the tenth century.
2. Define the terms: feudalism, benefice, fief, fealty, homage, investiture, vassal, patrimony, simony, vicus, patronage, suzerain.
3. What was the right of "immunity"?
4. What was the right of "seignory"?
5. What is to be thought of the pontificates of Sergius III, Leo VI, Stephen VII, John XI, and Benedict IX; do their actions militate against the Roman primacy or infallibility?
6. What was the nature of the *Privilegium Ottonis*?
7. Give an estimate of the character and learning of Gerbert.
8. Who was the first German Pope?
9. Sketch the attempts of Otto the Great to revive the Christian Empire.
10. What was the millennium?

BIBLIOGRAPHY

Feudalism in General.—Works: FUSTEL DE COULANGES, *Les origines du système féodal*, 1890; *Les transformations de la royauté pendant l'époque carolingienne*, 1892.—BOUTARIC, *Le régime féodal*, in *Rev. quest. hist.*, XVIII (1875).—J. FLACH, *Les origines de l'ancienne France*, I and II, 1886–1893.— LUCHAIRE, *Manuel des Institutions françaises*, 2nd Part, 1892.—Ch. MORTERT,

ginning of the fifteenth century, after the Great Schism had thrown a number of souls into a state of consternation and caused them to sigh for complete and general deliverance. It may well be that such persons imagined that Christians who lived in the tenth century had experienced the same aspirations. (See Dom Plaine, *Les terreurs de l'An Mil, Rev. quest. hist.*, t. XIII, 1873; J. Roy, *L'An Mil*, 1885; F. Duval, *Les Terreurs de l'An Mil*, 1908.)

art. "*Féodalité*," in *Grande Encyclopédie.*—LAVISSE, *Hist. de France*, II, ch. I. —LAVISSE and RAMBAUD, II, ch. I.—J. CALMETTE, *La féodalité* (Col. "Armand Colin"), 1923.—J. GUIRAUD, *Histoire partiale, histoire vraie*, I, ch. XX.—Msgr. LESNE, *Histoire de la propriété ecclésiastique*, t. II. *L'époque carolingienne*, 1922; art. "*Investiture*" in *Dict. d'Apol.*—*The Cambridge Medieval History*, Vol. V, *Contest of Empire and Papacy*, 1926. In two remarkable studies (*Episcopal Elections in France from the Ninth to the Eleventh Century*, 1891; *The Rural Parishes from the Fourth to the Eleventh Century*), Imbart de la Tour has demonstrated how the episcopal see became subject to the king, and the parish and monastery to the lord.

Italian Feudalism.—Sources: *Liber Pontificalis*, t. II, pp. 240 ff.—JAFFÉ, *Regesta*, I, pp. 443 ff.—Works: J. ZELLER, *Histoire d'Allemagne*, t. II and III; *Histoire résumée de l'Allemagne et de l'Empire Germanique.*—DUCHESNE, *Les origines de l'Etat Pontifical.*—LAVISSE and RAMBAUD, *Histoire générale*, I, ch XI.—DUCHESNE, *The Beginnings of the Temporal Sovereignty of the Popes* (transl. Arnold Harris Mathew).—WILLIAM BARRY, *The Papal Monarchy from St. Gregory the Great to Boniface VIII.*

John XII and Otto.—Sources: JAFFÉ, *Regesta*, I, p. 463–467.—LIUTPRAND, *Liber de rebus gestis Ottonis*, in *Mon. Germ. Hist., Script.*, III, pp. 340–346, and in *P. L.*, CXXXVI, col. 897–910.—*La Chronique de Benoit du Soracte*, in *Mon. Germ. Hist., Script.*, III, p. 714–719.—*Liber Pontificalis*, II, pp. 246–249.—*The privilegium*, in *P. L.*, CXXXVIII, col. 841–846, and in SICKEL, *Das Privilegium Ottos I für die römische Kirche*, Insbruck. 1883.— Works: A. HAUCK, *Kirchengeschichte Deutschlands*, III, pp. 220–236.— HEFELE-LECLERCQ, *Hist. des Conciles*, IV, pp. 777–816.—E. AMANN, art. "*Jean XII*," in *Dict. de Théol.*

John XIII.—Sources: *Liber Pontificalis*, II, pp. 252–254.—JAFFÉ, I, pp. 470–477.—Works: DUCHESNE, *The Beginnings of the Temporal Sovereignty of the Popes* (transl. Mathew).—HEFELE, *Hist. of the Councils*, IV.—HAUCK, *Kirchengeschichte Deutschlands*, III.—E. AMAND, art. "*Jean XIII*" in *Dict. de Théol.*

Otto III and Sylvester II.—Sources: OLLERIS, *Œuvres de Gerbert*, Clermont-Ferrand and Paris, 1867.—J. HAVET, *Lettres de Gerbert*, 1889.— Works: OLLERIS, *Vie de Gerbert*, Clermont-Ferrand, 1867.—P. COLOMBIER, *Etudes*, 1869.—U. CHEVALIER, *Gerbert*, in *La France Chrétienne dans l'histoire*, p. 143.—F. LOT, *Les derniers carolingiens* (954–981), (*Bibl. Hautes Etudes*, fasc. 87), 1891; *Etude sur le règne de Hugues Capet et la fin du X*[e] *siècle*, 1903.—PICAVET, *Gerbert, un pape philosophe d'après l'histoire et d'après la légende* (*Bibl. Ecole des Hautes Etudes, Sciences Relig.*), fasc. IX, 1897.— DUC DE LA SALE DE ROCHEMAURE, *Gerbert Sylvestre II, le savant, le faiseur des rois, le pontife*, 1921.

Henry II and Benedict VIII.—Sources: *Vita Henrici Imperat., Mon. Germ., Script.*, IV, 787 ff.—Works: HIRSCH, *Jahrb. des deutschen Reichs unter*

Heinrich II, 3 vols., Berlin, 1862–1875.—Sadée, *Die Stellung Heinrichs II zur Kirche*, Jena, 1877.—Lesêtre, *Saint Henri* (Coll. *"Les Saints"*), 1901.—H. Hemmer, art. *"Benoit VIII"* and *"Benoit IX,"* in *Dict. de Théol.*

The Gallican Revolution of 995.—F. Lot, *Les derniers Carolingiens* (954–991), 1891; *Etudes sur le règne de Hugues Capet*, 1904.—Pfister, *Robert le Pieux*, 1887.

I. The Monastic Reform: Cluny. The first reaction issued from a monastery which had succeeded in ridding itself of the overbearing influence of the secular power. The Abbey of Cluny in Burgundy had been founded in 910 by William of Aquitaine. In the very act of its foundation, the Duke had stipulated the principle which later on was destined to exercise such a saving influence: "I have deemed it prudent and wise to decree that the monks shall be free from any temporal domination, no matter whether such domination come from ourselves, our relatives, or even from the king." No one protested this decision in the land of Burgundy, the neutral zone between France and Germany, where the power of the king was counteracted by that of the emperor, and as a consequence, both were reduced to a minimum. Moreover, the monks themselves took every precaution to safeguard their freedom. On two successive occasions, as a preventive measure against intrusions, the abbot named his successor in the course of his own lifetime. Blessed Aymard named St. Mayeul, and he in turn named St. Odilo.

The importance of Cluny as an influence for good grew very rapidly. William of Aquitaine had entrusted to its first abbot, Berno, the direction of several new monasteries, notably those of Sauxillange, near Issoire (915), Déols in Berry (917), and Souvigny in Bourbonnais (921). During the administration of its second abbot, St. Odo, Cluny entered upon a period of great prosperity, thanks to many donations made by different lords. These donations included lands in the county of Mâcon, in the counties of Chalons and Lyons, in Bresse, and even in Provence. As early as 931, John XI approved the right of the monks freely to elect their abbot, at the same time authorizing Odo to spread the work of reform, "in these days when almost all monasteries are faithless to their rule." Later the good influence spread to Romainmoutier in Burgundy; to Aurillac, Tulle, and Sarlat in Aquitaine; and from there to Limoges, Solignac,

St. Jean-d'Angély, St. Allyre-de-Clermont, St. Chaffre-du-Monastier, and further to Fleury, St. Pierre-le-Vif at Sens, and St. Julien-de-Tours. St. Odo even journeyed to Italy, where Alberic, the son of Marozzia, entrusted to his care the direction of the monasteries of Rome and the surrounding country. He reformed Subiaco and an important monastery near Nepi. Very soon another reform movement, which centered around Gorze, for the dioceses of Metz, Toul, Verdun, Treves, and Liège, combined its efforts with those of Cluny, the result being that during the administration of St. Odo the good effects were felt throughout France and in Italy.

An influence of this kind was very effective. As a consequence of divisions of jurisdiction and authority into wellnigh infinitesimal parts, the system of almost complete isolation had come to be a menace for cloistered clerics, who were left without any defence against the secular power. In the interests of monachism it was imperative that its action as a body be speedy and subject to one dominant will. Now, in the monastic organizations of the West, the omnipotence of the abbot was accepted as an essential principle. In organizing the Congregation of Cluny, therefore, it was sufficient to extend the direct power of the abbot to all the monasteries. The title of abbot was suppressed in all dependent houses; the heads of these houses received the rather significant name of "prior," and were appointed directly by the abbot-general. The abbot entered into direct communication with monasteries affiliated with the mother institution by means of the general chapters, which studied the conditions of each community in particular, and designated two visitors for each province. He himself made frequent inspections of the different houses, as we learn from the lives of St. Mayeul (Majolus), St. Odilo, and especially St. Hugh, who journeyed from priory to priory. The statutes of the monastery of Cluny, drawn up by the monks Bernard and Udalric, familiarized all the houses of the Congregation with the customs and practices of the mother abbey.

Cluny sought also to emancipate itself from the tutelage of bishops, who claimed to be exercising an effective suzerainty over the abbeys. The monks were not backward in showing their resentment of episcopal interference, and by their austere lives protested most emphatically against the loose and worldly spirit of the hierarchy. They even began to question the right of bishops to make canonical visitations of the abbeys and worked to exclude them from their affairs as much as possible. In the many conflicts which arose as a consequence, the monks had the hearty support of the popes, under whose protection they had placed themselves, and who, being interested in reforming the Church, regarded the monasteries as the best instruments for that work. They were, moreover, afforded the powerful protection of the Capetian king, who also believed in their superior character. Many bitter strifes ensued: St. Odilo of Cluny had to oppose the bishop of Mâcon (1025); Foulco of Corbie, the bishop of Amiens (1049-1051), and the abbot of Reichenau, the bishop of Constance.

The monks finally triumphed and effected a reform that was destined to spread to the Church at large and to constitute a powerful aid to the papacy. Monasteries everywhere sought to affiliate themselves with Cluny; the Congregation had as many as seven provinces in France, and founded priories in Germany, Poland, Italy, and especially Spain. Other congregations began to vie with the Benedictines in zeal for the spiritual life and faithful observance of the divine and ecclesiastical laws, notably those of Hirschau (1071), very influential in Germany; Chaise-Dieu (1046); Cava in Italy (890); Sasso Vigno (1085); Sauve-Majour (1098), etc. In 982 *St. Romuald* established himself at Camaldoli in Arezzo, Tuscany, and erected a monastery equipped with thirty cells, each with a separate enclosure. This was the beginning of the Congregation of the Camaldolites, made up of hermits and cenobites. At Vallombrosa, not far from Camaldoli, *St. John Gualbert* founded a monastery the members of which lived at first under the Rule of St. Benedict, but later on embraced the cenobitic life. It was there that the monks first adopted the division of their members into choir religious and lay brothers.

England, too, received from France the principles of monastic reform. Before accepting the nomination to the archiepiscopal see of Canterbury (942), Odo begged to be clothed in the monastic habit brought to him by Abbo of Fleury. From that moment on he worked assiduously to spread the Benedictine Rule in the English monasteries. The greatest of all English reformers, however, was *St. Dunstan*. He was chancellor for a time at the court of King Eadred, but fell into disgrace as the result of many jealous connivings against him. He then withdrew to the monastery of Glastonbury, of which he was elected abbot in 940. He restored the monastery, which was badly in need of repairs, and made it the center of religious education for clergy and nobility. Called from his monastery to the see of Winchester, whence he was transferred in 959 to the archbishopric of Canterbury, Dunstan became the spiritual adviser of the young King Eadgar, and the real head of the government. At his instigation the King created no less than forty abbeys. Dunstan also convoked numerous important councils to enforce the canonical rule of celibacy among the clergy and guarantee the recruitment and election of an exemplary episcopate. Finally, the venerable Archbishop strengthened the relations between the Church in England and Rome, whither he himself went to receive the pallium. He died in 988.

II. The Reform under the Predecessors of Gregory VII. Clement II (1046–1047) had paved the way for a reform. At the Council of Rome (1047) it was decreed that "whoever received money to consecrate a church, ordain a cleric, or confer a benefice, an ecclesiastical dignity, abbey or provostship, would be excommunicated." Pope *St. Leo IX* (1048–1054) convoked another council in Rome for the same purpose, and himself travelled the length and breadth of Christendom to see to it that the papal enactments were carried out. In September, 1049, he presided in person at the Council of Mayence, and in October of the same year at that of Rheims. Moreover, he did not hesitate to enlist the aid of the secular powers, to wit, that of Henry I in France, that of Henry III in Germany, and that of Edward the Confessor in England. Under his successor, *Victor II,* numerous other synods were held to enforce these regulations, in particular at Châlons-sur-Saône and Toulouse in France, and at St. James of Compostella in Spain.

Several famous pulpit orators lent a helping hand. The most outstanding of these was *St. Peter Damian,* abbot of Fonte Avellana, later on bishop and cardinal. He travelled throughout Italy, Germany, and France preaching the moral regeneration of the clergy. His *Liber Gomorrhianus* reveals the extent of the scourge of immorality with a crudity of expression often untranslatable. This work was the signal of a sudden awakening of Christian opinion. In no other place perhaps was the response as generous as in the city of Milan, where the citizens established a confraternity called "Pataria," made up of simple folk who waged war on immoral clerics. They were headed by the two deacons, Ariald and Landulf, and for thirty years the anti-reformist party and the "Pataria" engaged in a continuous series of battles. In 1059, St. Peter Damian came to support the efforts of the reformers. His eloquence was such that Guido, archbishop of Milan, finally yielded, and both he and the principal members of his clergy solemnly promised to desist from simony and give up their incontinent habits.

These vices were too firmly rooted, however, for the work of reform to be accomplished in a day. For the results to be permanent, lay investiture, which was the real source of all these evils, had to be counteracted. And so, whereas St. Peter Damian opposed simony and concubinage by arguments that were chiefly moral in character, Cardinal Humbert, realizing that these evils were closely connected with lay investiture, attacked all three simultaneously in his treatise *Adversus Simoniacos* (1058). He compares the simoniacal cleric to a criminal who, in an attempt to carry away a young maiden already promised in marriage, endeavors to bribe her tutor with a sum of money. The maiden is the Church, the tutor, the prince who holds a church in order to sell it to the highest bidder. While not demanding the complete suppression of lay investiture as an institution, Cardinal Humbert insists on the culpability of those who sell ecclesiastical benefices. At the same time he points out that the only remedy for the evil is to subordinate the temporal to the spiritual power. His programme, therefore, was a rough outline of the reform instituted by Gregory VII.

III. Nicholas II and the Freedom of Papal Elections. The first step in this programme was to insure the freedom of the papal elections. A serious scandal furnished the occasion to effect this initial reform. After the death of Stephen IX (1057–1058) the Roman nobility and the laxer members of the clergy, supported by the powerful influence of the Tusculan party, chose John Mincius, Bishop of Velletri, who took the name of Benedict X. In the course of a regular election, however, Gerard, Bishop of Florence, was elected and ascended the papal throne as *Nicholas II*. Nicholas soon became master of the situation and published the famous edict of 1059, which settled once for all the manner of electing the Sovereign Pontiff. Henry IV retained the right to sanction the election, but it was regarded more as a personal favor. The very fact that the concession was made is clear proof that the papacy had already begun to emancipate itself from German tutelage.

IV. The Allies and Enemies of the Holy See: Normans and Greeks (Schism of Michael Cerularius). The moment was well chosen. At the death of Henry III (1054) the crown was placed on the head of a young boy, nine years of age, *Henry IV*. Hanno, Archbishop of Cologne, a devoted son of the Holy See, succeeded in having himself appointed as tutor to the young prince and began to take an active part in the government. The German party remonstrated in vain, and despite its repeated protests, Nicholas II again solemnly urged obedience to his decree. After his death the monk Hildebrand influenced the Roman faction to elect Anselm, Bishop of Lucca, who took the name of *Alexander II* (1061), but the German party struck back by electing under the direction of Henry IV, at the Synod of Basle, Cadalous, Bishop of Parma, who assumed the name of Honorius II. Hanno removed the young prince, Henry IV, from the influence of his mother, the Empress Agnes, who had sanctioned the election of Honorius, and taking the administration of the government into his own hands, called a council at Augsburg (1062) at which the election of Cadalous was declared null and void, and Alexander II proclaimed lawful pope.

The accord thus re-established was rather precarious, however, because all realized that Hanno would not always be there to protect the interests of Rome. Pope Nicholas II himself had already sensed the situation in his day and had begun to enlist the aid of powerful allies. In the opening years of the eleventh century, a host of Norman adventurers had offered their services to the Greeks of Sicily, who were constantly threatened by the Saracens. Chief among these adventurers were the sons of Tancred of Hauteville, lord of Coutances. Acting on a promise that they would receive in compensation the Island of Sicily, they gave battle to the Saracens and expelled them from the country. Upon being swindled out of their reward, however, they immediately attacked the Greek possessions in southern Italy. The allied forces of the Eastern Empire, the Holy Empire, and the papacy failed to expel them, and Pope St. Leo IX was defeated and taken prisoner at Civitate by *Robert Guiscard,* one of the sons of Tancred. The Normans, seeking to legalize their conquests, resolved to pay homage to the Holy See. Nicholas II acquiesced in the request to become their suzerain, and in return they swore that they would be faithful vassals and furnish him with troops to fight his enemies.

The papacy succeeded in enlisting the services of another even more faithful and more disinterested ally in the person of the pious Countess Matilda, who owned extensive feudal domains in the northern portion of Italy, on both sides of the Apennines, from Tuscany and the Gulf of Genoa as far as Mantua.

The invasion of southern Italy by the Normans had resulted in more intimate relations between the pope and the Greeks, in an effort to vanquish the common enemy, and the future held fair promise of a strong alliance between them, when *Michael Cerularius* plunged the Greek Church into schism. It was the secret ambition of this proud Patriarch to make the Oriental Church completely independent of Rome. As a first step in this direction he erased the name of the pope from the sacred diptychs. Then, realizing that the schism could not be of a lasting character unless it took a strong hold on the minds of the people, he set aside the complicated theological discussions that had been such a favorite weapon with Photius, and aimed more particularly at stressing certain liturgical and disciplinary differences that were apt to make an impression upon the crowd. He pushed to the front Leo of Achrida, Metropolitan of Bulgaria, and a monk by the name of Nicetas Stetathos, who in their writings revamped all the old objections against the Church of Rome, the practice of eating things strangled, fasting on Saturdays, omitting the Alleluia during the Lenten fast, but more especially using unleavened bread for the Holy Eucharist. After this preliminary press campaign, Cerularius issued orders that all the Latin churches in Constantinople be closed and anathematized their clerics, whom he dubbed "azymites." He found a thousand and one reasons for creating misunderstandings, and in his treatise against the Franks and the Latins enumerated no less than thirty-three grievances against the Catholic Church. These so-called grievances were ridiculous, but the multiplication of them could not fail to impress popular opinion.

Pope Leo IX summoned Cerularius to obedience and despatched Cardinal Humbert to Byzantium with orders to depose the Patriarch if he persisted in his revolt. The papal legate found it impossible to come to an agreement with Cerularius and solemnly excommunicated the Patriarch in the church of Santa Sophia. But the haughty prelate was not to be outdone, and so, taking advantage of his great influence, retorted by excommunicating the Pope and the Latins. But the Patriarch's days were numbered. In 1057 he deposed in his unbounded pride the Emperor Michael Strationicus and elevated to the throne in his place Isaac Comnenus. But even Isaac could not stomach his insolence, and in the very year of his elevation, exiled him to the island of Proconnesus, in the Sea of Marmora, where he died of ill-treatment (1059). His work survived him, however, and the dissensions created at the time of the Crusades are positive proof that it had already produced its desired schismatic effects. The remote origins of the schism, moreover, were very deep-rooted, to wit, Caesaro-papism, differences of language, and the contempt in which the Greeks held everyone and everything that hailed from the West.

TEXTS AND DOCUMENTS

DECREE OF THE SYNOD OF THE LATERAN ON THE ELECTION OF THE SOVEREIGN PONTIFF

Upon the death of the Pontiff of the Universal Roman Church, it shall, first of all (*imprimis*) be the duty of the Cardinal bishops to come together, and take the election [of a successor] seriously in hand; they shall next take joint action with the Cardinal clerics, and, finally, obtain the consent of the other clergy, as well as of the people, to their choice; guarding in advance against whatever might, in any way, be an occasion of bribery. If a fit person be found in the Roman Church, he is to be taken; if not, one may be sought elsewhere; provided, always, that the honor and reverence due to our beloved son Henry, at present reigning, or to any future emperor who shall have personally obtained the privilege from the Holy See, shall in no way be impaired. But if, owing to the perversity of bad and wicked men, an honest, fair, and free election cannot be had in the City [Rome], the Cardinal bishops, together with such of the clergy and Catholic laity as have a conscientious regard to duty, though few in number, may assemble where they conveniently can, and proceed to elect the bishop of the Apostolic See.

Should, however, any one acting in opposition to this our decree, promulgated with the concurrence of the Synod, secure his election, or his consecration, or his coronation by an uprising of the people, or by any unfair means whatever, he and his aiders and abettors shall be under perpetual anathema, cut off from the Church, and he himself be regarded as an antichrist, an invader and devourer of Christ's flock.

QUESTIONS

1. Which were the most important factors in effecting the monastic reform?
2. Who were the outstanding figures in this work of reform?
3. What was the origin and purpose of the Camaldolites?
4. Give a short account of the life and work of St. Dunstan.
5. List some of the achievements of St. Peter Damian.

6. Who was Cardinal Humbert?
7. Define Nicolaitism.
8. What was the outstanding event in the pontificate of Nicholas II?
9. Account for the sudden rise to power of the Normans.
10. Which were the initial steps in the Great Schism?

BIBLIOGRAPHY

Cluny.—Sources: Foundation Charter, in the *Bibliotheca Cluniacensis,* and in the *Recueils des Chartes de l'abbaye de Cluny,* published by A. BRUEL, 1876, I, p. 124.—*Consuetudines cluniacenses* in *P. L.,* CXLIX, col. 73 ff.— Works: LORAIN, *Essai historique sur l'abbaye de Cluny,* Dijon, 1859.—CU-CHERAT, *Cluny au XI⁰ siècle. Son influence religieuse, intellectuelle et politique,* Lyons, 1851.—PIGNOT, *Histoire de l'ordre de Cluny,* 1868, 3 vols.—CHAUMONT, *Histoire de Cluny,* 2nd edit., 1911.—Msgr. BAUDRILLART, *Cluny et la Papauté* in *Rev. prat. Apol.,* 1910.—E. SACKUR, *Die Cluniacenser in ihrer kirchlichen und allgemeingeschichtlichen Wirksamkeit bis zur Mitte des elften Jahrh.,* Halle, 1892–94, 2 vols.—SMITH, *The Early History of the Monastery of Cluny,* Oxford, 1920.—DOM A. DU BOURG, *Saint Odon,* Coll. "Les Saints," 1905.—DOM LHUILLIER, *Saint Hugues,* 2nd edit., 1923.—JARDET, *Saint Odilon,* Lyons, 1905. —DOM BERLIÈRE, *L'ordre monastique des origines au XII⁰ siècle.*—G. LETON-NELIER, *L'abbaye exempte de Cluny et le Saint-Siège. Etude sur le développement de l'exemption clunisienne des origines à la fin du XIII⁰ siècle,* 1924.— JOAN EVANS, *Monastic Life at Cluny,* 1931.

St. Romauld.—DOM J. BESSE, art. "Camaldules," in *Dict. de Théol.*— FRANKE, *Romuald von Kamaldoli und seine Reformtätigkeit zur Zeit Ottos III,* Berlin, 1913.

St. Dunstan.—W. E. BROWN, *Pioneers of Christendom.*—ART. "Dunstan, St." in *Cath. Encycl.,* Vol V.

The Investiture Quarrel in General.—Sources: JAFFÉ, *Regesta Pontificum Romanorum,* 1885, I.—WEILAND, *Constitutiones et acta publica imperatorum et regum,* I, in *Mon. Germ.*—*Libelli de lite imperatorum et pontificum sæculis XI et XII conscripti,* 3 vols., 1891–97, in *Mon. Germ.*—*Mon. Germ.,* SS. V and VI.—Works: A. SCHARNAGL, *Der Begriff der Investitur in den Quellen und der Litteratur des Investiturstreites,* 1908.—IMBART DE LA TOUR, *Les élections épiscopales en France du IX⁰ au XII⁰ siècle,* 1891.— MIRB, *Die Publizistik im Zeitalter Gregors VII,* 1894.—A. SOLMI, *Stato e chiesa secondo gli scritti politici de Carlomagno fino al concordato di Worms,* 1901.—J. DE GHELLINCK, *La littérature polémique durant la querelle des Investitures (Rev. quest. hist.,* 1913).—ESMEIN, *La question des Investitures dans les lettres d'Yves de Chartres,* 1889.—Msgr. LESNE, art. "Investitures," in *Dict. d'Apol.*—L. COMPAIN, *Etude sur Geoffroy de Vendôme,* 1891.— CAUCHIE, *La querelle des Investitures dans les diocèses de Liège et de Cam-*

brai, 2 vols., 1890–91.—ZELLER, *Hist. d'Allemagne.*—Msgr. WILLIAM BARRY, *The Papal Monarchy.*

The Pre-Gregorians.—A. FLICHE, *Les Prégrégoriens*, 1916; *La réforme grégorienne*, t. I: *La formation des idées grégoriennes* (*Spicil. Sacrum Lovaniense*), 1924.—DELARC, *Un pape alsacien, saint Léon IX.*—MARTIN, *Saint Léon IX.* (Coll. *"Les Saints,"* 1904).—D. R. BIRON, *Saint Pierre Damien* (Coll. *"Les Saints"*), 1908.—U. ROBERT, *Le pape Etienne IX*, Brussels, 1892.—J. GAY, *Les papes du XIe siècle et la chrétienté*, 1926.—E. AMANN, art. *"Léon IX"* in *Dict. de Théol.*

Michael Cerularius.—Sources: *Acta et scripta quae de controversiis ecclesiæ græcæ et latinæ saec. XI composita*, edit. C. Will, 1861.—*Lettre de Léon d'Achrida*, P. L., CXLIII, 929–932.—Works: J. HERGENRÖTHER, *Photius*, III, 710 ff.—W. NORDEN, *Das Papsttum und Byzanz*, Berlin, 1903.—L. BRÉHIER, *Le schisme oriental du XIe siècle*, 1899; *Les croisades*, pp. 44 ff.—JUGIE, art. *"Grecque (Eglise),"* in *Dict. d'Apol.*—S. VAILHÉ, art. *"Constantinople (Eglise de),"* in *Dict. de Théol.*—L. DUCHESNE, *The Churches Separated from Rome.*—BOUSQUET, *L'unité de l'Eglise et le schisme grec*, 1913.—ANTON MICHEL, *Humbert und Kerullarios*, Paderborn, 1925.—E. AMANN, art. *"Michel Cérulaire,"* in *Dict. de Théol.*

I. The Victory of Gregory VII over Henry IV. At the death of Alexander II, the archdeacon Hildebrand was nominated for the tiara by the vote of the people, and in order to comply with the decree of Nicholas II, the cardinals hastened to confirm the popular choice. The new Bishop of Rome was born at Soana in Tuscany, and educated at the Roman monastery of St. Mary of the Aventine. He was later called upon to direct the abbey of St. Paul and then entrusted with a diplomatic mission in France under Pope Leo IX. Hildebrand's influence assumed a universal character during the pontificate of Alexander II, but it is not true that he prompted the decree of 1059 regarding papal elections. Gregory was a true son of Cluny, imbued through and through with the spirit of reform. Above all he dreamed of completely emancipating the Church from the yoke of lay influence. And so, while urging absolute harmony between the priesthood (*sacerdotium*) and the empire (*regnum*), which, to use his own words, were "the two eyes of the world," he stressed the superior character of the sacerdotal, as contrasted with the royal, power. The latter, he pointed out, is purely human in origin and exercised merely in regard to human things. In his position as head of the ecclesiastical hierarchy, the Sovereign Pontiff is the judge of kings and emperors. It should not be thought, however, that the humble Gregory was ambitious to establish a universal monarchy; his conception of the theocratic form of government was merely intended to set limits to absolutism and to suppress the abuses and scandals caused by tyrannical rule.

The greatest of all these evils was lay investiture, since it was the root of simony and Nicolaitism. Gregory at once set himself to rid the hierarchy of this scourge. At a Roman synod held February 24-28, 1075, he promulgated this famous decree: "Whoever in future receives a bishopric or an abbacy from the hands of a layman, shall not be regarded as a bishop or an abbot. Similarly, if an emperor, a duke, a marquis or a count dares to confer an investiture in connection with a bishopric or any other ecclesiastical office, he shall be cut off from the communion of Blessed Peter." The lawful character of this decree was beyond dispute. Ecclesiastical goods bequeathed to the clergy in virtue of an irrevocable bequest, were nothing more than an appendage to their spiritual office. It is nevertheless true that the losses sustained by the princes were considerable, and perhaps no one was more profoundly affected by the decree than the Emperor Henry IV. Nowhere indeed did prelates appear richer than in Germany, nowhere were they more in the hands of the royal power, which used them to keep undisciplined lay vassals in subjection. Moreover, the kings of Germany regarded themselves as the protectors and directors of all Christendom. Their ambition was to possess not only the episcopal investitures in Germany, but also the papal investiture in Rome —all except the right of crowning the emperor, which they were willing to leave to the pope as the moral heir of Charlemagne. The battle that was about to be waged gradually expanded, until it finally issued more or less in a gigantic struggle between the priesthood and the empire.

Henry IV resigned himself in the beginning. Reared amidst dissensions of all kinds, prompted by lords who disputed the imperial power during his minority, he emerged a confirmed debauchee and despot when he finally ascended the throne. Very soon neighboring princes sought to shake off his yoke, and in Saxony they were already talking of electing Rudolph, Duke of Suabia, in his place. A precarious situation of this kind is ample explanation why Henry IV at first accepted the decree against lay investiture. He was anxious to secure the aid of Gregory VII, and with this end in view, despatched to him letters filled with sentiments of false loyalty. But the Emperor quickly changed his tactics when he had succeeded in defeating German feudalism; he knew, moreover, that he could count on the aid of a portion of the German clergy. In direct opposition to the papal decree, he himself nominated three prelates in Italy, gave the see of Bamberg to one of his protégés, and insisted on imposing the candidate of his choice upon the clergy and people of Cologne in spite of their protests. Gregory tried in vain to make him listen to reason. He sent him a letter overflowing with kindness and consideration, which Henry deliberately interpreted as a papal summons, demanding under threat of excommunication that he appear before an ecclesiastical tribunal in Rome. He refused to heed the Pontiff's exhortations, but instead, convoked a meeting of German bishops at Worms and proceeded to depose the Pope (January 24, 1076). The decree of deposition was sent to the Pope with the insulting statement: "Henry, king, not by usurpation, but by the will of God, to Hildebrand, who is no longer Pope, but a false monk. Having been condemned by the sentence of our bishops, and by our sentence, vacate the place which thou hast usurped." Gregory replied by pronouncing excommunication against Henry at a council held at the Lateran, and formally releasing the Emperor's subjects from their oath of allegiance.

Gregory's action in Germany had the effect of detaching many newly reformed bishops and members of the clergy from the imperial cause, and of encouraging the lay feudalists to renewed activity. In October 1076, the bishops and princes of the Empire met at Tribur near Mayence and decreed that Henry's fate should be decided on Candlemas day at Augsburg, at a council presided over by Gregory VII in person. Meanwhile Henry was to abstain from all exercise of the royal power.

Henry knew that he was lost if the Pope arrived to judge him publicly, and so advanced the day of his summons. In the dead of the winter of 1077, he crossed the Alps amid the greatest hardships, and finally arrived at the castle of Canossa, where Gregory, already on his way to Germany, was being entertained by his devoted friend, the Countess Matilda. On January 25 the King appeared before the ramparts of the castle in penitential garb and for three days voluntarily did penance within the precincts of the castle. "Won over at last by the persevering character of his repentance," wrote Gregory VII some time later, "we received him back into the grace of communion."

The outward appearances of the scene at Canossa may cause a prejudiced person to interpret it in terms of an insolent triumph of theocracy. It must be observed, however, that the penance imposed upon Henry had nothing extraordinary or arbitrary about it, and was quite in keeping with the disciplinary regulations of that period. Moreover, Henry IV subjected himself to it voluntarily. If Gregory VII sinned at Canossa, it was more from an excess of charity than from undue severity. He had his opponent in the palm of his hand and certainly could well have suspected the insincere character of his repentance and acted accordingly. A few weeks later, the Diet of Augsburg assured his complete triumph, and

Henry was deposed. Meanwhile, however, having been pardoned at Canossa, the deposed Emperor remained a dangerous enemy. Gregory VII did nothing more than allow himself to be swayed by Christian charity and kindness rather than by the harsh methods of a calculating politician, and he yielded to the entreaties of Countess Matilda and Hugh of Cluny, at the risk of estranging his own supporters in Germany.

II. **Triumph and Fall of Henry IV.** In order to regain possession of his throne, Henry IV had to await the decree of his solemn reconciliation, which was to be issued in the presence of a large assembly in Germany by the Pope himself. Encouraged by his followers, however, the King violated his promises. His opponents met at the Diet of Forchheim, declared him deposed, and elected as his successor his brother-in-law, Rudolph of Suabia. Gregory VII showed himself patient for two more years, until the day when Henry demanded that he recognize him or be resigned to see an antipope installed in his place. The Pope was then obliged to fulminate a double sentence of excommunication and deposition. Henry retaliated at the Synod of Brixen by setting up Bishop Wibert of Ravenna as antipope (1080).

The events which followed seemed at first to justify Henry's conduct. His rival Rudolph fell in the battle of Merseburg, and Henry immediately set out for Italy. After a siege of three months he gained possession of the City of Rome (1084), and had himself crowned Emperor in the Lateran Basilica by the antipope, Clement III, whom he had installed in the see of St. Peter. Gregory took refuge in the Castle of Sant' Angelo and was about to be taken prisoner, when his Norman vassal, Robert Guiscard, came to his rescue with a powerful army and forced the Germans to retreat. In the course of a dispute, however, which arose between the Normans and the Romans, the city was pillaged and set on fire, the flames extending from the Coliseum to the Lateran, and levelling an entire Roman quarter to the ground. Gregory VII was no longer safe in the midst of a people exasperated by the many misfortunes that had befallen him. He followed the Normans, when they withdrew from Italy, and spent the last months of his life at Monte Cassino, and at Salerno. It was here that he died, May 25, 1085. His last words, which constitute a fit epitaph for one of the greatest of the popes, were: "I have loved justice and hated iniquity, therefore I die in exile." He was canonized by Pope Paul V, in 1606.

Victor III, who succeeded him after a vacancy of eleven months, reigned only a short time (1086–1087). Six months later, Otto, Cardinal Bishop of Ostia, was elected pope under the name of *Urban II*. He remained faithful to the programme of Gregory, and at the Council of Melfi (1089) the prohibition to take the oath of allegiance to a lay suzerain was added to the prohibition to receive lay investiture. Henry IV still remained obstinate. In 1090 he invaded Italy a second time, but encountered the sturdy resistance of the Countess Matilda. Betrayed by his son Conrad, whom he had crowned king of the Romans at the age of nineteen, and accused of the basest crimes by his wife Adelaide, he retraced his steps to Germany. His second son, Henry, also turned against him. Finally, he was forced to abdicate and died in exile.

The prestige of the papacy, on the contrary, increased from day to day. At the Council of Clermont, where the decrees against lay investiture were renewed, Urban II armed the whole of Christendom (1095) and, thanks to the Crusaders, regained possession of his capital. His successor, Pascal II, witnessed the end of the imperial schism. Clement III died in 1100, and the reigns of his three successors were uneventful. The work of Henry IV seemed to have been completely undone.

III. Moral Reform of the Clergy. Gregory not only fought against simony, but also engaged in a bitter war against Nicolaitism. At a Roman council held in 1074, he issued the following decree: "Priests who have committed the sin of fornication are not to be permitted to celebrate Mass. . . . We also declare that the faithful may not, under any circumstances, assist at the Masses celebrated by such priests or receive the Sacraments at their hands. Our purpose in making these regulations is to move those who have become immune to the love of God or the dignity of their functions, by human respect and the censorship of the people." Gregory despatched legates to every country to see to it that these orders were carried out. Some of these legates were entrusted with a temporary mission, as was the case with Cardinals Peter of Albano and Odo of Ostia, or such fearless monks as St. Hugh of Cluny. Others received a permanent commission for a whole kingdom, and their duties in this regard were incorporated in those of their episcopate. This was the case with Altmann of Passau in Germany and of Amatus of Oloron and Hugh of Die in France. These legates convoked councils in the name of the pope, suspended and deposed clerics, and referred to Rome the cases of bishops who refused to carry out the papal decrees. They worked with extraordinary vigor and rapidity, but the resistance they encountered was at times no less energetic. Thus Altmann of Passau was threatened by clerics and almost stoned to death, a synod held at Paris protested vehemently, and the clerics of the city of Cambrai refused to heed any of the legate's exhortations.

Gregory's tenacity won out in the end, and ecclesiastical celibacy was slowly re-established. Urban II crowned his work at the Council of Melfi, where, not content with pursuing sinful clerics, he also punished their concubines, and in case they offered resistance, invested the rulers of the places where they lived with the right to carry them away into slavery. Under the administration of the same pope, but especially under that of Callixtus II, regulations were passed which ramified even into the domain of the Sacraments. The marriage of clerics in major Orders was declared null and void; and in the twelfth century the Councils of the Lateran (1123 and 1139) and the Synods of Pisa (1135) and Rheims (1148) confirmed this decision. If we compare the state of an ecclesiastical province in the middle of the eleventh century with the state of this same province at the end of the twelfth century, we become fully aware of the efficacy of the remedies applied.

IV. The Political Ideas of Gregory VII. The great merit of Gregory VII lay in his complete understanding of the deeper causes of the crisis. He was quick to perceive that only one way was open to emancipate the Church from the domineering influence of princes, and that was, to strengthen the authority of the pope. His plan of attack has given us the famous *"Dictatus Papae,"* a small collection of formulas inserted in the Register of Gregory, which determine not only the Roman prerogatives, but also the relations of the Holy See with secular princes. The same political ideas are to be found in his two letters to Bishop Hermann of Metz (August 25, 1076; May 15, 1081), where the spiritual primacy of the pope is set forth with all its political inferences. He agrees that two powers rule the world, the priestly power and the royal power, but insists that the latter must always be subject to the former. The popes, therefore, have the right to judge kings and emperors, and even to depose them, if they see fit: "When Christ gave to the blessed Peter the power of binding and loosing, he excepted no one and exempted nothing."

A supremacy of this nature, however, does not confer upon the pope any temporal sovereignty, and Gregory VII makes it very clear that it is not his intention to undermine the lawful authority of the secular rulers. "In matters which concern the service and fidelity due to kings," he wrote, "we have no intention to deny their rights nor to place any obstacle in their way." When the Gallicans ascribed to him the theory of "the purely human and diabolical origin of the State," they interpreted in an absolute sense words which he had used to stress the evil character of any established power which is exercised for the purpose of undermining the Christian faith.

There is no doubt that some over-zealous exponents of the political ideas of Gregory VII have exaggerated the papal theses. This is true, for instance, of the Alsacian monk Manegold, whose monastery at Lautenbach had been destroyed by the imperialists. He spent much time elaborating the contractual theory, according to which royalty derives its origin from a conditional agreement entered into between subjects who promise fidelity, and the king who binds himself to govern them in all justice. If the ruler is unfaithful to his promises, the subjects are, of course, released from their oath of allegiance.

In contradistinction to the political ideas of St. Gregory the Caesarists stress the divine origin of the monarchical power, basing their argument on Roman law, according to which sovereignty is derived from God by way of succession in such wise that one may neither condemn nor depose the king, nor, *a fortiori,* the emperor, who is vested with universal power over all peoples. Such is the power (*potestas*) inherited in direct line from Augustus and Tiberius, and to which applies the absolutist formula given by Sallust: *"Nam impune facere quod libet, id est regem esse"* (It is the privilege of the king to do as he pleases with impunity).

Besides attempting a solution of the problem of investitures, therefore, the Gregorian controversy brought to light two opposing and irreconcilable theories regarding sovereignty. According to the first theory, this power is of divine right and incapable of being lost; according to the second, it is essentially revocable. The triumph of the political ideas of St. Gregory inaugurated a new order of things, in which the lay powers accept or undergo the protection of the Church, instead of imposing their rule upon her. The reformers intended to restore the ancient right by re-establishing the freedom of canonical elections and making bishops and abbeys independent of their lay patrons or benefactors. In point of fact their efforts resulted in profound changes throughout feudal Europe. The Gregorian reform was more than a reform—it was a revolution, for it regenerated the entire Church and rendered her capable of directing Christendom without the assistance of the Empire.

TEXTS AND DOCUMENTS

GREGORY VII DEPOSES HENRY IV

Confident of my integrity and authority, I now declare, in the name of the omnipotent God, the Father, the Son, and the Holy Ghost, that Henry, son of the Emperor Henry, is deprived of his kingdom of Germany and Italy. I do this by thy [St. Peter's] authority and in defense of the honor of thy Church, because he has rebelled against it. He who attempts to destroy the honor of the Church should be deprived of such honor as he may have held. He has refused to obey as a Christian should; he has not returned to God from whom he had wandered; he has had dealings with excommunicated persons; he has done many iniquities; he has despised the warnings which, as thou art witness, I sent to him for his salvation; he has cut himself off from thy Church, and has attempted to rend it asunder; therefore, by thy authority, I place him under the ban. It is in thy name that I bind him with the chain of the anathema, that all people may know that thou art Peter, and upon thy rock the Son of the living God has built His Church, and the gates of hell shall not prevail against it.

> Translated in *Source Book for Mediaeval History* (Thatcher and McNeal), pp. 155–156.

QUESTIONS

1. On what grounds did Pope Gregory VII base his right to depose Henry IV?
2. Why has the triumph of the Church in the investiture quarrel been called a turning point in the history of civilization?
3. List the outstanding events in the quarrel between Gregory VII and Henry IV.
4. Write an estimate of the character of Pope Gregory VII.
5. What steps did Gregory VII take to reform the morals of the clergy?
6. Outline the political theory advocated by Gregory VII.
7. What is meant by the divine right of kings?

BIBLIOGRAPHY

Gregory VII.—Sources: *Works,* in *P. L.,* CXLVIII.—Works: DELARC, *Saint Grégoire VII,* 3 vols., 1890–92.—FLICHE, *Le règne de Philippe I,* 1912; *Grégoire VII* (Coll. *"Les Saints"*), 1922; *Les théories germaniques de la souveraineté* in *Rev. hist.,* CXXV, 1917, p. 1–67. *La réforme grégorienne,* t. II, *Grégoire VII* (*Spicil. Sacrum Lovaniense*), 1926.—CHALANDON, *Histoire de la domination normande en Italie et en Sicile,* 1907, 2 vols.—P. MONCELLE, art. *"Grégoire VII,"* in *Dict. de Théol.,* and in a general way the same bibliography as for the Investiture Quarrel.—J. GAY, *Les papes du XIe siècle et la chrétienté,* 1926.—E. VOOSEN, *Papauté et pouvoir civil à l'époque de Grégoire VII,* Gembloux, 1927.—A. H. MATHEW, *The Life and Times of Hildebrand, Pope Gregory VII,* London, 1910.—E. W. WILMOT-BUXTON, *The Story of Hildebrand, St. Gregory VII,* London, 1920.

Canossa.—Sources: LAMBERT OF HERSFELD, *Annales ad ann. 1076–1077,* *P. L.,* CXLVI, or in *Mon. Germ. Scriptores,* V.—Works: P. GUILLEUX, art. *"Canossa,"* in *Dict. d'Apol.*—J. GAY, *op. cit.,* p. 261.

Urban II.—PAULOT, *Un pape français, Urbain II.*—FLICHE, *Le règne de Philippe Ier; L'Election d'Urbain II* (*Revue Moyen Age,* 1916); *Leçons sur la crise religieuse de 1085 à 1088* (*Rev. des cours et conférences,* 1922–23).—RIANT, *Un dernier triomphe d'Urbain II* (*Rev. Quest. Hist.,* 1883, XXXIV, pp. 247–255).—J. GAY, *op. cit.*—RONY, *Election de Victor III* in *R. H. E. F.,* 1928, pp. 145–160.

The successors of Gregory VII adhered to his policies, although they used different methods in carrying them out. Gregorians and Imperialists had both proposed a solution to end the quarrel over investitures. For the Imperialists, the ecclesiastical function (*episcopatus*) is the business of the king, just like properties or revenues (*regalia*), and the bishop is a mere vassal, just like all other vassals. For the Gregorians the goods attached to a benefice belong to the Church, just like the ecclesiastical function itself, and the Church is the rightful owner of the one and the other. Both theories, therefore, imply that the spiritual and the temporal are so intimately connected that the investiture of the one goes with the investiture of the other. A Gregorian, Geoffroy de Vendôme, even went so far as to claim that investiture was "a sacrament," and that one should receive it only from a person who is able to confer consecration.

Towards the end of this century a more satisfactory solution was reached. In the opinion of several writers, Gregory VII had been too exorbitant in his demand that princes renounce all right to confer the investiture, and some went so far as to raise the question whether or not his teaching in this respect constituted a point of doctrine. Yvo of Chartres did not hesitate to answer this question in the negative, stating that the decree forbidding lay investiture was merely the outcome of circumstances and could be modified later to suit other circumstances. And so, while advocating strictly Gregorian principles on the relations between Church and State, he was willing to grant that an investiture that was concerned merely with temporal goods could be licit. His solution struck a happy mean between the solution of the Gregorians and that of the Imperialists, and ended by being generally accepted.

I. The Situation in Germany: Pascal II at Sutri (1111); Callixtus II at Worms (1122). Henry V, like his father, showed himself an obedient son of the Church as long as the imperial crown did not rest firmly on his head. But after he had become the undisputed master of the Empire (1109), he appeared in Italy, presumably to have himself crowned at Rome, but in reality with the intention of imposing his views on Pascal II. At this juncture the Pope, desirous to re-establish peace and harmony, proposed a solution to the problem which was as unexpected as it was unselfish. All the *regalia* were to be returned to the king, and the clergy were to take as their only means of support the tithes and voluntary offerings of the faithful.

By a sacrifice of this kind, Pascal II deprived the lay power of the right to confer the investiture, and set the Church free, while reducing her to poverty. This move exposed the Church to new dangers, for the loss of temporal goods left the prelates a prey to their enemies, and without any means of defence in the midst of an anarchical society. Moreover, the lay feudalism was not ready to admit that the Church could dispossess herself in this way to the distinct advantage of the king, already too powerful in the opinion of the barons. Finally, a number of laymen who held as fiefs lands belonging to episcopal sees, did not relish the idea of losing them, but were all for keeping the lords and dukes in power. And so, when the agreement was read in the Church of St. Peter's in Rome, it was received with protests. Thinking that he was caught in a trap, Pascal II refused to crown the Emperor. A brawl ensued between the Romans and the Germans, and Henry, infuriated, seized the person of the Sovereign Pontiff. A prisoner in the hands of the German Emperor and fearful for the life of his cardinals and clerics, Pascal II experienced a moment of weakness. He granted Henry V the right to confer the investiture with the crosier and the ring, on condition that the elections themselves should be free and unhampered. He then crowned the king, who returned to Germany.

The affair was not ended, however, for a council held at the Lateran declared that the concession made to Henry had been obtained by force; that it was not a *privilegium,* but a *pravilegium.* In France, the Council of Vienne declared that lay investiture was tainted with heresy and excommunicated the Emperor. In Germany the assembly of Gosslar anathematized Henry (1115). The Emperor then made a second expedition into Italy and seized most of the possessions of the Countess Matilda, but Pascal II had learned his lesson and refused him an interview (1116).

Gelasius II adopted the same attitude as his predecessor, and consequently Henry V set up an antipope in the person of Maurice Bourdin, who took the name of Gregory VIII (1118-1121). Gelasius fled to France and died at Cluny, January 29, 1119. His successor, Guy of Vienne, took the name of *Callixtus II*. He immediately convoked a council at Rheims, and sent legates to the Emperor to discuss peace terms. Henry displayed bad faith, however, and the Pope was forced to sever relations, pronounce excommunication against him, and release his subjects from their oath of allegiance. Public opinion pronounced itself in favor of the papacy. Callixtus II returned to Italy amidst scenes of great rejoicing, and the Antipope was taken prisoner. In Germany, the lay feudality issued a formal declaration to the effect that it would not obey the Emperor so long as he did not petition the Pope to lift the excommunication. Callixtus II showed himself willing to effect a reconciliation, and in 1122 the long struggle was finally settled by the *Concordat of Worms,* which was solemnly confirmed in 1123 by the Ninth General Council, *First Council of the Lateran.*

In this agreement both parties made important concessions. Since the bishop was the owner of both an episcopal see and a fief, it was agreed to confer upon him two investitures. The religious investiture with the crosier and the ring was to take place after the regular election, conducted by the canons of the cathedral Church and conferred by a prelate delegated by the pope; the feudal investiture with the sceptre and the sword was to be conferred by the emperor. A solution of this kind constituted a distinct triumph for the Gregorian ideas, since it emancipated the Church from lay servitude. The papacy, satisfied with this essential point, recognized the right of the prince to confer the temporal investiture in keeping with the political situation of the times. The thesis outlined by Yvo of Chartres was thus completely vindicated.

In France the quarrel was never quite so acute. Ecclesiastical lords did not have the same importance there as in Germany. Moreover, the investiture of episcopal sees and abbeys was divided between the kings and several great barons, like the counts of Champagne and Anjou, etc. The sacrifices which the lay power in France was constrained to make, therefore, were small in comparison with those made in Germany. On the other hand, the popes showed themselves very accommodating in the hope of securing the powerful assistance of the Capetian king against the emperor. It is true that, under the pontificate of Gregory VII, the legate Hugh of Die displayed a sense of justice that was somewhat rigid, and convoked councils at Autun and Poitiers (1077) to expedite the work of reform, but the Pope moderated his zeal. It is true also that Urban II engaged in an open conflict with Philip I, but his principal reason for doing so was to reprimand the King for his incestuous union with Bertrade, the wife of Count Fulco of Anjou. An agreement based on the principle of the separation of the two investitures was finally reached, when Pascal II, in order to escape from the persecution of Henry V, withdrew to France.

II. The Situation in England: St. Anselm's Conflict with William Rufus and Henry I Beauclerk. It might be well to observe that, in the mind of Gregory VII, the decree regarding investitures was not an end in itself, but a means to reform the clergy. This accounts for his not exacting that the decree be carried out in countries where civil authority co-operated to obtain acceptable episcopal nominations. This was the case in England under William the Conqueror (1066-1087), a friend of Lanfranc, Primate of England, who saw to it that clerical celibacy was everywhere strictly observed. But during the reign of William II, called Rufus, the whole situation underwent a profound change. William was a confirmed spendthrift and soon found himself obliged to replenish the royal coffers, which had been almost completely drained to satisfy his cravings for pleasure. He began to eye covetously the goods of the Church, and soon discovered that they could be of great assistance in achieving his purpose. In the first place, the revenues of a vacant bishopric could be legally collected by the king, and so William decided to leave several sees without incumbents; at his death one archbishopric, four bishoprics, and eleven abbeys were without titulars. In the second place, he sold those sees which he consented to fill to the highest bidder, going so far as to determine himself the price to be paid. In the third place, the royal investiture, according to him, reduced prelates to such a state of subjection that they could not transact any important business, and above all could not communicate with Rome, without the king's express permission. On the last two points William was drawn into a bitter conflict with *St. Anselm,* the successor of Lanfranc. The King reproached Anselm for not having furnished him with a large enough gift on the occasion of his appointment to the archiepiscopal see of Canterbury. He argued, moreover, that since he had not yet decided whether to take sides with Urban II or the imperial Pope, he could forbid the primate to journey to Rome to solicit the pallium. St. Anselm was betrayed successively by the assemblies of Rockingham (1095) and Winchester (1097), which had not the courage to offend the King, and so he finally decided to leave England. He assisted at the councils of Bari and Rome, which protested forcefully against lay investiture with the crosier and the ring. At the death of William Rufus, however, he returned to England (1100).

The new king, Henry I, was a cunning diplomat and at bottom more dangerous than his brutal predecessor. He demanded that St. Anselm render homage to him and consecrate only those bishops who were named by royal authority. The king and the primate referred the whole matter to Rome, and at the Assembly of London (1102) Anselm exhibited a papal letter which re-affirmed the interdict against lay investiture. Moreover, the clergy began to protest, and several bishops who had been nominated by the king resigned. To rid himself of Anselm, Henry suggested that he make a trip to Rome. But the events which followed turned to Henry's distinct disadvantage, for the Council of Rome excommunicated his advisers (1105), and his brother Robert rose up in rebellion against him. At this juncture Henry deemed it advisable to recall Anselm. An interview took place between them at Laigle in Normandy, and soon an understanding was reached, the terms of which were drawn up by the papacy itself. The Pope decided that former beneficiaries named by the King would not be molested, but that in the future bishops should be freely elected and then invested with crosier and ring. It was only after this ceremony that they would be required to do homage to the king. Freed for a time, the Church in England was placed in a position where it could enter into more intimate relations with Rome, for the appeal *ad limina,* the reception of legates *a latere,* and the ratification of elections by the papacy were one and all authorized.

It must be acknowledged, moreover, that the Norman kings rendered many services to the Church. Anxious to adorn England with several large abbeys, they appealed to the monks on the Continent, especially to those of Cluny and Citeaux, to the canons of St. Augustine, and to the Norbertines. The monks at once set themselves to cultivating the soil in this new land, and also to editing many valuable annals, which constitute a unique history of this period. Among others, we may cite the *Chronica* of Florence of Worcester (up to the year 1119); the *Historia Novarum* of Eadmer of Canterbury, a work of first importance as regards the Norman kings (1060–1122); the *De Gestis Regum Anglorum* of William of Malmesbury, supplemented by his *Historia Novella,* which runs as far as the year 1142.

III. The Conflict Between St. Thomas à Becket and Henry II Plantagenet. The Norman kings were succeeded in 1154 by the Plantagenets. The founder of this dynasty, Henry II, Duke of Anjou, promptly opened hostilities. He argued that ecclesiastical tribunals were not strict enough in regard to clerics and used this pretext to restrict the privileges of the forum. The assembly of Westminster decided that a royal official should be appointed for every ecclesiastical tribunal. The sixteen articles of the Assembly of Clarendon, better known as the "Constitutions of Clarendon," among other things state that clerics accused of any offence were to appear before the ecclesiastical court and the royal tribunal and that if they confessed or were convicted, the Church was to abandon them to the secular arm; that appeals in Church matters were to be made first to the archdeacon, then to the bishop, and finally to the archbishop; that no recourse to higher authority, such as that of the pope, could be permitted; that archbishops and bishops were obliged, like all the king's other vassals, to obey the royal officials and fulfill all the obligations of fief-holding; that bishops could not leave the kingdom without the king's permission and without taking an oath that they would refrain from any actions that would result in injury to the king and his kingdom; that vacant sees were in the hands of the king, who had the right to collect the revenues; that the election to a vacant see must be made in the king's chapel and with his consent; and, finally, that bishops-elect must take the oath of faithful vassals before receiving episcopal consecration.

To carry out these plans, the King reckoned on the aid of his primate and former chancellor, Thomas à Becket, who had, however, suddenly forsaken his worldly ways and embraced a life of rigid austerity; it was only with the deepest regret that he consented to countersign the Constitutions of Clarendon. He withdrew his approbation from them when he was reprimanded by the Pope and summoned to appear before the assembly of Northampton, forbade the bishops to take any part in his trial, and appealed his case to Rome. He himself appeared before the tribunal, vested in his pontifical robes, was found guilty of treason, and condemned. Taking advantage of a storm which broke out the following night, Thomas made his escape, and reached the Flemish coast. Henry was furious, swore that he would be avenged on the traitor, expelled from England all his kinsmen, and confiscated the domains of the abbey of Pontigny, which had afforded him protection. Thomas retorted by excommunicating all the king's partisans, and at the same time surrounded himself with powerful allies. Alexander III upheld him energetically, although he was averse to breaking entirely with Henry II, for fear that the latter would ally himself with Frederick Barbarossa. King Louis VII of France, who saw in Henry II a dangerous neighbor because he owned both Anjou and Guyenne, supported the contentions of the primate. Yielding to the entreaties of the French King, Thomas à Becket and Henry agreed to meet at Fréteval, July 22, 1170. Henry yielded, but in spoken words only, and authorized the Primate to return to England.

One of the Archbishop's first official acts was to excommunicate the bishops of London and Salisbury and to suspend the bishop of Durham and the archbishop of York. Henry was at one of his castles in Normandy at the time, and bursting into a violent passion exclaimed, "What a pack of fools and cowards I have nourished in my house, that not one of them will rid me of this insolent priest." Four knights who were present and heard the King's words, immediately rode to Canterbury, where they assassinated Thomas à Becket in his cathedral (December 29, 1170). Pope Alexander III demanded public reparation for the crime, and Henry did penance for his rash words, in the presence of the papal legates, in the cathedral of Avranches (May 22, 1172). He was asked to withdraw the Constitutions of Clarendon, promise not to prevent further appeals to the Holy See, and finally to acknowledge his indebtedness for his kingdom to the Pope, in the following terms: "I and my eldest son swear that we will receive and retain the kingdom of England from the Lord Alexander, Pope, and his Catholic successors, and we and our successors will not consider ourselves true kings of England until they have recognized us as Catholic kings."

TEXTS AND DOCUMENTS

The Concordat of Worms (1122)

"I, Callixtus, bishop, servant of the servants of God, grant to you, my beloved son Henry, by the grace of God august Emperor of the Romans, that the elections of bishops and abbots in the kingdom of Germany, which belong to said kingdom, take place in your presence, without simony and without violence of any sort. Should any differences arise between the parties concerned, you, acting with the advice and judgment of the metropolitan and the bishops of the province, will give your assent and lend your assistance to the most worthy party. The candidate will receive from you the *regalia* by the sceptre, without any constraint, except such as belonged to the Roman Church, and he in turn will fulfill towards you any duties which arise from the possession of such *regalia*. Any candidate who has already been consecrated in some other part of the Empire will receive from you the *regalia* by the sceptre, without any constraint, within the space of six months. In the event of your having to make complaints to me or seek my aid, I shall come to your assistance according to the obligations of my office. I hereby give you and all those who, throughout this quarrel, sponsor or have sponsored your cause, a sincere peace."

"I, Henry, by the grace of God, august Emperor of the Romans, for the love of God, the Holy Roman Church, and the Lord Pope Callixtus, as also for the salvation of my soul, leave to God and to His blessed Apostles Peter and Paul all investitures by the crozier and the ring, and hereby promise that, in all the churches of my kingdom or my empire, the elections shall take place according to the canonical regulations, and that the consecration of bishops shall be free and unhampered. I restore to the Holy Roman Church those goods and *regalia* belonging to St. Peter, which, from the outset of this quarrel until to-day, were taken from him either during the lifetime of my father, or during my own lifetime, and which are still in my possession. As to the goods which are not in my possession, I will do all in my power to see that they are faithfully restored. I shall return also, with the advice of princes and in conformity with the virtue of justice, the goods of other churches, princes, clerics, and private individuals, which they have lost in the course of this conflict and which are in my possession. As to those goods which are not in my possession, I will do all in my power to see that they are faithfully returned. I hereby accord a sincere peace to Pope Callixtus, to the Holy Roman Church, and to all those who sponsor or who have sponsored its cause. I will faithfully assist the Roman Church in the event of her calling upon me for aid, and will deal with her in all justice as often as I receive any complaint."

Monum. Germ. Hist., Leges, II, p. 76.

QUESTIONS

1. Discuss the respective merits of the solutions proposed by the Gregorians and the Imperialists to end the Investiture quarrel.
2. What is to be thought of the solution proposed by Pope Pascal II?
3. Why was the quarrel of the Investitures more acute in Germany than in any other country?

4. Which causes were responsible for the conflict between St. Anselm and William Rufus?
5. What service did the Norman kings render to the Church in England?
6. What is the importance of the "Constitutions of Clarendon"?
7. Discuss the character of St. Thomas à Becket.

BIBLIOGRAPHY

Pascal II.—Works: G. Peiser, *Der Deutsche Investiturstreit unter Kaiser Heinrich V. bis zum päpstlichen Privileg vom s. April 1111*, Berlin, 1883.—J. Röskens, *Kaiser Heinrich V. und Papst Paschalis*, 1885.—Zeller, *op. cit.*—B. Monod, *Pascal II. et Philippe I.* (*Bibl. Hautes Etudes*, fasc. 164), 1907.—A. Fliche, *Philippe Ier.*—Hefele-Leclercq, V, p. 465.

Callixtus II.—Sources: U. Robert, *Bullaire du pape Calixte II*, 2 vols., 1891.—Letters and *opuscula supposita*, P. L., CLXIII, col. 1093.—Works: U. Robert, *Histoire du pape Calixte II*, 1891.—F. Rocquain, *La cour de Rome, et l'esprit de Réforme avant Luther*, I, pp. 138-149, 1893.—H. Hemmer, art. "*Calixte II*," in *Dict. de Théol.*

St. Anselm.—Sources: *P. L.*, CLVIII and CLIX (edit. Dom Gerberon).—Works: Porée, *Histoire de l'abbaye du Bec*, Evreux, 1901.—Freeman, *The reign of William Rufus and the accession of Henry the First*, 2 vols., Oxford, 1882.—F. Ragey, *Histoire de saint Anselme*, 2 vols., 1890.—P. Richard, art. "*Anselme de Cantorbéry*," in *Dict. d'Hist.*—Green, *History of the English People*.—Bainvel, art. "*Anselme*," in *Dict. de Théol.*—J. J. Walsh, *The Thirteenth the Greatest of Centuries.*—Joseph Clayton, *St. Anselm*, 1933.

St. Thomas à Becket.—Sources: Robertson, *Materials for the History of Thomas à Becket*, 9 vols., London, 1875-85.—*Vitæ s. Thomæ*, P. L., CXC, 1-363 and 1070-1291; *Epistolæ*, ibidem, 369-671.—Mansi, XXI, 872.—Works: Morris, *Life and Martyrdom of St. Thomas Becket*, London, 1886.—Hutton, *St. Thomas of Canterbury*, London, 1899.—Dom Lhuillier, *Saint Thomas de Cantorbéry*, 2 vols., 1891-92.—A. du Boys, *Saint Thomas Becket d'après des documents récents*, Rev. Quest. Hist., 1882, XXXII, 353 ff.—L. Halphen, *Les entrevues des rois Louis VII et Henri II durant l'exil de Thomas Becket en France*, in *Mélanges Bémont*, 1913.—Lavisse et Rambaud, t. II, ch. XI.—Green, *History of the English People*.—W. H. Hutton, *Thomas à Becket*, Cambridge, 1926.—S. Dark, *S. Thomas of Canterbury*, London, 1927.—R. H. Benson, *Life of Thomas à Becket*.—Msgr. Demimuid, *St. Thomas à Becket*, New York, 1909.—Sidney Dark, *St. Thomas of Canterbury*.

FOURTH PERIOD

Christendom During the Twelfth and Thirteenth Centuries

SECTION I

Twelfth Century: From the Concordat of Worms to the Advent of Innocent III (1122–1198)

CHAPTER I

BEGINNINGS OF THE QUARREL BETWEEN GUELPHS AND GHIBELLINES

The Guelphs and the Ghibellines were two political factions which kept Italy in a constant state of division during the Middle Ages. The names originated in Germany and can be traced to the rivalry between the House of Welf (Bavaria) and the House of Hohenstaufen, whose ancestral castle was located at Waiblingen in Suabia. When the wars for the imperial crown in Germany and Italy were inaugurated by Otto of Bavaria and Philip of Suabia in the closing years of the twelfth century, the names of the rival parties were introduced into Italy. Guelfo and Ghibellino are the Italian forms of Welf and Waiblingen. The former name designated the partisans of the pope, and the latter the partisans of the German emperor. In the course of events the popes favored the growth of the Communes, so that the Guelphs became identified with the republican party. The Ghibellines represented the feudal lords of Teutonic origin. The cities of Italy were divided in their allegiance, Florence and Milan being Guelph, while Siena and Pisa were Ghibelline.

I. The Roman Anarchy: The Schism of Anacletus and the Republic of Arnold. After the death of Pope Honorius II (1124–1130) the Pierleoni and the Frangipani [1] fought each other to impose upon the Sacred College the candidate of their respective choice. Haimeric,

---

[1] The Pierleoni derived their name from Pietro Pierleone, the antipope Anacletus II; the Frangipani were an ancient Roman family who represented the opposing faction. (Transl.)

the chancellor of the late Pope, had Cardinal Gregory, a protégé of the Frangipani, elected in all haste under the name of *Innocent II*. Not to be outdone, the Pierleoni acclaimed Cardinal Peter pope by a partial vote of the Sacred College, and he assumed the name of Anacletus II. Having both money and protection on his side, the latter retained his hold on the City of Rome. Innocent II, expelled from Italy, appealed to the universal Church, stressing the fact that he had been elected before Anacletus and was more worthy of the office than his opponent. His cause was eloquently championed by St. Bernard, Abbot of Clairvaux, who at the assembly of Etampes succeeded in gaining over Louis the Fat, King of France, and later on Henry I, King of England, and the Emperor Lothaire II.

The Emperor re-instated Pope Innocent II in Rome, but was well rewarded for his deed by obtaining as a vassal of the Pope all the allodial or patrimonial possessions of the Margravine Matilda, which she, at her death, had bequeathed to the Holy See, together with the fiefs of the Empire inherited from her husband. The supporters of the Antipope however, still remained very powerful. From motives of personal interest, Roger, the Norman king of Sicily, took sides with the Antipope, after the latter had converted his duchy into a kingdom. These circumstances forced Lothaire to make a second journey to Italy. He had scarcely left the country, however, when Roger resumed hostilities. This time nothing could stop the Norman, neither the death of the Antipope in 1138, nor that of his successor, Victor IV, who reigned only two months, nor the *Second Council of the Lateran* (1139), which placed its seal of approval on the pontificate of Innocent II and excommunicated Roger (Tenth Ecumenical Council). He finally secured the recognition of his title of king by the Pope after a very disastrous campaign, in which Innocent II was taken prisoner by him.

At this juncture, several clusters of the population in Italy, whose ancestors had lived under the old Roman government, began to tire of the domination of the urban nobility and sought to shake off its tyrannical rule. Haunted by the memories of the ancient regime, recently revived by the study of Justinian's Code of Roman law, they began to group themselves into small but powerful republics. In 1143 one group took the capitol by assault, overthrew the consuls, and replaced them by a municipal council (*senatus*). Innocent II was powerless in the face of this revolution, which continued under the ephemeral reigns of his successors,

Celestine II (5 months) and Lucius (11 months). The latter was killed in a skirmish with the rebels.

The energetic *Eugene III* (1145-1153) succeeded in regaining possession of the City of Rome in the very first year of his reign, but a month later a revolt, enkindled by *Arnold of Brescia,* forced him to leave the city once more. Arnold cherished the dream of putting the finishing touches to the work of Pope Gregory VII and completely purging the Church of the vice of simony by doing away with all ecclesiastical property and suppressing the temporal power of the pope. He had already been condemned by the Council of the Lateran for advocating these theories from the pulpit in Brescia. After his appointment as tribune of the City of Rome, he directed the communal administration from 1147 to 1155 and wrote to the Emperor Conrad III to the effect that the commune would be a much more faithful vassal than the papacy. Meanwhile Eugene III had also sought the aid of Conrad. In 1149 he re-entered the City of Rome with the assistance of the King of Sicily, but was again expelled in 1150. Both he and his successor Anastasius IV appealed in vain for aid to the Germans.

Up to the twelfth century the administration of the City of Rome was left in the hands of the papacy. There was no senate and no Roman senators. It is true that the prefect of Rome was still invested with extensive judiciary powers, but he was a papal official, and the pope remained the supreme judge. After the revolution of 1144, the direction of the city passed into the hands of senators, who resided at the capitol and exercised legislative, executive, and judiciary powers, the power of declaring war and that of making treaties. If we except a short interval, under Innocent III, the importance of the senate continued to grow up to the middle of the thirteenth century, while the prefecture of Rome sank to a purely honorary rank by becoming the fief of the lords of Vico. The senate was invested with the right formerly exercised by princes to coin money and also collect the revenues from tolls and "tonlieus" (sums paid for a stand in a market) established by papal authority all around the City of Rome. The senate, too, administered the fund derived from fines imposed by the local tribunals.

In Rome, the mouthpieces of all these demagogic protests were the noblemen, a fact which accounts for their strength in that city. Besides their fortified castles in Campania, the barons possessed other strongholds in town, and, taken all in all, constituted an armed power with which any party would have to reckon. Chief among them were the Conti, the Savelli, the Colonna, the Poli, and the Vico families. And when the Church authorities protested against the blustering interference of these noblemen in papal elections, they immediately sought other fields, and began to meddle in the affairs of the Commune, seeking to have themselves appointed to the first positions. The result was that the local situation for the papacy was always precarious, for if the pope succeeded in subduing the emperor, he was almost simultaneously foiled by the insubordinate Romans. This was the situation which confronted Pope Alexander III, and it grew to such an extent that, in the thirteenth century, a decision was reached to elect only Roman or Campanian popes. They, being the descendants of the nobility, immediately raised their nephews to the plane of rich feudal barons, who could be depended upon to stand by them in need.

But if in a moment of wild fancy, occasioned by the memory of the glories of the ancient City of the Caesars, the Romans entertained dreams of an ideal republic, they were quickly disillusioned, for it soon became apparent to them that they could not live without the pope, since they were actually living on him.

II. The First Conflict Between the Papacy and Frederick Barbarossa under Hadrian IV. Henceforth the emperors intervened in the affairs of Rome only from motives of personal interest. Their aim was complete absolutism, and so, unable to check the uprisings of the turbulent feudal barons in Germany, they turned their eyes in the direction of Italy, claiming that they were invested with rights over this territory inherited from ancient times. An imperialism of this kind was strongly objected to by the popes, who realized that if the City of Peter became the property of the Caesars, Peter himself would be reduced to the level of a vassal and a chaplain. All those who were opposed to foreign domination adopted the same view and sided with the papacy, including the kings of Sicily, who were the feudatories of the Holy See, but above all the cities of Lombardy, which had become very jealous of their municipal rights.

Frederick Barbarossa (1152-1190) had been ruling Germany for only two years when *Hadrian IV* (Nicholas Breakspear, 1154-1159), the only Englishman to sit in the See of St. Peter, was elected to the papacy. The first clash between them occurred on the occasion of the Emperor's visit to Rome to receive the imperial crown. Frederick refused to hold the Pope's stirrup, as the Emperor Lothaire had done before him, for fear of passing for his vassal. He was, however, forced to yield in the end because Hadrian threatened not to crown him if he refused. His protest was very significant, for it gave everyone to understand that the Emperor was not *homo papae*. Moreover, Frederick demanded that a painting on which was inscribed the same epithet as applied to the Emperor Lothaire be destroyed.

The chief object of the conflict between the two powers, however, was the City of Rome, for when the Pope declared that he was its sole master, Frederick replied, "If it is not under my command, I am Emperor in name only." And so, if on the occasion of this first journey, there was no out and out break between them, it was because Frederick delivered the Sovereign Pontiff from the hands of the Roman insurgents and gave orders for Arnold of Brescia to be hanged, and Hadrian on his side agreed to place the imperial crown upon Frederick's brow. It remains true, nevertheless, that the Emperor on this occasion voiced ideas which savored of Caesarism and which later on resulted in open hostilities.

The Pope offended Frederick Barbarossa by making a treaty with William of Sicily without first conferring with the Holy See; the Emperor, on his part, offended Pope Hadrian by arresting the Archbishop of Lund, suspected of having sought to remove the churches of the northern part of Germany from the authority of the German Primate of Hamburg. At the Diet of Besançon, Cardinals Bernard and Roland Bandinelli presented to Barbarossa a letter from Hadrian, which alluded to the recent *beneficia* conferred upon the Emperor by the Pope, in particular the gift of the imperial crown (*coronae beneficium*). "It would have afforded us much pleasure," he wrote, "to have been able to confer upon Your Excellency even greater gifts (*beneficia*)." The Chancellor, Raynald of Dassel, maliciously translated the papal letter to the assembly as follows: "It would have afforded us much pleasure to have been able to confer upon Your Excellency even more important fiefs." The discussion waxed so hot that Otto of Wittelsbach rushed upon Cardinal Roland with brandished sword, and was prevented from ending the prelate's life only through the intervention of Barbarossa. The legates were ordered to quit the Empire, and the Pope wrote a second, very calm letter to the Emperor, in which the offensive expression was satisfactorily explained to mean "deeds of kindness" (*bona facta*).

But the despotism of the Emperor was bound to end in an open conflict. On the occasion of a second journey into Italy, Barbarossa, at the Diet of Roncaglia, suppressed the communal organization of the cities of Lombardy. Four eminent jurisconsults from Bologna declared that, according to Roman law, and more especially the Pandects recently rediscovered at Amalfi, Barbarossa had the right to exercise the power of the ancient Roman emperors and referred to him as ruler of the whole world. The despotic decisions of Barbarossa excited a general feeling of discontent among the Italian bishops, for being the holders of ecclesiastical fiefs, they feared they might become liegemen of the Emperor and be forced to take the vassals' oath. As a matter of fact, Barbarossa set out to exercise his authority in Corsica, a papal possession, where he proceeded to coin money, collect tolls and imposts, and levy a tax upon the possessions of the Roman Church. The Pope protested, but Barbarossa proposed arbitration, which the Sovereign Pontiff refused. The Emperor then endeavored to interest the Roman democrats in his views, while the Pope sought allies in Milan, Brescia, and Plaisance. Open war between the two powers was imminent.

III. The Open Conflict under Alexander III. Pope Hadrian IV died in 1159, and the Sacred College elected Cardinal Roland Bandinelli, who took the name of *Alexander III*. An imperialistic minority set up an antipope in the person of Cardinal Octavian, who assumed the name of Victor IV. The validity of Alexander's election was above dispute. The kings of England and France acknowledged it at the Council of Toulouse (1163), Spain and Ireland at the Council of Tours. Barbarossa alone upheld the claims of the antipope at the Synod of Pavia. His action resulted in open war between the priesthood and the empire. Alexander III was forced to quit Rome. He took refuge at Sens, where Louis VII gave him hospitality. Barbarossa made a third journey into Italy, gained possession of the city of Milan, and completely destroyed it. The death of Victor IV, in 1164, brought no change in the situation, for the Chancellor, Raynald of Dassel, caused to be elected in his place, Guido of Crema, who took the name of Pascal III. At the Diet of Würzburg (1165) the German princes and bishops declared themselves for the Pontiff supported by Barbarossa.

In November, 1165, Alexander III re-entered the City of Rome and was acclaimed as its liberator. He formed an alliance against Barbarossa with the king of Sicily, and also with Venice and the Lombardic League. Frederick made a fourth journey into Italy, seized Rome, and had himself crowned by the Antipope in St. Peter's, while Alexander III, disguised as a pilgrim, fled to Beneventum. At this juncture an epidemic broke out in Barbarossa's army, and he also was constrained to leave Rome. A Lombard alliance was organized to set the Roman peninsula free, and between the Tanaro and the Po a new fortress was built, named Alessandria in honor of the Pope. The Emperor besieged Alessandria on the occasion of a fifth journey into Italy, but was unable to reduce it. He was completely vanquished at the battle of *Legnano* (1176). Frederick then began negotiations with Alexander, which resulted in the Peace of Venice, 1177. The Emperor prostrated himself at the feet of the Pope under the archway of St. Mark's Cathedral in Venice and humbly pleaded for forgiveness. If his act of humiliation impresses us less than that of Henry at Canossa, his defeat was really more complete. The Peace of Venice stipulated that Frederick acknowledge Alexander as the true pope, the antipope was given a small abbey, and the bishops who had upheld him were granted forgiveness.

The papal victory resulted also in a triumph for the Lombards, who regained their communal rights. The Emperor concluded a six years' truce with them, which was followed by the Peace of Constance (1183). In this treaty he acknowledged the autonomy of the Communes and granted them the right to govern themselves. They in turn promised fealty to him, and obligated themselves to render minor services while he was in Italy. In the meanwhile the *Third Council of the Lateran* (Eleventh Ecumenical Council) convened (Lent 1179) and confirmed the Peace of Venice. To preclude any possibility of another schism, it was resolved to add an amendment to the decree of 1059 on papal elections. Henceforth a two-thirds' majority in the College of Cardinals was required for the valid election of a pope. The same council promulgated canons against simony, plurality of benefices, and the collation of benefices before the death of their incumbents. Pope Alexander III died August 30, 1181.

Frederick Barbarossa transmitted his ambitions to his son *Henry VI,* by arranging a marriage between him and Constance of Sicily, aunt of the Norman King William II, and sole heiress to the Norman kingdom. He thereby gave him to understand that the conquest of the Roman peninsula could be more effectively secured by approaching it from the south. Moreover, Barbarossa encouraged Henry to enlarge upon his own dreams and to plan the erection of a Mediterranean Empire that would reach into the East, and of which Germany and Italy would be nothing more than provinces. Popes Lucius III (1181-1185) and Urban III (1185-1187) both refused to crown Henry VI during the lifetime of his father. Clement III (1187-1191) finally promised to do so, when the Emperor resolved to head a Crusade. As a matter of fact, however, Henry VI was crowned emperor only after the death of his father, by Celestine III (1191-1198).

The agreement between the two powers was of short duration. With no regard at all for the promises made by his father, Henry VI refused to return to the Pope the lands bequeathed to the latter by the Countess Matilda, but instead, conferred the investiture of these possessions upon his brother Philip of Suabia, together with the title, Duke of Tuscany. Moreover, he created the German prince Conrad Duke of Umbria and gave to the High Seneschal, Markwal of Auweiler, the duchies of Romagna and Ancona. By these moves he hoped to prevent any league between Rome and the isolated communes of Lombardy. Finally, he claimed the kingdom of Sicily, and thus eliminated the second ally of the papacy in the Italian peninsula. He rendered himself even more odious by acts of unusual cruelty in the conquest of Sicily. After so speedily realizing his plans of conquest, the young Emperor died at the age of thirty. He had become partially reconciled with Pope Celestine III by organizing an army of Crusaders to re-conquer the Holy Land.

TEXTS AND DOCUMENTS

BARBAROSSA AT THE FEET OF ALEXANDER III

At Venice, which, inaccessible by position, maintained a sedulous neutrality, claiming to be independent of the Empire, yet seldom led into war by sympathy with the popes, the two powers whose strife had roused all Europe were induced to meet by the mediation of the Doge Sebastian Ziani. Three slabs of red marble in the porch of St. Mark's point out the spot where Frederick knelt in sudden awe, and the Pope with tears of joy raised him, and gave the kiss of peace. A later legend, to which poetry and painting have given an undeserved currency, tells how the Pontiff set his foot on the neck of the prostrate king, with the words, "The young lion and the dragon shalt thou trample under foot." It needed not this exaggeration to enhance the significance of that scene, even more full of meaning for the future than it was solemn and affecting to the Venetian crowd that thronged the church and the piazza. For it was the renunciation by the mightiest prince of his time of the project to which his life had been devoted: it was the abandonment by the secular power of a contest in which it had twice been vanquished, and which it could not renew under more favorable conditions.

BRYCE, The Holy Roman Empire, p. 171.

QUESTIONS

1. Account for the sudden rise of the Italian republics.
2. What was the plan of reform proposed by Arnold of Brescia?
3. What causes gave rise to the decision reached in the thirteenth century to elect only Roman popes?
4. What is the significance of the expression *homo papae?*
5. Enumerate the causes which led to the breach between Hadrian IV and Frederick Barbarossa.
6. What important decisions were reached at the Peace of Venice?
7. Discuss the early methods of electing the Sovereign Pontiff, and the merit of the changes instituted in the twelfth century.

BIBLIOGRAPHY

The Schism of Anacletus. Eugene III.—Sources: DUCHESNE, *Lib. Pont.*, II, p. 379–387.—WATTERICH, *Vitæ S. Pont.*, II, pp. 157.—JAFFÉ, *Reg.*, I, 823.—Works: HAUCK, *Kirchengesch. Deutschl.*, IV.—VACANDARD, art. *"Saint Bernard,"* in *Dict. Théol.; Histoire de saint Bernard,* 2 vols., 1897.— F. VERNET, art. *"Arnauld de Brescia,"* and art. *"Latran (IIe concile œcuménique de),"* in *Dict. de Théol.*—L. HALPHEN, *Etude sur l'administration de Rome au moyen-âge (751–1252).*

The Papacy and Frederick Barbarossa.—Sources: OTTO OF FREISINGEN (Pertz, t. XX).—JAFFÉ, *Reg.*, II, p. 102 ff.—WATTERICH, *Vitæ*, II.— DUCHESNE, *Lib. Pont.*, II, 388.—Works: ZELLER, *Histoire d'Allemagne*, III.— DU CHERRIER, *Histoire de la lutte des papes et des empereurs de la maison de Souabe*, I, 1858.—BRYCE, *The Holy Roman Empire.*—J. BIROT, *Le Saint Empire* 1900.—H. REUTER, *Geschichte Alexanders III. und der Kirche seiner Zeit*, 3 vols., 1860–1864.—G. BLONDEL, *Etude sur les droits régaliens et la constitution de Roncaglia*, in *Mélanges Fabre*, 1892.—F. CHALANDON, *Histoire de la domination normande en Italie et en Sicile*, 2 vols., 1907.—HAUCK, *Kirchengeschichte Deutschlands*, IV.—DOM POULET, *Guelfes et Gibelins*, I, *La lutte* *du Sacerdoce et de l'Empire* (1152–1250) (Coll. *"Lovanium"*), Brussels, 1922. —A. NOYON, art. *"Adrien IV,"* in *Dict. d'Hist.*—V. ERMONI, art. *"Alexandre III,"* in *Dict. d'Hist.*—KLEEMANN, *Papst Gregor VIII.*, Bonn, 1912.—T. F. TOUT, *The Empire and the Papacy*, London, 1903.

I. Causes of the Crusades. The Crusades were expeditions undertaken by Western Europe in the eleventh, twelfth, and thirteenth centuries to deliver Jerusalem and the tomb of the Saviour from the power of the Mussulmans. In these expeditions all nationalities were banded together into one vast army. It has been well remarked that the Crusades were "the external wars of Christendom."

Jerusalem had been in the possession of the Arabs for more than four centuries (636), although it had not unduly suffered from their rule. The Arabs looked upon it as a holy city, respected its monuments, and permitted pilgrims to make their devotions unmolested at its shrines. Haroun al-Raschid, Caliph of Bagdad (766–809), had even sent the Emperor Charlemagne the keys of the Holy Sepulchre. A change for the worse took place in the tenth century,[1] under the dynasty of the Fatimites; and the situation was completely transformed with the advent of the Turks, members of the yellow race, who subdued the whole of Asia Minor, and, in 1073, seized Jerusalem. Being religious fanatics, they persecuted the pilgrims.

Pope Gregory VII had conceived a plan to deliver the Holy Land from the domination of these tyrants, but his conflicts with Henry IV had forced him to lay it aside. Pope Urban II put the plan into execution. He convoked a council at Clermont, to discuss the reform of the French clergy (1095), and on the last day of that council, in the presence of a

---

[1] *The Byzantine Crusades in the Tenth Century.* It is important that we call the reader's attention to several remarkable expeditions undertaken by the Greeks in the tenth century, and in particular to those of Nicephorus Phocas, who seized several towns in northern Syria, and, later on, Antioch (968); and those of his successor John, who gained possession of Damascus (976) and advanced as far as the gates of Jerusalem. These expeditions were both national and religious in character, but were not undertaken by Christendom as such, their primary aim being to regain possession of provinces that had been lost to the Empire. It is this nationalistic concept of the movement which prevented the Greeks from understanding the true nature of the great Crusades. To their way of thinking, these expeditions were nothing more than attempts, on the part of the nations of the West, to encroach upon their possessions. (See G. Schlumberger, *L'épopée byzantine à la fin du xe siècle,* 3 vols.).

great multitude, recounted the sufferings of the pilgrims that visited Palestine. He closed with a stirring appeal in favor of an expedition to regain possession of the Holy Land. The Pope's discourse was received with great enthusiasm, and the cry went up from the lips of all those present, "God wills it! God wills it!" Applying to themselves the words of the Gospel, cited by Urban in his address, "If anyone will come after me, let him take up his cross and follow me," the recruits adopted as their insignia a cross made of red cloth, worn on the right shoulder and another worn on the breast. This accounts for the name, Crusaders, the word Crusade being derived from the Latin *crux,* meaning cross.

II. The First Crusade. Foundation of the Christian States. Pope Urban II now made a tour through the central and southern provinces of France for the purpose of raising an army of Crusaders. As a spiritual reward he promised all volunteers a plenary indulgence; as a temporal guarantee, he assured them of protection for their families and property while away from home. He also invited itinerant preachers to urge the movement upon the people, foremost among whom was Peter of Amiens, surnamed the Hermit. Peter was not present at Clermont and was not responsible, as several have maintained, for initiating the Crusade. He was none the less a most enthusiastic and eloquent propagator of the enterprise. If we are to believe his contemporary, Guibert of Nogent, "he travelled bare-footed and wore a long robe with a cowl. Bread was his only food and he never partook of wine. Something divine could be sensed in his slightest movements."

The announcement of this first Crusade was received enthusiastically everywhere—a fact easily explained by the deep-rooted faith of the people, their natural love of pilgrimages, devotion to relics, and the desire to gain the spiritual favors granted by the pope. The movement was fostered moreover, by the love of war and adventure so characteristic of knights, who saw in it a natural outlet for their desires and one that could be completely squared with their conscience.

Less than three months after the exhortation delivered at Clermont, from forty to fifty thousand persons of all ages and both sexes, enrolled from the ranks of the people, set out for the Holy Land without waiting for their lords, under the direction of Peter the Hermit and a knight known as Gauthier the Penniless. On the way their numbers were swelled by German, Flemish, and English pilgrims. The first Crusade was a motley crowd of peasants and adventurers, not an organized army; its pathway could be traced by the bodies of the dead left in its wake. Those who succeeded in reaching Constantinople, decided, against the advice of Peter the Hermit, to cross over into Asia, and were exterminated by the Turks near Nicaea.

Meanwhile the lords and barons had organized themselves into a Crusade, made up of four divisions, the trysting place of which was to be near Constantinople. The French from Southern France, under the direction of Raymond of Toulouse, were to cross into Northern Italy and proceed by the shore route of Dalmatia; the Normans of Italy, under the combined generalship of Tancred and Bohemond, were to embark at Brindisi, and traverse Albania and Macedonia; the French of the Ile de France, headed by Hugh of Vermandois, a brother of the king, were to follow the same itinerary; and Godfrey of Bouillon, Baldwin of Flanders, and the French from the North of France were to proceed by way of Germany and Hungary. Under the leadership of the Emperor Alexis Comnenus, who was planning with their aid to regain several places seized by the Turks, the Crusaders passed into Asia Minor. They gained possession of the town of Nicaea, defeated the Turks at Dorylaeum, and after a dreary march through the desert, during which they suffered all sorts of misfortunes and calamities and were constantly harassed by the enemy, they finally arrived at the gates of Antioch in Syria. After a siege of eight months they gained possession of the city, and defeated a Turkish army which had arrived to besiege them in turn. The route to Jerusalem now lay open before them. At the end of their strength, and dying of thirst, they attempted the heroic plan of storming this stronghold. An attack made Friday, July 15, 1099, at three o'clock in the afternoon, in memory of the death of Christ, was unexpectedly crowned with success. From Nicaea to Jerusalem the Crusaders had left in their path the bodies of six hundred thousand soldiers, and the two sieges of Antioch had cost them two hundred thousand more. When the cloud of battle lifted, their army was reduced to the pitiful number of forty thousand.

It was then decided to found the Latin Kingdom of Jerusalem and to offer the crown to Godfrey of Bouillon, the most popular, and at the same time the most unselfish, of the leaders of the Crusade. He refused to wear a diadem in the city where Christ was crowned with thorns, and accepted only the title of "Defender of the Holy Sepulchre." The

Christian conquests were gradually extended. With the aid of the merchants of Marseilles, Genoa, and Venice, the sea towns of Joppe, Acre, and Beyrut were taken, and in the interior the Crusaders gained possession of the entire country between the Jordan and the Red Sea.

To assure the results of this Crusade, military religious Orders were organized for the defence of the Holy Land. The three most important creations of this kind in the order of their institution were: the Knights of St. John of Jerusalem, the Knights of the Temple (or Knights Templars), and the Teutonic Knights. The Knights of St. John of Jerusalem were sometimes called Knights Hospitallers of St. John from the Hospital in Jerusalem where they were first housed, and where they received pilgrims and cared for the sick. The Knights Templars (1118) were organized at the Council of Troyes in 1128 by St. Bernard, who did much to spread the Order by a short treatise entitled, "In Praise of the New Knighthood." They derived the name, Knights Templars, from their original home in a portion of the royal palace at Jerusalem, near the ancient Temple. The Teutonic Knights appeared during the third Crusade (1191); they were organized by Germans and remained German in membership. This Order was later on transplanted to Europe, to engage in warfare with the pagan Slavs of Prussia.

The members of these three military Orders were divided into three groups: knights, priests or chaplains, and lay servants. They were each governed by a Grand Master, assisted by a Chapter. The Order itself was partitioned off into provinces, which corresponded to the different nations, and the provinces in turn were subdivided into bailiwicks, which comprised several houses or commanderies. Being monks, these knights were bound by the three vows of poverty, chastity, and obedience; being soldiers, they wore armor under a cloak, which, in the case of the Hospitallers, was black and adorned with a white cross, and in the case of the Templars, white and adorned with a red cross. Their rule obliged them to acts of bravery and heroism. The Templar could never refuse to give or consent to surrender. After the majority of the Crusaders had returned to their homes, these military Orders were transformed into a sort of permanent army, which, because of its knowledge of the country and of the ways of the enemy, proved to be a most valuable asset. They possessed many castles, such as those of Margat, Le Crac, and Tortosa, encircled by high walls and strongly fortified.

Unfortunately there existed in the constitution of these Christian States in the Orient elements which made for weakness. In the first place, there was no unity of government and no strong and firmly established royal dynasty. In the beginning there were four principalities, to wit, Jerusalem, Antioch, Edessa, and Tripoli, and the supremacy of Jerusalem over the other three was rather nominal in character. In the interior of each State the same feudal anarchy and a complete lack of any regular system of finances was in evidence. To this we must add the profound and almost continuous quarrels and dissensions with other Eastern countries. Established at Antioch, the son of Robert Guiscard, Bohemond, aroused the jealousy of the Emperor Alexis. Things came to a head in 1100, when Bohemond fell into the hands of the Turks, and the two armies which were sent to rescue him were exterminated. Alexis then demanded that the infidels surrender the prisoner. Bohemond, however, succeeded in making his escape and thereafter dreamed only of revenge. This gave rise to a lengthy war between the Normans and the Greeks. Under the reign of John Comnenus (1118-1143) the Byzantines succeeded in imposing their rule on Antioch. These unfortunate and continuous quarrels served only to maintain and intensify the Greek schism. Though a breach officially existed since the days of Michael Cerularius, an external peace was maintained by princely alliances, by pilgrimages of western peoples to Constantinople, and by the diplomatic relations established between Greece and the West. In the mind of the pope, the Crusade had been undertaken, in part at least, to renew friendly associations with the Byzantines and at the same time to compensate them somewhat for their former services. The undisciplined spirit of the Latins, the natural mistrust of the Greeks, and the cupidity of unscrupulous leaders were responsible for destroying an initial friendly understanding and gradually widening the gap between the West and the East. While these quarrels were taking place in the ranks of the Christians, the Turks were recuperating from their losses. The creation of a Latin Empire in the East had considerably weakened the Seljuks, who had been divided by rivalries among their chiefs, but when Zenghi, prince of Mossul, succeeded in effecting a concentration of their forces, serious disasters began to loom on the horizon for the Crusaders. Edessa was taken in 1144 and Jerusalem was once again threatened.

III. The Second and Third Crusades. The commotion caused by the capture of Edessa by the infidels occasioned the second Crusade. St. Bernard preached this Crusade, and his appeal was received as enthusiastically as that of Urban II. The French King Louis VII and the German Emperor Conrad III headed the expedition together, and although their forces were not as numerous as those of the first Crusade, they were better disciplined and recruited almost entirely from the military. The enterprise, however, proved a complete failure. Setting out for Palestine by land, through Hungary, Greece, and Asia Minor, the Crusaders tried to take Damascus, but they were unsuccessful, and so turned their eyes in the direction of Ascalon. But here, too, they were forced to retreat, and their hasty withdrawal had the disastrous effect of consolidating the Turkish forces.

For a long time the infidels had been threatening the Latin Kingdom from the northern boundary of Syria, especially since the Fatemite dynasty in Egypt had become extinct. After his successful victory over the forces of the second Crusade, Nurreddin succeeded in gaining possession of the valley of the Nile, where Amaury, King of Jerusalem, had made several vain attempts to establish his quarters. Nurreddin's successor, the formidable *Saladin,* thus found himself in a position to threaten the Latin Kingdom from both the North and the South. At this critical moment, more dissensions broke out in the Christian camp. Baldwin V died, and the right of succession was disputed by his mother, Sybil, and by Raymond of Tripoli. Sybil, who had contracted a second marriage with Guy of Lusignan, had him crowned at Jerusalem. Raymond was infuriated, and to avenge himself, delivered the city of Tiberias to Saladin. When Renaud of Chatillon, a powerful though secondary commander, with no regard for the general interests of the kingdom, foolishly aroused the anger of Saladin, the latter crushed the army of Guy of Lusignan at Hittin, July 4, 1187, and seized Jerusalem, July 17. Soon the Christians were left with only the cities of Tyre, Antioch, and Tripoli.

Upon receipt of this news, the Emperor Frederick Barbarossa, King Philip II of France, and King Richard the Lion-Hearted of England undertook a new Crusade. The German battalion broke up after the accidental drowning of Frederick while fording the river Self in Cilicia. The French and the English set out for Palestine by way of the sea, and thus avoided the countless battles which they would otherwise have had to wage with the peoples of lands through which they passed. Henceforth the sea route was the one followed in all Crusades. Richard on his way conquered the Island of Cyprus, which in the fourteenth century became the center of Christian corsairs. Despite the legendary feats of prowess of the English king, the Crusaders were able to take the seaport of Acre only after a siege of two years. The quarrelsome character of King Richard, who remained in Palestine after Philip returned to France, caused the failure of the expedition. Saladin was too much of a diplomat to create any further opposition; he realized that since the Latin possessions were reduced to a few seaports, they could do him no harm and might, moreover, be easily exploited later as commercial centers. He even went so far as to permit Christians to undertake pilgrimages to Jerusalem. Unfortunately, utilitarian motives began to appear among the Christians themselves, and the commercialism of the Venetians and the Genoese soon displaced the spirit of chivalry and knighthood. A German Crusade planned by Henry VI proved favorable to this new spirit, because it issued in the capture of several maritime ports. And so, at the end of the twelfth century, the Latin Kingdom had undergone a complete change, and interests had shifted to a different field. Only two of the four initial States still existed, Edessa and Tripoli, and the capital of the kingdom of Jerusalem was now Saint-Jean-d'Acre. On the other hand, two new States had been acquired, which became valuable ports of call for the Crusades that were to follow: the Isle of Cyprus, ruled by the Lusignans, and Little Armenia on the coast of Cilicia.

TEXTS AND DOCUMENTS

POPE URBAN'S PLEA FOR A CRUSADE

He [the Pope] dwelt upon the requests for aid which had come from the East, the sufferings of pilgrims and Christians there, and the need of giving assistance against the advancing Moslems. The evil private wars of Christian against Christian, which the Church was trying to curb, should be replaced by this holy war against the infidels, who could not hope to withstand the brave men from the West. The hardships of living in Europe would be exchanged for the pleasures of a land flowing with milk and honey. To those who took the cross, to their families and property, the Church extended its protection. Within the jurisdiction of the episcopal courts they could gain respite from their debts, a suspension of the payment of interest, and some exemption from feudal and secular control. For sinners the expedition offered the chance of a Plenary Indulgence. "You, oppressors of orphans and

widows; you, murderers and violators of churches; you, robbers of the property of others; you, who, like vultures are drawn to the scent of the battle-
field, hasten, as you love your souls, under your Captain Christ to the rescue
of Jerusalem. All you who are guilty of such sins as exclude you from the
Kingdom of God, ransom yourselves at this price, for such is the will of
God!" And, when Pope Urban had said these and very many similar things
in his urbane discourse, he so influenced to one purpose the desires of all
who were present that they cried out, "God wills it! God wills it!"

R. A. Newhall, *The Crusades*, p. 38.

QUESTIONS

1. Write an appreciation of the Crusades in general.
2. Account for the enthusiastic manner in which the movement was received
   by the people at large.
3. What was the purpose and organization of the military Orders?
4. Enumerate the causes which made for instability in the Latin Kingdom
   of Palestine.

BIBLIOGRAPHY

The Crusades.—General Bibliography. Collections: Bongars, *Gesta Dei
per Francos*, 2 vols., Hanover, 1612.—Michaud, *Bibliothèque des Croisades*,
4 vols., 1829.—*Collection de l'Histoire des Croisades*, published by the Acad.
des Inscriptions, *Historiens occidentaux*, 5 vols.; *Hist. orientaux*, 4 vols.; *Hist.
grecs*, 2 vols.; *Documents arméniens*, 2 vols.; *Lois*, 2 vols.—Publications of the
Société de l'Orient latin.—*Revue de l'Orient Latin.*—General Works:
Michaud, *Histoire des croisades*, 7 vols., 1824–29.—Kugler, *Geschichte der
Kreuzzüge* (Coll. *Oncken*), 1880.—Röhricht, *Geschichte der Kreuzzüge
im Umriss*, Innsbruck, 1898.—Heyck, *Die Kreuzzüge und das heilige Land*,
Leipzig, 1906.—Bréhier, *Les croisades*, 4th edit., 1921.—W. Norden, *Das
Papsttum und Byzanz*, Berlin, 1903.—Jorga, *Histoire des croisades*,
1924.—G. Schlumberger, *L'épopée byzantine à la fin du Xᵉ siècle*, 3 vols.—
For the Crusade of the Children, see W. Scott Durand, *Cross and Dagger*,
London, 1910.—Archer and Kingsford, *The Crusades*, 1894.—Harold Lamb,
op. cit.

First Crusade.—Sources: *Gesta Francorum et aliorum Hierosolymita-
norum*, edit. Le Bas.—Raimond d'Aguilers, edit. Robert le Moine.—Foucher
de Chartres, edit. *Hist. Occid. Crois.*, III, 311–485.—*Gesta Tancredi*, edit.
Hist. Occ. Crois., III, 537–601.—*Albert d'Aix*, edit. *Hist. Occ. Crois.*, IV, 265–
713.—*Robert le Moine*, edit. *Hist. Crois.*, III, 717.—*Baudri de Bourgueil*, edit.
Hist. Occ. Crois., IV, I–III.—*Guibert de Nogent*, edit. *Hist. Occ. Crois.*, IV,
I–III.—*Lettres d'Urbain II, P. L.*, t. CLI.—Works: Hagenmeyer, *Chronologie
de la première croisade* 1902, and *Rev. Or. lat.*, VI ff.—Chalandon, *Essais sur*

le règne d'Alexis Comnène, 1900; *Histoire de la première croisade jusqu'à l'élection de Godefroi de Bouillon*, 1925.—PAULOT, *Un pape français, Urbain II*, 1903.—CRÉGUT, *Le concile de Clermont et la première croisade*, Clermont, 1895.—HAGENMEYER, *Peter der Eremit*, Leipzig, 1879.—A. FLICHE, *Urbain II et la croisade*, R. H. E. F., 1927, p. 289-307.—LEIB, *Rome, Kiev et Byzance à la fin du XIe siècle* (1088-1099), 1924.—In a general way the works of W. Norden, Röhricht, and Bréhier.—HAROLD LAMB, *The Crusades*, 2 vols., New York.

The Latin Kingdom. The Military Orders.—REY, *Essai sur la domination française en Syrie pendant le Moyen-Age*, 1886; *Les colonies franques de Syrie aux XIIe et XIIIe siècles*, 1883.—DODU, *Histoire des institutions monarchiques dans le royaume latin de Jérusalem*, 1894.—CONDER, *The Latin Kingdom of Jerusalem*, London, 1897.—RÖHRICHT, *Geschichte des Königreichs Jerusalem*, Innsbruck, 1898.—DELAVILLE-LEROULX, *Les Hospitaliers en Terre Sainte et à Cypre* (1100-1310), 1904.—WILCKE, *Geschichte des Tempelherrenordens*, Halle, 1860.—PRUTZ, *Entwickelung und Untergang des Tempelherrenordens*, Berlin, 1888.—MADELIN, *La Syrie franque* (*Rev. des Deux-Mondes*, March 15, 1917).—THATCHER AND MCNEAL, *A Source Book for Mediaeval History*, New York, 1905.—F. C. WOODHOUSE, *Military Religious Orders of the Middle Ages*, New York, 1879.

Second and Third Crusades.—Sources: WILLIAM OF TYRE, edit. *Hist. Crois.*, I.—EUDE DE DEUIL, *De Ludovici VII profectione in Orientem, P. L.*, CXCV and WAITZ, *Mon. Germ., SS.*, XXVI, 60-73.—OTTO OF FREISINGEN, *Gesta Friderici imperatoris, Mon. Germ., SS.*, XX. 347.—For the third Crusade, AMBROISE, *Histoire de la guerre sainte*, edit. G. Paris (Unpublished documents of the Hist. of France, 1897).—Works: KÖNIG, *Balduin I. von Jerusalem*, Königsberg, 1884.—HAGENMEYER, *Chronologie de l'histoire du royaume de Jérusalem*, Baldwin's reign (1100-1108) (*Rev. de l'Orient Latin*, IX-XII).—VACANDARD, *Saint Bernard et la seconde croisade* (*Rev. quest. hist.*, XXXVII).—F. CHALANDON, *Jean II et Manuel Ier Comnène*, 1912.—SCHLUMBERGER, *Renaud de Chatillon*, new edit., 1923; *Campagnes du roi Amaury Ier de Jérusalem en Egypte au XIIe siècle*, 1906.—DE MAS LATRIE, *Histoire du royaume de Cypre*, I.—BRÉHIER, *Les croisades*, ch. V and VII; art. *"Amaury Ier," "Amaury patriache," "Amaury II,"* in *Dict. d'Hist.*

CHAPTER III

The Apostolic labors of SS. Cyril and Methodius among the Slavonic peoples in the ninth century had been confined to Bohemia and Moravia. Two pagan nations remained to be converted on the German boundary, the Hungarians and the Poles; and two others on the boundary of the Byzantine Empire, the Bulgarians and the Russians.

During the first half of the tenth century the Hungarians made so many incursions into Germany that Otto I resolved to wage war against them. He defeated their armies at the battle of Lech (955). These invasions helped the cause of Christianity, inasmuch as priests accompanied the thousands of prisoners brought back from Germany by the Magyars (Hungarians) and set out at once to convert them. Piligrim, Archbishop of Passau, showed himself well disposed towards an apostolate of this kind. The great military leader Geiza was converted to Christianity, and bishop St. Adalbert of Prague baptized his son, who later on became *King St. Stephen* (995-1038). Stephen crushed the uprising of the national pagan party at Veszprim and became an ardent propagator of the Christian religion among his people. He founded several episcopal sees, with the metropolitan at Gran. Sylvester II and Otto III officially recognized his kingdom, which he placed under the special protection of St. Peter. This accounts for the title of "Apostolic Majesty" used by the kings of Hungary. Under the reign of St. Ladislas (1077-1095) the last traces of paganism disappeared from the kingdom.

Meanwhile the great Polish leader Duke Miecislas (962-992) had received Baptism (966) and founded the archiepiscopal see of Posen. His son *Boleslaus I,* termed Chrobri (the Powerful), the national hero of the Poles (992-1025), was the true founder of the Church in Poland. Like St. Stephen of Hungary, he profited by the good will of Otto III and Sylvester II, and when the Emperor was solemnly received at Gnesen in 1000, established an archiepiscopal see in that city, with the suffragan sees of Colberg, Cracow, and Breslau. Boleslaus placed his kingdom under the protection of the Holy See and paid the "Peter's Pence." Union with Rome was to remain one of the distinctive characteristics of the history of Poland. Boleslaus II (1058–1079) walked at first in the footsteps of his father, but later gave himself up to a life of debauchery. And so when St. Stanislaus, Bishop of Cracow, called him to account and excommunicated him, he slew him with his own hand at the foot of the altar (1079).

The Bulgarians were neighbors of Byzantium, which they had already threatened in the second part of the ninth century. Princes Krum and Omortag scored several victories, and slaves brought back by them to Moesia introduced Christianity into that land. Their leader *Boris* (852–888) received Baptism in 864, and the Emperor Michael III was his godfather. Boris petitioned Pope Nicholas I (858–867) to send him missionaries, and the Pontiff answered his request by his famous *Responsio ad Consulta Bulgarorum*. Unfortunately, the revolt of Photius, which broke out a few years later, plunged this young Christian community into schism.

There was a Christian Church at Kiev in Russia as early as the tenth century. Olga, the widow of Grand Duke Oleg, received Baptism at Constantinople about 957; her grandson Vladimir (972–1015) was the Clovis of Russia. After coming to the assistance of the Greek Emperors Basil II and Constantine VIII and suppressing an uprising in Cappadocia, Vladimir asked the hand of their sister in marriage. They insisted, however, that he first receive Baptism, and he readily acquiesced. His conversion had the effect of strengthening the fidelity of his leading subjects, the Polianes of Kiev, many of whom had already embraced Christianity. But Russia was soon to become a sort of colony of Byzantium and together with the capital of the empire fell into schism.

To the Northeast of Christian Germany, on the shores of the Baltic Sea, lived the northern Slavs, and between the Elbe and the Oder, the Wends. The Wends had been defeated on several occasions by their neighbors, the Dukes of Saxony, who became Emperors Henry I and Otto I. These emperors established military stations in the land, and also created several dioceses: Havelburg and Brandenburg in the North, and the archdiocese of Magdeburg in the South. Taking advantage of the defeat of Otto II at Stilo in Southern Italy, the Slavs completely destroyed these nascent Christian communities in 983. True, some of the Slavonic princes and their retinues were led to embrace Christianity by contact with the German nobility, but the people resisted all the efforts of the missionaries. In the twelfth century it was realized that the only way to convert them was by colonization, and so the country was literally flooded with German immigrants. This step facilitated the establishment of parishes and monasteries on the right bank of the river Elbe, but spelled the complete destruction of the Slavonic element in those parts. *St. Norbert of Magdeburg* directed the work of evangelization with the aid of the Premonstratensians of Marienkloster (1129). Their missionary labors received the hearty support of the Prince of Brandenburg, Albert the Bear, founder of the Ascanian dynasty.

To the extreme North, in the country bordering upon Jutland and the North Sea, lived the Obotrites. Their prince, Gottschalk, was educated in a monastery and so undertook to convert his people to the true faith, with the aid of Bernard of Saxony and Archbishop Adalbert of Hamburg. He succeeded in establishing monasteries at Mecklenburg, Ratzeburg, and Lübeck. In the twelfth century the canon St. Vicelinus of Bremen continued the work of evangelization, but the real apostle of this country was Henry the Lion, Duke of Saxony, who by conquering the natives and colonizing the unsettled districts, won the population over to Christianity (1140). He founded the episcopal see of Mecklenburg-Schwerin (1149) and rehabilitated the sees of Oldenburg, Lübeck, and Ratzeburg.

More towards the East, between the Oder and the Vistula, lay Pomerania. This country was conquered in 1119 by Boleslas III of Poland, who converted its Duke Ratislas and his entire court. He enlisted the help of the German bishop, *Otto of Bamberg,* who, in the capacity of a legate, travelled the length and breadth of the land as far as the islands of the Baltic Sea (1124 and 1128) and established several churches in Pomerania, notably those of Stettin, Jullin, and Kammin. But because these regions were subject to the rival influences of the Germans and the Poles a conflict arose between the metropolitan sees of Magdeburg and Gnesen, the outcome being that Pope Innocent II placed the bishopric of Kammin under the direct jurisdiction of the Holy See. The work of evangelization continued, thanks to the efforts of the Saxon immigrants, and in the opening years of the thirteenth century several Cistercian and Premonstratensian monasteries were established.

Still more towards the East, between the Vistula and the Niemen, lived the Prussians. These people were savage pagans, who had put to death St. Adalbert in the tenth, and St. Bruno in the eleventh century. It was only in 1207 that the Cistercian monk, Christian, from the monastery of Oliva near Dantzig, resumed the active work of preaching among the Prussians. In 1217 he visited Pope Honorius III, who entrusted him with the mission of evangelizing the country, erecting episcopal sees, and preaching the Crusade. As the pagans, however, constantly sought to undermine his work, he attempted in vain to establish a military Order, that of the "Knights of Prussia," and called to his aid the Teutonic Order, first established for the Crusade in the Holy Land. The Grand Master of this Order, Herman of Salza, accepted his invitation, and with the assistance of the German Crusaders, the Teutonic Order undertook the conquest of the land, despite the implacable resistance of the Prussians (1231–1283).

Livonia, located on the Eastern shores of the Baltic Sea, was first evangelized by the Augustinian canon Meinhard, who had journeyed thither from Holstein. The great apostle of this country, however, was Albert von Buxhövden, who founded Riga. To help carry on the work of his apostolate, he established the "Order of the Swordbearers," approved by a Bull of Innocent III (1204). These Knights (*Schwertbrüder*) reduced the entire country to subjection. Soon, however, they were attacked by the Russians and forced to call the Teutonic Knights to their aid. They united with them in 1237, and in this way Prussia and Livonia became subject to the same masters. Pope Innocent IV created four episcopal sees, Kulm, Pomerania, Ermland, and Samland under the metropolitan jurisdiction of Riga (1243).

TEXTS AND DOCUMENTS

Russia Embraces Christianity

After his return to Kiev, the "Great Prince" caused his twelve sons to be baptized, and proceeded to destroy the monuments of heathenism. He ordered Perun to be thrown into the Dnieper. The people at first followed their idol, as it was borne down the stream, but were soon quieted when they saw that the statue had no power to help itself. . . . And now Vladimir, being surrounded and supported by believers in his own domestic circle, and encouraged by seeing that his boyars and suite were prepared and ready to embrace the faith, made a proclamation to the people, "That whoever, on the morrow, should not repair to the river, whether rich or poor, he should hold him for his enemy." At the call of their respected lord all the multitude of the citizens, with their wives and children, flocked to the Dnieper in troops, and without any manner of opposition received holy Baptism as a nation from the Greek bishops and priests. Some stood in the water up to their necks, others up to their breasts, holding their young children in their arms; the priests read the prayers from the shore, naming at once whole companies by the same name. . . . Vladimir erected the first church—that of St. Basil, after whom he was named—on the very mount which had formerly been sacred to Perun, adjoining his own palace. Thus was Russia enlightened.

MOURAVIEFF, *A History of Russia, passim.*

QUESTIONS

1. List persons who played an important part in the conversion of the Slavs and the Hungarians.
2. How did the conversion of the Slavonic peoples differ from that of the early nations of the Roman Empire?
3. What is the precise tenor of Pope Nicholas I's *Responsio ad Consulta Bulgarorum?*
4. Give some incidents in the life of St. Stanislaus, Bishop of Cracow.

BIBLIOGRAPHY

Conversion of the Slavs.—E. HORN, *Saint Etienne, roi de Hongrie* (Coll. *"Les Saints"*), 1899.—E. LAVISSE, *La marche de Brandebourg sous la dynastie ascanienne,* 1875.—MAX PERTBECH, *Die Statuten des Deutschen Ordens,* 1890.—W. KETRZYNSKI, *Der deutsche Orden und Konrad von Masovien,* 1903.—MAX OEHLER, *Gesch. des deutchen Ritter-Ordens,* 1908.—P. RICHARD, art. *"Allemagne"* in *Dict. d'Hist.*—LAVISSE and RAMBAUD, II, ch. XIV.—E. MAIRE, *Saint Norbert* (Coll. *"Les Saints"*), 1923.—PAUL FABRET, *La Pologne et le Saint-Siège du Xe au XIIe siècle* (Mélanges Monod), 1896.—BRIAND-CHAMINOV, *L'Eglise russe,* 1928.—A. VAMBERY, *The Story of Hungary,* New York, 1891.

CHAPTER IV

I. The False Reform: The Popular Anticlerical Heresy.
Simultaneously with heretical movements inaugurated by the learned, popular heresies made their appearance in the twelfth century. Sometimes these heresies were the work of devout souls, who, in their desire to reform the Church, advocated a complete social revolution; sometimes they savored strongly of the heretical teachings of Manichaeism. According to the localities in which they sprang up, these heresies translated themselves into ascetical practices, advocated open debauchery, or blossomed forth into brigandage.

Tanchelm, an illiterate and fanatical layman, sowed the seeds of revolution in the Netherlands. According to him, churches were nothing more than houses of prostitution, and priests did not consecrate the Body of Christ. "The Sacraments they give," he said, "have nothing holy about them; I alone, Tanchelm, together with my followers, constitute the Church, for I am God just like Christ, since I possess the plenitude of the Holy Ghost." In point of fact, Tanchelm was a monster, who wallowed in the grossest forms of lewdness. St. Norbert of Magdeburg succeeded in offsetting his teachings. The fanatic was assassinated in 1115, while attempting to reorganize his sect in Antwerp.

Peter of Bruis, who became notorious in Dauphiny and Provence, provinces of southern France, preached similar errors, contempt of the hierarchy, destruction of churches, etc. But his specialty was Iconoclasm. All crosses, he maintained, should be destroyed or burned, inasmuch as the cross is the instrument of Christ's torture and death. Putting these theories into practice, the Petrobrusians, as his followers were called, gathered together a huge pile of crosses, set fire to them and roasted meat thereon, which they ate on Good Friday. But while Peter of Bruis was burning crosses at St. Giles near Arles, he was seized by an angry mob, which had grown furious at his disrespectful treatment of holy things, and cast into the fire which he himself had lighted. An unfrocked monk of Cluny by the name of Henry of Lausanne succeeded to the headship of the sect and scored great success in Aquitaine, where St. Bernard bent every effort to undo his work.

The most eccentric of all these reformers was Eon de l'Etoile (*Eudo de Stella*). Applying to himself the words of the formula of exorcism: *"Per eum, qui venturus est judicare vivos et mortuos,"* he fancied that, because of the similarity between the name Eon and *Eum,* he was the Son of God and the judge of all men. In this capacity he travelled the length and breadth of Brittany, accompanied by a large number of followers, whom he called his angels or apostles, and engaged in pillagings and orgies of all kinds. He was finally seized by a bishop and summoned to appear before the Council of Rheims (1148), which condemned him to life imprisonment.

Italy also was ravaged by uncommissioned reformers. The trouble began when Manfred, Bishop of Brescia, in renewing the decrees against simony and the marriage of clerics, punished several guilty parties by confiscating their goods. These dispossessed clerics finally succeeded in ridding themselves of the Bishop, who was able to return to his diocese only through the intervention of Pope Innocent II and St. Bernard. At this juncture, Arnold, a cleric of Brescia, made bold to assert that the cause of all the evils in the Church was the wealth of the clergy. "Clerics who possess property," he said, "cannot be saved." And so, according to him, all ecclesiastical goods were to be returned to the secular power, which was to dispose of them in favor of laymen. Arnold had no trouble in rallying to his cause all those who profited by these sacrilegious thefts, including greedy and envious noblemen and plebeians enticed by the hope of sharing in the spoils. In the course of a journey undertaken by Bishop Manfred to Rome, Arnold stirred up the people and entrusted the administration of the city to two consuls. Manfred then appealed for help to the Council of the Lateran, which forbade Arnold to return to Brescia. Later on he sought to spread his revolutionary theories in Rome, but suffered the death penalty on the occasion of Frederick Barbarossa's first journey into Italy.

II. The True Reform: Monachism. The Chapters. The twelfth century witnessed a revival of the monastic life. In 1070 *Stephen Muret* founded the Order of Grandmont, which received the special approbation of Pope Gregory VII. Vividly impressed by the example of the hermits of Calabria, he resolved to live a similar life, establishing his headquarters on the side of a wooded hill near Limoges. His austerity attracted a number of followers, upon whom he enjoined the observance of the Rule of St. Benedict in all its severity. In 1170 the Order counted seventy monasteries, but in the fourteenth century it was torn asunder by schismatic movements, and finally disappeared at the time of the French Revolution.

Towards the end of the eleventh century, *St. Bruno* founded the Order of the Carthusians. He was born at Cologne, and after a brilliant course of studies at Paris, became master of the Cathedral School at Rheims, where he had as one of his pupils the future Urban II. Later he taught for a time in Paris. For many years, however, he had nourished the secret desire to lead an ascetical life in some solitary place, and so he repaired to Molesmes, where he lived under the direction of St. Robert, the future founder of the Order of Citeaux. Later on he settled in a wild and desolate valley, called La Chartreuse (Carthusium), situated within a few miles of Grenoble. A number of disciples followed him. They built a monastery, in which they met for liturgical exercises, but lived separately in small cells scattered round about. Their time was divided between prayer and manual labor, to which they also added the reading and copying of manuscripts. The statutes of the Order were formulated about 1130 by the fifth prior of La Chartreuse, Guido the Venerable. In the opening years of the thirteenth century the Order had a sub-order of women. At the time of the French Revolution it counted one hundred and seventy monasteries of men and thirty convents of women.

The Breton, *Robert of Arbrissel,* founded the abbey of Fontevrault in Anjou. This abbey comprised two monasteries, one for men and the other for women, and all inmates were subject to the Abbess of Notre-Dame-de-Fontevrault, Petronilla of Chemilly. The congregation at one time counted as many as sixty houses.

The greatest of all monastic revivals, however, originated at Citeaux. The founder of the new congregation was *St. Robert,* who at the tender age of fifteen entered the Benedictine monastery Moutier-la-Celle near Troyes. Upon his appointment to the abbacy he set out to reform the morals of his community, but failing to achieve success, withdrew to Molesmes, where a few hermits elected him their superior. Here, too, he encountered serious difficulties, which he was unable to overcome, and so established himself with about twenty faithful monks in the solitude of *Citeaux* in Burgundy. Neither St. Robert nor his two successors, Blessed Alberic and St. Stephen Harding, had dreamed of establishing a new Order, but the advent of a novice of renown was the signal for an extraordinary revolution in monastic ideas.

St. Bernard was born in 1090 at the Castle Fontaines near Dijon. At the outset he appeared to be a very reserved and excessively timid student. The memory of his mother, Aleth, whom he lost early in life, moved him to break loose from all worldly ties, and so he retired from the world in the autumn of 1111. Bernard was possessed of such a strong character and winning personality that he had no difficulty in inducing thirty of his companions to join him in solitude at Châtillon-sur-Seine. In the spring of 1112 all of them entered Citeaux. Bernard led a very austere life and inaugurated a monastic ideal far superior to any ever dreamed of by St. Benedict. His holiness, coupled with his eloquence and his miracles, prompted many others to follow in his footsteps. In rapid succession the following monasteries were founded: La Ferté (1113), Pontigny (1114), Clairvaux and Morimond (1115). These offshoots of Citeaux retained a special importance in later years; all subsequent foundations were constrained to place themselves under the jurisdiction of one of them.

St. Stephen Harding, the third abbot of Citeaux, had already drawn up the *Consuetudines* or "Customs of Citeaux," which regulated the internal administration of each house. To organize the Order he wrote the "Charter of Union," or, as it was more often called, "Charter of Charity," a collection of statutes for the government of all monasteries united to Citeaux. This charter was approved by Pope Callixtus II in 1119. According to these statutes, the abbot of Citeaux was the superior general of the Order, but as the concentration plan adopted at Cluny to escape lay interference was no longer necessary, each Cistercian monastery remained interiorly autonomous in accordance with the primitive spirit of the Rule. On the other hand, each monastery was subject to the jurisdiction of the Ordinary. Chapters and canonical visits made for unity in the Order. The annual chapters, in which all abbots had to take part, were vested with more extensive powers. They were permitted to interpret the *Consuetudines,* to render decisions binding in conscience, and to pronounce disciplinary sentences such as those which made for the suppression of abuses or those required to depose abbots. Their decisions were soon grouped together in a code.

Cluny was not in a state of decadence when *Peter the Venerable* was its abbot, but in establishing Clairvaux, St. Bernard wished to depart from Cluny on two essential points. Cluny possessed rich abbeys and sumptuous churches; to its way of thinking nothing could be too beautiful or too expensive for the service of God; St. Bernard enjoined upon his followers the observance of poverty in its strictest form. At Cluny intellectual work was stressed; at Clairvaux St. Bernard sought to have his monks engage mainly in manual labor. These differences became more accentuated as time went on, and the Cistercians engaged in more than one war of intrigue, but the sweet disposition of Peter the Venerable preserved harmony between the two Orders. Europe became dotted with Cistercian monasteries; in 1152 there were as many as three hundred and fifty of them, and at the end of the twelfth century this number had increased to five hundred and thirty.

Excessive attachment to wealth and property had brought about the decadence of canonical institution. Chapters had become the almost exclusive rendezvous of the younger sons of noble families. As a rule they entered upon their functions at the age of fifteen, with the title of *domicilli* or *domicillares,* and were first placed under the direction of the canon and master of the cathedral school. They did not receive major Orders, and many of them led worldly lives, paying priests to take their place in the recitation of the Divine Office. This was the manner in which the richest cathedral chapters were constituted, for instance, Notre Dame of Paris, St. Peter of Beauvais, Holy Cross of Orleans, and collegiate chapters like St. Genevieve of Paris and St. Martin of Tours.

Towards the end of the eleventh century a reform was attempted in this field. At first it was thought advisable to replace lax and degenerate canons by Cluniac monks, but the secular clergy quite naturally took umbrage at this. Moreover, the active ministerial life required by service in a cathedral or collegiate church did not agree with the cloistered life. A reform was effected in some chapters by imposing upon members a life in common within the precincts of the same monastery and under the rule of St. Augustine. This was the method followed by *Yvo of Chartres* at St. Quentin de Beauvais. It was difficult, however, to effect anything like a reform in chapters that had been almost completely laicized.

It was then realized that a good way out of the difficulty might be to found special communities of men who, by the severity of their rule and their complete detachment from worldly interests, would be on a par with the Benedictine abbeys. These special canons remained clerics, but pronounced the three vows of poverty, chastity, and obedience, and were subject to the direction of an abbot freely elected by themselves. Such was the origin of the abbeys of the canons regular. *William of Champeaux* founded St. Victor, which became a nursery of sacred orators and theologians. The most successful of all the foundations of canons regular was that of the Premonstratensians founded by *St. Norbert*. This contemporary of the great St. Bernard was born in 1082 at Xanten on the Lower Rhine and spent the early years of his life at the court of Henry V, as chaplain to the Emperor. Converted to a life of austerity after being miraculously saved from a thunderbolt, he made an attempt to reform the secular chapters of his native land, but was soon forced to admit that the task was hopeless. He then journeyed to Rheims and at a place not far distant from that city, in the very heart of the forest of St. Gobain, founded an abbey which he called *Praemonstratum*. Here, as at St. Victor, the canons regular were governed by a severe Rule. They lived in the strictest poverty, abstained entirely from meat, fasted practically all the year round, and lived on the products of their manual labor. They sought also to combine the active with the contemplative life and to fulfill the duties of monks as well as of parish priests. The new institution spread with astonishing rapidity, not only in France, but also in other countries. In less than thirty years after its foundation, the Order counted one hundred abbeys, and a century later one thousand monasteries of men and five hundred convents of nuns.

Many other congregations of canons regular originated at this time. We may cite that of the Lateran, that of St. Rufus near Avignon, that of the Holy Sepulchre at Jerusalem (1114), and that of the Cross, founded by Blessed Agnes of Bohemia (1236). We must call the reader's attention also to the Order of the Crusaders, founded by Theodore of Celles, a canon of Liège, at Clair-Lieu. They derived their name "Crosiers" ("Crusaders") from the fact that they wore a red and white cross on their black scapular. This Order spread rapidly in the Netherlands, France, England, and Germany, and was still quite prominent in the sixteenth century, as is attested by the fact that it obtained from Leo X the privilege to attach an indulgence of five hundred days to each Our Father and Hail Mary of the Rosary.

TEXTS AND DOCUMENTS

THE SOLITUDE OF CLAIRVAUX

The following description of Clairvaux is from the pen of William of St. Thierry, who composed it about 1140:

"At the first glance, as you entered Clairvaux by descending the hill, you could see that it was a temple of God; and the still, silent valley, in the modest simplicity of its buildings, bespoke the unfeigned humility of Christ's poor. Moreover, in this valley full of men, where no one was permitted to be idle, where one and all were occupied with their allotted tasks, a silence deep as that of night prevailed. The sounds of labor, or the chants of the brethren in the choral service, were the only exceptions. The orderliness of this silence, and the report that went forth concerning it, struck such a reverence even into secular persons that they dreaded breaking it, I will not say by idle or wicked conversation, but even by proper remarks. The solitude, also, of the place—between dense forests in a narrow gorge of neighboring hills—in a certain sense recalled the cave of our father St. Benedict, so that, while they strove to imitate his life, they also had some similarity to him in their habitation and loneliness.

As regards their manual labor, so patiently and placidly, with such quiet countenances, in such sweet and holy order do they perform all things, that, although they exercise themselves at many works, they never seem moved or burdened in anything, whatever the labor may be. Many of them, I hear, are bishops and earls, and many illustrious through their birth or knowledge; but now, by God's grace, all distinction of persons being dead among them, the greater anyone thought himself in the world, the more in this flock does he regard himself as less than the least."

Life of St. Bernard, Bk. I, Ch. 7.

QUESTIONS

1. Who were the Petrobrusians?
2. Whence do the Carthusians derive their name?
3. Are there any Carthusians in the United States?
4. Write a short appreciation of St. Bernard.
5. What are the present religious activities of the Premonstratensians?

BIBLIOGRAPHY

Small Sects.—Sources: VITA NORBERTI, Pertz, *Script.*, XII, 663; XIV, 770.—PETER THE VENERABLE, *Tract. contra Petrobrus.*, *P. L.*, CLXXXIX, 719.—Works: BÄUMKER, *Ein Traktat gegen die Amalricianer*, Paderborn, 1893.—On Peter of Bruis, see VACANDARD, *Rev. quest. hist.*, 1894, t. LV, pp. 67–72; and *Vie de saint Bernard*, II, p. 218–221.—F. VERNET, art. *"Bruys,"* in *Dict. de Théol.*—On Arnold of Brescia, see VACANDARD, in *Rev. quest. hist.*, 1884, t. XXXV, pp. 52–114.—F. VERNET, art. *"Arnauld de Brescia,"* in *Dict. de Théol.*

Carthusians.—Sources: D. LE COUTEULX, *Annales Ordinis Cartusiensis*, Montreuil, 1887–1889.—DE LE VASSEUR, *Ephemerides Ordinis Cartusiensis*, 1890–1893.—Works: D. S. AUTORE, art. *"Chartreux,"* in *Dict. de Théol.*

Cistercians.—Sources: *Exordium Ordinis Cist.*, *P. L.*, CLXVI, 150 ff.- *Exordium magnum Ordinis Cist.*, *P. L.*, CLXXXV, 995 ff.—MABILLON, *Annal. O. S. B.*, V, p. 367 ff., 377 ff.—Works: U. BERLIÈRE, *L'ordre monastique des origines au XII⁸ siècle*, ch. VI.—VACANDARD, *Saint Bernard.*—H. D'ARBOIS DE JUBAINVILLE, *Etudes sur l'état intérieur des abbayes cisterciennes au XII⁸ siècle*, 1858.—PH. GUIGNARD, *Les monuments primitifs de la régle cistercienne*, Dijon, 1878.—U. BERLIÈRE, *Les origines de Citeaux et l'Ordre bénédictin au XII⁸ siècle* (*Rev. d'hist. eccl.*, I, 1900, pp. 448–471; II, 1901, pp. 253–290).—DEMIMUID, *Pierre le Vénérable ou la vie et l'influence monastique au XII⁸ siècle*, 1905.—E. MAIRIE, *Les Cisterciens en France, autrefois et aujourd'hui*, 1922.—DOM A. LE BAIL, *L'Ordre de Citeaux. La Trappe* (Coll. *"Les Grands Ordres Religieux"*), 1924.

Reform of the Chapters.—D. MADELAINE, *Histoire de saint Norbert*, Lille, 1887.—E. MAIRE, *Saint Norbert* (Coll. *"Les Saints"*), 1922.—RICHOU, *Essai sur la vie claustrale et l'administration dans l'ordre de l'abbaye de Prémontré au XII⁸ et au XIII⁸ siècle* (Ecole de Chartres, 1875).—LAMY, *L'abbaye de Tongerloo depuis sa fondation jusqu'en 1263* (Collection of works published by the University of Louvain, fasc. XLIV).—FOURIER-BONNARD, *Hist. des chanoines réguliers de Saint-Victor*, 2 vols., 1904–08.—F. PETIT, *L'Ordre des Prémontrés* (Coll. *"Ordres religieux"*), 1927.

SECTION II

From the Advent of Innocent III to Boniface VIII (1198–1294)

CHAPTER I

THE PONTIFICATE OF INNOCENT III

Pope Celestine III died January 8, 1198, and was succeeded by Lothaire, a son of Count Frasmundo de Segni, who took the name of *Innocent III*. The new Pope was an expert theologian and canonist, and also a man of great piety. He had written one treatise "On the Holy Eucharist" and another "On the Contempt of the World." According to him the priesthood and the empire, in ruling Christendom, should be united by the closest bonds. But the priesthood is a spiritual power, whereas the empire is a material one. "Just as the moon receives its light from the sun," he said, "so the royal dignity is nothing more than a reflection of the papal dignity." In formulating this thesis Innocent III was not an innovator. The originality of his teaching lay in an attempt to carry out the plan in reference and opposition to all the great and mighty without exception. Upon his accession to the throne he found Europe far removed from the ideal he had of a Christian empire. Nations were at war with one another and refused to unite against their common enemy, the Saracens. The private lives of kings bordered on immorality, and the faithful had fallen prey to the whims of false reformers. Against all these insurgents without exception he inveighed with a force that was truly astonishing, never once compromising when principles were at stake.

I. **Innocent III and the Empire.** Thus the new Pope brought to the Roman question the steadfast resolution to uphold the rights of the papacy. His plan was to unite Christendom in one supreme attack upon the infidels, for he realized that peace would first have to be re-established in Italy and Germany, but that this was feasible only if the emperors abandoned their dreams of transalpine domination.

Rome, at the time, was in the hands of a very ambitious magistracy that was subservient to the Empire. Moreover, it was torn in all directions by the many factions which existed among the nobility; almost all the provinces of the Church were in the hands of German margraves set up by Henry VI. Innocent III effected quick and radical changes in this state of affairs. He took advantage of the vacancy of the Empire to have the prefect Peter de Vico and a new senator whom he placed at the head of the Roman municipality take an oath of submission to him. In the Patrimony of St. Peter, *i.e.,* in Sabina, Campania, and the Maritime Provinces, he despatched messengers to the barons, giving them the choice either to swear allegiance to him or be deposed from their offices; and in the cities of the Marches of Ancona, Romagna, and Tuscany, he constituted himself the head of the anti-Germanic independence movement. The seneschal of the Empire, Markwald of Anweiler, essayed in vain to maintain his position and reach an agreement with the Pope; he was soon constrained to quit Ravenna. Conrad of Urslingen, Duke of Spoleto, was also forced to capitulate before the threats of the insurgents, and in 1198, Innocent III made a triumphal journey into central Italy, delivered by him from all these factions. In southern Italy, Queen Constance, who had become the regent of Sicily and Naples at the death of her husband, Henry VI, obtained papal recognition, declared herself to be a faithful vassal of the Pope, and completely banished the Germans from her kingdom. In the closing months of the year 1198 she died, leaving her four-year-old son by will and testament in the care of Innocent III, who immediately despatched two cardinals to take charge of affairs. In this manner the entire peninsula was returned to the Italians and entrusted to the care of the papacy.

Meanwhile the Hohenstaufen, *Philip of Suabia,* brother of Henry VI, and *Otto of Brunswick,* of the house of Saxony, were engaged in a struggle for the right of succession in Germany. Both pretenders appealed their case to the Pope, who decided in favor of Otto. "Born of a race," the Pontiff said, "which has always persecuted the Church, Philip would only turn against the Church the weapon we placed in his hand." Moreover, it was believed that the accession of the brother of Henry VI might tend to strengthen the theory of an hereditary empire, in which papal ratification and the ceremony of royal consecration would soon be regarded as mere formalities, while the persistence of the same Caesarian ambitions would be permanently assured. It was these reasons which led Innocent III to favor Otto of Brunswick, who finally gained the upper hand, when his rival was assassinated in 1208.

Otto had scarcely been crowned by the Pope, however, when he began to show himself as haughty and overbearing as any Hohenstaufen. He set out to conquer the entire Italian peninsula, seized the States bequeathed to the papacy by the Margravine Matilda, claimed that all the States of the Church belonged to him, and prepared to take over also the possessions of the Pope's ward, Frederick II, in the two Sicilies. Innocent III remonstrated with, and finally excommunicated him. The Sovereign Pontiff also stirred up enemies against the Emperor: in Italy he aroused the suspicions of the Lombard cities, and in Germany he created a rival in the person of the young *Frederick* (Frederick II). The Pope's ward began by paying homage to him in his capacity of king of Sicily, and then entered Germany to receive the imperial crown at Mayence (1213). He had to wait, however, until Philip Augustus of France, who had accepted the Pope's invitation to rally to his support, had definitively crushed Otto. In the meantime the Pope had intimated to Philip that an offensive alliance between John Lackland of England (1199–1216) and Otto might prove disastrous to the French king. The decisive battle was fought between the contending parties at Bouvines, July 27, 1214, in which the papacy and the Capetian king scored a complete victory. Frederick II was now the undisputed head of the Empire (1216).

II. Innocent III and England: Conflict with John Lackland. In England, John Lackland continued the interfering policy of the Plantagenets, but being less skillful than his predecessors, drew down upon his head the hatred of the clergy and the nobility. His quarrel with the Church began at the death of Hubert Walter, Archbishop of Canterbury and Chancellor of the kingdom. To take his place, the monks of the cathedral in all haste elected their subprior Reginald, while King John nominated one of his tools, Bishop John Gray, of Norwich. For the sake of peace, Innocent III set aside both candidates and appointed as successor to the late archbishop the learned Stephen Langton, professor at the University of Paris and recently promoted to the dignity of cardinal. Foiled in his despotic plans, John Lackland confiscated the goods of the cathedral and evicted the monks. He then sought to levy a heavy tax on the clergy, despite the protests of the Archbishop of York, whom he finally condemned to exile. Innocent placed the entire kingdom under the interdict. Not to be outdone, the King threatened to exile any cleric who heeded the sentence. A number of bishops and priests fled to the Continent and many others were thrown into prison. As a last resort the Pope excommunicated John Lackland and absolved his subjects from their oath of allegiance. He then raised up a powerful enemy to John in the person of Philip Augustus, who immediately began to lay plans for an invasion of England. Frightened, John Lackland surrendered completely to the Pope, and not only conceded every disputed point, but, on May 15, 1213, declared himself *"tamquam feudatarius"* of the Pope and agreed to pay an annual tribute of one thousand marks to the Holy See. Two years later, John Lackland was forced by his rebellious barons to capitulate and sign the Great Charter of English liberties at Runnymede. The liberties of the Church were formulated in the first article: *"Ecclesia anglicana libera sit et habeat jura sua integra et libertates suas illaesas* (Let the Church in England be free and let her rights be complete and her liberties unhampered)." From that moment on, the kings of England never interfered in ecclesiastical elections. After several amendments were made to this document, the Great Charter (*Magna Charta Libertatum*) was ratified the day after the death of Innocent III by his successor Honorius III (November 12, 1216).

III. **Innocent III and France: The Divorce of Philip Augustus.** In August, 1193, Philip Augustus had married as his second wife, Ingeborg, a sister of King Canute III of Denmark. Almost immediately, however, he conceived a strange aversion towards her and sought to repudiate her. A council of bishops and barons, presided over by the King's uncle, the Archbishop of Rheims, convened at Amiens and annulled the marriage. When Ingeborg appealed her case to Rome, she was shut up in a convent and the legates sent by Celestine III were interned in the monastery at Clairvaux. In open defiance to the Pope, Philip Augustus then married Agnes of Meran, daughter of a Bavarian nobleman. As soon as Innocent III was elected to the papacy, he sent letters of protest to the King. "The Holy See," he wrote, "cannot leave persecuted women without defence; the dignity of king does not dispense you from your duties as a Christian." Philip Augustus refused to heed any exhortations, whereupon the Pope placed the entire French kingdom under the interdict (January 14, 1200). The King was beside himself with rage and sought to prevent the papal injunction from being carried out. But the discontent and indignation of his Catholic subjects soon obliged him to yield; he agreed to abide by the decision of an ecclesiastical assembly. The interdict was lifted September 7, 1200, and Philip Augustus made so complete a submission to the Pope at the Council of Soissons, that the bishops who convened there returned home without rendering any decision (1201). The King's conversion, however, was only on the surface; later on he subjected Ingeborg to another imprisonment and yielded finally only in the year 1213.

IV. Innocent III and the Eastern Question: The Fourth and Fifth Crusades. An uppermost thought in the mind of Pope Innocent III had always been to launch a universal Crusade, to free Palestine and all the Christian lands of the East. And so, at the very first opportunity, he issued orders to several preachers to announce a Crusade. Foremost among them was *Fulco,* curate of Neuilly, who rallied to the cause Theobald of Champagne, Louis de Blois, and Simon de Montfort. Neither Philip Augustus, who had been excommunicated on account of his divorce, nor Otto of Brunswick, who was engaged in a war with Philip of Suabia, took part in the expedition, the direction of which was entrusted to the Marquis *Boniface of Montserrat.* The Crusaders were well informed of the dangers that would beset them along the land route, and so resolved to embark from the coast of the Adriatic Sea. They appealed to the citizens of Venice to furnish them with ships, but the latter first exacted that they undertake a preliminary expedition against Zara, a rival port on the coast of Dalmatia. Zara, a Christian city, despite the repeated protests and prohibitions of Innocent III, was seized by the Crusaders.

But the Venetians had a much more formidable opponent to contend with in the Greeks than their rivals, the inhabitants of Zara, and for a long time the Doge Henry Dandolo had entertained the project of ending his differences with them by conquering the whole Byzantine Empire. At this juncture, a national crisis furnished him with the opportunity to meddle in their affairs. In the year 1095, Alexis III had deposed and blinded his brother Isaac Angelus. Alexis IV, the son of the unfortunate victim, journeyed to the West in search of help. The Crusaders were easily persuaded by his many attractive promises: to make them a gift of 200,000 silver marks, to return himself to the communion of the Church of Rome, to take part in the Crusade to the Holy Land, and to maintain a standing military organization of 500 knights in the East.

The orders of Innocent III to the Crusaders, not to allow themselves to be allured by these offers, arrived too late to prevent the disastrous expedition. In ten days the Christian army seized Byzantium, which was almost without defence (July 17, 1203) and re-established Isaac on his throne. The harmony thus obtained, however, was of short duration, and conflicts soon broke out between the Latins and the Greeks. Not having very much money, Isaac was unable to keep his part of the contract. Moreover, he had become very unpopular with the Greeks, and in the course of a national revolution was replaced by an adventurer, Alexis V, who forced the Crusaders to withdraw to their ships. The Crusaders' armies then attacked Constantinople, April 12, 1204, and after a desperate struggle captured the city, which they subjected to a hideous carnage. The Eastern Empire was abolished, a Latin Empire was erected in its stead, and Count *Baldwin of Flanders* was elected king. A number of duchies and marquisates divided the country among themselves, while Venice took as her share of the booty Crete and several other islands and ports in the Levant, which formed an uninterrupted chain from Venice to the Black Sea.

Innocent III could do nothing more than accept the *fait accompli.* Moreover, it was his opinion that the Church would win out in the end and secure invaluable assistance for the Crusade. His hopes were unfounded. Threatened on the European boundary by the Bulgarians, who overthrew and killed the Emperor Baldwin (1206), and attacked from the East by the Greeks, who had taken refuge at Nicaea, the Latin Empire finally (1261) crumbled to the ground without achieving anything for the cause of Christianity.

Innocent III's plans for the East had, therefore, completely failed. Another Crusade was inaugurated in 1212 by a young shepherd boy, named Stephen, from Cloyes near Vendôme, who travelled the length and breadth of the land crying out, "Lord God, deliver Christendom!" He assembled an army of children, women, and young girls, many of whom were sent back to their homes, but 1500 of whom succeeded in embarking at Marseilles. The latter either perished at sea or were sold to the Mussulmans by ship-owners from Marseilles. A similar expedition which set out from Germany was fortunately stopped by the bishop of Brindisi, who prevented the men from embarking.

To the very last day of his life Innocent III preached a Crusade which took place only after his death. This fifth Crusade was inaugurated at the Fourth Council of the Lateran, in 1215, and was first headed by Andrew II, King of Hungary. Later on, however, he withdrew his support because of the passive attitude of the barons of the Holy Land. The war was resumed by John of Brienne, titular King of Jerusalem, who attacked the Moslems in Egypt and seized the strongly fortified town of Damietta, the key city to the river Nile. The Crusaders should have proceeded immediately to Cairo, but a quarrel which ensued between the legate Pelagius and King John forced them to delay the attack. Taking advantage of this situation the Mussulmans destroyed the dikes of the Nile and opened the sluices of the river. The crusading army was forced to withdraw and evacuate Damietta. The fifth Crusade, therefore, also turned out to be a failure.

TEXTS AND DOCUMENTS

PRINCIPAL PORTIONS OF THE INTERDICT PRONOUNCED BY INNOCENT III

Let all the churches be closed; let no one be admitted to them, except to baptize infants; let them not be otherwise opened, except for the purpose of lighting the lamps, or when the priest shall come for the Eucharist and Holy Water for the use of the sick. We permit Mass to be celebrated once a week, on Friday, early in the morning, to consecrate the Host for the use of the sick, but only one cleric is to be admitted to assist the priest. Let the clergy preach on Sunday in the vestibules of the churches, and in place of the Mass let them deliver the Word of God. Let them recite the Canonical Hours outside the churches, where the people do not hear them; if they recite an epistle or a gospel, let them beware lest the laity hear them; and let them not permit the dead to be interred, nor their bodies to be placed unburied in the cemeteries. Let them, moreover, say to the laity that they sin and transgress grievously by burying bodies in the earth, even in unconsecrated ground, for in so doing they assume to themselves an office pertaining to others.

Let them forbid their parishioners to enter churches that may be open in the King's territory, and let them not bless the wallets of pilgrims, except outside the churches. Let them not celebrate the offices in Passion week, but refrain even until Easter day, and then let them celebrate in private, no one being admitted except the assisting priest, as above directed; let no one communicate, even at Easter, unless he be sick and in danger of death. During the same week, or on Palm Sunday, let them announce to their parishioners that they may assemble on Easter morning before the church and there have permission to eat flesh and consecrated bread. . . . Let the priest confess all who desire it in the portico of the church; if the church have no portico, we direct that in bad or rainy weather, and not otherwise, the nearest door of the church may be opened and confessions heard on its threshold (all being excluded except the one who is to confess), so that the priest and the penitent can be heard by those who are outside the church. If, however, the weather be fair, let the confession be heard in front of the closed doors. Let no vessels of Holy Water be placed outside the church, nor shall the priests carry them anywhere; for all the Sacraments of the Church beyond these two which are reserved are absolutely prohibited. Extreme Unction, which is a holy Sacrament, may not be given.

F. A. OGG, *Source Book of Mediæval
History*, pp. 382–383.

QUESTIONS

1. Give an estimate of the character and work of Innocent III.
2. What is the special importance of the Magna Charta for Church History?
3. Indicate the outstanding reasons for the failure of the Fourth Crusade.
4. What do you know about the Children's Crusade?

BIBLIOGRAPHY

Innocent III.—Sources: *P. L.,* CCXIV–CCXVII.—POTTHAST, *Regesta pont. rom.,* I, pp. 1–467.—General Works: HURTER, *Histoire du Pape Innocent III et de ses contemporains,* 3 vols.—LUCHAIRE, *Innocent III,* 6 vols.—*Cath. Encyl.,* art. *"Innocent III."*

Innocent III and Germany.—WINKELMANN, *Philipp von Schwaben und Otto IV,* 2 vols., 1873 and 1878.—HAUCK, *Kirchengeschichte Deutschlands,* vol. IV, *Die Hohenstaufenzeit,* 1902.—ZELLER, *Histoire d'Allemagne,* t. IV.—LUCHAIRE, *Innocent III, La papauté et l'Empire,* 1908.

Innocent III and England.—LUCHAIRE, *Innocent III. Les royautés vassales du Saint-Siège.*—W. STUBBS, *Constitutional History of England.*—GREEN, *History of the English People.*—ELSE GÜTSCHOW, *Innocent III. und England,* 1904.

Innocent III and France.—P. FOURNIER, *Les conflits de juridiction entre l'Eglise et le pouvoir séculier de 1180 à 1328.*—LUCHAIRE, *Innocent III. Les royautés vassales du Saint-Siège: Louis VII, Philippe-Auguste et Saint-Louis,* in *Histoire de France* by E. Lavisse, III, 1st Part, 1901.—J. DE LA SERVIÈRE, art. *"Divorce des princes et l'Eglise,"* in *Dict. d'Apol.,* fasc. IV, col. 116.

Innocent III and the Eastern Question.—Sources: VILLE-HARDOUIN, *La conquête de Constantinople,* edit. Natalis de Wailly.—ROBERT DE CLARI, *Chron. gréco-romanes,* 1873.—GÜNTHER, *De Pairis, P. L.,* CCXII, 222–255.—Works: RIANT, *Innocent III, Philippe de Souabe et Boniface de Montserrat*

(*Rev. quest. hist.*, XVII and XVIII, 1875); *Le changement de direction de la IVe croisade (ibid.*, XXIII, 1878).—HANOTAUX, *Les Vénitiens on-tils trahi la chrétienté en 1202?* (*Rev. hist.*, 1877).—NORDEN, *Der vierte Kreuzzug im Rahmen der Beziehungen des Abendlandes zu Byzanz*, Berlin, 1898; *Das Papsttum und Byzanz*, 1903, pp. 133–164.—LUCHAIRE, *Innocent III, La question d'Orient.*—BREHIER, *Les croisades*, ch. VII.

The Latin Empire.—DUCANGE, *Histoire de l'empire de Constantinople sous les empereurs français.*—GERLAND, *Geschichte der Kaiser Balduin I und Heinrich, 1204–1216*, Hamburg, 1905.—J. LONGNON, *Les Français en Grèce au XIIIe siècle* (*Correspondant*, Feb. 1917); *Les Français d'Outre Mer au Moyen Age*, 1929.

CHAPTER II

The anticlerical movement, which had remained in abeyance during the eleventh century, now assumed disquieting proportions. The loose state of morals which prevailed on all sides favored the rise and rapid expansion, at this particular time, of many extravagant and in some instances scandalous sects, nearly all of which had socialistic or anarchistic tendencies. We shall deal with each respectively.

I. The False Reform. 1. The Waldenses. *Peter Waldo* was a wealthy merchant of Lyons, who, grieved by the sudden death of one of his friends, and touched to the quick by the story of St. Alexis, resolved to lead the perfect life. He bequeathed part of his fortune to his wife and distributed the remainder among the poor. From that moment on his uppermost thought was to live the Apostolic life, the outstanding characteristics of which, to his way of thinking, were poverty and itinerant preaching. He began at once to discourse on the Word of God and gathered a few disciples, who, in order to carry out the injunctions of the Gospel literally, set out two by two, shod with sandals. Hence their name *Insabati*. The members of this small community lived on the charity of those whom they converted, a fact which accounts for their other name, "The Poor Men," or "The Beggars of Lyons." They were also called "Leonists" on account of the city of Lyons, in which they were founded, but preferred to go by the name of "The Humble Ones" (*Humiliati*). Their weapon of preaching was the Bible, which Waldo had had translated into French. Waldo failed, however, to receive papal approbation for his enterprise, and the members of his sect, being laymen, were forbidden to preach by the Archbishop of Lyons. They were also regarded unfavorably by the clergy. The Waldenses then became obstinate and grouped themselves into an Order. They rejected all hierarchical authority, claiming that merit alone confers the right to direct souls (*"magis operatur meritum quam ordo"*). According to them, the pope, bishops,

498

and priests were wielding a usurped power: in the spiritual domain they had not the right to administer the Sacraments, and in the temporal domain they had no privileges. This heresy obtained many followers in Burgundy, the Franche-Comté, and as far as Lorraine to the North, and Dauphiny, Provence, and Narbonne to the South. It even spread into Italy and had followers also in Germany, Bohemia, and Poland. The movement not only gained steadily in influence and importance, but outlived many others of a similar nature. Relegated finally to the high valleys of the Alps, the Waldenses continued to exist up to the sixteenth century, and are regarded as precursors of the Protestant Reformation.

2. **The Albigenses.** The Albigensian heresy reminds us forcibly of the Gnostic and Manichaean heresies. It was a product of the East. An Armenian by the name of Constantine of Samosata had revived Manichaean Gnosticism in the seventh century and spread that heresy in Asia Minor. His followers were called *Paulicians,* because they professed a high esteem for St. Paul. In the eighth century Leo the Armenian and the Empress Theodora sought to smother the movement in blood, but the Paulicians rallied to their cause the Saracens, engaged in many fierce battles in defence of their claims, and even defeated the combined Greek armies until Basil the Macedonian succeeded in crushing them (871). But small groups could still be found here and there in the Empire, notably in Thrace, whither a number of them had been transported. Later on the towns and villages of Bulgaria, a country but recently and imperfectly converted to Christianity, became infested with this heresy. In the second half of the tenth century, during the reign of the Czar Peter, *Bogomil* preached a form of Manichaeism there which admitted of many variations. At bottom, however, it advocated the same ancient doctrine, to wit, the constant struggle of the God of Evil, Satan, against the God of Goodness, who in this case, however, was called the Archangel Michael. The heresy met with great success, until the day when Byzantium intervened. In the opening years of the twelfth century, the Emperor Alexis I Comnenus (1081–1118) issued orders for the physician Basil, the head of the Bogomils, to be burned at the stake and all of his followers imprisoned. But the heresy continued to thrive under cover, especially in several monasteries. After the invasion of the Turks, the Bogomils of Bulgaria embraced Islamism in response to the preaching of Mahmoud Beddredin, an individual half-Turk and half-Christian.

The Bogomils would be of only remote interest to us if they were not, in a sense, the precursors of the Albigensian heresy. Manichaeism could originate from no other source than the East. In the seventh century, St. Gregory the Great called attention to its presence in Sicily, and in the eleventh century, the movement penetrated into southern France by way of Italy. Here it was called *Catharism* (καθαρός = pure), because its followers laid claim to a purity unknown to other men. It was also called Albigensianism, although Toulouse and not Albi was its main center. The basic teaching of Catharism was the dualism so dear to Manes: a principle of goodness which created the spirits, and a principle of evil which created matter. By force or ruse the evil principle seized a number of spirits and imprisoned them in matter. God, however, delivered them by sending His son, who was not a consubstantial son, but an angel. This angel being incorruptible, was not contaminated by the baseness of matter, and so the body with which he was clothed was not real, but apparent. It follows that he saved the world not by his sufferings, but by his preaching, instructing men to free themselves from the worship of the principle of evil and the tyrannical rule of matter. The logical consequence of all this was that honors, power, war, and marriage were sinful; that the body must be brought into subjection by fasting and mortification, and one should wish for death and bring it on if necessary by phlebotomy, by poison, or by what they termed the *endura* (Catharist suicide code), which consisted in starving oneself to death. Such a merciless system of morals was naturally not within the reach of all men, and so it was customary to distinguish two classes of Cathari: the "believers" and the "perfect." The latter were admitted to perfection by means of the *consolamentum* or Baptism of the Holy Spirit, conferred by the imposition of hands. They bound themselves to the observance of the moral teachings of their sect in all its strictness, and having severed all family ties, went about two by two preaching and administering the *consolamentum*. Ownership of private property was regarded as sinful, and the mass of believers lived a life in common under the direction of the perfect, promising to receive the *consolamentum* in danger of death. No wonder, then, that Professor Kurth, in speaking of this heresy, describes it as "a dark night which came down with the weight of lead and with the coldness of ice upon the mind and the heart, a chancre of death which ate at all the luminous and elevated faculties of the human soul, a deadly folly that choked the joy of living and made existence here below appear like a bad dream."

The heresy obtained great success in Languedoc, where its adepts assumed the name of Albigenses and turned persecutors. At Toulouse they almost constrained Catholics to conceal their faith. In the twelfth century the Church sought to suppress the movement by preaching, but Radulphus Ardens and St. Bernard met with very little success. "Even priests," wrote Raymond V of Toulouse, "have allowed themselves to be contaminated by this heresy; the churches are deserted or in ruins; the sword which pierces the heart will alone issue in a salutary warning." Nevertheless, the Church continued for thirty years to combat the evil effects of Albigensianism by peaceful methods; Innocent III himself worked untiringly to achieve this result for ten years (1198–1208).

At this juncture an event occurred which effected a complete change in the situation. After vainly entreating Raymond VI of Toulouse to take up arms against the heresy, the legate Peter of Castelnau excommunicated him in the name of the Pope. Peter was later on murdered by a follower of the Count on the banks of the Rhone. It was then that, all other means having failed, Innocent III resolved to proclaim a Crusade against the movement. Philip Augustus was in conflict at the time with John Lackland of England and refused to head the expedition. An army of about 200,000 Crusaders, recruited chiefly from among the nobility of the North of France, answered his invitation and took Simon de Montfort as their leader. The campaign undertaken against Roger of Beziers and Count Raymond VI of Toulouse dragged on amidst scenes of unspeakable cruelty for almost twenty years, and the fire of the religious struggle was enkindled still more by the rivalry between the North and the South and differences in customs and language. The southern provinces were completely devastated, and many unfortunate incidents occurred which are not imputable to the Church. It is not true, for instance, that the papal legate Arnold made this statement to Roger of Beziers: "Kill them all; God will recognize those who belong to Him." Simon de Montfort fell while besieging Toulouse (1215), but the heresy was finally suppressed. In 1229 the Council of Toulouse condemned it from the dogmatic point of view.

Many reasons account for the success which these exotic doctrines achieved in Southern France. In the first place, the nobility was the born rival of the clergy and willingly gave its support to a sect which advocated the complete suppression of ecclesiastical property. In the second place, the austere life of the "perfect" stood in marked contrast with the life of pleasure and loose morals of some clerics, and gave them great moral standing with the people. Their foremost concern was the apostolate, and to exercise it more efficaciously, they looked out for the material interests of the people. This fact accounts for a great number of the "perfect" being physicians. Finally, it not infrequently happened that the "perfect," being the recipients of gifts and bequests from their followers, handled large sums of money in the form of loans and alms. In the principal market-towns of Languedoc they opened workshops and engaged in crafts that gave them better access to the population. They trained apprentices in these places, who very soon became heretics like themselves.

3. The Amalricians. *Amalric of Bena* was one of the most outstanding and popular professors at the University of Paris, where he taught logic and exegesis. In the course of his lectures he set forth the theory that Jesus dwells in Christian souls in such a way that each member of the faithful is not only a member of Christ according to the common acceptation of that term, but an integral part of the Divinity. Formulated in this way, his theory bordered on Pantheism. He was condemned in 1206, but recanted his errors. He died of grief in 1209.

After the death of Amalric his disciples incorporated his teachings into a regular system of thought. According to them, the Trinity underwent a triple evolution, marked by a triple incarnation. During the first period, the Father alone became incarnate in the bosom of Abraham; during the second period, the Son became incarnate in Christ; and during the third period, the Holy Ghost becomes incarnate in the souls of all Christians, who are in this way divinized according to the Pantheistic teaching of Amalric. Quite naturally, the third period, which marked the incarnation of the Holy Ghost, began only with the Amalricians. The "Spirituals," as they were called, considered themselves as risen from the dead. This resurrection was understood in the true sense of the term, being nothing more than the life of the Spirit, and the substitution of the clear findings of science in place of the obscure notions of faith and hope, which must be henceforth discarded. Paradise was the contemplation of these new truths, and hell the ignorance thereof. Children born of a spiritual father and mother have no need of Baptism; Communion is nothing more

than the sharing by all in the same Spirit; while Penance is of no use
to those who know that God, being and doing all in all men, is as much
the Author of those acts which we call sins, as He is of all other acts. An
absolute Quietism of this sort naturally issued in complete disregard of
morality. The heresy was uncovered in 1209 and the sect tenaciously pursued. Its principal leaders were either burned or poisoned.

4. **The Suppression of Heresy: The Inquisition.** In the Middle
Ages, when religious beliefs were completely unified and the Church and
State were joint powers, heresy was regarded as a crime against society,
to be repressed by coercive means. Up to the middle of the twelfth century, however, ecclesiastical authority usually inflicted only spiritual penalties, such as excommunication, the interdict, etc. Less patient in their
attitude, the civil power by its sentences, and the discontented people by
their uprisings, foreshadowed the use of more violent means and, in fact,
lighted the first fires. During the second half of the twelfth century some
princes even went so far as to insist that the Church have recourse to
physical violence, and this is true not only of devout kings like Louis
VII of France, but also of princes like Henry II of England and Frederick
Barbarossa of Germany, who in the course of their lives rebelled against
the Church. The reason for their action is to be found in the fact that
heresy had ceased to be a mere discussion in the hands of misguided
schoolmen, and threatened to sway the masses by theories destructive of
the established order. At the Council of Verona, in 1184, Pope Lucius III,
in conjunction with Frederick Barbarossa, explicitly decreed the physical
punishment of heretics. Orders were issued not only to punish heretics
known to be such, but to ferret them out (*inquisitio*). The task was entrusted to the zeal of dependable bishops, and delinquents were required
to recant their errors or receive a punishment inflicted by civil authority.
But the action of the bishops was confined to their own dioceses, whereas
heresy sometimes spread out over extensive territories. Actively to combat
the evil, therefore, the bishops were constrained to meet periodically and
engage in lengthy discussions. The papacy soon realized that the business
of suppressing heresy would have to be entrusted to papal legates—an
authority which partook of its own character of universality. These legates were frequently selected from the ranks of religious who belonged to
the Mendicant Orders, Dominican or Franciscan Friars. The above facts
account for the existence of two Inquisitions: the first episcopal; the

second, legatine. The Anticatharist Councils of Narbonne (1227) and Toulouse (1229) completed the plan of organization, and for a period which lasted from 1225 to 1240 the ecclesiastical tribunal known as the Inquisition functioned in accordance with the wishes of popes, princes and bishops alike in every Christian country, with the exception of England.

The procedure adopted was as follows. As soon as it was decided to conduct an investigation in a heresy-ridden district, the inquisitor promulgated two edicts: the first, termed the Edict of Faith, addressed to the faithful and commanding them to denounce all heretics under pain of excommunication; the second, termed the Edict of Grace, addressed to the heretics themselves, summoning them to appear before the inquisitor and promising them forgiveness if they recanted their errors within the space of from fifteen to thirty days. When this time was passed, the suspicioned heretic was denounced as a suspect and kept under close observation or imprisoned to await trial. He then had the option of either remaining stubborn or repenting. In the latter case the inquisitor received his confession and imposed upon him, not a severe physical punishment like temporary or permanent incarceration or surrender to the secular power, but a suitable canonical penance, like a pilgrimage, assistance at the Divine Office, etc. If the heretic persisted in remaining stubborn, he could be further induced to yield by the fear of death, more or less close confinement, possibly emphasized by curtailment of food or torture, but above all, by friendly persuasion. When the procedure was ended, the inquisitor pronounced the sentence in a public and solemn assembly called for the purpose (*sermo generalis*).

The punishments inflicted were of various kinds. Some, as we have already stated, were canonical penances rather than corporal chastisements, such as scourgings, pilgrimages, or services to be rendered in the Holy Land; others affected the fortune of the condemned person, to wit, confiscation of his property, destruction of his home, fines, etc.; others, finally, were visited upon the individual himself, such as imprisonment or death at the stake.

Much has been written against the Inquisition. Like any human tribunal, it was sometimes presided over by cruel and rapacious judges, who were moved by the desire to profit by confiscations, but history shows that a great number of these judges were quite merciful. "The inquisitor," says Bernard Guy in his *Practica*, "must be a diligent and devout servant of religious truth. Amidst difficulties of all sorts, he must remain calm, never give vent to anger or indignation, never harden his heart to the extent of refusing delays or modifications of penalties according to circumstances."

The *Fourth Council of the Lateran,* convoked by Innocent III (1215), attempted a wholesome reform within the Church. No less than 412 bishops and 800 abbots or priors took part in its discussions. Besides condemning the errors of Joachim of Flora and the Albigenses, the Council adopted resolutions regarding ecclesiastical discipline, episcopal elections, and the selection of clerics. Bishops were requested to establish schools of grammar and theology for the instruction of clerics and poor students, and ordeals (direct judgments of God) were prohibited as well as duels. The many decisions reached by this Council forcibly remind one of the later Council of Trent. The Mendicant Orders, Dominicans and Franciscans, lent a helping hand to execute the reforms decreed by the Council.

II. The True Reform: The Mendicant Orders. *St. Dominic* was born at Calaroga in Old Castile, not far from the monastery of Silos (1170). He made his studies at the University of Palencia and, about 1194, became a canon of the cathedral church of Osma. He worked assiduously to reform the chapter by the aid of the Rule of St. Augustine and became prior in 1201. Shortly afterwards he accompanied his Bishop, Diego of Acebes, to Rome, and Pope Innocent III entrusted both with a mission among the Albigenses (1204). Dominic had several discussions with these heretics: at Servian, near Béziers, he argued with Baldwin and Thierry of Nevers; at Pamiers with Durand of Najac (1205-1207), and so forth. On all these occasions he met with little success, and so resolved to vary the methods of his apostolate. Seeing the need of safeguarding women converted from heresy against the evil influences of their own homes, he founded a convent for the education of young girls in Prouille, at the foot of the Pyrenees. His dealings with the Albigenses finally gave him the idea of founding an Order to supply the deficiencies of religious instruction among the faithful. The first weapon of these new religious, he insisted, would be poverty, to prove that it is possible to observe the evangelical counsels without denying the Church. To the "perfection" of Catharism, St. Dominic opposed that of Christianity.

The success with which his disciples met, was unprecedented, not only among the common people, but also among the educated, and their influence was strongly felt even in the universities. As early as 1218, John of Barastre bequeathed to the Order of Friars Preachers of Paris his mansion of St. James, and the members of the Dominican community of Bologna received St. Mary of Mascarella. A valuable recruit was Reginald, a former professor at the University of Paris. In and after 1221 the chapter of the Order created eight provinces. St. Dominic died in the same year. His successor, Jordan of Saxony, foresaw the day when all the members of the University staff would be Dominicans.

St. Francis of Assisi was born in 1182, the son of a wealthy clothier. In his early youth he indulged freely in pleasures, which were, however, never of a character to compromise his dignity or taint his honor as a Christian gentleman. After witnessing a vision at Spoleto (1204), he resolved to give up the ways of the world and journeyed to Rome as a beggar (1206). One day, while he was praying in the ruins of the little church of St. Damian, he heard Jesus Christ saying to him: "Francis, go and rebuild my house." He took these words literally and spent his entire fortune in rebuilding St. Damian's church. His action aroused the disapproval of his father, but Francis merely retorted by stripping himself in his presence of the very clothes he wore. He then set out on his new career as *"poverello"* and began to collect funds to repair fully the church of St. Damian, and later on the church of St. Mary of the Angels (Portiuncula). On February 24, 1209, he heard a priest preach on the words of Christ, "Take nothing for your journey, neither staff, nor scrip, nor bread, nor money, neither have two coats," gathered together a few disciples, among whom were Bernard of Quintavalle and Peter of Cattana, and imposed upon them the observance of strict poverty, penance, and preaching two by two. Innocent III verbally approved this mode of living in 1210. St. Francis then dreamed of converting the Mohammedans. He set out for Syria in 1211, but was forced back to port by a storm. In 1213 he tried again, following the route of Morocco, but this time sickness constrained him to retrace his steps. In 1219 he made a third attempt to leave for the Orient, but the complete failure of the fifth Crusade again forced him to return.

The only apostolate in which St. Francis succeeded was the one he undertook in Europe. He preached in Rome, Umbria, the Marches, and

Tuscany, and disciples flocked to him from all sides. With him absolute poverty was not merely a practice, but an essential principle underlying the very existence of an Order founded in direct opposition to the wealth and pleasures of the world. His followers clothed themselves with the garment of the poor, wearing a coarse, brown, woolen tunic with a pointed hood or capuche. They girded themselves with an ordinary knotted cord and went about barefooted and shod with only wooden sandals. They were known by the name of Friars Minor (*Fratres Minores,* abbr. O.F.M., *Ordo Fratrum Minorum*) and were required to practice poverty in its most rigorous form and follow the example of the beggar who depends entirely for his living upon public generosity. And since they preached more by example than by word of mouth, their influence was remarkable.

To act more directly on the masses by incorporating them into their great religious family through the Third Order, St. Francis also established a community of women, under the direction of his spiritual daughter, *St. Clare of Assisi,* but enjoined upon them complete seclusion and perpetual silence. This institute was called, "The Second Order of St. Francis," or "The Poor Clares." The latter accounts for the society founded for members who continued to live in the world, being called *"Third Order."* This Order furnished many pious Christians who could not sever their family ties with an opportunity to live a semi-religious life and share in the spiritual advantages of the Franciscan Order.

The Mendicant Orders soon aroused envy. The Dominicans, indeed, had succeeded in having themselves appointed to several chairs in the University, where their presence was strongly objected to by the lay professors. Moreover, the fruitful apostolate of Dominicans and Franciscans frequently aroused the hostility of the secular clergy. The theory was soon advanced that a mendicant friar could not exercise his ministry without the express permission of bishop and pastor. The question was agitated at several provincial councils and was finally settled by Pope Clement IV, who made episcopal authorization obligatory. Pope Martin IV confirmed this decision.

At the very outset, St. Francis had formulated a Rule written in the simplest language. He specified his thought more clearly in the Rule of 1223, approved by Honorius III. This new Rule required religious to renounce all right to property. The first disciples of St. Francis had accepted this stipulation, but more recent recruits declared that an ideal of that

kind was impossible of attainment. Francis was grieved by these misunderstandings, and withdrew to Mt. Alverna, where, on the feast of the
Exaltation of the Cross, September 14, 1224, he received the sacred stigmata
of the Passion. Two years later, when dying and singing about his sister,
Death, he drew up a testament in which he insisted on absolute austerity.
This action resulted in further agitation. Some of his disciples maintained
that the testament was just as binding on his followers as the Rule; others,
that it had no binding force whatever. In 1230 Pope Gregory IX took sides
with the latter party and created a *nuntius apostolicus,* who saw to it that
the religious received what they could not acquire by begging. This mitiga-
tion of discipline was looked upon as indispensable even by St. Antony
of Padua, but was greatly exaggerated by the ambitious *Brother Elias,*
who succeeded in deposing the General of the Order, John Parenti of
Carmignogna, and having himself elected in his place. His election marked
the beginning of a new era. He abandoned all the early practices, such as
hermitages, daily begging, etc., and issued orders for the construction of
magnificent churches, like that of the Holy Cross at Florence. He was
finally denounced and removed from office by Pope Gregory IX in 1239,
but became reconciled to the Church before his death (1253).

The partisans of extreme poverty, or "Spirituals," as they called themselves, continued their attack upon the "Community." Very soon they
declared themselves in favor of the ideas of Joachim of Flora. Joachim
was the saintly abbot of a Cistercian monastery in Calabria, who had
died in 1202, without being aware of the poisonous doctrines contained in
three of his writings: *The Concordance of the Old and New Testaments,
The New Apocalypse,* and *The Psalter of the Ten Cords.* He divided the
history of the world into three ages, corresponding to the three Persons
of the Blessed Trinity. In the first, which was the pre-Christian period,
the Father ruled, representing the power of the marriage state; in the
second, which is the Christian period, the Son rules, representing the
clerical state; in the third, that of the Holy Spirit, a new monastic Order
will convert the world. The "Spirituals" were not slow in recognizing
themselves in this new monastic Order. Between the years 1240 and
1260 their ideas made great progress. One of their number, John Burali
of Parma, became Superior General of the Order, and in 1250 another,
Fra Gerardo of Borgo San Donnino, wrote an *Introduction to the*

Eternal Gospel, in which he formulated the programme of *Neo-Joachimism.* According to this treatise the Catholic priesthood, including the papacy itself and the whole teaching of the New Testament, would be rendered void in a few years. Pope Alexander IV ordered the book to be burned (1254); its author was condemned the year after. The Superior General, John Burali of Parma, was forced to abdicate (beatified in 1777).

These dissensions were followed by a wise reaction, brought about by St. Bonaventure. The latter took into account several criticisms of abuses formulated by the "Spirituals," and in order to dissipate all misunderstandings, composed a new life of St. Francis and re-edited the Constitutions of the Order. In 1279 Pope *Nicholas III* clarified a number of disputed points of the Rule, especially those which had reference to the vow of poverty. He decreed that the property of the Order be henceforth held in the name of the Holy See, and that the religious have the use of it in conformity with their vow of poverty. Subsequently, Pope Martin IV designated pontifical legates to receive alms and draw up the necessary contracts. The concessions made by the Sovereign Pontiff, however, were abused. Under the leadership of *John Peter Oliva* the "Spirituals" raised their voice in protest and directly attacked the Bull of Nicholas III. According to Oliva, the Franciscans were entitled to the same use of all goods as the poor, and he proscribed anything which the poor could dispense with. This obligation continued to bind members of the Order who became bishops or cardinals. Throughout the bitter discussions in which he engaged, Oliva was guilty at times of mistakes in terminology and even doctrine, but he never once disputed the authority of the pope. In the fourteenth century his disciples exaggerated his ideas and rose in open revolt. And so it came to pass that the "Spirituals," who still constituted but one party in the Order of St. Francis, became the *Fratricelli,* who were heretics.

Some of the Benedictine monasteries had small brotherhoods of hermits under their protection, the most outstanding of which was at Montserrat in Spain, but there existed a number of isolated hermits whose lives were at times far from edifying. An effort was made during this period in Italy to group all the hermits together into local congregations. And so we have the John Bonists founded by the Blessed John Bon near Mantua (around 1209); the Brittinians in the Marches of Ancona; the Brothers of the Sack; the Congregations of Vallersuta, of St. Mary of Murcette, etc. Some of these congregations followed the Rule of St. Benedict, others that of St. Augustine, and still others had no rule at all. To put order into this chaos, Pope Alexander IV resolved to combine them all into one Order, which assumed the name of Hermits of St. Augustine. The principal heads of these congregations convened in Rome, elected a superior general, and divided their monasteries into four provinces. The new Order followed the Rule of St. Augustine and soon received Constitutions approved by the general chapters of Florence (1287) and Ratisbon (1290). The Order spread rapidly and in a comparatively short space of time counted 42 provinces, 2000 monasteries and 30,000 members. But in the fourteenth century its discipline had become very lax.

According to a tradition of the Carmelites, the founder of the hermits of Mt. Carmel was a certain Berthold, who lived in the twelfth century. They led the religious life under the patronage of the Prophet Elias, and in all probability followed the Rule of St. Augustine. Between 1206 and 1214 the patriarch of Jerusalem gave them a more suitable Rule. They possessed several monasteries in Palestine, the principal of which was that at Acre. In the thirteenth century, however, they decided to take refuge in Europe and established themselves in a number of large cities and also at the universities of Cambridge (1249), Oxford (1253), Paris (1259), and Bologna (1260). Pope Gregory IX had already ranked them among the Mendicant Orders, and the first chapter, held in England, elected St. Simon Stock superior general. Certain changes in the Rule made by Pope Innocent IV enabled the Order, which was contemplative in its foundation, to engage in activities similar to those of the Dominicans. This change resulted in a schism between those who favored such activities and the immediate successors of St. Simon Stock. The latter resigned their posts and withdrew into isolated monasteries. In the course of the fourteenth century more serious difficulties arose.

Canon 23 of the Council of Lyons (1274) confirmed the institution of the four great Mendicant Orders, to wit, the Dominicans, the Franciscans, the Augustinian Hermits, and the Carmelites, but being of the opinion that the great number of congregations had been one of the causes of confusion, suppressed all Orders which had appeared since the Council of the Lateran (1215) and had not received ecclesiastical approbation.

TEXTS AND DOCUMENTS

MOTIVES BEHIND THE INQUISITION

In the last analysis, the introduction and aggravation of the Inquisition was mainly influenced by two ideas, or, more correctly, the exaggeration of these two ideas. The Middle Ages by the power of the faith accomplished great things in all spheres of social life and art, produced saints, and erected architectural monuments before which we bow our head in awe and admiration. But this glowing faith concealed a danger which not all the men of that time were able to escape: I mean the danger of overdoing a good thing. This tendency to exaggerate led to fanaticism, which deadens the brain and petrifies the heart that loves the faith above everything, but does not glow with charity, having lost sight of the Apostle's dictum: If I had faith strong enough to transfer mountains, without love I should be nothing. Those who were thus affected loudly demanded the stake: many laymen even outdid the clergy, and so the Inquisition found open doors. Closely connected with the exaggerated enthusiasm for the faith was the overemphasis given to another idea, namely, that to the clergy belonged superiority and leadership in all domains of social, nay, even political life. Though the underlying idea was perfectly correct, when exaggerated it was bound to divert the ecclesiastical authorities from their own proper sphere and to urge them to adopt material measures which were not essential to their spiritual mission.

(Father Bernard Duhr, S. J., quoted in *The Fortnightly Review*, St. Louis, Mo., Nov. 1929, p. 279).

QUESTIONS

1. Indicate the causes of the false Reform.
2. Note the outstanding errors of the Albigensian heresy.
3. Justify the creation of the Inquisition as a means to uproot heresy.
4. What is meant by a mendicant Order? a contemplative Order?
5. Differentiate between orthodox and unorthodox poverty and austerity in the case of the Waldenses and the Franciscans.
6. Write a short appreciation of the life and labors of St. Francis of Assisi.

BIBLIOGRAPHY

Valdo.—HURTER, *Histoire d'Innocent III*, I. XIII.—T. GAY, *Histoire des Valdois.*

The Albigensian Heresy.—Sources: DE SMEDT, *Les sources de l'histoire de la croisade contre les Albigeois* (*Rev. Quest. Hist.*, 1874, XVI). —Works: ALPHANDÉRY, *Les idées morales chez les hétérodoxes latins au début du XIIIe siècle* (*Bibl. Ecole Hautes Etudes, sc. relig.*, XVI. fasc. I).—

Douais, *Les Albigeois, leurs origines, action de l'Eglise au XIIe siècle.*—Vacandard, *Les origines de l'hérésie albigeoise* (*Rev. quest. Hist.*, 1894. LV, p. 50–83).—Ch. Molinier, *L'Eglise et la société cathare* (*Rev. Hist.*, 1907, XCIV and XCV).—Jean Guiraud, *L'albigéisme languedocien au XIIe et au XIIIe siècle; Saint Dominique* (Coll. "*Les Saints*"), 1898; art. "*Albigeois*" in *Dict. d'Hist.*—F. Vernet, art. "*Cathares*," in *Dict. de Théol.*—Guilleux, art. "*Albigeois*," in *Dict. d'Apol.*—Luchaire, *Innocent III, La Croisade des Albigeois*, 1908.—Edm. Broeckx, *Le Catharisme, Essai sur les doctrines, la vie religieuse et rurale, l'activité littéraire et les vicissitudes de la secte cathare avant la croisade*, Louvain, 1916.—A. Chollet, art. "*Amaury de Bène*," in *Dict. de Théol.*—G. Bareille, art. "*David de Dinan*," in the same Dictionary. —A. Théry, *Autour du Décret de 1210*, t. I: *David de Dinan. Etude sur son panthéisme matérialiste*, Le Saulchoir, 1925.—Kurth, *The Church at the Turning Points of History.*

The Inquisition.—Sources: Bernard Guy, *Practica Inquisit. hœret.*, edit. Douais, 1886.—G. Mollat, *Manuel de l'Inquisition de Bernard Guy.*—*Processus inquisitionis*, an anonymous work composed around the year 1224, in Vacandard, *L'Inquisition*, 5th edit., 1914, appendix A.—Works: Alphandéry, *op. cit.*, 34–99.—Langlois, *L'Inquisition d'après les travaux récents*, 1902.— Lea, *History of the Inquisition.*—Molinier, *L'Inquisition dans le midi de la France au XIIIe et au XIVe siècle*, 1880.—Tanon, *Histoire des tribunaux de l'Inquisition en France*, 1893.—Th. de Cauzons, *Histoire de l'Inquisition en France*, 2 vols., 1909–1912.—Msgr. Douais, *L'Inquisition*, 1906.—E. Jordan, *La responsabilité de l'Eglise dans la répression de l'hérésie au moyen âge* (*Annales de Philosophie Chrétienne*, 1907).—Vacandard, *L'Inquisition*, 1914; art. "*Inquisition*," in *Dict. d'Hist.*—J. Havet, *L'hérésie et le bras séculier du Moyen Age jusqu'au XIIe siècle*, 1881.—Ch. Moeller, *L'Inquisition au XIIIe siècle, origine des bûchers*, in *Rev. Hist. Eccl.*, 1913 (XIV).—F. Vernet, *Latran* (3rd and 4th Councils of), in *Dict. de Théol.*—H. Pissard, *La guerre sainte en pays chrétien*, 1912.—J. Guiraud, *L'Inquisition*, 1929; art. "*Saint Office*," in *Dict. d'Apol.*—A. L. Maycock, *The Inquisition: From Its Establishment to the Great Schism*, New York, 1927.—H. Nickerson, *The Inquisition.*—Turberville, *Medieval Heresy and the Inquisition.*—Vacandard-Conway, *The Inquisition*, New York, 1908.

Dominicans.—Sources: Reichert, *Acta capitul. general. O. P.*, 9 vols., Rome, 1898–1904; *Litterae Encyclicae Magistrorum O. P.*, 1233–1376, Rome, 1900.—Balme and Lelaidier, *Cartulaire de S. Dominico*, Paris, 1893.— Douais, *Acta Cap. Provincialum Ord. Fr. P.*, Toulouse, 1894.—Works: J. Guiraud, *Saint Dominique* (Coll. "*Les Saints*"), 1898.—Danzas, *Etudes sur les temps primitifs de l'ordre de Saint Dominique*, 1st series, 5 vols., 1873– 1885; 2nd series, 1 vol., 1888.—A. T. Drane, *The History of St. Dominic*, New York, 1891.—Mortier, *Histoire des Maîtres généraux de l'ordre des Frères Prêcheurs*, 1903 ff.—Mandonnet, art. "*Frères Prêcheurs (La théologie dans l'ordre des*)," in *Dict. de Théol.*—Pourrat, *La spiritualité chrétienne,* vol. II, ch. VII.—Shahan, Guilday, Robinson, *Dominicans in Cath. Univ. Bull.,* Nov., 1916.—Guiraud-De Mattos, *St. Dominic,* London, 1901.—J. B. Reeves, *The Dominicans,* 1930.

St. Francis of Assisi.—Sources: Thomas de Celano, *Legenda prima* (*Acta Sanct.,* Oct., II, pp. 623–723); *Legenda secunda,* edit. Ed. d'Alençon, Rome, 1906.—*Légende des trois compagnons* (*Acta Sanct.,* Oct., II, pp. 742–798).—*Speculum perfectionis,* edit. Sabatier, 1898.—*Fioretti,* edit. Chaulin, 1901.—St. Bonaventure, *Legenda* (*Acta Sanct.,* Oct., II, pp. 742–798).— Works: Paul Sabatier, *Vie de saint François,* 26th edit., 1902.—G. Schnürer, *Franz von Assisi,* Munich, 1905.—J. Jörgensen, *Saint François.*—Lucien Roure, *Figures franciscaines.*—P. Edouard d'Alençon, art. *"Frères Mineurs,"* in *Dict. de Théol.*—A. Fierens, *La question franciscaine* (*Rev. d'hist. eccl.,* 1906).—Holzapfel, *Manuale Historiæ Ordinis Minorum,* 1906.—Beaufre- ton, *Saint François d'Assise,* 1925.—P. Gratien, *Histoire de la fondation et de l'évolution des Frères mineurs au XIIIᵉ siècle,* 1924.—L. Dubois, *St. Francis of Assisi, Social Reformer,* New York, 1905.—M. F. Egan, *Everybody's St. Francis,* New York, 1912.—Le Lemonier, *History of St. Francis,* London, 1894.—G. K. Chesterton, *St. Francis of Assisi.*—Bede Jarrett, *St. Francis of Assisi.*—Father Cuthbert, *St. Francis of Assisi,* 1927.—J. Jörgensen, *St. Francis of Assisi,* 1912.

Conflicts between the Mendicant Orders and the Seculars.— A. Van den Wingaert, *Querelles du clergé séculier et des ordres mendiants à l'Université de Paris,* in *France Francisc.,* 1922, pp. 257–281; 369–397; 1923, t. VI, pp. 47–70.—G. Glorieux, *Prélats français contre religieux mendiants* (1281–90), in *Rev. hist. Egl. de France,* 1924.—P. Gratien, *op. cit.*

Spirituals. Joachim of Floris.—Fournier, *Joachim de Flore, ses doc- trines, son influence* (*Rev. quest. hist.,* LXVII 1900, pp. 457 ff.—Gebhart, *L'Italie mystique,* ch. II, *Joachim de Flore,* 1890.—*Archiv für Litteratur und Kirchengeschichte des Mittelalters,* pp. 48–142, 1885.—F. Rocquain, *La Cour de Rome et l'esprit de Réforme avant Luther,* 3 vols.—G. Bondatti, *Gioachinismo e Francescanesimo nel Dugento,* Tip. Porziuncula, 1924.—E. Jordan, art. *"Joachim de Flore,"* in *Dict. de Théol.*

Augustinians.—Dom Besse, art. *"Augustin (Règle de saint),"* in *Dict. de Théol.*—Heimbucher, *Die Orden und Kongregationen,* 1896, I, pp. 443– 463.—P. von Schröder, *Die Augustiner-Chorherrenregel.*

CHAPTER III

**I. The Second Phase of the Quarrel between the Guelphs
and the Ghibellines: The Papacy and Frederick II.** As the ward
of the Pope and an enlisted Crusader, Frederick II seemed to be at once
the protégé and the protector of the Church. As the son of Henry VI,
however, he allowed himself to be moved by the haughty ambitions of
the Hohenstaufens, by seeking to subjugate the Italian Peninsula; and as
heir to the ambitions of his southern mother, Constance, he dreamed
of creating a Mediterranean Empire, the pivotal center of which would be
Sicily. From this remarkable point of strategy, war with the Pope and a
Crusade against the infidels—the two parties which stood in the path of
his imperialistic plan—became possible of achievement. Imbued with the
absolutistic maxims of ancient Roman law, impregnated with the most
subversive of Graeco-Arabic theories, and free from all scruples, Frederick II loomed up in the opening years of the thirteenth century as a
veritable fifteenth-century Italian. By the end he had in mind he was a
Caesar; by the means he took to attain this end, a Machiavelli.

Frederick had solemnly promised Innocent III to keep the Sicilian kingdom and the German Empire separate, in order to shield both the papacy
and the cities of Lombardy from serious danger. Despite this promise,
and under pretext of naming some one to take his place during the
Crusade, he had his son Henry, already king of Sicily, elected and
crowned king of Germany. Pope *Honorius III* was a saintly old gentleman, and had become attached to Frederick by an affection which was
almost that of a father for his son. Even while he was still Cardinal
Cencio Savelli, he had taken charge of the boy's education. And so he
did not oppose his action. Frederick began by postponing the time of his
departure, then suddenly decided that he would leave for the East, and
finally resolved to remain at home under the pretext that the state of af-

fairs in Germany did not permit him to make the expedition. Honorius III adopted a policy of *laissez-faire*.

At the death of the aged Pontiff things underwent a change. Cardinal Ugolino became Pope and took the name of *Gregory IX* (1227-1241). He was a nephew of Innocent III, and though well advanced in years, had the same energetic and inflexible character as his uncle. He summoned Frederick to keep his promises and depart for the Crusade. The Emperor embarked September 8, 1227, but returned three days later, pretending sickness. Gregory excommunicated him. Frederick then executed a master stroke. He set out suddenly for the East, hoping to regain the prestige of which the Pope had deprived him. The Crusade was a strange one, in which Saracen hirelings of Sicily and Teutonic knights marched side by side; at the same time it was an egotistical Crusade undertaken for the sole purpose of realizing the imperial programme of Frederick II. The King began by doing violence to a Christian State. At Cyprus, where the young King Henry ruled under the tutelage of his mother, Alix of Champagne, he claimed suzerainty over the kingdom, and when his action was protested, placed the island under martial law. Upon his arrival in Palestine he found the prince of Damascus engaged in open conflict with the Sultan of Egypt. He did not hesitate to take sides with the latter, promised to protect him against further invasions from the West, and agreed to leave the Turks free in their religious exercises. The Sultan was deceived by these promises, restored the cities of Jerusalem, Bethlehem, and Nazareth to the Christians, and the excommunicated King made his solemn entrance into the Holy City.

Meanwhile Pope Gregory IX had sought to play his rôle as the defender of Italy by reconquering Sicily, a vassal territory of the Holy See. With the assistance of the Lombards he invaded Apulia and advanced as far as Volturno. The expedition was headed by John of Brienne, upon whom Gregory IX had conferred the investiture of the two Sicilies to indemnify him for the loss of his rights to the kingdom of Jerusalem, usurped by Frederick. But the sudden return of the Caesar surprised his opponents, who were defeated and compelled to withdraw. Yielding, finally, to the entreaties of the Grand Master of the Teutonic Order, Herman of Salza, Gregory IX agreed to become reconciled with Frederick II and signed the peace of San Germano (1230).

Frederick, however, continued to adhere to his plan of reducing the whole of Italy. The communes of Lombardy, Tuscany, and Umbria resolved to league themselves against him, just as they had done in by-gone days against Barbarossa. Gregory IX owed it to himself to uphold them, all the more so as Frederick had just arbitrarily disposed of the papal fief, Sardinia, in favor of his natural son, Enzio. Thereupon Gregory IX excommunicated Frederick for the second time, an action which resulted in a bitter conflict between the papacy and the empire. Gregory felt very unhappy over all these quarrels and decided to convoke a council which would condemn Frederick. In answer to his call a number of bishops from France, England, and Spain embarked at Genoa, but their vessels were attacked by Frederick, who had the prelates conducted with silver chains to Pisa. The victorious King then arrived at the gates of Rome. Meanwhile the outrage inflicted upon the members of the hierarchy caused such a violent shock to Gregory, that he died shortly afterwards, at the age of 100 (1241). His death seemed to assure the triumph of Frederick II.

A phase in this terrific struggle between the two powers was the appeal which Gregory and Frederick alike made to the Christian peoples, and the angry correspondence which ensued between them. In the course of this correspondence both resorted to recriminations and personal and public accusations; the Pope in his encyclicals charging Frederick with perjury and blasphemy, and Frederick retorting by similar letters, in which he accused the Pope of shielding heretics. The Emperor went so far as to contemplate a schism and appoint as its head his own chancellor, Peter de Vinea, who would have been created patriarch.

Gregory IX was succeeded by Celestine IV, who reigned only seventeen days. The See of Peter then remained vacant for two years, during which time Rome fell prey to anarchical factions of all kinds. The cardinals finally assembled at Anagni and on June 25, 1243, elected Cardinal Sinibaldo Fieschi of Genoa, who took the name of *Innocent IV*. Negotiations were immediately opened between the new Pope and the Emperor Frederick II, but proved of no avail. The Pontiff requested in vain that the Emperor give up his claims to northern Italy. He was finally constrained to take the road of exile and convoked the Thirteenth Ecumenical Council at Lyons in the year 1245. At this council he disclosed the true character of Frederick and his base conduct. The Emperor was declared guilty of infidelity, debauchery, perjury, collusion with the

Saracens, injustices committed in the kingdom of Sicily, and, finally, of a sacrilegious warfare against the papacy. The sentence of excommunication fulminated by Gregory IX was maintained over his head; he was solemnly deposed from all the dignities of his office; Germany was invited to elect a new king, and the Pope requested to dispose of the kingdom of Sicily.

Far from submitting to the decisions of this council, Frederick II rose up in his pride and proffered all sorts of insults against the Pope. The quarrel turned to his distinct disadvantage, however, for in Germany his son *Conrad IV* was drawn into a number of conflicts with pretenders to the throne: Henry Raspe, Landgrave of Thuringia (1246), and Count William of Holland (1247–1256), raised up by the papal faction. After the promulgation of the sentence of Lyons the imperial cities of central Italy threw off their allegiance to Frederick and espoused the Pope's cause. Frederick himself suffered a smarting defeat at the hands of the Guelphs before the city of Parma; his own chancellor, Peter de Vinea, betrayed and, according to some, attempted to poison him. Frederick died suddenly at Fiorentino in Apulia and possibly became reconciled to the Church before the end (December 13, 1250).

The interests of the papacy required that *Alexander IV* (1254–1261) should oppose the rule of the Hohenstaufens. The new Pope immediately declared that that house had forfeited the throne and completely setting aside young Conradin, son of Conrad IV, tendered the imperial crown first to William of Holland and then, after a calculated delay, to Richard, Count of Cornwall, a brother of Henry III of England. The election of *Rudolph of Hapsburg* (1273) put an end to this long interregnum, and from that moment on the emperor ceased to be a dangerous enemy of the papacy. The ever increasing power of the nobility as well as that of the free cities constantly required Rudolph's presence in Germany, and, moreover, a costly experience had taught him how dangerous it was to cross the Alps. And so, when *Pope Gregory X* reclaimed the Romagna, the province was handed over to him without recourse to arms.

Thus the bitter strife between the papacy and the empire ended with a victory for the former. The expression is somewhat incorrect, however, because the papacy looked upon the empire as an allied and necessary power, and opposed not so much the empire itself, as the unbridled ambitions of certain of the Hohenstaufens. Moreover, the victory was only a negative one, for even after it was rid of the emperor, Italy did not enjoy peace. Guelphs and Ghibellines, according to their local interests in the various cities, took it upon themselves to continue the battle *intra muros*. At times it was the nobility against the popular party; at others, it was house against house; sometimes it was members of one household against other members of the same household. Italy was slowly drifting into anarchy, and the day was fast approaching when, no longer able to dwell in the City of Rome, the popes had to wander from Lyons to Anagni, and from Anagni to Perugia, until they finally began their long exile in Avignon.

II. The Crusades of St. Louis. While Frederick II was trying to tear Christendom asunder, King St. Louis of France was preparing to launch a Crusade. This purpose explains the peace negotiations which occurred intermittently in the long struggle between the papacy and the empire. The French king, indeed, showed himself ever ready to serve as arbiter and help settle the Italian question, in order to be in a better position to tackle the eastern problem. Of a sudden the danger assumed new and larger proportions, when the Mongolian hordes, who for a long time had lived in isolation, began to descend upon Europe under the leadership of the famous Genghis-Khan. Their steady march struck fear into the hearts of all. In 1216, Genghis-Khan entered Pekin, and in 1240 crossed the Hungarian boundary and advanced as far as the Adriatic Sea. The threat of these barbarian tribes was only transient, for of their own accord they turned their faces towards Asia, the home of their race; but the invasion had a direct effect upon Palestine, for a band of 10,000 Karizmians, fleeing before the Asiatic hordes, placed themselves under the command of the Sultan of Egypt, and in September, 1244, seized the city of Jerusalem.

The news of the fall of Jerusalem arrived in France when St. Louis was in danger of death. He made a vow that, should he recover, he would head a Crusade. At the same Council of Lyons which excommunicated Frederick II, the Pope issued orders for this Crusade, but France alone heeded the call. St. Louis embarked at Aigues-Mortes, spent the winter on the Isle of Cyprus, landed in Egypt, seized the port of Damietta, and marched on Cairo. After the hard-earned victory of Mansura, in which the French gave ample proof of both courage and imprudence, Louis was forced to make a disastrous retreat (1250), was taken prisoner and constrained to pay a high ransom and to give Damietta back to the infidels. The saintly king would not be discouraged, but remained four more years in Syria, during which time he rebuilt the fortifications of Acre, Jaffa, Caesarea, and Sidon. And even when the death of Blanche of Castile forced him to return to France, he still entertained the hope of some day going back to Palestine.

In France the capture and imprisonment of the King had stirred up a popular movement, "The Crusade of the Shepherd Boys," commanded by a mysterious chief, the Master of Hungary. People soon began to believe that a new Peter the Hermit had arisen in their midst. Setting out from Flanders, this man gathered along the route the scum element of the different towns and villages through which he passed, and his nondescript army soon began to indulge in abuses and excesses of all kinds. Indignant, the population of the center and West pursued them as they would robbers.

Their action sounded the death-knell of the Crusade. Genoa and Venice became involved in their egotistical rivalries, and in 1261 the Greeks put an end to the Latin Empire of Constantinople, while the brother of St. Louis, recently crowned king of the two Sicilies, was laying plans to undo their conquests. Meanwhile, more disastrous news was arriving each day from the Holy Land, for Bibars, Sultan of Egypt, succeeded in gaining possession one by one of several places in Palestine, including Antioch. And so it happened that, despite the slight enthusiasm displayed by his barons, St. Louis again resolved to head a Crusade. He embarked at Aigues-Mortes, July 1st, 1270, and landed at Carthage. His plan was to seize Tunis and make this city the center of his operations against Egypt. It was completely thwarted, however, by a plague which broke out in the army and caused the King's death (August 25). The Crusade which had barely begun, was thus brought to a sudden end. In vain did Gregory X resolve to undertake another expedition; in vain did the Council of Lyons endeavor to assist him by levying a tax on all ecclesiastical goods; for six years the Crusaders defaulted everywhere. Left to its own fate, the East fell prey to the power of the Mussulmans, who seized the last Christian centers, Tripoli and Acre, in 1291. The stupendous effort of the Crusaders had failed in its main purpose.

It must not be thought, however, that the Crusades were barren of all results. Undertaken by the popes, these movements naturally strengthened the papal authority, while the preaching of the Crusade furnished the Sovereign Pontiffs with the opportunity to intervene between Christian princes and exercise their jurisdiction over those who had enlisted. It is in this way that the advantages acquired by the popes were used to guarantee the common welfare of Christendom. Moreover, despite the fact that the Crusades had all the appearance of bold and daring offensives, they were in reality and from the very outset defensive wars. For if the Byzantine Empire had succumbed in the eleventh century, Europe would have been completely disrupted and unable to resist an invasion. By forcing the Mussulmans to defend their territory, therefore, the Crusaders gave a chance to the powers of the West to organize themselves, and when Islam resumed the offensive in the fifteenth century, it was immediately confronted with firmly established and highly organized States. European civilization, therefore, owes its independence to the Crusades. On the other hand, the knights of the West were brought under the influence of a more refined culture while engaged in their activities in Syria, and in addition, commerce with India, encouraged by the Crusades, effected a real transformation in the material lives of the Western peoples. The brilliant development of western civilization at the end of the twelfth century is the direct result of the Crusades. Finally, the Crusades brought out in men sentiments of honor, chivalry, and Christian generosity, which won for France, the land *par excellence* of the Crusades, a peerless prestige in the East (*Gesta Dei per Francos*).

We must, however, be on our guard against forming too ideal a picture of these movements. The Crusades did not retain during two centuries the uniform aspect of a heroic struggle. Quite frequently, indeed, the knights and the emirs were led by political necessity to set up and maintain relations, and even to enter alliances, and the Crusaders adopted eastern ways to the extent that many contracted marriage with baptized Saracens. And so, at a very early date, the Mussulmans were able to differentiate between the acclimated "Franks of Syria" and the "Franks beyond the Sea," who were only passing adventurers, capable of doing them no real harm.

The human side of these movements is brought out by the fact that generosity was often forced to yield to egotistical calculations. For while the ordinary run of men were still governed by the purest of intentions, those in higher places indulged in earthly dreams. This is particularly true of the expedition against Constantinople. Moreover, in the thirteenth century a new generation of Crusaders appeared on the horizon, so much so that, in the days of St. Louis the Crusade as a movement was openly opposed. "It is quite possible to serve God," was the common saying, "without quitting one's native land, by living on one's ancestral soil. It will be time enough to give battle when the Sultan invades our own country." The princes themselves took part in these expeditions only because they satisfied their dynastic ambitions. This was the sacrilegious attitude adopted first by the Ghibelline leaders Henry VI, Philip of Suabia, and Frederick II, and later on by the Guelph, Charles of Anjou. On the other hand, Venice was interested in the eastern question only in so far as it affected her colonies and commercial enterprises. It seemed the natural thing for her to provide the Saracen armies with supplies and furnish them with wood and iron to forge weapons against the Crusaders. Finally, in the fourteenth century the idea became fixed with European princes that a Crusade was an enterprise to be exploited and a rich mine for revenues. From that moment on they remained content to collect their tithes, so much so that when a Peter of Cyprus or a Manuel II Palaeologus canvassed Europe to obtain help, they were lavishly feted, but obtained no assistance whatever.

As for the Greeks, being sons of schism and extremely nationalistic in spirit, their only thought was to exploit the Crusaders. At the outset they would have liked nothing better than to discourage these movements and transform them into armies for the "Basileus," to enable him to reconquer his provinces in Syria. The policy of the Comneni during the entire twelfth century had no other purpose. In this way the soldiers of the pope helped to spread schism, for wherever the power of the "Basileus" was established, a Greek clergy and a Greek patriarch were substituted for the Latin clergy and the Latin patriarch. This fact explains why the Crusaders rejected any alliance with Byzantium, no matter how invaluable it might appear.

III. The Crusades of Spain. Missions of Africa and Asia. The Arabs of Africa who had established themselves in Sicily were constantly threatening the Italian peninsula. The Normans of lower Italy resolved to expel them once for all, and for this purpose a Crusade was headed by Roger, a brother of Robert Guiscard, which lasted no less than thirty-two years (1061–1093). This Crusade was marked by the victory of

Cerami in 1063, the occupation of Catania and Palermo in 1072, and that of Trapani in 1077. The capture of Girgenti and Noto in 1091 resulted in the complete conquest of the island. Roger II (1101–1154) united the two crowns of lower Italy and Sicily. This accounts for the origin of the kingdom of the Two Sicilies, which paid tribute to the Holy See, but fell into the hands of the Hohenstaufens and later of the Angevins.

The Caliphate of Cordova ruled over Mussulman Spain, but to the Northwest there existed two independent States, Asturia and Cantabria, which were re-united at a later date to form the kingdom of Leon. To the North, the March of Spain, organized by Charlemagne, gave rise to the kingdoms of Aragon and Navarra during the period of the Carolingian decadence. Finally, the kingdom of Castile was established in the upper basin of the Duro. For a long time the Christians were forced to remain on the defensive and fight off the incursions of the emirate, but in 1073 Alphonsus V, King of Castile, crossed the Tagus and, taking advantage of a number of dissensions which prevailed in the emirate, seized the city of Toledo. The Mussulmans called to their assistance first the Almoravides and then the Almohades of Africa. It was only under the pontificate of Innocent III that the three kings of Navarra, Aragon, and Castile scored the decisive victory of Navas de Tolosa (1212). From that time on the Moors were forced to take refuge in the extreme southern portion of the peninsula, where the Emir Muhamed Aben Alamar founded the *kingdom of Granada* (1238), which continued in existence until the end of the fifteenth century (1492).

In its struggle against Islam, Spain was greatly assisted by the French Crusaders. During the twelfth century military Orders were founded similar in character to those of the Holy Land, to wit, the Order of Calatrava 1158, Evora in Portugal 1162, Compostela 1175, established especially to protect pilgrimages to St. James, and, finally, Alcantara 1176. The stubborn resistance which the Spaniards were forced to display against Islam strengthened them greatly in their faith. At the same time it inspired them with a holy horror for the infidels and the heretics.

In Northern Africa a small Christian settlement continued to struggle for existence, but was fast becoming extinct. In the tenth century there were still some forty episcopal sees in that country, but in 1076 only three remained, as we are informed by a letter of Pope Gregory VII. And yet Gregory VII, Innocent III, Gregory IX, and Innocent IV put forth every effort to protect the Christians of Mâghreb by entering into friendly relations with the emirs. Moreover, there existed a number of Christians in Africa who had been transported to that land. They consisted principally of prisoners captured by the pirates or seized on the Mussulman marches. To proffer assistance to these poor unfortunates, and to redeem them from slavery, several religious Orders were founded. The Provençal John of Matha and Felix of Valois founded an Order which paid special homage to the Blessed Trinity by its garb, consisting of a white tunic adorned with a red and blue cross. The *Trinitarians* were also called Mathurins from the name of their chapel St. Mathurin in Paris. The center of their activities was Cerfroy. Very soon, however, they established houses throughout Europe: in France, Italy, England, and Spain, and at one time they had as many as 600 members, distributed through thirteen provinces. It is estimated that they freed as many as 200,000 slaves. In his famous letter of March 8, 1199, Pope Innocent III had authorized them "to redeem also pagan prisoners, so that by making exchanges they might free Christian captives from slavery."

The Languedocian, St. Peter of Nolasque and the Spaniard, Raymond of Pennafort, founded the *Order of Mercy*. The Trinitarians had remained content to redeem captives, but the Fathers of Mercy took a vow to serve as chaplains to these prisoners, to care for them, and even to take their place if they were in danger of apostatizing. Their apostolate was crowned with the greatest success. One of the disciples of the founder, St. Raymond Nonnatus, so distinguished himself by his zeal that the Bey of Algiers issued orders to pierce his lips with a red-hot iron and close them with a steel padlock.

Asia was evangelized exclusively by Nestorian heretics who had taken refuge in Persia. They penetrated into *China* with rich Armenian merchants, and were received with honor by Emperor Tai-Tsung of the Tang dynasty. A century later, Nestorianism attained such proportions throughout China that it assumed the rather pretentious title of King-Tsia (Brilliant Religion). An edict published in 845 attests the existence in that country of two thousand Nestorian monks. This edict was aimed principally at the Buddhists, but directly affected the Christians, inasmuch as they were members of a "foreign religion." After being on the wane for a while, Nestorianism regained its position of influence two centuries later, and in the twelfth century many Mongolian tribes were

Christian. There existed, moreover, a Nestorian kingdom, the rulers of which called themselves, so it is said, Presters John (priests, because they conferred Orders on all males). In point of fact the Prester John was located in Abyssinia. This Nestorian kingdom was destroyed by the never-to-be-forgotten invasion of Genghis-Khan, in 1206.

Genghis-Khan was instrumental in making Europe aware of the existence of Asia, but in justice to the Mongols it must be said that they showed themselves very liberal. Native Shamanism did not exclude other religions, not even Christianity, and so it was possible to attempt the work of evangelization in these lands. Pope Innocent IV was the first to show concern, and a missionary band led by the Minorite John of Piano Carpine repaired to the residence of the grand Khan at Kara Korum to assist at the election of a new "Son of Heaven." Another missionary band, under the direction of the Dominican Nicholas Ascelinus, journeyed to the camp of Batchu in Persia (1247), but came near being massacred because it did not bring any presents. Finally, at the request of St. Louis, Innocent IV founded a society of "Voyagers for Christ," recruited principally from among the Franciscans and the Dominicans.

It was only during the second half of the thirteenth century, however, that real missionary bands were organized upon receipt of the news from the Venetian, *Marco Polo,* just returned from a voyage to China, that the great Khan Kubalai was most affable and benevolent. The Superior General of the Franciscans, Bonagrazia de Persiceto, despatched thither a missionary band, headed by Brother John of Monte Corvino. After founding a Christian community at Melapore in India, he journeyed to Pekin, where, thanks to the protection of the Grand Khan Timur, he effected a number of conversions. His apostolate spread to all the larger cities of the province. When the Blessed Odoric of Pordenone landed at the Chinese port of Zayton, he found two Franciscan monasteries there, and when he arrived at Pekin, he was received by the Archbishop, *John of Monte Corvino,* and gladdened by the sight of the Grand Khan uncovering his head before the Cross when entering his capitol. Unfortunately, during the second half of the fourteenth century, a cruel civil war issued in the substitution of the Ming for the Mongolian dynasty, and a persecution was immediately started against the Christians.

Armenia was situated between Asia and the Byzantine Empire, and had fallen into the Monophysite heresy. The popes, however, especially Nicholas I, concerned themselves with its conversion. In 1080, Gregory VII vainly appealed in a letter to the Armenian Katholikos to return to the orthodox faith, but it was necessary to await the arrival of the Crusaders and the creation of the kingdom of Little Armenia in Cilicia on the shores of the Mediterranean Sea to establish better relations. By the middle of the twelfth century the Katholikos was drawing nearer and nearer to the papacy, and in 1198, under the administration of the Katholikos Abirard, union between Armenia and the Holy See was solemnly proclaimed at the coronation of King Leo II. The harmony thus established was brought to a sudden end, however, when Raymond Roupen, a nephew of Leo II, and Bohemond of Tripoli, disputed the right of succession to the see of Antioch. Rome's decision in favor of Bohemond infuriated Leo, who at once began a persecution against the Christians of Antioch. Innocent III was forced to excommunicate him. Not all the relations, however, between Armenia and the Holy See were severed by this unfortunate affair, for Gregory X invited the King of Armenia and the Katholikos to the General Council of Lyons (1274). But when the kingdom of Little Armenia became extinct (1375), the Armenian Church, torn asunder by interior strife, and threatened from the outside by the Mussulmans, began to wander farther and farther away from Rome. In the end, only a small nucleus of Roman Christians remained, thanks to the Dominicans, who had trained a congregation of native missionaries to promote reunion. These Brothers counted no less than fifty monasteries and seven hundred members, who wore the habit and followed the rule of St. Dominic. The theological discussions which arose during the fourteenth century regarding the Baptism of heretics unfortunately hampered their work.

A more stable conversion, directly resulting from the Crusades, was that of the *Maronites* of Mt. Lebanon and Anti Lebanon, who had joined the ranks of Monothelitism. In 1182, while Aimeric was patriarch of Antioch, they became reunited with Rome, and their patriarch assisted at the Council of the Lateran, in 1215. They have remained faithful to the teachings of Catholicism ever since.

IV. The Questions of Italy and the East at the End of the Thirteenth Century: The Papacy, the Greeks, and Charles of Anjou. The last refuge of the Hohenstaufens had been Southern Italy, where the young Conrad IV had been upheld by Manfred, a natural son of Frederick II, who achieved such great success that the barons of Sicily offered him the imperial crown. He was opposed by Edmund, a son of Henry III, King of England. At this time the papacy was in need of a powerful vassal in Southern Italy, capable of protecting it as the Norman dynasty had done in the past. Pope *Urban IV* (1261–1264), who was an energetic, intelligent, and fearless man, set aside the weak Edmund of England and substituted in his place *Charles of Anjou*, brother of St. Louis, who had the support of the entire French nobility. The followers of the Hohenstaufens in Sicily and in Rome were quickly ruined. Manfred was defeated at Beneventum (1266), and one of his nephews, *Conradin*, who had arrived from Germany to succeed him, suffered a decisive defeat at Tagliacozzo. He was taken prisoner and executed at Naples, and the race of the Hohenstaufens perished with him. The Angevin dynasty now obtained control in Italy. Charles of Anjou dreamed of setting up a vast Mediterranean empire, the chief centers of which would be Constantinople and Rome. To carry out this plan, he had recourse, not to force, but to diplomacy. When he pretended to intervene in the affairs of Byzantium, he used as his argument the Turkish menace; when he wished to impose his rule upon the Italian peninsula, he used as his pretext the anarchy prevailing there.

Constantinople had again fallen into the hands of the Greeks in 1261. Meanwhile, Charles of Anjou had married his daughter, Beatrice, to the heir of Baldwin II, the dethroned king of Jerusalem, and after gaining a foothold in Achaia and Epirus, dreamed of restoring the Latin Empire. He began to refer to his egotistical expedition as a Crusade, but the popes failed him. All hope for a Byzantine Crusade was lost when the papacy entered into a union with the Greeks. Negotiations for such a union were begun during the pontificate of *Clement IV* (1265–1268). At this Pope's death, however, Charles of Anjou engaged in intrigues to obtain the election of a pontiff favorable to his plans of conquest, and the resistance he encountered in the Roman Curia caused the Holy See to remain vacant for three years. *Gregory X*, who was finally elected in 1271, had the good sense to continue the policy of his predecessors. He submitted two plans for an understanding to Michael VIII Palaeologus: the submission of the Byzantine clergy and people in the presence of four papal legates, or the convocation of an ecumenical council. Michael preferred the latter plan, and in 1274 the Council of Lyons (Fourteenth General Council) decreed that a union be effected between the two churches under the following conditions: (1) acknowledgment of the Roman primacy; (2) right of appeal to the Holy See; (3) re-insertion of the pope's name in the diptychs. The union encountered strong opposition among the Greek clergy, enfeoffed to the cause of orthodoxy, but Michael, who was bent on settling the matter at all costs, had the more notorious recalcitrants arrested and thrown into prison. Priests, bishops, and even an old patriarch by the name of Germanus II, rallied to the cause of the papacy, as well as the famous theologian John Veccos. This union persisted during the short pontificates of the successors of Gregory X: Innocent V, Adrian V, and John XXI (1276-1277).

Nicholas III (1277-1280) began to antagonize the Greeks by placing more obligations upon them than were stipulated in the decrees of the Council of Lyons. He even spoke of sending a legate to Byzantium and papal nuncios to the principal cities to make sure that the Roman faith was duly respected. This Pope was a clever politician, and succeeded in counteracting the ambitions of the Angevins in Italy and ousting Charles of Anjou from the Roman senatorship. His plan was to set up in the northern portion of the Papal State a strong native principality that would serve as a fortified outpost.

Nicholas' successor, the French Cardinal Simon de Brie, took the name of *Martin IV* (1281-1285) and was completely devoted to the cause of the Angevins. Supporting the Eastern policies of Charles, he excommunicated Palaeologus as a heretic and schismatic, and in return the Basileus severed his connections, not with the papacy, but with Martin, whose name he ordered removed from the liturgical prayers. But soon the misfortunes visited upon the house of Anjou removed the last political motives which constrained the Byzantine rulers to prolong the union. In the East, the armies of Michael VIII routed the Angevin forces at Berat (Albania), and in the West the Sicilians, secretly stirred up by the inhabitants of Aragon and the Greeks, openly revolted and wrought a wholesale massacre of the French at Palermo (Sicilian Vespers, Easter Monday, 1282). Peter of Aragon, formerly acknowledged heir by Conradin, was proclaimed King of Sicily, and Charles of Anjou retained only his possessions in Southern Italy. Relieved now of all anxiety, Andronic II, son of Michael VIII, returned to schism.

TEXTS AND DOCUMENTS

Confession of Faith of the Council of Lyons (1274)

We make a faithful and devout confession that the Holy Ghost is eternally from the Father and the Son, not as from two distinct principles, but rather as from one principle. He proceeds not from two separate spirations, but from one spiration.

The Holy Roman Church enjoys supreme and full primacy and princedom over the whole Catholic Church, which, it truly and humbly acknowledges, it has received with the plenitude of power from Our Lord Himself in the person of Blessed Peter, prince or head of the Apostles, whose successor is the Roman Pontiff; and as the Apostolic See is bound before all others to defend the truth of faith, so also, if any questions regarding faith arise, they must be defined by its judgment.

QUESTIONS

1. Summarize the Hundred Years' War between the Hohenstaufens and the papacy in the form of a chronological table.
2. List the more important events in the struggle between Frederick II and the papacy.
3. What were some of the consequences of this struggle?
4. Give an estimate of the life and character of King St. Louis of France.
5. Enumerate some of the direct benefits which the Church derived from the Crusades.
6. Account for the foundation of the Order of the Trinitarians and that of the Fathers of Mercy.
7. Outline the successive stages in the Christian reconquest of Spain, up to the final defeat of the Mussulmans in 1492.
8. What were the Sicilian Vespers?

BIBLIOGRAPHY

Frederick II.—Sources: Huillard Bréholles, *Historia diplomatica Friderici secundi,* with an important introduction, 12 vols., 1852–1861.—Winkelmann, *Acta imperii inedita sæculi* XIII, 1880.—Works: G. Blondel, *Etude sur la politique de l'empereur Frédéric II en Allemagne,* 1892.—E. Winkelmann, *Kaiser Friedrich II,* 2 vols., 1889–1897.—Fr. W. Shirrmacher, *Kaiser Friedrich der zweite,* 4 vols., 1859–1865.—Fr. J. Biehringer, *Kaiser Friedrich II,* 1912.—Zeller, *Hist. d'Allemagne,* IV.—Bryce, *The Holy Roman Empire.*—Birot, *Le Saint Empire,* 1900.—Dom C. Poulet, *Guelfes et Gibelins,* I: *La lutte du sacerdoce et de L'Empire* (Coll. "*Lovanium*"), Brussels, 1922.—Arquillière, art. "*Honorius III,*" in *Dict. de Théol.*

Gregory IX.—Sources: Auvray, *Les registres de Grégoire IX*, 2 vols. have appeared, 1900, 1905.—*Mon. Germ., Epistulae saeculi XIII*, 1833, I.— Works: Balan, *Storia di Gregorio IX e suoi tempi*, 3 vols., Modena, 1872; *La prima lotta di Gregorio IX con Frederigo II* (1227-1230), Modena, 1871.— J. Felten, *Papst Gregor IX*, Freiburg, 1886.—K. Hadank, *Die Schlacht bei Cortenuova*, 1907.—A. Clerval, art. *"Grégoire IX,"* in *Dict. de Théol.*—H. Arquillière, *"Honorius III,"* in the same Dictionary.

Innocent IV. The Fall of the Hohenstaufen.—Sources: C. Höfler, *Albert von Beham und Regesten Papst Innocenz IV (Bibliothek des litterarischen Vereins in Stuttgart, XVI)*, 1847.—E. Berger, *Les registres d'Innocent IV*, 4 vols.—Works: A. Folz, *Kaiser Friedrich II. und Papst Innocenz IV.*, 1905.—Deslandres, *Innocent IV et la chute des Hohenstaufen*, 1907.—E. Berger, *Saint Louis et Innocent IV*, 1893.—E. Amann, art. *"Innocent IV,"* in *Dict. de Théol.*—F. Lenckoff, *Papst Alexander*, Paderborn, 1907.—V. Ermoni, art. *"Alexandre IV,"* in *Dict. d'Hist.*—Hauck, *Kirchengeschichte Deutschlands*, IV and V.—F. Vernet, art. *"Lyon (Ier concile de),"* in *Dict. de Théol.*

St. Louis and the Crusade.—Sources: Guillaume de Nangis, *Gesta Ludovici regis, Rec. Hist. de France*, XX, 312-465.—Joinville, *Natalis de Wailly*, 1881.—Geoffroy de Beaulieu, *Rec. Hist. de France*, XX, 3-26.— Works: Lecoy de la Marche, *La prédication de la croisade aux XIIIe siècle* (*Rev. quest. hist.*, July, 1890).—Le Nain de Tillemont, *Vie de saint Louis* (edit. Soc. H. de Fr.), 1847-51, 6 vols.—Wallon, *Saint Louis et son temps*, 1875, 2 vols.—Röhricht, *Der Kreuzzug Louis IX. gegen Damiette*, Berlin, 1890.—E. Berger, *Saint·Louis et Innocent IV*.—M. Sepet, *Saint Louis*, 1898, (Coll. *"Les Saints"*).—J. Paris, *Jean de Joinville* (*Hist. litt. de la France*, XXXIII, 1898).—Sternfeld, *Ludwigs des Heiligen Kreuzzug nach Tunis*, Berlin, 1896.—Bréhier, *Les Croisades*, ch. IX.—G. Goyau, *Saint Louis*, 1928.

Crusades in Sicily.—Amari, *Storia dei Musulmanni in Sicilia*, Florence, 1854.—Chalandon, *Histoire de la domination normande en Italie et en Sicile*, 2 vols., 1907.

Crusades in Spain.—Dozy, *Histoire des musulmans d'Espagne*, 4 vols., 1861.—Stanley Lane-Poole, *The Moors in Spain*, London, 1889.—Luchaire, *Innocent III, Les chrétientés vassales*, 1908.—J. Laurentie, *Saint Ferdinand III* (Coll. *"Les Saints"*).—Boissonnade, *Du nouveau sur la chanson de Roland*, 1923.—Lavisse and Rambaud, II, ch. XII.

Asia.—Works: Rémusat, *Biographie de Jean de Montecorvin (Biographie Universelle Didot)*.—Pisani, art. *"Asie (Missions catholiques de l'),"* in *Dict. de Théol.*—L. Bréhier, *Les croisades*, ch. V and X.—A. Thomas, *Histoire de la mission de Chine*, 1923.—For the Missions, see the excellent handbook of J. Schmidlin, *Katholische Missionsgeschichte*, Steyl, 1925 (transl. by M. Braun, S.V.D., Techny, Ill., 1934.)

Africa.—H. Froidevaux, art. *"Afrique,"* in *Dict. d'Hist.*—G. Deslandres,

l'Ordre des Trinitaires pour la rédemption des captifs, Toulouse-Paris, 1903.
Armenia.—E. Dulaurier, *Histoire, dogmes, traditions et liturgie de l'Eglise arménienne orientale,* 3rd edit., 1859.—Luchaire, *Innocent III, La question d'Orient.*—L. Petit, art. *"Arménie,"* in *Dict. de Théol.*—Tournebize, *Histoire politique et religieuse de l'Arménie.*—Kévork Aslan, *Etudes historiques sur le peuple arménien,* 1928.—For the Maronites, art. *"Maronite (Eglise),"* in *Dict. de Théol.*

Charles of Anjou and the Papacy.—Sources: J. Guiraud, *Registres de Grégoire X,* 1890-1898.—Langlois, *Les registres de Martin IV,* 1901.—Works: C. Jordan, *Les origines de la domination angevine en Italie,* 1910.—Cadier, *Essai sur l'administration du royaume de Sicile sous Charles I et Charles II d'Anjou (Bibl. Ecoles franç. Athènes et Rome, fasc. LIX.)*—Lavisse, *Histoire de France,* III.—A. Clerval, art. *"Grégoire X,"* in *Dict. de Théol.*—Vailhé, art. *"Constantinople (Eglise de),"* in *Dict. de Théol.*—Fournier, *Le royaume d'Arles,* 1891 (*passim*).—Dom C. Poulet, *Guelfes et Gibelins,* t. II, *La diplomatie pontificale à l'époque de la domination française* (1266-1378). —V. Grumel, art. *"Lyon (2ᵉ concile de),"* in *Dict. de Théol.*—E. Amann, art. *"Martin IV,"* in *Dict de Théol.*—C. Chapman, *Michel Paleologues,* 1926.

General Aspects of Christianity from the Eleventh to the
Fourteenth Century

CHAPTER I

THE PAPACY

I. Universal Influence of the Papacy. During these centuries
of profound faith the pope was looked upon as the supreme authority.
In expressing the relationship between the spiritual and the temporal
powers, Yvo of Chartres, Innocent III, and the Scholastics had recourse
to the significant comparison of the sun and the moon, the State receiving light from the Church, which quickens it with a higher supernatural
life. It was the pope who invested the emperor with his powers: "The
pope has two swords," says the *Schwabenspiegel;* "he retains the spiritual
sword and gives to the emperor the temporal one; when he mounts his
white steed, the emperor must hold his stirrups." The tiara was another
symbol of papal power. Formerly the popes had worn a white cap, but
in the opening years of the ninth century they adopted the tiara with
one crown, which was called the *regnum.* In the beginning of the fourteenth century the pope is represented with two crowns, and very soon
with a third, the *triregnum* (under Clement V, d. 1314). This tiara with
three crowns signifies the universality of the papal functions: primacy,
patriarchate, and temporal sovereignty.

As a consequence, civil rulers were amenable to the pope both as
private citizens and as public servants. When kings infringed upon the
moral order, whether by adultery, usurpation of church goods, or murder
of clerics, they were subject to canon law like the rest of the faithful,
and could be visited with excommunication. Philip I and Philip Augustus
were punished in this way for the crime of adultery; the emperors of
Germany for usurping church goods; and Boleslaus of Poland, Henry II

of England, and Raymond VI of Toulouse for the murder of St. Stanislaus
(1079), Thomas à Becket, and Peter of Castelnau, respectively.

For moral reasons the papacy intervened also in political questions
by virtue of the doctrine of indirect power. "The Sovereign Pontiff," said
Innocent III to Philip Augustus, "is bound by his office to procure peace
everywhere. Moreover, it is his duty to settle questions which regard to the
salvation or damnation of souls. Now it must be admitted that it is
detrimental to salvation to foster discord, to expose a country to all sorts
of calamities and to all the physical and moral miseries of war, and to
constrain churchmen to take up arms in a warfare for the king." In
matters pertaining to the Holy Empire this right to intervene is even
more strict. In his *Deliberation regarding the Status of the Empire,* written on the occasion of the dispute between Philip of Suabia and Otto,
Innocent III declared: "This question necessarily appertains to the Sovereign Pontiff, *principaliter et finaliter: principaliter,* because it was the
Holy See which transferred the empire from the East to the West;
finaliter, because it is the pope himself who confers the imperial crown."
The rights of the Sovereign Pontiff in this matter were opposed by the
Caesarian claims, the most outstanding exponent of which was Peter de
Vinea, the advisor of Frederick II. "It is ridiculous," he wrote, "to think
of subjecting to a law one who, by reason of his imperial dignity, is
exempt from all law (*qui legibus omnibus imperialiter est solutus*) and
to pretend to visit with temporal penalties one who has no temporal
superior." It is a well-known fact that jurists made every effort to have
the State absorb the Church and grant to civil princes an unrestricted
religious supremacy, which would give them the right to reform the
Church as they saw fit.

Against the political crimes of princes the popes often had recourse to
the interdict, which they inflicted upon an entire kingdom. "All churches
must be closed," stated the formula, "and no one may be admitted to
them except for the purpose of baptizing little children. Mass may be
celebrated only once a week, early Friday morning. On Sundays the
priests must omit Mass and instead preach the word of God; but they
must exercise this function outside at the entrance of the church. All
the Sacraments, including Extreme Unction, must be omitted, except
Baptism for newly born children and the viaticum for the dying." It
not infrequently happened that the people became exasperated and con-

strained their rulers to seek absolution. The pope could also release the subjects of a prince from their oath of allegiance, and even depose the king. Gregory VII adopted this line of conduct in regard to Henry IV (1080), Innocent III in regard to John Lackland (1212), and Innocent IV in regard to Frederick II (1245).

To secure their rights, the humbler folk placed themselves under the aegis of the Holy See. Monasteries desirous of escaping greedy and avaricious lords also secured the patronage of the popes by the payment of a small tax. It was in this way that Cluny succeeded in shaking off lay patronage. Oftentimes rulers, nay entire kingdoms, placed themselves under the protecting influence of the papacy. Thus Ramira I of Aragon, when threatened by his brother, declared himself the pope's vassal, and, in 1213, John Lackland promised to pay tribute to the pope and paid him the homage of his crown. In their international relations contracting parties swore to keep peace by an oath from which the pope alone could dispense, and Apostolic letters outlined the main points of the treaty. In the beginning of the fourteenth century, Boniface VIII ordered France and England to keep their terms of peace.

On the other hand, the supreme competency of the Holy See in matters of doctrine was more and more strongly emphasized. In the early days people had sometimes solemnly acknowledged that the popes were the guardians of the faith (Formula of Hormisdas, 516), and some had stressed their mission to carry on this function until the end of time. In the Middle Ages papal infallibility became a matter of public teaching. St. Thomas Aquinas rests his proof upon the words of Scriptures: *"Tu aliquando conversus, confirma fratres tuos,"* addressed by Our Lord to St. Peter, and upon the text of the First Epistle to the Corinthians, which requires unity in faith: *"Ut idipsum dicatis omnes, et non sint in vobis schismata."* Unity of this kind, however, is impossible without unity in doctrinal authority (*S. Theol.,* IIa, IIae, q. 1, art. 10). Finally, infallibility was implicitly acknowledged by the Council of Lyons in 1274 (can. "Majores"). Though not *de fide,* therefore, the doctrine is *prope fidem.*

II. Papal Administration: The Cardinals. Finances. The same Council of Lyons in its canon 2 laid down definite regulations regarding the function of cardinals in papal elections. On the tenth day after the pope's demise they were to meet in a room and remain absolutely sequestered from the rest of the world, whence the name conclave, *"cum* *clave,"* locked in with a key. After the first three days the cardinals received only one meal daily on the following five days, and when this period had lapsed, they were given only bread, wine, and water. The purpose of this regulation was to prevent protracted vacancies like that which preceded the election of Gregory X.

The popes referred a number of questions to the cardinals, and their gatherings replaced the annual Lenten synod held in Rome. The cardinals were often charged with trying major cases and were consulted on points concerning faith and morals and decisions of all kinds: canonizations, approbations of religious Orders, erections of universities and episcopal sees, grants of privileges and the government of the Papal States. The highest ecclesiastical dignitaries were selected from their number: Legates *a latere,* the General Inquisitor, the Grand Penitentiary, the Vice-Chancellor, and the protectors of Orders and countries. Their meetings with the pope were called consistories, and the cardinals were known as senators of the Holy See.

The organization of the Papal States, a complicated administration, and business transactions of all kinds with Christendom necessitated expenditures on the part of the papacy which far exceeded those of any other ruler. Rome commanded first of all the revenues of its own States, as we see from the *Liber Censuum* of Cencio Savelli, later Honorius III. Peter's Pence was another source of income. It was furnished by several countries, notably England. William the Conqueror had promised it to Gregory VII, and John Lackland had fixed the sum at 1000 marks. The other vassals of the Holy See acquitted themselves of this duty according to their means. The rents of Frederick II as king of Sicily amounted to 1000 pieces of gold. A third source of revenue was purely ecclesiastical in character, flowing from the right of protecting churches and monasteries, confirming bishops and abbots, despatching Bulls, etc. The popes also sought to regulate the levying of tributes (*Liber Censuum*), and for this purpose important investigations were conducted by the legates, Gonsalva in Spain (1213), the sub-deacon Peter Mark in southern France (1212), Brother Stephen in France proper, etc. Finally, the current expenses of the papacy, which were constantly mounting, forced the popes to seek new means of levying taxes. A first step in this direction was to reserve the nomination to benefices. And so, despite protests issuing from different nations, the papal treasury soon became powerfully centralized, reaching its full development at the time of the exile of the popes at Avignon.

TEXTS AND DOCUMENTS

The Doctrine of the Two Swords

There being but one faith and one Baptism, and the Church constituting but one body, there can necessarily be but one head. The invisible head is Jesus Christ; the visible head, His representatives, the successors of St. Peter. Christ has established two swords or powers in the Church—the one temporal, the other spiritual. The latter He has committed to the priesthood, the former to the kings; and both being in the Church, have the same end. The temporal power, being inferior, is subject to the spiritual, which is the higher and more noble, and governs the former as the soul does the body. Should the temporal power turn aside from its prescribed course, it becomes the duty of the spiritual power to recall it to its true duty. It is of faith that all men, even kings, are subject to the pope; for if kings were not subject to the censures of the Church whenever they sin in the exercise of the power committed to them, they would, as a consequence, be out of the Church, and the two powers would be essentially distinct, having, in that case, their origins in two different and opposite principles—an error not far removed from the heresy of the Manichaeans.

From the Bull *Unam Sanctam* of Boniface VIII.

QUESTIONS

1. Prove the validity of the temporal and indirect powers of the papacy.
2. State four ways in which the pope exercises and enforces his temporal power.
3. Which were the principal sources of papal revenues in the Middle Ages?

BIBLIOGRAPHY

The Papal Power.—E. W. Meyer, *Staatstheorien Papst Innocenz des III.,* Bonn, 1920.—E. Amann, art. *"Innocent III et Innocent IV,"* in *Dict. de Théol.* —F. Scaduto, *Stato e Chiesa negli scritti politici del 1122 al 1347,* Florence, 1882.—Carlyle, *A History of Medieval Theory in the West,* London.—L. Godefroy, art. *"Interdit,"* in *Dict. de Théol.*—E. Valton, art. *"Excommunication,"* in *Dict. de Théol.*; art. *"Divorce des princes et l'Eglise,"* in *Dict. d'Apol.*

Cardinals.—Goyau, *Le Vatican, les papes et la civilisation,* 2nd Part.— Choupin, art. *"Curie romaine,"* in *Dict. d'Apol.*—J. Forget, art. *"Cardinaux,"* in *Dict. de Théol.*—E. Jordan, *Le Sacré-Collège au Moyen Age,* in *Rev. des Cours et Confér.,* Dec., 1921, Jan.-March, 1922.

Papal Finances.—Sources: *Liber censuum de l'Eglise romaine,* published with a preface and commentary by L. Duchesne and Paul Fabre, 1895.— Works: P. Fabre, *Etude sur le Liber censuum de l'Eglise romaine (Ecoles franç. Athènes et Rome,* fasc. LXXXVI).—P. Kirsch, *Die Finanzverwaltung des Kardinalkollegiums im 13. und 14. Jahrhundert; Kirchengeschichtl. Stud.),* II, 4, Münster, 1895.

CHAPTER II

I. The Election of Bishops. The manner of proceeding in the election of bishops was the main point at issue in the quarrel over investitures, which ended in a complete victory for the papacy. In the twelfth century a reform in episcopal elections was effected, when Urban II barred from the episcopate all clerics who had not received one of the major Orders (Council of Beneventum, 1091; Council of Clermont, 1095). Moreover, the pope had already begun to acquire a sort of supervisory jurisdiction over the election of bishops. During the reign of Pascal II (1099–1118) the electoral body consisted of the bishops of the province, abbots of the diocese, clerics of the cathedral, a few laymen and delegates of the king, and finally the canons, who had the right to convoke the electors and cast the first votes. During the period which intervened between the Concordat of Worms and the Fourth Council of the Lateran (1122–1225) the cathedral chapters supplanted the other electors. This change was protested by the monastic element, and in 1139, Innocent II declared that the advice (*consilium*) of male religious (*religiosi viri*) should be taken. The canons, however, distinguished between *consilium,* which was simple advice, and the *electio,* or right to elect. Therefore, to retain their rights as electors, monks, rural archdeacons, and archpriests had no other alternative than to secure membership in the chapters by acquiring prebends. In 1215, canon 24 of the Council of the Lateran solemnly acknowledged that cathedral chapters alone had the right to elect the bishop. From that time on these chapters assumed more and more importance. The canons were regarded as the ordinary body of advisors to the bishop, who was bound to obtain their consent for the validity of such acts as the alienation of church goods or the introduction of new feasts into the diocesan liturgy. In the thirteenth century a number of chapters were directly subject to the metropolitan or to the pope, a state of affairs which rendered them almost completely independent of the Ordinary. This accounts for many unfortunate conflicts which arose between bishops and their canons.

Generally speaking, papal influence was making itself felt more and more in the dioceses. Quite frequently episcopal nominations depended entirely upon the pope. Innocent III, for instance, annulled a number of elections, substituted his own candidate in place of the one proposed by the canons, or even directly appointed the bishop. And while the right to confirm the election still belonged by law to the metropolitan, practically the majority of bishops-elect sought confirmation of their election from Rome, referring to themselves as "bishops by the grace of God and the Apostolic See." The right to transfer a bishop from one see to another, and to accept a bishop's resignation, also belonged to the Sovereign Pontiff. At a time when appeals to Rome were becoming more and more frequent, pontifical control proved very effective. Frequently prelates were summoned to Rome to justify their conduct or an investigation was entrusted to neighboring bishops and abbots.

Finally, the popes began to claim the right to confer benefices directly. Adrian IV (1154-1159), who inaugurated this practice, simply recommended his candidates; but his successors frequently enjoined their election, a step which more than any other fostered the promotion of deserving subjects. In 1245, however, protests against this procedure were formulated at the Council of Lyons. A little later several English bishops, notably Robert Grosseteste, complained bitterly because of the number of benefices conferred upon Italians. His action induced Alexander IV (1254-1261) to declare formally that no chapter could be burdened with more than four Apostolic *mandata*. Clement IV sustained the right of the Holy See to nominate to benefices *"apud sedem apostolicam vacantia,"* i.e., whose titulars had died in the place of residence of the Roman Curia; but he also decreed that the pope has full power to dispose of all ecclesiastical charges (*plenaria dispositio*).

II. Episcopal Auxiliaries. One person in the medieval hierarchy who frequently threatened to overshadow the bishop, was the archdeacon. Invested with extensive powers of jurisdiction, this dignitary made the canonical visitation in the place of the bishop and presided over the ecclesiastical tribunal with ordinary powers of jurisdiction. In an effort to limit his authority, the bishop often created several archdeacons with distinct territories or archdeaconries subdivided into archpresbyteries.

Despite these attempts to restrict the authority of the archdeacon, the senior archdeacon continued to reside in close proximity to the bishop and even became the grand archdeacon and first ecclesiastical official in the diocese (*major post episcopum*). Beginning with the twelfth century, however, removable vicars-general were appointed, who handled such important matters as marriage cases, simony, etc., leaving to the archdeacon only the less important functions. In this way the archdeacon ceased to be a rival of the bishop. His authority, which was controverted and contested by several councils, particularly that of Laval, in 1242, began to wane, until finally the Council of Trent suppressed the office altogether.

Other episcopal auxiliaries in the diocese were the bishops *in partibus*. At the time of the establishment of the Latin Kingdom of Jerusalem several dioceses were created there. After Palestine was lost, the episcopal titles were retained, because the popes refused to abandon hope of some day effecting a reconquest. Thus it happened that some bishops were without dioceses, because the territories over which they were appointed were in the hands of the infidel Turks. These bishops (*episcopi in partibus infidelium*) placed themselves at the disposition of the western prelates.

Below the higher clergy was a multitude of simple priests. In the twelfth century many parishes were incorporated in the territories of chapters and abbeys, and administered by a monk if they depended upon an abbey, and by an ecclesiastic designated for that purpose if they belonged to the chapter. This priest was not a pastor, but a mere vicar; he received only a meagre portion of the revenues, but had the right to the perquisites and free gifts of the faithful, called stole fees. The position of other priests was no less precarious, because the patrons, as proprietors of the parishes, looked upon the priest as a sort of tenant, who could be bled at will. In the opening years of the thirteenth century we meet with the term *fabrica,* used to designate the sum-total of the revenues of a church and administered by a committee to which laymen were admitted.

TEXTS AND DOCUMENTS

Power of Metropolitans

The metropolitan examined, confirmed, and consecrated the bishops of his province; he summoned them to synods, at which each one was bound to appear; to him were referred all complaints against a bishop and all disputes of the bishops among themselves; he appointed administrators of churches that had lost their bishop; no bishop could appeal to Rome against the will of the metropolitan, nor, without his permission travel beyond the province, send messengers, or alienate the goods of the Church. Upon the archbishop devolved the care of the entire province; in all ecclesiastical affairs he could be consulted; to him appeals might be made from the judgment of the bishop, and he was empowered, even without convening a synod, of his own authority to correct the errors or the crimes of a bishop.

DÖLLINGER, *Church History*, transl. Cox,
Vol. III, pp. 180–181.

QUESTIONS

1. Enumerate the three different stages in the election of bishops in the Middle Ages.
2. Which were the functions of the archdeacon?
3. Account for the origin of the so-called bishops *in partibus*.

BIBLIOGRAPHY

Episcopal Elections.—IMBART DE LA TOUR, *Les élections épiscopales dans l'Eglise de France du IXe au XIIe siècle*, 1891.—J. DOIZÉ, *Les élections épiscopales en France avant les Concordats* (*Etudes*, CVIII–CIX, 1906).—E. ROLAND, *Les chanoines et les élections épiscopales du XIe au XVIe siècle*, 1909. B. MONOD, *L'Eglise et l'Etat au XIIe siècle*, 1904.—K. EUBEL, *Hierarchia catholica Medii Aevi*, I, 2nd edit., 1913.—VIOLLET, *Les élections ecclésiastiques au Moyen Age* (*Rev. Cath. des Eglises*, 1907).—G. MOLLAT, art. *"Elections épiscopales,"* in *Dict. d'Apol.*

The Bishop's Auxiliaries.—ED. FOUNIER, *Le Vicaire général*, 1922.—J. FAURE, *L'Archiprêtre*, 1911.—E. GRIFFE, *Les origines de l'archiprêtre de district*, R. H. E. F., 1927, pp. 16–51.

CHAPTER III

I. The Officialities and their Competency. Although the bishop and the abbot may have had judiciary rights as possessors of fiefs, the expression "ecclesiastical justice" is to be understood of the special jurisdiction exercised not under the civil, but under the Canon Law. At the outset the bishop himself exercised his jurisdiction. He then called to his assistance the archdeacon, and finally, towards the end of the twelfth century, special delegates termed *officiales,* who could be deposed at will, and whose power ceased with the death, removal or resignation of the bishop. We meet with an institution of this kind at Rheims during the administration of the archbishops Henry and William (1162-1202); from Rheims it spread to the north and northwest of France. There were two distinct categories of *officiales:* the *principales,* who resided in the episcopal city and exercised jurisdiction over the entire diocese and for all cases; and the *foranes,* who issued decisions within a certain territory only, and from whose sentence an appeal lay to the bishop. The *officialis* was sometimes called *allocatus* or *judex episcopi,* and was more often than not a canon. He very soon became an important personage, surrounded by a number of auxiliaries (assessors, procurators, lawyers, notaries, etc.). In instituting proceedings, the *officialis* had the right to give a preliminary admonition, which enjoined upon all present to report what they knew of the crime.

The competency of these episcopal bodies in matters of ecclesiastical justice was far-reaching. We must distinguish between their competency for personal cases (*ratione personae*) and their competency for real cases (*ratione materiae*). Clerics were amenable to these courts in virtue of the privilege of the clergy (*privilegium clericaturae*). Several advantages accrued to them by reason of this privilege. Thus the personal property of a cleric was not subject to seizure in virtue of the juridical principle, "*mobilia sequuntur personam.*" The Church watched over the main-

541

tenance of this privilege. A cleric seized in the act of committing a crime could be arrested by the officers of civil justice, but had to be immediately turned over to the ecclesiastical court. The Council of Avignon (1279) excommunicated any civil officer who violated this rule. Nevertheless, the Church turned over to the civil courts any cleric who rendered himself unworthy of his office, either by attempting marriage or practising usury. This measure was necessary because a number of crafty and unprincipled merchants had adopted the habit of wearing the clerical tonsure in order to escape pursuit by the law. Crusaders, widows, orphans, and university students were also amenable to the *officiales,* as well as a few privileged laymen, who had agreed to subject themselves on certain points to the jurisdiction of the Church.

In real cases the competency of the Church extended to all spiritual causes pertaining to the Sacraments, vows, and ecclesiastical discipline. Legal actions relating to marriage were numerous (engagements, separation from bed and board, adultery, legitimization of children, and, above all, disposition of matrimonial goods). Lawsuits pertaining to ecclesiastical goods were also the affair of the officialities (benefices, almsgivings, tithes), as well as questions relating to last wills and testaments, which more often than not contained bequests for pious causes. In the domain of crime, offences against religion, sacrilege, blasphemy, witchcraft, and simony were also tried by the church court, as well as crimes committed in holy places and the violation of certain prohibitions made by the Church or institutions founded by her, *e. g.,* the Peace and the Truce of God. Akin to the question of crimes committed in a holy place was the right of sanctuary, in virtue of which any criminal who took refuge in a church or monastery could not be arrested. This right was extended when so-called "rings of salvation" were attached to the outer walls of a church or monastery, which the criminal had only to grasp, to escape pursuit by the law. Later on the *ius asyli* was still further extended, to thirty or sixty paces from the church or monastery, and finally to villages and cities placed under the protection of the Cross. These boundaries were frequently marked by crosses, which practice accounts for the origin of the French "Calvaries."

As a result, ecclesiastical cases were very numerous, all the more so, as custom gave everyone the right to arraign before the *officialis* persons who had made promises under oath. Oaths, indeed, formed the basis of feudal law. On this as well as on several other points, the line of demarcation between ecclesiastical and lay jurisdiction was not clearly defined. Moreover, ecclesiastical justice, being less partial and less venal, was often preferred to the justice meted out by the civil courts. And so, beginning with the twelfth century, princes began to complain that the competency of the church courts was too extended. Instances of such complaints are encountered in the struggle between Henry II and Thomas à Becket, and to a certain extent also in the struggle between the priesthood and the empire. In the thirteenth century the French barons began to organize against the episcopal officialities, and in 1204 addressed their complaints to Philip Augustus, who issued orders that these ecclesiastical institutions should not concern themselves with lawsuits pertaining to fiefs and quit-rents. In 1225, under the leadership of Peter de Dreux, surnamed Mauclerc, a conspiracy broke out, stirred up by the barons of the West, who sought to deprive churches of the right to settle questions pertaining to tithes, last wills and testaments, usury and agreements under oath. This conspiracy called forth bulls of condemnation from Honorius III and Gregory IX, against which the assembly of St. Denis violently protested (1235). In 1245 a new French league was formed in connivance with Frederick II, but Innocent IV excommunicated the confederate barons as well as all those who placed obstacles in the way of ecclesiastical justice when acting within its jurisdiction. The prudence of St. Louis succeeded, however, in quieting these continuous outbreaks.

II. **Canon Law.** The law applied by the ecclesiastical courts was termed Canon Law. Its sources were twofold, to wit, the canons of the councils and the decretals of the popes, codified at a very early date. Towards the end of the fifth century we meet with the collection of Dionysius Exiguus (Denis the Little); in the seventh century we have the *Collectio Hispana,* attributed to Isidore of Seville; towards the end of the eighth century, the *Codex Hadrianus,* sent by Pope Hadrian to Charlemagne; in the ninth century the so-called *Pseudo-Isidore;* in the tenth century, the collection of Regino of Prüm; and in the eleventh century, the *Decretum* of Burchard of Worms and the *Panormia* of Yvo of Chartres. These collections were spread everywhere, but labored under a twofold disadvantage: external criticism revealed the fact that not all the documents they contained were authentic; and internal criticism showed that contradictions existed between the old and new Canon

Law. A Camaldolese monk by the name of Gratian, who was a professor at the University of Bologna, resolved to remedy the situation by composing his *Concordantia Discordantium Canonum*. As the words indicate, this work is not a mere classification of texts, but an attempt to harmonize seeming contradictions. The author listed first the canons which harmonized, and then those which appeared at variance with one another. After that he cited texts which paved the way for harmony, and finally proposed a solution. Such as it was, this work, surnamed the *Decretum*, rendered invaluable service, despite the fact that it had no official sanction. It was accepted in all tribunals, cited in legal ecclesiastical documents, and adopted as the classical text in the faculties of law, which were soon called faculties of the *Decretum*.

It was not long, however, before new canons and new decretals had to be catalogued, and so, between 1190 and 1226, five collections were published as a sequel to the *Decretum*, comprising the decretals from Alexander III to Honorius III (1159–1226). These later collections were arranged according to a plan devised (1190) by Bernard of Pavia (*judex, judicium, clerus, connubia, crimen*). But the canonical collections still lacked unity, and therefore Gregory IX entrusted the task of editing them to the Dominican, Raymond of Pennafort, formerly professor at the University of Bologna. Raymond left the *Decretum* of Gratian intact, but amalgamated the *quinque compilationes* with two hundred new decretals, and arranged the whole according to the subjects treated and in chronological order, as suggested by Bernard of Pavia. He gave to this work the rather too narrow title of *Decretales Gregorii Noni,* and it later formed the second part of the *Corpus Juris Canonici*. The pope issued orders for this work to be used in the universities of Bologna and Paris.

Moreover, ecclesiastical students were forbidden to study the Pandects, because Christian law was at variance with ancient Roman law in several important questions. For while Roman legislation accepted the absolute axiom, *"Quidquid principi placuit, legis habet vigorem,"* Christian legislation proclaimed with St. Thomas that "the people are not made for the ruler, but the ruler for the people." Again, while the laws of the ancient city gave to the father a despotic right over his wife and children, papal law regarded marriage as a bilateral contract and protected the dignity of womanhood by such institutions as the dower and common ownership of property. Finally, the prescriptions of Canon Law tended to suppress duels and replace them by legal proceedings, which examined the griev-ances and endeavored to make a settlement. As may be seen, therefore, the ordinances of Christian law were dictated by highly moral motives.

III. The Papal Chancery. The affairs of Christendom were re-ferred to the papal chancery, composed of a chancellor, a vice-chancellor, and several notaries. It was divided into four bureaus: that of the minutes, where the summary, "minute" or first copy of the papal acts was made; that of the estreats, in which true copies and duplicates were drawn up to be sent to the parties involved; that of the bulls, where the acts were stamped with the seal or bull of the pope, a piece of flat lead bearing the name of the pope on one side and the effigies of SS. Peter and Paul on the other; and, finally, that of the register, where copies of all docu-ments were kept. Thus the greatest precautions were taken to preserve all papal acts and to insure their authenticity against forgers. Complicated and varied formulas were resorted to in drawing up these documents, and the manner of dating them, attaching the bull, etc., was governed by most exacting rules, which were adopted later on by the majority of European chanceries. No State, saving England, possessed better kept archives.

TEXTS AND DOCUMENTS

THE PEACE AND TRUCE OF GOD

The Peace of God was intended to protect certain classes at all times, the Truce to protect all classes at certain times. The Peace of God protected par-ticularly non-combatants, sacred places, and private property. It forbade the destruction or devastation of churches and monasteries, condemned theft and robbery committed by belligerents, and forbade all attacks on clerics, peasants, the poor, pilgrims, Crusaders, and even merchants on a journey.

The Truce of God prohibited war operations on certain days and during some seasons which seemed to recall in a more special manner events or mysteries of the life of the Saviour. All warfare was to cease from Wednesday evening to Monday morning, from the beginning of Advent to the Octave Day of the feast of the Epiphany, from the beginning of Lent to Low Sunday. These were the more general periods during which fighting had to be sus-pended. But the times differed frequently, according to localities. In all places, however, where the Peace and Truce of God were observed, general social conditions were bettered, life was rendered more tolerable, and property more secure. The most beneficial results followed, and the spirit of Christianity penetrated more and more all classes of society. It was impossible, however, to suppress war altogether, since the feudal lords would not surrender their cherished privilege of waging private war.

WEBER, *The Christian Era*, p. 191.

QUESTIONS

1. What were the functions of the so-called officialities?
2. Trace the history of the "Right of Sanctuary."
3. What are the origins of Canon Law?
4. What were the Pandects?
5. What is the significance of the principle: *"Quidquid principi placuit, legis habet vigorem"*?

BIBLIOGRAPHY

Officialities.—P. FOURNIER, *Les officialités au Moyen Age*, 1881.—SCHULTE, *Die Geschichte der Quellen und Litteratur des Kanon. Rechts*, 1875–1880.—A. TARDIF, *Histoire des sources du droit canonique*, 1887.—F. SENN, *L'institution des avoueries ecclésiastiques en France*, 1903.—CH. PERGAMENI, *L'avouerie ecclésiastique belge*, 1907.—R. GÉNESTAL, *Procès sur l'état de clerc aux XIIIe et XIVe siècles*, 1909.—P. FOURNIER, *Etude sur les fausses Décrétales* (*Rev. d'hist. ecclésiastique*, 1906–1907).—LAVISSE and RAMBAUD, *Histoire générale*, II, ch. V.—ED. FOURNIER, *Comment naquit l'official*, 1925, t. XLVII, p. 249–271.—R. GÉNESTAL, *Le Privilegium Fori en France du décret de Gratien à la fin du XIVe siècle*, 2 vols., 1924.

Corpus juris canonici.—J. LAURIN, *Introductio in corpus juris canonici*, Freiburg i. B., 1899.—A. TARDIF, *Histoire des sources du droit canonique*, 1887. —A. FRIEDBERG, *Corpus juris canonici. Editio Lipsiensis secunda* (in the Prolegomena) Leipzig, 1879, 1881.—F. X. WERNZ, *Jus Decretalium* (I, titr. XII, XIII and XV), 2nd edit., Rome, 1915.—PÉRIÈS, *La Faculté de Droit dans l'ancienne Université de Paris*, 1890.—J. BESSON, art. *"Corpus juris canonici,"* in *Dict. d'Apol.*

CHAPTER IV

I. Piety: Sermons and Mysteries. Medieval piety was both open and naïve. The people felt themselves completely at home in church, and to attract them thither, the clergy had recourse to two principal means: preaching and the mysteries. In the Middle Ages the sermon was used not only in religious ceremonies, but also in parliamentary gatherings, tournaments, fairs and markets, and at weddings and burials. Frequently, too, sermons were preached from a small movable platform in public places, and it sometimes happened that the assistants put questions to the speaker. With no fear of being accused of triviality, the orator quite willingly recounted fables and queer stories, punctuated here and there with quotations from the pagan classics to stress some moral obligation. This fact explains why, with few exceptions, these sermons, despite their great number, are just ordinary discourses and contain no information except on the history of contemporary morals. Among the greatest preachers were St. Bernard, Fulco of Neuilly, Stephen of Bourbon, Guibert of Nogent, Innocent III, St. Antony of Padua, St. Bonaventure, and St. Thomas Aquinas.

The "liturgical drama" also exercised considerable influence. At different times throughout the year, especially at Christmas and Easter, the principal mysteries of religion, in particular the Incarnation and the Passion of Christ, were represented in church. The actors in these mysteries were priests or clerics clothed with slightly altered priestly vestments. The dialogue consisted of short Latin sentences, written in prose, which merely paraphrased the Sacred Text. Thus the early liturgical drama was at bottom nothing more than a prolongation of the Divine Office. Very soon, however, transformations of all kinds were effected, and in the twelfth and thirteenth centuries, the "mystery" had the appearance of a modern play in verse. The representation of these mysteries, however, was transferred from the church to a nearby place, and endeavored to portray not

547

only the Passion of Christ, but also the lives of the Saints, arranged in touching but sometimes fantastic scenes. This was the semi-liturgical form assumed by the mysteries up to the fourteenth century, when they became completely secularized. The piety fostered by performances of this sort was directed either towards the veneration of the Saints or that of Our Lady. Each city possessed its own patron, whose feast was celebrated with great solemnity. New religious Orders were founded and dedicated to the Blessed Virgin Mary; cathedrals were erected in her honor; places of pilgrimage began to flourish; and hymns, canticles and collections of legends and miracles recounted the praises of her name.

II. Christian Institutions: Fraternities and Third Orders, Knighthoods and Guilds. The Middle Ages witnessed the rise of "fraternities" which, without forming a part of the then existing religious Orders, engaged in such works of the apostolate as the alleviation of the sufferings of the poor, the burial of the dead, and similar deeds of piety. Clerics, laymen and women were admitted indiscriminately to these fraternities, the majority of them having their own administration and the members living in about the same way. All wore the same garb, recited the same prayers, performed the same penances, received the Sacraments, assisted their fellow brethren, engaged in various good works, and met once a month. The more important of these associations, however, tended rapidly to combine with the regulars. In the beginning of the thirteenth century certain statutes seem to be inspired by Cistercian practices, but above all by the habits and customs of the Hospitallers. At the head of the confraternity was a "master," assisted by a treasurer, and a prioress, who ruled over the female members. Instances of such fraternities were the *Capuciati,* who were founded at Puy-en-Velay after Our Lady had appeared to the carpenter Durand Dujardin. They had for their mission to keep and procure peace. The *Capuciati* also pledged themselves to fulfill all their religious duties and not to gamble or enter taverns. Similar associations were founded in both the central and southern portions of France. At the outset, the Florentine Servites belonged to a *Confraternitas de Laudesi,* whose members, while remaining laymen and continuing to lead a secular life, performed certain practices of piety and distinguished themselves by their devotion to the Blessed Virgin. It was only later, under the direction of Bonfiglio, that they grouped themselves into a religious Order. The *Humiliati* of Lombardy also constituted a pious association, whose main purpose was prayer and preaching. They were rejected at first by Alexander III, but later on approved by Innocent III. There were also a number of confraternities of penitents, at Siena, Naples, Rome, and in several cities of Germany. By and by the confraternities became so numerous that frequently several of them existed even in smaller villages.

While some of these confraternities, like the Servites, embraced the clerical state, others retained their original character. This was particularly the case of the *Beghards* and the *Beguines,* who spread widely in the Netherlands. We must not, however, put faith in the legend that they were the spiritual offspring of St. Begga, a daughter of Pepin of Landen. There are four periods in the history of the Beghards and Beguines: (1) They were holy persons who lived in the world, but had no relations with one another: in the twelfth century the name Beguine was synonymous with bigot (*bigutta*). (2) Towards the end of the twelfth century the Beghards and Beguines adopted a community life in the world; *congregationes disciplinatae* of both sexes were founded at Liège under the direction of Lambert le Begue, as well as several congregations of women at Nivelles. (3) During the first half of the thirteenth century the Beguines began to lead a community life in cloistered cabins (*curtes*); these were the *beguinae clausae,* who finally imposed their rule of life on all Beguines in northern Holland and the land of the Walloons. (4) In course of time the Beguines assumed such importance that both civil and ecclesiastical authorities were constrained to group into autonomous parishes *curtes* which had banded themselves together. Beguinage parishes existed at Ghent, Bruges, Brussels, Antwerp, Bois-le-Duc, etc. The Beguines took a vow of perpetual or temporary chastity, and also promised obedience. They wore a special habit and vowed themselves to the care of the sick. The discipline of the Beghards was, as a general rule, less severe. We shall soon have occasion to show how, in these isolated centers, unorthodox doctrines thrived in secret, which called forth the condemnation of the Church at the end of the thirteenth and the beginning of the fourteenth century. However, orthodox Beghards and Beguines continued to exist.

At this juncture we must say a word about the *Third Orders.* St. Norbert founded a Third Order for persons in the world desirous of sharing in the merits of canons and canonesses. He gave them a rule, which reflects the Norbertine mode of life, and commanded them to wear a small white scapular. Kings and princes hastened to have their names inscribed on tablets which bore the title with the words, *ad succurrendum*. But the institution of the Third Order assumed its real proportions with the advent of St. Francis of Assisi. The religious movement inaugurated by him spread at the very outset to a group of disciples who imitated his form of life, then to a second group, represented by women who had vowed themselves to observe continence, and, finally, to a third group which included persons in the married state. While materially distinct, these three groups juridically constituted one fraternity, living under the same rule. The outstanding characteristic of the groups, which is found impressed on all three of them, was that of penance. The segmentation [1] of this Franciscan fraternity was effected in 1221, when the Order was organized by the Roman Church. It was then that the "Penitents" were given a special rule, drawn up by St. Francis and Cardinal Hugolinus. The second rule (1234) segregated the Friars Minor and placed them under the authority of the bishops, but the Bull *"Supra montem,"* of August 17, 1289, specified that the "Penitents" were to be governed by the Friars Minor and select their visitators from among them. It was not until 1285 that these "Penitents" were called for the first time *Tertius Ordo* (Third Order). Their ordinary obligations consisted in keeping three days of abstinence and two days of fasting per week, reciting the breviary or a certain number of Our Fathers daily, going to confession and Communion three times a year, and visiting the sick. The influence of the Third Order of St. Francis upon society in the thirteenth century cannot be overestimated. The Dominicans also grouped around their monasteries similar fraternities, which thrived particularly in Alsace. Munio of Zamora, superior general of the Dominicans, gave them a rule in 1285.

Despite these attempts to educate the people, manners and customs were still very unpolished. All too frequently the nobleman was at best a well-equipped thief, who made it his principal business to relieve merchants and travellers of their goods. The Church endeavored to intervene by stamping with a religious character the ceremony of conferment of arms, which transformed the young man into a knight. The candidate

---

[1] Some maintain that St. Francis founded the three Orders not by a process of segmentation, but successively and by way of addition. See F. Van der Borne, *Franziskanische Studien*, 1925.

prepared himself for the ceremony by a fast of twenty-four hours, one night spent in prayer (the vigil of arms), and confession and Communion. During the Mass he listened to a sermon on the duties of his state, to wit, the protection of widows and orphans, clerics and women of unblemished purity. Then came the blessing of the armor. The young aspirant pledged himself with his hands between those of his godfather, to fulfill all the duties of a true knight. The godfather then unsheathed his sword and struck him on the shoulder with the broad side of the blade, saying: "In the name of the Father, and of the Son, and of the Holy Ghost, I make thee a knight." Pagan in its origin, this institution was christianized as early as the eleventh century. Later on the Church surrounded it with all sorts of liturgical and symbolic formulas.

The twelfth century witnessed a thorough change in the social order. The agricultural and local economy, which up to that time had prevailed in the West, was replaced by an industrial and commercial exchange system, the result being that a number of corporate organizations sprang into existence, which reached their full development in the thirteenth century. This is attested by the "Book of Trades," composed by the provost of Paris, Stephen Boileau, at the instigation of King St. Louis. According to this writer, the guild comprised three classes of artisans: apprentices, journeymen, and masters (or employers). The principle of family life was in evidence in every workshop, and apprentices and journeymen boarded and roomed with their master, who acted as a sort of father to them and was bound in conscience to see to it that they faithfully performed their religious duties. Quite frequently the confraternity worked hand in hand with the guild, which grouped all the members of the same trade into a pious association or society for mutual assistance. Each confraternity rallied around the standard of its patron saint; the bakers adopting St. Honorius, the goldsmiths, St. Eligius, etc. Special Masses were celebrated on certain days, and sometimes the association possessed its own chapel. Several confraternities even went so far as to assume a quasi-religious aspect. Thus, a physician named William, with the help of several friends, founded at Paris a community house for students which went by the name of "Val des Ecoliers."

III. Christian Charity. Scourges were of frequent occurrence during the Middle Ages, particularly war, pestilence, and famine. The work of assisting the poor, however, was sufficiently organized to meet all emergencies. In the country districts, where the feudal regime continued to hold sway, the business of protecting the serfs was entirely in the hands of their lord. He was assisted in this task by the rural clergy, and above all by the monasteries, which as a rule had a hospice for travellers (*xenodochium*) and a hospital for the sick attached. In the cities there were the famous "maisons Dieu" (hospitals), first established in the tenth and eleventh centuries by the bishops and clergy, who gave them their regulations and inspected them periodically. In the twelfth and thirteenth centuries, when the feudal regime was in full force, the erection of "maisons Dieu" fell to the lot of the kings and lords. Finally, in the fourteenth and fifteenth centuries the commune, the aldermen, the commoners, and the confraternities were constrained to take the initiative in promoting works of charity.

The "maisons Dieu" were served by the different Orders of Hospitallers. We have very little information regarding their internal administration until the twelfth century, when the Rule of the hospital of St. John of Jerusalem was formulated by Raymond of Puis. This Rule was adopted by the three great Orders of Hospitallers, to wit, the Teutonic Knights, the Knights of the Holy Ghost, and the Knights of St. John du Haut-Pas, and, in 1212, imposed by a council of Paris upon all hospitals controlled by religious. The members of the congregations just mentioned were professed religious, bound by the three vows of poverty, chastity, and obedience. A decree of the same council of Paris forbade the custom of receiving persons together with their entire fortune with the proviso that they would be taken care of for the rest of their lives. Under the Rule of Brother Raymond, a sick person had to be treated like a lord (*quasi dominus*). Frequently the patients were quartered in a large hall, roofed with pointed arches, which adjoined the church, in such wise that it sufficed to open a wooden partition at the hours of prayer for the patients to be able to assist thereat. These institutions, therefore, were truly "maisons Dieu" (Houses of God). Annexed to this large hall were special rooms, together with the infirmary for grievously sick persons, and the maternity ward. It is not true that hygiene was unknown at this period. In return for services rendered them the sick were asked to make an alms of their prayers, the formula of which has been preserved: "O ye sick lords, pray for the fruits of the earth . . . and pray for the pilgrims, the Christian people, . . . and for those who are in the hands of the Saracens," etc.

Separate establishments existed for lepers, under the patronage of St. Lazarus, the patron of lepers. At the time of Louis VIII, in 1225, there were as many as 2000 hospitals for lepers in the kingdom of France alone. The Brothers and Sisters who attended the sick were grouped into a confraternity under the direction of the bishop, and as a general rule bequeathed all their goods to the "maladreries." Moreover, the Order of the Knights of St. Lazarus of Jerusalem was established to care for lepers after the Christians gained possession of the Holy Land, 1099–1113, with its mother-house located at Boigny near Orleans. From the thirteenth to the fifteenth century the Order of St. Lazarus numbered 3000 hospitals for lepers in Europe and Asia Minor. The lepers were examined by a board made up of the bishop and the aldermen, and were given the best of care. They lived in complete isolation, wore a piece of red cloth sewn on to the sleeve as a distinctive mark of their disease, and when they walked through the streets, had to make known their presence by shaking a small rattle. By these measures the dread disease was gradually stamped out.

A large number of charitable institutions had a special purpose. Thus the Order of the Holy Ghost, founded in 1160 by a commoner named Guy, and established in Rome under Pope Innocent III, pledged itself to care for foundlings. The Antonines were instituted by a hermit, named Gaston, from Dauphiny, who, under the special protection of St. Antony of the desert, cared for the sick and for pilgrims. The Brothers Pontiffs, who had charge of bridges and adjoining hospices, numbered several local communities, the most famous being that of Avignon, founded by St. Bénezet.

TEXTS AND DOCUMENTS

The Liturgical Mysteries

The earliest *tropes* have come down to us from the tenth and eleventh centuries. They are Easter and Christmas tropes. The Easter trope will serve as an illustration. After the Introit has been sung, three priests, clad in hooded mantles and carrying censers, slowly walk to the Holy Sepulchre, which may be seen on one side of the sanctuary. There two other priests, who take the part of the angels, sit vested in albs and hold palm branches in their hands. As soon as the three priests, representing the three Holy Women, approach the Sepulchre, the singing of the trope begins:

The Angels: Whom seek ye at this tomb, O Christian women?

The Holy Women: O ye inhabitants of Heaven, we seek Jesus of Nazareth, the Crucified.

The Angels: He is not here; He is risen, as He foretold. Go and proclaim the good news that He is risen from the dead. Alleluia!

All: The Lord is risen!

The Angels: Behold the place where they laid Him. (The Angels remove the cloth which covered the place of the sepulchre, and spread it out before the people.)

QUESTIONS

1. Trace the history of the mystery plays.
2. What was the fate of most of the early confraternities?
3. What was the chief heresy of the Beghards?
4. Account for the origin of the Third Order.
5. Which were the principal duties of a knight?
6. What was the purpose of the guilds?

BIBLIOGRAPHY

Medieval Piety. The Mysteries.—Sources: CESARIUS OF HEISTERBACH, edit. Strange, Cologne, 1851.—ETIENNE DE BOURBON, edit. Lecoy de la Marche, 1877.—*Le journal des visites pastorales d'Eudes Rigaud, arch. de Rouen,* published by Bonnin, Rouen, 1847.—Works: L. BOURGAIN, *La chaire française au XIIe siècle d'après les manuscrits,* 1879.—LEROY DE LA MARCHE, *La chaire française au Moyen Age,* 1886.—A. LUCHAIRE, *La société française au temps de Philippe-Auguste,* 1909.—CH. V. LANGLOIS, *La vie en France au Moyen Age,* 1908.—A. RAMBAUD, *Histoire de la civilisation française,* I, 5th edit., 1893.—O. DOBIACHE-RODJDESTVENSKY, *La vie paroissiale en France au XIIIe siècle, d'après les actes épiscopaux,* 1911.—PETIT DE JULLEVILLE, *Les mystères,* 2 vols., 1880; *Les mystères,* in *La France chrétienne.*—G. COHEN, *Histoire de la mise en scène dans le théâtre religieux français du Moyen Age,* 1906.—G. PARIS, *La littérature française du Moyen Age,* 1905.—DURIEZ, *La théologie dans le drame religieux en France au Moyen Age,* 1914; *Les Apocryphes dans le drame religieux allemand au Moyen Age,* 1914.—CH. V. LANGLOIS, *La vie en France au Moyen Age,* 4 vols., 1926-1928.—See also the articles on *"Mysteries," "Miracle Plays and Moralities,"* in *Cath. Encycl.*—KARL YOUNG, *The Drama of the Medieval Church,* 2 vols., Oxford, 1933.

Béguines.—FRÉDÉRICQ, *Note complémentaire sur les documents de Glascow concernant Lambert le Bègue,* 1895.—PIRENNE, *Histoire de Belgique,* t.

I, Brussels, 1912.—F. Vernet, art. *"Béghards,"* in *Dict. de Théol.*—Albanès, *Vie de sainte Douceline, fondatrice des Béghines de Marseille*, Marseille, 1879. Legrand, *Les Béghines de Paris*, 1894.—S. J. M. Philippen, *De begijnhoven*, Anvers, 1918.—P. Hoornaert, *Les Béguines de Bruges, leur histoire, leur règle*, Bruges, 1924.—Fr. Callaey, *Lambert, Bèges et les Béguines*, R. H. E., 1927, p. 254.—J. van Mierlo, *Les Béguines et Lambert li Bèges*, ibid., p. 785.

Third Order.—H. Lamy, *L'abbaye de Tongerloo, passim* (Recent works. by the University of Louvain, fasc. XLIV).—E. Maire, *Saint Norbert*, 1923.— Mandonnet, *Les origines de l'Ordo de Poenitentia* (Int. Congress of Catholics at Fribourg, 1897), Hist. sect., pp. 183 ff.; *Les règles et le gouvernement de l'Ordo de Poenitentia au XIIIe siècle*, 1902.—P. Sabatier, *Regula antiqua fratrum et sororum Poenitentiae*, 1901.—Frédégand, *Le tiers-Ordre de saint François d'Assise*, 1923.—Nesta de Robeck, *Among the Franciscan Tertiaries.* —B. J. Musser, *Franciscan Poets*, New York, 1933.

Knighthood.—Léon Gautier, *La Chevalerie.*—J. Flach, *Les origines de l'ancienne France*, II, 3rd Part, *La Chevalerie.*

Corporations.—Sources: R. de Lespinasse and Fr. Bonnardot, *Les métiers et corporations de la ville de Paris*, I. *Le Livre des métiers d'Ed. Boileau* (Coll. *"Hist. générale de Paris"*), 1879.—Works: Max Sabatier, *L'Eglise et le travail manuel*, 1895.—Martin de Saint Léon, *Hist. des corporations*, 3rd edit., 1922.—P. Viollet, *Les corporations au Moyen-Age*, 1900.— E. Dupont, *Corporations d'autrefois et syndicats d'aujourd'hui* (*Correspondant*, Feb. 10, 1883).—Levasseur, *Hist. des classes ouvrières*, 1900–1901.—Martin de Saint Léon, *Le compagnonnage*, 1901.—Fagniez, *Corporations et syndicats*, 2nd edit., 1905.

Charity and Maisons-Dieu.—Lallemand, *Histoire de la charité*, 4 vols., 1905–1912.—Léon le Grand, *Les Maisons-Dieu, leurs statuts au XIIIe siècle* (*Rev. Quest. hist.*, July 1, 1896).—Msgr. Prunel, *"Les Pauvres et l'Eglise,"* in *Dict. d'Apol.*—Neyron, *La charité chrétienne*, 1927.

CHAPTER V

After the tenth century the liturgy remained stationary. The process of unifying the different liturgies was undertaken during the Carolingian epoch by the Roman liturgy. The Celtic, Anglo-Saxon, and Gallican liturgies had ceased to exist, while the Ambrosian and Mozarabic liturgies were restricted to certain localities.

I. Liturgical Literature. A few liturgical writings are deserving of special mention. In the eleventh century there is the *Micrologus,* long attributed to Yvo of Chartres, but actually composed by Bernold of Constance. This work contains an exact description of the liturgy of those days. In the twelfth century we must single out Honorius of Autun, John Beleth, and Berold. Honorius of Autun made himself famous by his *Gemma Animae,* in which he gives a mystical explanation of the ceremonies and offices. He also composed a work entitled, *De Sacramentis,* or *Sacramentarium,* explaining the different ecclesiastical feasts. John Beleth, in his *Rationale Divinorum Officiorum,* explains the character of the Divine Office. Berold gives a minute description of the Ambrosian rite. In the thirteenth century Durandus of Mende composed a *Rationale Divinorum Officiorum,* a sort of liturgical compendium, which abounds in mystical and especially symbolical explanations.

II. Changes Effected in the Divine Office. The Breviary. The only important innovation made at this time was the change from the Office in choir to the private recitation of the Breviary. In the twelfth century John Beleth in his *Rationale* bitterly complained of the lukewarmness of priests in reciting the Office. Attempts had even been made to reduce the night Office to three psalms and three lessons. Gregory VII protested against this abuse and enjoined the recitation of the traditional number of psalms. There was also a tendency to reduce the number of lessons, although the monasteries continued to abide by the ancient custom. At Cluny, for instance, the monks recited the entire book of

Genesis in the course of a week, although many looked upon such readings as excessive. Moreover, the recitation of the Office in choir required the use of a whole library (psalter, antiphonary, responsorial, homiliary, etc.), and so portable Office books came into existence, called *breviarii,* which clerics used when they did not recite the Office in choir. In 1227 a council held at Treves stipulated that clerics must carry breviaries with them when travelling. The pope and the clerics of the Roman Curia were the ones who felt these inconveniences most, and not being able to recite the canonical Office daily in choir, were constrained to shorten it. In 1223 the Franciscans adopted the Breviary of the Roman Curia, but their general, Haymon of Faversham, made a number of corrections and suppressions approved by Gregory IX in 1241. Nicholas III (1277–1280) adopted this Breviary of the Friars Minor for the Roman Church, and it was definitively substituted in the place of the Office in use at the time of Charlemagne and Hadrian. This Office comprised five parts: calendar, psalter, *temporale,* proper and common of the Saints.

The outstanding characteristic of this reform was the importance accorded to the feasts of the Saints. All the feasts of Our Lady were raised to the degree of double-majors, just like Christmas and Easter, and also the feasts of St. Peter, St. John, and All Saints. The feasts of Apostles and Doctors, the feast of the dedication of the great Roman basilicas, and the two feasts of the Holy Cross were made double, while Sundays remained semi-double. All these feasts had nine lessons, the first six recounting the story of the Saint's life, and the last three being in the form of a homily. Towards the end of the twelfth century, 150 feasts of Saints had found their way into the Breviary and nearly crowded out the *temporale.* The insertion of these feasts was unfortunate, because it changed the essential characteristics of the Roman Office, the basis of which was the *temporale.* Finally, supplementary prayers, and notably the Office of the Blessed Virgin Mary, and that of the Dead, added considerably to the length of the daily Office, and rendered the task of reciting it quite onerous. This fact led some clerics to show preference for "superfluous prayers and acts of supererogation."

Several solemn feasts were created during this period. Already in the tenth century Stephen, bishop of Liège (903–920), had adopted the feast of the Blessed Trinity in his diocese; stimulated by Cluny during the twelfth century, it was soon accepted almost everywhere. The same is true of the feast of the Transfiguration, the rapid spread of which was due to the same monastic influence. The feast of the Immaculate Conception (Dec. 8), however, encountered serious resistance. Irish in its origin, it was acknowledged in England by Elsin, abbot of Ramsey (1080–1087), passed over into France, but met with strong opposition on the part of St. Bernard, who in a letter reproached the people of Lyons for not having first consulted Rome. Subsequent to revelations made to St. Juliana of Mt. Cornillon, a feast of the Blessed Sacrament was established at Liège in 1246, and confirmed in 1252 by the learned Dominican Hugh, cardinal legate in the Netherlands. After the famous Eucharistic miracle of Bolsena, otherwise known as the miracle of the Bleeding Host (1263), Urban IV made the celebration of this feast obligatory throughout the world, and St. Thomas Aquinas composed an Office for it. At the Council of Vienne (1311–1312) Clement V ratified this measure.

III. The Sacraments. The writers of the twelfth century were greatly concerned with the confusion in the list of Sacraments compiled by their predecessors. It was a relatively easy matter for them, however, to discern the cause of this confusion in a very imperfect definition of the word "Sacrament" itself. Hence their first act was to formulate a definition suited to all the Sacraments, and to the Sacraments alone (*omni sacramento solique*). They defined a Sacrament as an efficacious sign of grace. This definition was formulated with particular reference to Baptism, which is, in a way, the type *par excellence* of all the Sacraments. Hugh of St. Victor had already accomplished much in the direction of formulating this definition, although he mentions only three Sacraments: Baptism, Confirmation, and the Holy Eucharist. The credit for determining the exact number of the Sacraments belongs to Peter Lombard.

The manner of administering the Sacraments was, as a general rule, well determined. This is particularly true of Baptism. In the twelfth century the practice of baptizing by immersion became obsolete, and for practical reasons infusion was substituted in its place. The formula of the Sacrament, however, admitted of variations. St. Bernard held that the formula: "I baptize thee in the name of God and of the holy and true Cross," was valid, but by the thirteenth century absolute uniformity prevailed. However, two questions were still mooted regarding the Sacrament of Confirmation: Could the Pope give to a simple priest the right to confer this Sacrament; and was it necessary to receive the Sacrament fasting, as several synods ordained? Robert Pullen answered the first of these two questions in the negative; St. Thomas, in the affirmative.

Berengarius denied transubstantiation and thus undermined the dogma of the Real Presence. His error regarding the Eucharist was based on false philosophical principles (Nominalism), which led him to reduce all knowledge to sense experience. Now, if nothing exists except that which falls under the senses, the bread and wine remain substantially the same after the consecration, and no transubstantiation takes place. For the same reasons Berengarius should also have denied the Real Presence, because, according to him, every corporeal substance is subject to the laws of space, and the body of Christ being no exception to this rule, it is impossible for Him to be anywhere else but in Heaven. Christ is indivisible, and if He is present wholly and entirely in one host, He cannot at the same time be present on a thousand altars and in Heaven. It is true, Berengarius did not go so far as formally to deny the Real Presence, but his obscure and hesitant teaching certainly helped to undermine the dogma.

Berengarius formulated his errors in direct opposition to the realist theory of Paschasius Radbertus, the most brilliant exponent of which was Lanfranc, abbot of the monastery of Le Bec. Jealous of Lanfranc, who had defeated him in a philosophical tilt, and resentful because the school of Bec had eclipsed that of St. Martin of Tours, it seems he indulged in these innovations chiefly for the sake of notoriety. In 1049 Berengarius addressed a letter to Lanfranc, which drew down upon his head the censures of the Council of Rome (1050). Condemned once more, several months later, by the Council of Vercelli, the heresiarch was thrown into prison by order of Henry I, king of France, but obtained his freedom by bribery. At the Council of Tours, Hildebrand forced him to sign a profession of faith, the terms of which were too vague, however, to constitute a recantation. Summoned to Rome, Berengarius was condemned a third time and forced to subscribe to the following formula of faith: "The bread and wine offered at the altar are, after the consecration, not only a Sacrament, but the true body and the true blood of Jesus Christ." This formula admitted of no equivocation, and Berengarius claimed that it had been imposed upon him by force. In 1078 he was again summoned to Rome. Gregory VII dealt the death-blow to the heresy at the Council of the Lateran (Feb. 11, 1079), and Berengarius was again asked to subscribe to a most categorical formula. In forbidding anyone to molest either his person or his goods, or to call him a heretic, Gregory VII had made the unfortunate mistake of trusting too much in the good faith of this proud rebel, for scarcely had Berengarius returned to France, when he wrote against the formula which he had just professed in Rome. He was condemned for a fourth and last time at the Council of Bordeaux (1080), recanted his errors, and withdrew to the island of St. Cosmas, where he died reconciled to the Church. His case was the first instance of open revolt against the teachings of the Church in the West, a fact which has led some to regard him as one of the precursors of freethought.

Paradoxical as it may seem, the people in those ages of faith rather neglected the Holy Eucharist. The practice of administering Communion to children immediately after Baptism was gradually abandoned, and laymen approached the Holy Table only at rare intervals. The Fourth Council of the Lateran (1215) was obliged to re-state the precept of annual Communion and to enjoin its observance under severe penalties; it even complained that some priests said Mass only four times a year. On the other hand, as the result of a common tendency towards exaggeration prevalent in these times, some priests celebrated several Masses each day; others said a *missa sicca, i.e.,* without consecration or communion; others a *missa bifaciata* or *trifaciata,* by combining two or three Introits, Epistles, and Gospels; finally, there were those who celebrated the Mass of the Dead for persons still living, to hasten the hour of their demise and precipitate the judgment of God. All these abuses were severely condemned by the Church.

The practice of elevating the Host at Mass is of ancient origin. An *Ordo Romanus* attests its existence in Rome around the year 800, and we have a vestige of it in the "little elevation" which precedes the Paternoster. The elevation as we know it came into practice in the twelfth century. At the sound of the bell the people knelt down, but did not bow their heads; on the contrary, their devotion led them to look up at the Host. This fact accounts for that other practice of exposing the Blessed Sacrament in an ostensorium or monstrance, a custom existing in Germany in the fourteenth century. Quite frequently these monstrances were constructed in the form of Christ's body, and the Host placed behind a small glass in the upper center.

Annual confession was enjoined by the Fourth Council of the Lateran

(1215). Public penance, however, became more and more infrequent, and was imposed only on persons who had raised their hand against a bishop. According to the Council of Treves (1227), the cases reserved to the Holy See were violence done to the persons of clerics or monks, the burning of churches, the protection of excommunicated persons, and the forging of papal bulls. The penances enjoined were much more severe than they are to-day: prayers, alms, fasts, pilgrimages, entrance into a religious Order, participation in a Crusade, etc. Soon the practice of "redeeming" these penances assumed undue proportions, and the money thus collected was used not only for religious purposes, but also for works of public utility. The practice of granting indulgences also increased. They were often given to a crusader or to a person who equipped a crusader. Pope Innocent III granted a plenary indulgence to all who would assist in the construction of a bridge over the river Rhone, and Innocent IV to all who would help to erect the cathedral of Cologne. The bishops imitated this practice, and sometimes abused it. As a result, Innocent III (1215) was constrained to deprive them of the right of granting a plenary indulgence, and even to limit the right of granting partial indulgences.

IV. **Marian Liturgy.** The most beautiful prayers to the Blessed Virgin Mary date from the Middle Ages. The *Salve Regina* (Hail, Holy Queen), for example, originated at Puy and was brought into vogue by the Cistercians. St. Bernard is responsible for the addition of the last few invocations. The Hail Mary ended with the words: *"fructus ventris tui, Amen,"* but private devotion often enlarged upon the theme. The final prayer, as we have it, was added at a later date. The most popular of all devotions in honor of the Mother of God was the Rosary. In the Middle Ages a vassal made a practice of offering to his lord a wreath of roses as a token of his obedience, and so the mystics, who were the knights and servants of Mary, offered her wreaths and crowns of roses, whence the term, "Rosary." Moreover, the faithful took delight in imitating the monks, and so, not being able to wear the monastic habit, adopted a small scapular, which gave them the right to share in some of their merits. In the same manner, not being able to recite the entire psalter like the religious, laymen conceived the idea of replacing the 150 psalms by a crown or wreath of 150 Hail Marys. This was known as "The Psalter of Our Lady." In the year 1470, as the result of a vision, the Dominican Alain de la Roche conceived the idea of adding to the recitation of the

Hail Marys a short meditation on the life of Christ and the Blessed Virgin: whence the white roses to signify the joyous mysteries; the red roses to signify the sorrowful mysteries, and the golden roses to signify the glorious mysteries. The *Memorare* was not composed by St. Bernard, but inspired by his homilies (no. 8, from the fourth sermon on the Assumption, and no. 15, from the sermon for the Sunday within the Octave of the Ascension: *"Jam te, mater misericordiae"*).

TEXTS AND DOCUMENTS

THE ELEVATION OF THE HOST

It is not easy to state precisely at what epoch the elevation of the Host was introduced into the Mass. In the old liturgies, as we have seen, an elevation takes place at the end of the Canon—when the Priest, elevating a little both Host and Cup together, ends a prayer of doxology with the words *omnis honor et gloria.* This elevation, however, was not intended to challenge the adoration of the assistants. It was rather in honour of God. The usage of elevating the Host immediately after the Consecration is generally referred by the various writers who have searched through the monuments—such as Thiers, Mabillon, Du Chardon, Le Brun, etc.—to the twelfth century; and it seems to have been first adopted in France, and as a popular reply to the heretic Berengarius, who denied the Real Presence. It was sanctioned by the Holy See at the beginning of the thirteenth century by Pope Honorius III. As far as we can gather it seems to have been, at first, only one out of a variety of ways invented by the piety of particular priests or churches to show their detestation of heresy. But this particular rite was so well adapted to excite and respond to popular devotion that it spread everywhere, and by A. D. 1250 was certainly universal.

HEDLEY, *The Holy Eucharist,* pp. 260–261.

THE MEMORARE

Remember, O most pious Virgin Mary, that never was it known that any one who had recourse to thy protection, implored thy aid, or begged thy intercession, was left unaided. Filled with this confidence, I fly to thee, O Virgin of virgins, and my most tender Mother, for refuge, and, sighing under the burden of my sins, I throw myself at thy feet. Deign, O Mother of the Incarnate Word, graciously to hear my prayer. Amen.

QUESTIONS

1. What is the origin of the word "Breviary"?

2. Give the meaning of the terms: Psalter, Antiphonary, Responsory, and Homiliary.
3. What was the miracle of the "Bleeding Host"?
4. Why is Berengarius regarded as one of the precursors of freethought?
5. How do you account for the faithful of the Middle Ages not receiving the Sacraments frequently?

BIBLIOGRAPHY

Breviary.—P. Batiffol, *History of the Roman Breviary.*—S. Bäumer, *Histoire du Bréviaire*, 2 vols.

Immaculate Conception.—E. Vacandard, *Les origines de la fête de la Conception dans le diocèse de Rouen et en Angleterre (Rev. quest. hist.,* Jan., 1897).—M. Lesêtre, *L'Immaculée-Conception et l'Eglise de Paris,* 1904.—A. Noyon, *Les origines de la fête de l'Immaculée-Conception en Occident, Etudes,* 1904.—P. Doncoeur, *Les premières interventions du Saint Siège relatives à l'Immaculée-Conception, R. H. E.,* 1907-1908.

Berengarius.—Sources: *P. L.,* Cl, 63, 66.—Durand de Troarn, *Liber de corpore et sanguine Christi, P. L.,* CXLIX, 1375-1424.—Bernold de Constance, *De Berengarii damnatione, P. L.,* CXLVIII, 1458-1460.—Works: O. Delarc, *Les origines de l'hérésie de Bérenger (Rev. quest. hist.,* 1876, XX, pp. 115-155); *Saint Grégoire VII,* I, pp. 203-221, II, pp. 113-121, 293-327.—Fliche, *Philippe I.*—P. Renaudin, *L'hérésie eucharistique de Bérenger (An. cath.,* new series, Lyons, 1902. XL, pp. 415-447).—F. Vernet, art. *"Bérenger,"* in *Dict. de Théol.*—Ebersolt, *"Essai sur Bérenger" (Rev. hist. des religions,* 1903, XLVIII, pp. 1-42, 137-181).—Vernet, *Eucharistie du IXe à la fin du XIe siècle,* in *Dict. de Théol.*—R. Heurtevent, *Durand de Troarn et les origines de l'herésie bérengarienne* (Coll. *"Etudes de Théol. Hist."*).—Clerval, *Les écoles de Chartres au Moyen-Age,* 1895.—E. Amann and A. Claudel, art. *"Lanfranc,"* in *Dict. de Théol.*

Sacraments.—P. Pourrat, *The Theology of the Sacraments, A Study in Positive Theology.*—Lépicier, *Les indulgences. Leur origine, leur nature, leur développement,* 2 vols., 1903.—E. Dumoutet, *Le désir de voir l'hostie et les origines de la dévotion du Saint-Sacrement,* 1926.

CHAPTER VI

I. Philosophy in the Twelfth Century: The Controversy Concerning Universals. Up to the twelfth century, theology had remained content to rest its proofs on the arguments of the Fathers, which were copied almost literally. This slavish attitude seemed to be the only sure method of procedure. John Scotus Eriugena, in the ninth century, and Berengarius in the middle of the eleventh, had strayed from it and fallen into heresy as a consequence. Their example struck fear into the hearts of others and made them distrustful of the ways of philosophy. The great merit of *St. Anselm* lies in the fact that he inspired theologians with new confidence in the power of reason. Without setting aside the ancient proofs based on authority, he sought other arguments from metaphysics and dialectics. He developed many new viewpoints in his *Monologium,* a meditation on the Divine Essence, and in his *Proslogion,* in which he unfolds a new proof for the existence of God, based on the idea of perfection; but what gained for him a place next to St. Augustine and St. Thomas, was his successful attempt to direct a stagnant theology along more progressive lines.

It was at this juncture that the great philosophical disputations were inaugurated. The question of Universals, the fundamental ontological problem, was broached, and scholars began to ask themselves whether the Universal was merely a name (Nominalism), or whether it was more than a name, but at most a mere concept (Conceptualism); or, finally, whether and to what extent it was an objective reality (Mitigated or Absolute Realism).

The traditional realists in their writings commented with respect upon the views of Boethius, who maintained that the objects of our thoughts are not things in the same manner as they are in the intellect. In opposition to them the Nominalists maintained that only the existing individual is truly real; genus, species, man, humanity being empty conventional sounds (*flatus vocis*). A theory of this kind which professed belief only in sensible reality issued directly in sensualism. It was upheld by the Breton *Roscelin,* a scholar belonging to the Chapter of Compiègne, who, because of his courage and daring, met with tremendous success. He applied his theory of realism to the Holy Trinity itself, and, according to St. Anselm, claimed that the three Divine Persons are three separate and distinct beings, just like three angels, and that if custom permitted, one could even say, they are three Gods. His error was tantamount to tritheism or belief in a God who was a whole, made up of three parts. Roscelin was condemned by the Council of Soissons (1092). He first submitted to the decision, but afterwards reverted to his erroneous teachings, which he endeavored to spread in England and at Rome. It would appear that he amended his ways towards the end of his life. As a natural reaction to his teachings, *William of Champeaux,* a disciple of Roscelin, professed traditional Realism. His influence upon his time was considerable, for he taught in the cathedral school of Notre Dame, which later became the University of Paris. In the year 1108 he retired to the monastery of St. Victor, where he continued his career as a teacher, and was followed by an army of young students.

The Conceptualists held a middle course between the Nominalists and the Realists. According to them, concepts are definitions which express properties. These properties, however, do not correspond to distinct realities, as maintained by the Realists, but are only a general manner of defining an object which is apprehended under several different forms. A precocious teaching of this kind paved the way for Kantian subjectivism. For a long time it was claimed that *Abailard,* who was successively the pupil and the opponent of Roscelin and William of Champeaux, was the head of this school. In reality he was neither a Nominalist nor a Conceptualist, for while he is emphatic in his statement that the Universal exists in the individual, and only in the individual, he also insists on the function of abstraction in the genesis of our universal ideas. Therein lies his great merit, for he hastened the complete solution of the problem by transferring the discussion to the field of psychology. Abailard was less fortunate in theology, for in his attempt to refute the tritheism of Roscelin, he fell into the opposite error, and professed a sort of Trinitarian Conceptualism. According to him, many different concepts may be formed of the Blessed Trinity. In point of fact,

God has revealed three of these concepts to us of His own free will, namely, power, wisdom, and goodness. This is the whole mystery of the Trinity. At bottom, this heresy was nothing more than a revived form of the Modalism of Sabellius, in which the Father absorbs the other two Persons. Moreover, the method followed by Abailard was a dangerous one. Possessed of unlimited confidence and trust in the powers of reason, he declared that one can only believe what he has first understood (*nec credi posse aliquid, nisi primitus intellectum*). Abailard was refuted by St. Bernard, and after the Council of Soissons (1121) promised to amend his teaching. Later on, however, he succumbed to personal ambition and was condemned by the Council of Sens (1140). He then set out for Rome to explain his position to the pope, but on the way encountered Peter the Venerable, abbot of Cluny, who succeeded in pacifying him and offered him the hospitality of his monastery. He died in 1142 at Chalôns-sur-Saône, not far from Cluny.

After the condemnation of Abailard, the partisans of Realism again came to the front. *Gilbert de la Porrée,* bishop of Poitiers (1070-1154), pushed the doctrinal error to its very extreme, by setting up between God and the Divinity as real a distinction as the Thomists held between essence and existence in created beings. St. Bernard forced Gilbert to retract his errors. To solve the question of Universals it sufficed to show that the general representation of any individual being has a foundation in reality. It is impossible to name the writer who was first responsible for the adequate formulation of mitigated Realism in vogue towards the end of the twelfth century. Suffice it to say that the formula was hinted at by John of Salisbury († 1176). It must be observed that, in having recourse to these daring methods and rationalistic explanations, medieval writers always endeavored to respect the data of faith. They were bent on explaining truth, not on undermining it.

While these intellectual battles were being waged, *Peter Lombard* (1161) was composing his famous *Libri Quatuor Sententiarum,* a work comprising for the most part Patristic texts taken from the works of St. Augustine, St. Ambrose, and St. Hilary. The success with which this undertaking met was phenomenal, and for three centuries the "Book of Sentences" remained the text in use in the Schools.

II. Scholasticism in the Thirteenth Century. The thirteenth century was the golden age of medieval theology. Three causes made such a condition possible: (1) the creation of centers of theological culture, universities, and especially the University of Paris; (2) the arrival of new masters and the mendicant Orders in these universities; (3) the teaching of Aristotelianism by these Orders.

Towards the end of the twelfth century the Church was confronted with a serious Scholastic problem. The monastic schools and the schools of the canons regular tended to limit their teaching *intra muros;* the condition of the episcopal schools became rather unstable, dependent as they were upon the headmasters; and the school of Paris, famous for its course in the liberal arts and theology, together with the school of Bologna, renowned for its studies in Canon Law, threatened to monopolize the field. In vain the Third and Fourth Councils of the Lateran (1179–1215) attempted to reorganize the curriculum of studies by issuing orders for each episcopal see to have its own master of grammar, and each archiepiscopal see its own master of theology; the decree remained a dead letter in most cases. It was at this juncture that the papacy intervened and very wisely began to concentrate all its efforts upon the most outstanding schools.

Philip Augustus had conceded extensive privileges to students of the *University of Paris* in a charter dated 1200. Likening them to clerics, he exempted them from taxation, and also from sentinel duty. They were an autonomous body, and constituted a veritable "academic State." The University of Paris was amenable to ecclesiastical authority only. The intervention of the papacy soon transformed this institution into an official organ of the Universal Church. In 1215 the papal legate, Robert de Courçon, gave the University its first constitutions, but the opposition of the bishop still had to be overcome. Pope Honorius III took advantage of a misunderstanding which arose between the episcopal chancellor, Philip de Grève, and the University authorities, to exempt them from episcopal jurisdiction, the result being that licentiates were no longer required to take an oath of obedience to the bishop, who in turn had no further power to confine students to his dungeons. Moreover, to make it quite clear that the University was no longer the school of "Notre Dame," confined to the island of the City and subservient to the cathedral, professors were permitted to teach also on the left bank of the river, under the jurisdiction of the abbot of St. Geneviève (the Latin Quarter). It was in this way that the University of Paris, following the example of Cluny, became directly subject to the pope and an institution representative of the whole of Christendom. Henceforth the Sovereign Pontiffs began to look upon Paris as the official school of theology and abided by its judgment in the condemnation of heretics. Finally, by issuing orders to the Chapters to send their students to Paris, Honorius III gave everyone to understand that the University could confer the license to teach not only within the domain of the diocese, but also throughout Christendom, inasmuch as it was the mouthpiece of the Bishop of bishops. Professors of the University were forbidden to give instruction in civil law and requested to direct all their efforts to the ecclesiastical sciences. Thousands of young men began to journey to Paris, and grouped themselves into four nations: France, Picardy, Normandy, and England.

The mendicant Orders supplied the University with illustrious professors. St. Dominic was the first to establish an Order, of which the main duties were study and teaching, the Dominican foundation being essentially a school which taught the various branches of Holy Scripture and theology. The founder stipulated that each house should possess a doctor to instruct the religious and clerics, and larger monasteries, which went by the name of *Studia generalia,* one master and two bachelors. The *Studia generalia* established in Scholastic centers were soon affiliated with the universities themselves. In 1229, as the result of a conflict which arose between the bishop of Paris and the masters, the latter migrated to Angers and Oxford. Forced to replace them, the bishop called upon the Dominican, Robert of Cremona, who taught in the monastery of the Rue Saint-Jacques, and in this way the Friar Preachers gained entrance into the University. It sometimes happened that a secular master became a mendicant monk and transferred his chair to a cloister. This was the case with John of St. Gilles and Alexander of Hales. These newcomers were soon the victims of ever-increasing jealousy, and in 1253 the secular masters denied the mendicant masters the right to teach, because the latter would not join with them in a strike. They appealed, however, to the pope, who at once took sides with them. This was the signal for a never-to-be-forgotten conflict. Enlarging upon the points at issue, *William of St. Amour* published his *De Periculis Novissimorum Temporum,* in which he made bold to take exception to the principle of the monastic life and the usefulness of vows. In 1256 a papal Bull was issued, which sided with the mendicant Orders. William of St. Amour was condemned and forced to give up his chair, and St. Thomas avenged the Dominicans in his famous treatise, *Contra Impugnantes.*

The new personnel of the University introduced Aristotelianism into theology. The ecclesiastical writers of the thirteenth century may be divided into two classes: the pre-Thomists or Augustinians, and the Peripateticians of the Albertine-Thomist school.

Certain writers were willing to concede the many new lines of thought opened up by the study of Aristotle, but were reluctant to abandon the teachings of St. Augustine. A compromise was effected, which issued in a number of incoherencies. The school which thrived during this period of transition, counted several learned Dominicans, notably Hugh of Saint-Cher (✝ 1263), who composed a Commentary on the Sentences, and Robert Kilwardby, professor at Oxford and later on archbishop of Canterbury; but its most outstanding representatives were Alexander of Hales and St. Bonaventure. *Alexander of Hales* was an archdeacon of the Church in England, and received his doctor's degree at the University of Paris. He joined the Franciscan Order, and was directed by Pope Innocent IV to condense his teaching into a *Summa,* which, after being studied closely by sixty doctors from the University of Paris, was approved by a papal Bull. This work comprises a complete exposé of Catholic dogma in a series of questions, divided and subdivided in logical order. Alexander of Hales put forth two outstanding theories, later on termed Franciscan theories: the presence of matter and form in all contingent beings, and the plurality of substantial forms.

St. Bonaventure received his degree of master of theology at the same time as St. Thomas (1257) and later on was made General of the Franciscan Order. He remained faithful to the teachings of Plato and St. Augustine, and regarded philosophy as the handmaid of theology. He was above all a mystical theologian.

But the conservative followers of St. Augustine soon found themselves completely submerged by the Aristotelian movement. Several translations of the works of the Stagirite had been made by earlier writers under the patronage of Bishop Raymond of Toledo, the most famous of whom was Dominicus Gundissalinus. Moreover, the great Arabian philosophers, Avicenna, Averroës, and Avicebrol had adopted Aristotelianism. The teachings of the Stagirite, as interpreted by Averroës, had cast suspicion upon the system as a whole, because the Council of Paris in 1210 and later on (1215) the papal legate, Robert of Courçon, had prohibited the teaching of his metaphysics. In 1231, however, Pope Gregory IX decreed that the writings of Aristotle could be used, provided they were first expurgated. The work of ridding them of Averroistic importations and adapting them to the teachings of Catholic theology was accomplished by Albert the Great and St. Thomas Aquinas.

Albert the Great was born in 1206 and, while studying at Padua, was attracted to the Order of Friars Preachers by Jordan of Saxony. After being a lecturer in theology at Hildesheim, Freiburg i. B., Ratisbon, and Strasbourg, he began to teach in 1240 at the monastery of the Rue Saint-Jacques, Paris. At this very moment the Roman decree forbidding the use of the works of Aristotle in universities was lifted, and between the years 1245 and 1248 Albert the Great composed a sort of scientific encyclopedia, which placed within reach of western students all the teachings of Aristotle and the Arabian philosophers in their true light. This adaptation of the works of Aristotle received official approbation when, in 1256, Alexander IV directed Albert to refute Averroism. Albert, however, was only the frontiersman in this endeavor, for he did not dare to adapt the teachings of Aristotle to Catholic theology, which was still deeply imbued with Augustinianism. His disciple, St. Thomas Aquinas, continued to respect the teachings of the Augustinian school, but did not hesitate to substitute in their place the explanations afforded by Aristotle's metaphysics.

St. Thomas was born in 1225 in the fortress of Roccasecca, near Aquino, in the kingdom of Naples, and studied first at Monte Cassino and later at Naples. Despite the protests of his family, he entered the Order of St. Dominic, sat at the feet of Albert the Great at Cologne, and received the degree of doctor from the University of Paris. In 1261 he was called to Rome, together with the Flemish preacher, William of Moerbeke. Pope Urban IV commissioned William to translate Aristotle directly from the Greek, and St. Thomas to comment upon his teachings with due regard to the new translation.

Aristotelian metaphysics at once found a place in St. Thomas' own writings. In theology we must cite his commentaries on the *Books of Sentences* of Peter Lombard, on the *Divine Names* of Denis the Areopagite, on the *Trinity* of Boethius, and finally the *Summa Theologica*, the most finished and complete of all dogmatic treatises. His *Quaestiones*

Disputatae and his *Quodlibeta* are mixed treatises, containing both philosophical and theological subjects. His most outstanding apologetical works are the *Summa contra Gentiles* and the *Treatise against the Errors of the Greeks*.

But the followers of Averroes constituted a powerful party in the University of Paris, under the leadership of *Siger of Brabant*. St. Thomas returned to Paris in 1269 and immediately entered upon a lengthy discussion with them. In refutation of the *De Anima Intellectiva* of Siger of Brabant, he composed his treatise, *De Unitate Intellectus contra Averroistas*. The commotion caused by the appearance of these two manifestos was considerable and ended in the condemnation of Averroism by Stephen Tempier, Bishop of Paris. Four fundamental errors were scored in this condemnation: the denial of Divine Providence, the eternity of the world, the unity of intellect in all men, and the denial of human freedom. The pernicious doctrine of Averroism had threatened to effect a complete restoration of pagan thought within the Church, as serious in its consequences as was the Renaissance of pagan humanities for the people of the sixteenth century.

These errors were condemned in detail by the same bishop of Paris in 1277, but the verdict, issued three years to the day after the death of St. Thomas (March 7, 1274), also scored several of his own theories. Robert Kilwardby, bishop of Canterbury, likewise issued a series of condemnations which affected certain points of the Thomistic doctrine. St. Thomas was accused of an excessive love for philosophy, of contempt for the Fathers, and particularly of disregard for the teachings of St. Augustine. The most violent of the anti-Thomist pamphlets which appeared at this time, was the *Correptorium Fratris Thomae* by William de la Mare. However, the Dominicans came to the defence of their confrater, and to refute the attacks of Kilwardby and the masters of Oxford, Giles de Lessines wrote his famous treatise *De Unitate Formae* in the year 1278. The final decision was reserved to Rome, however, and after a thorough investigation of the miracles of St. Thomas by William of Tocco, who wrote the Saint's biography, John XXII canonized him, July 18, 1323. The canonization of the great Doctor put an end to all further controversy.

Finally, we must call attention to two famous eclectics, Blessed Raymond Lully and Roger Bacon. *Raymond Lully* was born at Majorca in

1215, and after leading a rather frivolous life, became a Franciscan tertiary. He was gifted with rare originality, and in his work, *Ars Magna,*
claimed to have found a method of universal science, based on syllogistic
reasoning. Raymond made bold to state that all truths, including the
mysteries of faith, are demonstrable by human reason. Another Franciscan, *Roger Bacon* (1210-1292), distinguished himself by his study of
the empirical sciences. Born in Somerset county, he studied first at Oxford
and then at Paris, where he imbibed a deep love for the linguistic and
mathematical sciences. Around the age of forty he entered the Franciscan
Order (c. 1251-1257) and was encouraged in his work by Clement IV.
His method was somewhat bold and aggressive, for he was not backward
in informing his contemporaries that syllogistic reasoning was inferior
to scientific experiment. Basing his theory on this same experiment, he
set out to shake to its very foundations the ancient physics of Aristotle.
Although some of his statements can be disputed, he is nevertheless a
pioneer genius.

III. Mysticism in the Twelfth and Thirteenth Centuries. The
mystical writers of this period may be divided into three groups: Benedictines, Victorines, and Franciscans.

The great Benedictine mystic of the eleventh century was *St. Anselm,*
abbot of Bec, and later on archbishop of Canterbury and primate of England (1033-1109). His principal treatise, *Meditations and Prayers,* may be
defined as a series of pious elevations of the soul on Christian dogma.
St. Anselm was at once a speculative and an affective writer, and begins
by expounding Catholic dogma as a theologian. Then, seized with the
beauty of the truth which he is describing, he concludes his subject with
a hymn of thanksgiving.[1]

The mysticism of *St. Bernard,* on the other hand, was entirely affective,
and its outstanding characteristic was devotion to the mysteries of the
earthly life of Our Lord and His first witnesses, Mary and Joseph. It
would be futile to seek in the writings of St. Bernard a didactic exposition of mystical theology, although he touched upon this subject in his
sermons on the Canticle of Canticles. In this work, however, he does not

---

[1] In connection with Benedictine mysticism we must mention the name of St. Hildegard.
She was at first a Benedictine recluse in the monastery of Diessenberg, and in 1147 founded
the abbey of Mt. St. Rupert, near Bingen, in the diocese of Mayence. She became famous for
her apocalyptic prophecies, and also for her visions, in which she imparted a superior sort of
dogmatic or moral teaching in the form of allegories. Her influence on the great personages
of her time was considerable.

treat his subject as a theorist—for he is completely ignorant of the neo-Platonic ideas so dear to St. Augustine and also of Scholastic philosophy—but from his own personal experience, which he includes in the framework of his allegorical commentary on this book of the Bible. Affiliated with his school were the three great mystics who brought fame to the monastery of Helfta, near Eisleben, in Saxony: St. Gertrude "the Great," St. Mechtild of Hackeborn, and another St. Mechtild, a Beguine of Magdeburg. St. Gertrude was born in 1256, and entered the convent of Helfta at the age of five. By order of Jesus Christ Himself she wrote an account of the different favors she received. In keeping with the school of mysticism of St. Bernard, the outstanding characteristic of these revelations is a tender and naïve devotion to the sacred humanity of Jesus Christ, and especially to the Sacred Heart.

The mysticism of *St. Victor* was much more theoretical in character: (1) It is based on a symbolic conception of the universe, which is like a mirror reflecting the divine thought; hence everything is explained in terms of allegory. A tendency of this kind was quite common to the writers of the Middle Ages, who composed veritable "mystical natural histories," in which plants and minerals are made the symbols of supernatural realities. Each one of the twelve precious stones, for instance, represents a special virtue. (2) Rising from the visible to the invisible, the Christian mystic is introduced to intuitive meditations, in which the divine truth is freed from sensible images. (3) Finally, contemplation, which forces the mystic to set aside the discursive method of reasoning, brings him into closer union with God. As representative of this school we must cite Richard of St. Victor. Convinced that a bond exists between the amount of knowledge and the degree of love one possesses, he made dialectics and metaphysics the handmaids of mysticism. His primary purpose was to nourish reason and so give it additional strength in the work of contemplation. His principal writings are: *Benjamin Minor, De Arca Mystica, De Trinitate,* and *Benjamin Major.*

The Franciscans of the thirteenth century gave to mysticism its true character. Enlarging on the mystical teachings of the school of St. Bernard, they stressed the humanity of Jesus Christ, and more especially His Passion. It was to the stigmatist of Assisi that the contemplatives of this century owed this "sorrowful joy," this "joy of the heart in the Holy Cross," to which they so frequently refer. Among Franciscan writers we must cite the biographers of the founder. The first in chronological order was Thomas of Celano, who wrote a *Legenda Prima*, a *Legenda Secunda*, and a *Tractatus Miraculorum*. He composed his *Legenda Secunda* with the aid of documents assembled by the Saint's companions. Perhaps the Legend of the Three Companions is related to this *Legenda Secunda*, parts of which are to be found in the *Speculum Perfectionis*, which dates back to the opening years of the fourteenth century. Previous to this, St. Bonaventure had collected the Franciscan sources in his *Legenda Major* (1261), called by this name to distinguish it from a more abbreviated legend, the *Legenda Minor*, which he composed in the interests of liturgy. Finally, Bartholomew Albizzi of Pisa (✝ 1401) wrote the *"Conformities,"* in which he proves that St. Francis was an exact replica of Christ Himself.

St. Bonaventure, the "Seraphic Doctor," was the greatest of all the Franciscan mystics. In his works he displays an affective piety which places outbursts of love above any theoretical and metaphysical contemplation. This explains why he regards beatitude as being less an act of intuitive vision than an act of beatific love. It accounts for his love of Jesus Christ, which was his inspiration in the treatises entitled, *Lignum Vitae* and *Vitis Mystica*. The *De Triplici Via* describes the three ways which lead to God: meditation, prayer, and contemplation. We must also cite the *Soliloquium de Quatuor Mentalibus Exercitiis*, the *De Perfectione Vitae ad Sorores*, a treatise on religious perfection, and the *Itinerarium Mentis ad Deum*, which points out the road one must follow in rising above creatures to the contemplation of the Godhead. A pseudo-Bonaventure, also a Franciscan of the thirteenth century, composed the famous *Meditations on the Life of Jesus Christ*, which is a mystical biography, based not only on the Gospel narrative, but also on private revelations, and even the imagination. In the following century Ludolph of Saxony, called "the Carthusian" (1300 to 1370), borrowed materials from the writings of St. Bonaventure to compose his Life of Christ. Blessed Angela of Foligno (✝ 1309) also belonged to the Franciscan school of the thirteenth century. She was a converted Magdalen and speaks of the Passion of Our Lord with poignant realism. Her frantic efforts at grandiloquence can be explained by the fact that she was quite conscious of her inability to describe what she had seen.

TEXTS AND DOCUMENTS

The Genius of St. Thomas

St. Thomas was primarily a theologian, and his metaphysics were chiefly built up around the mysteries of God. Not that this prevented him from using his great gifts to form a complete metaphysical system. He was naturally led to this from the fact that God, who is self-subsisting Being, in one sense coincides with the object of metaphysics, just as the sun coincides with the real image of it, which the astronomer sees in his telescope. He therefore made every effort to probe the mystery of God in philosophy, and as far as possible to explore His intimate truths. Not even the supreme mystery of the Trinity was beyond his speculations. He skirted round it and argued about it from outside, rather as a skilled mathematician invents formulae for unknown realities. God was impenetrable, but he could circle round Him and light up the frontiers; and in the penumbra, the God-fearing soul finds peace. . . .

Genius in metaphysics, he is possibly an even greater genius in moral theology. His very sanctity made it inevitable. Abounding charity urges the philosopher to mix with men, as Raphael walked with the young Tobias, showed him how to overcome the monstrous fish, and find the medicines he sought. St. Thomas thought in order to serve others, and his thought is coloured by this solicitude.

Sertillanges, *Saint Thomas Aquinas and his Work*, pp. 83–84.

QUESTIONS

1. How were the philosophers of the Middle Ages led to the discussion of Universals?
2. Define the terms: Nominalism, Conceptualism, Realism, Sensualism, Tritheism.
3. Why is Abailard called the precursor of Rationalism?
4. Account for the sudden rise to fame of the University of Paris.
5. What was the origin of the conflict between the seculars and the regulars at that University?
6. Which were the outstanding theories of Alexander of Hales?
7. Why were the writings of Aristotle forbidden at one time by Roman decree?
8. What was the principal teaching of Averroism?
9. What was the supreme achievement of St. Thomas?
10. Compare the mysticism of St. Anselm with that of St. Bernard.

BIBLIOGRAPHY

Scholastic Philosophy.—Th. Heitz, *Essai historique sur les rapports entre la philosophie et la foi de Bérenger à saint Thomas*, 1909.—B. Hauréau, *Histoire de la philosophie scolastique*, 3 vols., 1872–1880.—A. de Wulf, *History of Mediaeval Philosophy.*—Ueberweg, *Grundriss der Geschichte der Philosophie*, 4 vols., 1905–1909.—Picavet, *Esquisse d'une histoire générale et comparée des philosophies médiévales*, 2nd edit., 1907.—M. Grabmann, *Die Geschichte der scholastischen Méthode*, Freiburg i. B., 1909–1911.—W. Turner, *History of Philosophy.*—M. Grabmann, *Thomas Aquinas, His Personality and Thought* (transl. by V. Michel, O. S. B.).—H. Wilms, O. P., *Albert the Great*, London, 1933.—T. M. Schwertner, O. P., *St. Albert the Great*, 1932.

St. Anselm, Philosopher.—Sources: *P. L.*, CLVIII.—Works: Ragey, *Histoire de saint Anselme*, 1890; *Saint Anselme professeur*, 1890.—Domet de Vorges, *Saint Anselme* (Coll. *"Les Grands Philosophes"*), 1901.—Charles Filliatre, *La philosophie de saint Anselme, ses principes, sa nature et son influence*, 1920.—J. Bainvel, art. *"Anselme (arg. de saint),"* in *Dict. de Théol.* —Special no. of the *Rev. de Philosophie*, Dec., 1909.—Clayton, *op. cit.*

Roscelinus.—F. Picavet, *Roscelin, Philosophe et theologien*, 1911.

Abailard.—Sources: *P. L.*, CLXXVIII; edit. Cousin, 2 vols., 1859.—Works: Vacandard, *Vie de saint Bernard*, II, pp. 140–176; art. *"Abélard,"* in Dict. *d'Hist.*—Vigouroux, *Les livres saints et la critique rationaliste*, pp. 337–354, 1890.—De Régnon, *Etudes de théol. positive sur la Trinité*, II, pp. 65–85, 1892. —A. Hausrath, *Peter Abelard*, 1893.—Picavet, *Abélard et Alexandre de Halès*, 1896.—Kaiser, *Pierre Abélard, critique*, 1901.—Portalié, art. *"Abélard,"* in *Dict. de Théol.*—Th. Hatz, *La philosophie et la foi dans l'œuvre d'Abélard* (*Rev. des sciences philosophiques et théologiques*, Oct., 1907, pp. 703–726).

Gilbert de la Porée.—Berthaud, *Gilbert de la Porée, évêque de Poitiers, et sa philosophie*, Poitiers, 1912.—F. Vernet, *Gilbert de la Porée*, in *Dict. de Théol.*

Universities.—Sources: Denifle-Chatelain, *Chartularium Universitatis Parisiensis*, 4 vols., 1889; *Auctarium Chartularii*, 2 vols., 1894.—Works: Denifle, *Die Universitäten des Mittelalters bis 1400*, Berlin, 1885.—Rashdall, *The Universities of Europe in the Middle Ages*, 2 vols., Oxford, 1895.— Féret, *La Faculté de Théologie de Paris et ses docteurs les plus célèbres*, 7 vols., 1894 ff.—A. Luchaire, *L'Université de Paris sous Philippe Auguste*, 1898.—E. Jordan, *Les Universités*, in *La France Chrétienne*, 1896, pp. 267–280.—Mandonnet, art. *"Frères Prêcheurs (La théologie dans l'ordre des),"* in *Dict. de Théol.*—L. Delisle, *Les Ecoles d'Orléans aux XIIe et XIIIe siècles*, 1869.

St. Bonaventure.—Sources: *Opera omnia, edita studio PP. Collegii a S. Bonaventura ad Claras Aquas prope Florentiam*, 11 vols., 1882–1902.—

Works: G. Palhoriès, *Saint Bonaventure* (Coll. *"La Pensée Chrétienne"*), 1913.—Gilson, *La philosophie au Moyen Age* (Coll. *"Payot"*), I, ch. IV.— E. Smeets, art. *"Saint Bonaventure,"* in *Dict. de Théol.*—P. Léonard de Carralhoe Castro, *Saint Bonaventure* (Coll. *"Etudes de théologie historique,"* 1923).—Gilson, *La philosophie de saint Bonaventure*, 1924.—E. Clop, *Saint Bonaventure* (Coll. *"Les Saints"*), 1922.

Averroism.—Carra de Vaux, *Avicenne*, 1900; Gazali, 1902.—Picavet, *L'Averroïsme et les Averroïstes*, 1902.—Msgr. Chollet, art. *"Averroïsme,"* in *Dict. de Théol.*

Albert the Great and St. Thomas.—Sources: Albert the Great, *Opera*, edit. A. Borgnet, 38 vols., 1890–1899.—St. Thomas, *Opera jussu impensaque Leonis XIII edita*, Rome, 13 vols.—Works: Ch. Jourdain, *La philosophie de saint Thomas*, 1898.—A. Sertillanges, *Saint Thomas d'Aquin*, 2 vols. (Coll. *"Les Grands Philosophes"*), 1910.—P. Rousselot, *L'intellectualisme de saint Thomas*, 1908.—Durantel, *Le retour à Dieu dans la philosophie de saint Thomas*, 1918.—E. Gilson, *Le Thomisme*, Strasbourg, 1906; *La philosophie au Moyen Age* (Coll. *Payot*), II, ch. II.—P. Mandonnet, *Siger de Brabant*, 2 vols.; art. *"Frères Prêcheurs,"* in *Dict. de Théol.*—J. Zeiller, *L'idée de l'Etat dans saint Thomas d'Aquin*, 1910.—E. Gilson, *Saint Thomas d'Aquin* (Coll. *"Les Moralistes Chrétiens"*), 1925.—P. Petitot, *Saint Thomas d'Aquin*, Saint Maximin, 1925.—P. Kavanaugh, O. P., *Life and Labors of St. Thomas Aquinas.*

Raymond Lully.—Works: *Hist. litt. de la France*, XXIX.—Marius André, *Le Bx. Raymond Lulle* (Coll. *"Les Saints"*), 1903.—J. H. Probst, *Caractère et origine des idées du Bx. Raymond Lulle*, Toulouse, 1912.—E. Longpré, art. *"Lulle (Raymond),"* in *Dict. de Théol.*

Bacon.—Sources: Ed. Bridges, 2 vols., Oxford, 1897.—Works: E. Charles, *Roger Bacon*, Bordeaux, 1861.—H. Hoffmans, art. in *Rev. Néo-schol.*, 1906–1908–1909.—Feret, *La Faculté de Paris*, II.—De Wulf, *History of Mediaeval Philosophy.*—Delorme, art. *"Bacon,"* in *Dict. de Théol.*—Raoul Carton, *La synthèse doctrinale de Bacon; L'expérience mystique de l'illumination intérieure chez Bacon; L'expérience physique chez Bacon*, 1924.—Picavet, *Roger Bacon*, in *Rev. des Deux-Mondes*, 1914.

Mystics.—Sources: St. Anselm, *Méditationes*, P. L., CLVIII, 109–820; *Orationes*, 855–1016.—St. Bernard, *Sermones in Cantica Canticorum.* P. L., CLXXXIII.—St. Gertrude, edit. of the Benedictines of Solesmes; *Revelationes Gertrudianæ et Mechtildianæ*, 2 vols., Poitiers-Paris, 1875–1877.— Hugues de Saint Victor, P. L., CLXXVI.—Richard de Saint Victor, P. L., CXCVI.—St. Francis, see references above.—Works: Ragey, *Vie de saint Anselme.*—J. Bainvel, art. *"Anselme,"* in *Dict. de Théol.*—Vacandard, *Saint Bernard.*—E. Smeets, art. *"Bonaventure,"* in *Dict. de Théol.*—Edouard d'Alençon, art. *"Frères Mineurs,"* in *Dict. de Théol.*—F. Vernet, art. *"Gertrude la Grande,"* in *Dict. de Théol.*—General discussion in Pourrat, *La spiritualité chrétienne*, II. *Le Moyen Age.*—Dom Butler, *Western Mysticism.*—

FERRÉ, *"Les œuvres authentiques d'Angèle de Foligno,"* Rev. d'histoire francis-caine, July, 1924.—F. VERNET, art. *"Hugues de Saint Victor,"* in Dict. de Théol.—R. LINHARDT, *Die Mystik des hl. Bernhard von Clairvaux,* Munich, 1923.—*Le livre de la Bienheureuse Angèle de Foligno,* edit. by Paul Doncœur, 1926.—J. ANCELET HUSTACHE, *Mechtilde de Magdebourg,* 1926.—A. B. SHARPE, *Mysticism, Its True Nature and Meaning,* London, 1910.

CHAPTER VII

MEDIEVAL ART

I. Roman Art. Not until the eleventh century was there a renaissance of art, when the Roman style of architecture came into existence. The original feature of this style consisted in replacing the frame-work covering the basilicas by a barrel or arris-shaped vault. Several fanciful explanations have been suggested to account for this sudden change, chief among them being the fear of destruction by fire after the Norman invasions, and joy for having escaped the terrors of the year 1000. Perhaps the most satisfactory explanation is the Cluniac reform; in the midst of universal distress the arts had taken refuge in the abbeys and monasteries.

The first thing which commands attention in a church built in the Roman style, is the vault which covers the nave. It may be said that this vault is the key to the style of the edifice. Because it is difficult to construct a large semi-circular vault, if the nave is narrow, and because even a narrow vault exercises tremendous pressure and tends to push the walls apart, the latter are very thick, and, to preserve their force of resistance, have no windows. This fact accounts for the great nave being usually plunged in semi-darkness. To increase the resistance of the vault, it is sustained at regular intervals by binding arches, the function of which is sufficiently indicated by the name. These arches rest on columns or pillars set in the walls. On the opposite side of these so-called *dosserets,* and on the outside of the church, are the buttresses, massive pieces of masonry. But all these precautions did not appear sufficient to the Roman architects, for when the church had aisles, they transformed these buttresses into what have been called flying buttresses, which reinforced the vault of the great nave. Thus, as may easily be seen, the vault wrought a complete transformation in the proportions, lighting and appearance of the church edifice.

The idea which this style of architecture endeavors to convey is that of a firm and stalwart faith and complete recollection. The monastic origin

579

which this impression reveals, accounts also for the perfection of every detail, for the monks spared neither time nor pains. Their solicitude in this regard explains those exquisitely carved Roman capitals which we see in the cloister of Moissac, and also that lavish but truly scientific complexity in decoration which reminds us of Byzantine art.

There were different schools of Roman architecture. The school of Auvergne has given us Issoire, St. Nectaire and Notre-Dame-du-Port at Clermont, and has also inspired St. Sernin of Toulouse. The school of Poitou was famous for its richly decorated façades, and has bequeathed to us the masterpiece of Notre-Dame-la-Grande at Poitiers. The school of Périgord was noted for its use of the cupola, which lent an Oriental touch to all its churches. The outstanding church of this school is St. Front of Perigueux. The most daring of all schools was the school of Burgundy, which made bold to light up the nave by means of windows placed under the vault, and hence dispensed with the natural support afforded by the aisles, which were too low to reinforce the vault. The abbey church of Cluny was easily the most beautiful of all Roman churches. With its five naves, its two transepts, and its "quintuple tiara" of towers, it was in its day the greatest church in Christendom. The Rhenish school came into existence at a later date. Above all it conveyed the impression of strength, because of its square towers. In the interior its high vaults resembled a dome. The most beautiful examples of this school are to be found at Spires, Worms, Mayence, and Cologne.

II. Gothic Art. Among the inventions bequeathed by Roman to Gothic architects there is one concerning which we must say a brief word because of the confusion to which it has given rise. This invention is the broken or tierce-point arch, improperly called the ogive, a term reserved by archaeologists to the diagonal nerve or rib of the vault. The broken arch (vulgo: ogive), therefore, is a legacy of Roman to Gothic architecture, an indifferent form which antedates the ogival style and must not be included in its essential characteristics. The outstanding feature of the new style is the crossing of the ogives effected by two intersecting ribs, which support the Gothic vaults like a sort of brace, by resting them on the extremities of the drums. In this way the thrusts are definitely located at fixed points, where the outward flying buttresses nullify their action.

As a result, the entire edifice gains strength, slenderness, and audacity.

The pillars are transformed into slender columns, and the vault rises to heights previously unknown: 137 feet at Beauvais, 124 feet at Amiens, and 109 feet at Notre Dame in Paris. Very often the nave has three stories: the first made up of pillars and ogival arcades; the second comprising a gallery with triple arcades; and the third (clerestory) containing large windows, which supply the lighting absent from Roman edifices. The whole structure is surmounted by the vault. The plan differs from that of Roman architecture only in detail. It is the form of a Latin Cross with very short arms, each of which is terminated by a doorway or vestibule. The space thus created was sometimes used to perform certain ceremonies, such as the celebration of marriage.

For a long time it was thought that the creative innovations of Gothic architecture originated in Germany. Archaeological researches conducted during the course of the nineteenth century have proved, however, that the ogival transept was first used in the Isle de France, the most ancient attempt at this sort of architecture still in existence being the apsis of the Benedictine church of Morienval (Oise), which dates from the end of the eleventh century. And so the expression "Gothic," a term of contempt invented by the Italians of the Renaissance to designate this form of "barbaric" architecture, is entirely out of place. A more correct designation would be French architecture. The construction of the Benedictine church of Morienval was followed by a half century of earnest endeavors, which resulted in the choir of the abbatial church of St. Denis, designed by Suger and consecrated in 1144. Gothic architecture was officially inaugurated on this occasion. Literally dazzled by the splendor of this new form of art, the bishops and great French and foreign dignitaries who assisted at the ceremony at once set themselves to encourage its spread.

Roman architecture is essentially monastic in character, whereas Gothic is first and last an episcopal creation. No one places any faith today in the theory of Viollet le Duc, who maintained that Gothic is a lay art which originated with the communal movement. The true explanation is as follows. During the twelfth and thirteenth centuries, the bishop's power had been steadily increasing; he had surrounded himself with a large body of clerics and presided over a Chapter of great importance. He was also a rich proprietor and had at his disposal vast sources of revenue, which he used to build cathedrals. Frequently enough he was assisted in this work by munificent gifts from kings. Gothic architecture reached its height during the reigns of Louis the Younger, Philip Augustus, and St. Louis.

Because it was sponsored by the bishop, Gothic architecture was carried out not by monks, but by laymen. Organizations were formed, headed by a master, who was a veritable grand architect, and under whose direction technical information was imparted to apprentices through teaching which was a secret of the corporations. All crafts and trades were represented in these organizations, and unity of direction accounts for the logic which pervades their work. A whole course of instruction can be uncovered in the rich façades of cathedrals literally teeming with statues of all kinds, and also in the carved pulpits and stained glass windows. At times some particular subject receives special treatment. Thus Amiens is a Messianic cathedral and Notre Dame of Paris a church of the Virgin Mary. These monuments reflected "the whole of revelation" for the men of the Middle Ages. Everybody had a hand in their construction.

It is customary to distinguish three periods in the development of Gothic architecture. The first extends from the twelfth to the end of the thirteenth century, and is that of the primitive or lancet Gothic, so called because the windows are surrounded by a sharp ogive which gives the appearance of a lance or spear. Among the monuments typical of this style are St. Denis, Vézelay, Noyon, and above all the great cathedrals of Chartres, Paris, Rheims, Bourges, Amiens, the Sainte Chapelle and the cloister of St. Michael. The radiating style was inaugurated in the fourteenth century. It is characterized by enlarged windows, which expand into beautifully radiating roses. Rouen, Beauvais, and Strasbourg are typical examples of this period. Finally, the flaming style came into vogue, in which the mullions of the windows assumed the form of flames, and decorations became excessive. Some cathedrals, which required many years for their construction, bear the marks of all three periods.

TEXTS AND DOCUMENTS

Medieval Architecture

Architecture also provides remarkable examples of the primacy accorded by the art of the Middle Ages to the *intellectual and spiritual* construction of the work at the expense of material correctness, in regard to which the technical equipment and the theoretical knowledge of the old builders were inadequate. In the architecture of the Middle Ages geometrical correctness or anything approaching it is nowhere to be found; there is never a rectilinear alignment, never a right-angled crossing or symmetrical counterpart—irregularities and after-thoughts everywhere. The centring for the vault had to be specially prepared for each bay, even in the best constructed buildings of mediaeval art. The curves, especially in the ribs of the vaulting, are no more accurate than the alignment and the division of the bays. No more is the symmetry of their equilibrium. Keystones are not found in the middle of the arches or the vaulting—and sometimes the displacement is serious. . . . The right side of a building is hardly ever symmetrical with the left. . . . Everything is approximate in an art which is, nevertheless, very deliberate, but careless of exactitude. It may be that the sincerity and ingenuousness of such architecture owe their permanence of charm to this simplicity of construction.

MARITAIN, *Art and Scholasticism*, pp. 187–188.

QUESTIONS

1. Which are the outstanding features of Roman architecture?
2. Which are the leading characteristics of the Gothic style?
3. Account for the origin of Gothic architecture.
4. What religious ideas do these styles endeavor to convey?

BIBLIOGRAPHY

Christian Art.—REUSENS, *Eléments d'archéologie chrétienne*, 2 vols., Louvain, 1885–1886.—J. BRUTAILS, *L'archéologie du Moyen Age; Précis d'archéologie du Moyen Age*, 1908.—REVOIL, *L'architecture romane dans le Midi de la France.*—DE LASTEYRIE, *L'art roman.*—C. ENLART, *Manuel d'archéologie française. I. Architecture religieuse.*—DE LASTEYRIE, *Les origines de l'art gothique*, 1901.—E. MALE, *L'art religieux du XIIe siècle en France; L'art religieux du XIIIe siècle en France; L'art religieux de la fin du Moyen Age*, 2nd edit., 1922.—A. PÉRATÉ, *L'art chrétien au Moyen Age*, in *La France chrétienne.*—A. MICHEL, *Histoire de l'art.*—LOUIS GILLET, *Histoire des Arts*, in *Hist. de la nation française*, by G. HANOTAUX).—A. FABRE, *Pages d'Art Chrétien.*—R. DE LASTEYRIE, *L'architecture religieuse en France à l'époque gothique*, 2 vols., 1925–1926.—M. BAYET, *Les cathédrales françaises*, 1925.—A. FABRE, *Manuel d'art chrétien*, 1928.—EYGUN, *Romanesque Architecture*, 1933.—See also articles on *Romanesque* and *Gothic architecture* in *Cath. Encycl.*

PART III

Beginnings of the Modern Period

FIRST PERIOD

The Gallican Crisis

From the Advent of Boniface VIII to the Opening of the Council of Florence (1294-1438)

CHAPTER I

THE CONFLICT BETWEEN PHILIP THE FAIR AND BONIFACE VIII

After the death of Nicholas IV, the Holy See was vacant for two full years. The conclave which had gathered at Perugia threatened to protract the election for an even lengthier period of time, when Charles II, called the Lame, King of Naples, succeeded in imposing the candidacy of a hermit by the name of Peter of Morone, who was persuaded to leave his cell and assumed the name of *Celestine V*. The new Pope was not at all versed in the ways of Italian diplomacy, and allowed himself to be circumvented by Charles, who brought him to Naples, and at once devised plans to secure the appointment of a number of cardinals devoted to his cause. He even obtained the archiepiscopal see of Lyons for one of his sons, who at the time was only twenty-one years of age. Fortunately, Celestine soon became aware of his inability to cope with the situation, and expressed the wish to resign. The cardinals encouraged him in this intention, and it was canonically established that a pope could abdicate. Celestine V freely tendered his resignation in the presence of the Sacred College on December 13, 1294, and the conclave which convened at Naples within ten days elected Cardinal Benedict Gaetani, who took the name of *Boniface VIII*. It is not true that Boniface brought pressure to bear upon his predecessor to make him resign, and if he did keep him under close observation in the castle of Fumone, near Anagni, it was because he feared the secret plottings of discontented factions, who, by causing the Pontiff to change his mind with regard to his resignation, would have created a schism.

I. Pecuniary Immunity. Boniface VIII had a profound conviction of the grandeur of the papacy, which in his opinion was called upon to rule all Christendom and to impart salutary advice to all men, and above all, to kings. But the spirit of nationalism was at that moment on the increase and threatened to issue in complete and uncontrolled autonomy of the States. The new conception of things entertained by the king and the legists was about to clash with the old conception, that of the Pope and the canonists. The royal power incriminated itself first by encroaching upon the rights of the papacy. *Philip the Fair* (1285–1314) was in need of money. The royal administration required a veritable army of bailiffs, seneschals, provosts, etc. The luxurious manner of living at court added to the already long list of expenditures and, moreover, Philip was constantly engaged in warfare: the war of Aragon, the war against England, the war of Flanders followed in rapid succession. To remedy a financial situation which was becoming more and more serious, the King of France had recourse to every imaginable means. He despoiled bankers, Jews, Lombards or Knights Templar of their goods, struck counterfeit money, levied exorbitant taxes on serfs, commoners, and noblemen, and especially on clerics, who were less able to defend themselves. The Church made no systematic attempt to refuse the payment of these subsidies. As a matter of fact, in 1294 the provincial synods consented to pay double tithes for a period of two years. But even at that time there were several local protests, and many gave only conditional assent to the tax, the condition being, "with due regard to the rights of the pope." According to the traditional teaching, re-affirmed by the Council of the Lateran in 1215, no tax could be levied on the clergy without the pope's consent. This was a wise measure, inasmuch as it protected the Church against the exaggerated demands of the royal treasury. It happened that the purpose of the tax was not acceptable, that the sum demanded was exorbitant, or the manner of collecting it, odious. From this triple standpoint it was important not to acquiesce in the new financial demands of Philip the Fair. Beginning with the year 1294, the motive changed; for it was no longer the Crusade of Aragon against the usurper who had seized a vassal territory of the Holy See in Sicily, but a war with England, which Boniface VIII disapproved. Secondly, the sums exacted threatened to ruin the French clergy. Finally, the persons in charge of collecting the tax were brutal and avaricious laymen.

And so, when Philip the Fair convoked the bishops of France to Paris, in 1296, to solicit new tithes from the clergy, he was greeted with bitter complaints. The monks of Citeaux appealed to Rome by a protest in which Philip was compared to Pharao. Boniface VIII came to their rescue with the famous Bull *"Clericis laicos."* He threatened to excommunicate all rulers who levied taxes, as well as all clerics who paid taxes to any layman without papal permission. Philip felt that the Bull was aimed directly at him and retorted by forbidding any money to be exported from his kingdom. This was equivalent to cutting off all sources of revenue from the Pope and French beneficiaries employed outside of France, since it deprived them of their personal income. In his Bull *"Ineffabilis amor"* Boniface VIII explained his conduct in terms of unmistakable loyalty when he stated: "It was not our intention to forbid the clergy to come to your personal assistance and that of your kingdom, but only to do so without papal permission, because we had in mind the exorbitant demands of your agents upon ecclesiastical goods. If need be, the Holy See will come to your aid." As a matter of fact, when the bishops of the kingdom again met in Paris, on February 1, 1297, and begged the Sovereign Pontiff for permission to levy an ecclesiastical subsidy, Boniface consented. In his Bull *"Etsi de statu,"* issued July 31, 1297, he held firmly to the fundamental principle he had already enunciated, but went so far as to permit the King to decide for himself the cases in which taxation of the clergy was necessary.

It is true that difficulties arising in Italy forced the Pope to proceed with caution. Boniface had succeeded in holding in check the powerful Colonnas, who by force of intrigue had rallied to their cause all discontented factions. The latter comprised the partisans of the House of Aragon in Sicily, and also the Fraticelli, heirs of the "Spiritual" Franciscans, whom Celestine V had authorized to break with the "Conventuals" and form a congregation of hermits, but whom Boniface VIII had constrained to re-unite with their brethren. One of these high-strung individuals, Jacopone da Todi, so violently attacked Boniface in his pamphlets, that the Pope was forced to throw him into prison.[1] Cardinals James and Peter

---

[1] The Bollandists admit a later interpolation in the more violent invectives of Jacopone against Boniface VIII. Cfr. *Analecta Bollandiana,* XXVIII (1909), p. 233; see also *Miscellanea Ehrle* (1925), III, pp. 67–87.

Colonna headed the movement and began to circulate the charge that Boniface VIII had forced Celestine V to abdicate, and consequently his own election was null and void. The Pope found himself obliged to undertake a veritable crusade against the Colonnas, who finally had to submit, and whose fortresses, including that of Palestrina, were completely demolished. Moreover, on the occasion of the Jubilee of the year 1300, more than 200,000 pilgrims journeyed to Rome and paid homage to the Pope, so that Boniface VIII had no reason for believing that the situation had changed.

II. **Judiciary Immunity.** It was at this juncture that the administration of Philip the Fair caused a new conflict to arise between the King and the Pope. Bernard Saisset had been appointed to the newly erected see of Pamiers by Boniface VIII without the King's consent. The new bishop at once assumed the airs of a militant regionalist. There is no doubt that he was imprudent, and this fact accounts for his being accused of trying to stir up a local conspiracy. He was suddenly arrested during the night of July 12, 1301, and forced to appear before an assembly presided over by the King. The legist Peter Flotte delivered a virulent harangue, which resulted in the prelate being placed under the supervision of Giles Aiscelin, archbishop of Narbonne and metropolitan of the prisoner. A copy of the accusations was sent to the Roman Curia. Boniface VIII, however, saw only one thing in the whole procedure, namely, the violation of ecclesiastical immunity. In his Bull *"Salvator mundi,"* issued December 4, he gave orders to release the prelate and to allow him to plead his case in Rome. Simultaneously, another Bull, *"Ausculta fili,"* recalled the principle of the pope's supremacy over kings: "God has set us over kings, to build, plant, weed, and destroy." At the same time Boniface seized the opportunity to recapitulate all his grievances against the methods of the royal government: "You recognize no other judges than your own officials, and no other tribunal than your own, before whom you arraign both laymen and clerics with no regard at all for the tribunal of the papacy." He then convoked prelates and Chapters to a synod to be held in Rome, November 1, 1302, for the purpose of "correcting the King and promoting good government in France."

III. **The Bull "Unam Sanctam" and the Tragedy of Anagni.** Resolved to continue the fight to the bitter end, Philip and his legists set out to deceive public opinion on the questions at issue. In place of the papal Bull they substituted another, beginning with the words, *"Scire te volumus."* They also composed a reply written by the King: "Philip, by the grace of God, King of France, to Boniface, who calls himself pope, few or no greetings. It is important that your great stupidity know that we are not subject to your person in matters pertaining to the temporal order." It was then resolved to set up a national assembly in opposition to the Roman synod. Peter Flotte begged the members of three Orders to rally around the King, "to defend the liberties of the kingdom as well as those of the Church." Divided between their duties towards the Pope and their loyalty as French citizens, the clergy petitioned Boniface VIII to yield. His answer was that any bishop who would absent himself from the Roman synod, would be deposed.

The inevitable battle was waged on other grounds. On July 11, 1302, the French were defeated at Courtrai by the Flemish, and the position of the King being considerably weakened by this setback, he sought to open negotiations with Rome. To this end he permitted the bishops to convene with Boniface VIII, who, at the Roman Synod of All Saints, in 1302, issued the famous Bull *"Unam Sanctam,"* which was a complete reaffirmation of the ultramontane teachings. In this document he insisted "on the subjection of the sword to the sword, of the temporal authority to the spiritual power, for the Apostle has said, 'There is no power but from God: and those that are, are ordained of God.'" There was nothing revolutionary in this teaching. The comparison of the two swords had been used in the eleventh century by Godfrey of Vendôme, and had become classical. The conclusion stressed by Boniface VIII was perfectly logical: "It is the business of the spiritual power to set up temporal authority and to judge such authority if it is not what it should be. . . . We state, declare, and define that all creatures must be subject to the Sovereign Pontiff in order to be saved."

The King's *Responsiones* were both affected and insinuating, but Boniface VIII in his instructions to Cardinal Lemoine, who had been despatched to France as papal legate, signified in unmistakable language that unless the King would yield, he would be excommunicated. Philip's exaggerated sense of the importance of the State triumphed over the scruples of his Christian conscience, and he declared war. He was powerfully assisted in this political enterprise by William of Nogaret. On March 12, 1303, in the presence of an assembly of notables, the King read a hateful diatribe against the Pope, and proposed the convocation of a general council to try his case. Another meeting took place on June 13 and 14, at which William of Plaisians, a satellite of Nogaret, issued a pamphlet against Boniface crammed with calumnious accusations of the coarsest kind; *e. g.*: "Boniface does not believe in the immortality of the soul, nor in life eternal. He says that he would rather be a dog than a Frenchman, and has had statues of himself placed in different churches, so that people might adore him," etc. To these personal incriminations were added a number of political grievances. Boniface was held responsible for the hostility of the English against the French, for the loss of the Holy Land, and, finally, for the death of Celestine V, whom he had presumably forced to abdicate, etc. The bishops present at this assembly demanded that the Pope's case be referred to a general council. Meanwhile, a campaign was conducted throughout France to poison public opinion against him. The proceedings of the assembly were published everywhere by royal commissioners, who required that all subscribe to them. The only formal refusal was issued by certain religious, particularly the Cistercians. Boniface VIII was making ready to formulate his reply in the Bull *"Super Petri solio,"* by excommunicating Philip the Fair and releasing his subjects from their oath of allegiance, when Nogaret, together with the Colonnas, surprised the aged Pontiff in his palace at Anagni, September 7, 1303. Nogaret coolly explained to Boniface the crimes of which he was accused and the decision reached to arraign him before a general council. Sciarra Colonna openly insulted him. The Pope remained in the power of these ruffians for three days, but was finally rescued by his faithful followers, the citizens of Anagni, who arose with the cry: "Long live the Pope! Death to the foreigners!" Soon four hundred Roman horsemen arrived and conducted the Pontiff back to Rome. He died a few weeks later (October 11, 1303) as a result of the humiliation and ill-treatment to which he had been subjected.

Benedict XI (1303-1304) endeavored to settle all these difficulties in a peaceful manner. He stigmatized the direct authors of the assault perpetrated at Anagni, and cited William of Nogaret before his tribunal. Mindful, however, that he was "the legate of Him who forgives," the Pope annulled all sentences issued against the Colonnas and restored their goods. He absolved Philip the Fair from excommunication and his subjects from the censures pronounced against them. Benedict died a mysterious death after a reign of only one year.

IV. The Conflict of Political Theories in the Fourteenth Century. The struggle which we have just described, became even more complicated as the result of a doctrinal conflict which raged throughout the fourteenth century. The opposite views regarding the mutual relations of Church and State are of ancient origin, but they reached their climax during this period.

In an encyclical letter issued in 1245, Innocent IV had affirmed that the Church possesses universal power over all kingdoms. God, indeed, is the Master of the universe, and the pope, being His vicar on earth, as the successor of Jesus Christ, who is both true king and true priest according to the order of Melchisedech, has received not only papal, but also royal power, and not only the celestial, but also the terrestrial kingdom. This thesis in defence of theoretical papal imperialism was defended by James of Viterbo in his *De Regimine Christiano* (On Christian Government), dedicated to Boniface VIII. To his way of thinking, "the plenitude of both priestly and royal power belongs properly to the Bishop of bishops, the Sovereign Ruler of all consciences." In his *De Ecclesiastica Potestate* (On the Power of the Church), also dedicated to Boniface VIII, Giles of Rome states that "the extent of ecclesiastical power is such that it includes even private property. The possessor of a field or vineyard has a right to such a field or vineyard only if he possesses it under the authority of the Church, for by her right of eminent domain the Church consecrates private property." Similar ideas are found in the writings of Agostino Trionfo, and later on in the *De Planctu Ecclesiae* (On the Grievance of the Church) by Alvarez Pelayo.

It must not be supposed that this theory of the eminent domain of the Church was the result of an inordinate demand of pride. All its defenders, indeed, are careful to observe that the universal power possessed by the pope does not detract from the rights of temporal authority, but, on the contrary, strengthens this authority, provided the titular adopts the attitude of a vassal toward his suzerain. In last analysis these new rights of the papacy were stressed as an argument in favor of the pope's universal spiritual power and right to exercise moral control over Christendom, which was recognized throughout the Middle Ages, but had now become the subject of controversy.

Some theologians made an attempt to adopt a middle course in this matter. Thus John of Paris in his *De Potestate Regia et Papali* (On the Power of the King and the Pope) endeavors to establish that the dominion in temporal matters is neither essential nor contradictory in the Church, but may be conceded to her by a concession and with the permission of temporal rulers. In general, however, the thesis of the right of the State was violently opposed to that of papal supremacy. The author of *A Dialogue between a Cleric and a Knight* claims that the Church should be subject to the State, and the anonymous treatise *Rex Pacificus* (The Peace-loving King) expounds the same thesis. Peter Dubois in his *Summa Doctrina* demands that the kings of France take over the Papal States because they will be more efficiently administered, and in his *De Recuperatione Terrae Sanctae* (On the Recovery of the Holy Land) he regards the endeavor to establish peace in Italy through French intervention as the indispensable condition of a general Crusade. Divided between his Christian ideal and his admiration for ancient Rome, Dante concedes universal monarchy to the Emperor, while in his exaggerated Utopian dream he hopes that the "Holy Church" will return to the day when "Peter and Paul went about poor and barefooted." We shall soon have occasion to see how, taking advantage of the repeated conflicts of the Holy See with the "Spirituals" and Louis of Bavaria, Marsilius of Padua pushed these theories of the State to their logical conclusion in his bellicose treatise *Defensor Pacis,* which is impregnated with a ferocious hatred for the papacy.

In 1329, Philip of Valois resolved to settle the question of the relations between Church and State in a public debate, which has since been termed the "Disputation of Vincennes" (1329). Peter of Cugnières, an advisor to parliament, opposed ecclesiastical jurisdiction, while Peter Bertrand, the future Clement VI, defended it. Like all debates, that of Vincennes brought no solution, but when it was over, *"l'appel comme d' abus"* (the appeal as from an abuse) began to function. This consisted in bringing before parliament grievances directed against the acts of the clergy and the diocesan officials. It accounts for the frequent encroachments of judiciary authority in questions pertaining to the Church.

Towards the end of the fourteenth century these various conflicts became less and less acute, but the idea of the absolute independence of the civil power was more and more established. It was stressed especially in the writings of the publicists surrounding Charles V, such as, for instance, Nicholas Oresme, Philip of Mezières, and Ralph of Presle. The latter composed the *Dream of the Rod-Maker,* a dialogue between a cleric and a knight, who victoriously defends the independence of the secular power and the lay courts of justice. This work greatly influenced the development of Gallican ideas.

TEXTS AND DOCUMENTS

The Bull "Unam Sanctam"

The Bull begins with a long exposition, interspersed with many biblical comparisons, in support of the unity of the Church, which has only one head in the person of Jesus Christ, whom Peter and the popes have succeeded as visible heads. The metaphor of the two swords then introduces the passage to which so much importance has been attached:

"The Gospel informs us that there are in the Church, and in the power of the Church, two swords, the spiritual and the temporal. When the Apostles stated, 'Lord, behold here are two swords'—*here* meaning in the Church— He did not answer, 'It is too much,' but, 'It is enough.' We must admit that he who refuses to believe that the temporal sword is in the power of Peter, disregards the Word of the Lord, who said, 'Put up thy sword into its place.' Both swords, therefore, the spiritual and the temporal, are in the power of the Church, but the latter must be drawn for the Church, and the former by the Church; the first by the hand of the priest, the second by the hands of kings and soldiers, but with the consent and at the will of the priest. The sword must, however, be subjected to the sword, temporal authority to spiritual power, for the Apostle has said, 'There is no power but from God: and those that are, are ordained of God.' Now this order of things could not exist if one of the two swords were not subject to the other, and being inferior, linked through it to higher things, for according to St. Dionysius, 'the law of God is to the effect that lower things be linked with higher things by means of intermediaries.' It is not, therefore, in keeping, with the harmony of the universe that the order in things be parallel and immediate, but that the lowest things be subordinated to the highest. Now, it must be acknowledged that the spiritual power is superior in dignity and nobility to all temporal authority, for the simple reason that spiritual things transcend temporal things. The payment, blessing, and sanctification of the tithes, the collation of power, and even the activities of the government are evident proofs of this. For in all truth it is the business of the spiritual power to set up temporal authority and to judge it if it is not what it should be, and thus is verified the prophecy of Jeremias regarding the Church and the ecclesiastical power: 'Lo, I have set thee this day over the nations and over kingdoms to root up, and to pull down, and to waste, and to destroy, and to build, and to plant.'

"If temporal authority goes astray, therefore, it must be judged by the spiritual power, and if the spiritual power goes astray, it will be judged by a superior power, and if it be itself the supreme power, by God alone. It cannot be judged by man according to the words of the Apostle: 'But the spiritual man judgeth all things; and he himself is judged by no one.' Now, although this authority was given to a man, and is exercised by a man, it is not human authority, but rather a divine power conferred upon Peter by the Divine Logos Himself, the rock established for him and his confessors in Christ, whom he had confessed when the Lord said to Peter: 'Whatsoever thou shalt bind,' etc. Whoever opposes the power ordained in this way by God, opposes the order of God, unless he is of the same opinion as Manes regarding the two principles, an opinion which we stigmatize as false and heretical. For if we are to believe the testimony of Moses, it was not in the principles (*principia*) but in the principle (*principium:* beginning) that God created Heaven and earth. As a consequence we state, declare, and define that all creatures must be subject to the Sovereign Pontiff in order to be saved."

QUESTIONS

1. What was the occasion of the Bull *"Clericis laicos"*?
2. What was the tenor of this Bull?
3. What is meant by the phrase: *Ecclesiastical judiciary immunity?*
4. Which were the main points stressed by the Bull *"Unam Sanctam"*?
5. List the different events which directly led to the tragedy of Anagni.
6. In what sense does the Church possess universal power over all kingdoms, including the temporal order of things?
7. What was the *"appel comme d'abus"*?

BIBLIOGRAPHY

Boniface VIII. Benedict XI.—Sources: Digard, Faucon, and Thomas, *Les registres de Boniface VIII*, 2 vols., 1884–91.—G. Picot, *Documents relatifs aux Etats généraux et assemblées réunies sous Philippe le Bel*, 1902.—Grandjean, *Le registre de Benoit XI*, 1883.—Finke, *Aus den Tagen Bonifaz VIII.*, Münster, 1902.—Works: Dom Tosti, *Boniface VIII*, 2 vols.—Boutaric, *La France sous Philippe le Bel*, 1861.—Renan, *Etudes sur la politique religieuse du règne de Philippe le Bel*, 1889.—*Hist. litt. de la France*, t. XXV–XXVI, XXX.—R. Scholz, *Die Publizistik z. Zeit Philipps d. Schoenen u. Bonifaz VIII.*, Stuttgart, 1903.—Langlois, in *Hist. de France* by Lavisse, t. III. —Finke, *Benedict XI.*, Münster, 1891.—H. Hemmer, art. *"Boniface VIII"* and *"Benoit XI,"* in *Dict. de Théol.*—Dufourcq, *L'Avenir du christianisme, Histoire moderne de l'Eglise*, VII. *Le christianisme et la désorganisation individualiste* (1294–1527), 4th edit., 1925.—J. Rivière, *Le problème de l'Eglise et de* *l'Etat au temps de Philippe le Bel (Spicilegium Lovaniense)*, 1926.—M. M. CURLEY, *The Conflict between Pope Boniface VIII and King Philip IV, the Fair*, C. U. A., Wash., 1927.—TOSTI-DONNELLY, *Pope Boniface VIII and His Times*, New York, 1911.—N. WISEMAN, *Pope Boniface VIII*, in *Dublin Review*, 1844, reprinted in *Hist. Essays*.

Political Theories.—J. RIVIÈRE, *op. cit.*—ARQUILLIÈRE, *Etude des sources et édition critique du De regimine christiano*, 1927.—B. LANDRY, *L'idée de chrétienté chez les scolastiques du XIIIe siècle*, 1929.—O. MARTIN, *L'assemblée de Vincennes de 1329 et ses conséquences*, 1909.—CARLYLE, *A History of Medieval Theory in the West*, t. V, 1929.

CHAPTER II

The conclave which met at Perugia brought the two rival parties face to face. After eleven months of cavilling, the candidacy of Bertrand de Got was suggested, who, because he had shown attachment to Boniface VIII, was acceptable to the Italians. Bertrand de Got was a Frenchman and archbishop of Bordeaux. He had reached an amicable settlement with Philip the Fair, and so his election appeared to be the best means of effecting a reconciliation. He was elected June 5, 1305, and took the name of *Clement V*. The new pope was both kind and generous, but these qualities quickly degenerated into weakness. In the first place he feared that his independence would be compromised in the midst of the many Italian factions—at Rome, the Orsini and the Colonnas; in all the States, whites and blacks, Guelphs and Ghibellines; in the second place Philip the Fair urged him to remain in France. After residing at Bordeaux (1306) and Poitiers (1307-1308), he took up his abode at Avignon, in close proximity to the county of Venaissin, which had been a papal territory since 1229. Avignon itself did not belong to the papacy, but was acquired in 1348, when Clement VI purchased it from Queen Jeanne of Naples for the price of 80,000 gold florins. Clement V was of the opinion that his stay in France would only be temporary, and hence did not build himself a palace, but was content with a modest lodging in the house of the Friars Preachers.

I. The Papacy and France: The Trial of the Knights Templars. Philip the Fair took advantage of the situation and first of all obtained from his guest the retraction of the acts of Boniface VIII. Clement abrogated the Bull *"Clericis laicos"* and interpreted the Bull *"Unam Sanctam"* in a purely spiritual sense, which involved no new subordination of the King to the Roman Church. Goaded on by Nogaret, whose absolution was at stake, the King then demanded a dishonorable condemnation of the memory of Boniface VIII. In 1309, Clement V consented to an investigation, in which Nogaret accumulated against the victim of Anagni the worst kind of accusations, including debauchery, sacrilege, etc. Clement V rebelled against these methods of procedure, yet satisfied the King's desires for revenge on every point, save the formal condemnation of his predecessor. The King's intentions throughout the trial are said to have been upright; he was innocent of any ill-treatment to which the Sovereign Pontiff was subjected. Nogaret was absolved from excommunication *ad cautelam* and was asked to atone for his crimes by making a pilgrimage to the Holy Land. The general results of this victory of Philip the Fair cannot be overestimated. The political influence of the papacy was eclipsed by the absolutism of the King. The victory had a far more disastrous consequence, for by threatening Clement V with a libellous suit against the person of Boniface VIII, Philip extorted from him, in the trial and prosecution of the Knights Templars, more than he would have otherwise obtained.

The Knights Templars had been established to guard the Holy Land, but the original reason for their existence had ceased when the Christians were forced to evacuate Palestine in 1291. Subsequently they became the greatest bankers of their day and the royal treasure, together with the money of the rich, was securely guarded in their "temples," which were veritable strongholds. Moreover, they served the popes, and even the kings, in the collection of taxes. Their wealth caused much jealousy, and the secrecy which surrounded their meetings resulted in calumnies of all kinds. Taking advantage of a doubtful situation of this sort, Philip the Fair resolved to strike at the Templars and confiscate their goods. In 1306 he sounded Clement V on this point, and the Pope merely promised to investigate. But Philip was not satisfied. The royal council had the Grand Master, Jacques de Molai, arrested together with all Knights Templars, as guilty of heresy and all sorts of monstrous crimes (Oct. 12, 1307). A proclamation was drawn up by William of Nogaret, who accused them of taking an oath in their ceremony of profession to deny Christ, practise sodomy, worship an idol, and omit the words of consecration in the Mass. Subjected to the most atrocious tortures, the majority agreed to repeat anything their tormentors would suggest.

The whole matter seemed to be progressing to the King's satisfaction, when Clement V suddenly complained that the trial had been conducted with only his presumed permission. Shaken for a moment by the character of the admissions made by the Knights Templars to the point of issuing orders to Christian princes to arrest any of them who resided in their States, the Pope suddenly protested his former action at the news that several Knights, and especially Jacques de Molai, had solemnly retracted their statements. He immediately suspended the trial, summoned the affair to his own tribunal, and issued orders to Philip the Fair to transfer to him both the persons and goods of the accused. Nogaret then undertook to frighten Clement V by calumny, formulating against him accusations of simony and nepotism. In this way public opinion was exploited, and at the election to the General States of Tours, deputies were appointed who took sides with Philip the Fair. The Pope made a noble attempt to resist, but ended by yielding, at least partially. He consented to entrust the business of passing individual sentences upon Knights Templars to the bishops and ordinary inquisitors, according to the procedure formerly in vogue, but at the same time insisted that the matter of deciding the fate of the Order in general be placed in the hands of an ecumenical council, the preliminaries of which were to be handled by a pontifical commission.

From this moment on the prosecution of the Knights Templars was conducted along two distinct lines. Working under the direction of the Holy See, the pontifical commission refused to have recourse to torture, but permitted the Knights to give their testimony freely. The result was wholesale retractations of former admissions. "I wish to defend the Order," declared the accused, "I know nothing evil regarding it." Infuriated by this state of affairs, the partisans of the King resolved to expedite individual suits entrusted to the tribunal of inquisitors. Philip of Marigny, condemned without a hearing for having relapsed into heresy fifty-four Knights who had retracted their admissions before the pontifical commission. They were sentenced to be publicly burnt at the stake. Seized with fear, the surviving members of the Order immediately began to admit their guilt. In the month of October, 1311, the Council of Vienne could not make up its mind to ratify the sanction of the French inquisitors. It was useless, therefore, to hope for an out and out condemnation, but a suppression was effected, which satisfied the King. This was the tenure of the Bull "Vox in excelso." The Knights Templars who persisted in admitting their guilt regained their liberty; the others, including their Grand Master, Jacques de Molai, were condemned.

What is to be thought of the Knights Templars? There is no denying that their wealth had resulted in certain abuses, which necessitated a reform, but condemnations based on oral admissions obtained under torture are hard to justify. The rapaciousness of the administration of Philip the Fair accounts for this wicked trial and persecution. The King, however, did not derive all the profit he had expected from his enterprise. He received a grant of 200,000 pounds in Tours currency to balance the treasury, and 60,000 to defray the expenses of the trial. A papal Bull placed the goods of the Temple into the hands of the Hospitallers of St. John of Jerusalem, who put them to good advantage in their warfare against the Turks.

II. The Papacy and Germany: The Struggle with Louis of Bavaria. Clement V and Philip the Fair died in the same year, 1314. After the Holy See had remained vacant for two years and three months, because of rivalries between the Italians and the French, the latter succeeded in electing Cardinal Jacques Deuze of Cahors, Bishop of Porto, who took the name of *John XXII* (1316-1334). The new Pope was almost immediately drawn into a conflict with Germany. Two pretenders disputed the right to succeed Henry VII—Louis of Bavaria and Frederick of Austria. John XXII upheld the right of the papacy to settle all doubtful imperial elections, and declared that neither of the two aspirants to the throne should call himself *Rex Romanorum* until he himself had settled the dispute.

When Louis of Bavaria designated a vicar-general of the Empire for Italy, the Pope paid no attention to him, but left the administration of the peninsula to his legates and to Robert of Sicily. In Germany, however, nationalistic ideas were becoming more and more widespread, and people were beginning to object to the interference of the papacy in politics, demanding that these matters be settled, not by the Pope, but by force of arms. The battle of Mühldorf, September 28, 1322, proved favorable to Louis of Bavaria, who at once declared himself Emperor. On October 8, 1323, John XXII reminded Louis that his was the business of examining the person (*examen personae*) and consequently also approving the candidate elected (*approbatio electi*). Louis of Bavaria refused to yield and was excommunicated, March 23, 1324. His stand was the signal for a renewal of the conflict between the papacy and the empire.

Louis of Bavaria found powerful allies among some of the members of the Church. At that time the Franciscans were creating grave disturbances for John XXII, who in 1317 and 1318 had felt himself obliged to condemn the "exalted" members of the Order, *i. e.,* the same "Spirituals" who had opposed Boniface VIII. These men resembled the Montanists and based their prophecies and criticisms on the authority of Joachim of Floris and his disciples, Peter John of Oliva and Ubertino of Casale. They compared the Church, sunk in wealth and pleasures, to the city of Babylon, and the pope to the Antichrist. To their way of thinking the official priesthood should be replaced by a superior form of monarchism that would regenerate all Christendom. And so when, in the Bull *"Quorumdam exigit"* (Oct. 7, 1317), John XXII declared them to be in the wrong in their conflict with the "Conventuals," the "Spirituals" obstinately persisted in wearing their patched garb and denying the lawfulness of estovers. Things came to such a pass that John XXII, in two Bulls, *"Sancta romana"* (Dec. 30, 1317) and *"Gloriosam"* (1318), was obliged to excommunicate by name the Fraticelli, the Beguines, and the Brethren of the Poor Life. Pursued by the Inquisition, those who remained stubborn were imprisoned or burned at the stake.

Very soon a more serious conflict set John XXII at variance, not only with this group of "exalted" religious, but with almost the entire Franciscan Order. In the year 1322 a theological controversy arose as to whether or not Christ and His Apostles had practiced absolute poverty. John XXII summoned the matter to his own tribunal and was engaged in working out a solution and taking council, when, without awaiting the outcome, the general of the Friars Minor, *Michael of Cesena,* pronounced himself in favor of absolute poverty in a General Chapter of the Order held at Perugia, May 30, 1322. On November 12, 1323, by the constitution *"Cum inter nonnullos,"* John XXII condemned as heretical the declaration of Michael of Cesena, who was summoned to Avignon and closely guarded as a prisoner. Upon receipt of this news, a number of Franciscans inaugurated a violent press campaign against the Pope. Louis of Bavaria sponsored their cause and at Frankfort fulminated a sort of lay excommunication against the Pontiff residing at Avignon. In vain did John XXII place all Germany under the interdict; the Friars Minor were very popular and spent themselves in campaigning for the Emperor and preventing the execution of the papal sentence.

Louis of Bavaria was further assisted by *Marsilius of Padua* and John of Jandun, who in their treatise *"Defensor Pacis"* (The Defender of Peace) laid down the principles for a complete democratic reform of Christian society. In their theory the pope was only a bishop, just like all other bishops, or at most was vested with some sort of vague moral superiority over the others. The affairs of the Church, they claimed, should be administered by a council of delegates selected from among all the faithful. The president of this council would be the Emperor, *"fidelem legislatorem superiore carentem"* (a faithful human legislator with no superior.) In politics, therefore, the bishops of Rome were nothing more than usurpers, and if they required the imperial candidate to make over to them the Italian provinces, their action could only be construed as an intrusion. In 1326, the authors of this revolutionary libel took refuge at the court of Louis of Bavaria, who resolved to carry out their programme.

The Emperor at once undertook a triumphal journey through northern Italy, which was at that time in the hands of the Ghibelline lords. At Milan, he was crowned king of Italy, together with his wife Margaret of Holland (May 31, 1327), and shortly after entered Rome without encountering any obstacle. After the excommunicated bishops of Aleria and Castello had conferred the royal consecration upon him, he received the crown from the hands of Sciarra Colonna and the town syndics, who acted in the capacity of representatives of the Roman people. On April 14, 1328, it was resolved to bring John XXII to trial. Marsilius of Padua informs us that an assembly made up of a few clerics and a large number of laymen began by expressing doubts regarding his orthodoxy. By imperial verdict he was then deposed for the crime of lèse-majesté. A commission which claimed to represent the Roman people then elected a new pope, the Franciscan monk, *Pietro da Corvara,* who took the name of Nicholas V. As may be seen, the audacity of Louis of Bavaria far exceeded that of the Hohenstaufens, for he transformed the conflict between the papacy and the Empire into a battle for democracy. Very soon, however, the Roman populace rose up in rebellion (August 4, 1328). Louis was forced to quit the city and sojourned for a while at Pisa. Milan closed its doors against him, and so he had no alternative but to return to Germany. Seeing that his cause was hopeless, Pietro da Corvara threw himself at the feet of John XXII.

John XXII in turn seriously compromised his own position. In a sermon delivered December 15, 1331, he made bold to state that "before the resurrection of the body, the souls of the departed possess neither eternal life, nor beatitude properly so called, nor the beatific vision." For the same reason the damned and the devils themselves will be thrust into hell only after the end of the world. The partisans of Louis of Bavaria, Michael of Cesena, William of Occam, etc., at once cried, "heresy." But John XXII vindicated the papacy by declaring that he had spoken only in the capacity of a private theologian. Moreover, far from imposing his views upon others, he expressed himself as willing to consult the bishops and doctors regarding this question. At the point of death he retracted his statements in the presence of his cardinals in the following terms: "We confess that the souls of the departed, separated from their bodies and completely purified, are in Heaven, and that they see God face to face to the extent warranted by the state and condition of a soul separated from its body." His successor, *Benedict XII* (1334-1342), put an end to the controversy by defining in his Bull *"Benedictus Dei"* that the souls of the just who have no sins to expiate, "behold the Divine Essence face to face and in an intuitive manner" (January 29, 1336).

But the schism persisted in the domain of politics. Benedict XII showed himself willing to effect a reconciliation, but negotiations opened in the spring of 1335 and the autumn of 1336 proved of no avail. It was at this juncture that the German princes met at Rense (July 16, 1338) and formed what was called the Electoral Union (*Kurverein*). This agreement stipulated that "whoever had been lawfully chosen by the majority of the electors, was to be regarded as king of Germany, without there being any need of papal confirmation." Louis of Bavaria widened the breach between himself and the papacy by forcing his son, Louis of Brandenburg, to contract an irregular union with Margaret Maultasch, heiress to the kingdom of Tyrol and already married to John Henry of Bohemia. The new Pope, Clement VI (1342-1352), excommunicated Louis of Bavaria on April 13, 1346, and the German princes abandoned him to his own fate and elected in his place Charles of Bohemia, a protégé of the Pontiff. The death of Louis, October 11, 1347, brought the conflict to an abrupt end. But the Empire was fast moving towards a state of laicization. In 1354 the Golden Bull (*Bulla Aurea*) decreed that henceforth the election should be made by seven princes; three of them ecclesiastical, Mayence, Treves, and Cologne; and four lay, Bohemia, the Palatinate, Saxony, and Luxemburg. The medieval conception of a Christian Empire was rapidly disappearing and in its place jealous autonomous nations were surging into existence.

III. The Papacy and Italy: Albornoz, Urban V, and Gregory XI. The transfer of the Holy See to Avignon had left Italy without a protector. In the Patrimony anarchy was on the increase, fostered by the Orsinis, the Colonnas, and the Savellis, who were continuously at war and employed in their service hired assassins, who indulged in all sorts of crimes. In 1347 the people became so exasperated that they resolved to entrust their affairs to a tribune by the name of *Cola di Rienzi*. The first effect of this change was excellent, and peace and order were temporarily restored. In the beginning Clement VI was somewhat disturbed, but when Rienzi paid homage to him, he recognized his leadership. Unfortunately, this sudden elevation was too much for a man of low extraction, and completely turned his head. Intoxicated with the memory of the pagan classics, Rienzi dreamed of restoring ancient Rome. The poet Petrarch encouraged him in his design by saluting in him "the honor of the two Brutuses." Rienzi planned to combine all the kingdoms of Italy into one, with Rome as the capital, and in the presence of the representatives of the cities brandished his sword in the direction of the four points of the compass exclaiming: "All that is mine." Clement VI eventually excommunicated him, and a revolution broke out in Rome, December 15, 1347. The papal legate, Cardinal Bertrand de Deuse, re-established the former order of things. Two other tribunes, namely Cecconi (1352) and Baroncelli, had an ephemeral reign.

But the popes were constantly thinking of returning to Italy, and the successor of Clement VI, *Innocent VI* (1352–1362), worked untiringly to regain the Papal States with the assistance of the great warlike Cardinal Aegidius Alvarez *Albornoz,* who was a Castilian by birth, archbishop of Toledo, and a priest, soldier, and statesman all in one. He had been named legate to the Holy See at the time of the Crusade of Andalusia and had distinguished himself in the battle of Tarifa (1340). After Peter the Cruel had disgraced him, Innocent VI named him his legate in Italy (1353). The task entrusted to Cardinal Albornoz was an arduous one. In the Papal States as well as in northern Italy petty tyrants or great lords were everywhere in power, all of whom were licentious, crafty, and opposed to anything which savored of ecclesiastical intervention. Ruling over the Patrimony of St. Peter was the prefect, Giovanni di Vico; in the Marches, the

Ordelaffi at Forlì, at Faënza the Manfredi, and at Rimini, the Malatesta. To subjugate them, Albornoz was vested with supreme authority, which was, however, almost exclusively moral, because Innocent VI was not in a position to equip and maintain an expeditionary army. Albornoz began by forming an alliance with Archbishop Giovanni Visconti, the most powerful man in Italy, and master of Milan and Bologna. Confident now that he was not leaving any enemies behind, Albornoz headed a small army, swept down upon the Patrimony, and subdued by force the Prefect di Vico, whose submission brought about many others, particularly that of the cities of Narni, Terni, and Rieti. On September 30, 1354, Albornoz was able to convoke at Monte Fiascone a large assembly of barons and communes, who one and all took the oath of allegiance to the Church. It remained to regain possession of the Marches, a long strip of land on the coast which guaranteed the Papal States an outlet to the East by way of the sea, and an outlet into northern Italy by land. Albornoz defeated the petty tyrants of these regions, including Malatesta of Rimini and Ordelaffi of Forlì. Unfortunately, the intrigues of Visconti, who had grown alarmed at his success, and the jealousy of the papal entourage, drew down upon the great Cardinal two successive disgraces. His work remained incomplete, but was none the less considerable in character, for the Papal States were once again under the authority of the Sovereign Pontiff.

The time seemed ripe for the Pope to return to Italy, all the more so, as conditions in France made that country less and less fit as a place of papal residence. Taking advantage of the One Hundred Years' War, small groups of bandits kept the country in a perpetual state of terror. In 1357, the Provence was invaded by Arnold of Cervola and his henchmen. The whole Comtat was in a state of uproar, and Avignon was transformed into a veritable fortress. In 1358 and 1360, new troubles broke out, when the population, who had fled to Avignon, were devastated by famine and pestilence. The epidemic, which raged from March 29 to July 25, 1360, caused the death of no less than 1700 persons, among them nine cardinals. Towards the end of his pontificate, Innocent VI was seriously thinking of quitting France. His successor, *Urban V* (1362–1370), carried out this plan, despite the remonstrances of King Charles V and the French cardinals. His action was timely, for the long years spent under the administration of officials, most of whom were French, had exasperated the people. When Urban V re-entered Rome, Petrarch hailed his return as the end of a Babylonian Captivity. Meanwhile, underhanded hostile movements, climaxed by the revolt of Perugia, brought sorrow to the heart of the Pontiff. In vain did the Romans and Petrarch implore him to remain; in vain did St. Brigid warn him that if he returned to France, his death would quickly follow; in vain did Peter of Aragon insist that if the Pope departed from Rome, he would plunge the Church into a state of schism, because the sojourn of the Sovereign Pontiffs at Avignon, if prolonged, would create such a spirit of antagonism between the French and the Italians, that each nation would elect its own pope. Urban refused to listen to their entreaties, and returned to Avignon, where he died three months later, December 19, 1370.

From the very outset of his pontificate, *Gregory XI* (1370–1378), planned to return to Rome, but encountered new obstacles in the Florentines, who, jealous of the success of the Church and coveting the province of Tuscany, regarded the Pope as a rival and secretly instigated a movement to emancipate Gregory from French influence and to deport all Frenchmen from Italy. As a result, in the winter of 1375, a general insurrection broke out in Tuscany, the Papal States, and the Romagna. Gregory resolved to deal with the situation in all severity and placed Florence under the interdict. This measure was a distinct blow to the international trade of the city because it resulted in the suspension of payments, the seizure of merchandise, and the arrest of traffickers. *St. Catherine of Siena* intervened, asserting that in order to remedy the situation, "she would be willing, if this were possible, to sacrifice her life a thousand times." She even undertook a journey to Avignon. To her way of thinking, the immediate return of the Pope was the only solution of the problem, because it would dissipate all prejudices. Moreover, she reminded Gregory XI that Rome was traditionally the City of the Popes, referring to it as "a garden watered with the blood of the martyrs, which is still boiling and calling for others to follow in their footsteps." Despite the remonstrances of the French Court and the cardinals, Gregory XI re-entered Rome on January 17, 1377. Soon the Florentine League was dissolved, and the rebellious city, threatened with ruin, consented to negotiate with the papacy. When Gregory XI died, in March, 1378, a veritable European congress was in session at Sarzana to discuss plans for restoring peace to Italy.

IV. Centralization and Fiscal Administration at Avignon.

What are we to think of the stay of the popes at Avignon? In the first place, there is no denying that the joint entreaties of the Valois and the cardinals were one of the contributing factors in prolonging the exile. In the second place, the state of anarchy into which the entire Italian peninsula was plunged had made Italy an undesirable place of residence for the popes. Moreover, by sojourning at Avignon, they entertained the hope of putting an end to the Hundred Years' War. In this connection we must call attention especially to the efforts of Clement VI, who succeeded in drawing the Venetians and the Latins of the Orient (Cyprus and the Hospitallers) into a naval league against the Turks, who had established themselves on the coasts of Asia Minor and were infesting the Archipelago. The capture of Smyrna (Oct. 28, 1344) and the victory of Imbros (1347) completely rid the Mediterranean region of Turkish corsairs, but the rivalry which existed between Genoa and Venice, and the unfitness of the dauphin, Humbert of Vienne, generalissimo of the Crusade, prevented further successes.

Under the popes at Avignon the government of the Church became more and more centralized. Appeals to their tribunal were of frequent occurrence, and the Holy See began to take a deeper interest in the affairs of the religious Orders, enjoining reforms or placing them under the direct charge of Church dignitaries. Above all, the popes intervened more and more in the collation of benefices by multiplying reserved cases, *i. e.,* those in which the Sovereign Pontiff claimed the privilege of nominating the candidate. Enlarging upon a measure adopted by Clement VI, Boniface VIII claimed the right to nominate candidates to benefices of which the titulars had died in the vicinity of the papal court. Under John XXII, this reservation was extended and made to include all benefices which had lost their titulars by rejection at the moment of the election, by removal or by resignation, as well as all benefices of deceased cardinals and papal officials. Reservations of this sort were constantly multiplied, until, finally, Gregory XI claimed the exclusive right of nominating candidates to all patriarchal and archiepiscopal sees and all monasteries of men. Besides being vested in principle with the *plenaria dispositio,* the Holy See settled all disputes regarding illegal actions of ordinary collators of benefices in the choice of candidates and conflicts occasioned by episcopal and abbatial elections. In many Chapters discord was rampant and vacancies persisted, because of simoniacal intrigues and schisms. It was an easy matter, moreover, to find fault with the result of an election, as a numerical majority did not of itself suffice, but needed to be acknowledged by the *pars sanior*. We might add that in those days of discord it was imperative—especially in Germany and Italy—that all prelates nominated to office be specially devoted to the Holy See. As a general rule the papacy agreed to unite with the Chapters and approve the candidate selected by them; at times, when it was unable to secure the candidate of its choice for one benefice, it contented itself with nominating him for another; and not infrequently it acquiesced in the wishes of the king or the nobility. The autocracy which has been decried by many writers was not, therefore, such a flagrant evil. The real abuse originated in the cumulation of benefices. It was found practical to provide for the needs of the cardinals and officers of the papal court by conferring several benefices upon one man, the papacy even going so far as to designate the next titular in advance while the present incumbent of the benefice was still alive (*expectative*). The English clerics were particularly dissatisfied, because a large number of benefices had been granted to officials of the curia who were foreigners to that country.

The system of reserving certain benefices had a few direct financial advantages. (1) The prelates nominated by the Holy See had to acknowledge certain rights, to wit: (a) the *common services* gratuitously rendered to the Apostolic Chamber by the newly appointed bishops and abbots, which had become an obligatory tax in the thirteenth century; (b) the *minor services* rendered to the personnel of the Roman Curia; (c) the *sacra* paid on the occasion of episcopal consecration or benediction held at the papal court, and the *visitationes ad limina* or taxes due at the time of obligatory visits to the curia; (d) the *chancery rights*. To these taxes, paid to the seat of the Curia, must be added the *annates,* or revenues collected during the first year following the collation of a new benefice. (2) In the second place, the pope exercised the *ius spolii* at the death of a beneficiary, which entitled him to the furniture, treasury, and library of the deceased; he also collected the *vacantia* or fruits of the benefice accumulated during the interim. (3) In the third place, the Holy See occasionally levied tithes on ecclesiastical benefices, *i. e.,* extraordinary taxes, collected either for the purpose of organizing a crusade or carrying on wars in Italy. It also solicited the clergy for charitable donations (*subsidia caritativa*). It must be remembered, however, that the revenues formerly collected in Italy were not received by the popes at Avignon; that the powers tributary to the Holy See were becoming more and more lax in the discharge of their obligations, and that the popes had to maintain hirelings at their own expense. The centralization effected at Avignon was partly responsible for the anarchical reactions which reached their climax at the Council of Basle.

TEXTS AND DOCUMENTS

St. Catherine Begs Gregory XI to Return to Rome

Be valiant and not fearful; answer God who calls you to come and to fill and defend the place of the glorious pastor, St. Peter, whose successor you are. Raise the standard of the Holy Cross, for as, according to the saying of the Apostle Paul, we are made free by the Cross, so by the exaltation of this standard, which appears before me as the consolation of Christendom, shall we be delivered from discord, war, and wickedness, and those who have gone astray shall return to their allegiance. By doing thus, you shall obtain the conversion of the pastors of the Church. Implant again in her heart the burning love that she has lost. She is pale through loss of blood, which has been drained by insatiable devourers. But take courage and come, O Father; let not the servants of God, whose hearts are heavy with longing, have to wait for you. And I, poor and miserable as I am, cannot wait longer; life seems death to me while I see and hear that God is so dishonored. Do not let yourself be kept from peace by what has come to pass in Bologna, but come! I tell you that ravening wolves will lay their heads in your lap like gentle lambs, and beseech you to have pity on them, O Father.

Tommaseo, *Le Lettere di S. Catarina da Siena*, III, pp. 173–174 (transl. in Pastor, *History of the Popes*, I, p. 105).

QUESTIONS

1. Show that the reign of Clement V was one uninterrupted succession of mistakes and concessions to civil authority.
2. Give an impartial criticism of the Knights Templars.
3. List the principal grievances of Pope John XXII against the Franciscans.
4. How do you reconcile the theological statements of Pope John XXII with papal infallibility?
5. Describe the character of Cardinal Albornoz.
6. Which were the chief benefits derived from the sojourn of the popes at Avignon?

7. What is meant by the phrase "cumulation of benefices," and why did this practice constitute a serious abuse?
8. Which were the direct financial advantages of the system of reserving benefices?
9. What were the *"annates"*?

BIBLIOGRAPHY

Clement V. The Trial of the Knights Templar.—Sources: Bou-taric, *Notices et Extraits de documents inédits relatifs à l'histoire de France sous Philippe le Bel*, in the *Notices et Extraits des manuscrits de la Bibl. nationale*, t. XX (1862), pp. 83-237.—K. Schottmüller, *Der Untergang des Templerordens*, 2 vols., 1887.—Lizerand, *Le dossier de l'Affaire des Templiers* (Coll. *"Les classiques de l'Hist. de France au Moyen Age"*), 1923.—Works: H. Prutz, *Entwickelung und Untergang des Tempelherrenordens*, 1888.—H. Finke, *Papsttum und Untergang des Templer-Ordens*, 2 vols., 1907.—Ch. Lizerand, *Clément V et Philippe le Bel*, 1910.—Langlois, *Le Procès des Templiers*, in *Rev. des Deux-Mondes*, 1891, et *Hist. de France*, t. III.—P. Viollet, *Les interrogatoires de Jacques Molay*, 1909.—C. Lizerand, *Les dépositions de J. Molay*, 1913.—V. Carrière, *Hypothèses et faits nouveaux en faveur des Templiers*, in *Rev. hist. Eglise de France*, 1912 (III).—Hemmer, art. *"Clément V,"* in *Dict. de Théol.*—G. Mollat, art. *"Templiers,"* in *Dict. d'Apol.*—E. W. Schermerhorn, *Malta of the Knights.*

The Avignon Popes in General.—Sources: A. Coulon and Mollat, *Les registres de Jean XXII*, 1900 ff.—J. M. Vidal and G. Daumet, *Les registres de Benoit XII*, 1899.—E. Déprez, *Les registres de Clément VI et d'Innocent VI*, 1899.—P. Lecacheux, *Les registres d'Urbain V*, 1902.—*Vitæ paparum Avenionensium*, edit. Baluze, 2 vols., 1693, re-edit. G. Mollat, 1917.—H. Finke, *Acta Aragonensia*, 3 vols., 1907 ff.—*Œuvres de S. Vincent Ferrier*, edit. Fages, 1909.—Works: G. Mollat, *Les papes d'Avignon*, 3rd edit., 1920.—L. Bréhier, *L'Eglise et l'Orient au moyen âge. Les croisades.*—J. Guiraud, *L'Eglise romaine et les origines de la Renaissance*, 1911.—Dom C. Poulet, *Guelfes et Gibelins*, t. II: *La diplomatie pontificale à l'époque de la domination française (1266-1378)*, 1922.

Louis of Bavaria and the Papacy.—C. Müller, *Die Kämpfe Ludwigs des Baiern mit der römischen Curie. Ein Beitrag zur kirchlichen Geschichte des 14. Jahrhunderts*, Tübingen, 1879-1880.—P. Fournier, *Le royaume d'Arles et de Vienne*, 1891.—A. Leroux, *Recherches critiques sur les relations de la France avec l'Allemagne de 1292 à 1378*, 1882.—A. Baudrillart, *Des idées qu'on se faisait au XIVe siècle sur le droit d'intervention du Souverain Pontife en matière politique*, in *Rev. hist. et litt. relig.*, t. III (1898), pp. 193-223, 299-337.—Noel Valois, *Jean de Jandun et Marsile de Padoue*, in *Hist. litt. de la France*, t. XXIII.

John XXII.—Sources: A. Coulon and G. Mollat, *Les registres de Jean XXII*, 1900.—Works: E. Albe, *Autour de Jean XXII. Les familles du Quercy*, Rome, 1903-1906 (Extracts from the Annals of St. Louis of France).—J. Asal, *Die Wahl Johanns XXII*, 1910.—G. Mollat, *Jean XXII fut-il un avare* in *Rev. hist. eccl.*, t. V (1904), pp. 522-534; t. VI (1905), pp. 33-46; *L'élection du pape Jean XXII*, in *Rev. hist. Eglise de France*, t. I. (1910), pp. 34-49, 147-166.—N. Valois, *Jacques Duèse, pape sous le nom de Jean XXII*, in *Hist. litt. de la France*, t. XXXIV (1915), pp. 301-630.—Art. *"Jean XXII,"* in *Dict. de Théol.*—Mortier, *Histoire des Maîtres généraux de l'ordre des Frères prêcheurs*, t. II and III, 1905-1907.—For the Spirituals, see: F. Tocco, *L'Eresia nel Medio Evo*, Firenze, 1884.—Holzapfel, *Handbuch der Geschichte des Franziskanerordens*, Freiburg i. B., 1905.—F. Callaey, *L'idéalisme franciscain spirituel au XIVe siècle. Etude sur Ubertin de Casale*, Louvain, 1911.—Vernet, art. *"Fratricelles,"* in *Dict. de Théol.*—E. Jordan, art. *"Joachim de Flore,"* in *Dict. de Théol.*

Cola di Rienzo.—Rodocanachi, *Les institutions communales de Rome*, 1901;—*Cola di Rienzo, Histoire de Rome de 1342 à 1354*, 1888.

Albornoz.—Works: E. Filippini, *La reconquisita dello Stato della chiesa per opera di Egidio Albornoz (1353-1357)*, Rigoli, 1900 (Extr. from the *Studi Storici*, t. VI-VIII).—Art. *"Albornoz,"* in *Dict. d'Hist. et de géogr. eccl.*

The Return to Rome under Urban V and Gregory XI.—J. H. Albanès, *Abrégé de la vie et des miracles du bienheureux Urbain V*, 1872.—M. Chaillan, *Le bienheureux Urbain V* (Coll. *"Les Saints"*), 1911.—Mirot, *La politique pontificale et le retour du Saint Siège à Rome en 1376*, 1899.—E. Gebhart, *Moines et papes*, 1896.—M. Prou, *Etude sur les relations politiques du pape Urbain V avec les rois de France Jean II et Charles V*, 1887.—Comtesse de Flavigny, *Sainte Catherine de Sienne*, 1895.—Joergensen, *St. Catherine of Siena.*—J. Leclercq, *Sainte Catherine de Sienne, catholique romaine, la mystique de l'apostolat*, Brussels, 1921.—Comtesse de Flavigny, *Sainte Brigitte*, 1892.—A. Clerval, art. *"Grégoire XI,"* in *Dict. de Théol.*—E. de Lanouvelle, *Le bienheureux Urbain V et la chrétienté au milieu du XVe siècle*, 1929.

The Papacy at Avignon, France and the East.—E. Déprez, *Les préliminaires de la guerre de Cent Ans: La papauté, la France et l'Angleterre (1328-1342)*, 1902.—H. Denifle, *La désolation des églises, monastères, hôpitaux en France pendant la guerre de Cent Ans*, 2 vols., 1899.—Delachenal, *Histoire de Charles V*, 3 vols., 1909-1916.—G. Mollat, *Innocent VI et les tentatives de paix entre la France et l'Angleterre (1353-1355)*, in *Rev. hist. eccl.*, t. X (1909), pp. 729-743.—J. Gay, *Le pape Clement VI et les affaires d'Orient (1342-1352)*, 1904.—DeLaville Le Roulx, *La France en Orient au XIVe siècle. Expéditions du maréchal Boucicaut.*

Papal Finances.—G. Mollat and Ch. Samarin, *La fiscalité pontificale au XIVe siècle*, 1905.—A. Cleirgeac, *La curie et les beneficiers consistoriaux,*

1911.—J. Doizé, *Les finances du Saint Siège au temps d'Avignon*, in *Etudes*, t. CXI (1907), pp. 467–484, 639–654.—C. Daux, *Le denier de Saint Pierre*, 1907.—J. P. Kirsch, *L'administration des finances pontificales au XIVe siècle*, in *Rev. Hist. eccl.*, t. I (1900), pp. 274–296.—G. Mollat, *La collation des bénéfices ecclésiastiques sous les papes d'Avignon*, 1921.

CHAPTER III

I. Origin of the Schism: The Two Obediences. On the day after the death of Gregory XI, the citizens of Rome clamored for a Roman, or at least an Italian, pope. The Sacred College was divided on the issue, being composed of seven Limousin, five French, and four Italian cardinals. The French and the Italians had a common antipathy for the Limousins, and so suggested the name of Bartholomew Prignano, Archbishop of Bari, who, being a Neapolitan, was regarded as a compromise candidate. Manifestly, the main concern of the cardinals at this important moment was the question of personalities, for to elect a French pope was to condemn the Sovereign Pontiff to exile at Avignon. The Sacred College was greatly encouraged in its decision to elect an Italian when the vote was cast on Thursday, April 8th, by the shouts of the people storming the doors of the conclave. "Lords, make haste," was the greeting of the bishop of Marseilles; "you risk being torn to pieces if you do not hasten to elect an Italian or Roman pope." At this critical juncture the candidacy of the Archbishop of Bari seemed to be assured; fifteen out of the sixteen cardinals voted for him. Calm was now more or less re-established among the crowd as the cardinals, having partaken of their dinner, reappeared, and one of them made this sage observation: "Let us take advantage of the quiet that has been established, to re-elect the Archbishop of Bari. Are we still of the same opinion?" The majority of those present answered in the affirmative. The scene which followed is evident proof of the excited condition and threatening attitude of the mob. Ignorant of the outcome of the election, the crowd forced its way into the conclave. To satisfy them, the cardinals gave out the information that they had elected a Roman, the aged Cardinal Tibaldeschi. He was seized and invested with the papal insignia. Finally, the truth became known, and the next day, April 9, the cardinals paid homage to Prignano under the name of *Urban VI.*

In return for the favor conferred, the cardinals expected favors. But they were doomed to disappointment. Urban VI, a very undiplomatic and radical reformer, immediately informed them that they would have to moderate their high way of living. His reproaches were at times tantamount to personal insults. He even went so far as to call Orsini a fool. Meanwhile, Cardinal John de la Grange of Amiens arrived in Rome. He was a Benedictine monk and a shrewd diplomat, but Urban reproached him for his amicable relations with the insurgent prefect de Vico. A stormy altercation ensued. John grouped around his person the members of the discontented faction, who, not at all impressed with the valid character of the votes they had cast, began to doubt the lawfulness of Urban's election.

A spite that was excusable, coupled with an egotism that was quite unconscious, may have detached these cardinals from the party of Pope Urban and hurled them into an opposition that was all the more tenacious as it was rooted in well reasoned and probably sincere conviction. A plot was quickly formed, and the thirteen cardinals opposed to Urban VI repaired to Fondi, where they proceeded to elect the French Cardinal Robert, Count of Geneva, who took the name of Clement VII. A serious and loyal investigation was immediately undertaken by the assembly of the clergy of France at Bois de Vincennes, and the members present, together with King Charles V, declared themselves in favor of *Clement VII*. From this moment on the entire question assumed the proportions of a vast political conflict, in which both the papacy and Italy were at stake. The Francophile powers—Castile, Portugal, and Scotland—declared themselves ready to pay homage to Clement, while England, Flanders, and the Empire acknowledged obedience to Urban. The problem was an extremely complicated one, because up to that time the abettors of schism had been lay princes, the Hohenstaufens first, and then Louis of Bavaria. Now, however, ecclesiastical dignitaries were fomenting discord. Moreover, the circumstances which surrounded the election gave rise to interminable discussions, because there was no certain way of testing the different versions. It will be remembered that St. Catherine of Siena and St. Brigid declared themselves in favor of Pope Urban, while St. Vincent Ferrer and Blessed Peter of Luxemburg paid respect and obedience to the French Pope. Thus distracted, the Christian world was divided into two camps, and it was no uncommon sight to see two prelates or two abbots settle their right to a benefice granted by the pope of their choice by force of arms.

II. Futile Attempts to Restore Unity. Urban VI added to the difficulties of the situation by his personal conduct. Being of a vindictive disposition, he became completely absorbed in personal conflicts and used all his resources to combat his powerful neighbor, Queen Joan of Naples, who had espoused the cause of Clement VII. To finance his campaign, he went so far as to despoil churches and altars and entrusted to the ambitious Charles of Durazzo the charge of executing his sentences of revenge. Once the expedition was ended, however, Charles showed no further concern for Urban VI, who journeyed to the very gates of Naples to demand his rights. A battle ensued, and Urban was besieged in Nocera; he succeeded, however, in extricating himself. Seriously alarmed by these disquieting events, the cardinals resolved to appoint a guardian for the aged Pontiff. He discovered the plot, however, and issued orders for several of them to be tortured. His action brought discredit upon the Italian party, which soon grew too weak to end the schism. On the other hand, the Pope of Avignon could establish the lawfulness of his claim only if he became Pope of Rome. The only way open to him, therefore, was recourse to arms. With this purpose in mind, Clement VII linked his cause with that of the Angevins, to whom he promised to restore the city of Naples. Louis I of Anjou, and later on his son, Louis II, scored brilliant but ephemeral victories in Italy, which, however, failed to help the cause of Clement, and a league formed by John Galeas Visconti and his son-in-law, Louis of Orleans, also proved unsuccessful. These expeditions into Italy were not only disastrous, but also very costly. The clergy were complaining bitterly; people were growing tired of the schism, and so, when the open attack failed, it was resolved to settle the difficulty in another way.

In 1394, a referendum held by the University of Paris indicated that public opinion favored the voluntary withdrawal of both candidates. It was proposed that the two popes abandon their respective claims and that the cardinals proceed to hold a new election. But Clement VII was far from sharing that opinion, and when the University sought to persuade him to resign, he cried out: "That would be wicked, that would be fatal." *Benedict XIII* (1394-1417), his successor in the see of Avignon, showed himself more adroit by protesting his good will in the matter. He succeeded in rallying to his cause such eminent personages as Nicholas de Clamanges, who became his secretary, Peter d'Ailly, to whom he gave the see of Puy, and St. Vincent Ferrer. He then declared himself in favor of a middle course of action, or arbitration, and requested that he be permitted to have an interview with the Pope of Rome. But when he began to indulge in cavillings, the University resolved to settle the matter at all costs by demanding the resignation of both popes. Acting upon this advice, the clergy of France assembled in May, 1398, voted the withdrawal of their allegiance to the French Pope, and resolved to refuse any recognition to the authority of the Pope of Avignon until a reunion was effected. Bohemia, Hungary, and Navarre adopted the same attitude.

This step had unexpected results. The French court wanted not a victory for the Roman Pope, but the resignation of the two rivals. By nullifying the authority of Benedict XIII, withdrawal of obedience to him would increase the prestige of his rival, who was not affected by the French decision. The Jubilee of the year 1400 brought to Rome many pilgrims who, disregarding the question as to whom they owed obedience, came to gain the indulgence. Meanwhile, a scene more ridiculous than tragic was enacted at Avignon, where Benedict XIII was besieged in his palace for the purpose of forcing his resignation (1398-1403). In March, 1403, he succeeded in making his escape, and at the instigation of Nicholas de Clamanges and Gerson, a new assembly of the clergy of France re-affirmed obedience to him.

Meanwhile the schism threatened to continue indefinitely. On the Roman side, Urban VI (1378-1389) had been followed by Boniface IX (1389-1404), Innocent VII (1404-1406), and, finally, *Gregory XII* (1406-1415). Gregory at the very outset of his pontificate repeatedly declared that he was ready to meet Benedict XIII. The outcome was a comedy, for the two popes who set out to meet each other with the intention of abdicating together at Savona, purposely avoided a personal encounter, Gregory XII refusing to go beyond the city of Lucca, and Benedict XIII stopping at Porto Venere. This disloyal action drew upon the head of the Roman Pontiff the same vexations inflicted ten years before upon the Pope of Avignon. A party was organized against him within the Sacred College, and to cope with it he had to create four new cardinals favorable to his cause. It was an unfortunate move, for seven members of the opposing faction openly broke with him and appealed "from the ill-informed

Pope to a better-informed Pope, to Jesus Christ, to a general council, to the Pope of the future." Meanwhile Benedict XIII sustained another blow, when for a second time the clergy of France voted to withdraw their obedience from him.

The attempt to reach a solution by the voluntary withdrawal of the two rival popes having failed, the suggestion was made to settle the problem by means of a council. Roman cardinals and Avignonese cardinals who were at loggerheads with their respective candidates, held a conference (1408) at Livorno (Leghorn) and resolved to convoke a general council at Pisa. The two popes made a futile attempt to oppose their action by also convoking councils, the first at Perpignan, under the patronage of the king of Aragon, the second at Cividale in Frioul (1409); they were unable to prevent the cardinals from assembling a large number of followers. The *Council of Pisa* declared itself to be canonical in so far as its convocation was concerned, and also ecumenical and representative of the whole Church. As an explanation of this bold stand it was asserted that the two popes were outside the Church. They were not only abettors of schism, but also heretics, inasmuch as they had been guilty of undermining the faith in one, holy, Catholic, and Apostolic Church. The Council deposed both popes and elected another, Peter Philargos, Archbishop of Milan, who took the name of *Alexander V* (1409). He died the following year and was succeeded by Balthasar Cossa, who assumed the name of *John XXIII*. The Pontiff of Pisa rallied to his cause the Emperor, France, and England, while Benedict XIII retained Spain and Scotland, and Gregory XII received the allegiance of the majority of the Italian States. And so the Council which had met to reduce the number of Popes from two to one, increased it to three. The Popes of the three obediences were:

A. Rome

Urban VI (1378-1389)
Boniface IX (1389-1404)
Innocent VII (1404-1406)
Gregory XII (1406-1415)

B. Avignon

Clement VII (1378-1394)
Benedict XIII (1394-1417)

C. Pisa

Alexander V (1409-1410)
John XXIII (1410-1415)

D. Ending the schism: Martin V (1417-1431)

III. Anarchy in the Sphere of Ideas: Wicliffe and Hus. Confusion was steadily increasing in the sphere of ideas. This state of affairs was traceable to the influence of the University of Paris, which, in the absence of any certain authority, exhibited a tendency to become the great mouthpiece of Christendom. The Middle Ages admitted without discussion that the pope was the judge of all men, and amenable to none; in fact he was Jesus Christ Himself. The new doctors, on the other hand, clearly distinguished between Christ and the pope: "It is from Christ," they averred, "and not from the pope that the jurisdiction over bishops and priests is derived." The logical consequence of this teaching was that the subordination of the Church to the Holy See appeared to be purely accidental. The fallibility of the pope, the infallibility of the Church, the superiority of a general council over the pope are only a few instances of the new dogmas publicly taught from the university rostrum.

Foremost among the innovators must be ranked *William of Ockam,* often referred to as *the first Protestant,* according to whom the constitution of the Church is subject to change: it is absolutist, aristocratic or democratic, to fit the occasion. Different systems were reared upon this principle of opportunism, chief among which were those of Peter d'Ailly and John Gerson. *Peter d'Ailly* advocated the aristocratic system. He conceded the *magisterium* to the bishops, who are the nobility in the Church, but reserved doctrinal and scientific superiority to the doctors of theology and canon law. *John Gerson* professed a moderate democratic system and admitted pastors as well as bishops to ecclesiastical councils. There was, finally, the pure or exaggerated democratic system, also called multitudinarianism, according to which the teaching body of the Church consisted not only of priests, all of equal rank, but also of lay representatives elected by the people. Sheltered by the schism, these ideas developed rapidly. Constance witnessed the application of the aristocratic, Basle that of the democratic system.

Others went even farther and boldly rejected all external authority. These revolutionaries based their reform of the constitution of the Church on a theory of predestination, which substituted for the visible and hierarchical Church an invisible one, the members of which are not known. In the opinion of *Wycliffe,* all things are regulated by a divinely ordained necessity. Each and every being is constrained to perform each and every one of its acts. Those predestined to eternal glory may indulge in all sorts of sinful actions with impunity, because God obliges them to act in this way; whereas those predestined to eternal damnation pray in vain, because God has already resolved not to heed their prayers. Now, if this be the status of individual men, where is the Church? The answer to this question obviously is: The Church is in the souls of those predestined to eternal glory. The pope, cardinals, bishops, and priests may be numbered among this élite if, as individuals, they are among those predestined to eternal glory. In any case, they have no right to rule and govern the Church, because the Church, being essentially a spiritual institution, has no visible head. Away, therefore, with the hierarchy. The pope is the Antichrist, his partisans are idolaters, and the bishops and priests are co-equal and mere preachers without jurisdiction. Ecclesiastical authority cannot touch any person who is truly predestined, and hence no excommunication fulminated by it can cut anyone off from the Church. In this invisible society of predestined members, the Bible is the only source of faith, and Wycliffe undertook to translate it for the use of the common people. He also rejected most of the Sacraments, regarded the confession of sins as superfluous, Extreme Unction as a human invention, and the Holy Eucharist as involving only a moral presence of Christ in the substances of bread and wine. With the exclusive aid of Holy Scripture, the Church must resolve to undergo a complete and heroic reform, and resume the practice of Apostolic poverty. Thus Wycliffism contained the germs of a political and social revolution.

When Urban V, in 1366, demanded from Edward III the annual tribute of one thousand marks once promised by John Lackland, but not paid for thirty-three years, the heresiarch upheld the King in his refusal to meet this obligation. He also selected a few disciples from among the ranks of the lower clergy to bring out the contrast with "the wealthy Church, which had fallen into the power of the devil." Moreover, he stirred up a popular movement against the goods of the Church, especially the extensive possessions of religious, and in the heat of controversy even went so far as to condemn monasticism itself. In 1377, Wycliffe was summoned before an ecclesiastical tribunal, presided over by William Courtney, Bishop of London, but he was shielded by friends of the King. The high favor in which he was held in court circles also explains why he was protected against the Bulls of Gregory XI demanding his imprisonment. Finally, an assembly of bishops, before whom he was forced to appear, declared itself completely satisfied. The ever increasing audacity of Wycliffe, however, was to bring about his own ruin, for soon the chancellor of the University of Oxford issued orders for him to cease expounding his new theories. His party began to stir up the people and inspired a revolt, which culminated in acts of unprecedented violence.

Wycliffe's followers brought out a version of the whole Bible. His exact share is uncertain. Wycliffe entrusted the mission of expounding his teachings to priests clothed in russet-dyed sheep-skins, whence their name, "poor priests." The Catholics called them *Lollards,* sowers of tare (*lollium*). These heretics were partly responsible for the uprising of the peasants in England in 1381, as later the Anabaptists were responsible for the Peasants' Revolt in Germany in 1525. The insurrection, which was fomented in several different counties, had as its leader John Ball. The movement was clearly anarchical in character, one of its instigators, Jack Straw, even going so far as to propose a solution to the social question by killing off all lords, bishops, monks, and priests. To obtain a settlement of their grievances, the insurgents marched from all sides upon the city of London, where they murdered the Chancellor, John Sundbury, Archbishop of Canterbury. Wycliffe was suspected of being the abettor of this movement and arraigned before a synod of London by Archbishop Courtney (1382). He was forbidden to indulge in any further teaching, and forced to retire to the vicarage of Lutterworth, where he composed his principal work, the *Trialogus.*

Henry IV of Lancaster, who usurped the throne in 1399, resolved to wage war against the Lollards. In 1401 he signified his approval of the statute *De Haeretico Comburendo* (On the Burning of Heretics), which turned over to the secular arm any heretic found guilty by an ecclesiastical court. His son, Henry V (1413-1422), continued to pursue the Lollards and consented to the condemnation of their leader, John Oldcastle, despite the fact that the latter was a member of his own household. But England soon became engrossed in the cares and anxieties of the Hundred Years' War and the Wars of the Roses, and forgot its religious battles. The ideas of John Wycliffe, however, remained latent and were destined to reappear at the time of the Protestant Reformation.

The marriage of Richard II, King of England, with Princess Anne, daughter of the king of Bohemia, occasioned frequent relations between the two countries, and it was not long before Oxford students who had gone to study at Prague, introduced there the pernicious teachings of Wycliffe. *John Hus,* a professor at the University of Prague, placed himself at the head of the movement, sponsoring all the ideas of the English heresiarch, except his denial of transubstantiation. Being more of a tribune than a rhetorician, Hus spared no one, not even those in the highest stations. His principal grievances were against the clergy, a portion of whom he ensnared into error, and upon the remainder of whom he heaped attacks with an animosity that was at once obstinate and unbalanced. In his capacity of confessor to Queen Sophia, he succeeded in gaining powerful protectors at the court of the weak and voluptuous Wenceslaus. The conflict was intensified by a quarrel which involved two different nationalities. Bohemia was divided, as it is to-day, into two parties, one German and the other Czech. The former opposed Hus, the latter upheld him. Wenceslaus was deposed in 1400, and made use of all available means to regain his prestige with the people. In the Czecho-Hussite movement he discovered a force well worth exploiting. In the councils of the University of Prague, the Czechs had only one vote, as against three of the nations speaking the German language (Germany, Saxony, and Poland). The King reversed the proportions, giving three votes to the Czechs and only one to the Germans. The latter quitted Prague and founded the University of Leipsic. Their action spelled the complete triumph of the Hussite party at Prague. Measures of ecclesiastical discipline, such as the condemnation of all the writings of Wycliffe (1410), the excommunication of Hus (1411), and the interdict inflicted upon all places where he took refuge (1412), were in vain; sustained by civil authority and popular opinion, the movement assumed constantly larger proportions.

The excesses of the Bohemian Professor and his disrespect for any form of hierarchy soon effected a complete reversal. The action of John XXIII, the Pope of Pisa, who decreed a crusade against King Ladislaus of Naples and granted an indulgence to those who took part in it, provoked the protestations of the Hussites. The rejection of the doctrine of indulgences was a corollary of the teaching of Hus regarding predestination, just as it was later on in the case of Martin Luther. "If anyone is predestined," he said, "the indulgence can be of no avail, and if he is predestined, the Pope is in no position to know it." His partisans assailed with outrages all those who preached the indulgence in the churches, and a certain knight even went so far as to hang the papal Bull around the neck of a prostitute, who was then solemnly burnt at the stake. Wenceslaus was finally obliged to interfere. Three of the sectarians were beheaded, but Hus celebrated them as martyrs. Soon the Hussites themselves became indignant; several abandoned their master, chief among them being two professors, Stephen of Palec and Stanislaus of Znaim. Wenceslaus was then obliged to issue orders to Hus to leave the city of Prague, which had been visited with a censure of interdict as a consequence of his presence there.

TEXTS AND DOCUMENTS

THE CITY OF AVIGNON

Avignon was not only the sumptuous abode of the French popes, the city ringing with a thousand belfries; it was also a first-class fortress, of which the massive towers and battlemented walls, four yards thick, even to-day astonish the world. The ready pen and quick imagination of a child of Provence thus describes the city of the popes: "Nations drank at the Rhone," says Mistral; "churches, chapels, and oratories were counted there by the thousands. In continual motion the carillons of a hundred belfries resounded joyfully all through the town, and during the night the corners of the streets shone with illuminated madonnas. Astride of the rocky escarpment, the enormous castle that reaches the clouds flung into the sky the colossal mass of its seven hard stone towers, the mouldings of which looked like those of a habitation for giants. The colossal structure was reflected in the river that flowed below it, and its height commanded the vast surrounding plain. Striding over the swollen Rhone, like a road of triumphal arches, a stone bridge of unheard-of height and length linked together France and Provence, Villeneuve and Avignon. When the awful sounds of the mistral made themselves heard over the city, you would have said that God's breath was on its way to distribute the Pope's blessing amongst the nations."

The pontifical palace is to-day one of the wonders of medieval architecture and the glory of Avignon. "Both fortress and monastery, prison and palace, the provisional residence of the Popes is curiously like a faithful picture of the lot that befell the papacy in France, and its declension. It is at once a pontifical prison and a feudal castle of the period when the chiefs of Christendom took without blushing the rôle of vassal to the King of France, and the title of Count of Venaissin and Avignon."

Salembier, *The Great Schism of the West*, pp. 166–167.

QUESTIONS

1. Which events paved the way for the Great Schism of the West?
2. What is to be thought of the solution proposed by the University of Paris?
3. List in chronological order the principal steps in the Schism.
4. Which were the three systems of thought regarding the constitution of the Church inaugurated at this time by the University of Paris?
5. What in this respect was the teaching of John Wycliffe?
6. How was Wycliffism introduced into Bohemia?
7. Account for the founding of the University of Leipzig.
8. Summarize the principal teachings of John Hus.

BIBLIOGRAPHY

The Great Schism.—Sources: *Thierry de Niem, De schismate libri IV,* edit. Ehrle, 1890.—Nicolas de Clamengis, *De corrupto ecclesiæ statu,* in his works, edit. Lydius, Leyden, 1613.—*Œuvres de S. Vincent Ferrier,* edit. Farges 1909, 2 vols.; *De moderno Ecclesiæ statu,* edit. A. Sorbelli, 1910, etc.—Works: Salembier, *Petrus de Aliaco,* Lille, 1886.—Masson, *Jean Gerson, sa vie, son temps et ses œuvres,* Lyon, 1894.—L. Gayet, *Le grand Schisme d'Occident,* 2 vols., 1889.—Noel Valois, *La France et le grand Schisme d'Occident,* 4 vols., 1896–1902.—L. Salembier, *The Great Schism of the West,* New York, 1907.—M. Jansen, *Papst Bonifacius IX. und seine Beziehungen zur deutschen Kirche,* 1904.—A. Lafontaine, *Jehan Gerson,* 1906.—L. Salembier, art. "*Schisme d'Occident,*" in *Dict. d'Apol.*—G. Mollat, *Episodes du siège du palais des papes au temps de Benoit XIII, R. H. E.,* 1927, pp. 489–502.—J. L. Connolly, *John Gerson, Reformer and Mystic,* Louvain, 1928.

Wycliffe.—Trevelyan, *England in the Age of Wycliffe,* 1898.—J. Loserth, *The Beginnings of Wyclif's activity in Ecclesiastical Politics,* in *English Historical Review,* 1896.—Wattier, *John Wyclif, sa vie, ses œuvres, sa doctrine,* 1886.—J. Löserth, *Studien zur Kirchenpolitik Englands im 14. Jh.,* 1908.—A. Dakin, *Die Beziehungen John Wiclifs und der Lollarden zu den Bettelmönchen,* 1911.—For the sources, see *Wicliffe's Writings,* London, 1885 ff. J. Stevenson, *The Truth about John Wyclif,* 1885.

John Hus.—V. Kybal, *Etude sur les origines du mouvement hussite en Bohême,* in *Rev. d'Hist.,* t. CIII.—E. Denis, *Huss et la guerre des Hussites,* 1878; *Fin de l'indépendance de la Bohême,* 2 vols., 1890.—F. H. V. Graf Lützow, *The Life and Times of Master John Hus,* 1909.—E. J. Kitts, *Pope*

John XXIII and Master John Hus of Bohemia, 1910.—J. Löserth, *Hus und Wiclif*, 2nd edit., Munich, 1925.—P. Moncelle, art. *"Huss"* and art. *"Hussites,"* in *Dict. de Théol.*—E. Amann, art. *"Jérôme de Prague,"* in *Dict. de Théol.*—James Gairdner, *Lollardy and the Reformation in England*, 2 vols., London, 1908.

CHAPTER IV

I. End of the Schism: Martin V. Thus, in 1414, Christendom was threatened by two formidable evils: the Great Schism and the Hussite heresy. In the absence of anything like undisputed papal authority it was remembered that the Emperor was the born protector of Christendom. John XXIII, the Pope of Pisa, had failed in all his undertakings, and a council convoked by him in 1412 had been obliged to adjourn its meetings because of the insufficient number of delegates in attendance and failure to reach an understanding. Soon the Pope had the additional grief of seeing his ally, Ladislaus of Naples, betray him, march upon Rome, and completely pillage the city. Beside himself with fear, John XXIII appealed to the Emperor-elect *Sigismund*. The latter knew what the Pope had in mind, and came to his assistance. As head of the Holy Empire he longed for the end of the schism, and as future king of Bohemia he sought the extermination of the Hussite heresy. No course of action seemed better adapted to settle these difficulties than the convocation of a general council, and so Sigismund fixed the place of its meeting in the German city of Constance, imposed this choice upon the powerless John XXIII, and notified the other two popes, Gregory XII and Benedict XIII.

John XXIII had consented to have the Council convene, because he hoped that it would ratify his election as Sovereign Pontiff. Accordingly, he arrived in Constance, accompanied by a number of Italian cardinals, but only to discover that public opinion was very unfavorable to him. To counteract the influence of his party, it was decided to vote by nations, and in every instance to concede the right of suffrage not only to the prelates, but also to the procurators of the Chapters and universities, and the various delegates of the princes. This was, moreover, a concession to the ideas in vogue at the time. The Fathers of the Council listened to the

626

reading of an anonymous memoir containing monstrous accusations against the Pope of Pisa. For fear of being betrayed before the assembly, John XXIII solemnly promised to renounce his claims to the papacy for the peace of the Church, and then, thinking that his sudden departure would end the Council, he fled from the city to Schaffhausen, disguised as a groom. His action only served to increase the strength of the opposition. Goaded on by the members of the University, especially Peter d'Ailly and John Gerson, the Fathers composed the following articles in the fourth and fifth sessions: (1) "The Council of Constance, lawfully assembled in the Holy Spirit, constituting an ecumenical council and representing the militant Church, derives its authority immediately from God, and all, including the Pope, are obliged to obey its decisions in all that pertains to the faith, the uprooting of heresy, and the reform of the Church in head and members (*in his quae pertinent ad fidem et exstirpationem dicti schismatis et reformationem generalem Ecclesiae in capite et in membris*). (2) Whoever is so obstinate as to oppose the decrees of this Council, is amenable to punishment according to the laws and their enactments. (3) Because the authority of the Council is of the utmost utility and necessity to the Church, the sudden departure of John is manifestly a scandal and tantamount to a formal violation of all his promises. If, therefore, he does not abide by the decisions of the Council, he will lay himself open to the accusations of schism and even heresy. (4) Pope John XXIII and all those invited to the Council enjoyed complete freedom of action while at Constance."

If we consider merely the texts of these decrees, we are forced to admit that the superior attitude adopted by the Council in regard to Pope John was limited to the matter of the schism, which it sought to end. This was the interpretation accepted by many writers of that time, and by others of a later date. The opinions advanced by the Fathers of Constance, and their conduct, proved that they attached to these decisions a general and dogmatic significance. Their mistake was to establish as a rule applicable to all times the measures of expediency necessary to cope with existing extraordinary conditions. These decrees, however, are not dogmatic definitions, first, because of the opposition set up by a notable portion of the assembly, the preliminary act of protestation on the part of eleven cardinals and the voluntary absence of four others; secondly, because of the disorderly character of the vote, in which persons without any rights in the matter participated; and thirdly, because Pope Martin V never ratified them.

It was agreed to act at once on the different articles voted. John XXIII was deposed for having fomented the schism by his sudden departure and for other personal offences. Gregory XII renounced his right to the tiara of his own accord. Benedict XIII alone remained obstinate. In vain did Sigismund visit him at Perpignan to obtain his resignation, and in vain did the Spanish princes sever relations with him. He took refuge with three of his cardinals in the fortress of Peniscola, and persisted in calling himself the head of the Church. He was finally deposed in the same manner as John XXIII. The way was now clear, and on November 11, 1417, Cardinal Otto Colonna was elected pope and took the name of *Martin V*. The Great Western Schism was at an end.

II. The Condemnation of John Hus. The Council of Constance also passed sentence on John Hus. Thirty propositions taken from his works were anathematized; but he refused to recant his errors. He was given more than a month to retract, and eminent personages like Cardinal d'Ailly and the Emperor Sigismund did all in their power to shake his obstinacy. Hus was finally degraded, cut off from the Church, and handed over to the secular arm. He was condemned as an obstinate heretic and burned at the stake, July 6, 1415, together with his friend Jerome of Prague.[1] The Hussite party, however, remained quite powerful. It received assistance from Wenceslaus, who was goaded on by his jealousy against his brother Sigismund, and reckoned among its supporters many members of the nobility of Bohemia and Moravia. At Prague, all homes whose occupants were enemies of Hus were ransacked, clerics were ill-treated and expelled from their churches, and the archbishop was besieged in his palace and threatened with death. In a diet held at Prague, the Bohemian nobility drew up a letter of protest, addressed to the Council of Constance. They even formed a league, the members of which agreed to uphold freedom in the matter of preaching, to refuse to take notice of excommunications, and to obey episcopal

---

[1] The main object of the Emperor Sigismund in granting a written safe-conduct to Hus was to protect him during his journey to the city of Constance, whither he had been cited for cross-examination. The Emperor may have entertained scruples, therefore, when John was imprisoned before the time of his trial, but he certainly had no intention of protecting him by the safe-conduct in the event of his remaining obstinate. He had even made it clear to Hus that "should any heretic steadfastly refuse to recant his errors, he, Sigismund, would be the first to condemn him to be burned at the stake," and Hus had protested that this was not his understanding of the purpose of the safe-conduct.

authority only in so far as it was in conformity with the teachings of Scripture. The University of Prague also sponsored the cause of Hussitism, enjoining upon Christians to receive Communion under both species, according to the primitive custom of the Church. The Hussites adopted the chalice as their symbol, whence their name of *Calixtines* or Utraquists. Receiving little or no help from the King, the Catholics were almost helpless in the face of so strong an opposition. The Hussite party was headed by Nicholas of Pistna, John Ziska, and the ex-Premonstratensian, John of Selau. On Sunday, July 30, 1419, John of Selau, followed by enthusiastic partisans, marched in solemn procession through the streets of Prague. When they halted before the Senate Hall, a riot broke out, and the rumor was circulated that someone had thrown a stone at John while he was carrying the chalice. The furious Hussites then forced their way into the building, and, seizing seven of the senators, cast them headlong out of the window on to the pikes of the insurgents beneath. The whole city was thrown into an uproar, and King Wenceslaus was so overcome with indignation and grief that he succumbed to an attack of apoplexy. The advent of the Emperor Sigismund to the throne of Bohemia did not restore peace; he was forced to wage war against the exalted Hussite party, called Taborites, because they had established their headquarters in the city and fortress of Tabor, not far from the place where Hus had spent his exile. Ziska, the leader of the faction and the most famous general of his day, placed himself at the head of fanatical peasants armed with scourges and pikes, gave battle to the feudal armies, and was victorious on every occasion († 1424).

III. Reform of the Church: The Council of Siena. The question of the reform of the Church had been broached in the closing sessions of the Council of Constance, but when the commission appointed to investigate it failed to reach an agreement because of the differences among the nations, it was decided that decrees regarding the general reform of the Church should be issued, but that for the rest the Holy See would endeavor to come to an understanding with each nation by means of concordats. Accordingly, there was a German concordat, signed for a period of five years, an English concordat and a French concordat. The latter was made to include the Italians and the Spanish, but the Parliament of Paris refused to record it. These individual agreements regulated in particular the question of *annates,* appeals to Rome, provisions and indulgences (May and July, 1418). The decree on general reform (1) revoked in principle the cumulation of benefices and the exemptions granted since Gregory XI; (2) forbade to make over to the Apostolic Chamber vacant ecclesiastical benefices; (3) renewed the censures against simony and limited the right to collect tithes to cases of urgent necessity and upon the advice of the cardinals; and (4) formulated certain prescriptions relative to the garb to be worn by clerics.

All of these decisions were but abortive attempts at reform. Before separating, however, the Fathers of Constance issued the decree *"Frequens,"* regulating the periodical convocation of general councils: "Within a period of less than five years after the closing of this present synod, another general council shall be held; then a third within a period of seven years after the closing of the second; after which time general councils shall be convened at regular intervals of ten years" (Oct. 9, 1417). These decisions regarding the periodical convocation of councils seemed to have such force that Pope *Martin V* did not deem it wise to disregard them. Accordingly, he convoked a council at Pavia in April, 1423, which had to be transferred to Siena as the result of an epidemic. The leading ideas of the Council of Constance again became the object of discussion, the French nation proposing that the decrees of general councils be irrevocable and hence enjoy what might be termed a practical infallibility, and also that important decisions be not reached by the Holy See without the approval of the Sacred College. Martin V (1417–1431) was in no mood to capitulate, but, taking advantage of the many differences which had arisen among the delegates of the French nation regarding the election of the presiding officer, adjourned the Council. Before separating, however, the Fathers unanimously agreed to meet in the near future at Basle. The danger was at least deferred for seven years.

Meanwhile the papacy itself took up the matter of reform. For this purpose Martin V instituted a commission, made up exclusively of cardinals, and a thorough investigation conducted by this commission resulted in a papal constitution which enjoined various reforms. The cardinals were required to simplify their way of living, and bishops and abbots constrained to observe the laws of residence. It would not appear, however, that these decisions were strictly enforced, the simple reason being that too many persons would have had to suffer as a consequence. Public opinion seemed to expect very little from measures dictated by the papacy, but fixed its hopes upon a council. Martin V had to resign himself to convoke one, but in designating Cesarini as president, invested him with the right either to transfer or to dissolve the council. Thus the authority of the pope was safeguarded. Unfortunately Martin V was struck with apoplexy a short time afterwards, and died on February 20, 1431.

TEXTS AND DOCUMENTS

CONDEMNED PROPOSITIONS OF JOHN HUS

Of the thirty propositions taken chiefly from the *Tractatus de Ecclesia* of John Hus, the following are the most remarkable:

1. The members of the Church consist wholly of *praedestinati*, or those predestined to everlasting happiness, who can no more cease to be of her fold than the *praesciti*, or those foredoomed to eternal misery, can enter it.

2. There is no head of the Church other than Christ; and to say either that the Church militant has need of a visible head, or that Christ instituted such a head, is to assert what cannot be proved.

3. The papacy owes its origin solely to imperial favor and authority.

4. The claim of the Church to the obedience of her members is a pure invention of priests, and contrary to Holy Scripture.

5. When the conscience of a priest bears witness to his purity of motive and uprightness, he should not be deterred from preaching by papal injunction or frightened by sentence of excommunication.

6. Any one invested with temporal or spiritual authority, when satisfied by the witness of his conscience that he is in mortal sin, in that moment loses all power and jurisdiction over Christian people, and must lay down his office.

7. Holy Scripture is the sole source and rule of Christian faith.

QUESTIONS

1. What was the character of the decrees of the Council of Constance?
2. Who were the Utraquists?
3. Who were the Taborites?
4. Is the authority of the pope inferior to that of a general council?

BIBLIOGRAPHY

Council of Constance.—Sources: H. FINKE, *Acta Concilii Constanciensis*, Vol. I. *Akten zur Vorgeschichte des Konstanzer Konzils* (1410–1414), Münster, 1896; Vol. II, *Konzilstagebücher, Sermones, Reform und Verfassungsakten*, 1923.—RICHENTHAL (Ulrich von), *Chronik des Konzils*, edit.

Buck, 1882.—Works: Besides the works on the Great Schism, particularly Salembier, see Creighton, *History of the Papacy during the Period of the Reformation*, t. I; *The Great Schism, the Council of Constance*, London, 1882, —F. Rocquain, *La Cour de Rome et l'esprit de réforme avant Luther*, t. III, 1897.—Marmor, *Das Concilium in Konstanz*, Constance, 1898.—P. Bliemetz-rieder, *Das General-Konzil im grossen abendländischen Schisma*, 1904.—E. J. Kitts, *In the Days of the Councils*, 1908.—H. Finke, *Forschungen und Quellen zur Geschichte des Constanzer Konzils*, 1889.—A. Baudrillart, art. *"Constance,"* in *Dict. de Théol.*—E. Amann, art. *"Martin V,"* in *Dict. de Théol.*

CHAPTER V

I. The Question of Dissolution: Triumph of the Council.
The newly elected Sovereign Pontiff, *Eugene IV,* was a canon regular of St. George in Alga and a very energetic and austere man. At the time the council was to meet unforeseen obstacles suddenly arose, chief among which was the Austro-Burgundian war, which rendered the city of Basle difficult of access. As a consequence, only fourteen bishops and abbots were present at the first session, held July 2, 1431, and so Eugene IV decided to adjourn the council. At the same time he announced the convocation of a complementary synod to be held within the next eighteen months to discuss the eastern question (Bulls of Nov. 12, 1431). When the papal Bulls arrived at Basle, the assembly had already convened, Cesarini having presided at a solemn session, December 14. The Fathers resolved to resist the Pope's orders, in virtue of the decree of Constance: "The Council, lawfully convened in the Holy Ghost, declares that it may not be dissolved or transferred by any one, not even the pope, without the consent of the Council itself." The assembly sensed that it had the general approbation of the Catholic world, despite the fact that it still reckoned only a few scattered representatives, and the Emperor Sigismund wrote, saying: "Courage, we are with you even until death." Soon afterwards a few cardinals arrived at Basle, including Capranica, Louis Aleman, John de Rochetaillée, etc.; Cesarini himself adopted the creed of Constance, which he sought to impose upon the Pope. The Council held that its authority was supreme. In the third session the Fathers summoned the Pope to withdraw his Bull dissolving it, and to appear at Basle in person within the space of six months, "otherwise they themselves would provide for the needs of the Church."

Pope Eugene IV realized that it was necessary for him to negotiate, and despatched to Basle an embassy headed by John Berardi de Tagliacozzo, Archbishop of Tarento. The papal nuncio expounded the traditional thesis in straightforward language, stressing the fact that "even if the whole world thought differently than the Pope, the latter would still be in the right." Pope Eugene showed himself favorable to a reconciliation with the Fathers of Basle, authorizing them to solve the Hussite problem then and there, until the Council could be transferred to an Italian city, with which it would be easier for him to communicate. There is no doubt that these conditions would have proved acceptable, if the quarrel had been nothing more than a misunderstanding. Unfortunately, the trouble was more deep-rooted and essentially doctrinal in character. The Fathers, indeed, were bent on establishing as a dogma the supremacy of an ecumenical council in matters of faith and morals. "Let no one," they averred, "presume to think that a council lawfully convoked is subject to error. For if an admission of that kind were made, the whole Catholic faith would be shaken to its foundations, and nothing would be certain in the Church." A logical consequence of the infallibility of councils was that the pope was subordinated to the Council of Basle and all measures adopted by Eugene IV were adjudged illegal.

Feeble and sick, besieged by the Italian princes and abandoned by his own adherents, the Pope finally yielded. In his Bull *"Dudum sacrum,"* issued December 15, 1433, he revoked his former decree: "Since many grave misunderstandings have arisen as a result of our previous decree of dissolution, and lest these misunderstandings be further aggravated, we hereby decree that the General Council of Basle was lawfully convoked from the beginning, and revoke whatever we may have done to injure it." The Pope then approved the three ends for which the Council had convened: the extirpation of heresies, the restoration of peace to Christendom, and the reform of the Church, but made no mention of his approval of the theory of the supremacy of councils in matters of faith and morals. The Council was transformed into an ecclesiastical Babel, in which doctors, licentiates, simple bachelors, canons, religious and mendicant friars mingled indiscriminately: a heterogeneous multitude in which the vote of a simple cleric was equal to that of a bishop. It was not long before anarchy reigned supreme, and freedom was completely banished. All sorts of causes were introduced at Basle, the assembly being transformed into a sort of court of appeal, in which the Roman decrees were revised. Very soon it had its own curia: chancery, chamber, rota, and penitentiary. Then it set out to mimic Rome by levying taxes;

some bishops collecting from their lands subsidies, which they termed "caritative." In 1434, a demi-tithe was imposed on all Christendom, and later on the "quint denier" or one-fifth of the revenues of benefices. And yet, in the twentieth session (June 9, 1435), the Council voted the suppression of the *annates,* the principal source of revenue of the Holy See. Meanwhile new developments in the political situation furnished the Fathers with additional opportunities to voice their anti-papal sentiments. The Roman revolution sponsored the cause of the Visconti; Pope Eugene was held a prisoner in Rome, and after making his escape, was forced to withdraw to Florence. The Visconti then let it be known that he had acted in accordance with an order issued by the Council, and when the Emperor Sigismund begged the assembly to deny his statement, it refused to do so. Soon ambassadors from the Roman Republic appeared before the Fathers to institute proceedings against the Pope, stating that they had withdrawn from his obedience and were willing to place themselves under the jurisdiction of the Council. The Fathers listened to their plea without expressing the slightest indignation.

II. The Greek Question: Triumph of Eugene IV. Constantly threatened by the Turks, the Orientals had expressed themselves as willing to reach an understanding with Rome in a council. Their suggestion was that the assembly convene either at Byzantium or in a city of Italy in order to reduce the expenses. They even intimated that the best place would be St. Sophia. The Pope despatched Christopher Garatoni to Constantinople to discuss the project, and the plan was adopted. The Council of Basle, however, made it clear that it would favor as a meeting place only a city of the West. In vain did the Greeks endeavor to explain to the Fathers at Basle that the Pope's plan was the more practical; they had a feeling that their supremacy was at stake, and so held firm. To defray the enormous expenses of transportation, they placed a number of indulgences on sale, and when Pope Eugene IV refused to side with their scheme, they completely ignored him. Soon they became even more exorbitant in their demands. The Greeks had insisted that the town selected be somewhere along the Italian coast, to facilitate communications with the Orient. Fearful lest the influence of the papacy should become preponderant, the Fathers of Basle refused their approval, limiting the choice to either Basle, Avignon or a city in Savoy. At this juncture a schism broke out among the members of the Council—the majority subscribing to the views of Cardinal Louis Aleman, the minority, headed by Cesarini, acquiescing in the demands of the Greeks. In the twenty-fifth session, held May 7, 1437, each party tried to impose its decision. The decree of the minority was the only sensible one, and hence Eugene IV approved it, and by the Bull *"Doctoris Gentium,"* of September 18, 1437, transferred the council from Basle to Ferrara.

His action was the signal for a declaration of war. Already the Fathers of Basle had drawn up a long list of accusations against Eugene IV, including simony, nepotism, maladministration, and political abuses. He was given sixty days to justify himself (July 31, 1437), and after that time had elapsed, was declared contumacious (October 1). Cesarini attempted in vain to appease the infuriated assembly and quit the city of Basle, January 9, 1438. At this juncture several princes raised their voices in protest, including the Duke of Bavaria and the King of England. In France, at the request of Charles VII, the assembly of bishops retained twenty-three of the decrees of Basle, which later constituted the famous Pragmatic Sanction (July, 1438), but begged the King to intervene between the Fathers of Basle and those of Ferrara. In like manner, after first declaring himself neutral (March, 1438), Emperor Albert II convoked a diet at Mayence, which, while accepting several decrees of the Council, objected to its proceedings against Eugene IV, whose principal defenders were Nicholas of Cusa and the Spanish Dominican, Juan de Torquemada (March, 1439). Under the direction of Cardinal Louis Aleman, the Fathers of Basle continued the fight, and on May 16, 1439, adopted these three articles: (1) It is a truth of the Catholic faith that the holy general council has power over the pope and over all men; (2) it is also a truth of the Catholic faith that a general council, lawfully convoked, may not be dissolved, transferred, or protracted by the Roman Pontiff without its consent; (3) whoever shows himself obstinately opposed to these truths, must be declared a heretic.

As a consequence of these three articles, Eugene IV was declared a relapsed heretic and deposed, June 25, 1439. It must be observed that the decree of deposition was signed by three hundred clerics, only thirty-nine of whom wore the mitre. A few months later, an electoral college of thirty-two clergymen, chosen from among the members of the Council, elected a new pope in the person of Duke Amadeus VIII of Savoy, who was a widower and the father of a family, and had withdrawn to live in peace on his estate on the shores of Lake Geneva. Amadeus took the name of *Felix V,* and on June 24, 1440, made his solemn entrance into the city of Basle. He was recognized by his own hereditary States, by the kings of Aragon and Hungary, and by several German princes; but in agreement with a new assembly of the clergy, held at Bourges, September 2, 1440, Charles VII declared himself in favor of Eugene IV, at the same time expressing the wish that some future ecumenical council would restore peace to the Church. Felix V was soon drawn into a quarrel with the Fathers of Basle, who sought to impose their views upon him, and withdrew to Lausanne, while Eugene IV re-entered Rome. The Council of Basle ended in complete derision.

III. **The Hussite Question.** The only service which the Council of Basle rendered to the Church was in connection with the Hussites (1433). The representatives of this party demanded complete freedom in preaching, the prohibition of temporal goods by clerics, and Communion under both species. A mitigated Hussite party finally reached an understanding with the conciliar delegates who had come to Prague to discuss these matters, and Communion under both species was tolerated for Bohemia and Hungary (1433). These decisions were ratified at Iglau by the Emperor Sigismund, the delegates of the Council, and the plenipotentiaries of Basle, and went by the name of the *Treaty of Iglau.* The harmony thus re-established increased the power of mitigated Hussitism, which at the battle of Lipan (1434) completely crushed the Taborites, led by Procopius the Great. The Catholics of Bohemia were then divided into Calixtines (or Utraquists) and Subinists. The treaty of Iglau, however, was nothing more than a subterfuge for heretics, and hence was suppressed by Pope Pius II, who declared that the Council of Basle and the Emperor Sigismund had made the grants under pressure. A bitter conflict ensued between the Subinists and the Utraquists, fomented by George Podiebrad, King of Bohemia, but the preaching of St. John Capistran, from 1451 to 1452, and the advent of Ladislaus II to the throne of Bohemia, in 1472, finally put an end to Utraquism. The exalted Hussites or Taborites still remained. At first they were supported by the influence of Kokyzana, Archbishop of Prague, and the assistance of George Podiebrad, who had made over to them his manor at Licz. It was thither they withdrew in large numbers and assumed the name of *Bohemian Brethren.* Shortly afterwards, however, the Pope accused them of heresy, and Podiebrad was obliged to expel them from his kingdom. They then withdrew into the forests and mountains, and without abandoning hope, allied themselves with some of the Waldenses, who had settled on the Austro-Moravian border and boasted of validly ordained bishops descended in direct line from the Apostles. It was with the assistance of these Waldenses that the Bohemian Brethren secured a hierarchy. Later on they joined hands with Martin Luther and then lapsed into Calvinism.

TEXTS AND DOCUMENTS

POPES VERSUS COUNCILS

As for the conventicle that gathered at Basle in 1431, it was too often a mere mob: and what a singular and too often scandalous spectacle it presented to the world is well known. It dared to set the Lord of Ripaille, the anti-pope Felix V, against the true Pope Eugenius IV. Eugenius in turn summoned the synod of Ferrara to cope with that of Basle. There were not only two Popes, but two councils; and one might have imagined that things had reverted to the worst days of the Schism.

These excesses, which were as ridiculous as they were scandalous, did not, however, fail to have one result. They discredited the decree *Frequens*, which ceased to be applied, and they put at the same time an obstacle in the way of the periodical reunion of general councils, which could never be one of the ordinary means of government.

On the other hand, these deviations did not hinder further rebels from appealing to a later council against the Roman Pontiff. When a prince like Louis XI or Louis XIV desires to usurp the right of the Church, when bishops like those of 1682, such as Febronius and Gregoire, mean to shake off the papal yoke, when rebellious innovators put forth daring and incendiary propositions, when a doctor such as Döllinger refuses to believe in papal infallibility, all, despite the repeated vetoes of the Supreme Pontiffs, appeal to a future council as to a jurisdiction superior to that of the Pope.

SALEMBIER, *The Great Schism of the West*, pp. 381–382.

QUESTIONS

1. On what grounds did the Fathers of the Council of Basle claim supremacy for councils in matters of faith and morals?
2. May the action of Pope Eugene IV, and especially his Bull *"Dudum sacrum,"* be interpreted as approving their stand?

3. What were some of the direct consequences of this Bull?
4. What was the ultimate fate of the Council of Basle?

BIBLIOGRAPHY

The Council of Basle.—Sources: *Concilium Basiliense*, 7 vols., 1896–1910.—Works: CREIGHTON, *A History of the Papacy*, t. II. *The Council of Basel, the Papal Restoration* (1418–1464), London, 1882.—ROCQUAIN, *op. cit.*, t. III.—PASTOR, *History of the Popes*, I.—NOEL VALOIS, *La crise religieuse du XVᵉ siècle. Le pape et le concile* (1418–1450), 2 vols., 1909.—G. PÉROUSE, *Le cardinal Louis Aleman*, 1904.—M. BOULTING, *Aeneas Sylvius*, 1908.—E. VANSTENBERGHE, *Nicolas de Cues*, 1920.—A. BAUDRILLART, art. *"Bâle,"* in *Dict. de Théol.*—G. MOLLAT, art. *"Aleman,"* in *Dict. d'Hist.*—BRUCHET, *Le château de Ripaille*.

CHAPTER VI

I. The Pragmatic Sanction of Bourges. At the Council of Basle the "French nation" had shown itself more implacably opposed to the Roman Curia than any other group, although in all justice it must be said that this opposition was inspired rather by financial motives than by schismatic tendencies. Not wishing either to reject or accept *in globo* the decrees of the Council, Charles VII convoked an assembly of the clergy at Bourges, at which papal nuncios and delegates from Basle assisted (May 1, 1438). The assembly was forced to yield to the current ideas and acknowledged the supremacy of ecumenical councils in accordance with the teachings of Constance. Its chief concern, however, was with the collation of benefices which the Pope could no longer claim as his. Reservations, expectative graces, and annates were all suppressed, and instead it was decided that bishops and abbots should be elected by the Chapters and convents, as in the Middle Ages. The following amendment, however, was added: "The assembly sees nothing harmful in kings and princes intervening in elections by their pious prayers." From that moment on, the so-called free election of a candidate depended more on the king's attitude towards his candidacy. In nominating Jouvenel des Ursins to the see of Rheims, for instance, Charles VII wrote no less than four letters to the Chapter, and even went so far as to confiscate the temporal goods of bishops who refused to confer benefices upon the persons of his choice. Pius II stated the matter correctly when he declared in his Commentaries that the Pragmatic Sanction reduced bishops to the level of "slaves of the laity." Finally—and this offence was by far the most outrageous—the Pragmatic Sanction of Bourges, which was directed against Rome, was concluded without its consent. It was even decreed that "the work of Bourges should under no pretext be subject to the consent of the Pope." In the light of these facts it is easy to see how a reaction was inevitable. The new assembly of the clergy, which convened at Bourges in 1452, had its misgivings regarding the lawfulness of such an action, and to authenticate it, the legists produced an alleged Pragmatic Sanction by St. Louis, directed against the exactions of the Roman Curia, and in almost complete conformity with that of 1438. In 1461, Louis XI refused to acknowledge the Pragmatic Sanction, being manifestly prompted by the desire to obtain more ecclesiastical nominations and to deprive the lay patrons and the Chapters of their rights in the matter. In 1472, an agreement was reached between the papacy and the king to the effect that the Holy See would take into consideration the recommendations made by him. This was another step in the direction of the concordat of 1516, but in the eyes of the civil magistrates the Pragmatic Sanction remained the real Magna Charta of Gallican liberties.

II. German Concordats. The relations between Germany and the Holy See were also governed by concordats. The Emperor Albert II had at first adopted a neutral attitude towards the Council of Basle (March, 1438), but later on, following in the footsteps of Charles VII, he convoked a diet at Mayence, which abided by the decrees of the Council (March, 1439). When Eugene IV scored a complete victory in 1446, he deposed the archbishops of Treves and Cologne, who had sponsored the cause of the anti-pope, Felix V. At first the German princes protested his action at Frankfort on the Main, but later on, thanks to the shrewd methods of Aeneas Sylvius, secretary of the chancery of Frederic III, they reached an agreement, termed the *Concordat of the Princes*. The principal clauses subscribed to by Eugene IV pertained to the freedom of elections, the limitation of appeals to Rome, and the acknowledgement of the decrees of Constance regarding the supremacy of general councils. In the matter of the decrees of the Council of Constance, however, Eugene IV appended his name with the restriction, "as my predecessors have done." Moreover, in a secret Bull (*Bulla salvatoria*) he retracted in advance any concession "that would be detrimental to the Roman See." His successor, Nicholas V, showed himself disposed for a reconciliation, and the diet of Aschaffenburg (July, 1447) negotiated with him a new concordat, termed the *Concordat of Vienna* (February 17, 1448). In its broad outline this concordat upheld that of Eugene IV, stressing above all the matter of free elections. The Pope, however, was acknowledged to possess the right to nominate directly to benefices *apud sedem apostolicam vacantia*, as well as to the ordinary benefices of collegiate and cathedral churches, if they happened to become vacant during odd months. Moreover, in the event of a contested election, the Pope could intervene and impose a better candidate. The annates were suppressed and replaced by a reasonable tax, to be levied every two years. This concordat was not without its inconveniences. Insufficient acquaintance with the persons involved and situations of a local character exposed the pope to many serious mistakes in the selections he was called upon to make, but an even more serious evil were the ambitious claims of the German nobility. These two defects, coupled with the lack of anything like a priestly education among the German clergy, explain why sixty years later hundreds of titulars to benefices severed their relations with the Church and passed over into the camp of Martin Luther. It must be conceded, however, that this concordat made for a better understanding between the empire and the papacy.

III. The Administration of the Roman Church. Owing to the necessity of daily contact with the highly organized administration of the several nations, the papacy was compelled to equip its own administration in the most up-to-date fashion. The centralization effected in the course of the fourteenth and fifteenth centuries strengthened the papal administration, beginning with the sojourn of the popes at Avignon. At that time there were three principal institutions: the chancery, the Apostolic chamber, and the penitentiary. (1) The chancery comprised different bureaus, whose principal business it was to despatch papal letters. At its head was the vice-chancellor, and under him were several colleges of scribes, the most important of which was that of the abbreviators who outlined the papal Bulls, and in the fourteenth century were recruited from among the humanists. (2) The Apostolic chamber comprised the sum-total of the bureaus in charge of financial matters. At its head was the cardinal camerlengo, who was a real minister of finance. Under his direction, the Apostolic collectors gathered in all the taxes throughout Christendom, not only those imposed upon beneficiaries, but also the tithes and indulgences. Quite frequently their functions were also political and diplomatic in character. The cardinal camerlengo was the principal advisor of the pope, and subject to his orders secretaries transacted all political correspondence and drafted secret letters. (3) The penitentiary handled all matters pertaining to the withdrawal of ecclesiastical censures (excommunication, suspension, and interdict), the removal of irregularities preventing persons from exercising the sacred functions, and, finally, marriage dispensations, absolution from reserved cases, and indulgences. It was the intention of Pope Eugene IV to make the penitentiary, which he had completely re-organized, the instrument of his projected reforms. All these papal officials taken together constituted a veritable ecclesiastical class, termed the *curiales,* many of whom were married. Their presence in Rome transformed the city into a cosmopolitan metropolis. Because of the excessive solicitude for temporal matters on the part of the officials, the curia quickly degenerated into a more or less worldly institution, and the different officials themselves quite frequently upheld the Sacred College in its ambitious designs.

TEXTS AND DOCUMENTS

The Rehabilitation of Joan of Arc

By her victories at Orleans and de Patay, the Shepherdess of Domremy had saved France from the Anglo-Burgundian danger and caused Charles VII to be crowned king at Rheims. Seized later on at Compiègne, she had been condemned to be burned at the stake in consequence of the duplicity of the vice-inquisitor of France, Jean de Maistre (1431). Twenty years elapsed before the acts of her trial were re-examined, the first official investigation taking place in 1450, a complete report of which was sent to Pope Nicholas V. One year later, when the Pope despatched Cardinal d'Estouteville as legate to France, for the purpose of obtaining the withdrawal of the Pragmatic Sanction and the participation of the kingdom in the Crusade, the latter endeavoured to gain the King's favor by again broaching the question of the rehabilitation of the French heroine. D'Estouteville opened an investigation, in which he enlisted the services of the inquisitor general in France, the Dominican, Jean Brehal. The latter questioned the witnesses, and basing his evidence on the reports of two trustworthy lawyers, Paul Fontanus and Theodore de Lellis, composed a *Summarium,* or a sort of résumé of the leading accusations formulated by the judges of Rouen. With the aid of these data another report was drawn up and sent to Rome in the name of the mother and the brothers of Joan. The new Pope, Callixtus III, accepted the petition and appointed three commissioners to render a final decision: Jean Juvenal des Ursins, Bishop of Rheims, William Chartier, Bishop of Paris, and Olivier, Bishop of Coutances. To these three was added the inquisitor Jean Brehal. A new investigation was conducted, and Joan was solemnly rehabilitated at Rouen, July 7, 1456. The conclusions of Jean Brehal served as the principal basis for the decree of beatification issued many years later by Pope Pius X.

QUESTIONS

1. What is meant by "Expectative Graces"?
2. What was the purpose of the Pragmatic Sanction of Bourges?
3. When were concordats first instituted?
4. What was the common characteristic of all concordats with Germany?
5. List the different functions of the chancery, the Apostolic chamber, and the penitentiary.

BIBLIOGRAPHY

The Pragmatic Sanction and the Concordats.—Noel Valois, *Histoire de la Pragmatique Sanction de Bourges sous Charles VII*, 1906.—J. Combet, *Louis XI et le Saint Siège*, 1903.—R. Rey, *Louis XI et les Etats pontificaux de France au XVe siècle*, 1899.—De Beaucourt, *Charles VII et la pacification de l'Eglise*, in *Rev. quest. hist.*, 1888 (XLIII), pp. 390–419.—J. Salvini, *L'application de la Pragmatique Sanction sous Charles VII et Louis XI au chapitre cathédral de Paris*, in *Rev. d'Hist. de l'Eglise de France*, 1902 (III), pp. 121–48, 276–96, 421–31, 550–63.

Joan of Arc.—Petit de Julleville, *Jeanne d'Arc* (Coll. *"Les Saints"*), 1900.—R. P. Ayroles, *La vraie Jeanne d'Arc*, 1893–98.—Dunand, *Histoire complète de Jeanne d'Arc*, 3 vols., 1902; *Etudes critiques sur l'histoire de Jeanne d'Arc*, 3 vols., 1904–09.—G. Hanotaux, *J. d'Arc*, 1912.—U. Chevalier, *L'abjuration de J. d'Arc au cimetière de Rouen*, 1902.—Msgr. Touchet, *J. d'Arc*, 2 vols., 1921.—A. Lang, *The Maid of France*, New York, 1908.—For the sources, consult Quicherat, *Procès de condamnation et de réhabilitation de Jeanne d'Arc*, 5 vols., 1841–49.—Champion, *Le procès de J. d'Arc*, 2 vols., 1923.—M. R. Bangs, *Jeanne d'Arc, the Maid of France*, Boston, 1910.— F. C. Lowell, *Joan of Arc*.—D. Lynch, *St. Joan of Arc*.—Petit de Julleville, *St. Joan of Arc*, 3rd edit., London, 1923.—Ronnseil-Murphy, *St. Joan of Arc*, New York, 1925.—A. B. Paine, *Joan of Arc, Maid of France*, 1925.—H. Belloc, *Joan of Arc*.—M. Monahan, *My Jeanne d'Arc*, 1928.—See also, *For Joan of Arc: An Act of Homage from Nine Members of the French Academy*, Paris, 1930.

SECOND PERIOD

The Beginnings of the Renaissance
(1438–1517)

CHAPTER I

THE EASTERN QUESTION

I. The Turkish Menace and the Council of Florence. As early as the fourteenth century a new enemy threatened the orthodox East in the person of the Osmanli Turks. They had emerged from the ruins of the empire of the Seljuks, which had crumbled in 1294, and had established their headquarters in Asia Minor. Osman I gained possession of Brusa (1326) and later on his son Orkhan seized Nicomedia, Nicaea, and Gallipoli. It was not long before the Turks settled on the outskirts of Europe. In 1360, Amurath I captured Adrianople, and at the famous battle of Kossovo triumphed over all the Balkan States. Constantinople was thus encompassed on all sides, and the Byzantines, well aware of the danger which threatened them, appealed to Rome for assistance. Andronic III had already despatched the monk Barlaam to Pope Benedict XIII, to negotiate for the reunion of the two churches (1339), and the intervention of Clement VI resulted in the formation of a naval league between the Venetians and the Latins of the Orient, the capture of Smyrna (1344), and the victory of Imbros (1347). These successful attempts to ward off the danger, however, were transient, and so, when the Emperor John V was threatened by this new enemy, he journeyed to Rome in person and abjured the schism at the feet of Urban V, despite the fact that his people refused to follow him.

The West was finally aroused by the danger which once again threatened the whole of Christendom. Twelve thousand French soldiers, who comprised the élite of the nobility, and had at their head the Count of Nevers, joined with the Hungarians under King Sigismund, crossed the Danube, and invested Nicopolis, where they sustained a disastrous defeat, which was as much the result of their own foolhardiness as of the disciplinary maneuvers of the Turkish janissaries (1396). It was on this occasion that Philip de Mézières, who had dreamed all his life of establishing a military Order of knights for the conquest of the holy places, wrote his *Epistle of Laments*. The marshal Boucicaut (1366–1421) undertook several expeditions against the Turks, all of which were abortive, and everything would have been lost, had not a new Asiatic invasion been undertaken by the Mongols, who, sweeping down upon Asia Minor, completely routed Sultan Bajazet I at the battle of Angora (1402). But the victory of the Mongols was not followed by any lasting political change able to hold the Turks in check. After ten years of anarchy, the power of the Turks was again restored, first by Mohammed I, and then by his son Amurat II, who set out to extend their territorial conquests.

In the face of such imminent danger, several plans were outlined by John VIII Palaeologus, and presented successively to Martin V and Eugene IV. A nationalist party was formed at Byzantium, which suggested the convocation of a council to bring about a reunion of the Churches. The most opportune time to transfer the meeting-place to Bologna was when the first bitter conflicts broke out between the Pope and the Council of Basle, but the Fathers of the Council showed themselves steadfastly opposed to any such plan. Pope Eugene IV did not desist, however, but continued to negotiate with the Emperor. The city of Ancona was suggested, but it was pointed out that the transfer would involve much expense, and no understanding was reached. In view of all this, the most suitable place to hold the council seemed to be, as we have already indicated, St. Sophia in Constantinople. Christopher Garatoni, who had been despatched by the Pope to Constantinople to discuss the project, finally succeeded in having this plan adopted. In vain did the Greeks endeavor to explain to the Fathers that the Pope's plan was the more practical of the two; the Fathers of the Council had a feeling that the question of their supremacy was at stake, and so held firm. Very soon they became even more exorbitant in their demands. The Greeks, indeed, had insisted that the town selected be situated somewhere along the Italian coast, to facilitate communications with the Orient. Fearful lest the influence of the papacy should become preponderant, the Fathers signified their refusal, limiting the choice to Basle or Avignon or a city in Savoy.

We have already seen how, siding with a wise minority, Eugene IV ignored them and transferred the council to Ferrara, where the Greeks soon arrived.

While it may be true that the "Basileus" and the Byzantine patriots were eager to reach a settlement, it is equally certain that a few rebels were bent on making trouble. Their war-cry was the *"Filioque,"* and while refusing to enter into any theological discussion, they declared that it was forbidden to add a single word to the Creed, even to combat heresy. A break seemed imminent, when the Emperor resolved to ignore that issue and broach the basic dogmatic problem, namely, the procession of the Holy Ghost. The desire to reach an understanding, and the pressure brought to bear by the Emperor, explain the increasing influence enjoyed by the unionists. Moreover, it was decided that no further discussions should be held in public, but only by commissions, the delegates of which should be selected from among the unionists. These drastic decisions were reached at Florence, whither the council had been forced to adjourn because of a plague that had broken out at Ferrara. The discussion was led by Archbishop *Bessarion,* and was limited principally to matters of positive theology. The mooted question was which one of the two views was supported by the writings of the ancient Fathers. As favoring the insertion of the *"Filioque,"* the Latins cited two passages from St. Epiphanius and one from St. Basil; those opposed to this view had no difficulty in adducing passages from the writings of the Greek Fathers, in which it was asserted that the Paraclete proceeds from the Father, but were at a loss to find any in which it was denied that He also proceeds from the Son. It was an easy matter, however, for the subtle mind of the Greeks to find a way out of this difficulty, and they did so by refusing to acknowledge the authenticity of the citations adduced by the Latins. Setting aside, therefore, all patristic arguments, John of Ragusio shifted the controversy to the field of dogma. He asserted that the Roman Church acknowledged only one cause, and not two causes, of the procession of the Holy Ghost, the Son receiving from the Father two distinct things, to wit, His being and His power to produce the Holy Spirit. As may be seen, the position taken by John of Ragusio was no different from that taken by the Greeks. Finally, John Scholarios delivered a series of discourses which stressed the political necessity of a union, in view of the fact that the Turkish danger was becoming more and more threatening each day. It was pointed out, moreover, that the Pope had formally promised assistance to the Emperor.

An understanding was finally reached on the three questions at issue: that of purgatory, that of the leavened bread, and that of the primacy of the Bishop of Rome, and a decree of union was drafted, in which the *"Filioque"* and the primacy of the Pope were both acknowledged. On July 5, 1439, in the Cathedral of Florence, this decree was solemnly read by Cesarini in Latin and by Bessarion in Greek. Then all the Greeks, with the Emperor at their head, genuflected before the Pope, and kissed his hand. The Council completed its work of unification during the years which followed, by effecting the reconciliation of the Armenians (1439), the Jacobites (1442), the Monophysites of Mesopotamia (1444), the Nestorians of Chaldea and the Maronites of the Island of Cyprus (1444-1445). As a direct result, the prestige of the Holy See was greatly increased.

II. Failure of the Crusade and Capture of Constantinople. The majority of the Greeks had consented to unite with Rome only by force of necessity and with the hope of obtaining assistance. But the Crusade received help only from a tax levied by Pope Eugene IV on the lands of bishops, and as a consequence was forced to limit its assistance to countries directly threatened by the Turkish invasion. It was doomed to failure despite the heroism of King Ladislaus of Hungary, Scanderbeg, prince of Albania, and John Hunyadi, the "White Knight of Wallachia." The latter scored a brilliant victory over the Turks at Hermanstad (1439) and, pressing forward into Servia, defeated Sultan Murad II at Nissa. The Turks were then constrained to sign the treaty of Szegeddin, which restored to Hungary her supremacy over the Wallachians and the Serbs. Encouraged by these early victories, the Christians again took the offensive. Hunyadi invaded Bulgaria, but his army was defeated by forces three times as large as his at Varna, where the legate Cesarini met his death (1444). A second attempt on the part of Hunyadi to raise the blockade of Constantinople issued in the second defeat of Kossovo (1448), in which a Christian army of 17,000 men was completely wiped out after massacring 40,000 Ottomans.

The failure of the Crusade to achieve its purpose eliminated the political reasons which had induced the Greeks to acquiesce in the decree of union, and so the bishops withdrew their signatures. Fully aware of the danger, the new Emperor, Constantine XII Dragases, still hoped for an alliance with the Latins, and accordingly begged Pope *Nicholas V* to despatch theologians to his court, capable of persuading the Byzantine clergy. The Pope entrusted this mission to Cardinal Isidore, the former metropolitan of Kiev, and on December 12, 1452, the Henoticon (union) was solemnly proclaimed at St. Sophia in the presence of the Basileus and the papal legate. The hostility of the people, however, had in nowise abated and the phrase, "Rather the turban than the tiara," was the reply to every advance made by the Latins. Their prayer was soon answered, for after a siege of two months, Mohammed took Constantinople by assault, May 29, 1453. The débris of the Empire, including Athens, Lesbos, and Trebizond, quickly fell into the hands of this new conqueror. Pope Nicholas V appealed in vain to the western princes for help. The only echo to his prayer was voiced in 1454 at Lille, in the course of a gorgeous banquet, when a solemn vow called *"The Vow of the Pheasant,"* was taken by Philip the Good, Duke of Burgundy, the motive of which was nothing short of the complete extermination of the Turks. One hundred fifty knights, the flower of the nobility, repeated the vow after him, but the enterprise came to naught.

III. The Papacy and the Crusade after 1453. Henceforth the Turks infested all the countries bordering on the Mediterranean, and constantly threatened Europe. The papacy alone fully realized the seriousness of the situation. *Callixtus III* (1455–1458), the successor of Nicholas V, took an oath to sacrifice all the treasures of the Church, and even his own life, in order to keep the Turks in check. His efforts to combine the forces of the West proved of no avail, for Frederic III of Germany, Charles VII of France, and the Pope's own Italian subjects turned a deaf ear to his entreaties. At that time Mohammed II threatened to invade Europe by the three ways open to him: that of Hungary, which would enable him to penetrate into the very heart of Europe; that of Albania, which would give him access to northern Italy by skirting the coastline of Dalmatia; and, finally, that of the sea, which would pave his way to southern Italy, and Rome itself. At all three points, however, he encountered formidable adversaries. While he was besieging Belgrade, the gateway to Hungary, John Hunyadi succeeded in gaining admission to the city by following the course of the river Danube, and repelled the attack of the Sultan, who was wounded and forced to withdraw (1456).

In Albania, Scanderbeg took an invading army of Turks by surprise at Tomornitza, exterminating 30,000 men (July, 1457). As a reward for this signal victory the Pope conferred upon him the title, "General of the Curia for the war against the Turks." All these victories could be traced in part to the influence of Callixtus III, who had financed the Crusaders out of his own personal funds. The Pope now fitted out a fleet, which he entrusted to the legate Scarampo, who scored a brilliant naval victory at Mitylene, in which twenty-five Turkish vessels were captured (1457). Unfortunately, the inertia of the western princes prevented Christendom from reaping the full fruits of these victories. *Pius II* (1458–1464) convoked a congress at Mantua, but his eloquent display of indignation proved of no avail, and Cardinal Bessarion did not meet with any better success on the occasion of his visit to Germany. The city of Venice alone volunteered to proffer assistance, but its motive in doing so was purely utilitarian and commercial. In 1464, Pius II resolved to head an army against the Turks. Accordingly, he set out from Rome to Ancona, where the Venetian fleet awaited him. But the hardships of the journey and the distress at seeing his efforts wasted, hastened his death, which occurred August 14, 1464.

The efforts of *Paul II* (1464–1471) were equally futile. Scanderbeg journeyed to Rome to assist him, but the Italian States refused to advance him any money, and the German diet contented itself with empty promises. Nevertheless, Scanderbeg defended Croia, the key city to Albania and Europe, and held formidable Turkish forces at bay. When the Sultan heard of his death, he is said to have exclaimed: "At last Europe and Asia belong to me! Woe to Christendom! It has lost its sword and its shield!" (January 17, 1468). Soon the capture of Negrepont and Euboea increased the naval power of Mohammed. Rhodes was the only stronghold left in the eastern portion of the Mediterranean, and fortunately the Hospitallers stationed there succeeded in thwarting all the efforts of Mohammed under the leadership of their Grand Master, Peter d'Aubusson (1480). Paul II died as the result of fretting over the problem of the Turks, and his successor, *Sixtus IV* (1471–1484), appealed to all the western nations to sponsor a Crusade, but the labors of his legates, Bessarion in France, Capranica in Italy, and Marco Barbo in Germany and Austria, all came to naught. Nothing could distract the Italians from their own internal dissensions, until the day when the Turks brought the war to their very door by seizing Otranto. This was the signal for a revival of patriotism, and thanks to the bravery of the Italian fleet, Otranto was recaptured. Meanwhile, Mohammed II died, and a conflict arose between his heir, Bajazet, and his brother, Prince Djem. The latter was obliged to withdraw his claims, left the country, and became a valuable hostage in the hands of the Pope, who used him to force the Sultan to negotiate. Believing circumstances favorable, *Innocent VIII* convoked a congress in Rome to debate the question of a great Crusade (1490), but once again the western princes disregarded the plea. In the closing years of the fifteenth century, a Crusade in the eyes of princes was nothing more than a diplomatic argument to be exploited on all occasions (*materia christiana*). If there was question of concealing the true motive of armaments or the real purpose of a conference, it was stated that the purpose was to prepare a Crusade against the Turks. The papacy alone held firmly to the true ideal, and it must be admitted that its efforts were not all in vain. For the Turks were thus held in check at the most critical moments, so much so that the successors of Mohammed II, Bajazet II and Selim I, resolved to turn their forces against Africa and allowed Christian Europe a respite of thirty years.

TEXTS AND DOCUMENTS

EXTRACTS FROM THE DECREE OF UNION

Decree of the Holy Ecumenical Synod of Florence, Eugene, Bishop, Servant of the Servants of God, in perpetual remembrance, with the assent of our beloved son in Christ, John Palaeologus, the Illustrious Emperor of the Romans, and of the delegates of our venerable brethren, the Patriarchs and other representatives of the Greek Church.

Let the heavens rejoice and the earth break forth in songs of gladness. The wall of separation has fallen; the East and the West are not now, as in days past, two Churches, but one Church. Christ has again united them, and they are now bound together by the strong bonds of love and peace. The dreary days of schism are past, and the glorious splendor of a long-desired union brings light and gladness to all mankind. Who that is able now to make a worthy thanksgiving to Almighty God? Truly, this is the work of God, to be celebrated with heavenly song.

We define that all Christians must profess that the Holy Ghost is eternally from the Father and the Son, that He proceeds eternally from the One and the Other as from one principle and one and the same spiration (*spiratio*)

. . . We define, moreover, that the *Filioque* has been lawfully and reasonably inserted in the Creed.

Furthermore, we define that the Holy Apostolic See and the Bishop of Rome enjoy a primacy throughout the whole world; that the Roman Pontiff is the successor of Blessed Peter, Prince of the Apostles; that he is the true Vicar of Christ, the Head of the Universal Church, and of all Christians the Father and Teacher; that to him was given, in Blessed Peter, by our Lord Jesus Christ, the fullness of the power to feed, to rule, and to govern the Universal Church, as is also set forth in the acts of ecumenical councils and in the Sacred Canons.

QUESTIONS

1. What is the true teaching of the Church regarding the procession of the Holy Ghost?
2. Give some details of the life of John Hunyadi.
3. What was the "Vow of the Pheasant"?
4. List the principal causes of the failure of the Crusade against the Turks.

BIBLIOGRAPHY

The Turkish Peril.—GAY, *Le pape Clément VI et les affaires d'Orient (1342–52)*, 1904.—JORGA, *Philippe de Mézières et la croisade au XIVe siècle (Bibl. Ecole Hautes Etudes)*; "*Latins et Grecs d'Orient et l'établissement des Turcs en Europe (1342–62)*" in *Byz. Zeit.*, XV.—DELAVILLE-LEROUX, *La France en Orient au XIVe siècle*, 1885; *Les Hospitaliers en Terre Sainte et à Cypre*, 1904.—L. PETIT, art. "*Manuel II Paléologue*," in *Dict. de Théol.*— C. DAWSON, *The Making of Europe*, 1932.

The Council of Florence and the Crusade.—PIERLING, *La Russie et le Saint-Siège*, I, 1896.—VAST, *Le Cardinal Bessarion*, 1878.—A. VOGT, art. "*Florence*," in *Dict. de Théol.*—E. PEARS, *The Destruction of the Greek Empire*, 1903.—G. SCHLUMBERGER, *Le siège, la prise et le sac de Constantinople par les Turcs en 1453*, 1922.—THUASNE, *Djem-Sultan, fils de Mohammed II (1459–95)*, 1892; *Gentille Bellini et sultan Mohammed*, 1888.—PALMIERI, art. "*Bessarion*," in *Dict. de Théol.*

CHAPTER II

I. Sixtus IV (1471–1484). The papacy was also called upon to defend its rights in Italy, and while it is true that the day after the capture of Constantinople the Italian States signed the Peace of Lodi, subscribed to by Nicholas V and the cities of Venice, Milan, Florence, and Naples, in reality each was concerned only with its own interests. Florence, Naples, and Venice successively threatened the Papal States. Accordingly, for the last popes of the fifteenth century, Sixtus IV, Alexander VI, and Julius II, the Italian question held the first place.

Sixtus IV had been General of the Franciscans, and was a very austere character. Unfortunately, he displayed undue affection for his nephews, the most famous of whom were Girolamo Riario and Giuliano della Rovere, the future Julius II. Girolamo was put in charge of all political questions and, being very ambitious, plunged the papacy into expensive wars. Its great opponent at that time was Lorenzo de Medici, who was constantly engaged in intrigues to prevent an increase of the temporal power of the papacy. On two different occasions the city of Florence, due to his secret plottings, encroached upon the Papal States by taking possession of Imola in the Romagna and Citta di Castello in Umbria. In direct opposition to the pope's plan of organizing an Italian league against the Turks, Florence in 1474 had entered into an alliance with Venice and Milan for the purpose of isolating the papacy. To secure the complete victory of his anti-Roman policies, Lorenzo was willing to adopt any means, including even schism. "If the matter could be arranged without scandal," he is alleged to have said, "I would prefer three or four popes to one pope." To offset the attacks of this formidable opponent, Girolamo Riario did not recoil from the use of violent measures, and allied himself with the Florentine enemies of the Medici, namely, the Pazzi, a family of rich bankers, and with Francesco Salviati, whom Lorenzo was attempting to bar from the episcopal see of Pisa. When informed of the plot,

Sixtus IV volunteered his support, on condition that there should be no bloodshed. The conspirators ignored this clause and plotted an assassination. Taking advantage of the arrival in Florence of another nephew of the Pope, Cardinal Rafaello Sansoni Riario, they attacked Lorenzo as he was leaving the cathedral after solemn High Mass. But the plot failed; Archbishop Salviati and Pazzi were hanged, and the innocent Cardinal Riario was thrown into a dungeon. Sixtus IV blamed the conspirators, and protested against the imprisonment of the Cardinal. Later on, by his Bull *"Iniquitatis filius"* he excommunicated Lorenzo. However, the Florentines paid no attention to the Bull, but vowed their allegiance to Lorenzo as "the martyr of their country." A war ensued, in which the Pope had Naples for his ally. The Florentines were about to sacrifice Lorenzo de Medici, when the whole affair was compromised by the treason of Ferrante, King of Naples, who concluded a separate treaty with Florence (1480).

This gave rise to a second war against Naples. Its direct instigator was none other than Girolamo Riario, who, not content with Imola and a portion of the Romagna, dreamed of dethroning the King of Naples and assuming his place. This second war was a very undiplomatic move, because, to carry it on, an alliance had to be contracted with Venice, and the latter city had to be allowed to undertake the siege of Ferrara, an important stronghold which, situated at the mouth of the river Po, barred the way to the ambitions of the Republic. The papacy was seriously threatened, for Ferrante of Naples advanced as far as Marino, at the foot of the Alban mountains, while the Neapolitan fleet gained possession of Benevento and Terracina. Robert Malatesta, however, saved the situation by the victory of Campo Morto, but died shortly afterwards. Peace was signed, but Venice refused to acquiesce in its terms so long as she was not in possession of Ferrara. At a general congress held in Cremona the Italian powers resolved to ally themselves against her. Venice was on the point of being defeated, when the treason of Ludovico Moro, Duke of Milan, enabled it to win a victory. The Peace of Bagnola made over to the Republic Polesina (a territory situated at the mouth of the river Po), formerly in the possession of the duke of Ferrara, and thus compromised the safety of central Italy. Such was the sad outcome of the ambitions of Girolamo Riario.

The new Pope, *Innocent VIII* (1484–1492), was obliged to contend with the insolence of Ferrante, King of Naples, who had allied himself with his stepson, Mathias Corvin, King of Hungary. Once again the Neopolitans invaded the Papal States and threatened Rome, which was ·saved only by the composure of Cardinal Giuliano della Rovere, who had organized the defence. A treaty was signed, which Ferrante violated almost immediately, so that the Pope was forced to declare that he had forfeited his throne (1489). To bring him to terms, Innocent threatened to have the French intervene, and so Ferrante finally consented to negotiate with him (1492).

II. Alexander VI (1492–1503). Under the pontificate of Alexander VI the French danger loomed on the horizon. Charles VIII was an adventurous prince and, as heir of the house of Anjou, ambitioned the crown of Naples. He was invited to intervene by Ludovico Moro, who had seized the duchy of Milan from his nephew, John Galeas Sforza, husband of the grand-daughter of King Ferrante of Naples. On the other hand, Cardinal Giuliano della Rovere, an enemy of the Borgia Pope, appealed to Charles VIII, urging upon him the question of reform, and advising him to carry it into the very City of Rome, where a simoniacal Pope held sway. He was seconded by all the discontented factions in Rome, with Colonna at their head, who made haste to seize Ostia, the city's port of supply. Finally, the Dominican *Savonarola* of Florence foretold the complete restoration of the Church in Italy with the appearance of a new "Cyrus," who was none other than Charles VIII.

The French expedition resembled a military parade, and after a triumphal entrance into Florence, Charles VIII appeared before the City of Rome, which Alexander VI was unable to defend. But the French King was not at all anxious to depose Alexander, realizing that such action might plunge Christendom into the horrors of another schism. On the other hand, the Pontiff cleverly extricated himself from all difficulties by surrendering as a hostage Prince Djem, who died shortly afterwards, and then his own son, Caesar Borgia, who succeeded in making his escape. Finally, he conferred upon Charles VIII the investiture of the kingdom of Naples, but with the restrictive clause, *sine alterius præjudicio* (provided no one else is harmed), which was the equivalent of no promise at all. Thus he was soon able to form what was known as the *League of Venice,* with the cities of Milan and Venice, the Emperor Maximilian, and the King of Aragon, against the King of France, who had no other alternative but to withdraw in haste across the Alps (July 6, 1495).

Threatened by the turbulent Roman nobility (Orsini and Colonna) during the second part of his reign, and solicitous above all for the welfare of his children, Alexander VI resolved to change his tactics and seek the aid of France. His son, Caesar Borgia, journeyed to the court of Louis XII with a Bull granting the King a dispensation for his marriage with Anne of Brittany and the cardinal's hat for his favorite, George d'Amboise. An agreement was reached, in virtue of which the Pope pledged himself to assist Louis XII in the conquest of Milan, and in return Louis promised to assist the Pope in gaining possession of the Romagna. Due to this alliance, Caesar Borgia reduced the Romagna, with the exception of Bologna, and established a line of fortresses which, extending from Imola to Rimini, commanded the whole valley of the Po. When Louis XII began to ambition the conquest of the kingdom of Naples, Alexander VI again pledged his assistance, provided that, in return, the King would help him to subdue the turbulent Roman barons. Two duchies were created in favor of the Borgia, out of the possessions of the Colonna, the Savelli, and the Gaetani: that of Nepi and that of Sermoneta, which corresponded to the maritime province. Alexander VI, or, to be more exact, his son Caesar Borgia, was now master of central Italy, especially after a plot attempted by the last of the Roman barons grouped around the Orsini had utterly failed. Caesar Borgia drew the leaders of the conspiracy to Sinigaglia, and put them to death. To render his victory complete, he tracked the Orsini into their last two lairs, Cere and Bracciano. The young Borgia was making even more extensive plans, which included the conquest of Tuscany, when Alexander VI died, August 18, 1503. It is to be regretted that this Pope made so flagrant a misuse of his authority and subordinated his office to the interests of his family. It is none the less true that his scheming had the good effect of weakening the turbulent nobility which had for such a long time held the papacy in check.

III. Julius II (1503–1513). Cardinal Piccolomini, who took the name of Pius III, reigned only three weeks. With the assistance of Caesar Borgia, who sold him the Spanish votes, Cardinal Giuliano della Rovere was then elected and took the name of *Julius II*. He at once despatched Caesar into Spain and worked incessantly to regain from the Borgias their cities and castles. It was not long before this warlike Pope regained possession of the two principal cities of the Papal States, Perugia and Bologna, the first of which was under the despotic rule of the Baglioni, and the second under that of the Bentivogli. He then resolved to wage war against the city of Venice, which had begun to meddle in the affairs of the Romagna, stationed garrisons at Faenza, Cesena, and Rimini, occupied Ravenna and Cervia, and threatened Imola and Forlì. Through a series of patient and clever political moves Julius II finally succeeded in concluding the League of Cambrai with the Emperor Maximilian, Louis XII, King of France, and Ferdinand the Catholic. Venice was excommunicated and forced to yield after suffering a defeat at the hands of Louis XII at Agnadello (1509). It had to return to the Pope all usurped territories, and above all the fortified places which guarded the entrance to the Papal States (Ravenna, Faenza, Rimini). But Julius II was fully aware of the advantageous location of the city. Venice was a sort of sentinel, which guarded Christendom from the Turkish menace and protected Italy against German or French invasions. Moreover, the Republic was in constant dread of her former allies, the French, who occupied Upper Italy. The Pope's plan, therefore, was to rid Venice of these barbarians (*Fuori i barbari!*), and for this purpose he entered into an alliance with the Venetians and Ferdinand the Catholic. He was seconded by Matthaeus Schinner, Bishop of Sion, who obtained for him the assistance of 15,000 Swiss soldiers, and then turned his arms against the remaining members of the coalition of Cambrai, Louis II and the Emperor Maximilian.

The Pope's action greatly irritated Louis, who retorted by convoking a French synod at Tours, in which it was decreed that the Sovereign Pontiff had no right to make war on foreign princes and that, should he do so, these princes were at liberty to oppose him and completely disregard his censures. Julius II opened hostilities by forcing Chaumont, who had arrived to lay siege to Bologna, to withdraw his troops. He then occupied Mirandola, but had to withdraw at the approach of Trivulce and Gaston de Foix. Meanwhile a religious offensive was being organized, the cardinals of the French faction upholding Louis XII and the Emperor Maximilian, who appealed their case to a general council. They based their claims upon the decree *"Frequens"* of the Council of Constance, which stipulated that councils should be convoked at regular intervals (May 15, 1511). Completely exhausted by these trials and tribulations, Julius II re-entered Rome and almost succumbed to a serious illness. He recovered, however, and on October 5 of the same year, entered into a fresh coalition, known as the *Holy League,* with Ferdinand the Catholic of Spain, Henry VIII of England, Switzerland, and Venice. Heading the French troops, Gaston de Foix dispersed the Swiss forces, raised the blockade of Bologna, recaptured Brescia from the Venetians, and scored over the Spaniard, Raymond of Cardone, the victory of Ravenna, in which he was killed while pursuing the enemy (April 11, 1512). The French then occupied the whole of the Romagna.

The firm attitude of Julius II saved the situation, and very soon the French were expelled from Italy. The religious offensive also failed, the synod at Pisa, which convened in November, 1511, being attended by only three Italian cardinals and twenty-four French bishops. This synod decreed that a council was superior to the Pope, and Julius II was deposed ten days after the victory of Ravenna at Milan where, tired of the incessant wranglings of the Pisans and the French, the Fathers of the Council had adjourned their meeting (April 21, 1512). As early as May 3, however, the Pope retorted by convoking the *Eighteenth Ecumenical Council* or *Fifth Council of the Lateran*. The General of the Dominicans, Thomas de Vio, better known under the name of Cajetan, proved beyond question that the authority of the Pope was superior to that of a council, and the Fathers annulled the decisions of the schismatic prelates. In the interval between the second and the third sessions, the French troops of La Palice and Trivulce were forced to retreat, and the schismatic prelates had no other alternative but to follow them. Completely victorious, Julius II detached Parma and Modena from the duchy of Milan to protect the papal frontiers. He died February 20, 1513, as he was making preparations to rid the peninsula of the other barbarians—his former allies, the Spaniards. The best way to sum up the career of this warlike Pontiff would be to state that it was one continuous attempt to secularize the papal functions. It is none the less certain that Julius II saved the Papal States. After his death, the popes, despite many reverses of fortune, were always the masters of Rome. "There was a time," wrote Machiavelli, "when the most insignificant baron felt justified in contemning the Pope's authority; to-day that authority commands the respect of a king of France."

IV. Leo X (1513–1521): The Concordat of Bologna. Cardinal John de Medici, son of Lawrence the Magnificent, was elected Pope at the age of thirty-seven and took the name of *Leo X.* Upon learning that Louis XII had negotiated an alliance with Venice at Blois, in March, 1513, he concluded the Counter-League of Malines with the Empire, England, and Spain. Louis XII signed a treaty of peace with Leo X, after La Tremoille had been defeated at Novara by Swiss soldiers hired by the Pope, and finally dissolved the schismatic council, which had taken refuge at Lyons. The accord between the two powers was again compromised, when Francis I, the new king of France, resolved to gain possession of Milan, whereupon Leo X formed a new league with Spain, the Empire, the Swiss, Milan, and Florence. Meanwhile the Swiss forces, commanded by Cardinal Matthaeus Schinner, were defeated by Francis I at Marignan, and Leo X journeyed to Bologna to meet the King. A treaty was signed, the terms of which restored to Francis I Parma and Plaisance, which had been erected into independent principalities for his brother, Julian de Medici.

In the religious domain, Pope Leo X negotiated the *Concordat of Bologna,* which annulled the Pragmatic Sanction. While the latter was nothing more than a sort of civil constitution for the clergy, inspired by the theories of the Council of Basle, the agreement reached at Bologna was a real concordat or a synallagmatic treaty between Leo X and Francis I. The parts to be played by the King and the Pope in the collation of benefices were clearly defined. The elective method was completely suppressed, the king presenting his candidates for bishoprics and archbishoprics, monasteries and priories, which formerly enjoyed the canonical right of election, but the pope remaining free to accept or reject the candidates proposed. In cases where the pope rejected a candidate, a new one was to be proposed within the space of three months. When this period had passed, the pope was free to appoint the subject of his choice. To put the matter briefly, the king had the right of presentation and the pope the right of institution. The papal prerogatives were thus safeguarded, and the principles which had obtained for a century were repudiated. But because the king had an indirect hand in the collation of benefices, he retained his hold on the most tangible portion of the kingdom's fortune. The pope's right to benefices *apud sedem vacantia* (when the see is vacant) was acknowledged, and he also collected the annates and the dispensation fees. This Concordat was rejected by the ancient defenders of Gallicanism—the French Parliament and the University of Paris—and the King was obliged to issue a formal order to Parliament to record the agreement. The University appealed to a general council, but Francis I imposed silence. The Concordat of 1515 is of exceptional importance, because it regulated the relations between Church and State in France during the entire Ancien Régime. Many grievances have been formulated against it, and it must be admitted that the kings were guilty of more than one abuse in nominating candidates. Not infrequently prelates attached to the royal court and commendatory abbots, who were mere laymen, in their insatiable greed for money brought undue pressure to bear upon the monks. It must be observed, however, that these abuses are to be laid not at the door of the Concordat, but at that of the King. Moreover, the right of institution gave the Pope a sort of veto, which proved to be a most efficacious means of safeguarding the Church of France. The papacy owed to this document its victory during the troublesome days of the reign of Louis XIV.

TEXTS AND DOCUMENTS

THE CONCORDAT OF BOLOGNA

Three questions were solved by the Concordat of Bologna, concerning benefices, jurisdiction, and finances.

We are already acquainted with the system of benefices: some were elective, that is, conferred by the free choice of the Chapters; the others were collative, that is, conferred by the bishop or the patron. As for the former, a solution was already prepared by successive compromises, which would result in a system of appointment by the king and canonical institution by Rome. This solution constituted the fourth, fifth, and sixth articles of the Concordat. The king, however, could appoint only candidates meeting the canonical requirements, and the pope would refuse institution only in the case of men notoriously unfit or unworthy.

The régime of collative benefices had for a long time been troubled by the introduction of "exspectative graces" and "exspectative mandates," by which a collator or patron, even the pope himself, promised a person to confer a benefice on him in case of vacancy. The eighth article suppressed exspectative graces and reservations of all sorts. The Concordat also accorded an important place to university graduates and reserved a third of the benefices to them (eleventh article).

The solution of the question of jurisdiction was, like that of the benefices, prepared by precedence of procedure. The Concordat provided that "outside of major cases, expressly specified as such in the Canons, all cases should be brought before the judges of the parties, who by right, custom, or privilege, have jurisdiction over them." The Holy See remained the supreme court of appeal, but only after all intermediate jurisdictions had been exhausted.

The financial question, treated evasively, and probably by mutual agreement, in the Concordat of Bologna, was regulated by a Bull of October 1st, 1516. The pope fixed the manner of paying the annates. This was the most delicate question to be settled. The King of France, or rather Chancellor Duprat, allowed the pope to triumph in the matter of right, but in fact, as evinced by modern study of the reports of the chamber, this tax, which had become so unpopular, was henceforth paid only by a small number of benefices and for a trifling portion of their annual revenue.

The Concordat touched on the question of reform in a few articles: a prohibition against seculars holding benefices of regulars, and vice versa; strong measures against clerics living in concubinage; the establishment of a pulpit in each church where the Sacred Scriptures should be taught at least once a week.

QUESTIONS

1. Make out a chronological list of events pertaining to the Italian question.
2. Write a short appreciation of the character of Pope Julius II.
3. Distinguish clearly between the right of presentation and the right of institution of candidates to benefices.
4. What is the importance of the Concordat of 1515?

BIBLIOGRAPHY

The Italian Question.—PERRENS, *Histoire de Florence,* 1877 ff.—CH. YRIARTE, *César Borgia,* 1889.—H. FR. DELABORDE, *L'expédition de Charles VIII en Italie.*—J. KLACZKO, *Rome et la Renaissance, Jules II.*—KOHLER, *Les Suisses dans les guerres d'Italie de 1506 à 1512,* 1897.—PAQUIER, art. *"Innocent VIII,"* in *Dict. de Théol.* and art. *"Alexandre VI,"* in *Dict. d'Hist.*—A. RENAUDET, *Le concile gallican de Pise-Milan (1510–12),* 1922.—G. MOLLAT, art. *"Jules II"* and *"Léon X,"* in *Dict. de Théol.*

CHAPTER III

THE SPANISH QUESTION UNDER FERDINAND AND ISABELLA:
THE INQUISITION

I. The Maraños. A danger within the country itself was always threatening Catholic Spain, to wit, the influence and ever increasing number of foreign populations, chief among which were the Jews and the Moors. Wholesale deportation of these foreigners would have been a barbarian measure and might have entailed disastrous economic consequences. By their shrewd business methods, Jews had arisen to the highest places among the people, so much so that the great Spanish lords had not hesitated to replenish their family coffers by contracting alliances with them. As a consequence, men of Jewish extraction were to be found everywhere, even at court and among the members of the higher clergy. Under the wing of their powerful protection a number of Jews, who had been forced to embrace Christianity to escape popular vengeance, remained secretly attached to the Mosaic law, and were all the more dangerous as they mingled freely with the faithful. The danger was pointed out to the sovereigns at Sevilla in 1477 by the Dominican, Fray Alonso de Ojeda; and at the instance of the archbishop, a commission was entrusted with the duty of converting the heretics by preaching. The results were insignificant, however, and hence Ferdinand and Isabella requested Pope Sixtus IV to authorize the institution of a Spanish Inquisition. This tribunal differed from the general Inquisition, established in the course of the thirteenth century, only in the special end it sought to achieve, for it directed its efforts not against all heretics, but against one particular class of apostates: the Judaizers or *Maraños.*

The Inquisition was functioning at Seville as early as 1481, and later on extended its activities to Cordova and other Spanish cities. From a temporary institution it soon became a permanent organization, with a supreme council under the direction of a grand inquisitor, which office was successively held by *Torquemada,* prior of the Dominican monastery of Santa Cruz (1481–1499), Deza, Archbishop of Seville (1499–1506), and Ximenes, Archbishop of Toledo. The grand inquisitor was nominated by the king, but invested with spiritual jurisdiction by an Apostolic brief. The members of the supreme council were also political officials, and as such received their secular jurisdiction from the State; they were nominated to office, however, only at the suggestion of the grand inquisitor, who transmitted to them their spiritual jurisdiction. The Inquisition, therefore, was a mixed institution, and not, as has been pretended by De Maistre and Ranke, a purely political machine. To prove our contention, we have only to recall that the judges did not execute sentences involving capital punishment, but implored the mercy of the secular power in favor of the guilty by means of a petition and according to the prescriptions of Canon Law. It is none the less true that, because it was directly under the tutelage of the State, the Spanish Inquisition ran the risk of being engulfed by civil authority. Sixtus IV, in 1479, complained of the methods of procedure resorted to by Michael Morillo, who, by his own authority, removed the inquisitor of Valencia. It happened, too, that the kings made use of this tribunal to strike not only at the Maraños, but also at other enemies of the crown, and all important political lawsuits were amenable to its tribunal, provided they bordered on the religious.

Although the Spanish Inquisition was approved as an institution by Pope Sixtus IV, it was blamed by him for the irregular character of some of its methods of procedure. A brief issued August 2, 1482, decreed that: (1) decisions rendered upon appeal to Rome should overrule those issued in Spain; (2) penitents guilty of shameful crime must be absolved in private; (3) persons converted to Christianity must not be molested by the inquisitors, but permitted to enjoy the free possession of their goods. There is no doubt that excesses were committed, but they were far less numerous than has been maintained by anti-Catholic writers. Each tribunal of the Inquisition proclaimed at first what was known as the "delay of grace," a period during which apostates could request absolution. The tribunal was very forbearing and pronounced a sentence of capital punishment only as a last resort. Quite frequently, an *auto-da-fé* (*actus fidei* = an act of faith) was not synonymous with burning innocent victims, but with setting free those who had been falsely accused, or reconciling penitents with the Church.

It was not long before the Spanish Inquisition bore fruit, although it was soon realized that, in order to complete its work, it would have to direct its plan of attack not only against the Judaizers, but also against the Jews themselves. The Cortes of Toledo (1480) had already required them to confine themselves to their former district, and very soon they were expelled from Seville and Cordova. At last the Catholic kings of Spain published an edict banishing from Aragon and Castile all Jews who refused to receive Baptism (1492). There were many who preferred exile; those from Castile taking refuge in Portugal, those from Aragon and Catalaunia in Italy and the Barbary States.

II. The Moriscos. Meanwhile the Catholic kings had undertaken to wage war against the Mussulman kingdom of Granada, which, after ten years (1481–1492), was completely subjugated. The terms of capitulation granted to the Moors a generous civil and religious autonomy. But the addition of 400,000 Moors to the numerous Mussulmans who infested Valencia and Aragon created a new religious and national menace. In 1492 an uprising forced the Catholic kings to restrict the Moors of Granada to two faubourgs: Antequerula in the south and Abbaycin in the north. Two factions were now brought face to face. That which advocated the method of persuasion had at its head the grand inquisitor Torquemada, O.P., and that which advocated rigorous measures was under the leadership of Cardinal Ximenes, Archbishop of Toledo. When the latter arrived in Granada in 1499, he succeeded by means of both presents and threats in baptizing a large number of Moors, but soon an insurrection broke out in Abbaycin and spread throughout Andalusia. After the revolt had been suppressed, it was decreed that the Moors should choose between Baptism and exile, and to those who became Christians was given the name of "Moriscos." The faith of these new converts being somewhat doubtful, they were placed under the supervision of the Inquisition. The same logic in a method of defence which had struck first at the Judaizers and then at the Jews, extended the measures adopted at Granada as far as Leon and Castile, and a "Pragmatic" issued in 1502 condemned to exile all Moors who refused to receive Baptism. But the Inquisition, which had dealt so severely with the Judaizers, showed itself more lenient toward the Moriscos, and from the days of Hernando de Talavera to those of St. Thomas of Villanova, a number of holy men, spent themselves in the work of their conversion.

Finally, we must observe that, being indomitable in its faith and almost savage in its strength, the Spanish temperament understood methods of harshness better than any others. This explains why the Inquisition was so popular in the peninsula, where it took on the aspect of a Committee for Public Safety.

TEXTS AND DOCUMENTS

THE INQUISITION AND THE JEWS

In his learned studies in the *Histoire Littéraire de la France,* devoted to French Jewish writers of the fourteenth century, Renan reminds us that when the Jews were expelled from France by Philippe le Bel, who was desirous above all of appropriating their wealth in spite of Canon Law, they found an asylum in the lands which were to become papal (Avignon and le Comtat), in the county of Orange, in Provence and Catalaunia. "Toward the middle of the century," he adds, "we find Jewish students at Montpellier. Arabic was taught by them at Arles, Tarascon, and Perpignan. King Robert of Anjou was the inspirer of this. We find a great number of Hebrew writers who dedicated their works to him (for instance, Schemariah of Negropont), and it was for him that Calonymus made his translation into Latin." Among these Jews, patronized by Robert of Anjou, was Levi of Bagnols, the author of several philosophical works. "The Avignon Popes," says Renan, "greatly esteemed his astronomical works."

In these conditions the inquisitors had nothing to do with the Jews, except when by their writings they attacked the Church, or else when, having been converted, they became by their Baptism answerable to the Church in all that concerned the faith which they had freely adopted, and in particular, answerable for apostasy.

For just as in fact the Church recognized in the Jews the right to be and remain Jews freely, so also in the same measure she wanted to make sure that they should not insinuate their way into the Church by a simulated conversion. She feared to be corrupted by dangerous infiltration of foreign elements, and to expose her faithful to the deceits of enemies under the appearance of brethren. Hence she watched carefully the sincerity of converted Jews, and when she had reasons to suspect it, she applied to them the severe penalties intended for apostates; for the converted Jew who remained a Jew in his faith was a renegade to the faith of his Baptism, that is, an apostate. The inquisitorial measures taken against relapsed Jews were, therefore, the punishment of a deception, a means of defence against a dangerous Jewish penetration.

GUIRAUD, *The Medieval Inquisition,* pp. 168–169 (transl. E. C. Messenger).

QUESTIONS

1. What is the meaning of the term "Maraños"?
2. List the principal functions of the grand inquisitor.
3. Explain the phrase *auto-da-fé*.
4. What is the significance of the term "Moriscos"?
5. How do you account for the popularity of the Spanish Inquisition?

BIBLIOGRAPHY

The Concordat of 1516.—J. Thomas, *Le concordat de 1516*, 3 vols., 1910.—A. Baudrillart, *Quatre cents ans de concordat.*—Imbart de la Tour, *Les origines de la Réforme*, t. II.—Bourdon, *Le Concordat de 1516; négociations, réception en France*, 1902.—L. Madelin, *Les premières applications du Concordat de 1516* in *Mél. Arch. et Hist. de l'Ecole Française de Rome*, t. XVII (1897); *De conventu bononiensi*, 1898; *France et Rome*, 2nd edit., 1914. —G. Hanotaux, *Etudes critiques sur le XVIe et le XVIIe siècles en France*, 1886.

The Spanish Inquisition.—De Maistre, *Lettre à un gentilhomme russe sur l'Inquisition espagnole*, Lyon, 1837.—Ranke, *Fürsten und Völker*, Hamburg, 1827, t. I, p. 241.—Hefele, *Cardinal Ximenes.*—Mariéjol, *L'Espagne sous Ferdinand et Isabelle* (*Bibl. d'Hist. Illustrée*), 1802.—Pastor, *History of the Popes*, Vol. IV.—Dom J. Souben, art. *"Morisques"* in *Dict. d'Apol.*—John Guiraud, *The Mediæval Inquisition.*—Maycock, *The Inquisition from its Establishment to the Great Schism.*—See also references above.

I. The Literary Renaissance. The Renaissance was a transitional movement between the medieval and the modern world, marked especially by the revival of classical design in the arts and letters. It can be accounted for in part by the prestige of ancient Rome, which had remained the capital of the Christian world, the close resemblances between Italian and Latin, and renewed interest in Roman law. Laymen who until then had contented themselves with the study and writing of poetry, began to aspire to an intellectual function. *Dante Alighieri* (1265–1321) was a pioneer in this field, although his *Divina Commedia* is still a medieval work, the inspiration of which remains Christian throughout, despite the author's intense interest in politics. *Petrarch,* on the other hand, was the first of the humanists. He studied the writings of the ancient Latins as a moralist, but above all as a Christian. "When we read philosophical, poetical, and historical works," he is reported to have said, "the ear of our soul must always remain attentive to the Gospel of Jesus Christ." We must call attention to his *De Contemptu Mundi* (On the Contempt of the World) and *De Vita Solitaria* (On the Life of Solitude), in which he tells of his solitude at Vaucluse, so well suited to contemplation, his *De Sapientia* (On Wisdom), a eulogy of the faith, his *De Otio Religioso* (On Religious Tranquillity), a eulogy of the monastic life, and his *Triumphi* (Triumphs), an apologia of Christian chastity which completely conquers earthly passions.

But the literary Renaissance soon degenerated into paganism. The humanists advocated a sort of doctrinal and practical Epicureanism, and while careful not to oppose Catholic dogma too openly, made monks and clerics the chief objects of their satire. *Boccaccio* (1313–1375) blazed the trail in his *Decamerone,* which is nothing more than a collection of licentious tales. *Poggio Bracciolini* († 1459) composed his *Liber Facetiarum,* a conglomeration of filthy pleasantries. *Lawrence Valla* († 1457)

667

advocated the religion of pleasure in his *De Voluptate.* "I declare and insist," he says, "that pleasure is the only worth-while good, and I would even go so far as to say that there is no other good." He regarded the celibacy of priests and monks as a monstrosity (*De Professione Religiosorum*). The scandal reached its apex with *Antonio Beccadelli* († 1471), called the Panormite. His *Hermaphrodite,* which extols the most repellent vices of pagan antiquity, was publicly burned and the author excommunicated.

These writers, who possess no originality, and were at bottom nothing more than clever rhetoricians, enjoyed considerable favor with the princes. The majority of them belonged to the college of Apostolic secretaries, founded by the popes of Avignon to promote interest in arts and letters. It must be conceded that they rendered a real service to the papal chancery by drawing up its acts in perfect literary form, and that they were extremely clever at disguising their real opinions. It is to be regretted that the popes shared in the general infatuation. Nicholas V, who created the Vatican Library, where he assembled 5000 manuscripts, offered his protection to all writers, including even Valla. A slight reaction took place under Callixtus III and Pius II, and a very energetic one under Paul II (1464-1471). The latter limited the college of abbreviators of the curia, where the humanists held sway, and those who voiced their protests were grouped into a literary society called the Roman Academy, which was the rendezvous of all elements hostile to the papacy and favorable to paganism, heresy, and republicanism. Paul II had several of the members arrested, among them Pomponius Laetus and the satirist Platina. His purpose in doing so was to inspire them with fear of reprisals.

The Christian Renaissance had many illustrious representatives. Foremost among them was Cardinal John *Bessarion,* who in his well-known work, *In Calumniatorem Platonis* (Against a Calumniator of Plato), attempted to reconcile the Platonic theories with the teachings of Christianity. *Marsilio Ficino* (1433-1499) also vindicated the theories of Plato in his *De Religione Christiana* (On the Christian Religion) and his *Theologia Platonica de Immortalitate Animarum* (Plato's Theology on the Immortality of Souls). To these names should be added a whole list of learned cardinals: Albergati, Cesarini, Capranica, and, above all, Nicholas of Cusa. Their talents failed, however, to eclipse the popularity of the licentious humanists, who dragged public morals into the mire.

II. The Political Renaissance: Papal Nepotism at the End of the Fifteenth Century. The Renaissance was not merely a revival of classical design in the arts and letters; it was also and above all a complete renovation of the moral lives of the people, a new conception of the world, an original theory of society and public relations, a tradition of liberty in the association of the Christian with his Church. Under cover of civic disturbances, individualism had gained considerable prestige in Italy. It was personified in a special type, the head of the State or "tyrant," whose outstanding quality was force (*virtus*). The head of the State held firmly to the principle that the end justifies the means, and so, in dominating others, permitted himself to make use of deceit, trickery, and cruelty. Being an absolute master, he did not allow himself to be hampered by any moral law. To his thinking the satisfaction of one's passions is just another way of affirming one's personality. The mansions of princes were overrun with bastard offspring, and the example of immorality set by the heads of the States gradually found its way among the people, as attested by the many laws enacted during this period.

The influence of the Renaissance was also felt in Rome. The popes who occupied the See of Peter during the closing years of the fifteenth century had a strong tendency to regard themselves first of all as temporal princes, for whom simony and nepotism had become a political necessity. They came to look upon such means as essential, not only in their external relations with the Italian princes, but also to command the respect of the Sacred College. The latter institution, indeed, indirectly aimed at dominating the papacy and substituting in the place of the papal monarchy an oligarchy of cardinals. Beginning with the exile of the popes at Avignon, the cardinals held a very important place in Church administration. No decision was reached by the pope before he had consulted with them in private or public consistory. If it became necessary for him to settle some dogmatic question, they drew up memoirs (*vota*) or offered their advice. If it was a question of some political problem, they were pressed by the kings and princes of their nation, to whom they were obligated, as a rule, for their office. In the fifteenth century, the Sacred College attempted to dominate the papacy, after the councils had threatened to reserve the papal election to the teaching church at large. Each time the Holy See became vacant, the College of Cardinals enjoined upon the candidates proposed for office, conditions which aimed at restricting the rights of the future pope. It was thus that it reached an agreement with Cardinal Barbo, that he would seek the advice of the Sacred College in all matters, in the nomination to important functions and benefices, in the administration of the Papal States, and in questions pertaining to discipline and war. After he had become pope (Paul II), the Cardinal hastened to annul this agreement, so contrary to the divine right of the Sovereign Pontiffs. Sixtus IV and Innocent VIII also retracted promises made before their election to the papacy.

This state of isolation, into which the popes were forced by the coalition of the *purpurati,* partly explains and excuses what is commonly known as papal nepotism. The popes issued to lay nephews a *condotta,* or sort of permit to enroll hirelings for the protection of the Patrimony of St. Peter at the expense of the papal treasury. Quite frequently, too, the Sovereign Pontiffs conferred upon them, together with the papal standard, the title of *gonfalonieri* of the Roman Church. The senior member among them was a sort of minister of war, who occupied a place of honor at council meetings in which were discussed matters of general policy and difficulties that had arisen within the Patrimony. Moreover, the cardinals related to the pope were entrusted with the principal duties of the curia, generally the direction of some central bureau. Thus Rodrigo Borgia, a nephew of Callixtus III, was cardinal camerlengo for twenty years; Giuliano della Rovere, a nephew of Sixtus IV, was grand penitentiary; Giuliano de Medici, a nephew of Leo X, was chancellor, and all three became Sovereign Pontiffs. By these measures the popes of the fifteenth century succeeded in maintaining a personal hold on the political affairs of Italy.

Sixtus IV had inaugurated this regime by nominating cardinals of doubtful character, who were later on responsible for the scandalous election of Alexander VI. Sixtus also permitted his nephews, Girolamo Riario and Giuliano della Rovere, to dominate the political situation. His successor, Innocent VIII, who had had two children before his ordination, even went so far as to solemnize their marriage. The scandal culminated in the advent of *Alexander VI.* Pius II had already reproached him for a sylvan festival staged under his direction at Siena, and while a cardinal, he had had illicit relations with a Roman matron by the name of Vanozza de Cataneis, by whom he had four children. After he had been raised to the papacy (1492), Alexander provided liberally for his children. Joffre married Sancia, a natural grand-daughter of Ferdinand of Aragon. Juan, the oldest son, who was made duke of Gandia and given the duchy of Benevento, was mysteriously assassinated after returning from a nocturnal orgy. Alexander VI was filled with despair at the news, and spoke of reforming his life, but a few days later forgot all his promises and heaped favors on his other son, Caesar Borgia. After being made a cardinal, Caesar threw his purple to the dogs and by the grace of Louis XII became a duke and married Charlotte d'Albret, a daughter of the king of Navarre. Caesar Borgia was the real type of a cruel and debauched tyrant. He completely dominated his father, who spent all his efforts in building up his fortune. Lucretia, who has been discredited by all writers, was probably the best of the four. Possessed of no will of her own, she allowed herself to be married off according to the needs of the papacy, first to Giovanni Sforza, lord of Pesaro, then to a natural son of the king of the Two Sicilies, Alfonso of Bisceglia, who was assassinated by Caesar Borgia, and finally to Alfonso d'Este, son and heir of the Duke of Ferrara. There is no question that the scandals which occurred during this pontificate have been exaggerated. It is not true, for instance, that Alexander VI had incestuous relations with his own daughter, had a painting made of Giulia Farnese under the features of a Madonna, with himself kneeling at her feet, or slew Prince Djem with his own hand. It is but too true, however, that he continued his scandalous manner of living even after he had been elected Pope, made no effort to conceal his relations with Giulia Farnese, and had two more children—Juan, towards the end of 1494, and Rodrigo in 1503.

III. Girolamo Savonarola. Against such unparalleled excesses one eloquent voice was suddenly raised, that of Girolamo Savonarola, a Dominican friar, who had achieved extraordinary success as a preacher at Florence. His sermons converted the entire city; debauchees turned to pious occupations and women began to practice modesty in their attire. The ornaments laid aside by the fair sex were burned in huge "Vanity Piles"; Jewish money-changers were banished, usury was suppressed, and a bank established which made loans almost gratuitously. Savonarola acclaimed Christ as the Lord and King of Florence and sought to make the city the center of a reform movement which would spread to the whole Church. Being a rather high-strung man, however, and incapable of moderation, he inveighed against everything with a boldness that was almost unbelievable, advocating a theocracy like the one prevalent in the days of the Judges of Israel, but far more tyrannical. Moreover, he sought to promote reform by political means, placing his entire trust in "the new Cyrus," Charles VIII. Greatly disturbed by the political schemes of the fiery Dominican, Alexander VI attempted to silence him by two briefs (1495), and cited him before his tribunal in Rome. Savonarola, after he had obtained permission to resume his preaching through the inter- mediary of Cardinal Caraffa, violently denounced the corruption rampant in the Roman Curia and urged the convocation of an ecumenical council. He was again forbidden to preach, but this time refused to obey orders. As a result he was excommunicated, May 12, 1497, and on June 19 re- torted with his "Epistle to all Christians against the Excommunication surreptitiously obtained" against him; he continued to say Mass and to attack the Pope. Alexander VI then commanded the Florentines to sur- render Savonarola, or at least to prohibit him from preaching (February 25 and March 9, 1498). The friar retorted that he would abide only by the decision of a general council, and soon his popularity waned. His downfall became complete when he refused at the last minute to proceed with the trial by fire to which he had promised to submit. Arraigned before the government of Florence and judged by a board which included two representatives of the Pope, he was burnt at the stake and his ashes were thrown into the river Arno (May 23, 1498). His writings were subjected to a critical examination under Paul III, Julius III, and Paul IV, and declared free from error. His rebellious conduct, however, can- not be condoned.

TEXTS AND DOCUMENTS

ALEXANDER VI AND SAVONAROLA

The fiery Dominican was not afraid of attacking Alexander VI himself; he denounced him as simoniacal and appealed to a council. After an unsuc- cessful attempt to reduce him to silence by an offer of the red hat, the Pope forbade him to preach, and when this prohibition proved of no avail, he left him alone. As Pastor points out, Alexander acted in this matter with great moderation, his object being to allow Savonarola to alienate public opinion by his excesses and thus to bring about his own downfall. This is precisely what happened. When the friar refused at the last minute to proceed with the trial by fire to which he had promised to submit himself, he was ar- raigned and judged by the government of Florence, although the Pope as a matter of form cited him before his own tribunal. Condemned to death, he was burnt at the stake on May 23, 1498.

HAYWARD, *A History of the Popes*, p. 264.

QUESTIONS

1. Which were the causes that gave rise to the literary Renaissance?
2. Write a short appreciation of Dante.
3. Account for the gradual rise to power of the College of Cardinals.
4. What is the present-day organization of this institution?
5. Define nepotism and account for its existence in the Church of the fifteenth century.
6. What is to be thought of Girolamo Savonarola?

BIBLIOGRAPHY

Italian Humanism.—BURCKHARDT, *Kultur der Renaissance in Italien*, Leipzig, 1869.—J. GUIRAUD, *L'Eglise romaine et les origines de la Renaissance*, 3rd edit., 1922.—PASTOR, *op. cit., passim.*—P. DE NOLHAC, *Pétrarque et l'humanisme*, 2 vols., new edit., 1923.—E. RODOCANACHI, *Boccace*, 1908.—E. WASSER, *Poggius Florentius*, Leipzig, 1914.—MANCINI, *Lorenzo Valla*, 1891.—E. TATHAM, *Francesco Petrarca*, London, 1925.—F. VERNET, art. *"Ficin"* in *Dict. de Théol.*—A. PÉRATÉ, art. *"Renaissance,"* in *Dict. d'Apol.*—M. E. JERROLD, *Petrarca, Poet and Humanist*, London, 1909.

The Political Renaissance, Girolamo Savonarola.—GREGOROVIUS, *Stadt Rom im Mittelalter*, 2nd edit., t. VII and VIII.—DE MAULDE LA CLAVIÈRE, *La diplomatie au temps de Machiavel*, 3 vols., 1892.—THUREAU-DANGIN, *Vie de saint Bernardin de Sienne*, especially the Introduction.—A. CAPELLI, *Fra Girol. Savonarola.*—J. SCHNITZER, *Savonarola. Ein Kulturbild aus der Zeit der Renaissance*, 2 vols., 1924.—G. SCALION, *Girolamo Savonarola e Santa Catarina de Ricci*, Florence, 1924.—PETER DE ROO, *Materials for a History of Pope Alexander VI, his Relatives and his Time*, 5 vols., Bruges, 1924.—PASTOR, *History of the Popes.*—RODOCANACHI, *Une cour princière au Vatican pendant la Renaissance (1471-1503)*, 1925; *Le pontificat de Jules II*, 1928.—LUCAS, *Girolamo Savonarola.*—P. MISCIATELLI, *Savonarola* (transl. M. PETERS-ROBERTS).—P. VILLARI, *History of Girolamo Savonarola* (transl. L. HORNER).—W. VAN WYCK, *Savonarola*, New York, 1927.

General Aspects of Christendom Before the Protestant Reformation

It would be a serious mistake to regard the fourteenth and fifteenth centuries as periods of unrestrained debauchery, similar in character to the time which preceded the French Revolution. The faith in those days was still alive, as is evidenced by the increased number of religious societies and confraternities, the wide-spread practice of fasting, and the generous donations made to churches. Moreover, the Church continued to retain her hold upon the faithful through the twofold medium of the pulpit and the theatre. It is true, the theatre had become somewhat secularized; stage plays were no longer produced in church, and had departed from their former biblical simplicity, both in contents and setting. Nevertheless, they remained profoundly religious, the representations being ordinarily of paradise with its angels, and hell with its demons. A very popular play was the Mystery of the Passion by Arnould Greban, which in 35,000 lines marshalled before the eyes of the spectators the principal episodes of the New Testament. The Church actively concurred in the staging of these plays. The representation was sometimes preceded by the celebration of Mass, and frequently the canons played different parts. In a word, the "mystery" remained one of the chief means of edifying the people. Preaching was also very popular, especially when conducted by the Franciscans and the Dominicans; quite often the sermons were delivered in the public market-place. They were a mixture of sublime elevations of the soul and sound practical advice, expressed in a florid style which at times bordered on the trivial. The type of the preachers of this period was St. Bernardine of Siena.

The piety of the people, however, was inspired chiefly by fear, and dominated by the dread of death and judgment. The "Dance of Death" received much attention, and on the walls of cemeteries and churches, and even in the interior of dwelling houses, the "Eternal Reaper" was represented as mowing down popes and kings, noblemen and peasants, maidens and children alike. At times these tendencies led to exaggerated manifestations, such as, for instance, the processions of the so-called *"Flagellants."* The processions originated in Padua (1260), when confraternities of Flagellants suddenly appeared in Italy and rapidly spread across the Alps, through Hungary and Switzerland. The members wore large hats and a white mantle marked with red crosses, one in front, the other behind. With crosses and banners borne before them by the clergy, they marched slowly through the towns, stripped to the waist and with faces covered. In the course of these processions they formed a circle and scourged themselves with leathern thongs until the blood ran, while the "Master" intoned a canticle, which was taken up by the whole crowd. Occasionally these exhibitions were interspersed with extraordinary rites; sometimes the "Master" read a letter purported to have been brought by an angel from Heaven on December 25, 1348, in which the Blessed Virgin Mary promised the Flagellants the remission of all their sins. Clement VI severely condemned these practices and gave orders to imprison all who resisted his commands. As a result, the Flagellants disappeared, except in Thuringia and Saxony, where they degenerated into a sect of "Illuminati," who held that the Baptism of blood (flagellation) was more agreeable to God than the Baptism of water. In the opening years of the fifteenth century the Council of Constance was obliged to forbid public scourging. Another strange phenomenon was the rage for dancing which spread throughout the valley of the Rhine and the Netherlands. The people gathered *en masse* in market-places and even in churches to dance.

The true reform of the Church was hampered by endless wars, the disturbances occasioned by the Great Schism and the Council of Basle, and, finally, by worry over the Italian question which beset the papacy during the second half of the fifteenth century. The only serious attempt to remedy this situation was made by *Nicholas of Cusa,* whom Pope Nicholas V sent as legate to Germany. He convoked provincial councils, which set up synodal statutes on the reform of the clergy. He waged war particularly on concubinage and simony, prohibiting candidates to take an oath whereby they abandoned the revenues of churches to collators and patrons of benefices and contented themselves with a portion (*congrua*) thereof. With the aid of the congregations of Bursfeld and Windesheim, Nicholas of Cusa sought also to reform the monastic Orders and succeeded in enjoining upon nuns (*moniales*) the rule of strict enclosure. But this isolated effort, reminiscent of the one made on a former occasion by the legates of Pope Gregory VII, bore only passing fruits.

The period did, however, witness the efforts of a few zealous souls to reform the Church. The most outstanding among them was St. Bernardine of Siena, a popular orator in Italy, and St. Vincent Ferrer, who during the Great Schism travelled the length and breadth of Spain, France, and Italy, and finally died in Brittany, after preaching penance and the last judgment everywhere. In this connection we must also mention certain writings of scholars at the University of Paris, especially the *Canones Reformationis Ecclesiae in Concilio Constantiensi* (Canons regarding Church Reformation Formulated at the Council of Constance), and the *Capita Agendorum in Concilio* (List of Subjects to be Treated by the Council) by the Chancellor, Peter d'Ailly; the *De Simonia* (On Simony) and *De Emendatione Ecclesiastica* (On Church Reform) by another Chancellor, Gerson; the treatise *De Corrupto Ecclesiae Statu* (On the Corrupt State of the Church) and that *De Praesulibus Simoniacis* (On Simoniacal Prelates) by the rector, Nicholas de Clamanges. Finally, we must mention the *Liber de Reformatione Monasteriorum* (Treatise on the Reform of Monasteries) published in the Netherlands and attributed to John Buch, the writings of Denis the Carthusian at Ruremond, and those of his brother in religion, Jacob de Jüterborgk, *De Negligentia Praelatorum Libellus* (Short Treatise on the Negligence of Prelates) and *De Auctoritate Ecclesiae* (On the Authority of the Church). But no matter how authoritative the voices of these orthodox reformers, they were completely submerged by those of the humanists, whose lively and entertaining writings were more destructive than constructive: they foretold a reform, it is true, but a reform which would take place outside the Church and in opposition to her teachings.

TEXTS AND DOCUMENTS

PETRARCH ON THE BLACK DEATH

The following is taken from a letter of Petrarch to his brother, a religious at Monrieux, and the only survivor of a convent of thirty-five:

"Alas! my beloved brother, what shall I say? How shall I begin? Whither shall I turn? On all sides is sorrow; everywhere is fear. Would, my brother, that I had never been born, or, at least, had died before these times. How will posterity believe that there has been a time when, without the lightnings of heaven or the fires of earth, without wars or other visible slaughter, not this or that part of the earth, but well-nigh the whole globe, has remained without inhabitants.

"When has any such thing ever been heard or seen? In what annals has it ever been read that houses were left vacant, cities deserted, the countryside neglected, the fields too small for the dead, and a fearful and universal solitude spread over the whole earth? Consult your historians, they are silent; question your doctors, they are dumb; seek an answer from your philosophers, they shrug their shoulders and frown, and with their fingers on their lips bid you to be silent.

"Will posterity ever believe these things when we, who see, can scarcely credit them? We should think we were dreaming if we did not see with our eyes, when walking abroad, the city in mourning with funerals, and returning to our home, find it empty, and thus know that what we lament is real.

"Oh, happy people of the future, who have not known these miseries and perchance will class our testimony with the fables. We have, indeed, deserved these and even greater punishments; but our forefathers also have deserved them, and may our posterity not also merit the same."

A. PHILLIPPE, *Histoire de la Peste Noire*, p. 103.

QUESTIONS

1. Trace the history of the Mystery Play.
2. Account for the fact that the piety of the people in those days was inspired chiefly by fear.
3. Give a few incidents in the life of St. Vincent Ferrer.

BIBLIOGRAPHY

The **Reform** in the **Church.**—E. VANSTENBERGHE, *Nicolas de Cues*, 1920.—THUREAU-DANGIN, *Saint Bernardin de Sienne.*—FAGES, *Saint Vincent Ferrier*, 2 vols., 1893.—A. LAFONTAINE, *Jehan Gerson*, 1906.—L. SALEMBIER, art. *"Gerson,"* in *Dict. de Théol.*—G. BAREILLE, art. *"Flagellants,"* in *Dict. de Théol.*—M. GORCE, *Saint Vincent Ferrier*, 1923.

CHAPTER I

I. The Benedictines. The Benedictine Order had grown rather lax during this period, because of the many abuses of the nobility who had come to look upon the monasteries as family fiefs. As a consequence, young boys were admitted as candidates and entrusted with large benefices and important functions; men without a vocation gained access to the abbeys and refused to listen to the pleas for reform; and many abuses were committed in regard to the papal mandates appointing successors to benefices before they became vacant (expectative graces). To the above causes which made for laxity, must be added the voluntary or involuntary practice of admitting mendicant monks, especially Franciscans, to religious profession, when their sole purpose was to acquire regular benefices that would enable them to lead an independent and easy-going life. Finally, the spirit of the world was in evidence everywhere.

Benedict XII attempted to reform these conditions by his Bull *"Summi magistri"* of June 20, 1336, better known as *"Bulla Benedictina."* Its main purpose was to make for more coherence in that Order by grouping all the houses into thirty-five provinces, in which provincial chapters were to be held each year. Extraordinary officials were appointed to help re-establish monastic discipline. The *"Benedictina"* achieved only mediocre results. The only reform worth while was effected in a few scattered places by newly erected local congregations.

Already in 1312 Blessed Bernard Tolomei had founded, near Siena, in the solitude of Accona, a monastery which was soon known as Mt. Olivet. The congregation of Mt. Olivet was approved by John XXII in 1318, and again by Clement VI, in 1344, and founded in central Italy abbeys such as Gubbio and Foligno. Dom Louis Barbo inaugurated a congregation at St. Justina of Padua, which, after being approved by Martin V, in 1417, won over to the cause of reform all the monasteries of Italy, including the abbey of Monte Cassino, whose name it assumed in

1505. A congregation was modelled after it in Valladolid, Spain, in the course of the fifteenth century. This congregation finally absorbed all the Spanish abbeys and gave rise, first to the congregation of Portugal, with its Brazilian dependencies (c. 1560), and secondly to the English congregation which, during the period of the Reformation, established itself on the continent, especially in France.

The Councils of Constance and Basle made an attempt to reform the monastic life in Germany. To this end they re-inforced the obligation of convoking provincial Chapters every three years, according to the regulations laid down by the *"Benedictina."* These Chapters, however, were lacking in authority and hampered in their designs to legislate for all monasteries by the differences which existed in both discipline and liturgy. There were, however, attempts made at local reform, just as in Italy. The first of these were undertaken before the Council of Constance by the monastery of Castel, in the diocese of Eichstätt. It was quite natural for the German monasteries to base their reform on the reformed monasteries of Italy. The abbey of Subiaco, occupied since the middle of the fifteenth century by several German monks, was in possession of many customs particularly suited to the needs of the time. The fame of its prior, Abbot Nicholas of Matzen, led Albert of Austria to seek his aid. He established his headquarters at the abbey of Melk, and the customs of Melk were introduced into a number of other abbeys, not only in Austria, but also in Bavaria, due to the assistance of the bishops of Passau, Freising, and Salzburg. These abbeys grouped themselves into a sort of confederation, which was more moral than real, and assumed the name of the particular "observance" or "union."

The reform of Bursfeld, on the other hand, which aimed at grouping together the monasteries of Saxony, Thuringia, and the valleys of the Rhine and Moselle, resulted in the establishment of a real congregation. This congregation was organized by John Dederoth, abbot of Clus, to whom the duke of Brunswick appealed to reform St. Thomas of Bursfeld, not far from Münden on the Weser. With the assistance of the Council of Basle, which entrusted to him the mission of visiting and reforming the provinces of Mayence, Cologne, and Treves, he was able to exercise considerable influence. His successor, John Hagen, resolved to establish a union between the different reformed monasteries, based on disciplinary and liturgical conformity and the annual convocation of particular Chapters. After his appointment as papal legate to Germany, Nicholas of Cusa did all in his power to promote the interest of the congregation of Bursfeld. There was a time when it had as many as one hundred and thirty-six monasteries for men and forty-two for women.

II. The Mendicant Orders. The *Dominican Friars* also witnessed a period of decadence as early as the fourteenth century, due partially, in France, to the devastating influence of the Black Death, which had taken its toll of the members of many monasteries. A new regime was established under the name of "Conventuality," according to which religious were required to lead a more or less private life, while continuing as members of their respective monasteries. The benefices of the monastery were distributed among the brethren, and the conventual or territorial diet (assembly) was divided into regions or sectors, which comprised each so many towns and villages. Each region was provided for by one of the Fathers, who had a right to the benefices, part of which he was free to give to the monastery to defray general expenses. Quite naturally, the more important regions were entrusted to the best qualified religious, a fact which accounts for the division of the Dominican Order into a high and a low clergy.

When Raymond of Capua, the confessor of St. Catherine of Siena, became General of the Order, he resolved to work out a reform based on the following two principles: (1) No innovations were to be tolerated, but the former observances as found in the constitutions were again to be put into practice; (2) monasteries of the observance were to be established in each province to serve as regular nurseries for zealous religious; these religious were to be sent out from there into the other houses to revive monastic discipline. Invested with plenipotentiary powers by the General Chapter of Vienne (1388), Raymond published a reform decree, which was approved by Pope Boniface IX (1391). The center of this reform was the ancient monastery of St. Dominic in the city of Venice, to which Blessed John Dominici was appointed with the title of vicar-general. John re-established the ancient discipline at Chiogga, Citta di Castello, and in the monastery of SS. John and Paul (Zarepolo); and it was not long before Raymond of Capua enlarged his powers as vicar-general and placed him at the head of all the reformed Dominican houses in Italy (1396). Raymond of Capua was also assisted in his work of reform by Conrad of Prussia, who, after being appointed vicar-general for the Dominican houses in Germany, established the regular observance at Colmar (1391) Nuremberg (1396), and Utrecht (1397).

To avoid a split, Raymond of Capua had made it quite clear that the different monasteries would be free to accept or reject the reform. As a consequence, the vicars-general could do nothing with those who opposed them, and the reform was restricted to the monasteries of the observance. In an attempt to further the interests of the observance without detriment to unity, a new regime was adopted, that of the "Congregation," which, without territorial limits, set up reformed monasteries in the very heart of the different provinces. The "Congregation" was subject to a vicar-general elected by its members, who in turn was subject to the Master General. The Lombard "Congregation," inaugurated by Blessed John Dominici, furnished the model for all others. We should mention in this connection the "Congregation" of Holland, which became particularly prosperous, counting as many as sixty-seven monasteries for men and nine convents for women, not only in the Netherlands, but also in France and Germany. The French houses belonging to this "Congregation" detached themselves from it under Louis XII and grouped themselves into a Gallican congregation. The institution of "congregations" indicated a renewal of fervor in the Order of St. Dominic, a fact which is not marred by the petition sent to Pope Sixtus IV by the Master General, Leonard de Mansuetis, in which he begged the Holy See to grant to the Dominicans the ordinary and universal right of possessing in common rents and properties, claiming that a grant of this kind was indispensable on account of insufficient resources.

The Franciscan Order was still divided into two factions, and though the disturbances created by the "Spirituals" had subsided somewhat in the course of the fourteenth century, the heated controversy about poverty had not abated, and some members of the Order still insisted on the primitive observance of St. Francis. Under the direction of a lay brother, Paul Trinci of Foligno, the monastery of Brogliano became a real center of reform in Umbria and the Marches, and in 1415 as many as thirty-five monasteries had affiliated themselves with that monastery, chief among which was the Portiuncula. This reform obtained such outstanding recruits as St. Bernardine of Siena, who entered the Order in 1402, and St. John Capistran, who was admitted in 1414. The movement of the Observance also gathered momentum in Spain in the opening years of the fifteenth century with the assistance of such saints as Peter Regalado († 1456) and Didacus of Alcala († 1463). In France, the monastery of Mirabeau, near Poitiers, inaugurated a reform in the province of Touraine, which spread throughout the northern portion of the country. Benedict XIII made an attempt to shield these French Observants from the provincials by designating a vicar-general for the three provinces of Touraine, France, and Burgundy (1408), and upon request, the Council of Constance granted them the power to elect provincial vicars, who in turn nominated a vicar-general, to be confirmed by the Minister General of the Order.

The Order was thus slowly moving towards a division. In 1434, the Observants of Spain adopted the new mode of government, and finally, at the instance of St. John Capistran, Pope Eugene IV placed all Observants under the jurisdiction of two vicars-general, elected by them. The first of these ruled over what was known as the Cismontane provinces, where the reform was already established (Italy, Austria, Hungary, and Poland); while the second exercised jurisdiction over the other provinces, called Ultramontane (1443).

The goal of all Observants was to live according to the spirit of the Bull *"Exiit"* of Nicholas III, by renouncing all property. They necessarily found themselves at odds with the non-reformed members, or "Conventuals." To remedy this situation, Pope Leo X convoked a general chapter of the Order in 1517, and when the Observants requested him not to oblige them to unite with the Conventuals, he decided to combine all the reformed congregations under the title of "Friars Minor of the Regular Observance." These Friars Minor elected the Minister General of the whole Order, and the Conventuals lived apart under a Master General, whose election was confirmed by the Minister General (Bull *"Ite et vos,"* May 25, 1517). In this manner the division between the Conventuals and the Observants was consummated.

The *Carmelites* also passed through a period of decadence, due in part to the influence of wars, the Black Death, and the Western Schism, which created divisions within the Order, and in part to over-generous exemptions granted in favor of members of the universities. In 1431, Pope Eugene IV received a request from one of their Chapters to moderate the Rule. A few reforms were effected, but all were local in character. That of the Monastery of the Woods (*sylvarum*), near Florence, gave rise (1425) to the congregation of Mantua, which counted more than fifty monasteries; that of the Mount of Olives, near Genoa (1414), remained purely local; and the grouping of several monasteries in France, particularly those of Albi, Paris, Rouen, and Meaux, gave rise to the congregation of Albi, which was approved in 1513, but disappeared in 1584. The reform, therefore, remained incomplete, despite the zealous efforts of such superiors as Blessed John Soreth (1551–1571). It was during the generalship of the latter that the Carmelite nuns came into existence. Their origin can be traced to a community of Beguines at Guelders, who had asked to become affiliated with the Carmelite monks. Pope Nicholas V granted their petition and they adopted the Rule and constitutions of the Order, calling themselves Carmelites, but not changing their manner of living. They did not practice strict poverty and were not required to observe the rules of monastic inclosure in all their rigor. Their institute spread rapidly throughout the Netherlands, France, Italy, and Brittany, and derived great profit from the example of Blessed Frances d'Amboise, duchess of Brittany, who became a Carmelite nun in 1467. The task of imparting to the Order of the Carmelite nuns its true characteristics was reserved to St. Teresa.

The *Hermits of St. Augustine* also made an attempt in the direction of reform by means of their local congregations. In Italy, towards the end of the fourteenth century, Father Ptolemy of Venice founded the congregation of Illiceto, which numbered twelve monasteries. The foundation of La Carbonnière, in the kingdom of Naples, dates from this same period; it had fourteen houses. The congregation of Perugia, founded by the General Augustine of Rome (1419), numbered fourteen houses. The most flourishing of all foundations was that of Our Lady of Consolation at Genoa (1470), with thirty-one monasteries; that of Calabria (1507), with forty monasteries, and, finally, that of Lombardy (1431), which grouped together fifty-six monasteries, the most famous of which was Notre-Dame de Brou in the Diocese of Belley. Each one of these reformed congregations had at its head a vicar-general, who was subject to the authority of the Superior General. In Spain, the reform inaugurated by Father John of Alarcon (1430) won over to its cause all the monasteries of the kingdom of Castile, divided into four provinces: Toledo, Salamanca, Burgos, and Seville. In Germany, Simon Lindner and Andrew Proles inaugurated a reform which included a number of Ger-

man and twelve Bavarian monasteries (1493). These monasteries grouped
themselves into what was known as the Congregation of Saxony, whose
constitutions were formulated by the Chapter of Nuremberg and whom
Pope Julius II exempted from the jurisdiction of the Superior General
(1503). This congregation, which at one time was quite flourishing, was
brought into discredit by Martin Luther, who belonged to it before his
apostasy.

The mendicant Orders had to reckon also with the secular clergy.
In the thirteenth century, Clement IV and Martin IV had granted them
the right to preach everywhere, without first obtaining permission from
the bishops and pastors. Their conduct gave rise to frequent conflicts, and
for the sake of peace, Boniface VIII restricted the rights of the mendicant
Orders. They could not, without the permission of the Ordinary, hear
confessions, nor preach in parochial churches and administer the last
Sacraments without the permission of the pastors. Moreover, if they
conducted funeral services in their own churches, they were required to
pay one-fourth of the stipend received (*quarta funeralium*) to the parish.
These regulations, which were suppressed by Benedict XI, but again put
into force by Clement V at the Council of Vienne, failed, however, to
restore peace. During the pontificate of John XXII, John de Pouilly,
master of the University of Paris, taught that bishops and pastors derive
their jurisdiction immediately from God, and that, as a consequence, no
one, not even the pope, can deprive them of it. The logical conclusion
from such teaching was that absolution conferred by regulars, even
though they were in possession of Apostolic indults, was invalid. John
XXII summoned John de Pouilly to Avignon, where he was defeated in
a theological debate and forced to recant his statements. The Bull *"Vas
electionis,"* of July 24, 1321, formally condemned his errors.

Going to the other extreme, some mendicants made bold to state that
their powers in the matter of confession admitted of no limitations. Sixtus
IV, who was a former Superior General of the Franciscans, ardently
longed to end these conflicts to the advantage of the mendicant Orders.
He dispensed them from paying the *quarta funeralium* to pastors, and
granted them power to absolve from cases reserved to bishops (1474 and
1479). But this only made matters worse, and under Pope Leo X, the Fifth
Council of the Lateran (1516) was obliged to issue a number of stricter
regulations. Members of the mendicant Orders were informed that they

could neither bless a marriage nor administer the Last Sacraments without the pastor's permission; that they were subject to their own Ordinary in the matter of ordinations and the consecration of their churches, and, finally, that all parish churches served by them were subject to episcopal visitation. These new regulations quieted the animosity of the seculars.

In the fourteenth century, only one military Order remained in the East, namely the *Hospitallers of St. John*. After the capture of Acre, the last Christian stronghold in Syria (1291), they had taken refuge on the island of Cyprus. At a loss for more spacious quarters, their Grand Master, Foulques de Villaret, obtained authorization in 1308 to conquer the island of Rhodes, a strategic position of the first importance, then occupied by pirates. The Hospitallers established their headquarters at Rhodes (1310–1522) and remained the only force in the East officially at the service of the Crusades. At the time of the abolition of the Templars by Philip the Fair, the Hospitallers acquired their possessions. But the Order was torn asunder by internal strifes. In 1317, dissatisfied with the administration of their Grand Master, the courageous but prodigal Foulques de Villaret, the Knights substituted in his place Maurice de Pagnac. John XXII determined to handle the matter himself and took advantage of the existing situation to reform the Order. It was decided that priory Chapters must be held each year, that the same brother could not hold two commanderies at the same time, that the Grand Master could not consent to the alienation of real estate, etc.

The reform thus remained incomplete. In 1343, under the administration of Helion de Villeneuve, Clement VI threatened to dispose of the "Hospital" in favor of a more zealous Order. The Hospitallers are to be commended none the less for the courage which they displayed in their warfare against the Turks under the leadership of such masters as Foulques de Villaret, Hélion de Villeneuve, Jean de Lastic, Pierre d'Aubusson, and Villiers de l'Isle Adam. When they were finally forced to yield, in 1522, Sultan Soliman granted them permission to leave the island with military honors. They established their new headquarters at Malta, which had been bequeathed to them by Charles V, together with the islands of Gozzo and Comino (1530), and were expelled from there only in 1798.

III. New Religious Orders. This period also witnessed the establishment of several new religious Orders of men, most of which adopted the Rule of St. Augustine. The *Hieronymites* comprised four congregations: (1) The Spanish Hermits of St. Jerome, founded in 1367 by Peter Ferdinand Pocha de Guadalajara, chamberlain of Peter the Cruel, King of Castile († 1402), devoted their lives to study and preaching, and played an important part in Spain, where the king heaped great favors upon them. Charles V died in their monastery of St. Just (1558), and Philip II built the Escurial for their use. Cardinal Ximenes made use of their services outside the peninsula for the conversion of the Indians. (2) A reform of the Spanish Hieronymites, effected by Lopez de Olmedo, issued in the grouping together of seven monasteries, which returned to the earlier congregation in 1595. This same reform had penetrated into Lombardy, where it established seventeen houses, grouped together into an independent congregation, called the Hieronymites of the Observance, or of Lombardy. (3) The Italian Hieronymites, founded in 1372 by Blessed Peter of Pisa († 1435), established their headquarters at Montebello, whence they spread throughout Italy. At one time they numbered two provinces with forty-six monasteries. (4) The Hieronymites of the congregation of Fiesole, founded by Charles de Montgranelli, numbered forty monasteries. They were combined later by Clement IX with the congregation of Peter of Pisa.

The *Jesuates*, or Apostolic Clerics of St. Jerome, were a congregation of lay brothers, founded by Blessed John Colombini (1360), who followed the Rule of St. Augustine. They led austere lives, cared for the sick, especially persons infected with the plague, and buried the dead. They rendered signal services in Italy and southern France, where they founded a monastery at Toulouse (1425). Their name is derived from the salutation which they used in greeting one another: "Praised be Jesus Christ!" This congregation fell into complete decadence during the seventeenth century, and was suppressed by Clement IX (1668). The Jesuate nuns were founded by St. Catherine Colombini of Siena († 1387). Mention must also be made of the Hermits of St. Francis, who later became the *Minims*. They were founded by a former hermit from Calabria, St. Francis de Paola, whom Louis XI had called to his assistance and Charles VIII and Louis XII retained for the sake of his prudent counsels († 1507). The Order was approved by Sixtus IV and numbered as many as four hundred and fifty houses in 1474.

A number of religious institutes for women were also established at this time. Blessed Jane of Valois, a daughter of King Louis XI, and repudiated wife of Louis XII, founded the contemplative *Order of the Annunciation* at Bourges, in honor of the Blessed Virgin, which spread throughout France and the Netherlands. Another princess of royal blood, St. Brigid of Sweden, who rivalled St. Catherine of Siena in exhorting the popes of Avignon to return to Italy, founded the *Order of the Holy Saviour,* modelled on the ancient Order of Fontevrault. Each of the monasteries established by her was divided into two sections, one for men, the other for women, all under the authority of an abbess, who held the same position as that of the Blessed Virgin in regard to the Apostles. Urban V issued orders to segregate the two branches and erect a separate church for each. St. Brigid impregnated her Rule with the spirit of the Cistercian Order. The first convent established at Wadstena, near Linkoeping in Sweden, became famous and the *Brigittines* spread throughout Europe, even to Italy. St. Frances of Rome (1384–1440) founded at Rome, in 1425, the *Oblates della Torre de Specchi,* for the purpose of grouping together matrons and young girls of the nobility. They followed the Rule of St. Benedict, but did not take any vows. These Oblates were the precursors of the nuns of the Visitation. The new Orders of women displayed a craving for modern symbolism. The Annunciates wore an ash-colored garb as a sign of penance, a scarlet scapular out of love for the crucified Saviour, and a white mantle with blue cincture in honor of the virginity of Mary. The Brigittines wore above their black veil a sort of crown, made of white cloth and marked with five stripes of red woolen material, in memory of the five wounds of the Saviour.

The new Orders could not hope to achieve the success in the work of reform which had crowned the efforts of Cluny in the eleventh and those of the mendicant Orders in the thirteenth century. A movement in the Netherlands, however, was quite successful, owing to the initiative of *Gerard de Groote.* Gerard was born at Deventer in Holland (1340) and made his studies at the University of Paris, where he received the degree of Master of Arts. He possessed many rich benefices and was leading a rather worldly life, when a chance meeting with Henry van Kalkar, prior of the Carthusian monastery of Munnikhuizen, near Arnhem, led to his embracing the religious life. In 1379, he founded the *Sisters of the Common Life,* who, while not wearing any special habit or taking any vows, followed the religious life under the authority of a superioress elected each year. The institute assumed such proportions that, in the course of the fifteenth century, it numbered ninety houses. De Groote undertook the work of preaching in the Diocese of Utrecht, and grouped around himself a number of young clerics from the Chapter school of Deventer, who copied manuscripts under his direction. Soon he persuaded a canon of Utrecht, Florent Radewyns, to resign from his office and join the copyists of Deventer. Florent conceived the idea of grouping these clerics into a community and prescribing a rule of life for them, but without vows, properly so-called. His failure to enjoin vows upon the members of this new congregation prompted many attacks against it. Mathew Grabo, a Dominican, voiced these grievances at the Council of Constance, where the *Brothers of the Common Life* were defended by d'Ailly and Gerson. To offset these attacks, Gerard de Groote conceived the idea of a third institute, a monastery of canons regular, but he died in 1384, before he could realize his ambition. In 1387, however, a community of canons gathered together at Windesheim, between Deventer and Zwolle, their chief occupations being the recital of the Office in choir, manual labor, and above all the copying of manuscripts. At first they recruited their members from among the Brothers of the Common Life, and then won over to their cause other monasteries of canons. John Loeder was responsible for this movement spreading into Westphalia, and John Busch for its success in Germany; the prior John Mauburne was called to France, where he reformed and grouped together several Chapters, the most outstanding of which were St. Victor of Paris and St. Acheul of Amiens. In all, eighty-six monasteries of men and sixteen convents of women joined in the movement of Windesheim. We shall soon have occasion to call attention to the important influence exercised in the field of mysticism by these Canons Regular, who reckoned among their number the famous Thomas à Kempis. The intellectual influence of the Brothers of the Common Life was felt especially in their stupendous work of copying manuscripts, and if, contrary to the accepted opinion of their day, they did not at first possess any schools, but merely directed young men who followed the courses given in Chapter schools, towards the end of the fifteenth century they engaged in teaching and became a powerful influence in the development of a Christian humanism. Pius V indirectly suppressed them in 1568, when he abolished all congregations without vows.

TEXTS AND DOCUMENTS

The Benedictines and the "Commendam"

This was the period during which the great Benedictine houses were fully caught up into the feudal system, the abbots becoming feudal lords with results only too often deplorable. At this time, too, the evil system of "commendam" reached its greatest magnitude: the system whereby an extern, not a monk, often not an ecclesiastic, was nominated abbot of a monastery by some outside authority, pope or king or lay patron representing the founder of the monastery, to manage the property, administer the temporalities, carry out the feudal obligations, especially the military ones, and, above all, draw the greater part of the revenue of the monastery, only a portion, often inadequate, being assigned for the maintenance of the community and the upkeep of the monastic buildings. This vicious system, probably responsible in a higher degree than any other single cause for the decadence both spiritual and temporal of religious houses, was of early origin. We see it in the anxiety of Benet Biscop on his death-bed, depicted by Bede, lest his brother, a layman, should succeed him as abbot of Wearmouth. It seems to have existed in England also just before Dunstan's monastic revival; and on the Continent, already in the late Merovingian and early Carolingian times, the practice was a common institution, a secular lord being made abbot on account of the political and military importance of the abbeys, due to their great territories. After the conquest "commendam" never found place in England, thanks to the kings, who resisted all attempts at introducing it; so that Wolsey was the single English commendatory abbot. On the Continent the institution was widespread and most pernicious. In the Empire it was not universal; in Italy, after being widely prevalent, it was specially countered by the special constitution of the congregation of St. Justina, devised expressly in order to render it impossible; in France it was at its worst, becoming universal and going right up to the Revolution.

C. Butler, *Benedictine Monachism*, pp. 361–362.

QUESTIONS

1. What was the "Benedictina," and what results did it achieve?
2. What was a monastery of the Observance?
3. How did the Dominicans proceed to reform their Order?
4. Who were the "Friars Minor of the Regular Observance"?

5. Who were the "Conventuals"?
6. List some of the grievances of the seculars against the regulars at the time of the reform of the religious Orders.
7. List the principal duties of the Brothers of the Common Life.

BIBLIOGRAPHY

The Reform of the Old Orders.—M. Maréchaux, *Vie du Bx. Bernard Tolomei*, 1888.—Dom U. Berlière, *Le recrutement des monastères bénédictins aux XIIIe et XIVe siècles* (Acad. Royale de Belgique), 1924.—Dom U. Berlière, *La réforme de Melk au XVe siècle*, in *Rev. Bénéd.*, 1895, pp. 204-13, 289-309; *Les origines de la congrégation de Bursfeld*, in *Rev. Bénéd.*, 1899, pp. 360-69, 480-502.—Mortier, *Histoire abrégée de l'Ordre de saint Dominique en France*, 1920.—H. Dehove, art. *"Dominici (Jean),"* in *Dict. de Théol.*—P. Edouard d'Alençon, art. *"Frères mineurs,"* in *Dict. de Théol.*

New Orders.—Comtesse de Rambuteau, *Le bienheureux Colombini*, 1893.—Hebrard, *Histoire de sainte Jeanne de France*, 1890.—De Maulde, *Jeanne de France, duchesse d'Orléans et de Berry (1464-1505)*, 1883; *Alexandre VI et le divorce de Louis XII* (*Bibl. de l'Ecole des Chartes*, t. LVII, 1896).—Comtesse de Flavigny, *Sainte Brigitte de Suède*, 1892.—Dom Rabory, *Sainte Françoise Romaine*, 1884.—Comtesse de Rambuteau, *Sainte Françoise Romaine*, 1900.—G. de Bonnet-Maury, *De opera scholastica fratrum vitæ communis in Neerlandia*, 1889.—M. Schoengen, *Die Schule von Zwolle*, I. *Von den Anfängen bis zum Auftreten des Humanismus*, Freiburg i. B., 1898. —Acquoy, *Het Klooster de Windesheim en sijn invloed*, Utrecht, 3 vols., 1875-80.—A. Renaudet, *Préréforme et humanisme à Paris pendant les premières guerres d'Italie (1494-1517)*, 1916.—P. Debongnie, *Jean Monbaer de Bruxelles, abbé de Livry*, Louvain, 1928.

CHAPTER II

I. Dogmatic Theology: Scotism and Occamism. The four-teenth and fifteenth centuries marked the complete decadence of Scholastic philosophy. The causes of this decay were both internal and external. The internal causes were the condition of Scholastic philosophy itself, the unnecessary increase in the number of universities and other schools, the lack of personnel, and, finally, an uncouth and barbarous terminology, which bewilders the modern reader. The external causes were the political conditions of the time, above all a general relaxation of the spirit of serious study, constant interference on the part of rulers, who even went so far as to enjoin the teaching of Occamism on the new universities of Ingolstadt (1472) and Tübingen (1477). Three schools of philosophy fought for supremacy: Thomism, Scotism, and Occamism.

John Duns Scotus was born in the year that St. Thomas died (1274), and opposed his views successively at Oxford (1294), Paris (1304), and Cologne (1308). The danger which lurks in his system is its extremely voluntaristic tendency. Scotus explicitly taught that the will is superior to the intellect, an assertion which could, and actually did, lead to a complete denial of the ability of reason to know the truth. It would seem, moreover, that at the outset of his intellectual life there was a sort of contract drawn up between his own thoughts and the famous condemnation of 1277. Being a pastmaster in dialectics, he undertook a critical review of Thomism, subtly undermining the system with the aid of an extremely powerful dialectic. This abuse of logic led him to make a dangerous use of the argument *de potentia absoluta,* which introduces into theology the imaginative and hypothetical element under the formula: "It is not impossible that." Thus his method paved the way for that mania of endless and useless discussions and captious quibblings, which brought so much discredit upon the Scholastic system as a whole. The principal work of Duns Scotus is his Commentary on the Sentences of Peter Lombard, composed at Oxford, and later on published under the title of *Opus Oxoniense*. He summarized this work in Paris, and added to it a new Commentary, entitled *Reportata Parisiensia*. The treatise *De Rerum Principio* (Concerning the Beginning of Things), now attributed to Vitalis Dufour, and the *Theoremata,* which deal with metaphysical questions, are not from his pen. The Scotists of the fourteenth and fifteenth centuries, particularly Francis Mayron († 1325), who is known as *Doctor Acutus,* even surpassed Scotus in subtlety and rendered his method of philosophizing still more complicated.

Occamism sounded the death knell of Scholastic philosophy. Its author, William of Occam, was born in Surrey, about the year 1290. He joined the Franciscan Order and studied at Merton College, Oxford, where he lectured on the Sentences. He was not a disciple of Scotus, did not obtain the degree of master in theology, and did not teach in Paris. His principal works are: Commentaries on the Logic and Physics of Aristotle, a Commentary on the Sentences of Peter Lombard, the *Quodlibeta Septem,* and the *Centiloquium Theologicum.* To his way of thinking the individual and particular is the only real object, and we must never go beyond the data of sense experience. Concepts, therefore, are nothing more than names (Nominalism), mere words (Terminism), and general ideas have no counterpart in reality. This doctrine issued in a disquieting scepticism regarding metaphysical principles, and a determination not to transcend data of experience. All the proofs for the existence of God can inspire only probability, and the immortality of the soul must be relegated to the sphere of faith. Thus his empiricism inevitably led to Agnosticism. William of Occam remained a Christian nevertheless, and avoided the snares of scepticism through a sort of blind belief (*Fideism*), in which faith was something subjective, unreasonable, and incommunicable. His teachings were severely censured at Avignon as early as 1326, and shortly after condemned by the University of Paris (1339 and 1340). In 1346 Clement VI warned all students at the University against these *variae et extraneae doctrinae sophisticae* (various and extraneous sophistical doctrines), and in 1348 condemned the error of another Nominalist, Nicholas of Autrecourt, who denied the transcendental value of the principle of causality and declared that reason cannot prove the existence of God. William of Occam ended by throwing in his lot with the opponents of the temporal power of the pope, taking sides with Louis of Bavaria against John XXII.

Nevertheless, beginning with the middle of the fourteenth century, Occamism gained the ascendency at the University of Paris, and was taught by Peter d'Ailly and his pupil Gerson. The most outstanding of the Occamists were John Buridan, who advocated a sort of psychological determinism akin to that of Leibniz, and Marsile of Inghem († 1396), who made the first attempt to harmonize Nominalism with the metaphysics of Aristotle. The many differences which exist between the teachings of Marsile and those of his master prove that in his day Occamism was no longer a unified philosophy, to be reckoned among the great synthetic systems of the preceding era, but "a philosophy of dissolution and eclecticism." The *via antiqua* of the philosophers of the thirteenth century was thus supplanted by the *via moderna,* in which individual pride, breaking completely with tradition, wasted its efforts in inventing bizarre and heteroclite theories. Occamism retained its influence for a number of years. Luther affirmed that he had come to know of it through Gabriel Biel († 1495), a professor at the University of Tübingen. It eventually issued in that same *Fideism* which completely discounts the powers of reason, although in its method it abandoned the subtle arguments of dialectics for the authority of the Bible.

Thomism vainly attempted to react against these teachings, under the leadership of Peter de Palude († 1342), Hervé de Nedellec († 1323), and especially *John Capreolus* (1380–1444). Capreolus was called the prince of Thomists and composed the *Libri Defensionum,* in which he sought to offset the teachings of Scotism and Occamism by a sturdy presentation of the doctrine of St. Thomas. These writers, however, lacked the ability to adapt themselves to the new situation. Moreover, an excessive use of dialectics and the purely experimental method had undermined the authority of reason, which St. Thomas had proved to be in harmony with faith.[1]

Steering clear of the teachings of both Scotism and Nominalism, *Nicholas of Cusa* (1401–1464) based his system on the principle of the *coincidentia oppositorum,* which are solved only in God. "Our affirmations," he stated, "are no more true from the standpoint of reason than our negations"—a statement which would logically lead to both Agnosticism

---

[1] It must be observed, however, that the resolution on the part of such professors of the University of Paris as Buridan, Albert of Saxony, and Nicholas Oresme to limit their discussions to the field of experience may have paved the way for the great scientific discoveries made later on by Leonardo da Vinci and Galileo.

and Fideism. According to him, the infinite and the truth of things are beyond the scope of our intelligence, true wisdom being the knowledge of one's own ignorance (*docta ignorantia*). Despite such paradoxes and contradictions in his teaching, Nicholas of Cusa insisted in good faith that he was quite orthodox. His position is ample proof of the intellectual confusion prevalent at that time.

II. Moral Theology. Moral theology, which up to this time had formed one body with dogmatic theology, now became the object of special study. A large number of *Summae Casuum* began to appear, the majority of them being arranged in alphabetical order and discussing problems in casuistical form. The best known of these works was written by a friar minor from Asti, called *Astesanus* after his birthplace. This was soon followed by manuals for the use of confessors (*Confessionalia Interrogatoria*), the most outstanding of which were the *Manuale Confessorum* by the Dominican John Nider (✝ 1348) and the *Modus Confitendi* by Andrew Escobar (✝ about 1430). The real pioneer in this field was *St. Antoninus,* who in his *Summa theologica moralis* attempted to condense all the materials of Moral Theology. His work is divided into four parts. The first is distinctly philosophical in character and treats of the soul and its faculties; it is based almost entirely on the writings of St. Thomas. The second part is a discussion of the different species of sins. The third part describes the various social, religious, and ecclesiastical states, excommunication and censures, and is a valuable mine for Church historians dealing with fifteenth century conditions. The fourth part is concerned with the moral and cardinal virtues, and the gifts of the Holy Ghost. The *Summa* of St. Antoninus is not as well arranged as that of St. Thomas, but it is rich in material, and the juridical portion is so well developed that it has been termed *Juris Pontificii et Caesarei Summa.* For two centuries it was the only legal code in use, and the author exhibits throughout such a spirit of wisdom and consideration for moderate opinions, that he is sometimes called "St. Antoninus of the Counsels."

III. Holy Scripture. Great progress was made during this period in the study of Sacred Scripture. The study of the ancient languages developed. At the General Council of Vienne (1311) Clement V issued orders for the foundation of chairs for the teaching of Hebrew, Arabic, and Chaldaic in the residence of the popes and in the universities of Paris, Oxford, Bologna, and Salamanca. The Renaissance rendered great services in this direction by fostering the study of Greek; Reuchlin and Peter Niger distinguished themselves in this field in Germany. All these efforts were crowned by the appearance of the *Biblia Polyglotta Complutensis,* or Polyglot Bible of Alcala (1514–1517), edited by Cardinal Ximenes.

But the study of the ancient languages was merely a preparation for a better understanding of the literal sense of Scripture. The most famous biblical commentator in the fourteenth century was Nicholas of Lyra, O.M., a professor at the University of Paris. His principal work, entitled *Postilla,* is a commentary on the whole Bible in its literal sense and is written in clear and precise language, with very few digressions. Mystical explanations are given in a separate work, entitled *Moralitates.* Lyra's *Postilla* is in marked contrast to the allegorical commentaries of the Middle Ages, and he received the flattering titles of *Doctor Planus* and *Doctor Utilis.* The book was supplemented later on by Paul de Burgos, Patriarch of Aquilea, whose *Additiones* went through many editions. In the fifteenth century Alphonsus Tostat, professor at the University of Salamanca and Bishop of Avila, composed a *Commentarius in Libros Historicos V. T.* and an *Evangelium S. Matthaei,* in which the literal sense is given marked preference, but lengthier explanations are attempted. John Gerson formulated excellent hermeneutical principles in his *Propositiones de Sensu Litterali Scripturae Sacrae.* The mystical sense was not, however, completely disregarded, but is given large space in the commentaries of Denis the Carthusian, especially those on the Psalms, Job, Wisdom, the Gospels, and St. Paul.

Finally, the study of the Bible was ardently pursued in every Christian country—a historical fact which completely discredits the statement that Martin Luther revived interest in it as a "forgotten book." Many German and French translations appeared at this time, the first French Bible, called the Bible of St. Louis, meeting with phenomenal success. Subsequently other editions appeared, foremost among them the Bible of King John the Good and that of Charles V (translated by Ralph de Presles). The first complete edition of the Sacred Book was the Bible of Charles VIII, dedicated to him in 1487. Before the revolt of Martin Luther twenty popular translations of the Bible had appeared in Germany, and many *postillae* (a sort of complete prayer-book in the vernacular) were in evidence everywhere. Germany alone counted more than one hundred editions of such *postillae.*

TEXTS AND DOCUMENTS

An Appreciation of Duns Scotus

Scotus is frequently described as the Kant of Scholastic philosophy. He certainly resembles Kant in his refusal to accept without criticism any theory, no matter how universally received or how strongly supported by the authority of great names. The resemblance is accentuated by the fact that both Scotus and Kant are voluntarists, both maintaining that will is superior to intellect, and that human reason cannot demonstrate the truths which most vitally affect the destiny of man. But, remarkable as is the resemblance, the contrast is no less striking between the two philosophers. Kant appeals to the moral consciousness to prove the truths which reason cannot demonstrate; Scotus, on the contrary, appeals to revelation. Scotus places the supernatural order of truth above all philosophical knowledge, and consequently his criticism is partial and relative to the natural order of truth, while Kant's is radical and absolute. For Kant there is no court of appeal superior to the moral consciousness; for Scotus the supreme tribunal before which all truth is judged is divine revelation.

Scotus inaugurates an age of talent rather than of genius. The influence of St. Bonaventure, Albert, and St. Thomas seems to have silenced for a while the contentions which distracted the earliest Schoolmen. But now that the great constructive thinkers have disappeared, the intellectual knight-errantry of Abelard's day once more comes into vogue, and minds incapable of constructive effort devote themselves to analysis and controversy. It is among these lesser lights that Scotus, subtle and penetrating as his mind was, must be classed. For, while he excelled even the greatest of the Schoolmen in critical acumen, he was wanting in that synthetic power which St. Thomas possessed in so preëminent a degree, and which more than any other quality of mind stamps the writer or thinker as a *philosopher.*

Turner, *History of Philosophy,* pp. 391–392.

QUESTIONS

1. Enumerate the different causes of the decay of Scholasticism.
2. Define Occamism as a system of philosophy.
3. What is meant by the principle of the unity of opposites?
4. Was the Bible read before Luther?

BIBLIOGRAPHY

The Philosophical and Theological Movement.—E. Pluzanski, *Essai sur la philosophie de Duns Scot,* 1888.—B. Landry, *Duns Scot* (Coll. *"Grands Philosophes"*), 1922.—A Peltzer, *"Les 51 articles de Guillaume Occam censurés en Avignon en 1326,"* in *Rev. Hist. Eccl.,* t. XVIII (1922); pp. 240–270.—Art. *"Biel,"* in *Dict. de Théol.*—Salembier, art. *"Ailly,"* in *Dict. de Théol.*—J. Maritain, *Antimoderne,* ch. III. *De quelques conditions de la renaissance thomiste,* 1922.—M. de Wulf, *History of Mediaeval Philosophy.*—E. Gilson, *La philosophie au Moyen Age,* t. II. *De S. Thomas à G. d'Occam* (Coll. Payot), 1922.—Mandonnet, art. *"Antonin,"* in *Dict. de Théol.*—Morçay, art. *"Antonin,"* in *Dict. d'Hist.; Saint Antonin, fondateur du couvent de Saint-Marc, archévêque de Florence,* 1914.—P. Ephrem Longpré, *La philosophie de Duns Scot,* 1924.—E. Gilson, *Saint François d'Assise, son œuvre, son influence,* 1927, pp. 167–171; *Archives d'hist. doctr. du moyen âge,* pp. 89 ff. and pp. 146–149. See also Baudin, *Rev. Sciences Relig.* (1923), pp. 233 ff., 328 ff., and 508 ff.

Holy Scripture.—Cornély, *Cursus Scripturae Sacrae,* t. I: *Introductio generalis,* p. 660–667.—E. Mangenot, art. *"Polyglottes,"* in *Dict. de la Bible.* F. Vernet, art. *"Lyre,"* in *Dict. de Théol.*

CHAPTER III

I. In Germany. The Rhenish environment in which German mysticism of the fourteenth century finally blossomed forth, was prepared by an unusual growth of free religious associations, which included the Beghards and the Beguines, the Brethren of the Free Spirit, the Friends of God, etc. Unfortunately, all these associations lacked discipline and an organized hierarchy, and quickly degenerated into as many mystical heresies. Most of the harm seemed to come from the sect of the Brothers and Sisters of the Free Spirit, a sort of secret society, whose headquarters were located in Cologne, and whose influence was wide-spread in the valley of the Rhine. The teachings of this association were imbued with pantheistic and Averroistic tendencies, with the result that they finally issued in absolute Quietism. Acting in conformity with the wish of the German bishops, the Council of Vienne, in 1315, condemned the error of the Beghards, that "man in this present life is capable of acquiring such a state of perfection that he becomes impeccable and can make no further progress in grace. . . . Once he attains this state, his senses become so completely subordinated to his intellect that he can permit his body whatever he pleases." These errors account for the many degraded practices introduced under the guise of religious fervor. Another association of laymen, called Friends of God, strongly inveighed against the disorders of the clergy and exhibited tendencies towards Illuminism, but on the whole it was made up of souls who were anxious for religious reform.

The German mysticism which developed in this environment was intellectual rather than affective in character, for while the Franciscans sought to merge with the Godhead by the contemplation of Christ's Sacred Humanity, Eckhart and his school achieved the same result by metaphysical speculations, centering chiefly on the Divine Essence, the nature of the soul, and the union of the Saviour with the soul. Moreover, since German mysticism was intended for all men, it formulated its teachings in the vernacular and not in Latin. The head of this school, *John Eckhart,* was born at Hochheim in Thuringia about 1260. He entered the Dominican community at Erfurt, preached at Strasbourg, and taught at Cologne, but, towards the end of his life (1326), he was arraigned before the tribunal of Archbishop Henry on the charge of heresy. He appealed to the pope and died after recanting whatever might savor of error in his writings. It is impossible to obtain anything like a complete and direct estimate of these accusations, for the reason that only a small portion of Eckhart's works has come down to us. According to some, Eckhart was a friend of the Brethren of the Free Spirit and became involved in idealistic pantheism; the school which he founded adhered to these teachings, but made strenuous efforts to appear orthodox. According to others, in particular the learned Father Denifle, the obscurity of certain of his writings is responsible for Eckhart's falling into disrepute. According to another writer, some passages are manifestly pantheistic, but do not appear to fit in with the rest of his system; basically his teaching is orthodox. Nevertheless, certain propositions attributed to him were censured by Pope John XXII. The union between God and the human soul, of which he speaks, becomes so intimate at times that the two appear absolutely identical, as when he says: "We are completely transformed into God, and are changed into Him in the same manner as bread is changed into the body of Christ in the Holy Eucharist; I am thus changed into Him, because He makes me His being, and not merely His likeness" (Prop. 10). "The just man does all that God does, and he created Heaven and earth conjointly with God; he generated the Divine Word, and without this man, God could do nothing." (Prop. 13.)

Eckhart had two disciples, whose orthodoxy is beyond question: Tauler and Suso. *John Tauler* was born at Strasbourg about the year 1290 and, like Eckhart, entered the Order of the Dominicans. Like Eckhart, too, he labored mainly in the cities of Strasbourg and Cologne († 1361). The greater portion of his literary work consists of sermons, to which must be added a few didactic treatises, particularly his *Considerations on the Life and Passion of the Saviour.* Tauler is distinctly a speculative writer, a subtle and profound analyst. He has sometimes been compared with the famous English Oratorian, Father Faber. *Henry Suso,* on the other hand, is pre-eminently an affective writer. Born in 1295 at Neberlingen, on the shores of Lake Constance, he entered the Dominican community at

Constance at the age of thirteen, became the knight and lover of the Eternal Logos, with whom he contracted a spiritual marriage, and for whom he crucified his flesh. After his appointment as prior of Constance, his orthodoxy was questioned because of *The Book of Truth,* in which, strange to say, he strove to refute the errors of the Beghards and the Brethren of the Free Spirit. Removed from office by a general Chapter held at Bruges, in 1336, he spent the rest of his life in complete abandonment, and died at Ulm, in 1365. He related his trials and mystical graces to Elizabeth Staglin, a Dominican nun of the convent of Toss, who collected them and wrote his biography. His four principal works, the *Biography, The Book of Eternal Wisdom, The Book of Truth,* and *The Small Book of Letters,* were revised and grouped together by him in one work, entitled *Exemplar.* The most famous of his writings is *The Book of Eternal Wisdom,* which describes with poignant realism the sufferings of Jesus Christ, to which are opposed our mortal sins. The convents of the Dominican Sisters flourished under the influence of these mystics and became veritable nurseries of saints. We will mention only those of Toss, Unterlinden near Colmar, Adelhausen at Freiburg in Breisgau, Oltenbach near Zurich, and that in the Valley of St. Catherine, near Dissenhofen on the Rhine. Finally, we must call attention to the revelations of Christine Ebnerin († 1356), Adelaide Langmann († 1375), of the convent of Engelthal, and Margaret Ebnerin († 1371), of the convent of Medingen.

The Flemish mystic, *John van Ruysbroeck,* also belongs to the German school. While a canon of the church of St. Gudule in Brussels, he wrote against the sect of the Free Spirit. Later on, he retired with several companions to a place of retreat called Groenendael (*Viridis Vallis,* Vauvert, or Green Valley) in the forest of Soignes, where he modelled his life on the Rule of St. Augustine and composed his principal works. Among them are: the *Mirror of Eternal Salvation,* the *Book of the Seven Enclosures,* the *Kingdom of the Lovers of God* (wherein the purpose of the gifts of the Holy Ghost is clearly set forth), and, finally, the *Spiritual Espousals,* in which the three phases of the mystical life are fully described. Although his writings were attacked by Gerson and Bossuet, Ruysbroeck's orthodoxy is above suspicion. The Franciscan, Henry Halphius, or Henry of Herp, who was first provincial of the Franciscans of the strict Observance at Cologne, and later on guardian of the monastery at Malines, was a contemporary of Ruysbroeck and greatly influenced by his writings († 1478).

II. In the Netherlands. Here the Brethren of the Common Life inaugurated a reactionary movement in favor of a mysticism which was at once more affective and more practical. This movement was called *"Devotio Moderna."* The two outstanding authors of this school are Gerlac Petersen and Thomas à Kempis. *Gerlac Petersen* (1378-1411) is famous for his fervent *Soliloquy,* an interior monologue and a series of conversations with God, which bears a marked resemblance to the *Imitation of Christ.* It is incorrect to attribute the latter book to Gerson, because in the edition of his works published in 1488 it is explicitly stated that the work is not from his pen. The Italian Gersen, who is regarded as another claimant, probably never existed, and the name is only a faulty spelling of Gerson. Moreover, John Busch, the historian of Windesheim († 1479), in the second edition of his *De Viris Illustribus de Windesen* (1464), formally attributes the *Imitation* to *Thomas à Kempis.* Thomas was born in 1380 at Kempen, near Düsseldorf, in the Rhine Province, and after making his studies at Deventer, entered the monastery of Mount St. Agnes, near Zwolle in Holland, where he died in 1471. Thomas composed the *Imitation* according to a method used by the canons of Windesheim, who gathered together sentences and made collections (*rapiaria*) from them. The *Imitation,* indeed, is nothing more than a collection of maxims, colloquies, and prayers. Thomas à Kempis also composed a number of sermons and smaller works for the use of religious. Among them we may cite: *De Disciplina Claustralium, Epistola Devota ad Quemdam Regularem,* and *Sermones ad Novicios.* His works, like all the others written by members of the congregation of Windesheim, are imbued with a simple and practical spirituality, which enjoins the virtues of humility, patience, and regularity as the foundations of the Christian life.

Denis the Carthusian was also a native of the Netherlands (1402-1474). He was born at Ryckel, in the province of Limburg, and entered the Carthusian monastery of Ruremonde at the age of twenty. His work is a compilation of ascetical and mystical writings, which abound in practical counsels on contempt of the world, resistance to temptations, and the joys of union with God. It had a phenomenal success, comparable in many respects to that of the *Imitation.* This is particularly true of the

Speculum Conversionis and the *Speculum Amatorum Mundi.* St. Ignatius and St. Francis de Sales made considerable use of them in the sixteenth century.

Two famous doctors of the University of Paris launched a direct attack upon all false mystics: Peter d'Ailly in his two treatises *De Falsis Prophetis* (Concerning False Prophets), and the Chancellor Gerson in his *De Probatione Spirituum* (Concerning the Testing of Spirits). Gerson also composed a number of mystical treatises, the principal ones being: the *Mountain of Contemplation, Mystical, Speculative, and Practical Theology, Scholastic Exposition of Mystical Theology,* as well as several shorter treatises on the *Perfection of the Heart,* the *Simplicity of the Heart,* the *Alphabet of Divine Love,* etc. Following in the footsteps of his master, St. Bonaventure, he succeeded in setting up perfect harmony between affective and speculative spirituality. His last work, a *Commentary on the Canticle,* recalls St. Bernard.

Closely associated with the reactionary movement against speculative mysticism was the controversy of "learned ignorance" (*docta ignorantia*), which originated in the monasteries of Upper Bavaria and Lower Austria. The moot question was, whether thoughts were to be set aside as detrimental to true devotion, or whether the intellect was to be given a place in the practice of contemplation. The famous scholar, Nicholas of Cusa, pronounced himself in favor of the second alternative and very wisely stemmed the excessive reaction in the direction of agnostic piety.

III. In Italy. There was never any well-defined school of mystics in Italy, but there were a few staunch and able writers on the subject, the most outstanding of whom were St. Catherine of Siena, St. Catherine of Bologna, and St. Catherine of Genoa.

St. Catherine of Siena (1347–1380) was favored with a vision of Jesus Christ at the early age of six. After suffering incessant persecution at the hands of her family, because of her refusal to marry, she became a Dominican tertiary. Her life was one uninterrupted series of miracles, including ecstasies, the stigmata, etc., none of which, however, prevented her from caring for the sick with a devotion that was nothing short of heroic. The reader is acquainted with the part she played towards the end of the exile of the popes at Avignon. Her principal writings comprise *Letters* and a *Dialogue.* The former, addressed to all fervent souls who form what she termed her *"bella brigada,"* are imbued with sweetness, firmness, and practical sense. The *Dialogue* is an interview between the Eternal Father and St. Catherine. It comprises essentially three prayers, formulated by the Saint: the first for herself, the second for the world, and the third to obtain the reform of the clergy. This work contains an eloquent satire on the vices of the time. Catherine was first and last a speculative mystic and a true daughter of St. Thomas Aquinas. Blessed Raymond of Capua wrote her biography in Latin.

St. Catherine of Bologna was a Franciscan. After living at the court of Ferrara, she retired from the world, and was immediately beset with violent temptations, which ceased only when she entered the convent of the Poor Clares at Florence. She died in 1463 as abbess of a convent in Bologna. Her treatise entitled, *On the Seven Spiritual Weapons against the Enemies of the Soul,* is nothing more than an autobiography, written in Italian, in which, under the fictitious name of Catella, the Saint recounts her struggles, her efforts, and her spiritual favors. This work now goes under the title of *Revelations of St. Catherine.*

Born at Genoa, in 1447, of the illustrious family of the Fieschi, which gave to the world Innocent IV and Adrian V, *St. Catherine of Genoa* was married against her will to Julian Adorno, who made her very unhappy. She became a widow at the age of twenty-three, and spent the remainder of her life caring for the sick in a hospital at Genoa. St. Catherine was particularly impressed with the idea of divine purity, which constantly enjoins upon us greater and greater purifications. This is without doubt the motive which induced her to compose her famous treatise on *Purgatory,* in which she describes the torments of souls prevented by their sins from soaring towards God.

TEXTS AND DOCUMENTS

Blessed Henry Suso on "The Unspeakable Advantages of Meditation on the Divine Passion"

Behold, assiduous meditation upon My passion makes out of a simple man a master of high knowledge; truly it is a living book in which everything is to be found. How right blessed is that man who has it ever before his eyes and studies it! What wisdom, grace, consolation, sweetness, what cleansing from all imperfection, may not such a man obtain through the devout contemplation of My living Presence! Respecting which, listen to what follows. It fell out many years ago that a certain preacher in the beginning of his conversion had a bitter affliction of inordinate despondency, which, at times, so overpowered him that no heart which had not experienced it, could conceive it. And, as he once sat after dinner in his cell, his affliction was so great that he could neither study nor pray, nor perform any other good deed, except sitting there so sadly in his cell, and laying his hands in his lap, as though he meant only to take care of the cell, for God's sake, because he was no longer of any use in spiritual things. And, as he thus sat disconsolate, it suddenly seemed to him as if he heard these words addressed to him: Why dost thou sit here, arise and betake thee of My sorrowful Passion, and then wilt thou overcome thy own sorrow. And immediately he arose, for the words were the same to him as they came from Heaven, and he began to meditate on the sorrowful Passion of our Lord, in which all his own sorrow was lost so that he never felt it again in the same manner.

BL. HENRY SUSO, *Book of Eternal Wisdom,* pp. 90–91 (transl. R. Raby).

THE IMITATION OF CHRIST

The author of the *Imitation* knows little of Christ according to the flesh; he hardly mentions the Virgin Mary. But scarcely a book produced in the Middle Ages is more full of the interior life of Jesus within the soul. And neither the Middle Ages nor any other period has produced more books more simply human, more free from the peculiarities of the age which gave it birth. The *Imitation* would be sufficient—as would the *Summa contra Gentiles*—to acquit the literature of the Middle Ages of the unjust charge sometimes levelled against it, that it has always remained childish, never having managed to raise itself to the higher classical plane of those great works which touch the universal and permanent side of man. The fundamental restlessness of the created spirit, the persistent need of tenderness, the obstinate returnings of self-love, are here depicted with perfect simplicity and truth, without tricks of style or preciosity, and without subtleties or literary artifices. Everybody knows, too, those fine chapters, "of the familiar friendship of Jesus," and "of the wonderful effect of divine love." *Si quis amat, novit quid haec vox clamet!* In this last passage, the Latin of à Kempis has a certain pure and natural resonance which makes any translation sound very poor by comparison.

M. C. D'ARCY, S. J., *The Life of the Church,* pp. 191–192.

QUESTIONS

1. What is meant by Quietism and Illuminism, and how are they connected with mysticism?
2. How do intellectual and affective mysticism differ from each other?

3. Give an estimate of the mysticism of Eckhart.
4. Institute a comparison between the mysticism of John Tauler and that of Blessed Suso.
5. Give a literary appreciation of the *Imitation of Christ*.
6. Differentiate between the mystical teachings of the three St. Catherines.

BIBLIOGRAPHY

German Mystics.—DENIFLE, *Archiv für Litteratur und Kirchengeschichte des Mittelalters*, t. V, 349–364.—H. DELACROIX, *Essai sur le mysticisme spéculatif en Allemagne au XIVe siècle*, 1899.—F. VERNET, art. "Bégards, Béguines héterodoxes," "Frères du Libre Esprit," "Eckart" and "Eckart le Jeune," in *Dict. de Théol.*—THIRIOT, *Œuvres mystiques du B. Henri Suso*, 1899.—DENIFLE, *La vie spirituelle d'après les mystiques allemands du XIVe siècle.*—X. DE HORNSTEIN, *Le Bienheureux Suso*, in *Rev. Thomiste*, 1922; *Les grands mystiques allemands du XIVe siècle*, Lucerne, 1922.—RENÉE ZELLER, *Le Bienheureux Suso*, 1922.—J. PAQUIER, *Un mystique allemand au XIVe siècle. L'orthodoxie de la théologie germanique*, 1922.— Works of RUYSBRŒCK, transl. by the Benedictines of St. Paul de Wisques, 3 vols.—G. THÉRY, *Contribution à l'histoire du procès d'Eckart*, in *Vie spirituelle*, 1925–1926.

Dutch Mystics.—GERLAC PETERSEN, *Le soliloque enflammé*, 1921.— THOMAE HEMERKEN A KEMPIS, *Opera Omnia*, ed. Pohl, Freiburg i. B., 1902– 1918.—PUYOL, *L'auteur du livre De Imitatione Christi*, 1899.—A. DE BACKER, *Essai bibliographique sur le livre De Imitatione Christi*, Liège, 1864.—V. BECKER, *L'auteur de l'Imitation et les documents néerlandais*, La Haye, 1882.— SPITZEN, *Les hollandismes de l'Imitation*, Utrecht, 1884; *Nouvelle défense de Thomas à Kempis*, Utrecht, 1884.—K. HIRSCHE, *Prolegomena zu einer neuen Ausgabe der Imitatio Christi*, 3 vols., Berlin, 1873–1894.—DIONYSI CARTH., *Opera Omnia*, Montreuil-sur-Mer, 1896 ff.—S. AUTORE, art. "Denys le Chartreux," in *Dict. de Théol.*—VACANDARD, *Etudes de critique et d'histoire religieuse*, 4th series, *L'auteur de l'Imitation de Jésus-Christ*, 1922.—DOM J. HUYBEN, *Les premiers documents historiques concernant l'Imitation*, in *Vie spirituelle*, 1925–1926.—P. GROULT, *Les mystiques des Pays-Bas et la littérature espagnole du XVIe siècle*, Louvain, 1926.—P. DEBONGNIE, *Jean Monbaer*, Louvain, 1928.—BROTHER LEO, *The Imitation of Christ* (the Introduction records all that is known of Thomas à Kempis).—V. SCULLY, *Life of the Venerable Thomas à Kempis*, 1901.

CHAPTER IV

In the fourteenth century the sacramental liturgy had almost assumed its definitive form. The custom of baptizing by infusion was gradually introduced everywhere, and immersion restricted exclusively to the city of Milan. The practice of baptizing infants shortly after their birth was becoming more and more general. Communion was infrequent and Mass was celebrated all too rarely. The Synod of Ravenna (1314) complained that many priests never said Mass at all and demanded that they do so at least once a year; other councils (Tarragona, 1317; Toledo 1324) enjoined the celebration of the Holy Sacrifice two or three times a year. Nevertheless, some progress was being made along this line, thanks to the beneficial influence of the Brethren of the Common Life.

I. Different Kinds of Indulgences. The most important innovation in the domain of the Sacraments was the development of indulgences. The former penitential tariff was no longer applied for the purpose of imposing penances, but solely with a view of remitting punishments due to sin. As a consequence, the number of years and weeks remitted had no practical equivalent; they were, so to speak, securities with no current value that could be used on a large scale. Moreover, the popes were flooded with requests from monasteries and churches, from princes and bishops, and the low level of the faith called for less stringent regulations.

It was at this juncture that special indulgences came into being, notably the *Jubilee* and the *Confessionalia*. Towards the end of the thirteenth century the idea became wide-spread that the popes granted a jubilee under the form of a plenary indulgence at the beginning of each new century. This indulgence could be gained by making a visit to the churches of Rome. Pope Boniface VIII accredited this opinion by inaugurating the Jubilee for 1300 *"et in quolibet anno centesimo venturo"* (and for the first year of each succeeding century). The success of this favor surpassed all expectations. In 1343, Clement VI declared that the Jubilee would be celebrated every fifty years. Urban VI, in 1389, reduced the period to thirty-three and Paul II to twenty-five years. Finally, the custom was introduced of granting a Jubilee not only with the advent of a new pope, but also whenever a grave situation confronted the papacy. Towards the end of the fourteenth century, the English and the Portuguese were permitted to gain the Jubilee indulgences at home.

The *Confessionalia* or *Litterae Confessionales* were indults, granting the right to select a confessor who, together with other extraordinary privileges, had the power to remit sins and all punishments due to them. John XXII granted this privilege *in articulo mortis* (in the hour of death). Some of these *Confessionalia* contained the clause, *absolvas a poena et a culpa* (you may absolve from punishment and from guilt), a formula to be met with in other grants of indulgences, and one that has led several historians to denounce indulgences as an easy means of purging one's conscience. In point of fact confession was a necessary condition of gaining an indulgence, and it alone remitted the guilt; the indulgence properly so called never remitted anything but the temporal punishment due to sin. Moreover, the preachers of that time never ceased to inveigh against any other interpretation.

II. Abuses. It cannot be denied that the granting of indulgences often led to serious abuses. In the first place, the practice was frequently exploited for financial reasons. The popes of the fifteenth century, when in need of funds to carry on the warfare against the Turks or to uphold their reputation as patrons of the arts and letters, often resorted to indulgences as a means of raising money. Leo X borrowed enormous sums from such bankers as the Fuggers and the Fiescobaldi by guaranteeing the preaching of indulgences. These indulgences were of different kinds. Some were used to promote works of piety and assist charitable institutions (building of churches and hospitals, sponsoring of Crusades, etc.), while others were directed to needs of the temporal and general order (construction of ports, dikes, highways, etc.). Moreover, civic officers, princes, bishops, and city officials, in whose territories the indulgence was preached, often claimed a portion of the proceeds, the result being that agreements had to be made in the manner between them and the Holy See. Charles V obtained an indulgence for the Netherlands to defray the expenses of repairing the dikes, on condition that one-third of the proceeds go to the papacy and the remainder to the Emperor (1515). Finally, the preachers who were charged with promulgating an indulgence associated with themselves collectors who set up their desks in close proximity to the pulpit and the confessional, in such wise that the scene often resembled a county fair. It must be observed, however, that the poor were never required to pay.

To sum up. Indulgences were too frequently treated as a profitable business by three distinct parties: the pope, the civil authorities, and the collectors. We must not, however, forget the many services rendered by them. (1) From the standpoint of general interests, they hastened the return of social and economic prosperity after the period of depression caused by the One Hundred Years' War; (2) the granting of indulgences was always accompanied by the preaching of sermons and the hearing of confessions, and because the custom was a very popular one, it often issued in the same beneficial results effected by our present-day missions; (3) finally, during the fifteenth century indulgences were made applicable to the souls of the faithful departed; the legate Peraudi started this by preaching such an indulgence in Germany, in 1489, to promote public interest in the Crusade.

III. The Way of the Cross. Pilgrims and crusaders who undertook the journey to Jerusalem at an early period started the devotion of kneeling in prayer at the different spots to which tradition pointed as the principal scenes of the "Sorrowful Journey" of Christ. Soon Christians who found it impossible to go to Palestine substituted a devotion in place of the pilgrimage; and so, just as the Rosary became the psalter of the people and the scapular their religious garb, the spiritual pilgrimage took the place of an actual visit to the holy places. Blessed Suso saw the many advantages of such a substitution, and it was accorded a warm reception by the Flemish mystics. The number of stations, however, remained undetermined. Adam Kraft (1490) counted eight, others twelve, seventeen and even as many as thirty-four. The two works which exercised the greatest influence on the growth of this devotion were: the *Gheestelyck Perimagrie* of the Carmelite John Pascha, published at Louvain in 1563, and the treatise of the Franciscan Adrichomius, entitled *Jerusalem sicut Christi tempore floruit* (Jerusalem as it Flourished in the Time of Christ), published in 1584. The latter author mentions twelve stations in their present order, with only the last two missing. These two works helped to shape the devotion of the *Way of the Cross* in the West. It was finally judged necessary to modify the route of the "Sorrowful Journey" in the city of Jerusalem, so much so that the Franciscans were obliged to adapt the "stations" little by little to the piety of the faithful.

TEXTS AND DOCUMENTS

ACCUSATIONS AGAINST INDULGENCES

The accusations made against indulgences involve a threefold charge: First, that they are not of divine origin, but a pure invention of the Church; secondly, that the object of the Church in inventing them was only to lead the faithful into error; and, lastly, that they are mere useless contrivances with no practical result. All these accusations can be easily answered.

First, the power of granting indulgences is, as we have seen, a necessary corollary of the "power of the keys." Our Divine Lord's own behavior towards the adulterous woman, and St. Paul's towards the incestuous Corinthian, are clear proofs of this; and from the very beginning of the Church the pope and the bishops have used their power in analagous methods. Therefore, we have every right to place indulgences among those practices that owe their existence to the will and institution of Jesus Christ.

This being so, it is sheer absurdity to attribute to the Church, in making use of such a power, the motive of deceiving the faithful. Errors and abuses may certainly have crept in by degrees, as regards the mode of distribution; but it would be illogical to condemn the practice itself as false and deceitful, because it has been carried out in a spirit quite unlike what its Author intended, and indeed in actual opposition to His wishes.

As to the third accusation, respecting the futility of indulgences, we have already shown—and hope to show yet more fully—what good fruit they have borne, first, in the department of art, by prompting the erection of those magnificent cathedrals, numerous hospitals, and peaceful monasteries, which will ever remain a wonder to future generations; next, in the range of social interests, by bringing together men of so different countries and of so contrary habits to more perfect civilization and common sympathy, and generally by their influence in softening men's hearts; and above all, in the domain of faith, by impressing the deep truths of religion and promoting the spirit of prayer and the practice of good works.

LEPICIER, *Indulgences,* pp. 404–405.

QUESTIONS

1. On what grounds does the Church claim the right to grant indulgences?
2. What is the indulgence of the Jubilee, and how did it originate?

3. Enumerate the services rendered and the abuses occasioned by the granting of indulgences.
4. What are the present-day indulgences attached to the Way of the Cross?

BIBLIOGRAPHY

Indulgences.—A. FAUCIEUX (A. Chollet), *"Les Indulgences devant l'histoire et le droit canon"* in *Rev. des sciences ecclésiastiques,* 1887 and 1888.—H. C. LEA, *A History of Auricular Confession and Indulgences,* t. III. *Indulgences;* in reference to this work see Msgr. BOUDINHON, *"Sur l'histoire des indulgences, à propos d'un livre récent,"* in *Rev. hist. et litt. relig.,* 1898, t. III, pp. 435-55.—Msgr. N. PAULUS, *Johann Tetzel, der Ablassprediger,* Mayence, 1899.—SCHULTE, *Die Fugger in Rom (1495-1529),* Leipzig, 1904.—E. GÖLLER, *Der Ausbruch der Reformation und die spätmittelalterliche Ablasspraxis,* Freiburg i. B., 1917.—P. GALTIER, art. *"Indulgences,"* in *Dict. d'Apol.*—ET. MAGNIN, art. *"Indulgences,"* in *Dict. de Théol.*—H. THURSTON, *An Historical Study on the Way of the Cross.*—LEPICIER, *Indulgences.*

CHAPTER V

I. The Question of the Immaculate Conception. The problem of the Immaculate Conception was frequently discussed during this period. Through his constant use of what is known as the hypothetical method, Duns Scotus was led to treat this point of Mariology, and while not formally teaching the existence of the privilege, he defended its possibility. "It seems reasonable," he said, "to attribute to Mary what is more excellent." Many other doctors declared themselves against the privilege, notably among the Dominicans. They based their view on the authority of St. Thomas, who, according to them, had clearly stated his position in the matter. In 1387, one of them, John de Monzon, committed the twofold imprudence of scoring as heretical the opinion which defended the privilege, and of appealing to the authority of St. Thomas. Because he stubbornly persisted in teaching these views, fourteen propositions selected from his thesis were condemned by the University of Paris, and Peter d'Orgement, Bishop of Paris, forbade them to be taught under pain of excommunication. All candidates for university degrees were required to adhere to this condemnation. Nicholas Eymeric, another Dominican, who held the same exaggerated views, was severely censured by King John I of Aragon.

The Scotist and Franciscan reaction was also felt in the domain of worship. In the first half of the fifteenth century the feast of the Immaculate Conception was celebrated almost everywhere, and the Council of Basle—at a time, it is true, when it was already openly schismatic—raised the feast to the rank of a holyday of obligation, and issued orders for the composition of a special Office. Further confirmation of this devotion was given by Pope Sixtus IV, when, to offset the erroneous teaching of the Italian Dominican, Vincent Bandelli, who claimed that it was nothing short of impiety to make the Conception of Mary an exception to the general rule (1475), he successively approved two Offices in honor

711

of Mary Immaculate. When Bandelli continued to remonstrate, he was silenced by the Bull *"Grave Nimis,"* in which the Pope scored as "false and erroneous the views of those who look upon the feast celebrated in the Roman Church as intended to honor merely the spiritual conception or sanctification of the Blessed Virgin Mary, or accuse of heresy persons who hold to this pious belief."

II. The Angelus. It was during this period also that many devotions to the Blessed Virgin Mary assumed their final form. One of these was the *Rosary,* of which we have already spoken in connection with the preceding period. The concluding words of the Ave Maria, *"Nunc et in hora mortis nostrae,"* appear for the first time in a Carthusian breviary around the year 1350. In 1514, these words entered the breviaries of the Trinitarians and the Camaldolese, and in 1525, they are found in the breviary of the Franciscans. Very soon the practice of reciting them spread to the faithful laity. The *Angelus* originated in the fourteenth century with the practice of reciting one or several Hail Marys during the ringing of the curfew. We meet with this custom as early as 1296 in the city of Milan, where it had been introduced by Bonvicino de Riva, of the Order of the *Humiliati.* It was authorized in France by Pope Clement V, and in 1318 Pope John XXII granted several indulgences to those who recited three Hail Marys at the hour of the curfew. The ringing of the bells was intended to honor the mystery of the Incarnation and Salutation of the angel. Very soon the practice of reciting the Hail Mary in the morning was introduced, to honor more especially the sorrows of the Blessed Virgin at the foot of the Cross. According to St. Antoninus, this custom was prevalent in the middle of the fifteenth century. The ringing of the bells at noon is of more recent origin. In the beginning it was intended to honor the Passion of Our Lord, and was performed only on Fridays. Callixtus III (1456) and Louis XI (1472) helped to spread this devotion. The Pope enjoined the recitation of three Hail Marys to avert the Turkish peril; the King of France made their recitation obligatory throughout his realm to obtain the blessings of peace. An attempt to amalgamate the three devotions was made in the opening years of the sixteenth century, when, at the request of Briçonnet, Bishop of Meaux and abbot of St. Germain-des-Prés, Pope Leo X granted a number of indulgences to the faithful who would recite three Hail Marys on their knees in the morning, at noon, and in the evening. The present formula of the *Angelus* occurs for the first time in the *Officium Parvum B.M.V.* as revised by order of Pius V.

Two doctors of the University of Paris promoted the devotion to St. Joseph. The first of these, Peter d'Ailly, composed a treatise entitled, *De Duodecim Honoribus Sancti Josephi;* the second, Gerson, composed in French *Considerations on St. Joseph,* a series of meditations on the espousals of Our Lady and St. Joseph. At the Council of Constance this same scholar made an eloquent appeal to obtain the establishment of a feast in honor of St. Joseph. In Italy, St. Bernardine of Siena wrote a theological treatise on the devotion to St. Joseph. This movement resulted in the introduction of the feast of St. Joseph (March 19) into the Roman Breviary by Pope Sixtus IV.

TEXTS AND DOCUMENTS

The Bull of Sixtus IV

Pope Sixtus IV, by a Bull dated the 1st of March, 1476, exhorted all the faithful to observe with unusual piety and devotion the festival of the Immaculate Conception of that year. The occasion was as follows: In the beginning of that year there occurred a heavy fall of snow, which melted so suddenly and caused such an overflow of the rivers that people really believed that a second deluge had come upon the earth. Many lives were lost, there was a great loss of property and of works of art, and desolation reigned far and wide both in the city of Rome itself and in the country districts. And yet this frightful inundation was but the forerunner of a still more dreadful calamity. The plague broke out and in a few days the Eternal City became depopulated, for all those who escaped the epidemic fled beyond the walls of the city so acutely infected. In the hope of arresting the progress of the destructive elements and of saving some of the other portions of the country, and other Christian nations, the Supreme Head of the Church established the festival of the Immaculate Conception for the whole Catholic world and granted to the persons observing the day many indulgences.

B. Rohner, O.S.B., *Veneration of the Blessed Virgin,* pp. 104–105.

QUESTIONS

1. Explain the statement of Duns Scotus: *"Videtur probabile quod excellentius est attribuere Mariae."*
2. Give the origins of the *Angelus.*

3. Enumerate the reasons which finally induced the Church to define the dogma of the Immaculate Conception.

4. When was the Feast of St. Joseph originated?

BIBLIOGRAPHY

The Immaculate Conception and Devotion to Mary.—X. Le Bachelet, *"Saint Thomas, Duns Scot et l'Immaculée Conception,"* in *Recherches de science religieuse,* 1910, t. I, p. 601–16.—Msgr. Péchenard, *"L'Immaculée Conception et l'ancienne Université de Paris,"* in *Rev. du clergé français,* t. XLI (1905), pp. 225–83.—P. Doncoeur, *"La condamnation de Jean de Monzon par Pierre d'Orgemont, évêque de Paris,"* in *Rev. quest. hist.,* t. LXXXII (1907), pp. 176–87.—Mortier, *Hist. des Maîtres généraux de l'ordre des Frères Prêcheurs,* t. III, pp. 616–47.—X. Le Bachelet, art. *"Immaculée Conception,"* in *Dict. de Théol.*—Dom Berlière, art. *"Angelus et Angélique (Salutation),"* in *Dict. de Théol.*—O. R. Vassall-Phillips, C. SS. R., *The Mother of Christ,* London, 1922.

I. The First Renaissance in Italy. We must distinguish two successive attempts in Italy to revive popular interest in the arts: the first, called that of the Trecentists, was inaugurated by Giotto († 1337); the second, which we might term a "Religious Realism," the author of which was Masaccio. The first of these two attempts remained Christian in its inspiration. Giotto was in art what Dante was in literature—a link between the future and the past. He belonged to the past by the majesty of his conceptions, the virility of his faith, and the epic grandeur which flooded his soul; he was a prophet of the future inasmuch as he heralded the Renaissance proper by his spirit of inquisitiveness and his realism. No one has ever been known to carry the science of mimicry to such extremes. He decorated three churches: that of St. Francis of Assisi (*Communion of Magdalen, Resurrection of Lazarus,* and *Miracles of St. Francis*); that of the Madonna dell' Arena at Padua (*The Nativity, Adoration of the Magi,* and *Last Judgment*), and that of Santa Croce at Florence (*The Burial of St. Francis* and *The Banquet of King Herod*). He also inaugurated the great symbolic compositions which reveal the influence of Dante: *The Triumph of Faith* and the *Triumph of St. Thomas Aquinas,* the theme of which was resumed by Raphael in his *Disputation on the Blessed Sacrament* and *The School of Athens.*

The Dominican, Fra Angelico de Fiesole (1387–1455), revived the methods of the miniature-painters, employing their bright colors, gold backgrounds, and tints of rose and blue. The serene expression, supernatural beauty, and angelic naïveté of his figures compels our admiration, despite the simplicity of his technique. We should mention in particular his *Coronation of the Virgin* at the Louvre, *The Crucifixion,* in the convent of St. Mark, in which he brings out every expression with unsurpassed intensity, and the frescoes in the pope's private oratory (*Lives of St. Stephen and St. Lawrence*).

These first attempts to revive an interest in the arts in Italy were followed by a period of religious realism, heralded by Masaccio (1402–1443). In the opinion of a very distinguished writer, "he appears to be the first who discovered the path that leads to every excellence at which art afterwards arrived, and may, therefore, be justly considered as one of the great fathers of modern art." He blossomed forth in the Florentine school side by side with Lippi, Botticelli, and Ghirlandajo. *Fra Filippo Lippi* (1406–1469), who displays great ease in his work, coupled with a remarkable variety of expression, is famous for his frescoes in Prato (*Lives of St. John the Baptist and St. Stephen*). His pupil *Botticelli* (1444–1510) was gracious to a fault. It is plain from his painting that foreign types had a strange but chaste attraction for him. His best-known works are his *Virgins* in the Louvre, *Adoration of the Magi,* and *Allegory of Spring. Ghirlandajo* is noted for his serene simplicity, the beauty of his types, and the purity of his taste, as exemplified particularly in his great frescoes in the choir of Santa Maria Novella. The school of Padua stands above all for the cult of antiquity. Its outstanding representative is *Andrea Mantegna* (1430–1506), a learned and erudite painter, who by his vivid imagination again brought the treasures of ancient archeology to light. We may also cite *Perugino* (1446–1526), an eclectic, who taught Raphael; *Luca Signorelli of Cortona* (1441–1523), who by his dramatic power foretold the coming of *Michael Angelo* (*Last Judgment,* on the dome of Orvieto); and at Venice *Gentile* († 1507) and *Giovanni Bellini* († 1516), who, unlike the Tuscans, attached more importance to the harmonizing of colors and the right use of light than to beauty of design.

The two outstanding figures in the field of sculpture were Ghiberti and Donatello. *Ghiberti* (1378–1455) is famous for his two bronze doors of the baptistery in Florence, one of which represents in twenty-eight low reliefs different scenes from the New Testament; the other, eighteen subjects taken at random from the same source. We are particularly struck by the perfection of the work as a whole, its grave personages, all symmetrically arranged and most life-like. The works of Ghiberti, however, still savor of Gothic art and belong to a period of transition. The sculpture of *Donatello,* on the other hand, marks a veritable revolution, due to a realism in expression which is based on the study of nature and of ancient models. We must mention his *St. John the Baptist, St. George,* and the *Penitent Magdalen.* Among the Florentine sculptors of the

Trecento we may also cite *Lucca della Robbia* (1400–1482), who endeavored to harmonize the traditions of Christian idealism with the new realism. The great pioneer of Renaissance architecture was *Brunellesco* (1377–1444), who succeeded in combining the Greek line with the Roman arcade and the Byzantine cupola. In completing the Church of St. Mary of the Flowers, the cathedral of Florence, he connected four isolated naves by means of a cupola with eight sides. This church served as a model for many others.

II. The Renaissance in the Netherlands and in Germany.

While the Renaissance was well under way in Italy, it was just beginning in Flanders, fostered by the prosperous merchants of the great commercial cities of Bruges and Ghent, and by the liberal dukes of Burgundy. The center of this Renaissance was the city of Bruges, which was to Flanders what Florence was to Italy. The four outstanding artists were Van Eyck, Roger de la Pasture, Hans Memling, and Quentin Metzys. The most important work of *Van Eyck* is the great reredos of the *Mystical Lamb.* His work gives evidence of an ardent love of nature, displayed more particularly in care-free poses and gestures and a sense of truth which is at once precise and minute. His use of dryer oils gives to his paintings a richness which is most extraordinary. *Roger de la Pasture* (1406-1464), the founder of the Brabant school, is a more severe artist, although his portrayal of the dramatic sense is intense, especially in his profoundly human and compassionating figures of Christ. As instances in point we may cite *The Burial* (Berlin Museum) and *The Descent from the Cross* (Louvre), in which the rigidity and lividness of the mangled body produce a most poignant effect upon the spectator. Van Eyck excelled in scenes of grandeur; Roger de la Pasture, in the portrayal of pathos; and *Hans Memling* in grace and tender emotion. His outstanding works are: *The Reliquary of St. Ursula, The Adoration of the Magi, The Mystical Marriage of St. Catherine,* and *The Last Judgment.* Quentin Metzys (1466-1530) belonged to the school of Antwerp. His works are remarkable for the life which radiates in the faces, the sumptuous garb of the personages, and the brilliant yet soft coloring. The two most important are *Christ Surrounded by the Angels* and *Ecce Homo.* The influence of these Flemish painters was felt in all countries, in Germany as well as in France, in Spain as well as in Italy.

Cologne was the "Holy City" of Germany and the principal commercial centre of the Rhine country. Its clergy was strong and influential, and its citizens were wealthy and devout—two facts which account for its brilliant school of art. Its most outstanding artist was *Stephen Lochner* (✝ 1451), often referred to as the Fra Angelico of the Rhineland, and responsible for the masterpiece *Dombild,* or reredos of the cathedral (*Annunciation, Adoration of the Magi*). We should mention also his *Virgin of the Rosebush* and his *Virgin of the Violets.* The school of Augsburg is represented by *Hans Holbein the Elder* (1470–1517?) and his son, *Hans Holbein the Younger,* who in his works combined the realism of the German school with an idealism of the loftiest sort. His masterpiece is the *Madonna of the Burgomaster. Albrecht Dürer* was a native of Nuremberg, and the founder of the German Renaissance. He was more of a sculptor than a painter, blending in his works scrupulous observance of nature with a wealth of imagination. His principal works are *The Feast of the Rosary,* the *Saints Adoring the Trinity,* an *Apocalypse,* a *Life of the Virgin* in nineteen settings, a *Small Passion* in thirty-six and a *Great Passion* in twelve settings.

German sculpture was productive of a great number of works of art in the fifteenth century, chief among which were choir-stalls and reredos displaying a realism that is both minute and picturesque. Three great masters belong to the school of Nuremberg, to wit, Adam Kraft, Veit Stoss, and Peter Vischer. Kraft (✝ 1505), who is best known for his *Way of the Cross,* exhibits great dramatic power. Veit Stoss, who has a greater sense of delicacy and grace, in his *Crown of Roses* portrayed the seven joys of the Virgin Mary in seven medallions, joined together by a crown of roses. Peter Vischer (✝ 1529) carved the reliquary of St. Sebaldus, surmounted by three baldachinos, which, in turn, are supported by four pairs of pillars. Midway on these pillars are the figures of the twelve Apostles, and on the summit, the twelve prophets. The inscription carved on this work of art attests the strictly religious character of the German school: "This work was undertaken for the sole glory of God Almighty, and in honor of the prince of heaven, St. Sebaldus, with the help of alms contributed by devout people."

III. The Second Italian Renaissance. The closing remark of the last paragraph unfortunately does not apply to the second Italian Renaissance, dominated by the three figures of Michael Angelo, Leonardo da Vinci, and Raphael. They were preceded by *Bramante d'Urbina,* the greatest architect of the Renaissance period, who attained fame at the age of sixty, when Pope Julius II asked him to remodel the Vatican and reconstruct the ancient basilica of St. Peter. To connect the different parts of the Vatican, he built two groups of buildings, faced with two-storied *loggie,* which enclosed a stadium used for tourneys. He did not live to carry out his plans for the church of St. Peter (✝ 1514), which called for a central cupola with the four arms of a Greek Cross, each terminated by a rounded apsis. The artists who were successively employed in this work modified it considerably, but the influence of Bramante continued throughout western architecture. The central cupola was retained as well as the decorations by means of columns and friezes in the Roman style.

Michael Angelo Buonarotti (1475–1564) was primarily a sculptor. Pope Julius II employed him to construct and adorn his tomb. The monument was never completed, the most impressive part of it being the statue of *Moses Seated,* which represents the great Jewish leader as stern, domineering, and over-bearing. The same Pope called upon Michael Angelo to decorate the Sistine Chapel, the ceiling of which he painted with a power and grandeur that are truly biblical (*The Creation of the World, of Man, of Woman, Adam and Eve,* etc.). At a later date Pope Leo X commissioned him to continue the work on St. Peter's in Rome, which he crowned with a magnificent cupola. His powerful imagination expressed itself in Titanic creations.

Leonardo da Vinci was a sculptor, an architect, a painter, and an engineer. He excelled, however, above all as a painter, for whom art was something mental (*"cosa mentale"*). And so, when he attended to reality as such and studied the anatomy of the human body, not stopping at voluptuousness in his passionate quest for a model, he always endeavored to bring out the psychological traits of his characters on the canvas. His painting of *The Last Supper* is a picture in which all the persons represented express their reaction to the words of Christ: "Behold, one of you will betray me." Among his works we must cite the *Magdalen* (Palace Pitti), the *Virgin of the Rocks, St. John the Baptist* (Louvre), and *Herodias* (Gallery in Florence).

While Leonardo da Vinci and Michael Angelo left a deep personal impress upon their works, *Raphael* (1483–1520) seems to have spent all his genius in creating the most general mode of expression and the most impersonal type of beauty, in which all the harsh and rugged features of personality are happily blended. Raphael raised classical beauty to its highest perfection. His activity was nothing short of prodigious. In the stanzas of the Vatican he dealt with both philosophical (*Disputation on the Blessed Sacrament, The School of Athens*) and historical subjects (*Heliodorus Expelled from the Temple, Attila Halted by St. Leo*). He also painted a whole series of madonnas, the first of them being tender and candid, the last, glorious and majestic. The most famous among them are *The Virgin of the Chair* (Florence) and *The Madonna of St. Sixtus* (Dresden).

From this moment on, the study of form for its own sake, apart from any truly Christian inspiration, held the stage. And so, while *Fra Bartolommeo,* the spiritual son of Savonarola, was a real contemplative who depicted moral beauty with all due sobriety (*Descent from the Cross, Coronation of the Virgin,* in the Pitti Palace), his pupil, *Andrea del Sarto* (1446–1531), represented the saints in languishing postures amidst a profusion of light and bright colors (*Charity*). Pagan tendencies of this sort became even more pronounced in the case of the Venetian painters Giorgione and Giovanni Palma de Bergamo, who represented on canvas madonnas and mistresses indiscriminately. And if *Tizian,* who is sometimes quite sensuous, was able to give expression to religious sentiments, it was because of the extraordinary flexibility of his talent (*Burial of Christ,* in the Louvre). With the advent of *Correggio,* who inaugurated the study of the affectionate and the pretty, religious painting degenerated into insipid affectation, caressing gestures, and engaging smiles (*Mystical Marriage of St. Catherine,* in the Louvre; *Madonna of St. Jerome,* at Parma).

IV. **The Renaissance in France.** The Renaissance did not assume the same proportions in France before the wars with Italy, although two brothers of Charles V, Philip the Brave, Duke of Burgundy, and John of France, Duke of Berry, had taken the initiative. The first of these two employed in his service the painter Claus Sluter, of Holland, who created the tomb of Philip the Brave, the statues in the doorway of the chapel in the Carthusian monastery of Champmol, the *Well of Moses,* and the base of a calvary for the cloister of this same monastery, which is adorned with the famous statues of Moses, Daniel, and Isaias. The realism of this artist is most powerful. The Duke of Berry ordered the execution of the magnificent "Hours," which are masterpieces of miniature painting.

The school of Tours, which began in the fifteenth century, produced two great artists: John Foucquet (1415–1480), a miniaturist of the first order, who introduced into his religious scenes all the leading personages of the time with their familiar poses, costumes, and mannerisms (Book of Hours of the Knight Stephen); and the Breton, Michael Colombe († 1512), who, though influenced to some extent by the Italian Renaissance, remained faithful to the tradition of the old Gothic masters and inaugurated an idealized form of French sculpture which is at once grave and elegant (Tomb of Duke Francis II of Britany, at Nantes, and St. George Crushing the Dragon, in the Louvre). He created sepulchres and burial scenes (church of St. Saviour in la Rochelle), in which ten or more life-size persons are grouped around the figure of Christ. A large number of these may be found in French churches of the fifteenth and sixteenth centuries, the most famous among them being St. Mihiel and Solesmes.

TEXTS AND DOCUMENTS

THE CATHOLIC CHURCH AND ART

As art has always been the product and the manifestation of a definite cultural period, so in its most highly specialized achievements and in certain of its most distinguished products it occurs, not synchronously with the crest of social and cultural attainment, but after the driving energy has ceased to function with power. This is particularly true of music and painting, the two most abstract and personal of the arts. During the great thirteenth century, while architecture and sculpture were attaining heights at least equal to anything that had gone before, and far greater than what has since been achieved, painting, except in the minor art of illumination and possibly in fresco, though these vestiges being now wholly obliterated, there is no progress whatever, until the very end of the century. It was not until the appearance of Cimabue, about 1290, that any advance was made beyond the rigid formulae of the Byzantine precedent, but from then on, particularly after Giotto, with his humanism and naturalism, the progress was headlong in its impetuosity. It was a purely secular movement and a secular art, so far as its creators were concerned, but it was eagerly seized on by the Church that realized at once its didactic and emotional power, and to the end, three centuries later, it was the ecclesiastical power that gave the new art its strongest backing, as it offered through religion itself the most stimulating subjects and the most powerful motive force.

CRAM, *The Catholic Church and Art,*
pp. 87–88.

QUESTIONS

1. Write a short appreciation of the art of Fra Angelico.
2. List the principal differences between the Renaissance in Italy and that in the Netherlands.
3. Institute a comparison between Michael Angelo, Leonardo da Vinci, and Raphael.

BIBLIOGRAPHY

Renaissance in Art.—J. Guiraud, *op. cit.*, 1911.—E. Muntz, *Histoire de l'art pendant la Renaissance*, 3 vols., 1889–95; *Les précurseurs de la Renaissance en Italie*, 1882; *Raphaël, sa vie, son œuvre et son temps*, 2nd edit., 1886. —A. Michel, *Histoire de l'art.* t. IV, 1906–09.—G. Lafenestre, *La peinture italienne*, 2 vols., 1891; Venice, 1897; Florence, 1895.—H. Cochin, *Le bienheureux fra Giovanni Angelico Fiesole* (Coll. *"Les Saints"*), 1906.—L. Scott, *Brunellesco*, 1902.—L. Palustre, *L'architecture de la Renaissance*, 1892.—C. Perkins, *Les sculpteurs italiens*, 1891.—A. Alexandre, *Donatello*, 1906.—J. Klaczko, *Rome et la Renaissance, Essais et Esquisse, Jules II*, 2nd edit., 1909. —A. J. Wauter, *La peinture flamande* (*Bibl. de l'Enseignement des Beaux Arts*).—G. Lafenestre, *Saint François d'Assise et Savonarole, inspirateurs de l'art italien*, 1911.—A. Schmarsow, *Hubert und Jan Van Eyck*, Leipzig, 1924. —Friedländer, *Die altniederländische Malerci*, 3 vols., Berlin, 1924–1925.— L. Dimier and L. Réau, *L'histoire de la peinture française depuis les origines jusqu'à la fin du XVIIIᵉ siècle*, 5 vols., 1925–1927.—M. Hubert, *La sculpture française du moyen âge et de la Renaissance*, 1926.—A. Venturi, *A Short History of Italian Art* (transl. E. Hutton), 1926.—J. Pijoan, *An Outline History of Art*, 3 vols., (transl. R. L. Roys), 1927.

APPENDIX

CHRONOLOGICAL CHARTS

SYNOPTIC CHARTS

SECOND CENTURY

MARTYRS	EMPERORS	POPES	EVENTS
	The Antonines		
100 St. Clement, Pope	Nerva 96–98	St. Clement 88–97	112 Trajan's answer to Pliny.
107 St. Ignatius of Antioch	Trajan 98–117	St. Evaristus 97–105	125 seq. Gnostic heresies: Basilides and Saturninus.
119 St. Alexander I . . . St. Symphorosa and her seven sons	Hadrian 117–138	St. Alexander I 105–115	
		St. Sixtus I 115–125	
155 St. Polycarp	Antoninus 138–168	St. Telesphorus 125–136	140 Valentine.
		St. Hyginus 136–140	
177 The Martyrs of Lyons St. Cecilia . .		St. Pius I 140–155	155 Marcion in Rome
St. Felicitas	Marcus Aurelius 168–180	St. Anicetus 155–166	c. 172 Montanism.
	Commodus 180–192	St. Soter 166–175	St. Victor and the Easter Controversy.
		St. Eleutherus 175–189	
		St. Victor I 189–199	

THIRD CENTURY

MARTYRS	EMPERORS	POPES	EVENTS
202–203 SS. Felicitas and Perpetua	**The Severi (193–235)** Septimius Severus ..... 193–211 Caracalla .... 211–217 Heliogabalus .... 218–222 Alexander Severus 222–235	St. Zephyrinus .... 199–217 St. Callixtus .... 217–222 Hippolytus, antipope .. 217–235 St. Urban I .... 222–230 St. Pontian 230–235	Controversy regarding unforgivable sins.
St. Pontian	**The Imperial Crisis (235–285)** Maximinus .... 235–238 Attempt at a Senatorial Empire (the 2 Gordiani Philippi) 238–249	St. Anterus .... 235–236 St. Fabian .... 236–250 St. Cornelius 251–253	250 The schism of Felicissimus at Carthage. 252 The schism of Novatian in Rome.
St. Hippolytus St. Antherus	Decius 250–253	Novatian, antipope ... 251	253–257 Controversy regarding the Baptism of heretics.
St. Fabian	Valerian .... 253–260 The Provincial Emperors 260–268	St. Lucius .... 253–254 St. Stephen I .... 254–257 St. Sixtus II .... 257–258 St. Dionysius 259–268	262 Council of Rome against Sabellius. 264–269 Three Councils of Antioch against Paul of Samosata.
258 St. Cyprian St. Stephen St. Sixtus II. St. Lawrence	Claudius II .... 268–270 Aurelian .... 270–275 Last attempt at a Senatorial Empire ...... 275–284 **The Restoration Under Diocletian (285–312)** Diocletian 284–305	St. Felix I .... 269–274 St. Eutychian .... 275–283 St. Caius 283–296	

FOURTH CENTURY

EMPERORS	POPES	RELIGIOUS EVENTS
306–337 Constantine.	314–335 St. Sylvester.	313 Edict of Milan.
		318 Arius denounced as a heretic.
		323 Defeat of Licinius.
		325 First Ecumenical Council of Nicaea.
	336 St. Mark.	328 Athanasius, Bishop of Alexandria.
337–361 Constantius.	337–352 St. Julius I.	336 Death of Arius. Athanasius in exile.
	352–366 St. Liberius.	342–343 Council of Sardica.
		351 First Council of Sirmium.
		355 Caesaro-papist meddling of Constantius at Milan.
		357 Second Council of Sirmium.
		358 Ancyra. Third Council of Sirmium.
		359 Council of Seleucia-Rimini.
		360 Heresy of Macedonius.
361–363 Julian the Apostate.	366–384 St. Damasus.	373 Death of St. Athanasius.
363–364 Jovinian.	384–399 St. Sircius.	381 Second Ecumenical Council of Constantinople.
364–378 Valens.		385 Execution of Priscillian at Treves.
379–395 Theodosius the Great.		394 Beginning of the Origenist controversy.
395–408 Arcadius.		

FIFTH CENTURY

EMPERORS	POPES	THE EAST	THE WEST
395-408 Arcadius.	399-401 St. Athanasius I. 401-417 St. Innocent I.	401 Theophilus of Alexandria excommunicates Origen. 402 His fight against St. John Chrysostom. 403 First exile of Chrysostom. 404 Second exile of Chrysostom. 407 Death of Chrysostom.	
418-450 Theodosius II.	417-418 St. Zosimus. 418-422 St. Boniface I. 422-432 St. Celestine I.		410 Sack of Rome by Alaric. 411 Triumph of St. Augustine over the Donatists. 412 Council at Carthage against Celestius. 414 Councils at Jerusalem and Diospolis against Pelagius. 416 Councils at Carthage and Mileva against the Pelagians. 417 Condemnation of Pelagius by Innocent I. 418 Pope Zosimus and Pelagianism.
	432-440 St. Sixtus III.	420 Nestorius appears on the scene. 429 St. Cyril opposes Nestorius. 430 Condemnation of Nestorius at Rome. 431 Third Ecumenical Council at Ephesus. 433 Reconciliation of Cyril with the Antiochians. 440 Death of Nestorius. 440-461 St. Leo I the Great. 444 Death of St. Cyril. 448 Eutyches appears on the scene.	
450-457 Marcian and Pulcheria.		449 Robber Synod of Ephesus. 451 Fourth Ecumenical Council at Chalcedon.	452 Attila halted by St. Leo.
457-474 Leo I	461-468 St. Hilary. 468-483 St. Simplicius.	476 Encyclicon of Basiliscus. 477 Anti-encyclicon of Basiliscus. 482 Zeno's Henoticon.	

SIXTH CENTURY

THE FRANKS	THE LOMBARDS	THE GREEKS	THE PAPACY
Conversion of Clovis ... 496	Hormisdas' Formula ... 519	Advent of Justinian ... 527	St. Hormisdas ... 514–523
Vouillé ... 507	Murder of John I ... 526		St. John I ... 523–526
Epaom ... 517	Death of Theodoric ... 526	Beginning of the Question of the Three Chapters ... 544	Vigilius ... 537–555
		The *Iudicatum* of Vigilius ... 548	
		The Fifth General Council ... 551	Pelagius ... 556–561
		The *Constitutum* of Vigilius ... 551	

SEVENTH CENTURY

THE ENGLISH	THE GERMANS	THE GREEKS	THE PAPACY
St. Augustine in England .. 596	Columban at Constance ... 612	The Hegira 622	St. Gregory the Great .. 590–604
Baptism of Ethelbert 597	St. Gall 613	Capture of Mecca 630	Honorius I 625–638
Death of St. Augustine 604		Death of Mohammed 632	
		Capture of Jerusalem 637	
		The Ecthesis 638	
		The Type 648	St. Martin I 649–653
		Martin in exile 653	
		Martin at Byzantium 654	
		Martin martyr 655	
	Wilfrid in Frisia 678		St. Agatho 678–681
		Synod in Rome 680	
	Willibrord in Frisia 690	Sixth General Council 680–681	

EIGHTH CENTURY

VIII CENTURY	THE GERMANS	THE FRENCH	THE PAPACY	THE EAST
714		Charles Martel (714–741).		
715			St. Gregory II (715–731).	
719	St. Boniface missionary.			
723	St. Boniface bishop.			
726				First iconoclastic edict of Leo the Isaurian.
730				Second iconoclastic edict.
731			St. Gregory III (731–741).	
732	St. Boniface metropolitan.	Poitiers.		
740				
741	St. Boniface at Mayence.	Pepin the Short (741–768).	St. Zacharias (741–752).	Death of Leo the Isaurian.
748				
752			Stephen II (752–757).	
753				Conciliabulum of Hiera under Copronymus.
755	St. Boniface martyr.			
756		Bequest of Pepin.		
757			St. Paul I (757–767).	
768		Charlemagne (768–814).	Stephen III (768–772).	
772	War with Saxons.		Adrian I (772–795).	
774		Bequest to the Pope.		
785	Baptism of Widukind.			
787				Seventh Council of Nicaea.
795			St. Leo III (795–816).	
800		Charlemagne Emperor.		
809				Council of Aix convoked to discuss the Filioque.
814		Death of Charlemagne.		

NINTH CENTURY

THE BARBARIANS	THE FRANKS	THE GREEKS	THE PAPACY
	Coronation of Louis at Rheims 816	Leo Bardas. Persecution 813–820	Stephen IV 816–817
	Louis the Pious 817–840		Pascal I 817–824
	Division 817		
	Council of Aix-la-Chapelle 817		
	Reform of St. Benedict of Aniane 817		
		Michael the Stammerer. End of persecution .. 820–829	Eugene II 824–827
			Gregory IV 827–844
		Theophilus. Persecution 829–842	
		Theodora. End of Iconoclasm 842	
	Treaty of Verdun 843		Sergius II. The Saracens 844–847
	Hincmar, archbishop .. 845–882		St. Leo IV. The Leonian city 847–855
	Council of Mayence against Gottschalk .. 848	Photius, patriarch ... 858	St. Nicholas I 858–867
		Council of Constantinople 859	
St. Ansgar in Denmark 826		Basil recalls Ignatius .. 867	Hadrian II 867–872
St. Ansgar in Sweden 829		Eighth General Council of Constantinople .. 869	John VIII 872–882
	Charles the Bald, Emperor 875–877	Death of Ignatius. Photius patriarch 878	
St. Methodius in Bulgaria .. 861		Council of Constantinople 879	
Death of St. Ansgar 865	Charles the Fat, Emperor 882–887	Photius deposed 886	Stephen V 885–891
		Death of Photius 891	

TENTH CENTURY

Popes	Emperors or Kings of Germany	Events in Italy
Benedict IV 900– 903	Louis III, the Child .. 900– 911	Victory of Garigliano 916
Leo V 903		
Christopher 903– 904		
Sergius III 904– 911	Conrad I 911– 918	
Lando 913– 914		
John X 914– 928	Henry I 919– 936	
Leo VI 928– 929		
Stephen VII 929– 931		
John XI 931– 936		
Leo VII 936– 939	Otto the Great 936– 973	
Stephen VIII 939– 942		
Marinus II 942– 946		
Agapetus II 946– 955		First journey of Otto I to Rome 962
John XII 955– 963		*Privilegium Ottonis*
		Second journey of Otto I to Rome ... 963
Leo VIII 963– 965		Condemnation of John XII
		Election of Leo VIII
Benedict V (antipope) ... 964		Third journey of Otto I to Rome 964
John XIII 965– 972		Otto II consecrated co-imperator ... 967
Benedict VI 972– 974		Marriage of Otto II and Theophania ... 972
Boniface VII (antipope) ... 974	Otto II 973– 983	
Benedict VII 974– 983		
John XIV 983– 984	Otto III 983–1002	
John XV 985– 996		
Gregory V 996– 999		
John XVI (antipope) ... 979– 998		
Sylvester II 993–1003		

ELEVENTH CENTURY

EMPERORS	POPES	HISTORICAL EVENTS
Henry II 1002–1024	Sylvester II 999–1003	
	John XVIII 1003–1009	St. Romuald founds the Camaldolese 1012
Conrad II 1024–1029	John XIX 1024–1033	
Henry III 1039–1056	Benedict IX 1033–1045	The Truce of God 1041–1042
	Clement II 1046–1047	
	Damasus II 1047–1048	
	St. Leo IX 1048–1054	
	Victor II 1054–1057	Beginning of the Eastern Schism 1054
Henry IV 1056–1106	Nicholas II 1058–1061	Decree of Nicholas II governing papal elections 1059
	Alexander II 1061–1073	Conquest of England by the Normans ... 1066
		Death of St. Peter Damian 1072
	St. Gregory VII 1073–1085	Council of Rome 1074
		Assembly of Worms 1076
		Canossa 1077
		Henry IV at Rome 1084
		Death of Gregory VII 1085
	Victor III 1086–1087	
	Urban II 1088–1099	Council of Soissons against Roscelinus ... 1092
		Council of Clermont 1095
		First Crusade 1096

TWELFTH CENTURY

EMPERORS	POPES	THE WEST		THE EAST	
Henry IV 1056-1106	Pascal II 1099-1118	Death of St. Anselm	1109	Clermont	1095
Henry V 1106-1125		St. Bernard enters religion	1113		
	Gelasius II 1118-1119			Foundation of the Knights Templar	1118
	Callixtus II 1119-1124	Foundation of the Premonstratensians	1120		
		Concordat of Worms	1120		
		Ninth Ecumenical Council (I. Lateran)	1123		
Lothaire II 1125-1137	Honorius II 1124-1130				
Conrad II 1138-1152	Innocent II 1130-1143	Schism of Anacletus 1130-1138			
		Tenth Ecumenical Council (II. Lateran)	1139		
		Death of Abailard ..	1142	Fall of Edessa	1144
Frederick I Barbarossa 1152-1190	Eugene III 1145-1153	Death of St. Bernard	1153	Second Crusade	1147
		Execution of Arnold of Brescia	1154		
	Hadrian IV 1154-1159				
	Alexander III 1159-1181	St. Thomas à Becket, archbishop	1162		
		Constitutions of Clarendon	1164		
		Death of St. Thomas	1170		
		Legnano	1176		
		Ninth Ecumenical Council (III. Lateran)	1179		
	Lucius III 1181-1185			Jerusalem seized by Saladin	1187
				Third Crusade	1189

THIRTEENTH CENTURY

EMPERORS	POPES	THE WEST	THE EAST
Frederick II 1197–1250	Innocent III 1198–1216	Innocent III protects Otto IV 1204	Fourth Crusade 1202
			The Latin Empire 1204
		Foundation of Prouille ... 1206	
		Murder of the legate Castelnau 1208	
		Crusade against the Albigenses 1209	
		Bouvines 1214	
		Magna Charta 1215	
		Twelfth Ecumenical Council (IV. Lateran) 1215	
	Honorius III 1216–1227	Death of St. Dominic 1221	
	Gregory IX 1227–1241	Death of St. Francis 1226	Fifth Crusade 1228
	Innocent IV 1243–1254	Thirteenth Ecumenical Council (I. Lyons) 1245	Sixth Crusade 1248
			Capture of Damietta 1249
Conrad IV 1250–1254		Death of Frederic II 1250	
The Interregnum .. 1254–1273	Alexander IV 1254–1261		End of Italian Empire 1261
	Urban IV 1261–1264		
	Clement IV 1265–1268	Death of Conradin 1268	Seventh Crusade. Tunis .. 1270
Rudolph of Hapsburg 1273–1291	St. Gregory X 1271–1276	Fourteenth Ecumenical Council (II. Lyons) 1274	
	Nicholas III 1277–1280		
	Martin IV 1281–1285	The Sicilian Vespers 1282	Loss of Acre 1291

FOURTEENTH CENTURY

EMPERORS	POPES	THE WEST	THE EAST
Andronicus II 1282–1328	Boniface VIII 1294–1303	The Bull "Unam Sanctam" 1302	
	Benedict XI 1303–1304	The Tragedy of Anagni 1303	
	Clement V 1305–1314	Trial of the Knights Templar 1307	
		The Popes move to Avignon 1309	
		Council of Vienne .. 1311–1312	
Andronicus III 1328–1341	John XXII 1316–1334	Canonization of Thomas Aquinas . 1323	
John V 1341–1376	Benedict XII 1334–1342	The "Benedictina" .. 1336	Formation of the "Naval League" 1344
			Capture of Smyrna 1344
			Victory of Imbros 1347
			Emperor John V abjures schism 1349
	Innocent VI 1352–1362	The "Bulla Aurea" .. 1354	Capture of Adrianople by Amaruth I 1360
John V (second time) 1379–1391	Urban VI 1378–1389	The Great Schism of the West 1378–1417	
Manuel II 1391–1425			

FIFTEENTH CENTURY

EMPERORS	POPES	THE WEST	THE EAST
Manuel II 1391–1425		Council of Constance 1414–1418	
	Martin V 1417–1431	Death of John Hus 1415	
		End of the Great Schism of the West 1417	
John VIII 1425–1448	Eugene IV 1431–1447	Council of Basle 1431–1440	
		Condemnation of the Hussites 1433	
		Pragmatic Sanction of Bourges 1438	
			Decree of Union 1439
Constantine XI, Dragases 1448–1453	Callixtus III 1455–1458		Capture of Constantinople 1453
	Innocent VIII 1484–1492	Spanish Inquisition .. 1481	
	Alexander VI 1492–1503	Death of Savonarola 1498	

ECUMENICAL COUNCILS

DATE	PLACE	PURPOSE	MOTIONS
325	Nicaea.	Condemnation of Arianism.	Adoption of a suitable and precise Creed in which the expression *consubstantialis Patri* was inserted to define the relationship of the Son to the Father.
381	I. Constantinople.	Condemnation of Macedonius.	Addition to the Creed of the following formula: "We believe in the Holy Ghost, who reigneth and quickeneth, who proceedeth from the Father, and must be honored like Him, who hath spoken to us through the prophets."
431 451	Ephesus. Chalcedon.	Condemnation of Nestorianism. Condemnation of Monophysitism.	Adoption of a Creed which stated: "We confess one and the same Christ Jesus, the Only-begotten Son, whom we acknowledge to have two natures, without confusion, transformation, division or separation between them. The difference between these two natures is not suppressed by their union; on the contrary, the attributes of each nature are safeguarded and subsist in one person."
551	II. Constantinople.	Condemnation of the Three Chapters.	
680–681	III. Constantinople.	Condemnation of Monotheletism.	"We also proclaim two natural volitions and wills in Him and two natural operations, without division, without change, without partition and without confusion, according to the teachings of the holy Fathers; and not in any sense of the term two natural wills opposed to each other, as wicked heretics have averred, but a subordinated human will, which, far from being at variance with the divine and all powerful will, is humbly subjected to it."
787	II. Nicaea.	Condemnation of Iconoclasm.	The Fathers define in exact words the veneration due to images. It is an adoration of honor and not latreutic adoration, which is due to God alone.
869–870	IV. Constantinople.	Condemnation of Photius.	
1123 1139 1179 1215	I. Lateran II. Lateran III. Lateran IV. Lateran	Disciplinary decisions.	

ECUMENICAL COUNCILS

DATE	POPES	PLACE	DATE	PURPOSE
1243-1254 1271-1276 1305-1314	Innocent IV. Gregory X. Clement V.	I. Lyons. II. Lyons. Vienne.	1245 1274 1311-1312	Condemnation of Frederick II. Union of the Greeks. Procession of the Holy Ghost. Trial of the Knights Templar. Condemnation of the Beghards.
1417-1431 1431-1447	Martin V. Eugene IV.	Constance. Ferrara-Florence.	1414-1418 1438-1445	Condemnation of John Wicliffe and John Hus. Return of the Greeks, the Armenians and the Jacobites to unity.
1513-1521 1534-1549 1550-1555 1559-1565	Leo X. Paul III. Julius III. Pius IV.	V. Lateran. Trent. 1) Sessions I-XII. 2) Sessions XIII-XX. 3) Sessions XXI-XXIV.	1545-1547 1545-1563 1551-1552 1562-1563	Sacred Scripture. Original Sin and Justification. Sacraments. Baptism and Confirmation. Holy Eucharist. Penance. Extreme Unction. Holy Communion and Holy Mass. Holy Orders. Matrimony. Purgatory. Veneration of the Saints. Indulgences.
1566-1572	St. Pius V.	Roman Catechism. Roman Breviary. Roman Missal.	1566 1568 1570	
1846-1878	Pius IX.	Vatican.	1869-1870	On Faith. On the Church. Proclamation of papal infallibility.

CHRONOLOGICAL TABLES

THE POPES

1	Saint Peter	67(?)
2	Saint Linus	67–76(?)
3	Saint Anacletus	76–88(?)
4	Saint Clement I	88–97(?)
5	Saint Evaristus	97–105(?)
6	Saint Alexander I	105–115(?)
7	Saint Sixtus I	115–125(?)
8	Saint Telesphorus	125–136(?)
9	Saint Hyginus	136–140(?)
10	Saint Pius	140–155(?)
11	Saint Anicetus	155–166(?)
12	Saint Soter	166–175(?)
13	Saint Eleutherus	175–189
14	Saint Victor	189–199
15	Saint Zephyrinus	199–217
16	Saint Callixtus I	217–222
	Saint Hippolytus	217–235
17	Saint Urban I	222–230
18	Saint Pontian	230–235
19	Saint Anterus	235–236
20	Saint Fabian	236–250
21	Saint Cornelius	251–253
	Novatian	251–258
22	Saint Lucius I	253–254
23	Saint Stephen I	254–257
24	Saint Sixtus II	257–258
25	Saint Dionysius	259–268
26	Saint Felix I	269–274
27	Saint Eutychian	275–283
28	Saint Caïus	283–296
29	Saint Marcellinus	296–304
30	Saint Marcellus	308–309
31	Saint Eusebius	309 or 310
32	Saint Miltiades	311–314
33	Saint Sylvester I	314–335

34	Saint Mark	336
35	Saint Julius I	337–352
36	Saint Liberius	352–366
	Felix II	355–365
37	Saint Damasus I	366–384
	Ursinus	366–367
38	Saint Siricius	384–399
39	Saint Anastasius I	399–401
40	Saint Innocent I	401–417
41	Saint Zosimus	417–418
42	Saint Boniface I	418–422
	Eulalius	418–419
43	Saint Celestine	422–432
44	Saint Sixtus III	432–440
45	Saint Leo I	440–461
46	Saint Hilary	461–468
47	Saint Simplicius	468–483
48	Saint Felix II (III)	483–492
49	Saint Gelasius I	492–496
50	Saint Anastasius II	496–498
51	Saint Symmachus	498–514
	Lawrence	498–505(?)
52	Saint Hormisdas	514–523
53	Saint John I	523–526
54	Saint Felix III (IV)	526–530
55	Boniface II	530–532
	Dioscorus	530
56	John II	523–535
57	Saint Agapetus I	535–536
58	Saint Silverius	536–537
59	Vigilius	537–555
60	Pelagius I	556–561
61	John III	561–574
62	Benedict I	575–579
63	Pelagius II	579–590
64	Saint Gregory I	590–604
65	Sabinianus	604–606
66	Boniface III	607
67	Saint Boniface IV	608–615
68	Saint Deusdedit	615–618
69	Boniface V	619–625
70	Honorius I	625–638
71	Severinus	640

110	Marinus I	882–884
111	Hadrian III	884–885
112	Stephen V	885–891
113	Formosus	891–896
114	Boniface VI	896
115	Stephen VI	896–897
116	Romanus	897
117	Theodore II	897
118	John IX	898–900
119	Benedict IV	900–903
120	Leo V	903
121	Christopher	903–904
122	Sergius III	904–911
123	Anastasius III	911–913
124	Lando	913–914
125	John X	914–928
126	Leo VI	928–929
127	Stephen VII	929–931
128	John XI	931–936
129	Leo VII	936–939
130	Stephen VIII	939–942
131	Marinus II	942–946
132	Agapetus II	946–955
133	John XII	955–963
134	Leo VIII	963–965
	Benedict V	964
135	John XIII	965–972
136	Benedict VI	972–974
	Boniface VII	974
137	Benedict VII	974–983
138	John XIV	983–984
139	Boniface VII	984–985
140	John XV	985–996
141	Gregory V	996–999
	John XVI	997–998
142	Sylvester II	999–1003
143	John XVII	1003
144	John XVIII	1003–1009
145	Sergius IV	1009–1012
146	Benedict VIII	1012–1024
	Gregory	1012
147	John XIX	1024–1033
148	Benedict IX	1033–1045

149	Sylvester III	1044
150	Gregory VI	1045–1046
151	Clement II	1046–1047
152	Damasus II	1047–1048
153	Saint Leo IX	1048–1054
154	Victor II	1055–1057
155	Stephen IX	1057–1058
	Benedict X	1058–1059
156	Nicholas II	1058–1061
157	Alexander II	1061–1073
	Honorius II	1061–1069
158	Saint Gregory VII	1073–1085
	Clement III	1080–1110
159	Victor III	1086–1087
160	Urban II	1088–1099
161	Pascal II	1099–1118
	Theodoric	1100
	Albert	1102
	Sylvester IV	1105–1111
162	Gelasius II	1118–1119
163	Callixtus II	1119–1124
	Gregory VIII	1118–1121
164	Honorius II	1124–1130
	Celestine II	1124
165	Innocent II	1130–1143
	Anacletus II	1130–1138
	Victor IV	1138
166	Celestine II	1143–1144
167	Lucius II	1144–1145
168	Eugene III	1145–1153
169	Anastasius IV	1153–1154
170	Hadrian IV	1154–1159
171	Alexander III	1159–1181
	Victor IV	1159–1164
	Pascal III	1164–1168
	Callixtus III	1168–1178
	Innocent III	1179–1180
172	Lucius III	1181–1185
173	Urban III	1185–1187
174	Gregory VIII	1187
175	Clement III	1187–1191
176	Celestine III	1191–1198
177	Innocent III	1198–1216

178	Honorius III	1216–1227
179	Gregory IX	1227–1241
180	Celestine IV	1241
181	Innocent IV	1243–1254
182	Alexander IV	1254–1261
183	Urban IV	1261–1264
184	Clement IV	1265–1268
185	Saint Gregory X	1271–1276
186	Innocent V	1276
187	Hadrian V	1276
188	John XXI	1276–1277
189	Nicholas III	1277–1280
190	Martin IV	1281–1285
191	Honorius IV	1285–1287
192	Nicholas IV	1288–1292
193	Saint Celestine V	1294
194	Boniface VIII	1294–1303
195	Benedict XI	1303–1304
196	Clement V	1305–1314
197	John XXII	1316–1334
	Nicholas V	1328–1330
198	Benedict XII	1334–1342
199	Clement VI	1342–1352
200	Innocent VI	1352–1362
201	Urban V	1362–1370
202	Gregory XI	1370–1378
203	Urban VI (Rome)	1378–1389
	Clement VII (Avignon)	1378–1394
204	Boniface IX (Rome)	1389–1404
	Benedict XIII (Avignon)	1394–1424
205	Innocent VII (Rome)	1404–1406
206	Gregory XII (Rome)	1406–1415
207	Alexander V (Pisa)	
208	John XXIII (Pisa)	1410–1415
209	Martin V	1417–1431
	Clement VIII	1424–1429
	Benedict XIV	1424
210	Eugene IV	1431–1447
	Felix V	1439–1449
211	Nicholas V	1447–1455
212	Callixtus III	1455–1458
213	Pius II	1458–1464
214	Paul II	1464–1471

215 Sixtus IV	1471–1484
216 Innocent VIII	1484–1492
217 Alexander VI	1492–1503
218 Pius III	1503
219 Julius II	1503–1513
220 Leo X	1513–1521

ROMAN EMPERORS
The Julio-Claudian Family
(14–68)

Tiberius	14–37
Caligula	37–41
Claudius	41–54
Nero	54–68

The Flavians
(68–96)

Galba-Otho-Vitellius	68
Vespasian	69–79
Titus	79–81
Domitian	81–96

The Antonines
(96–192)

Nerva	96–98
Trajan	98–117
Hadrian	117–138
Antoninus	138–161
Marcus Aurelius	161–180
Commodus	180–192

The Severi
(193–235)

Septimius Severus	193–211
Caracalla	211–217
Macrinus	217–218
Heliogabalus	217–218
Alexander Severus	222–235

The Imperial Crisis
(235–285)

Maximinus	235–238
Puppienus and Gordianus	238
Philip the Arab	244–249
Decius	250–253
Gallus and Volusian	251–253
Valerian	253–260
Gallienus	260–268

Claudius II		268–270
Aurelian		270–275
Tacitus		275–276
Probus		276–282
Carus		282–284

Restoration under Diocletian
(284–312)

Diocletian	284–305
Galerius	305–311
Maximinus	308–313

BYZANTINE EMPERORS
The Constantinian Dynasty

Constantine the Great	313–337
Constantius II	337–361
Julian the Apostate	361–363
Jovinian	363–364
Valens	364–378

The Theodosian Dynasty

Theodosius I the Great	379–395
Arcadius	395–408
Theodosius II	408–450
Marcian	451–457
Leo I	457–474
Zeno	474–491
Anastasius	491–518

The Justinian Dynasty

Justin I	518–527
Justinian I	527–565
Justin II	565–578
Tiberius II	578–582
Mauritius	582–602
Phocas (Usurper)	602–610

The Dynasty of Heraclius

Heraclius	610–641
Constantine III and Heracleonas	679–695
Constans II	642–668
Constantine IV Pogonatus	668–685
Justinian II Rhinotmetus	685–695
Leontius (Usurper)	695–698
Tiberius III (Usurper)	698–705
Justinian II	705–711
Philippicus	711–713
Anastasius II	713–716

Theodosius III	716–717
The Isaurian Dynasty	
Leo III	717–740
Constantine V Copronymus	740–775
Leo IV	775–780
Constantine VI	780–797
Irene	797–802
Nicephorus (Usurper)	802–811
Staurakios	811
Michael I	811–813
Leo V the Armenian	813–820
Michael II the Stammerer	820–829
Theophilus	829–842
Michael III the Drunkard	842–867
The Macedonian Dynasty	
Basil I	877–886
Leo VI the Wise	886–912
Alexander	
Constantine VII Porphyrogenetus	913–959
Romanus II	959–963
Nicephorus II Phocas	963–969
John I	969–976
Basil II the Bulgarochtone	976–1025
Constantine VIII	1025–1028
Zoe	1028–1050
Constantine IX Monomachus	1042–1054
Theodora	1054–1056
Michael VI Stratiotikos	1056–1057
Dynasty of the Dukas and the Comneni	
Isaac I Comnenus	1057–1059
Constantine X Dukas	1059–1067
Romanus IV Diogenes	1067–1071
Michael VII Dukas	1071–1078
Nicephorus III (Usurper)	1078–1081
Alexis I Comnenus	1081–1118
John II Comnenus	1118–1143
Manuel I Comnenus	1143–1180
Alexis II Comnenus	1180–1183
Andronicus I Comnenus	1183–1185
Dynasty of the Angeli	
Isaac II	1185–1195
Alexis III	1195–1203
Isaac III and Alexis IV	1203–1204

Alexis IV Musurphus (Usurper)	1204
*Latin Emperors of Constantinople**	
Baldwin of Flanders	1204–1205
Henry of Angre	1206–1216
Peter de Courtenay	1217
Yoland	1217–1219
Robert II de Courtenay	1221–1228
Baldwin II	1228–1261
Greek Emperors of Nicaea	
Theodore I Lascaris	1204–1222
John III Vatatzes	1222–1254
Theodore II Lascaris	1254–1258
Leo IV Lascaris	1258–1259
Michael VIII Palaeologus	1259–1261
Dynasty of the Palaeologi	
Michael VIII	1261–1282
Andronicus II	1282–1328
Andronicus III	1328–1341
John V	1341–1376
John IV Cantacuzene (Usurper)	1341–1355
Andronicus IV (son of John V)	1376–1379
John V (second time)	1379–1391
John VII (son of Andronicus IV, usurper)	1390
Manuel II	1391–1425
John VIII	1425–1448
Constantine XI Dragases	1448–1453
EMPERORS OF THE HOLY ROMAN EMPIRE	
Charlemagne	800–814
Louis I the Pious	814–840
Lothaire I	840–855
Louis II	850–875
Charles II the Bald	875–877
Charles III	881–887
Guy of Spoleto	891–893
Lambert of Spoleto	892–898
Arnulph	896–899
Louis III the Child	900–911
Louis III of Provence	901–902
Conrad I	911–918
Berengarius of Frioul	915–924
Henry I	919–936
Otto the Great	963–973
Otto II	973–983

Otto III	982–1002
St. Henry II	1002–1024
Conrad II	1024–1039
Henry III	1039–1056
Henry IV	1056–1106
Henry V	1106–1125
Lothaire II	1125–1137
Conrad III	1138–1152
Frederick I	1152–1190
Henry VI	1190–1197
Otto IV	1198–1215
Frederick II	1215–1250
Conrad IV	1250–1254
The Great Interregnum	1256–1273
Rudolph of Hapsburg	1273–1291
Adolph of Nassau	1272–1298
Albert I of Austria	1298–1308
Henry VII of Luxemburg	1308–1313
Louis of Bavaria	1314–1347
Frederick of Austria	1314–1330
Charles IV of Bohemia	1346–1378
Wenceslaus of Bohemia	1378–1400
Robert of the Palatinate	1400–1410
Sigismund of Hungary	1410–1437
Albert II	1438–1439
Frederick III	1440–1493
Maximilian I	1493–1519

KINGS OF FRANCE
Carolingians

Pepin of Heristal	678–714
Charles Martel	715–741
Pepin the Short	741–768
Charlemagne	768–814
Louis the Pious	814–840
Charles the Bald	843–877
Louis II the Stammerer	877–879
Louis III	879–882
Carloman	879–884
Charles the Fat	885–887
Eudes	887–897
Charles III the Simple	898–922
Robert I	922–923
Ralph	923–936

Louis IV	936–954
Lothaire	954–986
Louis V	986–987

Capetians

Hugh Capet	987–996
Robert the Pious	996–1031
Henry I	1031–1060
Philip I	1060–1108
Louis VI the Fat	1108–1137
Louis VII the Younger	1137–1180
Philip Augustus	1180–1223
Louis VIII	1223–1226
St. Louis IX	1226–1270
Philip III the Brave	1270–1285
Philip IV the Fair	1285–1314
Louis X the Quarreller	1314–1316
John I	1316
Philip V the Tall	1316–1322
Charles IV the Fair	1322–1328

Valois

Philip VI of Valois	1328–1350
John II the Good	1350–1364
Charles V the Wise	1364–1380
Charles VI	1380–1422
Charles VII	1422–1461
Louis XI	1461–1483
Charles VIII	1483–1498
Louis XII	1498–1515

KINGS OF ENGLAND
Norman

William I the Conqueror	1066–1087
William II Rufus	1087–1100
Henry I	1100–1135
Stephen of Blois	1135–1154

Plantagenet

Henry II	1154–1189
Richard I the Lion-Hearted	1189–1199
John Lackland	1199–1216
Henry III	1216–1272
Edward I	1272–1307
Edward II	1307–1327
Edward III	1327–1377
Richard II	1377–1399

House of Lancaster

Henry IV	1399–1413
Henry V	1413–1422
Henry VI	1422–1461

House of York

Edward IV	1461–1483
Edward V	1483
Edward VI	1483–1485

Tudors

Henry VII	1485–1509
Henry VIII	1509–1547

INDEX